Managing Product and Service Development: Text and Cases

Stefan Thomke

Harvard Business School

Boston   Burr Ridge, IL   Dubuque, IA   Madison, WI   New York
San Francisco   St. Louis   Bangkok   Bogotá   Caracas   Kuala Lumpur
Lisbon   London   Madrid   Mexico City   Milan   Montreal   New Delhi
Santiago   Seoul   Singapore   Sydney   Taipei   Toronto

The McGraw·Hill Companies

McGraw-Hill
Irwin

MANAGING PRODUCT AND SERVICE DEVELOPMENT: TEXT AND CASES

Published by McGraw-Hill/Irwin, a business unit of The McGraw-Hill Companies, Inc., 1221 Avenue of the Americas, New York, NY, 10020. Copyright © 2007 by The McGraw-Hill Companies, Inc. All rights reserved. No part of this publication may be reproduced or distributed in any form or by any means, or stored in a database or retrieval system, without the prior written consent of The McGraw-Hill Companies, Inc., including, but not limited to, in any network or other electronic storage or transmission, or broadcast for distance learning.

Some ancillaries, including electronic and print components, may not be available to customers outside the United States.

This book is printed on acid-free paper.

1 2 3 4 5 6 7 8 9 0 DOC/DOC 0 9 8 7 6

ISBN-13: 978-0-07-302301-4
ISBN-10: 0-07-302301-9

Editorial director: *Stewart Mattson*
Executive editor: *Scott Isenberg*
Executive marketing manager: *Rhonda Seelinger*
Project manager: *Harvey Yep*
Senior production supervisor: *Sesha Bolisetty*
Designer: *Cara David*
Lead media project manager: *Brian Nacik*
Cover design: *Chris Bowyer*
Typeface: *10/12 Times New Roman*
Compositor: *Interactive Composition Corporation*
Printer: *R. R. Donnelley*

Library of Congress Cataloging-in-Publication Data

Thomke, Stefan H.
    Managing product and service development: text and cases / Stefan Thomke.
        p. cm.
    Includes index.
    ISBN-13: 978-0-07-302301-4 (alk. paper)
    ISBN-10: 0-07-302301-9 (alk. paper)
        1. New products—Management—Case studies. 2. Product management—Case studies. I.
Title.
HF5415.153.T485 2007
658.5—dc22

                                                                                    2005056173

www.mhhe.com

Table of Contents

About the Author

Stefan Thomke, an authority on the management of technology and product innovation, is Professor of Business Administration at Harvard Business School. He has worked with U.S., European, and Asian firms on product and technology development, organizational, and strategic issues. Since joining the Harvard faculty in 1995, Professor Thomke has taught MBA and executive courses on technology and operations management, product development, R&D and innovation management, and operations strategy, both at Harvard Business School and in individual company programs in the United States and abroad. For several years, he was faculty chairman of the Executive Education Program *Leading Product Development,* which helps business leaders in revamping their product development processes for greater competitive advantage. Professor Thomke is currently faculty co-chairman of the doctoral program in Information, Technology and Management (I,T&M), a collaboration between HBS and Harvard's Faculty of Arts and Sciences.

Professor Thomke's research and writings have focused on the process, economics, and management of experimentation in innovation. An important part of his research examines the impact of new and rapidly advancing technologies (such as computer simulation and prototyping) on the economics of innovation in general, and product development performance and organization in particular. He is a widely published author with more than three dozen articles, cases, and notes published in books and leading journals such as *California Management Review, Harvard Business Review, Journal of Product Innovation Management, Management Science, Organization Science, Research Policy, Strategic Management Journal,* and *Scientific American.* He is the author of *Experimentation Matters: Unlocking the Potential of New Technologies for Innovation* (Harvard Business School Press, 2003), which shows how new technologies provide firms with an opportunity to take innovation to a new level if they are willing to rethink their product development and business models from the ground up. Professor Thomke is also an editor of *Research Policy,* an international journal devoted to research policy, management, and planning, and he serves on the editorial boards of several other leading management journals.

Professor Thomke holds B.S. and M.S. degrees in Electrical Engineering, an S.M. degree in Operations Research, an S.M. degree in Management from the MIT Sloan School of Management, and a Ph.D. degree in Electrical Engineering and Management from the Massachusetts Institute of Technology (MIT), where he was awarded a Lemelson-MIT doctoral fellowship for invention and innovation research. Before joining the Harvard University faculty, he worked in electronics and semiconductor fabrication and later was with McKinsey & Company in Germany, where he served clients in the automotive and energy industries.

Preface

This book introduces you to the design, management, and improvement of product and service development organizations and processes, and how these can be effectively learned. It not only explores an array of best management practices, tools, and frameworks, it also introduces approaches holding promise for the future. The book is based on my Harvard Business School elective course, "Managing Product Development (MPD)," which I taught from 1997 to 2003[1]. Some material is also featured in a one-week HBS executive education program, "Leading Product Development," which I have participated in and led for many years.

For the past decade, my course development and research activities have addressed the managerial aspects of product development. Having been trained as an electrical engineer, however, I have understood, and emphasized to students and managers alike, the technological and scientific challenges of complex development projects. Designing such projects is no trivial task; managing them may be harder still. My hope is that such work is understood and appreciated—for it is through the efforts of scientists, engineers, and managers that new products are created and customers' lives are changed.

A key theme in this book, and the course it is based upon, is the importance of learning by doing. Cases, class discussions, and team activities (focused on creating prototypes of new product/service offerings) all have been designed to complement each other. The aim is a healthy balance between theory, real-world problems and the management challenges they suggest, and hands-on experience. At HBS, the culmination was a Design Fair, where MPD students showcased their efforts and crowds gathered to applaud the results.

I do hope that my enthusiasm for the exciting and important field and *practice* of product development is contagious. The organizations in this book create and develop computers, drugs, cars, food flavors, software, videogames, banking services, and many more products and services that affect us deeply. The processes by which they do so can lead to spectacular successes or disappointing failures, both financially and in the lives of customers. Such differences in outcomes can often be attributed to the quality of general and functional management practice. Product development is not just about engineering or R&D departments—it is a company-wide activity, demanding the efforts of people from marketing to manufacturing. The fortunes of all of us rest in their abilities.

---

[1] The course's predecessor was *Developing and Managing Technology* and was renamed when my colleague Marco Iansiti became coursehead. In 1997, I taught the course with Professor Iansiti, who had developed the teaching material before I took over as coursehead in 1998. Over the next five years, I replaced most of the course materials and developed three new modules that became the foundation of this book.

Acknowledgments

Many people have contributed to the development and success of the material in this book. Writing the case studies would have been impossible without the generous support of many talented managers who not only donated time to teach me about their challenges but had the courage to share their problems openly. We are deeply indebted to these men and women for allowing us to write about their clean and dirty laundry, in the hope that others would learn from it.

I am also grateful to many students in MBA and executive programs where I have tested and refined the material for this book. They patiently read and discussed my articles and cases, listened to new research, and their comments, questions, and criticism have taught me what does and does not work in teaching product and service development.

Along with my students, I would like to thank my HBS colleagues who have tested the case studies and teaching notes, and provided me with invaluable feedback. Many thanks to: Rob Austin, Kent Bowen, Richard Bohmer, Alan MacCormack, Clay Christensen, Lee Fleming, Marco Iansiti, Dorothy Leonard, Gary Pisano, Sandra Sucher, and Steve Wheelwright. Marco in particular helped me to get started in MPD and encouraged me to revise the course entirely. At other schools and organizations, the following people contributed and tested some of the material: Paul Adler at the University of Southern California, Sara Beckman and Hank Chesbrough at UC Berkeley, John Ettlie at the Rochester Institute of Technology, John Heugle at austriamicrosystems, Nitin Joglekar at Boston University, Vish Krishnan at UT Austin, Christoph Loch at INSEAD, Earl Powell at the Design Management Institute, Kamalini Ramdas at the University of Virginia, Don Reinertsen of Reinertsen & Associates, Gary Scudder at Vanderbilt, Steven Sinofsky at Microsoft, Christian Terwiesch at the University of Pennsylvania, Phil Thomas at the Indian Institute of Management, and Eric von Hippel, Michael Cusumano and Rebecca Henderson at MIT. The book also benefited from nine anonymous reviewers and the support of Scott Isenberg, Lee Stone, and Beth Baugh at McGraw-Hill.

Barbara Feinberg worked with me on the design of the course and its pedagogy, and of this book. Her experience, encouragement, and advice have been invaluable. Ashok Nimgade helped write many of the cases studies. His creativity, intelligence, and wit not only made the interviewing and case-writing process fun but also resulted in much better case studies than if I had tried to write them alone. Thanks to you both.

Most of all, I am indebted to my family. It is difficult to find words for all the love and support they have given me. The prime contributor has been my wonderful wife, Savita. Developing the case studies, articles, and teaching notes required extensive travel and writing time, which inevitably led to neglecting some responsibilities at home. She not only "covered" for me but – along with our children Arjun, Vikram and Anjali – was always encouraging and understanding, even when I complained about the work. Over the years, she must have learned that my temporary frustrations are signs of healthy progress, and I dedicate this book to her.

Stefan Thomke
Boston, Massachusetts
July 6, 2005

Managing Product and Service Development introduces you to the critical elements of designing and developing innovative products and services, and specifically to how these are managed. These elements include the pivotal role played by experimentation, prototyping, and learning; product/service development process design and improvement; the understanding and integration of customer needs; development strategy and project management; and the powerful challenge of designing and managing development networks. Along the way you will encounter many of the best management practices, tools, and frameworks currently in use as well as new approaches just now being deployed.

The materials you will analyze and discuss are drawn from product and service development courses that have been offered at the Harvard Business School over the past years. Nearly all the cases were written for the latest version of this course. Intentionally, the case particulars cut across functional boundaries, for the focus is squarely on the managerial skills and capabilities needed for effective practice. So while many situations you encounter emphasize the role of (new) technology, you will approach these as a manager, not as a technologist. All technology introduced is fully explained as part of the case situation. If you happen to be a technologist, however, the managerial perspective will be enriching! But it's important to note that this managerial perspective is not undifferentiated. Depending on the situation, you will be assuming the role of team manager, project manager, functional manager, general manager, or CEO.

This array of roles suggests how fundamental product and service development is to firms at every level, and how excellence in its management is critical to competitiveness. No longer an issue solely for in-house R&D departments, product and service development has become the focal point of the entire organization. That focus remains true even when many "traditional" development activities no longer take place in-house, i.e., when these have been dispersed across a firm and/or outsourced to other organizations (this point is addressed in the third module). Indeed, when the work of development is distributed, the premium placed on its management—at all levels—increases exponentially.

Moreover, it's no longer "product" development that's the issue; services are core to nearly every firm's portfolio of offerings. Indeed, the line between product and service is increasingly hard to draw. Consider Apple. For more than 20 years, it has been considered a product company—it "makes" computers, operating systems, and associated "products." But what is Apple today? It's the creator of the ubiquitous iPod. In one sense, of course, the iPod as a device qualifies as *product*. But it operates with (and, indeed, cannot operate without) iTunes Music Store, which is specifically referred to as an online *service*. So, what is the iPod? A product? A service? A hybrid? Has Apple become a "service company"? Does it matter? What's really important is that it's all been hugely successful!

1

Because the old hard-and-fast distinctions between product and service have blurred to the point of interchangeability, the emphasis in *Managing Product and Service Development* is on how *development* is best achieved and managed in today's hypercompetitive global reality. Organizations live and die based on their ability to innovate, and that ability is directly linked to their skill in experimentation and problem solving (explored in the first module) and executing on the learning from those activities with precision and speed (the topic of the second module).

Specifically, *Managing Product and Service Development* will help you learn:

- How experimentation, learning, and prototyping fuel the development and improvement of products and services, processes, and systems.
- How to design and manage development systems that maximize learning.
- How to unlock the potential of new experimentation technologies for productivity, innovation, and value creation.
- How to design structured and flexible development processes.
- How to integrate customers and new technologies into product development processes.
- How to manage and leverage product platforms.
- How to design, build, and manage development networks.

CONTENT AND STRUCTURE

Managing Product and Service Development is divided into three modules, followed by an optional development project in which you can "learn by doing." (The project is briefly described at the end of this introduction.) The learning, from the cases and readings and from class discussion (and the project as well), is cumulative. That is, each session introduces new ideas, while reinforcing the topics you've debated in previous sessions. In this way, even though you will be plunged into what may look like amazingly different circumstances (e.g., an America's Cup race and a company that makes "flavorings" for food products), in fact you are encountering best practices that cut across all situations. By the end of the course, you will be able to see these commonalities and discuss them cogently.

Figure 1 indicates the variety of industries that the book material highlights. Preceding the material in each module is an overview Module Note describing the broad themes you will be learning about and discussing in class. Below is a brief summary of the modules, followed by an introduction to all those themes. (The Module Notes develop each module's topics in greater detail.) These themes bind the book together as a whole.

Module One: Building Capabilities for Experimentation, Learning, and Prototyping

In the sessions that make up this module, you will learn how product and service development should be structured and organized as a cross-functional process essential to value creation. Equally important, you will see that development activities fully leverage the power of experimentation. You will also be introduced to development *systems* whose successes are predictable and repeatable, as well as factors that cause other systems to fail. A pivotal component of the book—how experimentation is transformed by new technologies—is introduced toward the end of the module.

FIGURE 1
Industries
Covered in the
Book

Aerospace

Telecommunications

Computers

Videogame
Software/Hardware

Design Services

Specialty
Chemicals

**Managing Product &
Service Development**

Sports
Competition

Automotive

Banking/Financial
Services

Pharmaceuticals/
Biotechnology

Medical Products
and Services

Computer
Software

Module Two: Development Process Design and Improvement

This module discusses the theory and practice of designing (and redesigning) and improving processes for the development of products and services. You will quickly see that there is no single "best way"—no silver-bullet approach; rather, a good process design needs to match its purpose, environment, and project economics. The importance of "designing" user input into a process is emphasized right off the bat in the opening session of this module, where the notion of "lead users" is introduced. And user input is again brought front and center in the final case situation, but for a very different purpose: a radical rethinking of innovation that shifts product design almost entirely to customers themselves. Between these situations, you will see how new experimentation technologies fundamentally alter organizations using them. If processes, structures, and the organizations themselves fail to adapt to the reality of these technologies, they fail to harness the power experimentation provides. When that adaptation occurs, however, innovation soars.

Module Three: Managing Development Networks

This final module addresses the management of development networks at three levels: between firms (e.g., R&D alliances), within firms (e.g., distributed development), and between products (e.g., product platforms). Product/service development is undergoing significant changes, and the development activities you will encounter in this module represent a trend that will only intensify. Complex projects today draw on design resources separated in time and space, around the globe, and you will meet a diverse array of projects in Japan, India, Germany, as well as the United States. The challenge of managing such complexity is not trivial. Those who master the skills, however, will be at a distinct competitive advantage for the foreseeable future.

TABLE 1	Themes	Module 1	Module 2	Module 3
Linking Themes with Modules	1. Managing Experimentation in the Development of Products and Services	♦	♦	
	2. The Impact and Integration of New Experimentation Technologies	♦	♦	
	3. The Design and Improvement of Structured and Flexible Processes		♦	
	4. The Role of Customers in Product Development		♦	♦
	5. Managing Development Networks within and between Organizations			♦

MAJOR THEMES

Managing Product and Service Development is built on a broad research base and best-practice illustrations. Five major themes thread throughout the book, as shown in **Table 1.**

Theme 1: Managing Experimentation in the Development of Products and Services

The importance of experimentation is powerfully underscored throughout the book, particularly in the first module. While everyone realizes, at some level, that no product or service, much less an innovative one, exists without some kind of "testing" in the background, how such experimentation happens, and how it relates to product development itself, is not so familiar. The importance of experimentation is seen not simply at the level of testing, i.e., making sure that what has already been designed will work, but also at the level of determining what might work in the first place. Further, experimentation can be used to ask "what if?" questions. Regardless of their specific purpose, and most crucially, experiments generate learning. What works—and why? And what *doesn't* work—and why? Only through organized, managed, and systematic experimentation can these questions be both asked and answered and the information gained through the process put to good use.

What this really means is that experimentation is a primary way of resolving uncertainty, and the book introduces four categories of uncertainty that experimentation helps to alleviate. The first is *technical*: this relates to solutions (e.g., materials or physical changes) that have not been combined or tried before. What happens if components are reduced in size, for instance? Does the product still work? A second uncertainty concerns *production*. What happens when something works in the laboratory, in prototypes, but now must scale up to much larger quantities? Can that be done—at all? Can it be done cost-effectively, with excellent quality intact?

Then there is *need uncertainty*. What do customers really want?! How do we know? How do they know? Customers cannot always specify or even articulate what it is that they want or need. And finally, *market uncertainty* takes us to a broader competitive level. Is the innovation contemplated a "disruptive" one?[1] Will the company bet on it, or be reluctant to take the risk?

Fundamentally, experimentation, like product development itself, can be regarded as a "four-step cycle": design, build, run, and analyze.[2] During the *design* step, individuals or teams determine what they expect to learn from the experiment and define the experimental activities to be carried out and analyzed. During the *build* step, physical or virtual prototypes and testing apparatus—models—needed to conduct that experiment are created. During the *run* step, an experiment is conducted either under laboratory conditions or in a real setting. Finally, in the *analyze* step, results are examined, compared against expectations, and interpreted in light of those expectations. It is during this step that most of the learning occurs, forming the basis of experiments in the next cycle (if these are needed). It's at this point that you determine whether the experiment worked, failed, or needs more work—and what has been learned en route. If "more work" is needed, you try again, modifying the design of the experiment, the conditions of the experiment, and/or even the goal originally aimed at, drawing upon the learning that has been generated so far.

Although every experiment by definition yields information, whether that information is taken advantage of—in the form of learning—is another matter. Ideally, learning from experiments is directly reused, and a formal process of experimentation—comprising the cycle above—helps ensure that. But even if such learning happens, how can the *rate* of learning increase? Can experiments be designed such that even more can be gained from the process? In fact, well-designed experiments, regardless of their particular purposes, have several factors in common, all of which will affect learning: fidelity, cost, iteration time, capacity, sequence, signal-to-noise ratio, and the extent to which variables are changed. The Overview for Module One details them further.

Theme 2: The Impact and Integration of New Experimentation Technologies

Experimentation, no matter how intrinsic it is to product creation and development, was expensive to undertake in a pre-simulation/modeling-technology world; the more complex the product, the more costly it became to develop physical prototypes that aimed to replicate the product's intentions. In fact, experiments often turned into a kind of hold-your-breath *tests,* as everyone hoped the results would "prove" that what was envisioned actually worked. Even in such all-or-nothing settings, the experiment (test) yielded learning, but at what cost and stakes! Today much of this drama can be eliminated. It is now possible to experiment in increments, revisions (iterations), and modifications, using a vast array of new technologies. It is possible to consider a "failed" experiment a success—you may, and often do, learn more from failure than from quick hits.

New technologies for experimentation are notable for several reasons: they cost less to buy and deploy; they enable multiple "views" of ideas, both early and late-stage, through modeling techniques; most importantly, they allow more experimentation *capacity* to be

---

[1] See Clayton Christensen, *The Innovator's Dilemma* (HBS Press, 1997).

[2] See Stefan Thomke, *Experimentation Matters* (HBS Press, 2003), Chapter 3. Similar building blocks to analyze the design and development process have been used by other researchers. The Module One overview chapter has a detailed discussion of what these steps entail and how they can be managed.

created. That is, it's now possible to run more experiments, in more and different settings, than ever before—and more cheaply. Meanwhile, the individual experiment can be staged to create more learning, more efficiently. All this happens because the results of technology-based experiments are almost instantaneously revealed, and can be assessed—and modified, if need be—almost as instantaneously, and shared over multiple settings.

This seemingly positive impact, however, no matter how evident in terms of experimentation itself, has profound consequence on organizations accustomed to other approaches to experimentation vis-à-vis product development. You will see many firms, in an array of situations, grappling with the problems that arise when the implications of new technologies for experimentation confront them. The power that's offered—speed, low cost, experimentation capacity increases, "learning from failure"—these and more, at the same time, imply profound organizational challenges.

How does an organization go about dealing with this challenge? What does it take? New people (i.e., replace the "traditionalists" with the "radicals," on the assumption that they'll be more receptive to new ideas)? New processes? New systems? Different incentives? You'll meet organizations wrestling with these questions. Another route is to *integrate* new technologies into existing routines. What has been built up, organizationally and procedurally, is not, in this approach, considered ipso facto wrong; rather, it's that the new ways of looking at experimentation can enhance tried-and-true routines. Not easily, of course, but it's possible. Because the orientation of the book is the manager's perspective, you will confront these issues by taking on multiple managerial roles—and experience yourself how they have been resolved.

Theme 3: The Design and Improvement of Structured and Flexible Processes

Experimentation, whether conducted with "old" or "new" technologies or in some integrated form, is a core part of a larger system: product and service development. Another critical element of product development is the design and organization of the *process* that development projects follow. In other words, what results "from" experimentation goes "into" a process of development.

By far, the most favored process is called "stage-gate" (or phased development). The rationale behind this approach is to have a series of milestones ("gates") that govern the sequential progress of the project; senior management essentially arrives at these points to advise (on the schedule, progress) and consent to the resources allocated (or, of course, to deny them). Uncertainty is increasingly eliminated, it is assumed.

And yet, as you shall see in several situations, this very attempt to eliminate uncertainty (recall the variety of forms it can take) can literally "freeze" the endeavor. Whatever was determined to be the best product—even if it resulted from all the new experimentation technologies on the planet, all skillfully employed—could be foiled if "the process" insists on being rigid. What happens if a competitor threatens to put forth something better, more appealing, cheaper? At the same time, can a process be *designed* to be sufficiently flexible such that every contingency is accounted for? Is there any way to be *structured and flexible*? This is something you will have to figure out. What's the difference between a process design that is rigid and one that is structured? How can a so-called flexible process design not be chaotic in execution? And most important, how can processes—of any stripe—be improved? A clue is found in **Figure 2,** which shows different approaches to increasing

FIGURE 2
Achieving
Increased
Development
Flexibility[3]

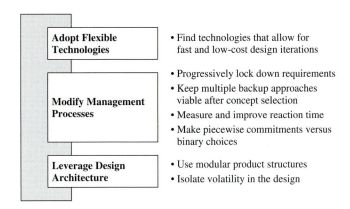

Adopt Flexible Technologies	• Find technologies that allow for fast and low-cost design iterations
Modify Management Processes	• Progressively lock down requirements • Keep multiple backup approaches viable after concept selection • Measure and improve reaction time • Make piecewise commitments versus binary choices
Leverage Design Architecture	• Use modular product structures • Isolate volatility in the design

flexibility. Subsequent module overviews, supplementing investigations of the book's material, will provide more insight.

Theme 4: The Role of Customers in Product Development

So far, we've been within the firm. Where is the customer in all this? No product, no matter how well "experimented with" or "processed" has a lock on customers from the outset. Customers, existing and/or potential, must have some kind of input at the outset for there to be some guarantee that what all this effort aims at will in fact succeed. Yet firms are not so good at determining what "their" customers—or any customers—want. Not only do they often fail to understand what (potential) customers want from new products, they often don't integrate what (existing) customer data about previous products could reveal. This is not simply ineptitude. Customer information, regardless of origin, is messy, complex; it is expensive to gather, collate, and analyze. Who's to be studied? Why? How? Does what someone, much less a mass of customers, bought *then* predict what will be bought *now*? Who knows? "Market research" is supposed to answer these questions, yet it rarely does—effectively.

In fact, *Managing Product and Service Development* puts the customer *within* product development—not as some outsider to be catered to (if possible), but as an intrinsic influence in determining what happens and how. Two approaches to this role are explored in particular. The first approach leverages *lead users*—companies, organizations, or individuals that are well ahead of market trends and have needs that go far beyond those of the average user. Considerable research on such lead users suggests that they are not only willing to experiment, but even to prototype product solutions when they are not commercially available. In other words, lead users are interested in solutions to problems that are not yet articulated by the rest of us.

A second approach is even more radical in its implications: involving customers *directly* in the "innovation process" itself. What if customers (individuals or organizations) could dream up their own variations, their own custom products? Instead of having the supplier "provide," the customer would "create." In fact, this is a long-standing approach taken by chip manufacturers in the custom-design arena—a decades-old practice. Chip manufacturers

[3] For more information, see the Module Two article "Agile Product Development: Managing Development Flexibility in Uncertain Environments," *California Management Review* 41, no. 1 (Fall 1998) by Stefan Thomke and Don Reinertsen.

pioneered the concept of *design toolkits*.[4] Moreover, the toolkit approach has been taken up in various settings—as is detailed in the second module overview, and as is illustrated in material you will encounter in classroom discussions.

What's particularly interesting in the toolkit approach is that experimentation—so front-and-center in product development within the firm—now moves beyond it. Clearly, to do this means making some pretty drastic changes to boundaries—both thinking about them and deciding where and how they should and can be moved. The third module, which focuses on development networks, will help clarify some of the challenges involved in both design and management.

Theme 5: Managing Development Networks within and between Organizations

It's a rare product development organization that operates in isolation, even if it doesn't take the toolkits approach. Whether it's a geographical dispersion of personnel, an array of outsourcing activities, or various alliances, most firms are implicated in arrangements that take them beyond their own four walls. From the R to the D, product and service development is increasingly a networked phenomenon. Multiple boundaries are crossed—even if these do not, as yet, directly involve customers or other firms. How do we think about these? How do we organize for them? How can they be managed?

Managing Product and Service Development distinguishes between the issues involved in organizing for internal networks and those involved when more than one firm is implicated. In the first situation, the interdependencies are at once internal to the firm and yet across time zones, "cultures," languages, customs, and a host of factors usually not so evident. In the second situation—spanning firm boundaries—there are inevitably contractual difficulties, again not so easy to predict at the outset. Yet the potential benefits from such cross-fertilization are large, and in any case, that is the route that's being taken.

While there are many possible solutions to the challenges of boundary-crossing, this book introduces a powerful lever: that of product platforms, increasingly used for networks within companies. As you will see, particularly in the third module (but in fact throughout the situations you encounter), organizations increasingly aim to address multiple market segments as inexpensively as possible. Traditionally, platforms are devised for "families"—a new product is designed in order to have several or many derivative follow-ons. You will read more about this approach in the Note before the third module's materials.

Central to achieving such leverage is the development of a product platform. Typically, platforms establish the basic architecture for a set of follow-on derivative projects that are much narrower in scope.[5] By spending substantial resources on platforms up-front, derivative projects can be completed at much lower cost and time and aimed at very specific market segments. The benefits of platforms come in multiple ways: (a) the development effort of platforms can be amortized over many derivatives; (b) more derivatives can cover more

---

[4] For more information on the approach described, see Stefan Thomke and Eric von Hippel, "Customers as Innovators: A New Way to Create Value," *Harvard Business Review,* April 2002, and Chapter 7 in Stefan Thomke, *Experimentation Matters* (HBS Press, 2003).

[5] Steven Wheelwright and Kim Clark, *Revolutionizing Product Development* (The Free Press, 1992), have a detailed discussion on how companies can leverage product platforms in their development organizations.

profitable market niches that otherwise would be too costly to address; and (c) the platform/derivative portfolio planning process adds strategic focus for management.

Product platforms are not the only way organizations aim to enhance their internal networks. Many large companies are creating global R&D sites and distributing development work across them. This intention has immediate appeal. The hope is to take advantage of time zone differences—development around the clock—and to be as close as possible to customers and markets. Lower labor and operating costs are an obvious spur as well. And yet, as appealing as this is, managing global networks, even within a single company, is by no means simple. Just because everyone works for the firm doesn't mean that everyone thinks the same way. It isn't just a matter of people speaking different languages, something all organizations are more or less prepared for. Rather, different "world views" need to be taken into account.

Such differences are even more acute when networks span companies. Again, the appeal is obvious; an "innovation network" comprising interdependent "components" would seem to make product platforms even more advantageous—the whole would be greater than the sum of its parts. Of course, there are deep challenges to be met in order for this dream of synergy to be realized. The fact that in many cases "components" are being developed simultaneously means that if there are problems in one area, many others are immediately affected; the entire network can grind to a halt. A major aspect of these cross-firm networks is the need for sophisticated contact to ensure that, as much as possible, potential problems are foreseen—at least in the abstract—and contingency plans built in.

****

Overall, you will see that the themes sketched above (and addressed in more detail in the module overviews) arise throughout the book, though each module has a specific focus. The *first* shows how development activities should be designed, organized, and led to fully leverage the power of experimentation. It addresses many issues for successfully managing experimentation activities, ranging from structured experimentation to managing experimentation processes under technological change. The *second* module covers the core aspects of development processes, including flexibility, speed, structure and the integration of new technologies. The *third* module introduces the increasing importance of distributed development networks within companies, among companies, and between products.

Optional Theme 6: Student Projects—Learning by Doing

When taught at Harvard Business School, the Managing Product and Service Development course was accompanied by project work. Students, in teams, design and develop products and services, either on their own or in conjunction with company sponsors. At the end of the semester, the class puts on a Project Fair to (proudly) exhibit their product and service development accomplishments. The power of having project work parallel classroom discussion is that teams are actually *experiencing* what is being grappled with in case situations as the course proceeds.

At the same time, projects are optional—*Managing Product and Service Development* was designed to work either with student projects as part of a course or without them. Because the learning is cumulative, with new situations both reinforcing previous learning and introducing new ideas, the sum total of learning is comprehensive and coherent.

Module **One**

Building Capabilities for Experimentation, Learning, and Prototyping

Experimentation, learning, and prototyping are integral to the development—and innovation—of products and services. New products and services don't drop from the sky—formally or informally, they've been through activities of trial and error, of learning about what does and does not work, of prototyping, of more learning, of improvement, and of more learning. Eventually, the outcome is "developed"—the product/service result is now ready for the ultimate experiment: whether it will sell to customers. Sometimes this is a billion-dollar hit; sometimes it literally explodes.

Experimentation, learning, prototyping, however, don't—or shouldn't—drop from the sky, either. The purpose of this module is to make that point clear: experimentation itself is a process, one that product development organizations need to be capable of executing. At the same time, these organizations have to be organized to *receive* the learning that comes from experimentation. In other words, experimentation *should feed into* product development itself. The learning that is the "product" of experimentation must be integrated into the "product" that's the focus of development.

This module focuses on what experimentation is, what it looks like, how it's been "operationalized" for better or worse in a variety of situations. As you will see, in some cases, experimentation is made equivalent to "testing"; in other situations, it's been pursued for its own sake. All cases in this module, however, raise the issue of how organized (and managed) experimentation can be integrated into product (service) development itself: organizationally, managerially. In other words, just as experimentation is an organized (managed) process that must integrate with product development, product development processes must be organized (managed) to incorporate it.

The second module will get deeply into product and service development processes themselves and examine and analyze various approaches and their strengths and weaknesses. But the critical issue, the one that starts us off here in this first module, is how intrinsic experimentation is to *any* development process—it should be organized, managed, and *integrated* in itself. It is critical to understand, off the bat, just what "experimentation" is, and how it has its own logic. Appreciating this will better help you when you turn to the "logic" of development processes in the next module. The themes (below) detailed in this module note outline much of that experimentation "logic." You will face the explicit issue of "integration" in cases to come.

For their part, the situations portrayed in this module highlight the role of experimentation in critical events; these represent the complexities product and service organizations face as they struggle to understand just how powerful experimentation can be—or the dangers that happen when that is ignored. Some cases are "classic"—e.g., the dramatic problems encountered before and after the Challenger Shuttle explosion. That case, which opens the module, provides the ultimate lesson in how important integrating experimentation into "development" is. Similarly classic but with a more positive result is the second case, about Apple's Power Book. In both cases, and in the subsequent situations, the strengths and weaknesses of integration efforts are exposed as people attempt to design and develop products and services while simultaneously organizing activities for experimentation as they go along.

The stakes are raised as the module proceeds, because an array of technologies for experimentation now exists, e.g., computer simulation and other IT-mediated tools. Not only do these new technologies promise to further magnify experimentation's influence on innovation and product development by increasing and accelerating possibilities for learning, they challenge existing approaches to managing the process of experimentation itself. If not thoughtfully integrated into the larger span of product development activities, such technologies can actually threaten ongoing operations. The Eli Lilly case illustrates this well.

In sum, this module stresses the intrinsic importance of *organized* experimentation: what it consists of (as outlined in the themes of this note); what it looks like in various situations (as illustrated in the cases). You should "take away" the following:

- Experimentation is not a random walk of trial and error ("let's see what turns up") or the organization of One Big Test ("we've put a zillion dollars in this project, let's make sure it works"). There is an *integrity* to experimentation that needs to be understood.
- At the same time, such an experimentation process needs to be coordinated with the objectives of a product development organization and integrated into its process activities. This implies mutual accommodation.
- The process of experimentation and the process of development are neither mutually exclusive nor arranged hierarchically. Development doesn't trump experimentation (much less vice versa) "when the chips are down." The only way that experimentation is effective is if it is incorporated into development; the only way development can flourish is if it is structured to embrace experimentation.

The result of this learning should prepare you for the next set of cases in Module Two— you should be armed with an understanding of how organizations can create "capabilities" for experimentation, but to do so they also have to assess, and modify if necessary, their own "'capabilities" for development.

MODULE STRUCTURE

There are six cases and two readings in this module. The material emphasizes, through the variety of situations presented, the critical importance of experimentation to innovation and product development. Whether the "product" is in fact a service (as in the Bank of America case), a laptop (the Apple Power Book case), or consulting (IDEO), the ability to take advantage of the learning that comes from experimentation proves to be critical to success (the Team New Zealand case). In fact, this module intentionally introduces you to such diverse—yet representative—situations in order to make that point. See the **Exhibit** on page 26 for a synopsis of the cases.

THEMES

Three major themes are highlighted in this module. The research background supporting the themes draws from ongoing work on managing experimentation and learning as well as on the challenges introduced by technological change.[1]

Theme 1: Importance of Experimentation to Learning, Prototyping, and Product Development

No product has been successfully developed without an equally successful process of experimentation preceding it. Major development projects can involve thousands, if not hundreds of thousands, of ongoing attempts to figure out what does, and what does not, work. Product development—much less *new* product development—happens on the back of experimentation. Why is this so? Experimentation generates learning, and that in turn generates insight into both the aim of the experiment and how it was carried out. At the outset, "the product" is an idea, with some assumptions about how it can be realized. Only through organized testing—experimentation—can the possibilities be either realized or rejected. As such, a key purpose of experimentation is the resolution of uncertainty.

In fact, no product can *be* a product without its first having been an idea subsequently shaped through experimentation: to *learn,* through rounds of organized testing, whether the product concept or proposed technical solution holds promise for addressing a new need or problem—in short, to deal with multiple possibilities. The information derived from each round is then incorporated into the next set of experiments, until the best product ultimately results. In short, new products and services do not arrive fully fledged but are nurtured through an experimentation process that takes place in laboratories and development organizations. All such groups have an experimentation process, but not every group organizes that process to invite innovation; not all processes can efficiently resolve uncertainty, but all organizations aim toward that goal.

Indeed, according to academic research on R&D organizations, project teams spent an average of 77 percent of their time on experimentation and related analysis to resolve

---

[1] Some of the material in this section comes from Stefan Thomke, *Experimentation Matters: Unlocking the Potential of New Technologies for Innovation* (Harvard Business School Press, 2003).

uncertainty.[2] But uncertainty is not a uniform phenomenon. *Technical uncertainty* arises from the exploration of solutions (e.g., materials) that have not been used before, or have not been combined in "this" way before, or miniaturized in such a way before. *Production uncertainty* exists when we do not know if a technical solution that works well in proto-types can also be produced cost-effectively or at high quality. What may work in small quantities may not be feasible when production ramps up; the entire manufacturing process itself may need to be revised.[3] At every stage of R&D, technical and production uncertainty exists and needs to be managed, in part through a systematic process of experimentation.

Beyond technical and production uncertainty, rapidly changing customer demands create *need uncertainty,* another critical reason for rigorous experimentation. Customers are rarely able to fully specify all of their needs because they either face uncertainty themselves or can-not articulate their needs for products that do not yet exist.[4] If they have neither seen nor used such a product before, they themselves will have to experiment before arriving at a recom-mendation. Finally, when innovations are "disruptive," as research has shown, *market uncer-tainty* can be so significant that firms are reluctant or unable to allocate sufficient resources to the development of products for those markets.[5] To successfully harness the opportunities of such disruptive technologies, managers rely in part on experimentation.

Overall, experimentation is combined with an emphasis on up-front efforts that include setting specifications and establishing "game plans." The up-front notion has a long heritage in research and writings on how product development is effectively designed and managed.[6] The emphasis on experimentation here, and on the new technologies that can enhance its power, continues in that tradition. Yet while experimentation (and other "up-front" activities) is grasped as important in itself, it is not always understood in relation to product develop-ment. So your challenge in analyzing the material in this module is to understand how exper-imentation (as an up-front activity)—and the learning that stems from it—makes an impact on product development and how it is to be managed. How does learning that ideally arises "early and often" have an impact on product development—and its management?

A related question is: How does an organization deal with the failure that is an inevitable consequence of "early and often"? Many experiments "fail" as part of product development efforts because, first, they are intended to be "up-front" activities, and, second, because of their preliminary nature, experiments relate to the uncertain nature of the undertaking itself. When teams begin the development of products or services—especially novel or

---

[2] Thomas Allen, *Managing the Flow of Technology* (Cambridge, MA: MIT Press, 1977), Chapter 4.

[3] Gary Pisano, *The Development Factory* (HBS Press, 1997), Chapter 2.

[4] See Eric von Hippel, *The Sources of Innovation* (New York: Oxford University Press, 1988), pages 102–106.

[5] Clayton Christensen, *The Innovator's Dilemma: When New Technologies Cause Great Firms to Fail* (HBS Press, 1997).

[6] For example, see Stefan Thomke and Takahiro Fujimoto, "The Effect of 'Front-Loading' Problem-Solving on Product Development Performance," *Journal of Product Innovation Management,* March 2000. The importance of up-front efforts in product development has been addressed in a number of books, includ-ing Kim Clark and Takahiro Fujimoto, *Product Development Performance* (HBS Press, 1991); Marco Iansiti, *Technology Integration* (HBS Press, 1997); Dorothy Leonard-Barton, *Wellsprings of Knowledge* (HBS Press, 1995); Gary Pisano, *The Development Factory* (HBS Press, 1997); Stefan Thomke, *Experimentation Matters* (HBS Press, 2003); and Steven Wheelwright and Kim Clark, *Revolutionizing Product Development* (The Free Press, 1992).

FIGURE 1-1
Experimentation as Iterative Cycles

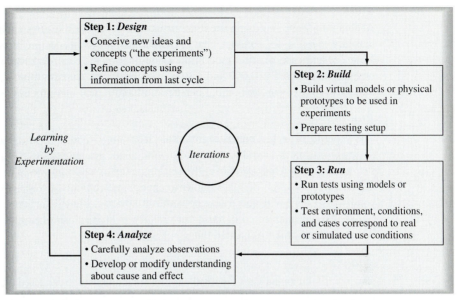

complex ones—they rarely know whether a particular concept will work as imagined. That means they have to find ways of rapidly discarding dysfunctional ideas while retaining those that show promise. At the same time, the "dysfunctional ideas" themselves have generated knowledge and should, as such, have value—again, knowing what doesn't work is as important as knowing what does. Keeping track of "failed" ideas is, therefore, critical. The learning, in other words, comes not only from experiments themselves but from a library, in essence, of what did—and, critically—what did *not* work.

A final issue: experimentation should be an *iterative process*. New technologies for experimentation, e.g., simulations and other modeling techniques, make this possible given their economics; it is now feasible to run multiple experiments for the cost of a single one just a few years ago.

Specifically, experimentation comprises four-step iterative cycles (see **Figure 1-1**):[7]

Design

During this step, individuals or teams define what they expect to learn from the experiment. Existing data, observations, and prior experiments are reviewed, new ideas are generated through brainstorming, and hypotheses are formulated based on prior knowledge. The team then selects a set of experiments to be carried out in parallel and analyzed.

[7] See Stefan Thomke, *Experimentation Matters* (HBS Press, 2003, Chapter 3). Similar building blocks to analyze the design and development process have been used by other researchers. For example, Herbert Simon, *The Sciences of the Artificial* (MIT Press, 1969, Chapter 5), views design as a series of "generator-test cycles." Kim Clark and Takahiro Fujimoto, *Product Development Performance* (HBS Press, 1991), and Steven Wheelwright and Kim Clark, *Revolutionizing Product Development* (The Free Press, 1992, Chapters 9 & 10), use "design-build-test" cycles as a framework for problem-solving in product development. In my research, I modified these blocks to include "run" and "analyze" as two explicit steps that conceptually separate the execution of an experiment and the learning that takes place during analysis.

Build

At this point, one builds physical or virtual prototypes and testing apparatus—models—that are needed to conduct that experiment. In yacht design shown in the Team New Zealand case, teams would build a one-quarter scale (20-foot) version of the boat at an expense of about $50,000 and several months of construction time. It wasn't unusual to build five to six boats in parallel per iteration and repeat this process three to four times.

Run

The experiment is then conducted in either laboratory conditions or a real setting. In yacht design, for instance, wind tunnels and towing tanks simulate the varying conditions of the sea, giving designers control over the settings. Storms and high waves can be created without having to wait for the real weather to change. Of course, the trade-off is that laboratory conditions aren't real and a test apparatus is often designed for certain purposes. True errors may go undetected or false "errors" show up because of unique conditions under which the experiment is carried out.

Analyze

The experimenter analyzes the result, compares it against the expected outcome and adjusts his or her understanding of what is under investigation. It is during this step that most of the learning can happen, forming the basis of experiments in the next cycle. At a minimum, the developer will be able to disqualify failed experiments from the potential solution space and continue the search. In many cases, however, an error or a failed experiment can help someone to adjust mental, computer, or physical models to reflect what has been observed. The result will be a deeper understanding and less uncertainty about cause and effect.

If the results of a first experimental cycle are satisfactory, you stop. However, if (as is usually the case) analysis shows that the results of the initial experiment are not satisfactory, you may elect to modify the experiment and "iterate"—try again. Modifications may involve the experimental design, the experimental conditions, or even the nature of the desired solution. For example, a researcher may design an experiment with the goal of identifying a new cardiovascular drug. However, experimental results on a given compound might suggest a different therapeutic use and cause researchers to change their view of an acceptable solution accordingly. Experimentation iterations like those noted above are performed by individuals and teams that are often divided across different functional departments; in large development projects such as automotive development, there can be tens of thousands of such cycles—even very small projects can involve hundreds of iterations. How firms link experimentation activities to major process phases, system stages, and development tasks is therefore an essential part of effective management practice. As projects progress and designs mature, cycles tend to include models of increasing fidelity, gradually moving toward functional prototypes and pilot vehicles. These models, in turn, are used to test decisions affecting design appearance, function, structure, and manufacturability.

Theme 2: Development Systems That Maximize Learning from Experimentation

The objective of any experiment, as has been repeatedly stressed, is to learn *from* the experiment. Information gleaned ultimately (ideally) leads to the development of new products, processes, and services that will benefit the firm. The rate at which companies

TABLE 1-1
Factors That Affect Learning by Experimentation

Factor	Definition
Fidelity of experiments	The degree to which a model and its testing conditions represent a final product under actual use conditions
Cost of experiments	The total cost of designing, building, running, and analyzing an experiment, including expenses for prototypes, laboratory use, etc.
Iteration time (all four steps)	The time from conceiving an experiment to when the analyzed results are available to the experimenter (step 1)
Capacity	The number of same fidelity experiments that can be carried out per unit time
Sequence	The extent to which experiments are run in parallel or series
Signal-to-noise ratio	The extent to which the variable of interest is obscured by experimental noise
Type of experiment	The degree of variable manipulation (incremental versus radical changes); no manipulation results in observations only

can learn by experimentation will depend on many factors that demand strategic clarity, managerial commitment, and organizational flexibility. These do not result in "innovation" overnight, but they do eventually. While learning from particular experiments can be affected by multiple firm-specific influences, there are several *factors* common to learning across all experimentation (see **Table 1-1**) and thus product development systems have to be designed and organized for it. That is, these factors dictate, in general, how learning-through-experimentation occurs.

How these factors are traded off is a paramount focus in several cases you will encounter. How accurate should their models be? What is the best way to speed up iterations? How should "noise" be controlled, how much experimentation capacity can they afford, and how much risk should experimental changes entail?

Fidelity of Experiments

Experimentation often makes use of simplified versions (models) of the eventually intended test objects and/or test environment. For example, aircraft designers usually conduct experiments on possible aircraft designs by testing a scale model of that design in a "wind tunnel"—an apparatus that creates high wind velocities that partially simulate the aircraft's intended operating environment. The value of using models in experimentation is twofold: to reduce investment in aspects of the "real" that are irrelevant for the experiment, and to control some aspects of the "real" that would affect the experiment in order to simplify analysis of the results. Thus, models of aircraft being subjected to wind tunnel experiments generally include no internal design details such as the layout of the cabins—these are both costly to model and typically irrelevant to the outcome of wind tunnel tests, which are focused on the interaction between rapidly moving air and the model's exterior surface.

Of course, while models and prototypes are necessary to run experiments, they do not represent reality completely (if they did, they would be the reality they are to represent). *Fidelity* is the term used to signify the extent to which a model does represent a product, process, or service in experimentation. Perfect models and prototypes, those with 100 percent fidelity, are usually not constructed because an experimenter does not know or cannot economically capture all the attributes of the real situation, and therefore could not transfer them into a model even if doing so was desired. Lower fidelity models can be useful if they are inexpensive and can be produced rapidly for "quick and dirty" feedback, which is often good enough in the early concept phase of product development, when experimentation itself is in "early development." However, as the experimentation process itself unfolds, higher fidelity models become increasingly important, first because the learning from experiments is increasingly vital to understanding how close to a solution the effort is, and second, because modeling errors can get "carried along."

Cost of Experiments

Conducting an experimental cycle typically involves the cost and time of using equipment, material, facilities, and engineering resources. These costs can be as high as millions of dollars in the case of a prototype of a new car used in destructive crash testing. They can be as low as a few dollars for a chemical compound used in pharmaceutical drug development and made with the aid of combinatorial chemistry. In general, firms facing high experimentation costs will be more reluctant to try radically new ideas or to depart significantly from existing know-how. They will also try to economize; many design changes will be combined in a single experiment, which will make learning more difficult. There will be fewer "errors" vis-à-vis the number of "trials" to learn from.

Consider the four-step experimental cycle in Table 1-1. The cost of building (step 2) an experimentation model depends critically on the available technology, the thoroughness of knowledge about the phenomena, and the degree of accuracy the underlying model is intended to portray. For example, modern computer-aided design (CAD) tools sometimes have an interface to computer software that converts a design directly into a simulation model. In such cases, building a model is relatively inexpensive: the cost primarily represents the investment in conversion tools, which is fixed, and the time required to operate them, a variable cost. Furthermore, experimentation models can have varying degrees of fidelity with respect to reality. As noted, the rationale for using "incomplete" models in experimentation is to reduce investments in "real" aspects that are irrelevant to the experiment and to simplify the analysis of the test results (step 4). Sometimes a model is incomplete because one cannot economically incorporate all relevant aspects of the "real" or does not know them. The incompleteness of a model, however, can lead to design errors when it is replaced by higher fidelity product or process models in the real use environment for the first time.

Iteration Time

People learn most efficiently when their action is followed by immediate feedback.[8] (Imagine how hard it would be to learn to play the piano if there were a long delay between striking a key and hearing the note.) Yet, far too many experimenters must wait days, weeks, or months before their ideas can be turned into testable prototypes. Time passes, attention

---

[8] The importance of feedback in learning has been noted by numerous management scholars. Examples include David Garvin, *Learning in Action* (HBS Press, 2000); Dorothy Leonard-Barton, *Wellsprings of Knowledge* (HBS Press, 1995); Stefan Thomke, *Experimentation Matters* (HBS Press, 2003); and John Sterman, "Modeling Managerial Behavior: Misperceptions of Feedback in a Dynamic Decision-Making Experiment," *Management Science* 35 (1989).

FIGURE 1-2
Waiting for a Resource

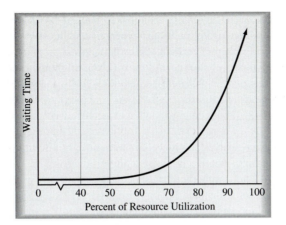

shifts to other problems, and when feedback finally arrives, momentum is lost and the link between cause and effect is severed. But in many circumstances it takes time to ensure that results are accurate: giving misleading feedback is even worse than giving no feedback. Finding the right balance between speed and reliability in providing feedback is crucial to effective experimentation.

Capacity

The ability to provide rapid feedback to a developer is in part affected by an organization's capacity for experimentation. Not surprisingly, when the number of experiments to be carried out exceeds capacity, the waiting time will grow very rapidly and the link between action and feedback is severed. What often surprises people, however, is that the waiting time in many real-world queues increases substantially even when we're not using our total capacity. In fact, the relationship between waiting time and utilization is not linear—queuing theory has shown that the waiting time typically increases gradually until a resource is utilized to around 70 percent of capacity, and then the length of the delays surges (see **Figure 1-2**).[9] Moreover, when people expect long delays, they tend to overload queues, slowing down the system even further. More experiments are submitted in the hope that one makes it through quickly, but without any sense of how it may affect the overall innovation process. Or simply, firms often lack the right incentives and organization to remove queues and speed up experimentation.

Sequence

Most large-scale experimentation involves more than one experiment, and, as we have seen, usually requires multiple iterations within that effort. When the identification of a solution involves more than a single experiment, the information gained from previous trials may serve as an important input to the design of the next one. When learning from one cycle in a set of experiments is incorporated into the next cycle, experimentation has been conducted

[9] This property of queuing systems often surprises managers even though it can be found in most operations management textbooks. For a very insightful discussion of queuing theory and its application to product development, see Don Reinertsen, *Managing the Design Factory* (The Free Press, 1997, Chapter 3).

sequentially. By contrast, when there is an established plan of experimental cycles that is *not* modified by the findings from previous experiments, the experiments have been performed in parallel. For example, you might first carry out a preplanned array of design experiments and analyze the results of the entire array. You might then run one or more additional verification experiments, as is the case in the field of formal design of experiments (DOE) methods. The experimentation cycles in the initial array are viewed as being carried out in parallel, while those in the second round have been carried out in series with respect to that initial array.

Parallel experimentation clearly can proceed more rapidly, but it does not take advantage of the potential for learning between and among trials. As a result, when parallel experimentation is used, the number of trials needed is usually much greater—but it's usually possible to get "there" faster. In comparison, getting "there" takes longer with a sequential approach: the number of trials conducted depends very much on how much a firm expects to learn between each round. For example, trying one hundred keys in a lock can be done one key at a time, or all keys at once, as long as enough identical locks are available. Since little can be learned between experiments, a sequential strategy would, on average, require fifty trials and thus cost only half as much—but also take fifty times longer.[10]

Signal-to-Noise Ratio

Experiments can be distorted when "noise"—variables other than the one being tested—influences results in ways that can't be controlled or measured. You will see in the following cases that managing noise was a major challenge, and various strategies were undertaken to do so. What's important in this effort is determining, first, whether what is being tested (the "signal") *is* something that can be defined in the absence of "noise," and second, whether the signal-to-noise ratio can be assured in different settings. This is not a trivial pursuit!

Type of Experiment

Not all experiments, structured or trial-and-error, are alike. Tweaking independent variables usually results in smaller changes in output—the kinds of changes that are desired in the incremental improvement of product and processes.[11] Alternatively, large variable manipulations or the introduction of new variables can foster a much wider search, thus increasing the probability of discovering more radical improvements and, at the same, inviting more failures. More radical experiments can point us in new directions and take us into unknown territories that may or may not result in more radical innovations—one has no way of

---

[10] The formal trade-off between sequential and parallel experimentation strategies is modeled and discussed in Christopher Loch, Christian Terwiesch and Stefan Thomke, "Parallel and Sequential Testing of Design Alternatives," *Management Science* 47, no. 5 (May 2001); and Stefan Thomke, Eric von Hippel and Roland Franke, "Modes of Experimentation: An Innovation Process and Competitive Variable," *Research Policy* 27 (1998).

[11] An exception is highly nonlinear systems where small changes in independent variables can result in large changes in dependent variables. Optimizing such systems can be challenging but experience has shown that increasing robustness, rather than a single point performance optimization via Monte Carlo-type methods, appears to be promising (e.g., in improving automotive crash safety). However, in many areas of engineering design, this will require much more experimentation capacity than is available to development teams today.

knowing in advance. As a result, real-world innovation needs to strike a healthy balance between incremental and radical experimentation.

Theme 3: Impact of New Technologies on Experimentation Strategies

Despite the critical role that experimentation plays in innovation, complex experiments have traditionally been costly and time consuming to run, and companies have been leery of dedicating resources to provide for them. Two interrelated consequences followed. Experimentation capacity has been constrained, and the number of experimental iterations has been limited. More subtly, the notion of "experimentation" has been confined to verification; testing, to arrive at the end of development programs, is designed and managed to find late-stage problems, or to assure the "success" of the process itself. And when the test itself becomes a high-profile event, such as the preliminary evaluation of a new and expensive weapon system, companies regard a successful outcome as one that results in *no new information or surprises and, hence, in no learning at all.*

Thus, given the costs and time heretofore associated with running experiments—as much as experimentation itself can generate learning—*"good failure"* can be a consequence, too. As we have seen, "failure" is a prime source of information, enabling experimenters to quickly sort the "what works" from the "what doesn't"; such efforts also stockpile knowledge, along with the bits and pieces available for future inspiration. Indeed, in the absence of "learning from failure," because of experimental capacity constraints and/or the number of iterations possible, experimentation itself can become a bottleneck to innovation.

Greater capacity for experimentation can be generated in two ways. New technologies and process innovations can make experimentation cheaper to perform overall. Alternatively, individual experiments can be made more efficient. Statistical methods for designing experiments have focused primarily on the latter option and have had a big impact on industrial R&D.[12] By manipulating multiple variables in a single experiment, while maintaining integrity in its statistical analysis, scientists and engineers can get more learning out of their experiments than their professional peers did in earlier times. However, even more structured methods cannot overcome all the limitations that scarce experimentation capacity poses in itself. That's where new information-based technologies come in.

These technologies slash experimentation cost and time, thereby not only bringing much-needed capacity aboard but also making "what if" ("blue sky") experiments possible. Until now, such efforts have been prohibitively expensive even if their long-term value was acknowledged. What if an airplane, a car, a drug, or a business was designed in a particular way? Not only could such technologies potentially provide new knowledge about how nature works but they could also fundamentally change how the fruits of that effort are harvested in innovations, process improvements, and ultimately, the new technologies themselves.

It's vital to appreciate how these technologies allow more learning more rapidly so that results (positive or negative) can be incorporated into further rounds of experiments at less expense. This is a fundamental shift in product development. While we all know that the cost of computers and related equipment and products has decreased, we do not immediately see

---

[12] Douglas Montgomery, *Design and Analysis of Experiments* (Wiley, 1991) is a good overview on the history and techniques of the statistical design and analysis of experiments.

the impact of this economic effect elsewhere—much less with experimentation. The economics change more than how experiments are run; the fact of lower costs influences what can be done—the "what if" possibilities noted above.

Thus, some technologies can make existing experimental activities more efficient, while others introduce entirely new ways of discovering novel concepts and/or solutions. Advances in some fields, such as computer simulation, are relevant to a wide variety of applications. Others, such as the scanning tunneling electron microscope, are germane to only a narrow range of applications—although the range of application for a given technique often broadens significantly over time. Nevertheless, a quick review of computer simulation techniques suggests what these advances in experimentation technologies actually imply.

Experimentation via computer simulation involves representing experimental objects and experimental environments in digital form, rather than in the form of physical objects tested within physical environments. As such, the interaction is within a computer in a type of virtual experiment. The advantages of substituting virtual experimentation via computer for experimentation with real physical objects are significant. For example, studying automobile structures via real car crashes clearly is quite expensive and requires a lot of time—a crash prototype can cost in excess of $1 million and often take a year to build and test.[13] In computer simulation, however, once the proper digital models have been created, a virtual car crash can be run again and again under varying conditions at very little additional cost per run. And a real car crash experiment happens very quickly, so the experimenter's ability to observe details is typically thwarted, even with high-speed cameras and well-instrumented cars and crash dummies. In contrast, a computer can be instructed to enact a virtual car crash as slowly as one likes; any structural element of the car (or minute section of a structural element) can be zeroed in on. It is thereby possible to observe the forces acting on that element and its response to those forces during the crash. Thus, computer simulation not only decreases the cost and time of an experimental cycle but can increase the depth and quality of analysis, leading to improved learning and ultimately to products of higher quality.

The ability to substitute a simulation for a "real" experiment requires, of course, more than the development of advanced computer equipment. It also demands the development of simulation models that are accurate for a given experimental purpose. Often, a simulation model is not fully accurate in ways that later turn out to matter. When this is recognized, virtual and physical experiments may be conducted in some combination so as to combat this source of error. (For example, auto designers supplement data gathered from virtual car crash experiments with data from real crash experiments using real cars, in order to assure themselves that the results of the virtual experiments also hold in the real world.)

At the same time, methods for conducting physical experiments are also advancing, e.g., in the building of prototypes. Complex three-dimensional objects used to require days or weeks of fabrication work in a machine shop. Many such shapes can now be made rapidly—in a few hours—by using computer-controlled machining equipment and/or equipment for creating objects via rapid prototyping technologies. Similarly, physical

---

[13] Stefan Thomke, Michael Holzner, and Touraj Gholami in "The Crash in the Machine," *Scientific American,* March 1999, explain how crash simulation has the potential to revolutionize automotive development.

FIGURE 1-3
Growth of
Computer
Performance
and Solvable
Problems[15]

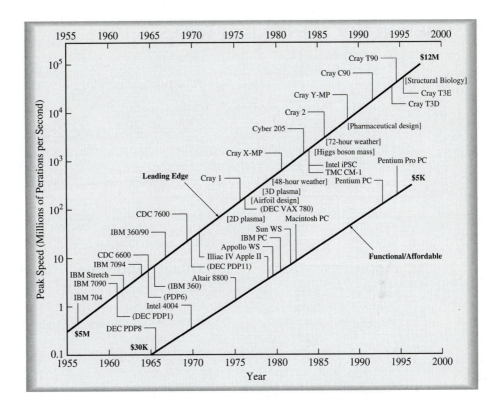

prototypes of complex electrical circuitry, custom integrated circuits, used to take months to create via "full custom" methods, and weeks to create via "Application-Specific Integrated Circuits" (ASIC) technology. Now, designers can create customized circuits in minutes at their desks or lab benches with so-called "Field Programmable Gate Arrays" (FPGAs).[14]

As the cost of computing keeps falling, thereby making all sorts of complex calculations faster and cheaper, and as new technologies emerge, virtually all companies are discovering that they have a greater capacity for rapid experimentation to investigate diverse product concepts (see **Figure 1-3**). Financial institutions, for example, now use computer simulations to test new financial instruments. In fact, the development of spreadsheet software itself totally changed financial modeling; even novices can perform many sophisticated "what if" experiments that were once prohibitively expensive.

[14] See Stefan Thomke, "Managing Experimentation in the Design of New Products," *Management Science* 44, no. 6 (1998); and Stefan Thomke, *Experimentation Matters* (HBS Press, 2003), (HBS Press, 2003), Chapters 2 and 7.

[15] Growth of computer technology since 1955, showing advances in average commercial performance and milestone events. Problems that are solvable in reasonable times at the indicated level of computer performance are shown in brackets. Approximate system prices are shown in dollars at the time. For more information, see Stefan Thomke, *Experimentation Matters* (HBS Press, 2003), page 29.

DESCRIPTION OF CASES AND ARTICLES

The three module themes will be addressed in the various teaching cases and readings. The following summary of the material will prepare you for what you can expect to learn.

The Final Voyage of the Challenger

This case is a historical account of the events that led to the space shuttle Challenger disaster. It provides an opportunity to examine the development of the shuttle rocket booster system and the critical interactions among scientists, engineers, and managers immediately before the tragic January 1986 launch. The case serves as an excellent study of complex product development processes by focusing on critical managerial challenges in product design, technical problem solving, testing, and managerial decision making. The role of experimentation is dubious here—it's captured in the notion of "testing." But testing is *not* equivalent to experimentation, a critical lesson of this case.

Apple PowerBook: Design Quality and Time to Market

In this case you will explore how the PowerBook was developed, particularly how the company managed prototyping and experimentation. Because it's your first "deep dive" into how experimentation and product development were intentionally combined, the lessons are thought-provoking. On the one hand, going from zero to a billion dollars in one year (what the PowerBook achieved) with one product is not trivial. On the other hand, the process by which that happened was hardly structured—and as such, neither sustainable nor replicable. A question left hanging is whether making the process more structured in fact lessens the creativity involved. The following case (IDEO) faces that issue squarely.

IDEO Product Development

IDEO, one of the world's leading product development firms, has a distinct and structured approach to innovation along with a determinedly creative culture. It is, therefore, a wonderful example of how innovation and organization can be joined. The case emphasizes IDEO's prototyping and experimentation processes, using the design of the Palm V handheld computer as a lens on the firm's product development operation. Unlike the haphazard process Apple employed in the PowerBook, the Palm project was a marvel of discipline—such that IDEO was asked to take on the rapid-fire development of a competing handheld. This project had to be completed in half the time of the Palm V and incorporated novel features.

Bank of America

Experimentation is not invariably about imagining exotic new products; it can be about creating seemingly mundane services to accommodate customers in settings where these in fact become novelties. Moreover, experimentation itself can be a short-lived phenomenon. In the Bank of America situation, the aim was to experiment with an array of amenities that, on the surface, were hardly revolutionary: TV monitors, complimentary coffee, "greeters." These services, however, were conceived of as temporary, introduced under careful conditions, monitored, tweaked, and either retained or rejected on the basis of that assessment. Going into extensive detail, the case shows how Bank of America carefully thought through its design and execution of experiments, all to be undertaken "live" in twenty-five bank branches in Atlanta, Georgia. That is, all experiments were run on actual customers, during working hours, and performed by bank employees. Included in the case is an analysis of the factors critical to any and all experimentation efforts (these are also listed previously within "Major Module Themes"), whether the experiments are run "real time" (as in the bank branches), in product development labs (as in Apple and IDEO), or as part of the lavish competition that is the America's Cup (the following case). The *Harvard Business Review* article "R&D Comes to Services" reinforces the lessons from this case study and shows how learning from experimentation is achieved in a service setting.

Team New Zealand

This case describes the design and development of Team New Zealand's yacht, *Black Magic,* for the 1995 America's Cup competition. Prior to this time, Cup entrants depended on highly experienced designers and rounds of small-scale physical prototypes to explore their "competitive advantage." For the 1995 competition, however, the "state-of-the-art" allowed many syndicates to deploy simulation technology for experimentation as well. The case shows various approaches to this deployment. With high stakes, exhausting trials, and a fight to the finish, the case is an exciting ride—as a race and as a demonstration of rapid learning that is taken advantage of within a system that includes boat design, sailing expertise, and crew enthusiasm. Once again, therefore, how experiments are organized, in themselves and as a system, is reinforced. The *Harvard Business Review* article "Enlightened Experimentation: The New Imperative for Innovation" explains how companies can leverage new experimentation technologies by changing their process, management, and organization of innovation. Following such an integrative approach to product development gave Team New Zealand a competitive advantage and accounted in part for winning America's Cup.

Eli Lilly and Company: Drug Development Strategy

In 1995, Eli Lilly has discovered a promising anti-migraine drug candidate using conventional research methods, but the compound has the typical 10 percent chance for passing grueling FDA-monitored clinical trials in order to gain market approval. Meanwhile, two scientists have been applying combinatorial chemistry, a new and still untried method for rapidly synthesizing new drug candidates, to make analogues of this current lead compound. Whereas a traditional chemist might take 7–10 days to make one candidate compound at a cost of $5,000–10,000, combinatorial chemistry allows a chemist to synthesize several thousands of compounds per month at a dramatically lower cost per candidate. The case series presents difficult product development choices (should Lilly release the leading compound to clinical trials or revise it further?) and also addresses the potential opportunities and threats of new technologies to development organizations and how their integration should be managed.

EXHIBIT
Themes of
Cases in
Module

Module 1: Building Capabilities for Experimentation, Learning, and Prototyping	
The Final Voyage of the Challenger	• Course and module overview • Introduction to complex development systems • Preview of the role of testing in managing uncertainty
Apple PowerBook: Design Quality and Time to Market	• Introduction to the power of product design • Prototyping methods and cultures • Interaction between products and development processes
IDEO Product Development	• Understanding systems for product innovation • Managing prototyping and experimentation • Processes for predictable and repeated product innovation
Bank of America	• Introduction to service development and innovation • Learning from experimentation: theory and practice • Managing failure in organizations • Article: "R&D Comes to Services" (*Harvard Business Review*)
Team New Zealand	• New technologies (CAD/CAE) and experimentation • Prototyping strategies • Integration of technologies into design processes • Reading: "Enlightened Experimentation" (*Harvard Business Review*)
Eli Lilly and Company: Drug Development Strategy	• Managing complex and risky development processes • The impact of new technologies on the economics of experimentation • New process paradigms and organizational change

The Final Voyage of the *Challenger*[1]

FLIGHT OF MISSION 51-L[2]

The ambient[3] air temperature at launch, 11:38 a.m., measured at ground level approximately 1,000 feet from the 51-L mission launch pad 39B, was 36 degrees Fahrenheit. The description of flight events is based on visual examination and image enhancement of film from NASA-operated cameras and telemetry[4] data transmitted from the *Challenger* to ground stations.

Time (Seconds from Lift-Off)

−6.566 *Challenger*'s liquid fuel main engines ignite in sequence and run to full thrust while the entire Shuttle structure is still bolted to the launch pad. This bends the Shuttle assembly forward from the bolts, and, when it springs back to vertical, the Solid Rocket Boosters' restraining bolts are explosively released. The maximum structural loads on the aft (rear) field joints (see **Exhibit 1** and **Exhibit 2** for details of the Space Shuttle and its

---

[1] This case is based on publicly available sources, especially Joseph Trento, *Prescription for Disaster* (1987); Trudy E. Bell and Karl Esch, "The Fatal Flaw in Flight 51-L," *IEEE Spectrum*, February 1987; and on a manuscript by former U.S. Navy Test Pilot and HBS MBA 1989, John T. Tartaglione. All the quotes and exhibits are from *Reports of the Presidential Commission on the Space Shuttle Accident* (1986).

[2] For Space Shuttle flights one through nine, NASA used the designation STS (Space Transportation System). After STS-9 NASA changed the method on numbering missions: Each flight was since designated by two numbers and a letter, e.g., 41-B. The first digit indicated the fiscal year of the scheduled launch ("4 for 1984), the second digit identified the launch site ("1"—Kennedy Space Center, Florida, "2"—Vandenberg Air Force Base, California), and the letter corresponded to the alphabetic sequence for the fiscal year ("B"—the second mission scheduled).

[3] Term used to denote surrounding environment.

[4] In this case, very accurate measurement of linear distance to an object by measuring the time required by a radar signal to echo back from the object.

Harvard Business School Case No. 9-691-037. Copyright 1990 President and Fellows of Harvard College. All rights reserved. For information: permissions@hbsp.harvard.edu.

This case was prepared by Oscar Hauptman and George Iwaki. HBS cases are developed solely for class discussion and do not necessarily illustrate effective or ineffective management.

main systems) of the Solid Rocket Boosters (SRB)[5] occur during the release "twang," exceeding even those of the maximum dynamic pressure period experienced later in flight.

0.000 Solid Rocket Motor ignition command.

+0.678 Strong puff of gray smoke spurts from the vicinity of the aft field joint of the right Solid Rocket Booster (SRB). The vaporized material streaming from the joint indicates incomplete sealing within the joint.

between +0.836 and +2.500 Eight more puffs of darker smoke spurt from the same area of the joint.

+2.733 Last smoke is seen from the aft field joint.

+7.734 *Challenger* transmits: "Roll Program."

Houston: "Roger, roll *Challenger*."

Challenger main engines are throttled to 104 percent.

+19.869 Main engines are throttled down to 94 percent.

+35.389 Main engines are throttled down to 65 percent.

+37 until +64 *Challenger* encounters several wind shear conditions, which creates forces on the vehicle with relatively large fluctuations. These are immediately sensed and countered by the guidance, navigation, and control systems. The steering system of the SRB responds to all commands and wind shear effects; the wind shear causes the system to be more active than on any previous flight.

+45.000 Three bright flashes, each lasting less than 0.033 seconds, appear downstream of *Challenger*'s right wing (similar flashes have been seen on other flights).

+51.870 Main engines are throttled up to 104 percent.

+58.788 A very small flame (detected on image-enhanced film) appears on the right SRB in the area of the aft field joint.

+59.262 Visible flame (plume) appears on the right SRB in the area of the aft field joint.

+60.014 Pressure differential develops between the right and left SRB. Telemetry data indicate right SRB pressure is lower, confirming leak in the area of the field joint.

+62.000 The left SRB starts to counter the yaw[6] and pitch[7] caused by reduced thrust from the leaking right SRB. During the next nine seconds the Shuttle control systems work to correct anomalies in pitch and yaw rates.

+62.404 Peak yaw rate response to wind shear.

+64.660 An abrupt change in the shape and color of the plume indicates mixing with leaking hydrogen from the External Tank; telemetry indicates changes in the hydrogen tank pressure, confirming the leak.

+64.705 A bright sustained glow develops on the underside of the *Challenger*.

+65.000 Houston transmits: "*Challenger*, go at throttle up."

Challenger: "Roger. Go at throttle up."

+72.000 Telemetered data indicate a wide variety of flight systems acting against the forces destroying the *Challenger*.

---

[5] Solid Rocket Booster (SRB) or Solid Rocket Motor (SRM) can be used interchangeably.
[6] Angular rotation of an aircraft about a vertical axis.
[7] The angular motion of an aircraft or ship from the vertical.

+72.200   Lower strut linking SRB and External Tank is severed or pulled away from the weakened External Tank permitting the right SRB to rotate around the upper attachment strut.

+73.124   White vapor pattern is blooming from the side of the External Tank bottom dome. The structural failure of the External Tank culminates with the entire aft dome dropping off. This releases massive amounts of liquid hydrogen from the tank and creates a sudden forward thrust of 2.8 million pounds, pushing the External Tank upward into the intertank structure. At about the same time, the rotating right SRB impacts the intertank structure and the lower part of the liquid oxygen tank.

+73.137   The structures fail with white vapor appearing in the intertank region. Within milliseconds there is massive, almost explosive burning of the hydrogen streaming from the failed tank bottom and the liquid oxygen breach in the area of the intertank.

+73.618   Last telemetry data received from *Challenger*.

+74.130   Last radio frequency signal from *Challenger*.

At this point in its trajectory, while traveling at Mach 1.92 at an altitude of 40,000 feet the *Challenger* is totally enveloped in the explosive burn. The burn of the propellants occurs as the Shuttle exits the oxygen-hydrogen flames; the reddish-brown colors of the fuel burn are on the edge of the main fireball. The Orbiter, under severe aerodynamic loads, breaks into several large sections that emerge from the fireball—the main engine/tail section with the engines still burning, one wing of the Orbiter, and the forward fuselage trailing a mass of umbilical lines pulled loose from the payload bay.

BACKGROUND OF THE SPACE SHUTTLE

The Space Shuttle concept was developed by the National Aeronautics and Space Administration (NASA) in the late 1960s and early 1970s as a reusable and efficient means of space transportation during the austere fiscal environment of the early 1970s. In September 1969, two months after the initial lunar landing, a Space Task Group chaired by the Vice President of the United States offered a choice of three long-range plans:

1. An $8–10 billion per year program involving personnel for a Mars expedition, a space station in lunar orbit, and a five-person Earth-orbiting station serviced by a reusable ferry, or Space Shuttle;
2. An intermediate program, costing less than $8 billion annually, that would include the Mars mission;
3. A relatively modest $4–5.7 billion a year program that would include an Earth-orbiting space station and the Space Shuttle as its link to Earth.

In March 1970, President Nixon made it clear that, while he favored a continuing active space program, funding on the order of Apollo was not possible. He instead opted for the Shuttle-tended space base as a long-range goal, but deferred going ahead with the space station pending development of the Space Shuttle vehicle. Thus the reusable Space Shuttle, earlier considered only the transport element of a broad, multi-objective space plan, became the focus of NASA's near-term future.

After considering an array of potential designs, NASA went back to the drawing board in 1971 aware that development cost rather than system capability would probably be the determining factor in getting a green light for the Shuttle development. Conceptual design and development decisions to justify the Space Shuttle were made on a cost-benefit analysis basis. In January 1972 Dr. Oskar Morgenstern and Dr. Klaus Heiss of the Princeton-based organization Mathematica produced a widely cited cost-benefit analysis of the Space Shuttle program that predicted that the shuttle could orbit payloads for as little as $100 a pound. The main premise of the study was an assumed flight rate of 60 launches per year with full payloads of 65,000 pounds. After lengthy negotiations among the Office of Management and Budget (OMB), White House, and NASA, the Space Shuttle program was scaled from significantly higher earlier estimates to a total program cost of $5.1 billion. In the process, the more expensive all-liquid-fuel design was replaced by a mixed solid (SRB) and liquid (External Tank) system. Werner von Braun (the "father of the American space program"), among others at NASA, questioned the use of solid rocket boosters on grounds of safety and controllability.

The design that emerged is the Space Shuttle as it is known now: a three-element system composed of the Orbiter, an expendable External Fuel Tank carrying liquid propellants for the Orbiter's engines, and two recoverable solid rocket boosters.

NASA divided managerial responsibility for the space shuttle program among three of its field centers. The Johnson Space Center in Houston, Texas, was assigned the management of the Orbiter. The Marshall Space Flight Center (MSFC) in Huntsville, Alabama, was responsible for the Shuttle's main engines, the External Tank, and the Solid Rocket Boosters. The Kennedy Space Center (KSC) on Merrit Island, Florida, was responsible for assembly of the Shuttle's components.

By August of 1972 NASA began to award major contracts for the delivery of the Space Shuttle. Rockwell International Corporation's Space Transportation Systems Division got the design and development of the Space Shuttle Orbiter. The development and fabrication of the External Tank went to Martin Marietta Denver Aerospace. Rocketdyne, a division of Rockwell, was selected to develop the Orbiter Main Engines.

DEVELOPMENT OF THE SOLID ROCKET BOOSTER

Morton Thiokol Wins the Contract

Proposals for the solid fuel rocket motor design and production for the shuttle program were solicited by NASA in 1973 from Aerojet Solid Propulsion Co., Lockheed Propulsion Co., Morton Thiokol, and United Technologies. The NASA Source Evaluation Board composite rating of Morton Thiokol's proposals was tied for second and third with United Technologies. This consisted of being rated fourth on design, development, and verification; second on manufacturing, refurbishment, and product support; and first on management. In a December 12, 1973 report the NASA officials indicated that Morton Thiokol's "cost advantages were substantial and consistent throughout all areas evaluated" (Thiokol bid $100 million lower than the next competitor). They also singled out Thiokol's joint design for special mention:

> The Thiokol motor case joints utilized dual O-rings and test ports between seals, enabling a simple leak check without pressurizing the entire motor. This innovative design feature increased reliability and decreased operations at the launch site, indicating good attention to low cost (design, development, testing, and engineering) and production. We noted that the

board's analysis of cost factors indicated that Thiokol could do a more economical job than any of the other proposers in both development and the production phases of the program; and that accordingly, the cost per flight to be expected from a Thiokol-built motor would be the lowest.

Aerojet Solid Propulsion Co. criticized several weaknesses of a segmented design to support its own single case design: "Acceptance of the integrity of the O-ring is largely a matter of faith."

Nevertheless, the cost-plus-award-fee contract, estimated to be worth $800 million, was awarded to Thiokol on November 20, 1973, with the board's summarizing: "We concluded that the main criticisms of the Thiokol proposal in the Mission Suitability evaluation were technical in nature, were readily correctable, and the costs to correct did not negate the sizable Thiokol cost advantage."

The design envisioned by Thiokol, which, in contrast to the other bidders, had never built anything on the scale of the SRB, was of 149-foot-long tubes, 12 feet in diameter; each SRB weighed 2 million pounds, or one thousand tons (see Exhibit 2 for SRB details). The boosters were to be assembled from four segments, shipped from Utah, at the launch center. Because the SRBs were very heavy and could be damaged in transit, some at NASA tried to push for the contractor to locate its production facility right at Kennedy Space Center.

Solid Rocket Booster Design

The Thiokol design for the shuttle SRMs was based on the segmented design of the Titan III solid fuel rocket motor. The Titan III was designed and produced by United Technologies in the 1950s for the Air Force for the single-use transportation of space satellites without personnel. Unlike the Titan, Thiokol's SRMs were designed for multiple firings—up to 20 times.

Joint Design

In contrast to a single case design, a segmented design requires mating numerous case segments' joints at each point of connection (see **Exhibit 3** for details of the joint). In both the Titan's and the Shuttle's joints a tang on the rim of one segment slips into a clevis on the rim of the next, and the two segments are fastened together by pins. Joint sealing is provided by rubber O-rings, installed during assembly.

Despite their many similarities, the Thiokol's SRMs and the Titan's motors had some significant design differences. The tang portion of the Thiokol joints was longer in order to accommodate two O-rings instead of one, resulting in different flexibility of the tang. At the same time, because the shuttle's joints contained a primary and a secondary O-ring, while the Titan's joints contained single O-rings, the former were perceived by NASA and Thiokol as redundant, and, consequently, more reliable. Joe Kilminster, Thiokol's Vice President of Space Booster Programs (see **Exhibit 4** for organizational structure), believed in the implicit safety margin of the redundancy:

> We felt we could only be in a *more* safe condition having two O-rings there than with a single O-ring. In an overall sense, the comfort zone, if you will, was expanded because of the fact that the shuttle joint was so similar to the Titan joint, and its many uses had shown successful operation. That's why a lot of—I guess "faith" is the right word—was based on the fact that the Titan had had all these tests and successful experience.

Repeated comparisons were made to the successful Titan III joint in documents supporting the shuttle's SRMs. This faith in the design translated directly to a classification system used by NASA in which designs are classified by their risk to the mission (see **Exhibit 5** for NASA's safety classification system).

Thiokol's O-rings differed from Titan's in their production. Even though both were Viton rubber, while the Titan's O-rings were molded in one piece, the Shuttle's O-rings were made of five sections, glued together. The vendor had to routinely make repairs to voids and inclusions in the rubber received from the material supplier. Surface inspections were performed by Thiokol and the vendor before assembly.

The Putty

The joint seal design included a zinc chromate putty, to be applied to the insulation face of the primary O-rings prior to assembly; it was intended as a thermal barrier between the combustion gases and the O-rings. Thiokol engineers believed the putty to be plastic, so that under the pressure of the combustion gases it will force the primary O-rings into the gap between the tang and the clevis, creating what was dubbed "pressure actuation of the O-ring seal." This pressure actuation sealing was required to occur very early during the SRM ignition, because the gap between the tang and the clevis could increase during ignition.

Horizontal Assembly

Thiokol started testing the SRMs in the mid-1970s. Booster inspection and 11 static tests were conducted on the horizontal Solid Rocket stack at Thiokol and they required horizontal assembly of the boosters. As a Thiokol engineer described it: "We were concerned very much about the horizontal assembly that we had to do to do the static tests. The Titan had always been assembled vertically, and so there had never been a larger rocket motor to our knowledge that was assembled horizontally."

The horizontal assembly required changes in tolerances of the segments to create a larger gap between the tang and clevis. For reasons of test fidelity, the design of the flight SRMs was identical to the SRMs designed for the static tests.

SRM TESTS AND PROBLEMS

Pre-Flight Tests

One of the early critical pre-flight tests was the 1977 "hydroburst" test, during which the SRM case was pressurized with water to half the expected pressure of an ignited motor. According to Arnold Thompson, during these tests "joint rotation" was discovered. This meant in technical terms that the clevis and tang bent away from each other, the joint was opening rather than closing, reducing pressure on the O-ring, and, consequently, reducing joint sealing. Thiokol reported these results to Marshall Space Flight Center, but, believing that the problem was not critical, did not schedule either additional tests or corrective action.

Reaction from Marshall was rapid and alarmed. On September 22, 1977, Glenn Eudy, Chief Engineer at Marshall for the SRMs, wrote a memorandum to Alexander McCool, Director of Structures and Propulsion Laboratory. Eudy pointed out that the clearance between the tang and clevis, already increased from the Titan specification to allow easier assembly, became excessive, and did not allow enough squeeze on the O-rings to ensure their sealing. Eudy wrote that:

> . . . Some people believe this deficiency must be corrected by some method such as shimming[8] and perhaps design modification to the case joint for hardware which has not been final machined. . . . I personally believe that our first choice should be to correct the design in a way that eliminates the possibility of O-ring clearance. . . . Since this is a very critical SRM issue, it is requested that the assignment results be compiled in such a manner as to permit review at the . . . Director's level as well as project manager.

After seeing the data from the same hydroburst test another Marshall engineer, Leon Ray, wrote a report on October 21, 1977, titled "Solid Rocket Motor Joint Leakage Study." Ray wrote that failure to change the Thiokol design would be "unacceptable," and made recommendations similar to Eudy's analysis.

After a lengthy exchange of memos and visits to the O-ring manufacturers, the design was modified: To tighten the joints' fit and increase the squeeze in the O-rings, the larger tolerances were counteracted by putting metal shims between the outer walls of the tang and the clevis.

The rationale for retaining the Thiokol's joint design (written by a Thiokol engineer and attached to the Critical Items List) explained that ". . . the joint concept is basically the same as the single O-ring successfully employed on the Titan III Solid Rocket Motor." While the report cited the Titan's excellent history, the leak and hydroburst tests, and the static motor firings, it noted that certain test results indicated "that tang-to-clevis movement [joint rotation] will unseat [move out of normal position] the secondary O-ring at operating pressures."

The final report by a NASA committee for verification-certification of September 15, 1980, stated that the original hydroburst, along with lightweight case tests underway at the time, satisfied the recommendations of Ray's report.

Test Flights

The continuous budgetary pressure forced NASA to reduce the planned five-Orbiter fleet to four. This, combined with technological uncertainties, delayed the initial orbital test flights by more than two years. The first Shuttle test flights were conducted from the Dreyden Flight Research Facility, California, in 1977. The test craft was the Orbiter Enterprise, a full-size vehicle that lacked engines and other systems needed for orbital flight. The purpose of these tests was to check out the aerodynamics and flight control characteristics of the Orbiter in atmospheric flight. Mounted piggy-back atop a modified Boeing 747, the Enterprise was carried to altitude and released for a gliding approach and landing at the Mojave Desert Test Center. Five such flights were made.

Extensive ground tests followed between 1977–1980, including vibration tests of the entire assembly at Marshall. Main engine test firings were conducted at the National Space Technology Laboratory in Mississippi and on the launch pad at Kennedy. By early 1981, the Shuttle was ready for an orbital flight test program, carefully designed to include more than 1,000 tests and data collection procedures. Originally intended as a six-mission program, the orbital test series was reduced to four flights.

---

[8] A shim is a thin strip of material, used singly or multiplied, to take up space between clamped parts.

On April 12, 1981, Orbiter Columbia was successfully launched with astronauts John Young and Robert Crippen aboard. Its main payload was a flight instrumentation pallet containing equipment for recording temperature, pressure, and acceleration level at various points around the Orbiter. In addition, there were checkouts of the cargo bay doors, altitude control system, and orbital maneuvering system. With the landing of STS-4 on July 4, 1982, the orbital flight test program came to an end with 95 percent of its test objectives accomplished. The interval between flights was reduced from nine to four months, then to three. NASA declared all Space Shuttle flights after STS-4 "operational" in the sense that payload requirements would take precedence over spacecraft testing, and would require larger crews.

Problem Detection and Joint Reclassification

In December 1982, after the erosion of the primary O-ring detected on the November 1982 flight of STS-5, the joint was reclassified from "Redundant components, the failure of **both** could cause loss of life or vehicle" (Criticality 1R) to "Loss of life or vehicle if **the component** fails" (Criticality 1). The revised Critical Items List noted: "Leakage of primary O-ring seal is classified as a single failure point due to possibility of loss of sealing at the secondary O-ring because of joint rotation after motor pressurization (see **Exhibit 6** for reclassification documents)."

The failure effect summary read: "Actual Loss—Loss of mission, vehicle, and crew due to metal erosion, burn through, and probable case burst resulting in fire and deflagration."

However, this reclassification was not communicated throughout the Thiokol organization. While the field joint had been classified as Criticality 1 since 1982, most of the problem reporting paperwork generated by Thiokol and Marshall continued to list it as Criticality 1R, perhaps leading some managers to believe that redundancy still existed. Roger Boisjoly, Staff Engineer at the Thiokol SRB program, explained: "The working troops—and I consider myself one of the working troops—had no knowledge of the thing being changed to a Criticality 1. So far as we were concerned, we had two seals that were redundant."

The first O-ring problems to cause real alarm happened February 3, 1984, on the 10th shuttle flight (41-B), when O-rings on both nozzle joints showed erosion. Thiokol personnel reported this erosion soon afterward at an early Flight Readiness Review (see **Exhibit 7** for Flight Readiness Review Levels) for the next flight. The field joint erosion on STS-2, as well as signs of heat damage to an O-ring in STS-6, were then brought up for the first time at a Flight Readiness Review.

The Marshall Problem-Assessment System Report on the mission noted: "Remedial action—none required," and added, "Possibility exists for some O-ring erosion on future flights." Thiokol's computer analysis, based on empirical data from tests on mock-up parts, indicated that O-rings would still seal even if eroded by as much as 0.09 inch—nearly one-third of their diameter. Thiokol reported: "Therefore, this is not a constraint to future launches." This view led Larry Mulloy (engineering degree), manager of Marshall's SRB project, to introduce the concept that a certain amount of erosion was actually acceptable, along with the notion that the O-rings carried a margin of safety.

At the Level I Flight Readiness Review briefing for the thirteenth flight (41-G) on September 26, 1984, Mulloy referred to "allowed erosion." At a meeting on February 12, 1985, Mulloy and Thiokol personnel spoke of the observed blow-by (leakage of combustion gases) of O-rings in two field joints as an "acceptable risk" (see **Exhibit 8** for a sample of Shuttle Projects Office Board summary of action items and problems).

Meanwhile, the worst seal failure yet had taken place on mission 51-B, launched April 29, 1985. The primary O-ring on one nozzle joint eroded away by 0.171 inch, two-thirds of its diameter, while the secondary ring was eroded by 0.032 inch—the first instance of erosion to a secondary O-ring. Soot and grease on the booster showed that hot gases had blown past the primary seal in the nozzle joint, indicating that for some two minutes into the flight the O-rings had not sealed at all. Upon receiving the report of the 51-B primary ring failure, Mulloy and the Marshall Problem Assessment Committee placed a "launch constraint" on the shuttle system. A typical launch constraint includes all open (unresolved) problems coded Criticality 1, 1R, 2, 2R until they are resolved or evidence of sufficient rationale to conclude that a problem will not occur on the flight vehicle during pre-launch, launch, or flight. The SRM system contained numerous Criticality 1 items primarily because the SRM had few redundant features. There were some 706 critical items that had been identified on the SRM since 1978 (see **Exhibit 9** for SRM critical items list chronology).

After the launch constraint was imposed, Mulloy waived[9] it for each Shuttle flight after July 10, 1985.

Thiokol's O-Ring Task Force

In July 1985, Thiokol set up an internal task force to solve the O-ring problems. However, the task force was slow in getting started. Boisjoly was getting frustrated for not getting support from Kilminster (master's in mechanical engineering): "He [Kilminster] felt, I guess, that we were crying wolf. We were fighting all the major inertia in the plant, just like everyone else, and yet we were supposed to be this tiger team to get a very severe problem solved."

In a memorandum to Robert Lund (mechanical engineer), Vice President of Engineering, dated July 31, 1985, Boisjoly noted the group's "essential nonexistence," adding that the consequences of not dealing with the seal problems "would be a catastrophe of the highest order—loss of human life" (see **Exhibit 10** for full text). By October 1985, Robert Ebeling, Manager SRM Igniter and Final Assembly, wrote to Allan McDonald, Director SRM: "HELP! The seal task force is being delayed by every possible means. . . . This is a red flag."

On December 4, 1985, after discussing erosion to both nozzle joints on flight 23 (61-B), Mulloy noted that the "SRB joint O-ring performance [was] within [our] experience base." Since the risk of O-ring erosion was accepted and almost expected, it was no longer considered an anomaly to be resolved before the next flight.

LAUNCH DECISION OF MISSION 51-L

Delays

Bad weather and Kennedy Space Center work schedule slippage lingering from the delayed launch of mission 61-C delayed mission 51-L beyond its initial launch date of January 22, 1986. Rescheduled for January 27, the launch was temporarily halted due to an exterior hatch handle problem, which was resolved early on during the launch sequence. However,

---

[9] A waiver is a short-term, intermediate NASA procedure acknowledging that a specific problem has been identified and diagnosed not to jeopardize the forthcoming mission. Two hundred and thirteen items were waived for mission 51-L, 18 of them on the SRMs alone.

the launch was later delayed once more as a result of unfavorable wind conditions at Kennedy.

In the meantime, on January 23, 1986, the entire problem of erosion to both nozzle joints and the field joints had been officially "closed" by Marshall's problem-reporting system.

Preparations

On January 27, 1986, 1:00 p.m. (EST)[10], Larry Wear, NASA's SRM Projects Office, Marshall Space Center (see **Exhibit 11** for the list of participants of the teleconferences and their titles and affiliations) had asked Boyd Brinton, Morton Thiokol's Manager Space Booster Project, whether Morton Thiokol had any concerns about predicted low temperatures and about what Morton Thiokol had said about cold temperatures' effects following January 1985 flight 51-C. Brinton telephoned Thompson and other Morton Thiokol engineers in Utah to ask them to determine if there were concerns based on predicted weather conditions. Ebeling and other engineers were notified and asked for evaluation.

2:00 p.m.

Mission Management Team Meeting, NASA Level I and II readiness was centered around the temperature at the launch facility and weather conditions predicted for launch at 9:38 a.m. on January 28.

4:00 p.m.

Ebeling called McDonald in Florida to get the predicted temperature data around the time of launch. He called back with data—temperature around 26 degrees—and requested Ebeling to involve Lund and to prepare the engineers for a teleconference that he would set up.

5:15 p.m.

McDonald called Cecil Houston, MSFC Resident Manager at KSC, informing him that Morton Thiokol engineering had concerns regarding O-ring temperatures. Houston indicated that he would set up a teleconference with MSFC and Morton Thiokol. Then he called the NASA chain of command (Judson Lovingood) and asked to set up the teleconference. Lovingood called Stan Reinartz at MSFC and set up the teleconference for 5:45 p.m.

First Teleconference

Started at 5:45 p.m. with numerous participants at KSC, MSFC and Utah. Concerns regarding temperature effects on the O-rings were discussed, with Morton Thiokol expressing the opinion that launch should be delayed until noon or later. Another teleconference was set up for 8:45 p.m. to transmit the data to all the parties and to have more personnel involved. McDonald relayed the news of the teleconference back to Ebeling in Utah and requested that they fax copies of any relevant charts and information before the conference.

More Preparations

At 6:30 p.m. Lovingood called Reinartz and told him that if Morton Thiokol persists they should not launch. He also suggested to inform Aldrich, Manager, National Transportation

[10] All times are given in EST—Eastern Standard Time.

Systems (Level II) of the teleconference to prepare him for Level I meeting and the possibility of another delay.

7:00 p.m.

Reinartz and Mulloy visited Dr. William Lucas, Director MSFC, and Jim Kingsbury, Director of Science and Engineering, MSFC, in their motel room to inform them of Morton Thiokol's concerns and the planned teleconference.

Second Teleconference

From 8:15 p.m. 14 Morton Thiokol manager and engineers huddled around a conference table in Wasatch, Utah. At 8:45 p.m., after the various documents were prepared and faxed, a three-way teleconference was initiated with MSFC and KSC. The three groups were clustered around speakerphones through which they spoke and listened. This caused some confusion about location and identity of speakers.

The Thiokol engineers in Utah took the lead, presenting the hastily prepared documents they had just faxed, which outlined their concerns about the effect of the low temperatures on the O-rings (see **Exhibit 12** for originals of main text). Boisjoly and Thompson reviewed the accumulated history of the static and flight tests, describing the data of erosion and blow-by of the primary O-ring. The effect of the primary O-ring blow-by on the performance of the secondary O-ring was also discussed. Some details of the technical data were exchanged between the engineers.

Boisjoly emphasized that the effect of lower temperatures on the O-rings would slow the sealing reaction of the primary O-ring, resulting in greater amounts of hot gas released past the primary seal and, possibly, erosion of the secondary seal. Boisjoly and Thompson attempted to convince Marshall, Kennedy, and Thiokol teams of the danger in launching outside of the temperature of their experience base. "A launch at low temperature is . . . away from the direction of goodness. I cannot quantify it but I know that it is away from the direction of goodness," argued Boisjoly.

Marshall and Kennedy people concentrated on the information faxed to them about the previous coldest launch, on January 1985, (51-C, motor number SRM-15), which seemed, at least qualitatively, to have the worst blow-by of any previously observed—it showed deep and black soot deposit and arcing of the primary O-ring in the field joint. Boisjoly was queried about more supporting data, but was unable to quantify the negative impact of the observed soot from the blow-by on previous launches. He referred to the plot from the previous seven launches that exhibited signs of O-ring erosion (**Exhibit 13**), but was unable to demonstrate a correlation between temperature and O-ring erosion from the chart, because severe erosion also happened at 75 degrees; Boisjoly repeated his negative qualitative assessment of the O-ring erosion.

Lund summarized the discussion and made it clear that the engineering people would not recommend a launch below 53 degrees Fahrenheit: "Within our experience base, we should not operate any solid rocket motor at any temperature colder than we have previously operated one, which was 51-C."

At that point in the conference, NASA's Mulloy burst out over the network, "My God, Morton Thiokol! When do you want me to launch—next April?" He contended that Morton Thiokol was inappropriately attempting to establish a new Launch Commit criterion at the last minute before a launch.

Hardy (at Marshall) seconded Mulloy's apparent incredulity at Morton Thiokol's recommendation but declared that he would not fly without Morton Thiokol's concurrence.

Reinartz (at Kennedy) commented that the SRMs were qualified from 40 to 90 degrees Fahrenheit, and that the 53 degrees recommendation was consistent with that range. Houston (at Kennedy) interrupted, commenting that the early morning temperature at Kennedy would not reach the fifties until Thursday (two days later).

The NASA people began to question the interpretation of the data. They cited several previous launches that had occurred at cold temperatures before 51-C. McDonald commented about the static tests history, which Boisjoly had just described, and indicated that he had strong reservations about the conclusiveness of Boisjoly's data, leading many in the teleconference network to interpret these reservations as being opposed to a "no launch" decision.

Kilminster (in Utah) was again queried by NASA about the recommendation of his engineering staff, and he stated that he would not go against the recommendation of his people. NASA then asked Morton Thiokol to reassess the data based on the controversy brought up during the teleconference. At this point, around 10:30 p.m. Eastern Standard Time, Morton Thiokol asked for a five-minute caucus offline to discuss the situation.

CAUCUSING OFFLINE

At Thiokol

Approximately ten engineers participated in the caucus along with Jerry Mason, Senior Vice President Wasatch Operations (aeronautical engineer); Kilminster; Calvin Wiggins, Vice President and General Manager Space Division (degree in chemistry); and Lund. Mason set the tone of the caucus by declaring that a management decision was necessary (see **Exhibit 14** for Boisjoly's recall).

During the caucus Boisjoly and Thompson continued to vigorously press their case but there was a feeling in the room that Boisjoly had not conclusively demonstrated a correlation between temperature and O-ring's blow-by. Boisjoly was frustrated and ill at ease from the tone of the meeting, and from being unable to quantify his technical judgment about the criticalness of temperature. He felt that there was a determination to launch, with the burden on the engineers to prove without reasonable doubt that it was not safe to do so. During the caucus, not a single positive statement had been made by the engineering staff for a launch.

Mason and the other vice presidents (Kilminster, Lund, and Wiggins) huddled at the end of the conference table opposite Boisjoly and Thompson. Mason repeated his statement that a management decision was necessary. He turned to Lund and asked him to take off his engineering hat and put on his management hat. From that point on, the managers formulated the arguments for their decision to launch, excluding inputs from Boisjoly and Thompson.

At Kennedy Space Center

When Morton Thiokol in Utah went off the network, a conversation ensued between McDonald, Reinartz, Mulloy, Houston, and Buchanan. McDonald challenged Reinartz's rationale that SRM was qualified at 40 degrees to 90 degrees and Mulloy proposed a late afternoon launch when temperatures would be above the 53 degrees benchmark. NASA officials cited weather problems related to an afternoon launch.

APPROVAL

Around 11:05 p.m., Morton Thiokol came back on line. Kilminster and Lund reversed their earlier recommendation against the launch, citing the inconclusive nature of the data. Kilminster then described the rationale for the decision to approve the launch.

When Kilminster finished his explanation, Hardy (at Marshall) asked him to put the recommendations in writing and send it by fax to both Kennedy and Marshall.

11:15 to 11:30 p.m

McDonald continued to argue for delay, and indicated that if anything happened he would not want to have to explain to the Board of Inquiry. He indicated that he would cancel the launch due to: (1) O-ring problem at low temperature, (2) booster recovery ships heading into wind toward shore due to high seas, and (3) icing conditions on launch pad. He was told by Mulloy and Reinartz that it was not his concern and that his concern would be passed on in advisory capacity.

At 11:45 p.m. Kilminster faxed a signed technical memo.

MTI Assessment of Temperature Concern on SRM-25 (51L) Launch

0   Calculations show that SRM-25 o-rings will be 20° colder than SRM-15 o-rings

0   Temperature data not conclusive on predicting primary o-ring blow-by

0   Engineering assessment is that:

    0   Colder o-rings will have increased effective durometer ("harder")

    0   "Harder" o-rings will take longer to "seat"

        0   More gas may pass primary o-ring before the primary seal seats (relative to SRM-15)

            0   Demonstrated sealing threshold is 3 times greater than 0.038" erosion experienced on SRM-15

    0   If the primary seal does not seat, the secondary seal will seat

        0   Pressure will get to secondary seal before the metal parts rotate

            0   O-ring pressure leak check places secondary seal in outboard position which minimizes sealing time

0   MTI recommends STS-51L launch proceed on 28 January 1986

    0   SRM-25 will not be significantly different from SRM-15

[signature]

Joe C. Kilminster, Vice President
Space Booster Programs

Morton Thiokol Inc.
Wasatch Division

Information on this page was prepared to support an oral presentation
and cannot be considered complete without the oral discussion

EXHIBIT 1 Space Shuttle Systems

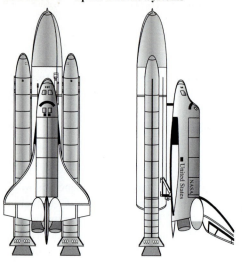

Artist's drawing depicts Space Shuttle stacked for launch in view from dorsal side of Orbiter (left) and from the left side of stack.

Mechanical Subsystems

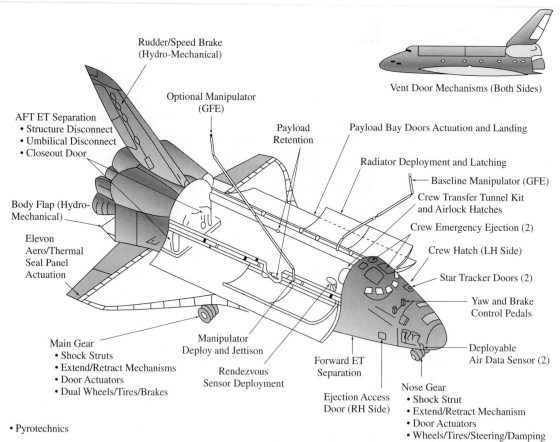

Rudder/Speed Brake (Hydro-Mechanical)

Optional Manipulator (GFE)

Vent Door Mechanisms (Both Sides)

AFT ET Separation
• Structure Disconnect
• Umbilical Disconnect
• Closeout Door

Payload Retention

Payload Bay Doors Actuation and Landing

Radiator Deployment and Latching

Baseline Manipulator (GFE)

Crew Transfer Tunnel Kit and Airlock Hatches

Body Flap (Hydro-Mechanical)

Crew Emergency Ejection (2)

Crew Hatch (LH Side)

Elevon Aero/Thermal Seal Panel Actuation

Star Tracker Doors (2)

Yaw and Brake Control Pedals

Main Gear
• Shock Struts
• Extend/Retract Mechanisms
• Door Actuators
• Dual Wheels/Tires/Brakes

Manipulator Deploy and Jettison

Rendezvous Sensor Deployment

Forward ET Separation

Deployable Air Data Sensor (2)

Ejection Access Door (RH Side)

Nose Gear
• Shock Strut
• Extend/Retract Mechanism
• Door Actuators
• Wheels/Tires/Steering/Damping

• Pyrotechnics

Artist's drawing depicts Space Shuttle stacked for launch in view from dorsal side of Orbiter (left) and from the left side of stack.

EXHIBIT 1
(*continued*)

**Space Shuttle
Lightweight External Tank**

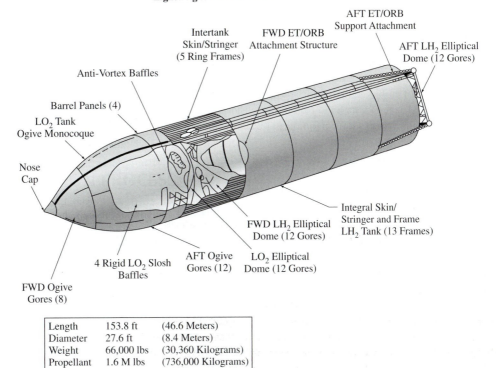

Length	153.8 ft	(46.6 Meters)
Diameter	27.6 ft	(8.4 Meters)
Weight	66,000 lbs	(30,360 Kilograms)
Propellant	1.6 M lbs	(736,000 Kilograms)

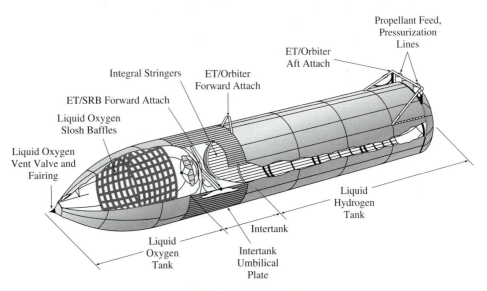

Partial cutaway drawing of External Tank shows oxygen tank
at left, intertank to its right and hydrogen tank at right.

EXHIBIT 2
SRB Details

Cutaway view of the Solid Rocket Booster showing Solid Rocket Motor propellant and aft field joint

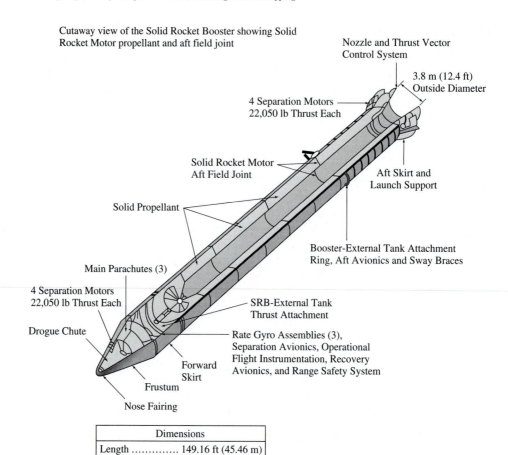

Nozzle and Thrust Vector Control System

3.8 m (12.4 ft) Outside Diameter

4 Separation Motors 22,050 lb Thrust Each

Solid Rocket Motor Aft Field Joint

Aft Skirt and Launch Support

Solid Propellant

Booster-External Tank Attachment Ring, Aft Avionics and Sway Braces

Main Parachutes (3)

4 Separation Motors 22,050 lb Thrust Each

SRB-External Tank Thrust Attachment

Drogue Chute

Rate Gyro Assemblies (3), Separation Avionics, Operational Flight Instrumentation, Recovery Avionics, and Range Safety System

Forward Skirt

Frustum

Nose Fairing

Dimensions	
Length	149.16 ft (45.46 m)
Diameter	12.17 ft (3.70 m)

EXHIBIT 3

Joint Design

Comment on Clevis and Tang joint:

A case-to-case joint. The tang end of the motor segment is aft. It is lowered into the clevis for the assembly. There are two O-rings and two O-ring grooves (.305 to .310 inches) that are in the clevis. There are 177 pins (in comparison, the Titan III had 237 pins), each high strength steel, one inch in diameter, going around the circumference, that secure the joint in place. A zinc chromate asbestos-filled putty (Randolph Type-2) acts as a thermal barrier. Also, there are 180 shims (32-36 thousandth inch) at each pin to ensure adequate squeeze on the two O-rings.

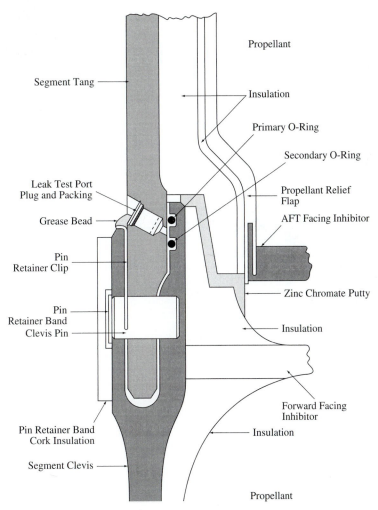

Solid Rocket Motor cross section shows positions of tang, clevis and O-rings.
Putty lines the joint on the side toward the propellant.

EXHIBIT 3
(continued)

Comment on O-ring:

DuPont Viton fluorocarbon material, 0.280 inch in diameter, plus 0.005, minus 0.003. Seals under compression and by pressure extrudes into a gap. Mil Spec: −30 degrees to +500 degrees Fahrenheit. Single-use item. Manufacturer: Parker Seals.

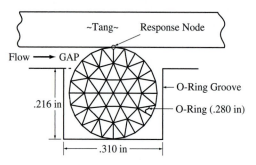

(a) O-Ring Model in Groove (Undeformed)

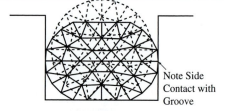

(b) O-Ring Compressed 0.035 Inches

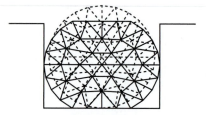

(c) O-Ring Compressed 0.046 Inches

(d) O-Ring Compressed 0.064 Inches
(Steel to Steel Contact)

EXHIBIT 4   Excerpts from Thiokol's Organizational Chart

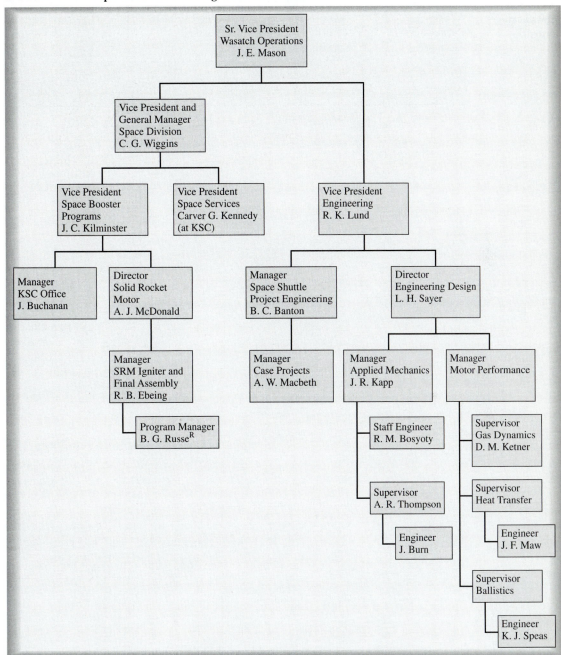

EXHIBIT 5
NASA Safety
Classification
System

Level	Description
Criticality 1	Loss of life or vehicle if the component fails.
Criticality 2	Loss of mission if the component fails.
Criticality 3	All others.
Criticality 1R	Redundant components, the failure of both could cause loss of life or vehicle.
Criticality 2R	Redundant components, the failure of both could cause loss of mission.

EXHIBIT 6   **Joint Criticality Reclassification Documents**

SRB CRITICAL ITEMS LIST

Sheet: 1 of 2

Subsystem SOLID ROCKET BOOSTER	Criticality Category __1__ Reaction Time immediate to sec.
Item Code 10-01-01 *Case, P/N (See Retention Rationale) Item Name (Joint Assys, Factory P/N 1U50147 Field: 1U50747	Page: A-6A Revision:
No. Required 1 (11 segments, 3 Field joints, 7 plant joints)	Date: December 17, 1982
FMEA Page No. A-4 of MSFC-RPT-724	Analyst: Garber
Critical Phases: Boost	Approved:

Failure Mode & Causes: Leakage at case assembly joints due to redundant O-ring seal failures or primary seal and leak check port O-ring failure.

NOTE: Leakage of the primary O-ring seal is classified as a single failure point due to possibility of loss of sealing at the secondary O-ring because of joint rotation after motor pressurization.

Failure Effect Summary: Actual Loss - Loss of mission, vehicle, and crew due to metal erosion, burnthrough, and probable case burst resulting in fire and deflagration.

RATIONALE FOR RETENTION

Case, P/N 1U50129, 1U50131, 1U50130, 1U50185, 1U51473, 1U50715, 1U50716, 1U50717

A. DESIGN

The SRM case joint design is common in the lightweight and regular weight cases having identical dimensions. The SRM joint uses centering clips which are installed in the gap between the tang O.D. and the outside clevis leg to compensate for the loss of concentricity due to gathering and to reduce the total clevis gap which has been provided for ease of assembly. On the shuttle SRM, the secondary O-ring was designed to provide redundancy and to permit a leak check, ensuring proper installation of the O-rings. Full redundancy exists at the moment of initial pressurization. However, test data shows that a phenomenon called joint rotation occurs as the pressure rises, opening up the O-ring extrusion gap and permitting the energized O-ring to protrude into the gap. This condition has been shown by test to be well within that required for safe primary O-ring sealing. This gap may, however, in some cases, increase sufficiently to cause the un-energized secondary O-ring seal to lose compression, raising question as to its ability to energize and seal if called upon to do so by primary seal failure. Since, under this latter condition only the single O-ring is sealing, a rationale for retention is provided for the simplex mode where only one O-ring is acting.

The surface finish requirement for the O-ring grooves is 63 and the finish of the O-ring contacting portion of the tang, which slides across the O-ring during joint assembly, is 32. The joint design provides an OD for the O-ring installation, which facilitates retention during joint assembly. The tang has a large shallow angle chamfer on the tip to prevent the cutting of the O-ring at assembly. The design drawing specifies application of O-ring lubricant prior to the installation. The factory assembled joints have NBR rubber material vulcanized across the internal joint faying surfaces as a part of the case internal insulation subsystem.

A small MS port leading to the annular cavity between the redundant seals permits a leak check of the seals immediately after joining segments. The MS plus, installed after leak test, has a retaining groove and compression face for its O-ring seal. A means to test the seal of the installed MS plug has not been established.

The O-rings for the case joints are mold formed and ground to close tolerance and the O-rings for the test port are mold formed to net dimensions. Both O-rings are made of high temperature, low compression set fluorocarbon elastomer. The design permits five scarf joints for the case joint seal rings. The O-ring joint strength must equal or exceed 40% of the parent material strength.

B. TESTING

To date, eight static firings and five flights have resulted in 180 (54 field and 126 factory) joints tested with no evidence of leakage. The Titan III program using a similar joint concept has tested a total of 1076 joints successfully.

EXHIBIT 6 *(continued)*

SRB CRITICAL ITEMS LIST		Sheet 2 of 2

Subsystem: SOLID ROCKET MOTOR	Criticality Category 1R	Reaction Time Immediate to Sec.
Item Code: 10-01-01	Page: A-36	
Item Name: 1U51473 (Joint Assys, Factory, P/N 1U51768, Field: 1U50747)	Revision:	

Case, P/N 1U50129, 1U50131, 1U50130, 1U50169, 1U50185,

RATIONALE FOR RETENTION (CONT'D)

A lightweight case joint verification test (TWR-12690) has demonstrated the secondary seal performance with a purposely pre-failed primary O-ring and demonstrated three pressure cycles on the primary seal with one cycle to 1.40 times maximum expected operating pressure.

C. INSPECTION

The tang -A- dia. and clevis -C- dia. are measured and recorded. These diameters control the radial spacing between tang and clevis. The depth, width and surface finish of the O-ring grooves are verified. The segment finish of the tang is also verified. The O-ring seal mating surfaces of the forward and aft segments are verified for flatness and surface finish. The following characteristics are inspected on each O-ring to assure conformance to the standards.

- o Surface voids and inclusions
- o Mold flashing
- o Scarf joint mismatch or separation
- o Cross section
- o Circumference

Each assembled joint seal is tested per STW7-2747 via pressurizing the annular cavity between seals to 50 ± 5 psi and monitoring for 10 minutes. A seal seating pressure of 220 psi, with return to 0 psig, may be used prior to the test. A pressure decay of 1 psig or greater is not acceptable. Following seal verification by QC, the leak test port plug is installed with QC verifying installation and torquing.

D. FAILURE HISTORY

No known record of failure due to case joint seal leakage on segmented 156" or Titan IIIC motors.

No failures in the four development and three qualification SRM motor test firings.

EXHIBIT 6 (*continued*)

```
┌──────────────────┬────────────────────────────┬──────────────────────────┐
│ IPCIX            │                            │                          │
│ V 02?C5          │   SPACE TRANSPORTATION SYSTEM │ IPAGE    1  OF    1     │
├──────────────────┤         LEVEL I            ├──────────────────────────┤
│ ICR NO.          │      CHANGE REQUEST        │ IORIGINATOR              │
│  422106L         │                            │ I LA3/J. B. Jackson Jr.  │
├──────────────────┼────────────────────────────┴──────────────────────────┤
│ ELATED CHANGES   │ ITITLE                                                  │
│ I S22106L        │      SRB Critical Items List (CIL) Requirements        │
└──────────────────┴────────────────────────────────────────────────────────┘
```

ISYSTEM/ELEMENT(S) AFFECTED:

/ / Shuttle System	/ / System Software	/ / Payloads
/ / Orbiter	/ / Crew-Related GFE	/ / Operations
/ / Space Shuttle Main Engines	/ / Shuttle Carrier Aircraft	/ / Other(Specify)
/ / External Tank	/ / IUS	
/X/ Solid Rocket Booster	/ / Spacelab	
/ / Launch and Landing		

IDESCRIPTION OF CHANGE: / / Mandatory / / Improvement /X/ Other(Specify) Waiver

This change identifies Criticality 1 critical items which do not meet the fail safe
requirements of Paragraph 2.8 of the Space Shuttle Program Requirements Document,
Level I, dated June 30, 1977. These critical items contain 3 new items and 5 items which
were previously approved Criticality 1R by Level II Change Request S02106G and are now
being reclassified Criticality 1.

SUBSYSTEM – SOLID ROCKET MOTOR

Subsystem – Electrical and Instrumentation

CRITICALITY	ITEM NUMBER	ITEM	FMEA NO.
1	1U50129	Case	10-01-01
1	1U50130		10-01-01
1	1U50131		10-01-01
1	1U51473		10-01-01
1	1U50185		10-01-01
1	1U50715		10-01-01
1	1U50716		10-01-01
1	1U50717		10-01-01

IRECOMMENDED EFFECTIVITY: STS-6 and subs

WEIGHT IMPACT:	SCHEDULE IMPACT:	COST PER FLIGHT IMPACT:
None	None	None

COST	PROJECT|FY	|FY	|FY	|FY	IREMAINDER	ITOTAL
IDDT&E						
IPROD.						
IOPS. NONE						

IREASON FOR CHANGE:
Critical items which do not meet Level I fail-safe requirements require submittal per
NASA Headquarters letter MHR-7 dated February 21, 1979, which states that all waivers to
Level I redundancy requirements be submitted to the Level I PRCB for review and approval.

IFORWARDING AUTHORIZATION	ISIGNATURE	IDATE
/X/ Space Shuttle		
/ / Other(Specify) PRCBD S22106L		3/2/83

ILEVEL I ACTION	ISIGNATURE	IDATE
/X/ Approved		28 MAR
/ / Approved with Revision,		'83
See Pages _____		
/ / Disapproved		

EXHIBIT 7
Flight
Readiness
Review
Protocol

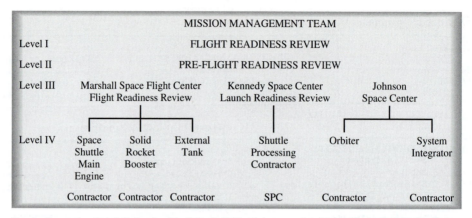

Note: Readiness reviews for both the launch and the flight of a Shuttle mission are conducted at ascending levels that begin with contractors. In the initial notice of the review, the Level I directive establishes a Mission Management team for the particular mission. The team assumes responsibility for each Shuttle's readiness for a period commencing 48 hours before launch and continuing through post-launch crew egress and the safing of the Orbiter. On call throughout the entire period, the Mission Management Team supports the Associated Administrator for Space Flight and the Program Manager.

A structured Mission Management Team meeting—called L-1—is held 24 hours prior to each scheduled launch. Its agenda includes closeout of any open work, closeout of any Flight Readiness action items, a discussion of new or continuing anomalies, and an updated briefing on anticipated weather conditions at the launch site and at the abort landing sites in different parts of the world. It is standard practice of Level I and II officials to encourage the reporting of new problems or concerns that might develop in the interval between the Flight Readiness Review and the L-1 meeting, and between L-1 and launch.

EXHIBIT 8   **Shuttle Projects Office Board Summary of Action Items and Problems**

Shuttle Projects Office Board (February 12, 1985)

Chart 61

A41–0174

SUMMARY OF ACTION ITEMS

ACTION	DESCRIPTION	STATUS	REMARKS
SRM 1	PROVIDE SRM EXIT CONE ENVIRONMENT FOR DESCENT	CLOSED	AEROTHERMAL & ACOUSTIC ENVIRONMENT PROVIDED TO MTI FOR ANALYSIS OF EXIT CONE BREAKUP
SRM 2	PROVIDE THE DESIGN MARGIN OF SAFETY OF NOZZLE EXTENSION FOR ASCENT FLIGHT	CLOSED	SPECIAL TOPIC
SRM 3	PROVIDE ADDITIONAL DATA REGARDING SIC CASE JOINT O–RING EROSION	CLOSED	SPECIAL TOPIC
SRM 4	EXPAND DM–7 FWC INSULATION DEBOND RATIONALE RE: STEEL CASES	CLOSED	SPECIAL TOPIC
SRM 5	EXPAND RATIONALE RE: NOZZLE EXIT CONE FAILURE TO DEFINE THE ENVIRONMENT THAT CAUSED FAILURE	CLOSED	SPECIAL TOPIC
SRM 6	EXPAND STS 51–C O–RING EROSION RATIONALE RE: INTEGRITY OF SECONDARY SEAL	CLOSED	SPECIAL TOPIC

Chart 62

$..:–9176

PROBLEM SUMMARY

PROBLEM	CONCERN	RESOLUTION	SPECIAL TOPIC
● EVIDENCE OF HOT GAS PAST PRIMARY O–RINGS ON 2 CASE JOINTS (PREVIOUSLY OBSERVED ON NOZZLE JOINT)	MISSION SAFETY	ACCEPTABLE RISK BECAUSE OF LIMITED EXPOSURE AND REDUNDANCY (REF. STS 41–C FRR)	YES
● DM–7 FWC HAS A DELAMINATION IN THE INTERNAL INSULATION WHICH COULD BE THE RESULT OF A GENERIC PROCESS PROBLEM COMMON TO STEEL CASES	MISSION SAFETY	FWC UNIQUE	YES
● BREAKUP OF –403 AND –404 RINGS IN LEFT HAND SRM EFFECT ON ABILITY TO EVALUATE NOZZLE EROSION	MISSION SAFETY	RECONSTRUCTION VERIFIES NOMINAL EROSION	YES
● DIMENSIONAL DISCREPANCY ON STS 51–E LEFT HAND NOZZLE RESULTS IN LESS THAN SPECIFIED MINIMUM O–RING SQUEEZE	MISSION SAFETY	ACCEPTABLE RISK. WITHIN SUCCESSFUL TEST AND FLIGHT EXPERIENCE BASE	YES
● APU SN 149 FUEL PUMP SHAFT SEAL LEAK OUT–OF–SPEC	MISSION SAFETY	REMOVED, RETESTED, REINSTALLED, TEST O.K.	NO
● AFT BSM/SN 1000045 DAMAGED BY FRANGIBLE NUT PRE–TENSIONER DEBRIS	MISSION SAFETY	REMOVE & REPLACE 1V/SN1000060	NO
● APU CONTROLLER CAPACITOR FAILURES ON ORBITER APU	MISSION SAFETY	CHANGE OUT AFT IEA'S	YES

EXHIBIT 9
SRM Critical Items List Chronology

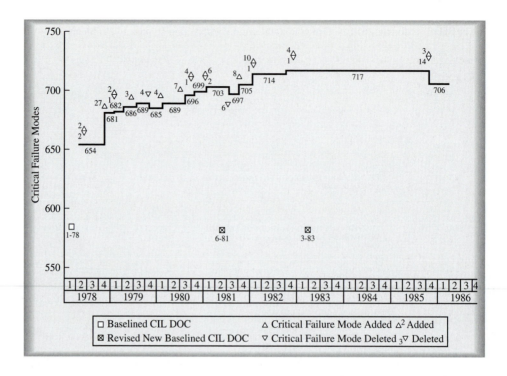

EXHIBIT 10
Memo from Boisjoly to Lund

July 31, 1985

SRM O-ring Erosion/Potential Failure Criticality

This letter is written to insure that management is fully aware of the seriousness of the current O-ring erosion problem in the SRM joints from an engineering standpoint. The mistakenly accepted position on the joint problem was to fly without fear of failure and to run a series of design evaluations which would ultimately lead to a solution or at least a significant reduction of the erosion problem. This position is now drastically changed as a result of the SRM 16A nozzle joint erosion which eroded a secondary O-ring with the primary O-ring never sealed.

If the same scenario should occur in a field joint (and it could), then it is a jump ball as to the success or failure of the joint because the secondary O-ring cannot respond to the clevis opening rate and may not be capable of pressurization. The result would be a catastrophe of the highest order—loss of life.

An unofficial team with leader was formed on July 19, 1985 and was tasked with solving the problem for both the short and long term. This unofficial team is essentially nonexistent at this time. In my opinion, the team must be officially given the responsibility and the authority to execute the work that needs to be done on a non-interference basis (full time assignment until completed).

It is my honest and very real fear that if we do not take immediate action to dedicate a team to solve the problem with the field joint having the number one priority, then we stand in jeopardy of losing a flight along with all the launch pad facilities.

EXHIBIT 11   **Teleconferences Participants**

NASA Marshall Space Flight Center (MSFC)

1. George B. Handy, Deputy Director, Science and Engineering
2. Judson A. Lovingood, Deputy Manager, Shuttle Projects Office
3. Leslie F. Adams, Deputy Manager, SRB Project
4. Lawrence O. Wear, Manager, SRM Project Office
5. John Q. Miller, Technical Assistant, SRM Project
6. J. Wayne Littles, Associate Director for Engineering
7. Robert J. Schwinghamer, Director, Material and Processes Laboratory
8. Wilbur A. Riehl, Chief, Nonmetallic Materials Division
9. John P. McCarty, Deputy Director, Structures and Propulsion Laboratory
10. Ben Powers, Engineering Structures and Propulsion Laboratory
11. James Smith, Chief Engineer, SRB Program
12. Keith E. Coates, Chief Engineer, Special Projects Office
13. John Schell, Retired Engineer, Materials Laboratory

Present at Kennedy Space Center (KSC)

14. Cecil Houston, MSFC Resident Manager, at KSC
15. Stanley R. Reinartz, Manager, Shuttle Projects Office
16. Lawrence B. Mulloy, Manager, SRB Project

Morton Thiokol Wasatch Division

1. Jerald Mason, Senior Vice President, Wasatch Operations
2. Calvin Wiggins, Vice President and General Manager, Space Division
3. Joe C. Kilminster, Vice President, Space Booster Programs
4. Robert K. Lund, Vice President, Engineering
5. Larry H. Sayer, Director, Engineering and Design
6. William Macbeth, Manager, Case Projects, Space Booster Project Engineering, Wasatch Division
7. Donald M. Ketner, Supervisor, Gas Dynamics Section and Head Seal Task Force
8. Roger Boisjoly, Member, Seal Task Force
9. Arnold R. Thompson, Supervisor, Rocket Motor Cases
10. Jack R. Kapp, Manager, Applied Mechanics Department
11. Jerry Burn, Associate Engineer, Applied Mechanics
12. Joel Maw, Associate Scientist, Heat Transfer Section
13. Brian Russell, Manager, Special Projects, SRM Project
14. Robert Ebeling, Manager, Ignition System and Final Assembly, SRB Project

Present at MSFC

15. Boyd C. Brinton, Manager, Space Booster Project
16. Kyle Speas, Ballistics Engineer

Present at KSC

17. Allan J. McDonald, Director, SRM Project
18. Jack Buchanan, Manager, KSC Operations

EXHIBIT 12
Documents
Faxed from
Thiokol Before
the January 27,
1986,
Teleconference

BLOW BY HISTORY

SRM -15 WORST BLOW-BY

   e 2 CASE JOINTS (80°), (110°) ARC

   o MUCH WORSE VISUALLY THAN SRM-22

SRM 22 BLOW-BY

   o 2 CASE JOINTS (30-40°)

SRM-13 A, 15, 16A, 18, 23A 24A

   o NOZZLE BLOW-BY

EXHIBIT 12 (*continued*)

FIELD JOINT   PRIMARY O-RINGS   SRM 25

o   A TEMPERATURE LOWER THAN CURRENT DATABASE RESULTS
     IN CHANGING PRIMARY O-RING SEALING TIMING FUNCTION

o   SRM 15 A — 80° BLACK GREASE BETWEEN O-RINGS
                    ARC
     SRM 15 B — 110° ARC BLACK GREASE BETWEEN O-RINGS

o   LOWER O-RING SQUEEZE DUE TO LOWER TEMP

o   HIGHER O-RING SHORE HARDNESS

o   THICKER GREASE VISCOSITY

o   HIGHER O-RING PRESSURE ACTUATION TIME

o   IF ACTUATION TIME INCREASES, THRESHOLD OF SECONDARY
     SEAL PRESSURIZATION CAPABILITY IS APPROACHED

o   IF THRESHOLD IS REACHED THEN SECONDARY SEAL MAY
     NOT BE CAPABLE OF BEING PRESSURIZED

EXHIBIT 12 *(continued)*

CONCLUSIONS:

o TEMPERATURE OF O-RING IS NOT ONLY PARAMETER
CONTROLLING BLOW-BY

SRM 15 WITH BLOW-BY HAD AN O-RING TEMP AT 53°F
SRM 22 WITH BLOW-BY HAD AN O-RING TEMP AT 75°F
FOUR DEVELOPMENT MOTORS WITH NO BLOW-BY
WERE TESTED AT O-RING TEMP OF 47° TO 52°F

DEVELOPMENT MOTORS HAD PUTTY PACKING WHICH
RESULTED IN BETTER PERFORMANCE

o AT ABOUT 50°F BLOW-BY COULD BE
EXPERIENCED IN CASE JOINTS

o TEMP FOR SRM 25 ON 1-28-86 LAUNCH WILL
BE   29°F   9 AM
      38°F   2 PM

o HAVE NO DATA THAT WOULD INDICATE SRM 25 IS
DIFFERENT THAN SRM 15 OTHER THAN TEMP

RECOMMENDATIONS:

o O-RING TEMP MUST BE ≥ 53°F AT LAUNCH

DEVELOPMENT MOTORS AT 47° TO 52°F WITH
PUTTY PACKING HAD NO BLOW-BY
SRM 15 (THE BEST SIMULATION) WORKED AT 53°F

o PROJECT AMBIENT CONDITIONS (TEMP & WIND)
TO DETERMINE LAUNCH TIME

EXHIBIT 13
Plot of Flights with O-Ring Incidents versus Joint Temperature

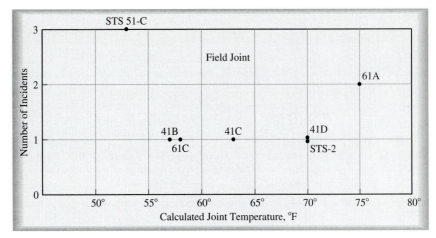

Note: Incident is defined as O-ring erosion, (gas) blow-by, or excessive heating.

EXHIBIT 14
Excerpt from the Testimony of Roger Boisjoly to the Roger's Commission

Source: Testimony of Roger Boisjoly in the *Report of the Presidential Commission on the Space Shuttle Accident*, Volume 5 (1986), p. 783.

Okay, the caucus started by Mr. Mason stating a management decision was necessary. Those of us who opposed the launch continued to speak out, and I am specifically speaking of Mr. Thompson and myself because in my recollection he and I were the ones that vigorously continued to oppose the launch. And we were attempting to go back and rereview and try to make clear what we were trying to get across, and we couldn't understand why it was going to be reversed. So we spoke out and once again tried to explain the effects of low temperature. Arnie [Thompson] actually got up from his position which was down the table, and walked up the table and put a quarter pad down in front of the table, in front of the management folks, and tried to sketch out once again what his concern was with the joint, and when he realized he wasn't getting through, he just stopped.

I tried one more time with the photos. I grabbed the photos, and I went up and discussed the photos once again and tried to make the point that it was my opinion from actual observations that temperature was indeed a discriminator and we should not observe the physical evidence that we had observed. I must emphasize, I had my say, and I would never take away any management right to take the input of an engineer and then make a decision based upon that input, and I truly believe that.

Apple PowerBook: Design Quality and Time to Market

Apple Computer, Inc. launched the development of a portable computer late in 1985. None of the portables in the market had been successful, and Apple's goal was to address its competitors' shortcomings: passive and underlit screen displays, very short battery life, and limited performance. Apple did not compromise in its search for solutions. Graphical user interfaces, which Apple had pioneered in desktop computers, required more speed, higher resolution, and more sophisticated displays than could be provided by the passive matrix displays used by its portable competitors. Unwilling to forego its leadership in front-of-screen performance, Apple insisted on having an active matrix display in its first portable. Finding a display supplier with a reliable manufacturing process delayed introduction by twelve months. A full performance Mac Portable was introduced in late September 1989 at a list price of $4,999.

The Portable successfully addressed its objectives, but the initial backlog of orders collapsed before Christmas. Although the battery ran for 8–12 hours, the product weighed nearly 17 pounds while Compaq's full-function LTE, introduced just six weeks later, weighed seven. Apple soon had a huge inventory of unsold Portables. Randy Battat, then Vice President of Worldwide Product Marketing, commented, "We had been concerned about competition but I think we felt we had a lot of inherent competitive advantages that would outweigh weaknesses in other areas. We didn't recognize how fast the market

Courtesy of the Case Study Research and Development Program at the Design Management Institute.
© Copyright 1994 The Design Management Institute. All rights reserved.

This case was prepared by Dr. Artemis March of the Design Management Institute as a basis for class discussion rather than to illustrate either effective or ineffective handling of an administrative situation.

Many thanks to Bob Brunner and the people at Apple Computer for their openness in discussing their experiences of the PowerBook project, and especially to Jon Krakower, whose long memory and extraordinary commitment to this project made it possible to tell a coherent story; to Bill Evans of Bridge Design, who conducted many of the interviews and provided early orientation to the project; and to Earl Powell, President of DMI, who conducted interviews and envisioned the possibility of the larger program of which this case is one part.

was moving." Had the Portable come out two years earlier, the consensus was that it would have been a smashing success. But, as one manager noted, "When you put a Portable next to an LTE, you had to say, 'Where were we?'"

The Mac Portable brought into sharper focus a growing recognition within the company that major changes were needed in the way it was organized and how it operated. One manager summarized the company: "Apple is not 'time to market.' It's more 'time to perfection.'" Time to market was described as being alien to a culture that "shipped no product before its time." Yet Apple was now challenged to gain entry into the notebook market in 18 rather than 48 months.

In October 1991, Apple introduced the PowerBook 140/170, a seven-pound notebook, and immediately had a runaway success. Originally envisaged as a temporary placeholder, the PowerBook sold 400,000 units in its first year, becoming a billion-dollar business overnight.

THE PORTABLE COMPUTER MARKET

Portable computers were originally conceived as "second computers" that would be particularly useful to salespeople, consultants, and others who worked extensively outside their offices. The "portables" of the middle '80s were in truth "luggables," such as Compaq's 28-pounder, introduced in 1983. Price-performance continued to improve, while technology advances made it possible to shrink the size and reduce weight. When portables also became battery-operable, their range of use and customer base broadened considerably. Factory sales of portables were $2.3 billion in 1988, and jumped to $3.3 billion the following year.

By the end of the decade, four segments were emerging, based on weight. "Portables" weighed over 11 pounds; "laptops," 7–11 pounds; "notebooks," less than 7 pounds; and "handhelds," under two pounds. Notebooks were projected to become the leading segment. Prices ranged from $1000–$6000. The high-end models contained more powerful microprocessors, and were full-performance computers.

APPLE COMPUTER, INC.

Product Strategy

Apple Computer, Inc. was founded in 1977 by two young entrepreneurs with a passionate commitment to their physical product. Apple dramatically changed the personal computer (PC) market in 1984 when it brought out the Macintosh (Mac). The Mac introduced a graphical user interface (GUI), which allowed users to perform numerous functions by pointing at objects (icons) on the screen with a device commonly called a "mouse." Despite Apple's proprietary operating system and its incompatibility with IBM/Microsoft DOS, the Mac was enormously successful. Its user-friendly interface made computer users owners out of nonusers, while its graphics capabilities soon gave Apple a leading position in the areas of desktop publishing and presentation graphics. Apple's share of the PC market was second only to IBM's.

Apple's basic strategy was to develop user-friendly, differentiated products based on its proprietary technologies. These products commanded a price premium, which gave Apple the high gross margins that allowed it to reinvest in R&D, and continue to develop very attractive products. Successful implementation also required growth. But growth and high margins had become more difficult to achieve as the desktop computer industry matured, the number of competitors proliferated, competition became more price-based, and differentiation harder to achieve.

Organization

In 1989, Apple's activities were organized as functions and departments. No resources were dedicated to particular projects; each department supported all projects. Product Development (i.e., engineering), Product Design, Worldwide Product Marketing, and Manufacturing all reported to Jean-Louis Gassée, president of Apple Products. "Engineering" at Apple meant electrical engineering. The centralized engineering organization housed both hardware and software. (See **Exhibit 1.**)

With this departmental organization, project managers could not, as Jon Sedmak put it, "make decisions stick." Formerly with Texas Instruments, and more recently a project manager at Apple, Sedmak described some of the frustrations. "You had to deal with other departments that had other things to do on numerous projects. You had to get consensus not only with the product design engineers that were working on your stuff, but also their boss and their boss's boss. Everything went up. When John-Louis [Gassée] was here, he controlled industrial design; so ID would kick things up to John-Louis and then they would come down again."

Industrial Design at Apple

During the period in which the Portable and PowerBook were developed, mechanical engineers and industrial designers were part of a single centralized department called product design. Headed by Richard Jordan, its role was to create the product enclosures that housed the electronics and interfaced with the user.

When Jordan first approached Robert (Bob) Brunner to take over management of the design group, Apple had only five designers, and did 90 percent of its design work through outside consultants. Brunner, who was then 31 and had worked with Apple for two years as a consultant, turned down the offer. "It wasn't right for me or for Apple. With such a skeletal staff, there really could be no direction-setting."

Subsequent discussions generated a different offer—to create a strong internal group that would chart Apple's strategic direction in design. Brunner accepted the position as manager of the Industrial Design Group (IDG) in November 1989; he reported to Jordan. "I came to Apple because it has great products, and is driven by product design. People here are very visually oriented. They rally around objects, and the company centers around physical objects. Design is embedded in the culture. I sometimes say I have a staff of 10,000." Brunner noted as well the architectural environment that Steven Jobs, one of the company's founders, had created for Apple. "We are surrounded by a very high-quality physical environment."

PORTABLES

Product Divisions

In the months following the Portable's introduction, senior managers became committed to the idea of reorganizing the company by product divisions and business units. Early discussions favored sub-dividing the company by high-end and low-end products, but by the spring of 1990, this was rejected in favor of a more sustainable organizational difference between desktops and portables. This decision was made at a time when Apple had virtually no portable business; Mac Portable had been written off, and nothing else had yet been developed. A portable program was under way, however. (See **Exhibit 2.**)

Twister

Senior industrial designer Gavin Ivester had been asked to undertake some concept studies in June of 1989. Ivester was "volunteered" for this project because he had pointed out some of the Portable's design problems, and was subsequently tagged as "Mr. Portable." Working with two outside design groups, Ivester was guided by the concept of the "mobile Mac." Aiming at a 3.5 pound notebook that "you carry with you all the time," his slender models incorporated a level of miniaturization that "didn't quite exist. I went to see all the technology experts at Apple to see what was coming." Ivester's series of five studies, called "Twister," drew on these next-generation technologies such as a 2.5 inch hard drive, midas trackpad, and touch-screen. (See **Exhibit 3.**) The 3.5 pound target was established in conjunction with a marketer who made up some wooden blocks in a range of weights, and through testing, found the break point for "carry with you all the time" to be 3.5 pounds.

Companion

In August 1989, Apple began to formalize its next step in portables by launching a three-year program called "Companion." The program gave some of Apple's best and most experienced engineers and designers the opportunity to completely rethink portables from scratch. Their overall product objective was to create an ultra-light, ultra-small notebook. The product would be risky because it would incorporate several new technologies to achieve the needed degree of miniaturization.

Enhancing the Portable

Despite the Portable's size and weight, many hoped it would hold Apple's place in the portable market for a couple of years until the much more miniaturized Companion could be developed. Their hopes were pinned on high demand from Apple's installed base. A second portable project got underway in August to enhance the 15.5" × 14" × 4" Portable. It would maintain the same weight and look as the Portable, but add backlighting, upgrade the power of its 68000 microprocessor to a 68030, and modify the main logic board; the latter entailed a considerable electrical engineering effort.

DEFINING THE NOTEBOOK CONCEPT

Some, including John Sculley, chairman and CEO of Apple, were not satisfied with this portable program. Concern mounted as the Portable's failure in the market became evident. Late in 1989, engineering was asked if it could pull in Companion within a year. It could not. Could the Portable be shrunk to notebook size? Simply entering the market required a product that weighed no more than seven pounds, in a package no more than 9" × 11" × 2.5", and that used an 030 chip. It would have to use existing technologies to get to market in 18 months. Jon Sedmak, who was managing the Portable enhancement project, was asked to oversee the exploration of this notebook concept as well. During a subsequent meeting, people kept writing TTM (meaning "time to market") all over the board. A latecomer misread the board and asked, "What is this 'TIM'?" The name stuck; people immediately began calling the project TIM.

ID Models

In January, Bob Brunner and Gavin Ivester led a small group of Apple designers in an exploration of component layouts for TIM. Their configuration studies moved component blocks around, producing at least eight primary models of internal configurations. They used two kinds of 3D models—foam to show scale and form, and crude hard models to give a better sense of size and weight. All of these designs were "clamshells" (i.e., top and bottom halves that opened and closed like a briefcase), and used a trackball of indeterminate size to control the cursor. A front-and-center trackball arrangement predominated. Some models had an internal floppy disk drive, and some had an external floppy module. The designers explored how a modular floppy would be attached, e.g., by snapping into the side or docking on the bottom. (See **Exhibit 4.**)

While the clamshells were more conventional than Twister, both concepts drew on Apple's existing design language, called "Snow White." Brunner described this language as "rectilinear, light, ordered, and strong." This "language of the desktop" had been applied across all Apple product lines, and the designers were feeling its constraints. Brunner described the situation: "Snow White was predictable, and making it harder to innovate. It lacked extensibility."

Trackball

Portables required a device to control the cursor; the standard approach was to do this through the keyboard. Because of its GUI, Apple was the first company to be faced with solving the ergonomic/space/weight problems of building a pointing device into a notebook. The Portable had used a trackball—a freely rotating, round device that had previously been used in video game arcades as well as high-end workstations. By rolling the trackball, the user controlled the position of the cursor. By pressing on the trackball buttons, the user made a selection.

For the Portable, Apple had designed a 33 mm trackball that could be configured by the dealer for either side of the keyboard. The size of a trackball had many implications. A large diameter enhanced fine motor control of the cursor, but it took up more space and was heavier, and was thus more difficult to integrate. Its diameter affected its height, a factor which had to be considered in relation to the height of the keys and the depth of the display, for the display closed over both the keyboard and trackball when the notebook was closed.

Krakower's Concept

Another person who had been dissatisfied with the timetable of the portable program was Jon Krakower, an electrical engineer who was passionately committed to making Apple a major competitor in the notebook market. He had begun his graduate work in architecture, and had a deep and abiding interest in design. Although the narrowest definition of his role had to do with board design and layout, he was better known as a system integrator—someone who made sure that all the boards, electricals, mechanicals, and software worked together, and could be manufactured easily.

Krakower felt that Apple was already two years behind in portables, and if it didn't get a competitive notebook out in 18 months, it would miss the window of opportunity and might never get another chance. He also felt that Apple's product would have to be clearly differentiated from the competition's, and that ergonomics should be a priority in its distinctiveness. On his own initiative and time, he began thinking about a concept for a small, light package whose pointing device was ambidextrous. His first notion of what that might be took the form of a paper model made from marketing materials for the Portable at its New York introduction to the press in September. Its central feature was a large, centered trackball. (See **Exhibit 5.**)

A centered trackball located in front of the keyboard addressed the needs of left-handers as well as making it possible for users to control the cursor with their thumbs without moving their hands away from the keyboard's home-row position. But what about the space on either side of the trackball? Krakower began to envisage a "palm rest" that would support the user's hands. By pushing the keyboard further out from the user as well as providing support in its own right, the palm rest reduced the user's lateral wrist angle when working in a cramped space, and more closely approximated the normal distance and angles between a user and a desktop keyboard.

Early in 1990, Krakower put together a working model of his design. (See **Exhibit 6.**) He cut up a Portable, devised a palm rest, put the trackball in the middle, and started showing it informally, beginning with peers and first-level management, and later, second and third-level management. Many within senior management thought it looked strange, and that it might give Apple a second black eye in the portable market. In addition, many product designers seriously doubted that it was possible to be competitive on size and weight with a large trackball, full-size palm rests, and a built-in floppy disk drive.

To validate the concept and ease management concerns, Krakower set up a temporary user test facility where he videotaped 45 subjects using a modified version of his original model that allowed him to vary the size of trackball and of palm rest. In addition to this test data, he also produced documentation showing how the size/weight goals could be attained through using proper module placement, a multitiered PCB/cable partitioning scheme, and the latest miniaturization techniques in component packaging technology.

Integrating the Trackball

Brunner recalled, "The biggest challenge that we faced initially was the integration of the pointing device. How could we integrate it without growing the box, or doing some ugly appendage? This is where we kept hitting the wall." One day around the middle of February, Krakower stopped by and suggested a solution. Brunner recalled, "Then Jon said, 'Wait a minute, we can just push the keyboard back, pull the battery forward into the left front corner and the hard drive forward into the right front corner, and there you go. You can drop the trackball right in between the batteries and the hard disk." This layout had the further advantage of locating two of the heaviest components in front; this created a forward center-of-gravity, a critical consideration for wheelchair users and an attraction for mobile users when balancing the unit on their lap.[1]

Floppy Drives

The issue that next came into focus was whether or not to have an internal floppy drive. The LTE and most other competitive products used an internal floppy. An internal floppy

---

[1] Gavin Ivester, "Shrinking the Mac Wrap," *Innovation*, Fall 1992.

added weight to the product, and competed with other components for interior space. If Apple chose an internal floppy, it could match the size/weight norms for notebooks; but if it chose an external floppy, it could possibly gain an edge for lightness. Many people at Apple felt—and some quite strongly—that an internal floppy was not necessary; those people included Gavin Ivester; John Medica, director of CPU engineering; Rodger Mohme, project leader for Companion; and Bruce Gee who later became the marketing manager for PowerBook.

Krakower believed it was critical that Apple's notebook have an internal floppy drive because "in an immature market, people thought they couldn't get by without it." Brunner and Sedmak also favored an internal floppy for TIM. Some of ID's models had floppies built in, and some didn't. Brunner created most of the former, and Ivester most of the latter. Building on Krakower's partitioning scheme, Brunner found a way to incorporate the floppy so that it took up very little additional space. The partitioning scheme divided the main PC board into two boards and stacked them, leaving enough space under the keyboard for the drive. This proposal, which was considered daring, was not ideal for manufacturing, but the space benefit could be argued to outweigh the additional costs.

Design Review

Toward the end of February, an early morning meeting was held to review the ID designs for TIM. Brunner, Ivester, Medica, Sedmak, Krakower, and Gee were present. The biggest decision on the table was whether or not to have an internal floppy. The ID designs were compared with one another. Krakower also presented his model to show that the amount of additional space consumed by an internal floppy and a large trackball could be designed to be very minimal, and summarized the advantages and disadvantages of each choice on a handout. (See **Exhibit 7.**) While some of the others were skeptical, particularly about the "wasted space" of palm rests, Brunner thought the large trackball and full-size palm rest were viable, and that ID could make it look right. He recalled, "We in ID tend to like radical solutions, but most of the group still had a fairly conventional image in their mind of what the product should look like, which was Compaq's LTE." It required a strong lobbying effort on the part of both Brunner and Krakower before people's perceptions began to change.

Brunner quickly designed a new model with full-size palm rests. (See **Exhibit 8.**) On March 6, Sculley was shown this and other ID models, as well as some of the Twister designs. From a pure design standpoint, he liked some of the soft, sculptural forms of the latter, but for TIM, he preferred Brunner's latest model using the internal floppy and full-size palm rest. He favored the large trackball because the trackpad was about the same size, and TIM would be able to accept the trackpad when it was ready. Brunner noted that, "After the Sculley meeting, we didn't explore other configurations. There was no time. We were looking for the final design."

Gee later noted, "Going with an internal floppy was the smartest decision we made. A machine was not perceived as full-functional unless it had a built-in floppy drive." Brunner retrospectively commented on the early commitment to the product concept: "When we began our usability tests in April, we were already committed to what we were going to do; all we were doing was refining it. Such an early commitment was exclusive, I think, to this project. We knew we were behind, and we felt we had nothing to lose. Therefore, we made a commitment to that concept without a lot of data backing it up."

TIM: FORMING A PROJECT

In the spring of 1990, several things happened that had an impact on TIM. Gassée, who had taken a strong and active interest in ID and been its de facto head, announced his retirement. Apple decentralized into product divisions in April. Both engineering and product marketing were decentralized while product design was not. John Medica was asked to form, lead, and build the new Portable engineering group. His role would be to drive the successful product development of all portable programs. He was described by one of his colleagues as "the brightest young rising hardware manager" in the company. Medica selected Jon Sedmak as the project manager for TIM. Sedmak also continued overseeing the Portable enhancement project until it was cancelled in September.

For the duration of the PowerBook project, both ID and the mechanical designers continued to report to Jordan. Product design remained centralized, with the understanding that it would co-locate the mechanical designers in the divisions, and that industrial designers would spend about three days per week with their projects. Co-location was considered especially critical for portables because, as Medica put it, "everything is so integrally intertwined. You have to get portable people tightly coupled, all breathing the same air, talking the same talk." Strong resistance to co-location was expressed during the April–May time frame, but began to settle down in the following months. Because of the tight coupling needed for miniaturized products, product design reported to the portable division, yet served other product divisions as well. (See **Exhibit 9.**)

Project Objectives

Sedmak declared that TIM was to be the smallest, lightest, and quickest portable Apple could do; everything else was negotiable. One manager recalled Sedmak's directives to him when he joined the team: "10,000 a month, presence in the market-place, place holder till the real product gets out there." Brunner described Sedmak's focus: "He had his priorities straight in his mind: to get the product to market, make sure it was competitive in size and weight, and everything else was last."

Acquiring Resources

In March, the team consisted of Sedmak, Krakower, Ivester, Gee, a senior EE, a coordinator, and a product design manager. Sedmak's first priority was to try and get engineering resources. TIM was at priority level six (out of seven levels, where one was the highest level). Other desktop programs and Companion had higher priorities, and Companion had already taken what several people described as the "A-team" talent. TIM was able to secure either junior people with little experience, or people from desktop who had no experience in portables. As one manager put it, "You might have product design experience, but it is very different when it comes to doing low weight and getting a very small package." The mechanical designers began joining TIM during the May–June period. They included two product designers, a draftsperson, and a fourth who did both. Part-time representation was secured from other departments.

Decision-Making

The major decision-making forum was the team leaders' weekly meeting with Sedmak. Their first major decision was to find a balance between battery life and the weight of the product. Every hour of battery life increased weight by half a pound. A three-hour, seven-pound target was agreed upon.

DESIGNING THE PRODUCT

During the next several months, ID worked with Krakower on board size and layout, and with Apple's user testing lab to further validate the ergonomic principles and refine the details of the keyboard/trackball/palm rest design.

Product Core

During the January–June time period, Krakower put together a package of drawings that included outlines of the six PC boards, their connector/cable partitioning, module placements, and top level assembly sequence. He noted, "even though we didn't have the product design resources on board, we couldn't let the time slip by." His work also reflected his broad interpretation of what it meant to be a technical lead or system integrator. The role was ambiguously defined as handling the logic boards and their interfaces. Typically, projects partitioned things very cleanly; the systems integrator worked with the architect to make sure the board designs were implemented while another group handled the interfaces. By contrast, Krakower took a broader approach, working on the interrelationships among all the components interfacing with the boards. He later commented on this approach: "This was Apple's first real attempt at shrinking the development schedule to less than half that of previous first-generation products. The need for the technical lead to take a strong, multidisciplined, proactive approach to engineering was certainly crucial then and is becoming more and more important with shorter design cycles and limited resources. The technical lead has to make sure there isn't a cross-functional disconnect somewhere."

When the product design manager joined the team in late April, he felt that his mechanical engineers should have the opportunity to design from scratch. Schooled in the Apple tradition of designing rugged, snap-together plastics, he brought this same approach to designing portables. After a month's effort, his product design team concluded that Krakower's approach was indeed the only way to do it without increasing the size and weight of the product.

Design and Test

Design alternatives began to be tested in April, and continued through August in a concentrated series of seven usability tests-design cycles. The process was iterative; as Ivester noted, "It was designing to test and testing to design." Learning from one round of tests was incorporated into design changes that were tested in the next round. Gee recalled, "Brunner's organization was coming up with these different designs. We would sit and brainstorm with them about what they had learned last time and what they wanted to do next time."

Ireng Wong of the user test lab ran most of the test research. She encouraged the designers and other team members to sit behind one-way mirrors, to watch videotapes of the tests, and to attend user feedback sessions. Tests were conducted with Apple employees whose hand size ranged from very large to very small, and whose height ranged from very tall to very short. Wong wrote up reports after each round of testing.

The test results clearly supported the core concept of centering a large trackball. Wong, Ivester, Krakower, and their colleagues worked on many design details, such as: size of trackball; number of trackball buttons; placement of trackball buttons; depth and width of the keyboard; width of the palm rest; whether the palm rest should be flat or slanted, and, if the latter, at what angle. Discussions were extensive and sometimes heated. Ivester pointed out that:

> The biggest challenge was to design trackball buttons which would be easy to understand, physically comfortable, and efficient. The ongoing user testing proved very helpful in finding the right balance, since these goals conflicted to some extent. For comfort and efficiency, buttons both above and below the ball seemed to work well. Users could move the trackball with one thumb and click the top button with the other, leaving the hands positioned over the home row of the keyboard. For fine pointing work, it was better to drop the hand down, moving the ball with the index finger and clicking the bottom button with the thumb of the same hand. But having two mouse buttons was not the Macintosh way, and it caused some confusion. To counter the confusion, we needed to communicate that the buttons have the same function.

Several designs were tried, and multiple inserts were built that could be placed into the test models. (See **Exhibit 10.**) People found the three-button designs to be especially confusing. Ivester explained the final design. "The two buttons were designed to occupy the same amount of space, with the largest button surfaces placed where fingers naturally reach when using the ball. The bottom button's lower edge is curved to help it clear the palms when typing. The top button's top edge has a similar curve to help communicate that the buttons have the same function." The buttons themselves were designed through ID models, and sanded to get them to feel just right.

When the machine was flat on a desk, people felt as if they were typing downhill. This sensation was accentuated when the palm rest was tilted. The designers revised the palm rest to a flat position, while also shortening the keyboard to reduce the reach. In addition, they incorporated wheel-like feet or lifters in the rear corners of the machine. (See **Exhibit 11.**) When the notebook was on a person's lap, the lifters could be left folded up, but they could be rotated down to raise the keyboard to a more comfortable position for typing on a flat surface.

Portability and Object Value

These months of iterative testing and design led to an evolutionary shift in the meaning and execution of the product concept. Brunner looked back upon the emergence of the themes of portability and object value:

> To be competitive, we had certain size and weight specs we had to meet. This was driving the TIM program. We were assuming that it was just a catch-up maneuver, not a way of moving ahead. Where we felt we could win and take leadership was by integrating hardware, software, and industrial design, because those are the things that we have or take more seriously than anybody else in the industry.
>
> But we were still looking at TIM as a small computer. We made models of a small computer, but we weren't thinking usability scenarios or emotional content. On the Companion project, we had begun thinking about usability, and what people really want in a portable product. As we built and tested more models for TIM, we started thinking more about its environmental aspects. As we got further into TIM, we could begin to see real advantages to what we were coming up with, and we began to develop this idea of true

portability versus the mobile desktop. This is where we began to build upon the idea of integration as being more than hardware and software; it meant viewing the product from a portability point of view.

Portability referred to usability in a variety of mobile environments, which might range from a dining table, a lap, or an airline tray to a hotel bed. The design had to have the flexibility to deliver consistent performance across environments. The designers also began to recognize the usability advantages of a full-size palm rest and its implications for portability.

Portability was very intertwined with a second emergent theme, that of object value. Notebook users didn't just sit down, flip a switch, and start working. They carried their notebook around with them, used it on their laps, they opened and closed its case, and took batteries in and out. A notebook was not a piece of business equipment that someone operated; it was a personal object with which they formed a relationship. Bruce Gee recalled: "When we first started on the program, it was, 'Build a small notebook computer.' It wasn't, 'Build the most ergonomic notebook computer.' Through the use of testing, we began to push ergonomics as a key differentiation. So rather than being a small Macintosh, it became a great notebook that has an easy-to-use operating environment, and by the way it is a Macintosh."

Shrinking the Design

While the designers and researchers were iteratively evolving the ergonomics of portability, Sedmak, Krakower, and the mechanical designers were shrinking the design, millimeter by millimeter. They zealously rooted out every extra millimeter taken up by components and plastics. This approach came to be known as "millimeter madness." While everyone agreed that TIM's footprint and size had to shrink, Battat felt that this millimeter approach "missed the whole emotional connection." Brunner cautioned against taking it too far. In a memo to the team in May, he acknowledged the need to reduce TIM's size but pointed out that, "In the end, few buyers will care about a few millimeters of footprint, but rather the *perception* of size and mass in their eyes . . . ID [has the ability to alter] perceived size and mass . . . [so] ID may come back [to you] with some designs that increase slightly the X or Y overall dimensions, but will decrease the *perception* of size to the human eye." [emphasis added] In his view, the customer was less concerned with millimeters than with the question, "Does it fit in my briefcase?"

Led by Krakower's PCB component miniaturization efforts, the product designers took the width down from about 10 inches to 9.3 inches, and reduced the height by about .25 inch. The result, in Sedmak's view, was that by mid-August, "We finally figured out the right size and what we needed to do."

Low-Cost TIM

Apple managers originally anticipated that TIM would have a low-cost (LC) version, differentiated by its microprocessor; TIM would use the 68030 chip, and TIM LC the 68020. After exploring new LCD technologies in the May–June period, the team decided to delay the schedule by four weeks so that it could offer both the old and new technologies, with a price differential of around $1000. TIM would have an active matrix display and

EL backlighting, and TIM LC would use a passive display with either no backlighting or a less expensive lighting technology. In the meantime, Gee noted, "We learned that people did not want the 020, just the 030." Gee discussed the implications of customer-driven design changes. "If you are building a line, you want something in the middle that is less than the top. We started with 020 in the middle and 030 at the top. But when everyone wanted the 030, how could we differentiate two 030 machines? By processor speed and displays. We had to build a faster 030 for the high-end machine, and at the time we didn't know if it was feasible." The team decided that the active matrix 170 model would be used with a very powerful 25 Mhz 68030 chip. Low-cost TIM would have a passive display, and use a less powerful 16 Mhz 68030, it became the model 140.

DESIGN QUALITY AND TIME TO MARKET

Because of the intense pressure to miniaturize the notebook and get to market as soon as possible, it became obvious to everyone that compromises would have to be made in its design. The pressure was particularly intense on mechanical engineering, which was continually on the critical path. To this was added Gassée's very public view that mechanical engineers in the U.S. lacked the ability to miniaturize to requisite levels of size and quality. Thus, mechanical engineering's needs tended to dominate TIM's development. Its response to other group's needs was, as Brunner put it, "We'll do it if we have time." For example, the quick, low-risk way to meet shielding requirements meant that parting lines were not what ID would have liked.

The approach taken by the first product design manager was to get "first article" parts off of tools as quickly as possible, and then refine them. Brunner observed, "Apple is normally a front-ended loaded process. We usually do several rounds of engineering models and refinements before going to tooling. In this case where we did it the other way, we missed some big things, and had to jump back into the process in a big way after tooling." Few early indications of the scope of these issues were given by "first builds," or engineering proveouts, in October 1990. First builds were expensive prototypes that were machined to look and feel like the final product.

New Product Design Manager

Medica replaced the product design manager with Tom Bentley in November. Bentley not only knew manufacturing, but also had an appreciation for design, for the look and feel of a product, and was experienced with leading edge design methodology tools. Upon his arrival, Bentley thought TIM looked like the "project from hell. . . . Management was putting their energy into other programs. The directors were micro-managing design and telling the design team how to implement. Most of the designers had never done a plastic part before. Everything was line-to-line fit. I got there two months before first articles, and first articles came back with all these issues appearing out of the woodwork."

Prototype Builds

By line-to-line fit, Bentley meant that the inexperienced designers had not taken manufacturing tolerances into account. Therefore, some of the plastic parts did not fit precisely or line up as they should have because of tolerance stack-up. But it was not until parts were made from tooling, rather than machined, that it became evident that many refinements were still needed before TIM met Apple's design standards. First articles were the first of some fifteen prototype builds over a seven-month period; each build revealed new issues.

150 Items

By late February 1991, Bentley compiled a list of nearly 150 items that were problems or less than satisfactory. Many of the items were fit and feel issues with the product and enclosure parts: doors and latches that were too difficult to open; hinges that creaked or latches that rattled; a sharp edge on the I/O door; a CAPS LOCK key that did not click down or have a light. Some were aesthetic: the power plug hole was too large and ugly, the gap around the trackball buttons too large. Some were functional issues such as connector interferences, or EMI issues that required shielding, grounding, gaskets, or some other fix. Some were significant for product integrity, such as the addition of a shroud around the display to seal up the unit when closed, and the addition of ribs to strengthen the thin-wall structure in certain key areas.

Dissatisfied with the quality but mindful that tooling was already being cut, Bentley asked Sedmak and his team leaders which five or ten items needed to change in order to get the product out the door. People had difficulty deciding. Bentley insisted that they prioritize the problems, but in every meeting, the list of number-one-priority items seemed to grow rather than to shrink. In the end, the team decided to change all 150 items.

Resources

The scope of what had to be done in such a limited time was way beyond what five product designers could do. TIM would require a great infusion of resources.

Medica explained what this meant:

> It was not until well after the PowerBooks had been introduced that Product Design for portables actually reported directly into our group. During development of the 170, Product Design—which includes the actual mechanical product designers, the tooling engineers, and the CAD designers—reported to a functional engineering manager. He managed all of Apple's product design across imaging, desktops, and portables. I had to influence him to steal resources from other groups, and have them come back and work for us. It was apparent to him that he had no choice but to take resources from Companion and move them over to PowerBooks.

For six to eight weeks in the March–April 1991 period, TIM commandeered the resources of the entire portable design organization—22 engineers. Bentley described it rather colorfully from his perspective:

> I stopped the prima donna group [i.e., Companion] that had been told they were the center of the universe. I said, "Stop. Sorry, Rodger, but I am taking your entire team. Sorry, John [the manager of the PowerBook 100, a joint venture with Sony that began in August 1990], I am taking your entire team. I am gutting your department and taking everyone over until we get this done. We are going to learn what it takes to ship the product no matter what the costs."

An incremental million dollars in tooling costs was incurred to make hundreds of tooling changes. Bentley believed that through this experience, "People gained a real good sense of portables. If you haven't designed a portable before, you are not used to the things that happen. You can't design with normal clearances. All the moving parts on PowerBook were redesigned at least four times."

NOTEBOOK DESIGN AND MANUFACTURING

The team's broadest design challenge was learning and understanding what it meant to design a portable as compared to a desktop product. The PowerBook's development was an extended lesson in learning what it meant to design a seven-pound notebook from the ground up.

Apple DFM Philosophy

Apple normally designed thick wall plastic parts that snapped together easily; its design-for-manufacturability (DFM) policy was to use no screws. It designed zero-draft parts, which meant it routinely invested in expensive tooling that yielded beautifully molded products. These design practices also made manufacturing's life easier, but added weight and size to products. Because the Portable's designers had abided by these rules, their product became much bigger and heavier than the market would accept.

Because of its need to meet much more stringent size/weight requirements, the Power-Book was the first Apple product that was allowed to violate these rules. It could not be designed with desktop clearances. Heavy plastic structures and thick walls were out of the question. Thin walls were necessary, as were positive fasteners. TIM had 50–75 parts, and over 40 screws. Routing complexity of PC boards was much greater than for a desktop; boards were more closely stacked and required header connections. TIM had more subassemblies, and much more labor content.

Manufacturing Expectations

Sedmak described the "established rhythm at Apple" as one in which "it took three to four years to do a product; the design team waited nine months, and did another. A three-month slip was not that big a deal. It was important, but it wasn't, 'boy, we've got to make it.' Now we are having to move at a speed that is straining the entire corporation. Manufacturing sites are having to move at a speed that they are not comfortable working at because their infrastructure was put there by a different design cycle."

The Fremont plant was designated to build the PowerBook. The people there had never built a portable. When Bentley took a prototype over there, they said, "You're crazy. We can't build this thing. It has 47 screws in it." Bentley recalled, "It was exactly the same thing with the manufacturing organization as it was with the design organization. People didn't know what the rules were, what the standards were. Apple is 100 percent snap-together parts, which means we can use 80 percent temps on the line."

One way that Sedmak dealt with manufacturing's discomfort with portables was to bring competitive products to team leader meetings, and proceed to take them apart. They all had thin walls and positive fasteners. Compaq had even resorted to going to a Japanese company to assemble its first high-volume model. When the LTE was taken apart, Fremont manufacturing took it as a kind of challenge. Resistance gradually lowered, and there was acknowledgment that, in Sedmak's view, "We had no choice. If we wanted to be in this business, we had to do this."

POWERBOOK INTRODUCTION

By the end of 1990, marketing was working on TIM positioning and pricing. Early in 1991, it began thinking about naming TIM, and about treating it differently from a Macintosh. Based on formal research, marketing began calling it PowerBook.

Market Projections

Initial sales forecasts were low—perhaps 100,000 units the first year, and, at most, 150,000. That changed very dramatically and very quickly during the spring and summer. Even with first plastics, Gee recalled, "the level of excitement was incredible. People were just amazed that we could get something that small. Once they got their hands on it, we had to pry their hands loose at the end of the presentation." His boss, Neil Selvin, elaborated on what was coming back from usability testing, focus group presentations, and customers of the early prototypes:

> What hit people was the ergonomics. The DOS clones all looked alike. They had squared corners and looked clunky. They had clip-on mice or trackballs that you had to use with a long stringy cable. Control over the screen from one application to another was very weak. There was an immediate attraction to PowerBook. The center-mount trackball, the palm rest, the keyboard's being moved back, the slope and tilt of the screen, the slider bars for adjusting keyboard tilt—all these little things that made it comfortable.

Ramp Challenge

As a result, over a period of several weeks beginning in March 1991, marketing estimates for quarterly sales went from 50,000 to 75,000, then 100,000, and finally 175,000. Even the 50,000 estimate caught Sedmak's attention because, compared to the Portable, this meant a huge ramp. Sedmak and Bentley began holding weekly "ramp challenge" meetings, primarily with the factory and Apple's critical suppliers. Working through all the problems took nearly a year, and for many months Bentley had one of his product designers with a beeper on the line at all times on both shifts. He would beep Bentley at home or wherever he might be; if they couldn't get the line up in half an hour, they called in the manufacturing manager.

Verification Testing

Some of the most important problems were revealed through Production Verification Tests (PVT) at the plants during June and July. Problems showed up with virtually every subassembly. Sedmak described why PVT was so important:

> It is fairly typical of the electronics business that when you go through your builds, you are only building a couple hundred units, and usually the subassemblies are being put together by engineers. They often build them on prototype lines and use premium components because you haven't turned your vendor loose yet so that you can see where the process really goes. So when you finally do turn them loose, and build them on a regular line with regular production people, you get surprised.

By June 1991, however, TIM was a first-level priority, had enormous visibility in the corporation, and got whatever help it needed. Sedmak described the pressure as "ferocious." "You find problems and you have no options and you are up against the wall. Our active matrix display went into production in May so that we would not be short. But if we found a problem in June or during PVT test, we already had 30,000–40,000 displays in inventory. If you want to change something then, you are talking big time scrap heaps."

Product Launch

The PowerBook 140/170 was announced October 20, 1991. Within two weeks, Apple was backlogged by 140,000 units. During the first 12 months in the market, over 400,000 were sold, generating over one billion dollars in revenue for Apple. (See **Exhibit 12.**)

RETROSPECTIVES AND LEARNING

Apple had been concerned that in doing a notebook, it would have to make a flimsy, non-Apple quality product to get to the size and weight required by the market. When its engineers looked at competitors' portables, their response had been, "We can't do a product like that. That is not Apple quality." Brunner felt that TIM had been "a real learning experience for Apple in coming to grips with what traditional Apple quality means in this time to market environment. TIM helped us to do this even though it was occasionally painful." He elaborated:

> During development, time was king. When we got some of the first units back, we realized that there were some areas that had been cut. We went back and did a lot of refinement that we normally wouldn't have had to do in order to meet Apple quality. I think initially we let the timing push us and then we came back later and said, "Wait a minute, this is too far on the other side of the line. We've got to come back and fix some of these things because it just won't be good enough." It was a valuable lesson for every portable program I have been involved in since. We definitely learned our lessons about what is good acceptable quality and what are the compromises that we have to make to get something out.

Design refinement and correction of the 150 items was the difference between, as Medica put it, "something that I would be proud of versus a piece of junk." Retrospectively, he mused, "If we hadn't done them, I believe the PowerBook would not have been nearly as successful. I think the PowerBook is about the whole customer experience—the ease of use, the ergonomics, the elegant design, the fit and finish, the performance." He also believed that the long-term effects of TIM's pulling major resources during the second calender quarter of 1991 had been beneficial. He explained,

> At the time, people on the Companion project felt they were being significantly shortchanged. It wasn't a popular decision, but we had no choice because we had to deliver the 100, 140, and 170 in October.[2] In hindsight, it actually made the Duo [the Companion team's first product] a better product because most of the Duo team had never done a portable before. They had only done an eight-to-ten piece part design for desktops. On TIM, they got involved in a fifty-part piece design with all the secondary operations, vendor-related issues, and factory-related issues when everything had to come together. They learned a hell of a lot. It was a great training ground, and subsequently, the Duo didn't go through nearly the pain that we did on the original 140 and 170.

[2] The PowerBook 100 was a joint venture with Sony. It was a miniaturized version of the Portable, using a 6800 chip and weighing 5.5 pounds. Apple lacked the engineering resources to do this low-end notebook concurrently with TIM, TIM LC, and Companion.

Bentley believed that design—what he described as the look and feel of the product—was responsible for 95 percent of the "people essence" of the PowerBook. During its first year in the market, he went to a trade show where he took apart and played with 72 portables; he found PowerBook to be unquestionably the best, 20 percent above the rest.

Battat shared his view of the importance of design to PowerBook's success. "I think customers have an emotional attachment to PowerBooks, and that has nothing to do with size and weight and meeting their performance expectations. In some cases, it may be bigger than it needs to be because there are curves in it. But those curves are what helps generate emotions. Unfortunately, you can't prove it."

Organizational Maturation

In Bentley's view, the responsibility of the product design manager in a program was to look at problems and escalate those that people would care about. But on TIM,

> We didn't have the experience level to flag and escalate such issues. People couldn't look at a hinge and say, "We are going to have problems with that hinge," or, "That latch doesn't look like it's going to work." Since then, we have built these capabilities. The marketing guy now would take things out and test them, and come back and say, "These 20 of the 150 need to change, and these 70 people don't care about."

The idea of empowering and supporting project managers was increasingly in the air during and after the 1990 reorganization. It took time, however, before it was understood well enough to become translated into practice. Used to the "champion model," many senior middle managers interpreted "supporting" as meaning that problems that could not be resolved by the project manager should be brought upstairs to them. This had been formalized under Gassée; if the senior managers could not agree, then the matter had to be referred to Gassée. One manager commented on his frustrations with this process, "You could never go to John-Louis with a problem; you always had to go to him with a solution. You had to get consensus before you went in there, or he would rip you up. Then you had to get on his calendar." After Gassée's departure later that year, directors still resolved a lot of issues, but did so more quickly, while project managers began assuming more authority.

PowerBook's Impact on Design

In Brunner's view, "The two most powerful things about the PowerBook design are its design for portability so it can be used in a variety of environments, and its object appeal." He recalled that, "Industrial Design was driving the notion of 'object value,' and got definite support from product marketing. Most manufacturers were treating their portables as extensions of their desktop environment, as business equipment, rather than as personal objects. A lot of our focus on the product detailing came from our sense of its object appeal." This experience with portability had also affected how Apple thought about design language. Brunner continued:

> Prior to the PowerBook, we looked at good design as being policy. It was not tailored to the products or the individual, but an aspect of Apple philosophy. The result was homogenous design. So when we did me Portable, we took the same Apple rules and applied them. But as we got into the PowerBook and started thinking about portability, we were using design to move the product out in a certain direction toward certain people. This has changed our thinking about design language. We have more freedom now in terms of form, color, detail, and layout to define, to move towards a certain customer group.

Bob Brunner, Director, Industrial Design

When Robert (Bob) Brunner was first approached to take over management of Apple's ID group, Apple had only five designers, and did 90 percent of its design work through outside consultants. Brunner, who was then 31 and consulting to Apple, didn't find this appealing, nor did he think it right for Apple unless the charter became one of forming a strong internal group to chart Apple's strategic direction in design. When this charter was accepted, he joined the company in November, 1989. "I came to Apple because it has great products, and is driven by product design. People here are very visually oriented. They rally around objects, and the company centers around physical products. Design is embedded in the culture. I sometimes say I have a staff of 10,000."

In fact, Brunner now has a staff of 21 who do about 60 percent of Apple's design work. Inside ID people are used for direction-setting products. A few are assigned to a specific product line, and have a strategic responsibility to take that line somewhere. The others are part of the model shop, or of the design studio, a captive, creative pool of talent that crosses all areas. By thus leveraging his design resources, Brunner aims to keep headcount down and creativity up. Apple has long-term relationships with numerous external designers who are used for follow-on products, as a source of fresh ideas, and as a problem-solving resource.

The PowerBook, for which ID began making sketches and models a few weeks after Brunner's arrival, was a learning experience for everyone associated with it. "We had certain size and weight specs we had to meet, and that was driving the program. We were assuming that it was just a catch-up maneuver, not a way of moving ahead. But as we got into it, we began to develop this idea of true portability versus the mobile desktop. We felt we could win and take leadership through integrating hardware, software, and industrial design, because those are the core things that we have and take more seriously than anybody else in the industry. We began to build upon the idea of integration as being more than hardware and software; it meant viewing the whole product from a portability point of view."

This experience with portability has affected how Apple thinks about design language. "Prior to the PowerBook, we looked at good design as being policy. It was not tailored to the products or the individual, but an aspect of Apple philosophy. The result was homogenous design. So when we did the Portable, we took the same Apple rules and applied them. But as we got into the PowerBook and started thinking about portability, we were using design to move the product out in a certain direction toward certain people. This has changed our thinking about design language. We have more freedom now in terms of form, color, detail, and layout to define, to move towards a certain customer group."

This freedom is particularly pronounced in the "outer ring" of Apple's design language. "We used to be very retentive about design language, but now I look at it like rings of a tree. We have core systems, monitors, and displays that need to be very consistent. Then we move out into the second ring to things that are related to the Macintosh brand, such as printers and portables. In the third ring are consumer products that are not directly related to computers; these we should design for the specific application and our target customers."

One of Brunner's major challenges is to address Apple's triple messages of innovation, cost, and time to market. To meet cost pressures, "we have had to learn to scale our process." By that he means that ID must leverage its time/resources wisely; it cannot overinvest in incremental products, or those having limited market potential. To insure innovation, "you have to keep the pressure on, do design studies, do early explorations. And if you want things fast, then you have to do more work in advance. A high percentage of that will wind up in the dumpster, but that is the price of innovation. And you need to allow for quality think time—'grave time'—on the project itself."

PowerBook was designed primarily in the language of Snow White. Brunner observed that it "looked like a module for the desktop," yet its curves and dark color began the transition toward "Espresso," Apple's new design language. Brunner described "Espresso":

> Its global themes are curvature, central symmetry—or an axis of symmetry, but it's usually a central axis—complex surfaces that catch the light and are comfortable to hold (like the new mouse), surface tearing and bulging, overt expression of function, and general detail consistency. At this global level, the design language itself serves as a unifying theme to define Apple as a whole. Espresso is also flexible and scaleable. That means that the attributes and goals of the product itself define the final implementation of the language.

Brunner also added that, "Randy [Battat] asked me not too long ago whether we could do another PowerBook and I said no. It would be much harder because at that point we had nothing to lose. Now that we are successful, we have to say, 'Wait a minute, that is radical. We better go out and test that.' It's healthy to find a balance, because we could have fallen on our face if the concept had been too radical."

EXHIBIT 1
Apple's Organization, November 1989

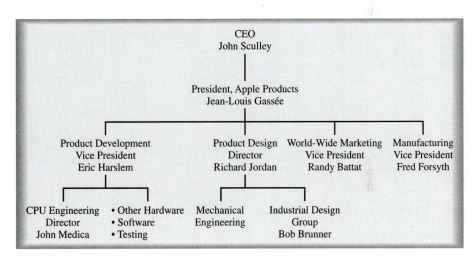

EXHIBIT 2 **PowerBook Design Timeline**

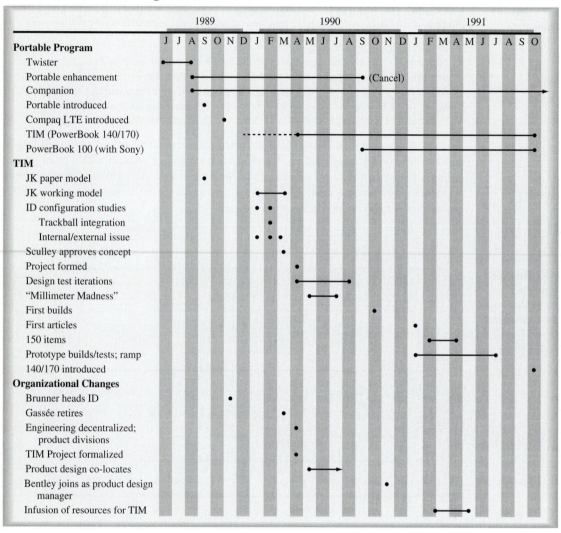

EXHIBIT 3
Twister Model,
Summer 1989

EXHIBIT 4
ID Models for TIM, January–February 1990

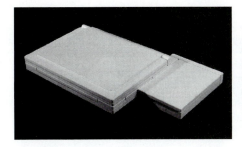 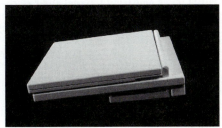

EXHIBIT 5
Krakower's Paper Model, September 1989

EXHIBIT 6
Krakower's Working Model, January–March 1990

EXHIBIT 7   Comparing Internal and External Floppies

	Modular Floppy		Integrated Floppy	
	Advantages	**Disadvantages**	**Advantages**	**Disadvantages**
1. Feature Set	Provides customer option to remove floppy drive.	Customer perception of less than full-function machine; does not keep pace with competition.	Full Waimea feature set, minus internal PDS card capability.	None
2. ID Volume Dimensions	Fits with 9.5" × 11" form factor, max height—52mm.	None	Fits within 9.5" × 11" form factor, max height—52 mm; same size as floppyless model.	None
3. Weight	Unit is about 0.75 lb. lighter than other model (all other factors being equal) outside case.	None	Will weigh-in at 7 lbs., +/−0.25 lb.; very competitive for a full-function '030/386 laptop in '91.	NONE:-> with the machine being transported in the carrying case, the overall package weighs less.
4. PC Board(s)	One continuous 10.5" × 3.8" rectangle; good for routing and production handling.	Only 79 sq. in. (top & bottom).	Total of 138 sq. in. of routable area (top & bottom); 75 percent more area.	Requires two PC boards; 4.0" × 4.75" two-sided SMT board stacked on top of motherboard.
5. ASIC Integration Requirements	None	Requires massive integration, including TAB on bottom side.	Requires no further ASIC integration; can use Waimea 84-pin PLCC chip set as is.	None
6. Ergonomics	TBD	Unproven 1.5" palm rest feature; unproven mini-trackball design.	Tested 3.85" palm rest feature; with sample of 45 subjects; proven trackball design.	Needs further ergonomic testing.
7. Product Design	TBD	Thicker reinforced walls required to support HDA, inverter, modem above PCB; schedule risk due to modular floppy design issues.	Internal plastic support walls minimized, resulting in reduced design and tooling lead times and less plastic weight.	None
8. Battery	None	4.4" × 10" flat battery is not user friendly nor very rugged; costs more and is heavier than SLA block.	Standard 2.4 Ah mono-block style cartridge SLA battery is rugged and easily inserted by customer.	None
9. Floppy	Can be dismounted at will.	Increases susceptibility for mechanical damage to machine; bad aesthetics on right side regardless of whether floppy is attached.	One less thing to worry about; frees up room in carrying case for spare battery, power adapter, etc.	None
10. Trackball	TBD	Schedule risk due to new design; requires further ergonomic testing; difficult to use in lap position.	A slightly reduced version of current Portable trackball can be used; test subjects prefer larger trackball.	None

EXHIBIT 7   (*continued*)

	Modular Floppy		Integrated Floppy	
	Advantages	**Disadvantages**	**Advantages**	**Disadvantages**
11. RAM/ROM Expansion	None	Only one slot available for RAM expansion; customer must take unit to dealer for installation.	Two identical slots available; allows for ROM expansion as well as 8 MB of RAM; customer installable cards.	None
12. Modem	None	Customer must take unit to dealer for installation; difficult to design modem to fit mechanical outline.	Easily installed by customer; RJ11 connectors readily accessible on left side of machine.	None
13. Carrying Case	None	Overall weight and size of case (with machine and floppy inside) will be greater than other model.	Size and weight is less than other model's case because of modular floppy's metal/plastic housing and extra padding/pocket requirements.	None

EXHIBIT 8
Brunners's Winning Design, Late February 1990

EXHIBIT 9
April 1990
Decentraliza-
tion

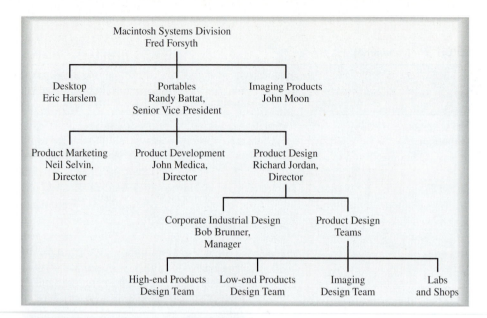

Macintosh Systems Division
Fred Forsyth

Desktop
Eric Harslem

Portables
Randy Battat,
Senior Vice President

Imaging Products
John Moon

Product Marketing
Neil Selvin,
Director

Product Development
John Medica,
Director

Product Design
Richard Jordan,
Director

Corporate Industrial Design
Bob Brunner,
Manager

Product Design
Teams

High-end Products
Design Team

Low-end Products
Design Team

Imaging
Design Team

Labs
and Shops

EXHIBIT 10
Trackball
Inserts for
User Testing

EXHIBIT 11
Rear Lifters to
Tilt Keyboard

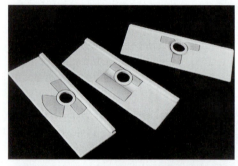

EXHIBIT 12
Production
Model,
PowerBook
140/170

Case **1-3**

IDEO Product Development

"I should have had café latte," thought Dennis Boyle as he was sipping his strong espresso at Peet's coffeehouse, just around the corner from his office. Many designers and engineers from his company, IDEO, one of the world's largest and arguably most successful product development firms, often gathered here and talked. It was late summer 1998 in Palo Alto, the heart of California's Silicon Valley, and Boyle gathered his thoughts for a meeting with David Kelley, the head and founder of IDEO.

Boyle had just led his group at IDEO through the development of 3Com's Palm V hand-held computer, which designers and managers at both firms already considered a success-ful product with very large commercial potential. Now he was being asked to design the competing Visor product by the very same individuals he had worked with previously. The only twist was that these clients themselves now worked at Handspring, a new venture whose goal was to come out with a fully compatible, slightly smaller, and less expensive palm-size computer that could easily add functionality. 3Com had even licensed out operating software to Handspring.

Although working on the Palm V challenged IDEO's engineering skills, working with Handspring promised to challenge the very manner in which it operated. It operated on the principle of getting all team members to "fail often to succeed sooner"—a creative process that often looked to outsiders like "spinning wheels." The process usually generated a foun-tain of absurd-appearing but innovative ideas before the final answer and product miracu-lously came through a process of discipline and fast decision-making.

The IDEO philosophy melded Californian iconoclasm with a genuine respect for new ideas and invention. For over two decades, the firm contributed to the design of thousands of new products ranging from the computer mouse to the stand-up toothpaste dispenser. Along the way, it had also become the largest award-winning design firm in the world (see **Exhibit 2**). IDEO came to national prominence when ABC's *Nightline* illustrated its

Harvard Business School Case No. 9-600-143. Copyright 2000 President and Fellows of Harvard College. All rights reserved. For information: permissions@hbsp.harvard.edu.

This case was prepared by Stefan Thomke and Ashok Nimgade. HBS cases are developed solely for class discussion and do not necessarily illustrate effective or ineffective management.

innovation process by showing its designers re-engineer a decades-old icon, the supermarket shopping cart, in just five days.

Now Boyle had to decide whether he should suggest to Handspring's management to add more time to a development schedule that was less than half of what it took to design the stunningly beautiful and innovative Palm V. Boyle's group feared that an overly aggressive development schedule would require them to bypass many of the early development stages that the firm was particularly good at and, at the end, deliver a product that could be so much better if they just had more time.

HISTORY OF IDEO

[David Kelley] and the company he heads, IDEO of Palo Alto, has designed more of the things at our fingertips than practically anyone else in the past 100 years, with the possible exception of Thomas Edison.

—San Francisco Examiner[1]

It was desperation caused by recalcitrant furniture during a college move that drove David Kelley to enter the Carnegie-Mellon campus workshop in search of a saw. The sights and sounds of the strange new world captured the fancy of the electrical engineering major from Ohio. For a while, in fact, he considered switching majors to fine arts but stayed with engineering. The internal switch that flickered on, however, would lead Kelley to leave engineering jobs at Boeing and NCR to embark on the journey that, according to *Fortune* Magazine, would make him "one of the most powerful people in Silicon Valley." But the first thing Kelley would ever actually design of consequence was a telephone that could only ring one number: his own. He presented this to his college girlfriend.

In 1975, Kelley joined the Stanford University program in product design. These were heady days with Kelley finding that "In Silicon Valley everything was new . . . there were no preconceived notions."[2] Through part-time consulting experience, Kelley found to his surprise that most consulting firms consisted of specialists, with technological companies lacking clear access to a general product development firm. In 1978, amid the Silicon Valley boom, Kelley gave up writing his Ph.D. thesis. (Nonetheless, even without a formal Ph.D. he would become a professor at Stanford University.)

Kelley went on to form and run David Kelley Design for the next decade. IDEO started in 1991 when David Kelley Design merged with two companies: ID Two, led by renowned designer Bill Moggridge, and Matrix, started by Mike Nuttall. The name IDEO came to life when Bill Moggridge scanned his dictionary for suitable names and liked "ideo-" (a Greek word which meant "idea") as it formed the foundation of many important combined words such as *ideo*logy and *ideo*gram. Kelley, whose company was larger than the other two combined, took over as chief executive of the new firm.

The merger brought under one umbrella all services client companies needed to design, develop, and manufacture new products: mechanical and electrical engineering, industrial design, ergonomics, information technology, prototype machining, and even cognitive psychology. IDEO thus pioneered the design version of "concurrent engineering"—a fusion of

---

[1] R. Garner, *San Francisco Examiner*, May 23, 1994, p. B-1.

[2] L. Watson, "Palo Alto Product Designer Finds Business Booming," *The San Francisco Chronicle*, August 3, 1992, p. C3.

art and engineering to produce aesthetically pleasing products that were also technically competent.[3] As an example of the utility of concurrent engineering, consider how the decision to add air vents to a computer to prevent overheating might detract from the product's streamlined aesthetics if the designers and engineers failed to work together closely.

The hardest places to practice concurrent engineering, quite understandably, were in devices involving compact and complex design such as automotive components, medical instruments, and small computing devices where small changes would have often unforeseeable ripple effects on components far removed. IDEO, with its equal emphasis on design and engineering, took up many of these challenges. In contrast, its leading competitors historically had stressed industrial design over engineering.

Major IDEO clients included Apple Computer, AT&T, Samsung, Philips, Amtrak, Steelcase, Baxter International, and NEC Corp. IDEO's thirst for variety led it to complete thousands of projects, including 50 projects for Apple Computer (including its first mouse), ski goggles, the Avocet Vertech Skiers watch, and a large variety of medical instrumentation. The company also participated in Hollywood film projects, creating scale-model submarines for *The Abyss* and a 25-foot mechanical whale for *Free Willy*. In the 1990s, IDEO won more industry awards than any other design firm worldwide (see **Exhibits 2** and **4**).

In the late 1990s, IDEO employed over 300 staff and maintained design centers in Boston, Chicago, San Francisco, London, Palo Alto, Grand Rapids, New York, Milan, Tel Aviv, and Tokyo. The sites were chosen for their stimulating locations. Although all centers operated independently, seeking business locally, they exchanged a high volume of e-mail and often shared talent as needed. Over the years, while his employees focused on designing client products, Kelley increasingly found himself designing and re-designing IDEO. "I'm more interested in the methodology of design . . . ," according to Kelley. "I'm the person who builds the stage rather than performs on it."

Part of this stage-building involved studying the IDEO environment in new ways. Instead of merely relying on employee surveys, the company also studied workplace interactions through suspended video cameras in order to optimize office design.[4] IDEO also sought to improve its own design processes by reviewing all completed projects. According to Kelley, "We pick the things each client does well, and assimilate them into our methodology. We're not good at innovating because of our flawless intellects, but because we've done thousands of products, and we've been mindful."[5]

With corporate downsizing of the 1990s, IDEO and other design firms flourished as companies outsourced more design projects. IDEO's fees generally ran from as little as $40,000 to over $1 million, depending on the scope of the project. The privately held company remained tightlipped about revenues, but in 1996 was known to have revenues of $40–$50 million. Revenues came from about 30 percent each in medical, consumer, and telecommunications/computers with an additional 10 percent from industrial products.[6]

---

[3] J. Lew, "Of Mice and Miatas: Design Shops Shape Our Lives," *San Francisco Examiner*, August 12, 1992, p. 4.

[4] P. Roberts, "Live! From Your Office! It's . . . ," *Fast Company*, October 1999.

[5] T. S. Perry, "Designing a Culture for Creativity," *Research Technology Management*, March 1995, v. 38(2), pp. 14–17.

[6] R. Rosenberg, "By Design, These Firms Take On Other Companies' Products," *The Boston Globe*, May 11, 1997, p. C1.

IDEO came to national prominence when it allowed ABC to televise a segment showing its designers meeting the challenge of re-engineering the commonplace shopping cart—a virtually unchanged icon for the past several decades, despite its creaky and obdurate wheels and often unwieldy basket—in just five days. The IDEO design replaced the traditional large basket with a system of baskets that allowed consumers to use the shopping cart as a "base camp" for shopping. Innovative new wheels allowed greater maneuverability in the store. Hooks on the frame would allow for bagged items to be transported out to the parking lot. The lack of a central basket removed much of the incentive for stealing the shopping carts.

DESIGN PHILOSOPHY AND CULTURE

If a picture is worth a thousand words, a prototype is worth ten thousand.

—IDEO innovation principle

Central to IDEO's design philosophy was the role of prototyping. According to Tom Kelley, general manager and David Kelley's brother, "we prototype more than our clients suspect, and probably more than our competitors." Frequent prototyping served as the most important way for his company to communicate with clients, marketers, experts, and end users. Prototypes ensured everyone was imagining the same design during discussions about a product. All IDEO offices had shops staffed by highly skilled machinists to rapidly produce both simple and sophisticated prototypes. Quite often, according to Whitney Mortimer, a Harvard MBA who joined the firm in the late '90s, "the real 'aha's' in product development occur here."

But in the early stages, perfecting a sophisticated model was considered a waste of time. "You learn just as much from a model that's wrong as you do from one that's right," according to engineer Steve Vassallo. Thus, designers and engineers themselves created early prototypes from readily available material such as cardboard, foamcore, Legos, and Erector sets.

Rapid prototyping at IDEO followed the three "R's": "Rough, Rapid, and Right!" The final R, "Right," referred to building several models focused on getting specific aspects of a product right. For example, to design a telephone receiver, an IDEO team carved dozens of pieces of foam and cradled them between their heads and shoulders to find the best shape for a handset. "You're not trying to build a complete model of the product you're creating," per Vassallo. "You're just focusing on a small section of it."[7]

Quick and dirty prototyping allowed for a greater number of iterations. "By our method," David Kelley claimed, "you could never design a VCR you couldn't program. [Researchers at larger companies] are afraid of looking bad to management, so they do an expensive, sleek prototype, but then they become committed to it before they really know any of the answers. You have to have the guts to create a straw man." At IDEO, these straw men were repeatedly knocked down, a process that left IDEO's staffers with thick skin. "Failure," Kelley felt, "is part of the culture. We call it enlightened trial and error."[8]

In an allied process, IDEO sought to generate as many ideas as possible early in the design process through almost daily brainstorming sessions. A much-used paraphrased

[7] T. S. Perry, "Designing a Culture for Creativity," *Research Technology Management*, March 1995, v. 38(2) pp. 14–17.
[8] Ibid.

quotation from Einstein epitomized the playfulness of the early stage: "If at first an idea does not sound absurd, then there is no hope for it." The entire process resembled a funnel, with several ideas at the top, three or four at the base, and only one making it all the way through. People were generally not upset if their idea did not become the definitive solution since the act of clipping off ideas brought the entire team closer to the solution—similar to legendary baseball batter Babe Ruth who outlined his strategy once as, "Every strike I make gets me closer to a home run." In addition, discarded ideas were archived and sometimes kept for possible future products.

Sometimes in the course of a project, when progress appeared to come to a standstill, the leader could call for what has come to be known as a Deep Dive® approach. In this process, the team would focus intensively for an entire day to generate a large number of creative concepts, weed out weak ideas, and start prototyping based on the top handful of solutions.

To an outsider, however, the entire process could appear messy. "The nature of the organization is very much like David Kelley's mind," says Arnold Wasserman who was part of IDEO's innovation strategy group. "Both are seriously playful and messy. And both are comfortable with confusion, incomplete information, paradox, irony, and fun for its own sake."[9]

The inherent inability to precisely predict the innovation process' outcome, time, and cost made it extremely important to keep clients involved. At the beginning of a new project, IDEO would submit cost and time estimates to potential clients. As a project unfolded and designers came up with innovative ideas and concepts, project managers had to ensure that those concepts were within agreed upon budgets and timelines. However, designers often aimed for perfection, which could potentially lead to cost and time overruns—also known as "creeping elegance" in design circles—and clients needed to be aware of those opportunities for further innovation and the cost and time involved. As a result, IDEO required very frequent client meetings where all those issues would be discussed.

After a visit to the company's Palo Alto office, business writer Tom Peters likened IDEO to a veritable playground. In his words, "IDEO is a zoo. Experts of all flavours co-mingle in offices that look more like cacophonous kindergarten classrooms. . . . Walk into the offices of IDEO design in Palo Alto, California, immediately you'll be caught up in the energy, buzz, creative disarray and sheer lunacy of it all. Breach the reception area at XYZ Corp . . . and you'll think you've walked into the city morgue."[10]

In keeping with its playroom atmosphere, on Mondays all company branches held "show-and-tells" where designers and engineers could showcase their latest insights and products. Also, of increasing importance to designers was IDEO's "Tech Box," the company's giant "shoebox" for curiosities and interesting gadgets meant to inspire innovators. Designers could rummage through the contents and play with the switches, buttons, and odd materials in search of new uses. The Tech Box included some 300 objects ranging from an archery bow based on pulleys to heat pipes that would turn uncomfortably hot almost the moment they were placed in a cup of hot water.

The culture itself reflected the importance that management attached to creating a democracy of ideas. Most design firms had less than two dozen employees. Growing IDEO to 300 employees involved keeping each unit small. Thus, growth was achieved by budding

[9] R. Garner, *San Francisco Examiner*, May 23, 1994, p. B-1.
[10] T. Peters, "The Peters Principles," *Forbes ASAP*, September 13, 1993, p. 180.

out smaller design studios whenever one appeared to grow too large. Much quoted was David Kelley's confident assertion in 1990 that "This company will never be larger than 40 people."[11] Following an amoeboid growth strategy, even in a small section of Palo Alto, found the company in possession of nine different buildings in the late '90s.

Employees were encouraged to design their own workspace to reflect their own personalities. Some strung up their bicycles on pulleys. Rolling doors could quickly seal offices for privacy. Staffers kept personal possessions in portable bookshelves and cabinets so that moves between projects could be accomplished rapidly. One studio suspended the wing of a DC-3 airplane with a blinking red winglight from the ceiling.

In keeping with Silicon Valley informality, the company discouraged formal titles and did not mandate a dress code. Management encouraged employees to leave their desk and walk around, especially during mental blocks. "It's suspicious when employees are at their desk all day," according to general manager Tom Kelley, "because it makes you wonder how they pretend to work." IDEO paid high rent for its prime Silicon Valley location so as to encourage stimulating interactions between employees. Free, unlocked loaner bicycles at the Palo Alto lobbies also facilitated movement between each building. Designers were encouraged to talk to one another or even call a brainstorming session through e-mail.

Management rarely fired employees. "We do a better job of managing good employees than of weeding out lower performing employees," David Kelley admitted. "But with small studios, there's literally nowhere to hide for noncontributors." High-performing employees were rewarded by being given more challenging projects to lead. Each employee was assessed through peer review sessions, with peers chosen by the employee. Management also sought to reward high performers through more shares in its client venture capital base.

Through much of the 1990s, turnover, at less than 5 percent per year, was shockingly low by Silicon Valley standards. The company typically recruited young individuals out of its own internship programs. Recruiting was a long process, entailing meeting with ten staff members, often over lunch. A disproportionate number of recruits came from Stanford University, where Kelley continued to serve as a professor.

An individual could work on one large project as a principal or on as many as three to four projects as a contributor. IDEO was a flat organization to an extreme. All work was organized into project teams, which formed and disbanded for the life of a project. As a result there were no permanent job assignments or job titles. There were no organization charts or titles to distract from the quality of the work. Project leaders often emerged on the basis of personal excitement about a project. Motivation from peer pressure also spurred employees to put in 50- to 60-hour weeks in creative endeavors.[12]

The lack of hierarchy also avoided the problem of promoting designers and engineers into administrative positions and out of their first love: creating products. But the "no-policy policy" could make for confusion among new recruits. Even proponents of the IDEO culture, including veteran Larry Shubert, admitted that "The culture is partly to be comfortable with ambiguity and confusion. . . . We err on the side of autonomy. There's some discomfort, yes."[13]

---

[11] B. Katz, "A Leadership Style," *Perspective*, Fall 1999.

[12] T. S. Perry, "Designing a Culture for Creativity," *Research Technology Management*, March 1995, v. 38(2) pp. 14–17.

[13] S. Orenstein, "The Doyen of Design," *Stanford*, May/June 1996, pp. 74–79.

But growth appeared to bring its own changes. According to Jeff Smith, president of the Palo Alto-based Lunar Design and an admirer of IDEO, "How well they're able to remain creative and not become bureaucratic and politicized will be very interesting. There's rumor of politics and agendas. . . ." Even David Kelley admitted some increase in bureau-cratization. "People are talking about it like it's a company. 'Is it o.k. to invite my wife to this?' Nobody ever asked me that before . . . Or, 'Is it o.k. if I go home and mow the lawn this afternoon?' Of course, it's o.k."[14]

By the late 1990s, however, the turnover had crept up to 10 percent as the promise of unparalleled high-tech wealth at Internet-based firms beckoned employees. To counter the trend of increasing attrition, IDEO sought to redo its compensation strategy, planning to do more equity deals and seek royalties.

IDEO'S INNOVATION PROCESS

It is inconceivable that the head guy in any organization will know all the answers.

—David Kelley, IDEO founder

If prototyping was central to IDEO's design process, brainstorming was central to its methodology. The two processes, actually, went hand in hand, with brainstorming sessions leading to rapid prototyping or vice versa. The goal was to quickly create a whirlwind of activity and ideas, with the most promising ideas developed into prototypes in just days. The firm followed several principles of brainstorming: stay focused on the topic; encourage wild ideas; defer judgment to avoid interrupting the flow of ideas; build on the ideas of oth-ers (since it was usually more productive than seeking glory for one's own insights); hold only one conversation at a time to ensure that introverts also got their say; go for quantity (very productive brainstorming could generate 150 ideas in 30 to 45 minutes); and be visual, since sketching ideas would help people understand them.

Throughout a single project, the project leader might hold brainstorming sessions, or "brainstormers." No more than eight invitees attended these sessions, which ran under the above rules. IDEO personnel viewed invitations to these sessions as a sign of worth and rarely turned them down. In an organization whose lobbies sported large bowls of M&M chocolates, David Kelley once said "brainstormers are the candy. . . . You are in the middle of a project, handling endless details, and then you get invited to a brainstormer, where you get to have all sorts of good ideas and leave with no responsibility for them. It's cathartic, to dump your ideas."[15]

IDEO's product development process followed several phases (see Exhibit 3 for details). In **Phase 0 ("Understand/Observe")**, the team sought to understand the client's business and immersed itself in finding out about the feasibility of a product. This involved inhaling everything ever written about the planned product and potential users. By the end of this process, team members tacked to the project center walls pictures and diagrams summariz-ing major discoveries about the marketplace and users. In the closely related **Phase I ("Visualize/Realize")**, the team ended up choosing a product direction based on ideas,

---

[14] Ibid.

[15] T. S. Perry, "Designing a Culture for Creativity," *Research Technology Management*, March 1995, v. 38(2) pp. 14–17.

technologies, and market perceptions. The team also gained an understanding of the product context through a gallery of envisioned characters using the product in their daily lives. By the end of Phase I, through close coordination with the client, the team would have rough three-dimensional models of a product and a general idea of the manufacturing strategy to be utilized.

In **Phase II ("Evaluating/Refining")**, the team enhanced design prototypes through testing functional prototypes. Emphasis shifted over the course of this stage from human factors and ergonomics to engineering. Phase II culminated with a functional model as well as a "looks like" design model. Then in **Phase III ("Implement/Detailed Engineering")**, the team completed product design and verified that the final product worked and could be manufactured. Although engineering efforts predominated, continuous low-level involvement with design team members occurred. By the end of this phase, the team delivered a fully functional design model, tooling databases, and technical documentation. Finally, in **Phase IV ("Implement/Manufacturing Liaison"),** the team ensured smooth product release to manufacturing as the product moved from the shop floor to the client's factory lines.

But despite the phases delineated above, IDEO had mixed feelings about formalizing any aspect of the innovative process. According to European director Tim Brown, "It's a delicate balance between process and innovation. . . . It's no good if you crank the handle and you know exactly what is going to come out the other end. You also have to be prepared to fail a lot. The great thing about a prototype culture like ours is that we have lots of spectacular failures. We celebrate that."[16]

Nonetheless, armed with the tools of rapid prototyping, brainstorming, and a well-honed product development process, the company viewed itself as being able to provide value to virtually any client. The very diversity and experience of its personnel ensured that it would rarely encounter entirely new problems. Occasionally, however, the company found itself swimming out of familiar water. Once, for instance, the governor of Hawaii asked IDEO about how the state should proceed with its economic reforms.

THE PALM V PROJECT

Never go to a client meeting without a prototype.

—"Boyle's Law" (per Dennis Boyle of IDEO;
not to be confused with the law of pressure and
volume named after seventeenth century physicist Robert Boyle)

In the mid-1980s, with the advent of Apple Computer's Newton pad, handheld computing got its start and met its near-demise. This revolutionary feature-laden product proved ahead of its time, with consumers frustrated by the sometimes slow and inaccurate handwriting recognition system that was meant to replace the tyranny of the cumbersome keyboard. Users also found the system large and inconvenient. It took until March 1996 before anyone could successfully introduce another general-purpose handheld computing device. This honor belonged to California-based engineer-visionary Jeff Hawkins, whose "Palm Pilot" found almost immediate consumer acceptance. Key to Hawkins' success was the development

---

[16] D. Dearlove, "Innovation from the Chaos," *The Times* (U.K.), August 13, 1998.

of critical technologies, including the so-called Graffiti program for handwriting recognition and "syncing," the capability to synchronize data between a handheld computer and a home computer.

Hawkins possessed a maniacal focus on product simplicity. This led him to hone his vision by carrying a crude wood prototype the size of a deck of cards in his pocket while envisioning how typical customers might use the product through the course of a day. Sometimes he would sit through staff meetings scrawling imaginary notes onto the inert wood screen of the prototype. The end result proved a product meant to compete with paper rather than with larger computers. Although it could just store addresses, telephone numbers, a calendar, and a to-do list, it did so rapidly and conveniently.

For all its apparent simplicity, the Palm Pilot became the fastest-selling computer product ever.[17] Hawkins and his staff achieved their feat of design and engineering while working during a period of corporate upheaval that saw their parent company change from Palm Company to U.S. Robotics to 3Com. Understandably, the Palm Pilot success story attracted other start-ups and entrants to the new field, leading to handheld devices touting features such as vibrating alarms, voice recording, increased memory, and so on. One advertisement for the competing Everex Freestyle palm-sized computer, after listing several new features, warned: "Palm Pilot beware!"[18] Microsoft itself was expected to enter the field with a new product that would leapfrog current products by offering eight megabytes of memory.

At the Palm division, while many engineers pondered new ways to retain market share, Hawkins recalled thinking, "Who cares. I don't need eight megabytes; I can't even fill up two. Let's show the world that this isn't about speeds and feeds. . . . It's about simplicity."[19] To avoid being caught up in the battle over new features and minutiae, the Palm division under Hawkins' leadership sought an entirely new approach, one that would also hopefully draw in more female users into a market of predominantly male businessmen.

Palm eventually turned to IDEO to fulfill Hawkins' vision. Within IDEO, the choice of project leader fell naturally to Dennis Boyle, a senior project leader and studio manager who had left his mark on the company with a stream of successful products and the institution of the Tech Box, a natural outgrowth of his tendencies since childhood (to the chagrin of this mother) to collect curios of all sorts in shoeboxes. For Boyle, the fit was natural: the very moment he first saw the Palm Pilot he knew "this will make a big difference" and proceeded to use it, add it to his collection, and discuss it at staff meetings. Palm was to remain Boyle's main client for the duration of the project, with a majority of his billable time dedicated there.

For Hawkins' and Boyle's teams, inspiration came from the sleek Motorola StarTac mobile phone that was introduced in 1996 at the price of $1,000—at a time when many mobile phone makers started giving away their products in return for user subscription fees. Hawkins recalled that, "The StarTac was a radical departure. It looked different, beautiful. It also commanded outrageous prices. We wanted to do the same thing."[20] Other products that inspired the IDEO team, and which Boyle kept in his briefcase, included a metal Canon minicamera, Pentax opera glasses, and a telescoping pair of eyeglasses in a thin metal case used as emergency back-up eyewear.

---

[17] P. E. Teague, "Special Achievement Award: Jeff Hawkins," *Design News*, March 6, 2000, p. 108.

[18] D. Roth, "Putting Fluff over Function," *Fortune*, March 15, 1999.

[19] Ibid.

[20] Ibid.

Each of these small and elegant products made the existing line of Palm Pilots appear stodgy in comparison. This was not surprising given that the computer world had generally ignored design in favor of technical bells and whistles that catered to men. Men, after all, comprised the majority of computational gadget users at the time. This mindset was successfully challenged by Apple Computer, which true to its "Think Different" advertisement campaigns, came up with its translucent turquoise iMac computers. Apple President Steve Jobs declared, "For most consumers, color is more important than megahertz."

With similar thoughts in mind, Boyle's team outlined plans for a slimmer, sleeker version of the existing Palm Pilot. This called for reducing the thickness from the current 19 mm to 11 mm and the weight by one-third. According to Janice Robert, the 3Com vice president in charge of the Palm division at the time of the Palm V release: "We want to appeal to people not just on the rational level but the emotional level."[21]

The team started work on what would become the Palm V project late in 1996.[22] At the outset of the "Understand Phase" (**Phase 0**), which lasted 10–12 weeks, the IDEO team realized that despite the popularity of the Palm III, little data existed on user preferences. Boyle therefore started creating his own observational database by purchasing dozens of the Palm Pilots and giving them to colleagues, business friends, spouses, physicians, and representatives from other walks of life.

The rapidly developing obsession of Boyle's team with Palms spread throughout the company: over 200 IDEO staff members throughout the company eventually started using Palms. Feedback through e-mail or through casual hallway conversations quickly started reaching Boyle's team. The team thus became aware of problems concerning the product's susceptibility to breaking after being dropped, rigidity of the case, placement of the battery and memory doors, and location of the stylus holder.

In March 1997, **Phase I** (visualize and realize) started. At the outset, only three to four IDEO designers and engineers were involved. At the project's height of activity, as many as a dozen staffers would become involved. The diverse team included nationalities ranging from as far afield as Taiwan, the Netherlands, and Israel. Boyle deliberately tapped the talent of two female design engineers including senior designer Amy Han in hopes of achieving insights that would attract more female users into a marketplace where 95 percent of the existing Palm users were men.

Han and her colleague Trae Niest, in turn, obtained feedback from 15 other female colleagues. As a group, they challenged the conventional wisdom that handheld devices, in general, had to be square with block edges and colored a mundane gray. Even the advertisements promoted a corporate monolithic blandness, with, for instance, depictions of businessmen slipping Palms into gray suit pockets. The findings and insights of Han and her group led the industrial designers to make the new product more curvy, with tapering edges. The new project bore the code name "Razor," which indicated the goal of Hawkins' team at Palm to create a "razor thin" product.

The IDEO team met weekly with the Palm division to ensure a constant stream of feedback. Boyle made sure the team never went to a client meeting without a prototype of some type or another. The prototypes varied from being as simple as a keypad button to mockups

---

[21] Ibid.

[22] Many viewed the parallels in nomenclature between the Palm III, V, and VII and the BMW 3, 5, and 7 series as 3Com's tribute to BMW's internationally heralded automotive product line.

of subtly different-sized LCD panels to styluses of varying thicknesses, lengths, and contours (see **Exhibits 5** and **6**). This process helped ensure that even the smallest of details would be considered. As a result, for instance, the team designed both sides of the device to accommodate a wide variety of potential add-on covers and styluses. Even left-handed individuals would find the dual rail system accommodating.

To ensure a very thin product, the design teams realized early in the process that traditional batteries would have to give way to thinner rechargeable lithium ion batteries. However, it was not clear, considering recharging times and use patterns, that lithium ion would work in this design. The Palm team under Frank Canova, director of hardware engineering, and IDEO spent much of the first half of 1997 corralling reluctant battery makers to cooperate in this venture. Another sticky issue confronting the entire team concerned the use of anodized aluminum for creating the thin casing—a choice of material based on the limitations of plastics—given that U.S. manufacturers had little experience working with this material. As a result, the Palm V team faced the dual challenge of communicating with Asian manufacturers while simultaneously using anodized aluminum to create the technically difficult thin complex surfaces.[23]

By May 1997, conceptualization and realization of the Palm V project gave way to **Phase II** (evaluation and refinement). This stage involved computer-aided design (CAD) engineering to help create accurate industrial models resembling the proposed end product. In this phase, designers and engineers incorporated observed usage patterns to allow users to recharge the Palm for only brief periods of time without shortening battery lives. The team moved toward a final model, choosing solutions, vendors, and sources. Every part of the mechanical model was machined out as close as possible to the final mass-produced parts. By the end of Phase II, some 20–25 prototypes had been created (see **Exhibit 6**).

In the fall of 1997, **Phase III**, implementation (detailed engineering), started. Every component was engineered to be functional in terms of the electronics and software. Some three to five production prototypes were created. A number of each of these prototypes were built for drop testing to develop the sturdiest possible electronics. Testing was also undertaken to meet government regulations. By the end of Phase III, prototype models could exceed $30,000 each. The team kept refining those models until just one or two final contestants remained. At the same time, the Palm team grew by leaps and bounds, particularly in the realm of production as well as product promotion. Through regular meetings of increasing sizes, and through a flurry of e-mail exchanges, responsibilities gradually shifted away from IDEO.

One of the most bothersome problems confronting the team involved binding the complex 11mm-wide unit together without a single screw (screws being considered aesthetically and mechanically undesirable by the IDEO designers). The team ultimately committed to using a binding device never before used for handheld computers: industrial glue. At a most inopportune time, however, 3Com's modem card gluers—the only available personnel with experience in using industrial glue—left the company. The remaining team ended up experimenting through trial and error with several different adhesives and bonding parameters before arriving at a satisfactory solution (see Exhibit 6).

By end of **Phase IV**, implementation (manufacturing liaison), and expected late fall 1998, "Razor" would be released to production. The Palm division planned to retain some

[23] D. Roth, "Putting Fluff over Function," *Fortune*, March 15, 1999.

IDEO personnel for another six months—the amount of time projected for gearing up for market release in February 1999. During this period, pilot production would work on smoothing processes at the production line to ultimately allow for manufacturing up to 5,000 units a day. This was crucial: each day's loss of a production line's output would cost the company a few hundred thousand dollars. Many problems still remained for the Palm manufacturers to address including cracks in the display, electrostatic charge, docking problems, cover imperfections, supplies procurement, and component switching. An aggressive schedule would compound problems that would otherwise be considered routine for products of this complexity. Hundreds of personnel were expected to become involved at the manufacturing sites in Utah, Japan, and Singapore as well as at dozens of vendor sites in Hong Kong, Taiwan, California, Texas, and Singapore.

THE HANDSPRING PROJECT

In July 1998, both Hawkins and his business partner, Donna Dubinsky, a Harvard MBA who had run the business side of Palm, resigned from 3Com on amicable terms to set up shop in Palo Alto. Part of the reason for the move was the desire for greater autonomy. Despite the success of the Palm line, 3Com as a whole was not doing well enough to reward personnel with stock. The goal of the new company was to come out with a fully compatible, slightly smaller, and less expensive clone of the palm-size computers. A technical motivation behind the new company was to address the Palm's inability to easily add functionality.

Hawkins had already scaled back to part-time work at Palm Computing to turn his attention to a long-time interest of his: writing a book on how the brain works. The temptation to interrupt the academic project to take another pass at building the perfect palm-size device was irresistible for someone universally hailed as the "father of a new industry." In quick order, Hawkins and Dubinsky were joined by the original Palm team of a dozen engineers. People enjoyed working with Hawkins, who, in Boyle's words was "by and large an even-keeled, predictable, normal person despite being a brilliant innovator."

Just a few weeks after starting up, Dubinsky and Hawkins, now chief product officer at Handspring, signed a licensing agreement with 3Com for the right to use the Palm operating system. This agreement would provide any product they developed compatibility with the myriad applications already available for Palm devices. Once again, Hawkins would turn to IDEO for designing a new product.

In July 1998, Hawkins asked Boyle for a proposal. Hawkins felt that the proposed device should be able to easily link-up through so-called "ROM cards" for games, pagers, cell phones, Global Positioning System receivers, voice recorders (the product would have a tiny built-in microphone), wireless modems, MP3 music players, graphing calculators, digital cameras, and even cardiac monitors. A solution for how to do this came to Hawkins when he spotted his child's Nintendo Game Boy, which allowed for changing games simply by inserting interchangeable game cartridges. This led to the so-called "Springboard" slot on the back of the product, which would allow the user to plug in a variety of matchbook-size modules. Hawkins' ten-year-old daughter actually proposed the product name "Visor"—short for "advisor."

The IDEO-Handspring team wanted the modules to be simple to use, with the device operating the moment a module was inserted. Some two dozen third-party developers expressed interest in developing add-on devices for the proposed Visor. Even without a concrete plan, funding flowed easily from venture capitalists eager to duplicate Palm's success with a device that could set a new trend in handheld computing. Publicity, too, would come easily, even in a field replete with new handheld devices. For the meantime, however, the media was kept guessing.

Apart from product features such as price, memory, and colors, the Visor team saw little need for market research. According to Dubinsky, "We felt we understood the marketplace pretty well. After all, we invented the product and the category . . . . You can't test the concept of a slot; it's too major."[24] The new project, however, was launched at a time when skeptics noted that people used hand-held devices primarily for mundane tasks such as storing addresses and personal calendars, rather than for complex tasks such as accessing e-mail. "People don't want a combination device," according to Ken Dulaney, mobile computing market research specialist at the Gartner Group. "Every time you try to get a computer to do many things, it ends up doing none of them well."[25]

Hawkins and Dubinsky insisted that the Visor's cost be kept to $150—a price far below the $300 commanded by the original Palm Pilot in 1996 and the $450 commanded by the Palm V at its market launch. This price was intended to attract a wider following and consistent with Handspring's strategy of getting a product with the new standard into many hands as quickly as possible. As a result, Hawkins and Dubinsky pushed for a product launch deadline of late 1999, just in time for the holiday gift-giving season and several months less than their already ambitious prior deadline of spring 2000. This would entail a product development cycle of about ten months before handing off the product to production in March-April 1999.

Boyle was not worried about meeting this challenging deadline because IDEO could meet difficult deadlines, even if at the eleventh hour and fifty-ninth minute. Furthermore, the team under Boyle had already encountered and worked smoothly with most of the Handspring team through dozens of prior meetings and other encounters during the Palm V project. IDEO and Handspring shared in common a belief in quick prototyping and a consumer-centered mentality. In Hawkins' words, after all, "I'm not down on engineering, but I'm really down on technology for technology's sake. . . . I don't say 'Put the biggest, meanest CPU in here.' I say, 'Make this work well for the consumer.' "[26]

The Handspring project would also require Boyle's team to keep the rest of IDEO, not to mention the rest of Silicon Valley, in the dark about the project. This would make for uncomfortable moments, especially during informal hallway conversations with colleagues, some of whom were still working on the Palm V project.

What concerned Boyle much more, however, was having to sacrifice the IDEO emphasis on innovation and design in order to meet the client's goal. Because of the time and price pressures, Hawkins' proposal would imply running with only "tried-and-true" technology; IDEO would not be able to indulge in the early phases of its legendary development process that differentiated it from other product development firms. Visor would have to sacrifice style and settle on an inexpensive plastic housing, and on AAA batteries instead of the rechargeable lithium-ion battery found in the Palm V.

---

[24] K. Hafner, "One More Ultimate Gadget," *The New York Times*, September 16, 1999, Late Edition, p. G1.

[25] Ibid.

[26] R. Merritt, "Palm Pilot Designer Steers Fresh Course in Handhelds." *Electronic Engineering Times*, October 25, 1999.

If they had twice the time, Boyle was confident that his team could help create a killer product that would match the Palm V in design excellence and capability. Should he and Kelley try to persuade Handspring to postpone the Visor launch, allowing the team to follow all the steps of IDEO's legendary innovation process? Or should they just accept the client's request for a very aggressive schedule that would not allow his team to fully engage in early experimentation? He wrestled with these thoughts as he finished his espresso and walked back to the studio to meet David Kelley.

EXHIBIT 1
Important Milestones

ca. 500 B.C.	Documentation of Egyptian papyrus prototypes for paper, which millennia later remains medium of choice for personal data storage.
1978	David Kelley receives master's degree from Stanford's product design program. Eventually starts up his own company, David Kelley Design.
Mid-1980s	With the advent of Apple Computer's Newton, handheld computing gets its start and meets its near-demise.
1991	IDEO started through a merger between David Kelley Design, ID Two, and Matrix.
1996	Annual IDEO revenues reach $40–50 million.
March	Engineer-visionary Jeff Hawkins' handheld "Palm Pilot," meant to replace papyrus derivatives rather than computers, finds immediate consumer acceptance.
Fall	IDEO starts work on the Palm V project, which bears the code name "Razor."
1997 March	Phase I ("Understand") starts on the Palm V project; by May Phase II ("Evaluation and Refinement") starts; by fall, Phase III ("Implementation") starts.
1998 Summer	Handspring project starts at IDEO when Jeff Hawkins asks Dennis Boyle for a proposal for proposed handheld computing device with revolutionary "Springboard" slot.
Fall	Phase IV ends; "Razor" will be released to production. Gearing up for market release starts.
1999 February	First Palm V shipments expected.
October	Shipment of Handspring Visor planned by Hawkins and Dubinsky, in time for Christmas shopping season.

EXHIBIT 2
**Leading Design
Firms and
Corporations
with Industrial
Design
Excellence
Awards**

Source: Business
Week's 1999 Design
Awards, Industrial
Designers Society
of America.

Design Firms	1995–1998 Awards
IDEO	32
ZIBA Design	20
Fitch	18
Frogdesign	12
Altitude	11
Pentagram	10
Design Continuum	10
Lunar Design	9
Herbst Lazar Bell	7
Hauser	6
Ralph Applebaum Associates	6

Corporations	1995–1998 Awards
Apple	9
Black & Decker	13
Compaq	9
Samsung Electronics	7
Hewlett Packard	5
NCR	9
IBM	5
Microsoft	7
Philips Electronics	6
Thomson Consumer Electronics	7

EXHIBIT 3   **IDEO's Product Development Process Phases**

PHASE 0: Understand/Observe

This phase helps the team determine feasibility of designing a product. It involves understanding everything about a new client and its business. Thus, to design a new home entertainment remote control, for instance, the team might study the history of remote controls and the companies involved in designing them. It would research everything from the cost structure of remote controls to the associated panic incidence of "where is the remote control?" syndrome. The team would buy every different kind of remote controls on the market to take apart in a fashion more gentle and controlled than exhibited by frustrated owners.

In addition to meeting with representatives from marketing and manufacturing, the team might also observe people at home on their couches attempting to use remotes. On the topic of consumer observations, IDEO head David Kelley once noted: "That's where most of the good ideas for a new project come."[27] Although this phase was typically the least expensive part of an entire project, product developers at most companies spent little time here for fear of duplicating efforts of marketing or R&D. By the end of Phase 0, the team created a feasibility record along with major discoveries about the marketplace and users.

PHASE I: Visualize/Realize

In the "Visualize/Realize" phase, the product development team visualized potential solutions through tangible prototypes to the point where a product direction was chosen. Although it involved similar activities as Phase 0 (in fact, Phases 0 and I were often combined), it was more product-focused. This intensive stage required close coordination of efforts with the client to ensure constant feedback. By the end of Phase I, the team aimed for having rough three-dimensional models of a product, an understanding of the context in which the product would be used, and an outline of a manufacturing strategy.

The team combined ideas, technologies, and market perceptions with observations of real world users to investigate potential needs that the product could fill. To do this, IDEO eschewed the traditional reliance on statistical data collected by the marketing team in favor of storyboard depictions of lives of several potential users. Use of these fictional characters concretized the product development process. For instance, while designing a better remote system, the IDEO team might conjure up characters like "Jughead, the constantly eating couch potato" or "Archie, the swinging bachelor" or "Moose, the klutz," or "Veronica, the princess." Observations of Jughead or Veronica might lead to thoughts about how to avoid spillage of food or nail polish into the buttons; observations of Moose might lead to ideas about developing drop-proof remotes; observations of either Archie or Veronica on a weekend night might lead to design of a remote with large "glow-in-the-dark" buttons that could hastily be programmed with just one hand in a darkened room.

PHASE II: Evaluate/Refine

The purpose of this stage was to develop functional prototypes and resolve technical problems as well as problems users faced. The emphasis shifted over the course of this stage from human factors and ergonomics to engineering. Concurrent engineering often occurred, through filling in previously unspecified features using an iterative process. This process, of course, required constant communications between various subgroups to ensure that the final outcomes would mesh well together.

By the end of Phase II, a functional model as well as a "looks like" design model was delivered. The industrial design solutions eventually became documented using CAD tools. With finalization of technical specifications, detailed engineering could occur.

PHASE III: Implement (Detailed Engineering)

During this phase, the team completed product design and verified that the product worked. It validated the manufacturability and performance of the final product. Although engineering efforts predominated, continuous low-level involvement with design team members occurred. For designers, frequent visits to the machine shops during this phase provided a reality check. By the end of this phase, the team delivered a fully functional design model, tooling databases, and technical documentation. Testing might also be undertaken in this phase to meet government regulations. The team also started selecting vendors.

PHASE IV: Implement (Manufacturing Liaison)

In this phase, the team resolved issues involving the final design to ensure smooth product release to manufacturing as the product moved from the shop floor to the client's factory lines. The team still supervised production of tooling, regulatory approvals, and construction of pilot runs of the manufacturing line. Testing of manufacturing feasibility was crucial: each day's loss of a production line's output might cost the client company a substantial amount in lost revenues. By the end of this phase, the product would be formally handed over to the client.

Source: IDEO.

[27] R. Garner, *San Francisco Examiner,* May 23, 1994, p. B-1.

**EXHIBIT 4
Sample of
Products
Developed
by IDEO (see
www.ideo.com
for more
products)**

Source: IDEO.

Product: Apple Mouse
Year: 1983
Client: Apple Computers
Function: Input device for the Apple Lisa and MacIntosh computers

Product: Vertech Alpine/Ski
Year: 1994
Client: Avocet
Function: Sports wristwatch with altimeter; records total feet of ascent or descent per session

Product: Oral-B Squish Grips
Year: 1996
Client: Oral-B
Function: Soft-handled kids' toothbrushes

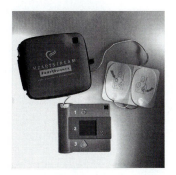

Product: Heartstream ForeRunner
Year: 1996
Client: Heartstream (now Agilent)
Function: Portable defibrillator for cardiac arrests

EXHIBIT 5   From Concept to Production: Prototyping and Experimentation During the Palm V Project

Left to right:
Low-density foam study
High-density foam study
Phase I industrial design prototype with stylus
concept

Left to right:
Machined engineering prototype
Final industrial design prototype
Preproduction prototype

Source: IDEO.

EXHIBIT 6 "Enlightened Trial and Error" at IDEO: Families of Palm V Prototypes

Early Industrial Design Form Studies

Preliminary Modem Concept Prototypes

Foam, Wood, and Mechanical Prototypes of HotSync Cradle

Source: IDEO.

Prototypes Used for Button Location and Feel Experiments

EXHIBIT 6 **"Enlightened Trial and Error" at IDEO: Families of Palm V Prototypes** (*continued*)

Stylus Retention and "Experiential" Mechanical Prototypes

Cover and Stylus Attachment Concept Prototypes

First Articles from Production Case Stampings

Source: IDEO.

Experimentation to Determine Optimum Glue Bonding Temperatures

Case **1-4**

Bank of America

The banking industry is ripe for innovation. We need to grow through value creation and excellent service that is appreciated by customers as opposed to price alone.

—Milton Jones, president, Georgia Banking Group

"I wonder if we're being 'overrewarded'!" exclaimed Warren Butler to Amy Brady, the executive responsible for Bank of America's Innovation & Development (I&D) Team in Atlanta, Georgia. As an executive in the consumer bank's quality and productivity group, Butler led innovation and process change in Brady's group, which was responsible for testing new product and service concepts for the bank's branches. In the company's elegant 55th floor conference room on a day in May 2002, the two prepared for a team meeting on an important strategic decision that would affect how experimentation would be done in the I&D Market.

Seeds of change were in the air at Bank of America. Indeed, earlier in the day, Butler had escorted an astonished visitor, a European banking executive, on a tour of some two dozen real-life "laboratories" in Atlanta. Each was a fully operating banking branch, yet in every location new product and service concepts were being tested continuously. Experiments included "virtual tellers," video monitors displaying financial and investment news, computer stations uploading images of personal checks, and "hosting stations." (See **Exhibit 1** for a selection of experiments carried out in a single branch.)

Currently, the I&D team had 25 bank branches in Atlanta in its experimentation portfolio. Senior management, however, had now offered them additional branches across the country that could expand experimentation capacity by nearly 50 percent. This offer appeared a vindication of the I&D Market project, which had been launched as an experiment itself only two years earlier. This reward posed some tough questions. Would increasing the size of its innovation laboratories aid or inhibit the group's ability to develop new products and services? What would be the effect on the group itself? The issue of whether it was a dedicated research and development (R&D) operation or not had yet to be resolved. And, finally, what kinds of expectations would be placed on the group if its size were to increase so dramatically?

Harvard Business School Case No. 9-603-022. Copyright 2002 President and Fellows of Harvard College. All rights reserved. For information: permissions@hbsp.harvard.edu.

This case was prepared by Stefan Thomke and Ashok Nimgade. HBS cases are developed solely for class discussion and do not necessarily illustrate effective or ineffective management.

BANK OF AMERICA: A PIONEER IN BANKING

> Many innovative banks have gone out of business, often because they deviated from the "best practices" followed by most.
>
> *—Rick Parsons, executive vice president, Strategic Projects*

When Bank of America was formed in 1998 through a merger between California-based Bank of America and NationsBank of North Carolina, it could be proud of a long and rich history that spanned more than 150 years. Under its last CEO, the colorful but controversial Hugh McColl, the company had gone on a three-decade-long acquisition binge that resulted in a truly nationwide bank. In the fitting end to an era of hunting, McColl left his last annual meeting wearing cowboy boots and jeans on his way to a turkey shoot in Texas. Toward the end of the twentieth century, Bank of America was the second-largest national bank with nearly 4,500 banking centers in 21 states, more than any other financial services company and with most of them in the high-growth belts of the South and the West Coast (see **Exhibit 2** for a map of the bank's regional market share). In the United States, the bank served 27 million households and 2 million businesses and processed more checks per day than the Federal Reserve System. Globally, it boasted over 140,000 employees across 190 nations, over $8 billion in annual revenues, $360 billion in deposits, and some $600 billion in assets (see **Exhibit 3** for key financial data).

Yet, increasing competition ensured that Bank of America could not rest on its laurels. Like many of its successful peers, its growth had been driven by cost reduction and consolidation. From 1985 until 2000, the number of U.S. banks had dwindled from around 14,000 to about 7,000. These still large numbers—especially when compared with there being only six major banks in Canada—reflected the highly competitive nature of the U.S. banking industry as well as its regional focus. Driving consolidation had been a realization that while service was local, products were national. Despite this realization, however, banks continued viewing financial services as commodities, and this bottom-line orientation did not make for an industry rife with innovation. In the estimation of Butler, a senior vice president and industry veteran, "People's expectations for banks are very low; in fact, they're used to being treated badly by banks."

To meet the challenges of an increasingly competitive environment, Bank of America had started decentralizing its national operations and encouraged branch managers to undertake more responsibilities. According to reengineering expert Michael Hammer, however, the era of acquisitions had left the bank with "the loopiest organizational structure I'd ever seen"—organized partly by customer, partly by geography, and partly by product (see **Exhibit 4** for a section of the bank's organization). As CEO Kenneth Lewis put it, "We'd talk about customer satisfaction, then go out and buy that next bank."[1]

For the new century, however, things would change. *Fortune* magazine observed:

> The hunter will become a farmer. "Organic growth" is the strategy, reduced earnings volatility and greater profitability the goals. The plan is to make more money from essentially the same customers by selling more services. In the huge Consumer & Commercial bank, which generated 65 percent of earnings, that means getting a bigger

---

[1] T. A. Stewart, "BA: Where the Money Is," *Fortune,* September 3, 2001.

"share of wallet" by encouraging consumers to consolidate their banking and—the Holy Grail—bring their portfolios over from Fidelity and Merrill Lynch.[2]

Few banks, however, had formal efforts under way that would generate the continuous stream of new products and services needed to grow organically. Only in recent years did banks start filing for patent applications. When innovation occurred, it did so only in specific areas: the Fifth/Third Bank in Ohio, for instance, innovated on the cost side, while Washington Mutual (WAMU) innovated on the service side. Many large banks had pockets of innovation that quite often simply remained that—pockets.

WAMU, one of the more innovative U.S. banks, had aggressively started opening traditional as well as experimental branches, sometimes directly across the street from Bank of America's I&D Market branches. Taking a cue from retailers such as department stores as well as coffee retailer Starbucks, WAMU started its Occasio pilot program. A concierge at the front entrance and several casually dressed roving sales representatives carrying mobile handheld computer devices answered customer questions. Several strategically placed teller stations replaced the traditional monolithic teller counter. Play areas for children also provided parents more time for banking. The first five Occasio branches opened in Las Vegas in April 2000, and customers opened checking accounts at twice the rate of regular branches.[3] For most banks, however, little sense of urgency existed.

THE STATE OF INNOVATION IN BANKING

> Our banking branches haven't really changed much in the last hundred years. If Jesse James brought his gang here, he'd still know where to go for the cash.
>
> *—Al Groover, senior process design consultant and I&D Team design lead*

One of the first actions Lewis took when becoming CEO was to consult several outside executives in areas from e-commerce to process management on what they considered to be "best management practice." "Process and competence will win," insisted Lewis, who also announced a Six Sigma quality program to reduce errors and streamline processes. In his focus on operational excellence, Lewis tried to rectify a situation that, according to a leading financial consultant, could be best described as "banks are very good at being mediocre at a lot of different things."[4]

Innovation, too, would require a revolution. That banks traditionally downplayed product and service development was reflected by a near universal lack of R&D departments. The comforting, stolid shadow of the three-piece-suited banker, after all, still loomed over most large banks. New products and services in the banking industry, if and when they came, generally arose from marketing departments, which lacked the formal processes, methodologies, and resource commitments that companies in many other industries took for granted. In fact, even inspired senior executives with sufficient initiative could, through relatively informal channels, bring their own ideas to test markets. Although banks had IT departments, these primarily supported ongoing infrastructure changes in technology and software.

---

[2] Ibid.

[3] WAMM Web site at <http://www.wamunewsroom.com>.

[4] T. A. Stewart, "BA: Where the Money Is," *Fortune*, September 3, 2001.

In the late 1990s, however, several converging forces led Bank of America to launch its formalized system for product and service development, the I&D Team. First, along with other industries, the bank began appreciating the value of continuous experimentation and testing in its efforts to grow through innovation. Second, Internet fever had nurtured a spirit of innovation everywhere, including the banking world. Third, banks began realizing that value creation had to be based on the voice of the customer to grow revenue and deepen customer relationships.

Bank of America initially viewed the emerging Internet as a way to overcome geography. This led to a strategy of moving customers out of branches. As a result, according to Butler, "Sometimes we were downright rude in our attempts to get people out of our branches. But eventually we realized that people like dealing with people and therefore branches were our strongest base." Frank Petrilli, president of TD Waterhouse, the country's second-largest discount brokerage, also acknowledged that "branches are a crucial customer acquisition tool which solicits 30 percent to 50 percent of our clients through the 160 offices in the U.S. The branches are continuous advertising outlets, allowing us to spend only $58 per new account, compared with our online competitors that have cost up to $250."[5]

The question then became how to change the role of the branches to balance customers' needs for a human touch with the bank's desire for cost-efficient, high-technology-based transaction platforms. The strategists at Bank of America realized that such a balance could not be found overnight; nor, in a world of changing technologies, could solutions ever prove permanent. A dynamic test bed for experimenting with new banking concepts had to be found.

THE INNOVATION & DEVELOPMENT TEAM VISION

The Innovation and Development Market is a test bed for creative ideas to increase customer satisfaction and grow revenues.

—Amy Brady, senior vice president, I&D Team executive

Every day, Bank of America processed 3.8 million transactions—including more checks than the entire Federal Reserve System. A typical noncommercial customer entered a branch every nine days and used an ATM nearly three times a week.[6] Thus, even a 99.9 percent success rate would still mushroom into over one million mistakes a year and expose consumers to problems ranging anywhere from paycheck deposit errors to bill mispayments. It was feared, therefore, that "experiments" and "mistakes" would be considered synonymous. Yet if consumers wanted Swiss-watch precision for their money, they also craved Mediterranean warmth for their service experiences. At about the same time that WAMU was taking a page from successful retailers to create more inviting bank branches, so too was Bank of America thinking about how to experiment with the human dimension of its bank branches as well as the human-technology interfaces. To reduce risks of large-scale failure, the bank confined its experimentation to a set of bank branches eventually called the "I&D Market."

In the controlled environment of these laboratory branches, routine transactions could be handled efficiently while customers' wishes for a good experience could be studied and experimented with. The bank could explore myriad questions: Could people's waiting time in line be made more tolerable? Was there even a need for lines? Could technology-inexperienced

[5] *American Banker*, October 7, 1999.
[6] T. A. Stewart, "BA: Where the Money Is," *Fortune*, September 3, 2001.

customers relate well to using keyboards and other devices? How best could staff members coach customers about Internet banking options? The goal was to boost customer and staff satisfaction at bank branches, which would ideally boost revenue growth within a given customer base while secondarily lowering staff turnover.

The original idea for the I&D Market came from different sources, including several senior executives. "Proceeding with the Innovation & Development Market project was a no-brainer," according to Rick Parsons, one such executive. "What was trickier were issues such as execution and budgeting of the project. For execution-level leadership, we assigned Amy Brady, Rob Johnson, and Warren Butler, all managers with good track records of getting results on a day-to-day basis."

The team sought to establish a process whereby ideas could be generated, collated, and queued up for systematic, objective evaluation (see **Exhibit 5** for its product and service innovation process). For the few ideas that made it through this "filter," experiments would be designed and planned for the I&D Market branches. Successful experiments—determined on the basis of consumer satisfaction or revenue growth—could then be recommended to senior management for a national rollout.

To set up the new system for innovation, little upfront financial investment was required, as many team members worked part time on the project. Soon, however, the team grew to roughly a dozen managers, who often worked evenings and weekends. The 2001 budget allocation was $11 million, of which only $6.3 million was spent on the team's experiments. Management considered this allocation generous, even for a company with $8 billion in revenues. The company's senior leadership resisted any attempts to carve out a "president-level" special budget for the innovation and process change team, arguing that, instead of enabling it to become another cost center, the group's funding should be tied directly to the performance of the 25 I&D banking centers. These branches also "brought their own checkbook" and paid for part of the experiments themselves.

Intensive initial debates had centered on whether the new group should operate as a stand-alone R&D center. Those in favor argued that a specific budget for new products and service development would protect the team from the day-to-day responsibilities of running a bank. Without such protection, the risk always existed that short-term market pressure would stifle long-term thinking and opportunities. It would also prevent comparisons between new concepts and mature products or even help prevent premature testing in live conditions. Thus, products and services under development could incubate properly without risking premature termination. After all, no automobile company would want a customer to walk up to one of its dealers and drive away with an untested prototype car. And finally, creating an R&D group charged to tinker allowed for much more organizational focus on innovation rather than a group that was supposed to also show operating results.

Many executives, however, felt that a separate R&D center would run the risk of becoming "too hypothetical and impractical." Some feared that results from the I&D Market might then not prove duplicable elsewhere. Marrying experiments with real-world banking facilities would thus decrease cycle time for rollout. As Jones reflected on the thinking of the bank's senior leadership: "We were really looking at being able to execute fast—so making a separate R&D center is harder. Furthermore, ideas in some R&D centers never get a chance to see the light of day."

But the issue of dual operating and innovation responsibility was hardly settled. As one employee in a feedback seminar put it succinctly, "We are building a plane as we are flying it." Indeed, the issue was still up in the air in May 2002.

THE VISION AT WORK: ATLANTA'S I&D MARKET BRANCHES

For a variety of reasons, Bank of America settled on Atlanta as the site for its I&D Market. The bank branches there boasted the most advanced communications infrastructure, with T1 and broadband communication lines installed. Atlanta also represented a "stable" market, with the bank's last major acquisition there in 1996. Finally, Atlanta lay a stone's throw from the bank's national headquarters in Charlotte, North Carolina.

Of its 200 branches in Atlanta, Bank of America initially gave 20 to the I&D Team. This hardly proved an imposition on the Mid-South Banking Group. The locations generally came from richer neighborhoods where customers were more computer literate and interested in a wider range of services. The I&D Team also replaced the conventional "one size fits all" mentality with three different types of branches configured to satisfy varying customer needs: "express centers," where consumers could quickly perform routine transactions; "financial centers," where consumers could access more complex technologies and more highly trained associates for a wider range of services; and "traditional centers," which provided conventional banking services, albeit with enhanced processes and technologies (see **Exhibit 6** for a brief description of the banking centers). The Atlanta I&D Market included five express centers, five financial centers, and fifteen traditional centers.

The group unveiled its first remodeled branch—a financial center—in the posh Buckhead section of Atlanta at a cost of about $1 million, mostly for technology. The other branches were remodeled to one of the three branch types and reopened shortly thereafter. Customers entering any financial center were greeted by a host at the door—an idea taken from department and clothing stores. Customers no longer needed to sign in to see bank officers. At freestanding low kiosks, associates stood ready to perform transactions such as opening accounts, creating loans, retrieving copies of old checks, or, in some instances, even selling stocks and mutual funds. None of these associates had private offices. Customers could visit an "investment bar" with computers where, once online, they could bank, check personal portfolios, or just surf the Internet. Customers waiting for tellers could pass the few minutes in line watching television news monitors above the tellers' desks or observing electronic stock tickers running along another wall. Some branches featured "investment centers" where customers, sipping complimentary coffee, could lounge on couches reading magazines, newspapers, or financial journals or hook up their personal computers.

All these nontraditional items were, in fact, experiments. The flat-panel monitors above the tellers, for instance, represented part of the "Transaction Zone Media" experiment (detailed in a later section); the instant retrieval of old checks comprised the "ImageView" experiment; the investment centers and complimentary coffee, too, came under experimental scrutiny. All branches closely monitored customer reactions to these innovations through a variety of means, including customer satisfaction surveys and statistics on such factors as revenue growth, deposit growth, and number of services used by each customer.

Prior to introducing these experiments into the I&D Market branches, the team actually rehearsed how the activity should occur. So, in a "prototype center" in Charlotte, North Carolina, people acted out how the host would behave as he or she handed off customers to specialists. They choreographed how a bank associate (not a specialist) might spend only 30 minutes with a customer to set up a mortgage. To maximize the fidelity of these prototype rehearsals, actual specialists mimicked the intervening steps. When all the kinks were worked out in this rehearsal process, the experiment was launched in the "living laboratory." The Walt Disney Company designed and taught them a "Bank of America Spirit" program—demonstrated in theme parks and taught through seminars as a service approach to other industries—which was a principal motivator of the team.

The staff at local branches put the "Bank of America Spirit" into action in different ways. They got to know their customers better, more personally. And the results were impressive. Bank teller Kemaly Jacques recalled: "One customer had been boycotting our branch for the past three months because of poor service; now he swears he won't go anywhere else." The host, a key figure who guided customers as they entered the branch toward appropriate services, became a great success story, though at the outset the role confused some customers, particularly those with complex transactions. "Where do I sign in?" many would ask. Host Kilah Willingham, who had worked her way up the organization from teller to loan officer, described the host's role as follows:

> I spend up to five minutes probing customer needs. I also intercept people going toward the old-fashioned tellers and usher them toward our innovative stations [where "experimental" technologies were offered]. A lot of customers are wary of technological change, for instance, of having the camera on them at the virtual personal banker station. My role is to make them comfortable here. I like not knowing what's coming up next; it keeps me on my toes.

During the early months, however, planning and running experiments tied up tellers and associates in meetings for almost 30–50 percent of their time (later this would drop to about 25 percent). On one occasion, a fill-in teller, providing temporary coverage during one of the meetings, mistakenly gave a customer a "dye pack," a fake wad of dollar notes meant for use only during robberies. As the customer walked out, the wad started smoking in his pocket and exploded. The Bank of America Spirit, however, persevered. Hosts and tellers emerging from the meeting showed their service experiments to firemen arriving at the scene. "This is so cool!" cried out one fireman before opening an account.

EXPERIMENTATION, LEARNING, AND MEASUREMENT

At the end of the day, the most critical aspect of experimentation and learning is measurement. Measurements will defend you if done right; otherwise they will inhibit you.

—*Milton Jones, president, Georgia Banking Group*

Of the many difficulties the team faced, one of the thorniest was resolving "how to" questions: how to gauge success of a concept, how to prioritize which concepts would be tested, how to run several experiments at once, and how to avoid the novelty factor itself from altering the experimental outcome. Moreover, according to Butler: "While we were building R&D capabilities, those controlling the purse strings thought we were doing just a one-time experiment." Thus, the problem list included one last addition: how to defend the I&D Market itself from budget cuts.

The team selected concepts to be tested on the basis of available funding, business fit, and business case. To some extent, just continuing with the evaluation process served as a natural filter for ideas. But with many ideas and concepts that needed formal testing, according to team managers Joann Donlan and Mark Lewis, "Even top-priority experiments need prioritization." As a result, the team started assigning priorities (high, medium, or low) based on the assumed impact to customers, and Brady and Butler made the final decisions about which product or service concepts to actually test. By May 2002, more than 200 new ideas had been generated, of which 40 made it to testing, 36 were successfully implemented and measured, and 20 were recommended or had been already rolled out nationally. Only four experiments eventually failed—and one of these became a "redefined" concept.

Central to the team's innovation process was how quickly people could learn from experiments, and measurements played an important role. The group amassed considerable experience and mastery of the subtle factors that affected learning.

High-Fidelity Experiments

The team sought to ensure that its experiments mirrored reality, or possessed high "fidelity." Concepts that worked only inside their branches, after all, had little value to senior management interested in the scale effect of national rollouts. But high fidelity also meant high cost and commitment, which was hard to justify when ideas were at an early stage. Sometimes, low-fidelity tests using small focus groups gave the team an alternative during the very early stages of idea assessment. Experiments requiring minimal human intervention, such as news monitors over the teller's counter, for instance, would likely work just as well in regular branches as in I&D Market branches. But not all innovations might transfer perfectly in the course of a nationwide rollout. For instance, would staff in a regular branch provide the hand-holding and attention required to initiate technophobes to a virtual teller? In such cases, the insistence by upper management that experimentation occur in a live banking situation helped ensure high fidelity and confidence in the team's learning.

Minimizing the Effect of Noise

Isolating the effect of a particular experiment on a bank branch's performance meant being clear on what that effect was *in itself*, minus "noise" factors. Such noise could arise from a variety of sources such as seasonal performance fluctuations and changing market or even weather conditions. To minimize the effect of noise on learning, the team made heavy use of two techniques, *repetition of trials* and *experimental controls*. First, repeating the same experiment at one branch or running it simultaneously at different branches averaged out the effect of noise and thus reduced the possibility of obscuring the changes that teams were interested in observing and measuring. It would also ensure that success of a given concept would not rely on factors unique to a given branch. Second, pairing up two similar branches, one with an experiment (the "intervention") and the other running under normal conditions (the "control"), enabled the team to attribute differences between the branches primarily to the intervention itself. It could draw on controls from the I&D Market, or even from other branches in Atlanta or nearby regions such as North Carolina. The best controls, however, were likely the very same I&D Market branches themselves in a before-and-after type of experiment; if properly done, this would help factor out the so-called *Hawthorne effect*. The Hawthorne effect referred to the implications of actually participating in an experiment and how that might affect its outcome. The team was aware this was possible, given the direct and indirect pressure on staff to perform. Willingham acknowledged, "We are spoiled. We get special corporate shirts, we get parties; every quarter we have special 'let's talk' sessions. We associates can even contact the regional manager if we need. Other associates envy us. So we had better do well."

Rapid Feedback

The cycle time for any given experiment carried out by the I&D Team was specified at 90 days. This did not include a preliminary "washout" period of a couple of weeks during which the novelty for both staff and customers hopefully subsided. Obviously, shorter turnaround time for feedback would help experimenters learn and prepare modified experiments more rapidly. Occasionally, it became quickly evident after the first few days if a concept would flop or succeed. Only rarely, however, did the team remove flops prematurely. On one occasion the team canceled a mortgage loan program after just a 30-day trial, primarily because getting credit approvals took far too long. The early termination allowed for quicker revision of this experiment, leading to a successful mortgage program.

Increased Experimentation Capacity

The number of experiments a single branch could run depended on available floor space and personnel, among other things. Less capacity would force the team to cram more experiments into one branch. If no capacity remained, the team could be forced to do things sequentially, which, in turn, would slow the entire concept-evaluation process. If the team succumbed to the understandable temptation of cramming too many experiments in a single branch, it would be hard to analyze the contribution of each individual experiment— another signal-to-noise problem. A single branch might have as many as 15 active experiments running at any given time. If customers loved an experiment, however, it was left in the branch even after the 90-day trial period. This being the real world, after all, the branches could not simply pull the plug on something customers had grown to relish. Measurement team leader Scott Arcure admitted, "We often worry about changing too many chemicals in the mix and wonder about which one made it explode. As bankers, we're not experts at this type of measurement." The team planned to bring in a statistics expert to help sort out the effects of multiple variables. One of the bank's outside research partners suggested moving to an entirely different market for further experiments. But the group was focused on its Atlanta market. With the customer satisfaction percentage higher than in traditional bank branches, some felt that capacity still remained for assessing additional experiments. In any case, Arcure warned that "the Hawthorne effect would spike again in any new bank branch."

More Learning Comes from More Radical Experiments

The biggest problem with experimenting in a real-world laboratory was balancing innovation with a need for bottom-line success. Pursuing radical innovations would allow the team to explore entirely new possibilities; an incrementalist approach, however, allowed for improving current banking processes. Successful radical innovations would bring glory to the team. But home runs came at the cost of strikeouts. With its future not ensured, the team could simply not take outrageous chances. Many tests thus ended up validating ideas that were likely to succeed. Team members readily acknowledged such to be the case for host stations Transaction Zone Media and Bank of America Spirit. According to Teri Gann, a former regional executive, "Interestingly, and not surprisingly, many of our successes, such as the host station, have been simple and low cost." The biggest impact so far came from Bank of America Spirit—technologically, a nonrevolutionary program transplanted wholesale from Disney. While the original vision called for a 30 percent failure rate, the actual rate in the first year hovered close to 10 percent.

Butler commented, "We're trying to sell ourselves to the bank. If we have too many failures, we just won't be accepted. Currently, we may have failure *within* concepts, but not failure *in* concepts."

"We might tweak a process, but everything conforms to the status quo," observed Wells Stanwick, Bank of America manager of channel strategy. "Could we try out a more radical concept such as providing branch offices similar to attorney offices in large office buildings for wealthy customers?" Deborah McAdams, banking center manager, agreed: "Let's do something really innovative, such as trying out loan machines similar to automatic teller machines like they do in Japan. When I mention this, some people aren't sure if I am joking."

Concepts that appeared intuitively obvious did not always prove so in reality. Such was the case for innovation and for financial payback. Team leaders wondered if a "breakthrough" product should be measured through its degree of innovation or through financial payback or both. According to Brady, "Our metric should be how an innovation affects the bottom line two years out, rather than looking for instant feedback [through customer satisfaction]." Problems with assessing innovation soon surfaced. What might appear radical to one person, for instance a "mobile teller" to a technophobe, might prove less radical from a purely technical standpoint.

Nor did the innovation team take financial performance into account, largely because of an anticipated lag of eighteen months to two years in going from concept to rollout beyond Atlanta. The I&D Market, instead, would settle on the proxy measure of consumer satisfaction. Many team members recognized the shortcomings of their measurement process. Gann stated, "I believe we're doing the wrong thing by measuring the I&D Market staff on productivity, not innovation." But, she added, "You can't chase two rabbits at the same time." Some team members pointed to WAMU as a possible benchmark, for it was "a competitor willing to change and willing to raise the bar."

THE TRANSACTION ZONE MEDIA EXPERIMENT

A good example of the bank's new innovation process at work was the Transaction Zone Media (TZM) experiment. Internal researchers, who "intercepted" some 1,000 customers at bank lines, noted that after about three minutes the gap between actual and perceived wait time rose exponentially. Two focus groups with sales associates and a formal analysis by the Gallup organization provided further corroboration—and the TZM experiment was born. The team speculated, based on published psychology literature, that "entertaining" clients through television monitors above the lobby tellers would reduce perceived wait times by at least 15 percent.

The team chose one enhanced "traditional center" for the TZM experiment and another one as a control branch so it could maximize learning from the experiment. In the summer of 2001, the team installed monitors set to the Atlanta-based news station CNN over teller booths in the branch. The team then waited for a week's washout period to allow the novelty to wear off before measuring results for the subsequent two weeks.

Results from the TZM-equipped branch showed that the number of people who overestimated their actual wait times dropped from 32 percent to 15 percent. During the same period, none of the other branches reported drops of this magnitude. In fact, the control branch saw an increase in over-estimated wait times from 15–26 percent (see **Exhibit 7** for results from the experiment). Though these were encouraging results, the team still had to prove to senior management that TZM could positively affect the corporate bottom line. To do so, the team relied on a model that used the easily measurable "customer satisfaction index" (based on a 30-question survey) as a proxy for future revenue growth.

Prior studies indicated that every one-point improvement in a customer satisfaction index corresponded to $1.40 in added annual revenue per household from increased customer purchases and retention. A banking center (branch) with a customer base of 10,000 households would thus increase its annual revenues by $28,000 should the index increase by just two points. Percentages generally ranged in the mid-80s in Atlanta's I&D Market and in the high 70s to low 80s nationally. The team measured an overall 1.7 percent increase after installation of the TZM monitors. Sufficiently encouraged, it entered a second phase, to study and optimize the impact of more varied programming, advertising, and sound speaker parameters.

While the benefits of the TZM program were laudable, the team now had to consider whether they outweighed the costs. Studies indicated that it would cost some $22,000 to install the special TV monitors at each I&D Market branch. For a national rollout, the estimated economies of scale would bring costs down to about $10,000 per site.

INCENTIVE AND COMPENSATION ISSUES: TELLERS DO NOT LIKE CHANGE

Another thorny "how to" issue the team faced was how to motivate its staff. Could—and should—the performance of employees who were part of continuous experimentation be measured and rewarded conventionally?

At the Atlanta branches, Bank of America tellers earned about $20,000 a year; annual turnover averaged about 50 percent. The next step up from teller was sales associate; people in this job helped customers start up savings or checking accounts, fill out mortgage applications, notarize documents, and entice customers with new services. At I&D Market branches, some associates could serve as hosts—making many decisions without bringing in the branch manager.

Some 30–50 percent of associates' compensation derived from performance bonuses based on a decade-old point system that used sales quotas—where points varied according to product, customer satisfaction, local market demographics, as well as managerial discretion. Given this system, associates were tempted to ignore customers' actual needs. "For instance, they would encourage customers to open up a checking account, which yields one point, rather than a savings account, which yields none," said an internal financial consultant.

For the first several months, the I&D Market maintained the conventional incentive scheme. The sales associates seemed to relish the additional pressure. But it soon became apparent that they would have to spend as much as a quarter of their time in special training sessions, not to mention "alternate" time working as hosts, an experiment that yielded no bonus points. The staff, thus, began feeling disadvantaged by their rewards as hosts, since they faced the same monthly quota of points despite having less time with customers as part of an actual selling activity.

For some, however, being part of the experiment proved reward in itself. "I would not go back to my old job," said one associate who looked forward to working every morning. "It would be like stepping several years back in terms of technology and service." Annual "Bank of America Spirit" motivational sessions with vibrant music and motivational speakers reinforced this sense of exclusivity. Yet cracks in the prevailing incentive scheme began showing. "Let's be realistic," one sales associate admitted, "you can't be happy all day long; sometimes you have to fake it."

In January 2001, senior management switched associates in all 25 branches to fixed-incentive compensation. Most of them welcomed the change, which added to the feeling of being special. It also represented a commitment from top management to the experimentation process. But not all staff thrived under the new fixed incentives. One executive complained that "those in the I&D Market branches now thought they didn't have to chin to the same level as others." Another manager had to reassign an associate "since that person now sat passively at a desk; the team mentality of working for the customer proved foreign to her."

With all the attention and resources dedicated to the I&D Team, some senior executives echoed a growing impatience that it was time "to pay the piper." Resentment from personnel in other conventional branches might also have fueled this feeling. The group already enjoyed more resources than other branches, and there was a fear that different incentive schemes would remove them further from the daily realities of banking. There was also uncertainty whether the concepts tested in prototype form would work nationally because of different market conditions. As Allen Jones, a regional executive, pointed out, "If a test is successful only under fixed-incentive schemes, then we can't roll it out elsewhere." With growing discomfort, senior management switched the staff back to the old point-based incentive system after just a six-month trial.

Not surprisingly, with this about-face the behavior of the staff reverted as well. Hosts, for instance, became reluctant to send customers over to insurance agents because they got no points for such referrals. On two occasions, in fact, supervisors witnessed a host undertake entire transactions just to make his points quota rather than direct customers to associates. The about-face also led one staff member to question Brady about senior management's commitment to the I&D Market vision. What concerned Brady and Butler the most, however, was the impact of incentives on the learning and quality of in-branch experiments.

FIRST-YEAR PERFORMANCE

I see the following challenges for the I&D Market: ownership, evaluation, and continued support in a changing environment. The solution is to highlight successes, have a good batting average, rapid experimentation cycles, and maintain awareness at senior management level.

—*Milton Jones, president, Georgia Banking Group*

By traditional banking measures, the I&D Market performance appeared less than stellar. Overall deposit growth in 2001 stood at just 0.5 percent, compared with 3.7 percent growth in other Atlanta branches. In terms of revenue, however, I&D branches did about 10 percent better than traditional branches. Some experiments proved quite effective; for instance, a "loan solutions" experiment generated an extra $700,000 in the first quarter in all 15 participating I&D branches combined. With all additional costs factored in, however, the I&D Market was not, at least on a pilot scale, a winning proposition. The team therefore wondered about how senior management would react to its performance in an environment where many programs throughout the bank were being axed. Were comparisons with traditional benchmarks fair, given its mission of being the bank's product and service development laboratory?

Despite just a slight rise in customer volume, many associates observed a larger spike in customer satisfaction, with some customers now coming from longer distances just to bank at the new branches. Another promising trend not captured by traditional measures involved personnel turnover. Except for an initial turnover spike, annual teller turnover had dropped from 50 percent over the past three years to 28 percent. In the last quarter of 2001, annualized teller turnover had dropped to as low as 20 percent, but it was unclear how much of this stemmed from employment uncertainties in the aftermath of the terrorist attacks on September 11, 2001.

At the same time, some senior executives viewed the I&D Market as the crown jewels of the Atlanta branches. The bank offered tours of its gleaming prototype facilities to customers, Bank of America executives, visitors from other industries, and even competing banks. "Everyone's eyes are on us," admitted Allen Jones. "Just last week, one of the bank's top executives visited us."

In 2001 the I&D Team received an additional five branches as part of a corporate reorganization that would increase each regional manager's branch portfolio. While these measures increased operating budgets, they did not boost the research budget for experimentation and testing. Brady and Butler wondered how to deal with the unexpected "reward." Some people even suggested leaving these five new branches untouched to serve as additional experimental controls. Ultimately, the five branches joined the ongoing experimental portfolio, bringing the total to twenty-five.

The new branches added much-needed experimentation capacity. Operationally, however, taking on additional branches stretched the team's efforts thin, since it required staff retraining and the setup of additional experiments, let alone all the minor logistics of managing branches that literally involved running among them all day long. With the potential drag of these branches on overall portfolio performance, the team also worried about increased corporate pressure for positive results.

A VOTE OF CONFIDENCE?

"We had a good first year," Brady said as the last of the small group took their seats at the conference table overlooking downtown Atlanta. "[The year] 2001 was our year to prove the I&D Team vision; 2002 is our year to grow up. At the end of this year I will have to restate our case, but hopefully to double funding." The I&D Team had been one of the few projects to survive companywide cuts, albeit with a smaller budget. "We still make a small profit in our branches," Brady added, "and potentially, this could cover our salaries, but it is too early to say."

Next, Brady explained how the bank's senior leadership had offered the group yet another "reward" of additional branches across the country. These branches could expand experimentation capacity by some 40–60 percent and take the strain off the 25 branches that were piling up so many experiments. But only about half the team responded to the news with smiles—just as Brady and Butler had expected. The team had debated almost since inception the use of external control branches from North Carolina or even other Mid-Atlantic or East Coast regions. Some felt that geography did not matter in this Internet age, as long as demographics, customer profiles, and size of banking centers were comparable. Others, such as Stanwick, disagreed: "The prospect of using, say, North Carolina branches as controls for our Atlanta Innovation and Development Market scares me to death."

Those in favor of taking on the new branches pointed to the limited experimentation capacity and the increasing testing backlog. In 2002 alone, 26 new experiments were added to about 25 ongoing tests carried over from 2001, bringing the number of active experiments to more than 50 (see **Exhibit 8a** for the group's growing idea pipeline). They argued that more experimentation capacity allowed for faster evaluation of ideas through the running of more tests simultaneously and reduced feedback times because of potentially lower capacity utilization (see **Exhibit 8b**). Alternatively, the bank could run fewer simultaneous experiments and obtain cleaner and more reliable results. They further noted that the team by now had gained much experience in running experiments. In any case, it took the same time to design concepts for one center as for ten. Having a larger portfolio of branches might also make scale-up and national rollout of successful concepts easier and quicker. By making a big splash within the corporation, the I&D Team could win greater prominence. Because the offered branches were underperformers, the team would look good in case of turnarounds but lose little if these new branches failed.

Those against taking on the additional branches argued that the current 25 branches (or even fewer) in the portfolio were optimal. Taking on five branches within Atlanta had been difficult enough. Ten additional branches would be difficult to manage even if they were all in Atlanta. How much harder would it be for Atlanta managers, who were already stretched thin, to simply march into another branch and say, "Hi, we're here to test." Specifically, some pointed out that associates in other states such as California appeared more individual than team oriented. Experience had also shown that associates would need to spend a quarter of their time undergoing additional training. In Atlanta, increased demands on tellers and associates had led to an initial rise in turnover (before eventually declining). Who could predict teller and associate turnover in a different geographic area? Some executives further noted that a larger I&D Market would increase the drag on the balance sheet, potentially stifling innovation. Too large a market might also confuse customers using more than one branch. Brady and Butler jotted down the rapidly flying ideas. Soon they would formulate a recommendation to the bank's senior leadership about whether to accept new branches into its experimentation portfolio.

One thing that stuck in both their minds was, ironically, "failure." In particular, the need for failure so as to generate more learning. Failures had been few and far between so far—indeed, the last failure was that of a mortgage loan experiment whose post-mortem analyses indicated "red tape" as the cause, that is, too much paperwork at the back end. Hardly a "revolutionary" experiment, thought Brady; hardly something—even if it had worked—remarkable. For both Brady and Butler, the words of their superior, Jones, an enthusiastic champion of their efforts, rang loud: "So far, most of our experiments have been successful. Perhaps we don't fail often enough."

EXHIBIT 1
Examples of Selected Experiments in Atlanta's Buckhead Financial Center

Source: Bank of America.

EXHIBIT 2 Bank of America's Regional Deposit Market Position and Share (Consumer and Commercial Banking)

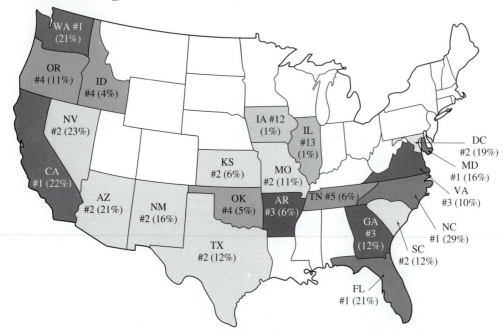

Source: Bank of America Web site, <www.bankofamerica.com>. Deposits are as of June 2001.

EXHIBIT 3
Selected
Financials and
Operating
Data (Dollars
in Millions,
Except
Per-Share
Data)

Source: Compustat.

Bank of America Year	2001	2000	1999
Cost of goods sold	22,290	27,351	20,906
Selling and administrative expenses	12,718	12,255	12,281
Research and development expenses	n.a.	n.a.	n.a.
ROA	1.1	1.2	1.2
ROE	14	15.8	17.8
Market value	98,158	74,025	84,179
Total interest income	38,293	43,258	37,588
Total interest expenses	18,003	24,816	19,086
Net interest income	**20,290**	**18,442**	**18,237**
Provision for loan losses	4,287	2,535	1,820
Net interest income after provision for loan losses	**16,003**	**15,907**	**16,417**
Other Income	8,564	9,920	9,996
Salaries, occupancy, and equipment	12,718	12,255	12,281
Depreciation	1,732	1,784	1,917
Total other expenses	**14,450**	**14,039**	**14,198**
Pre-tax income	**10,117**	**11,788**	**12,215**
Income taxes	3,325	4,271	4,333
Income before extraordinary items & discontinued operations	**6,792**	**7,517**	**7,882**
Earnings per share basic from operations	4.8	4.77	4.77
Earnings per share diluted from operations	4.71	4.72	4.68

EXHIBIT 4   Section of Bank of America's Organizational Chart

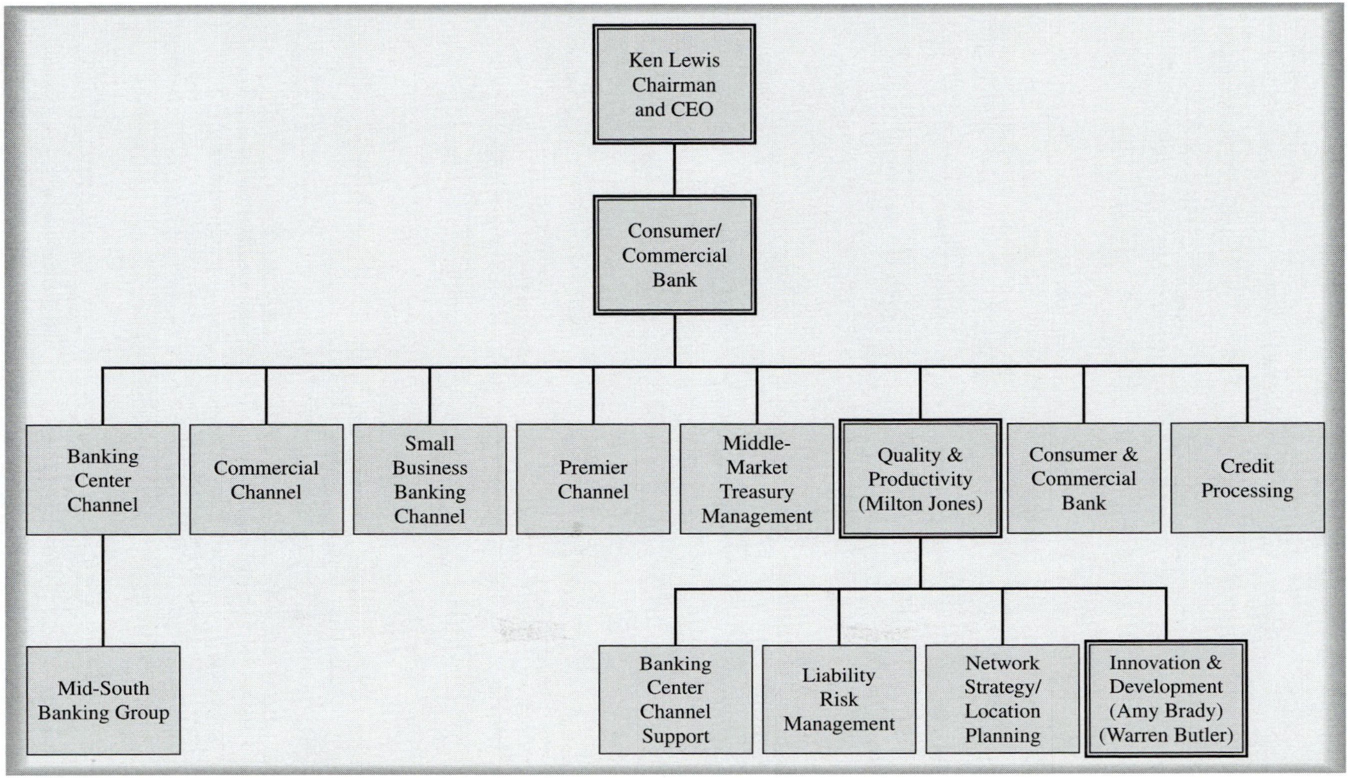

```
                        Ken Lewis
                        Chairman
                        and CEO
                            |
                       Consumer/
                       Commercial
                          Bank
                            |
        +----------+--------+--------+----------+----------+----------+----------+
        |          |                 |          |          |          |          |
     Banking   Commercial       Small      Premier    Middle-    Quality &  Consumer &  Credit
     Center     Channel        Business    Channel    Market     Productivity Commercial Processing
     Channel                   Banking                Treasury   (Milton Jones) Bank
        |                      Channel                Management
     Mid-South
     Banking Group

                    +----------+----------+----------+----------+
                    |          |          |          |
                 Banking    Liability  Network    Innovation &
                 Center     Risk       Strategy/  Development
                 Channel    Management Location   (Amy Brady)
                 Support               Planning   (Warren Butler)
```

Source: Bank of America.

119

EXHIBIT 5   The I&D Market's Product and Service Innovation Process and Activities

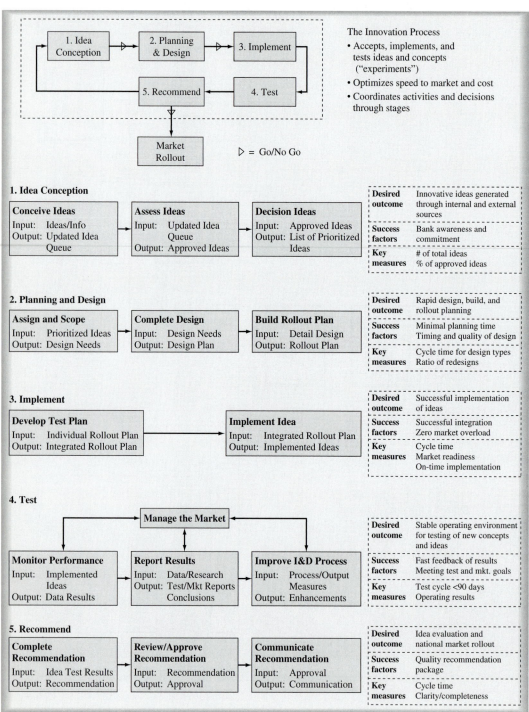

The Innovation Process
• Accepts, implements, and tests ideas and concepts ("experiments")
• Optimizes speed to market and cost
• Coordinates activities and decisions through stages

▷ = Go/No Go

1. Idea Conception

Conceive Ideas	Assess Ideas	Decision Ideas
Input: Ideas/Info Output: Updated Idea Queue	Input: Updated Idea Queue Output: Approved Ideas	Input: Approved Ideas Output: List of Prioritized Ideas

Desired outcome	Innovative ideas generated through internal and external sources
Success factors	Bank awareness and commitment
Key measures	# of total ideas % of approved ideas

2. Planning and Design

Assign and Scope	Complete Design	Build Rollout Plan
Input: Prioritized Ideas Output: Design Needs	Input: Design Needs Output: Design Plan	Input: Detail Design Output: Rollout Plan

Desired outcome	Rapid design, build, and rollout planning
Success factors	Minimal planning time Timing and quality of design
Key measures	Cycle time for design types Ratio of redesigns

3. Implement

Develop Test Plan	Implement Idea
Input: Individual Rollout Plan Output: Integrated Rollout Plan	Input: Integrated Rollout Plan Output: Implemented Ideas

Desired outcome	Successful implementation of ideas
Success factors	Successful integration Zero market overload
Key measures	Cycle time Market readiness On-time implementation

4. Test

Manage the Market

Monitor Performance	Report Results	Improve I&D Process
Input: Implemented Ideas Output: Data Results	Input: Data/Research Output: Test/Mkt Reports Conclusions	Input: Process/Output Measures Output: Enhancements

Desired outcome	Stable operating environment for testing of new concepts and ideas
Success factors	Fast feedback of results Meeting test and mkt. goals
Key measures	Test cycle <90 days Operating results

5. Recommend

Complete Recommendation	Review/Approve Recommendation	Communicate Recommendation
Input: Idea Test Results Output: Recommendation	Input: Recommendation Output: Approval	Input: Approval Output: Communication

Desired outcome	Idea evaluation and national market rollout
Success factors	Quality recommendation package
Key measures	Cycle time Clarity/completeness

Source: Bank of America.

EXHIBIT 6
Banking Branches in the Innovation and Development Experimentation Portfolio

Source: Bank of America.

Financial Centers (5):

Provide ability to advise across product line with expanded people, technology, process, and environment capabilities

Express Centers (5):

Provide fast, friendly, convenient access for routine transactions with self-directed options and teller services

Traditional Centers (15):

Provide traditional banking products and services with enhanced processes and technology

EXHIBIT 7
Data from Transaction Zone Media (TZM) Experiment

Source: Bank of America.

The TZM Experiment:

Flat-panel monitors above bank tellers broadcast news for people waiting for service.
Do such customers perceive shorter waiting times to service?
Are such customers more satisfied with their banking experience?

Actual versus Perceived Waiting Time
(Customers who wait > 5 minutes)

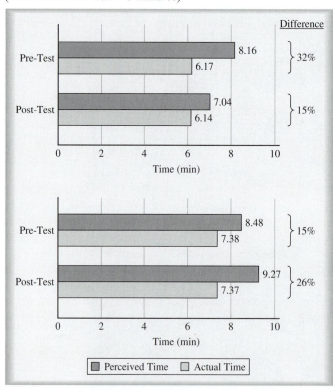

Experimental Site:

Prior to installation of TZM, customers who waited longer than five minutes significantly overestimated their waiting time (32 percent).
After installation, overestimates for the same customer group dropped to 15 percent.

Control Branch:

No experimental intervention was carried out during the observation period.
Control branch had very similar customer demographics to experimental site.
During the observation period, overestimates actually increased from 15 percent to 26 percent.

EXHIBIT 8A
List of Product or Service Concepts Waiting to be Tested

Source: Bank of America.

Process Measure	January	February	March	April	May	*Total*
Inflow of new ideas before assessment*	13	5	27	3	27	75
Ideas put on hold/reactivated	(4)	(1)	4	0	0	(1)
Assessments completed	(10)	(6)	(1)	(4)	(6)	(27)
— recommended for design/testing	10	6	1	4	6	27
— not approved	0	0	0	0	0	0
Ideas moved to design/testing	**10**	**6**	**1**	**4**	**6**	**27**
New ideas discontinued (before or during assessment)	(7)	(7)	(1)	(20)	(5)	(40)
Change in idea backlog**	−8	−9	+29	−21	+16	+7

*New ideas come from brainstorming workshops, employee input, etc.
**The January 1, 2002, backlog of new ideas awaiting a decision (assessment or discontinuation) is about two months.

EXHIBIT 8B
Waiting for a Resource

Source: S. Thomke, "Enlightened Experimentation: The New Imperative for Innovation," *Harvard Business Review*, February 2001.

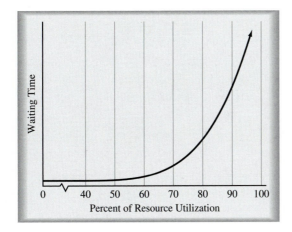

According to queuing theory, the waiting time for a resource increases gradually as more of the resource is used. But when the utilization passes 70 percent, delays increase dramatically.

Article

R&D Comes to Services: Bank of America's Pathbreaking Experiments

At the heart of business today lies a dilemma: Our economy is increasingly dependent on services, yet our innovation processes remain oriented toward products. We have well-tested, scientific methods for developing and refining manufactured goods—methods that date back to the industrial laboratories of Thomas Edison—but many of them don't seem applicable to the world of services. Companies looking for breakthroughs in service development tend to fall back on informal and largely haphazard efforts, from brainstorming, to trial and error, to innovation teams. Such programs can produce occasional successes, but they offer little opportunity for the kind of systematic learning required to strengthen the consistency and productivity of service development—and innovation in general—over time.

The challenges in applying the discipline of formal R&D processes to services are readily apparent. Because a service is intangible, often existing only in the moment of its delivery to a customer, it is difficult to isolate in a traditional laboratory. And since many services are tailored to individual buyers at the point of purchase, they can't be tested through large samples. As a result, experiments with new services are most useful when they are conducted live—with real customers engaged in real transactions. Live tests magnify the cost of failure, however; an experiment that doesn't work may harm customer relationships and even the brand. Live experiments are also harder to execute and measure. Once you leave a laboratory and enter the hurly-burly of a commercial setting, the whole notion of experimental controls has to be rethought. The noise can drown out the signal,

Stefan Thomke is professor of technology and operations management at Harvard Business School in Boston. He is the author of three other HBR articles, including "Enlightened Experimentation: The New Imperative for Innovation" (February 2001), and the book *Experimentation Matters: Unlocking the Potential of New Technologies for Innovation* (Harvard Business School Press, 2003).

making it hard to determine whether the variable you're testing for is the one that actually causes the effect you observe.

Given such challenges, it's no surprise that most service companies have not established rigorous, ongoing R&D processes. But now there is an important exception to that rule. Over the past three years, Bank of America has been running a series of formal experiments aimed at creating new service concepts for retail banking. The company has turned a set of its branches into, in effect, a laboratory where a corporate research team conducts service experiments with actual customers during regular business hours, measures results precisely and compares them with those of control branches, and pinpoints attractive innovations for broader rollout.

Bank of America's program is a work in progress—it is in itself an experiment. Refinements have been made at every stage of its development. Some of its elements have proved successful; some haven't. But through its successes and its failures, the effort has revealed an enormous amount about what a true R&D operation might look like inside a service business.

THE GROWTH CHALLENGE

The end of the twentieth century was a time of rapid consolidation in the U.S. banking industry, and Bank of America was an eager participant. Through a three-decade M&A effort, culminating in a $60 billion merger with NationsBank in 1998, the bank transformed itself from a regional West Coast operation into one of the country's largest national banks, operating some 4,500 banking centers in 21 states and serving approximately 27 million households and 2 million businesses. But as the twenty-first century dawned, Bank of America, like other large U.S. banks, faced a new challenge: With the opportunities for further acquisitions narrowing, it would need to find ways to grow organically, to expand its existing business by attracting more customers and fulfilling a greater share of their banking needs.

When Kenneth Lewis became the bank's chief executive in 1999, he saw that winning the battle for customers would require fresh approaches to service development and delivery. The old modus operandi of the banking industry—provide the same services in the same ways as your competitors—was a recipe for stagnation. But Lewis faced a major obstacle in achieving his vision: The bank had never made innovation a priority, and as a result, it lacked any formal infrastructure for developing new services. Innovation, Lewis saw, would require a revolution in thinking and in practice.

The instrument of that revolution was the Innovation & Development (I&D) Team, a corporate unit charged with spearheading product and service development at the bank. The team's immediate goal was to pioneer new services and service-delivery techniques that would strengthen the bank's relationships with branch customers while also achieving a high degree of efficiency in transactions. Recognizing that service innovations should be tested in the field, I&D Team members, together with senior executives, decided to take an unprecedented step in the conservative banking industry: They would create an "innovation market" within the bank's existing network—a set of branches that would provide, as bank executive and I&D Team leader Amy Brady put it, "a test bed for creative ideas to increase customer satisfaction and grow revenues." The test market, the team realized, would have to be large enough to support a wide range of experiments but small enough to limit the risks to the business.

The bank settled on Atlanta as the site for its innovation market. Atlanta represented a stable region for the bank—its last major acquisition in the area occurred in 1996—and it was near the national headquarters in Charlotte, North Carolina. The Atlanta branches were also technologically advanced, even equipped with broadband communication lines. Twenty of Bank of America's 200 branches in Atlanta were initially dedicated to the innovation market, most in wealthier neighborhoods with sophisticated banking customers interested in a wide range of services. (Five more branches were later added to the project.) The managers of each of these branches agreed to work closely with the I&D Team in carrying out the research effort, and they also agreed to provide much of the required funding out of their own budgets in order to get the early benefits of the resulting innovations. Integrating the program into normal operations at the branches was a risky step—experiments, after all, necessarily carry the potential for disruption—but the team saw it as essential. Only by carrying out experiments under realistic conditions—organizationally, operationally, and economically—could the I&D Team ensure the reliability of the results.

DESIGNING EXPERIMENTS

The I&D Team quickly realized that it would be very difficult to conduct a diverse array of experiments within the confines of a traditionally designed bank branch. Experiments require frequent changes in practices and processes, which neither the branch employees nor the physical facilities were prepared for. So the team decided to reconfigure the 20 Atlanta branches into three alternative models: Five branches were redesigned as "express centers," efficient, modernistic buildings where consumers could quickly perform routine transactions such as deposits and withdrawals. Five were turned into "financial centers," spacious, relaxed outlets where customers would have access to the trained staff and advanced technologies required for sophisticated services such as stock trading and portfolio management. The remaining ten branches were configured as "traditional centers," familiar-looking branches that provided conventional banking services, though often supported by new technologies and redesigned processes.

The group unveiled its first redesigned branch—a financial center—in the posh Buckhead section of Atlanta in the fall of 2000. A customer entering the new center was immediately greeted at the door by a host—an idea borrowed from Wal-Mart and other retail stores. At freestanding kiosks, associates stood ready to help the customer open accounts, set up loans, retrieve copies of old checks, or even buy and sell stocks and mutual funds. An "investment bar" offered personal computers where the customer could do her banking, check her investment portfolio, or just surf the Internet. There were comfortable couches, where she could relax, sip free coffee, and read financial magazines and other investment literature. And if she had to wait for a teller, she could pass the few minutes in line watching television news monitors or electronic stock tickers. What that customer probably wouldn't have realized was that all of these new services were actually discrete experiments, and her reactions to them were being carefully monitored and measured.

To select and execute the experiments in the test branches, the I&D Team followed a detailed five-step process. The critical first step was coming up with ideas for possible experiments and then assessing and prioritizing them. Ideas were submitted by team members and by branch staff and were often inspired by reviews of past customer-satisfaction studies and other market research. Every potential experiment was entered into an "idea portfolio," a spreadsheet that described the experiment, the process or problem it addressed, the customer segments it targeted, and its status. The team categorized each experiment as a high, medium, or low priority, based primarily on its projected impact on customers but also taking into account its fit with the bank's strategy and goals and its funding requirements. In some cases, focus groups were conducted to provide a rough sense of an idea's likely effect on customers. By May 2002, more than 200 new ideas had been generated, and 40 of them had been launched as formal experiments.

Once an idea was given a green light, the actual experiment had to be designed. The I&D Team wanted to perform as many tests as possible, so it strove to plan each experiment quickly. To aid in this effort, the group created a prototype branch in the bank's Charlotte headquarters where team members could rehearse the steps involved in an experiment and work out any process problems before going live with customers. The team would, for example, time each activity required in processing a particular transaction. When an experiment required the involvement of a specialist—a mortgage underwriter, say—the team would enlist an actual specialist from the bank's staff and have him or her perform the required task. By the time an experiment was rolled out in one of the Atlanta branches, most of the kinks had been worked out. The use of the prototype center reflects an important tenet of service experiments: Design and production problems should be worked out off-line, in a lab setting without customers, before the service delivery is tested in a live environment.

GOING LIVE

An experiment is only as good as the learning it produces. Through hundreds of years of experience in the sciences, and decades in commercial product development, researchers have discovered a lot about how to design experiments to maximize learning. We know, for example, that an effective experiment has to isolate the particular factors being investigated; that it must faithfully replicate the real-world situation it's testing; that it has to be conducted efficiently, at a reasonable cost; and that its results have to be accurately measured and used, in turn, to refine its design. (An overview of the qualities of good experiments is provided in the sidebar "Learning Through Experiments.") These are always complex challenges, and, as Bank of America found out, many of them become further complicated when experiments are moved out of a laboratory and into a bank branch filled with real employees serving real customers in real time. To its credit, the I&D Team thought carefully about ways to increase the learning produced by its experiments, with a particular focus on enhancing the reliability of the tests' results and the accuracy of their measurement. As Milton Jones, one of the bank's group presidents, constantly reminded the team: "At the end of the day, the most critical aspect of experimentation and learning is measurement. Measurements will defend you if done right; otherwise they will inhibit you."

Learning Through Experiments

The objective of all experiments is to learn what does and does not work. Experiments should be designed not so much to maximize their odds of success but to maximize the information and insights they produce. The rate at which companies can learn by experimentation will depend on many factors, some of which will be unique to a given company. But there are seven factors that tend to be common to all experiments.

Factor	Definition
Fidelity	The degree to which a model and its testing conditions represent a final product, process, or service under conditions of actual use.
Cost	The total cost of designing, building, running, and analyzing an experiment, including expenses for prototypes, laboratory use, and so on.
Iteration time	The time from the initial planning of an experiment to when the analyzed results are available and used for planning another iteration.
Capacity	The number of experiments that can be carried out with some fidelity during a given time period.
Sequence	The extent to which experiments are run in parallel or series.
Signal-to-noise ratio	The extent to which the variable of interest is obscured by other variables.
Type	The degree to which a variable is manipulated, from incremental change to radical change.

Minimizing the Effect of Noise

Experiments can be distorted when "noise"—variables other than the one being tested—influences results in ways that can't be controlled or measured. Managing noise is a particular challenge in service experiments conducted in business settings. At the bank branches, for example, extraneous factors like seasonal fluctuations in demand, changing market conditions, staff turnover, or even bad weather could alter customers' perceptions and behavior, distorting the results of the tests. To temper the effects of noise, the I&D Team made heavy use of two techniques, *repetition of trials* and *experimental controls*. Repeating the same experiment in the same branch served to average out noise effects, and repeating the same experiment in different branches helped the team determine which factors were unique to a given branch. Setting up a control branch for each experiment—one with similar characteristics and customer demographics to the branch actually conducting the experiment—enabled the team to further isolate the variable being tested. If the team members wanted to test, say, a new piece of software for making transfers between accounts, they would install the software on the terminals at one express center but not on the terminals at another, similar express center. In this way, any differences in customers' performance in carrying out a transfer at the two branches could be attributed to the change in the software. The team was able to draw control branches not only from the three different types of branches in the innovation market but also from other branches in Atlanta and in nearby regions.

Achieving High Fidelity

In the development of products, experiments are often, for cost or feasibility reasons, conducted with models or prototypes. This always raises a question of fidelity: How reliable is the model in representing the real world? That question becomes, in some ways, less of a concern in service experiments like Bank of America's. While real-world testing has the drawback of amplifying noise, it has the advantage of increasing fidelity. But the bank did have to grapple with the cost issue. Achieving high fidelity required substantial investment—in bank remodeling, personnel training, technology, and the like. By requiring that the experiments be funded out of the branches' operating budgets, the bank imposed fiscal discipline on the program: Branch management would naturally demand that experiments have a high likelihood of providing attractive returns. To attain high fidelity, the bank also had to deal with the so-called Hawthorne effect. A well-documented phenomenon, the Hawthorne effect refers to the way that people who know they are under observation—such as those participating in an experiment—tend to change their behavior and thus distort the results. The I&D Team was aware that such distortion was possible—given the direct and indirect pressure on branch staff to perform well in the experiments—and that it could damage the fidelity of the experiments. Here, too, the careful use of controls helped. By comparing the results of experiments susceptible to the Hawthorne effect to the results achieved by control branches within the innovation market, the team was able to filter out some of the effect. The team also instituted "washout periods." Measurements of an experiment's results did not begin until a week or two after its start, allowing time for any novelty effects to wear off among the staff.

Attaining Rapid Feedback

People learn best when they receive immediate feedback on the results of their actions. (Imagine how hard it would be to learn to play the piano if there were a long delay between striking a key and hearing the note.) But, in many circumstances, it takes time to ensure that results are accurate—giving misleading feedback is even worse than giving no feedback. Finding the right balance between speed and reliability in providing feedback is crucial to effective experimentation. The I&D Team specified that every experiment would run for 90 days (not including the washout period) before it could be adjusted or discontinued based on the results generated. The team believed that three months would provide enough time to gain reliable measures without unduly delaying modifications. In practice, there were some exceptions to this rule. The team revamped, for example, a mortgage loan experiment after just 30 days, primarily because it became clear that it was taking much too long to get credit approvals. The quick revision of this experiment paid off by leading to the launch of a successful new mortgage program.

Once an experiment was completed and measured, a decision had to be made about whether it was a success and warranted a broader rollout. This required a straightforward, two-part analysis. First, performance data from the test locations and the control branches were analyzed to determine whether the experiment had enhanced customer satisfaction, revenue generation, productivity, or any other relevant measure of performance. Second, a cost-benefit analysis was carried out to ascertain whether the performance gain outweighed the expense required to introduce the new process or technology throughout the broader

The transaction zone media (TZM) experiment provides a useful example of how Bank of America's innovation process works. The experiment had its origins in an earlier study in which market researchers "intercepted" some 1,000 customers standing in bank lines and asked them a series of questions. The study revealed that after a person stands in line for about three minutes, a wide gap opens between actual and perceived wait times. A two-minute wait, for example, usually feels like a two-minute wait, but a five-minute wait may feel like a ten-minute wait. Two subsequent focus groups with sales associates and a formal analysis by the Gallup organization provided further corroboration of this effect. When the I&D Team reviewed the data, they realized there might be opportunities to reduce perceived wait times without reducing actual wait times. Psychological studies have revealed, after all, that if you distract a person from a boring chore, time seems to pass much faster. So the team came up with a hypothesis to test: If you entertain people in line by putting television monitors in the "transaction zone"—above the row of tellers in a branch lobby—you will reduce perceived wait times by at least 15 percent.

Because long waits have a direct impact on customer satisfaction, the team gave the transaction zone media experiment a high priority. In the summer of 2001, the bank installed monitors set to the Atlanta-based news station CNN over the teller booths in one traditional center. Another traditional center serving a similar clientele was used as a control branch. After a week's washout period, the team began to carefully measure actual and perceived wait times at the two branches. The results were significant, as shown in the chart "Actual Versus Perceived Waiting Time." The degree of overestimation of wait times dropped from 32 percent to 15 percent at the test branch. During the same period, the control branch actually saw an increase in overestimated wait times, from 15 percent to 26 percent.

Although these were encouraging results, the team still had to prove to senior management that the installation of television monitors would ultimately boost the bank's bottom line. The team knew, from prior studies, that improvements in the bank's customer-satisfaction index (based on a standard 30-question survey) correlated with increases in future sales. Every one-point improvement in the index added $1.40 in annual revenue per household, mainly through increased customer purchases and retention. So a branch with a customer base of 10,000 households would increase its annual revenues by $28,000 if the index increased by just two points. The team carried out a statistical analysis of the test branch's results and projected that the reductions in perceived wait times would translate into a 5.9-point increase in overall banking-center customer satisfaction.

While the benefits were substantial, the team had to consider whether they outweighed the costs of buying and installing the monitors. The team determined that it would cost some $22,000 to upgrade a branch in the Atlanta innovation market but that, for a national rollout, economies of scale would bring the per-branch cost down to about $10,000 per site. Any branch with more than a few thousand households in its customer base would therefore be able to recoup the up-front cost in less than a year. Encouraged by the program's apparent economic viability, the team recently launched a second phase of the TZM experiment, in which it is measuring the impact of more varied television programming, different sound levels, and even advertising.

branch network. To date, the program has posted strong results: Of the 40 experiments conducted as of May 2002, 36 were deemed successes, and 20 had been recommended for national rollout. But, as we'll soon see, this high success rate posed its own challenges for the I&D Team. (For a detailed discussion of one of the bank's successful experiments, see the feature box "In the Transaction Zone.")

Actual Versus Perceived Waiting Time

Bank of America's I&D Team asked customers who had waited in line more than five minutes: *How long have you been waiting?*

Experimental Site

Before the implementation of Bank of America's transaction zone media experiment, customers who waited longer than five minutes significantly overestimated their waiting time (32 percent). But after the installation of TV monitors in the bank lobby, overestimates for the same customer group dropped to 15 percent.

Control Branch

In this same testing period, no intervention was carried out at the control branch, which had demographics very similar to those of the experimental site. Overestimates at this site actually increased from 15 percent to 26 percent.

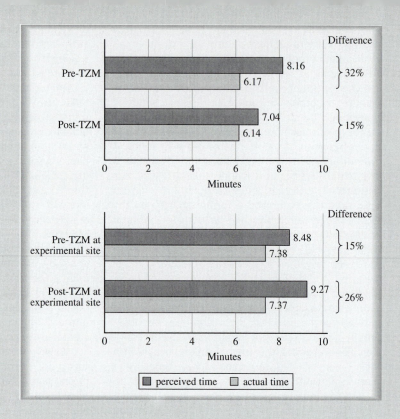

REWARDS AND CHALLENGES

Bank of America has reaped important rewards from its experiments. The initiative has generated an unprecedented surge of creative thinking about branch banking, as manifested not only in the dozens of innovative proposals for service experiments but in the establishment of the three very different models of physical branches. Within the innovation market, customer satisfaction has improved substantially, and the experimental branches have attracted many new customers, some of whom travel considerable distances to do their banking at the new centers. More broadly, many of the experimental processes and technologies are now being adopted throughout the bank's national branch network, with promising results.

As important as the business benefits is the enormous amount of learning that the bank has gained. Carrying out experiments in a service setting poses many difficult problems. In grappling with the challenges, the bank has deepened its understanding of the unique dynamics of service innovation. It may not have solved all the problems, but it has gained valuable insights into the process of service development—insights that will likely provide Bank of America with an important edge over its less adventurous competitors.

Let's look more closely at some of the toughest challenges the bank has faced. First of all, carrying out experiments in a live setting inevitably entails disruptions. Customers may at times be confused by unfamiliar processes, and employees may be distracted as they learn new ways to work. During the early months of the Bank of America program, for example, the I&D Team found that tellers and other staff members had to spend between 30 percent and 50 percent of their time in meetings and training sessions related to the experiments. Branches often had to bring in temporary workers to take up the slack, a practice that sometimes introduced problems of its own. Although employees spent less time in training and meetings as they became used to the program, they continued to feel added time pressure throughout the experiments. Any company pursuing a similar experimentation initiative will need to plan staffing requirements and work schedules carefully.

In addition to the new demands on their time, Bank of America employees also faced different and sometimes conflicting incentives, which raised some hard questions about compensation. Sales associates at the branches traditionally earned between 30 percent and 50 percent of their total pay from performance bonuses tied to a point system. An associate would earn points for meeting various sales quotas, and the number of points would vary according to, among other things, the products sold, the branch's customer-satisfaction levels, and local market demographics.

For the first several months of the I&D program, the test branches maintained the conventional incentive scheme. At first, sales associates seemed to relish the additional activities—their involvement in the program made them feel "special" (as a number of them put it), and they made extra efforts to get the experiments up and running. But the time pressures inevitably took their toll on the associates. They soon realized that all the time they had to dedicate to meetings and training reduced their opportunities to earn bonus points. In a number of branches, moreover, associates had to take turns greeting customers as the host—an activity that, again, offered no chances to earn points. Because their monthly sales quotas hadn't changed, some associates became frustrated with the new arrangement. When acting as the host, for example, some associates would leave their post to help a client open an account (and to gain the associated bonus points) rather than refer the client to another specialist as the experiment's design dictated. The desire to earn points conflicted with the desire to participate in the experiments.

To address this unanticipated effect of the program, senior management abandoned the traditional bonus system in the test branches in January 2001, switching all associates to fixed incentives based on team performance. Most associates welcomed the change, which amplified their feeling of being special while also underscoring top management's commitment to the experimentation process. But, again, not all staff members thrived under the new scheme. Without the lure of points, some associates lost their motivation to sell. Resentment from bank personnel outside the innovation market also intensified as a result of the special compensation program. One bank executive pointed out that "those in the I&D branches now thought they didn't have to chin to the same level as others." Doubts about the broader applicability of test-market findings also grew. As Allen Jones, a regional executive, said, "If a test is successful only under fixed-incentive schemes, then we can't roll it out elsewhere."

In response to the problems, senior management switched the staff back to the old point-based incentive system after just six months. Not surprisingly, tensions between earning bonus points and assisting in experiments quickly returned. Further, the about-face disheartened some staffers, leading them to question management's commitment to the program. The bank's difficulties over determining incentive pay underscore the problems inherent in having employees participate in a corporate innovation initiative while also pursuing their everyday jobs: This is an unavoidable consequence of real-time experimentation. In the long run, the best solution will likely turn out to be a hybrid bonus system, one that includes both individual sales commissions and a fixed, team-based component. But every company will have to go through its own testing period to arrive at the balance that is right for its people and that doesn't undermine the fidelity of its experiments. It's important to note, also, that staff turnover in the test branches dropped considerably during the program. The difficulties employees faced paled in comparison to the enthusiasm they felt about participating in the effort.

Another challenge Bank of America struggled with was managing its capacity for experimentation. Any laboratory has limits to the number of experiments it can carry out at any time, and if that capacity isn't carefully planned for, feedback slows and learning diminishes. The bank had to manage capacity both in individual branches—one branch sometimes had as many as 15 active experiments—and across all the branches undertaking experiments. If the capacity of the entire market was not well managed, too many experiments would have to be performed at a single branch, increasing the amount of noise surrounding each one. And if the team were to run out of capacity, it would be forced to do tests sequentially rather than simultaneously, which would delay the process.

Conducting the experiments in a commercial setting added another wrinkle to capacity management. If customers loved a new service, branch managers would naturally demand that it be continued beyond the 90-day trial period. This being the real world, after all, the branches could not simply pull the plug on something customers had grown to relish. But that made it more difficult to start new experiments—the noise from the continuing experiments would begin to obscure the results of the new ones. Scott Arcure, who led the I&D Team's measurement efforts, admitted, "We often worry about changing too many chemicals in the mix and wonder about which one made it explode. As bankers, we're not experts at this type of measurement." The team ultimately decided to bring in a statistics expert to help it sort out the effects of multiple variables.

Finally, there was the issue of failure. In any program of experimentation, the greatest learning comes from the most radical experiments—which also have the highest likelihood of failure. In a laboratory, radical experiments are routinely undertaken with the expectation that they'll fail but still produce extraordinarily valuable insights, often opening up entirely new frontiers for investigation. In the real world, however, there are inevitably pressures to avoid failures, particularly dramatic ones. First, there's the fear you'll alienate customers. Second, there's the fear you'll damage the bottom line, or at least shrink your own source of funding. Finally, there's the fear you'll alienate top managers, leading them to pull the plug on your program.

The I&D Team felt all these pressures. Although it knew the value of radical experiments, it also knew that extravagant failures in a live setting could put its entire effort at risk. As a result, the team tended to take an incrementalist approach, often pursuing experiments that simply validated ideas that were likely to succeed. Although the team's original plan called for a 30 percent failure rate, the actual rate in the first year was just 10 percent. The team turned out to be much less adventurous than it had hoped to be. As Warren Butler, a bank executive and team leader, explained, "We're trying to sell ourselves to the bank. If we have too many failures, we just won't be accepted. Currently, we may have failure *within* concepts, but not failure *of* the concepts." In the tradition-bound and risk-averse world of banking, it's no surprise that the team would end up erring on the side of caution. And the conservatism of some of the experiments should not obscure the radical nature of the overall program. Any service company designing an experimentation program will have to carefully weigh the risks involved against the learning that may be generated.

* * *

For hundreds, if not thousands, of years, systematic experimentation has been at the heart of all innovation. Advances in products, the tools that make them, and the value they create for both producers and consumers have emerged through carefully designed and executed experiments. Similar advances in services have lagged because, as we have seen, experimentation in a live setting entails particular challenges. But however daunting they may initially seem, the challenges can be met, as Bank of America's effort suggests. In just a few years, the bank has achieved important benefits that are having a real impact on its business and its future. By applying the lessons from the bank's experience to their own businesses, other service companies will be able to make the transition from haphazard to systematic approaches to innovation—from guesswork to true R&D.

Case 1-5

Team New Zealand

Doug Peterson leaned back in his chair and twisted the cap off another Steinlager. The Wharf Cafe had grown crowded and smoky since the meeting had started. "We really have to get ourselves a proper conference room next time," he thought, as he stared out over a misty, gray Auckland harbor.

It was late May 1994. Peterson had been working on the design of New Zealand's 1995 America's Cup yacht for over a year. As lead designer, he had conceived the original concept and recruited the design team, which, for the first time, was making extensive use of sophisticated computer-aided design and simulation tools. Now, as the team assembled for its weekly review after the day's sailing, the time had come to commit to the construction of the new yacht.

Peterson pondered the decision they faced. The budget allowed for two yachts to be built; however, there were several strategies they could take with regard to their design. Should they build two yachts with *similar* hull and keel designs, so they could vary the details of the keel design and race them against each other to assess potential improvements? Should they build two yachts with hulls optimized for *different* sailing conditions? Or should they build one yacht now, but delay building the second, waiting until after another round of prototype tests, while they experimented with the first one on the water? The decision they made in the next hour would profoundly affect their chances of winning in San Diego and becoming only the second team in 145 years to win the Cup from the Americans.

THE AMERICA'S CUP

In 1851, the Royal Yacht Squadron of England offered a silver trophy, called the "Hundred Guinea Mug," to the winner of a sailing race run around the Isle of Wight, a small island off the south coast. Open to all nations, the race attracted fifteen English entries and only one foreign challenger—the eventual winner, America. The Hundred Guinea Mug thereafter became known as the America's Cup, in honor of its first winner, and when the last surviving

Harvard Business School Case No. 9-697-040. Copyright 1996 President and Fellows of Harvard College. All rights reserved. For information: permissions@hbsp.harvard.edu.

This case was prepared by Alan MacCormack and Marco Iansiti. HBS cases are developed solely for class discussion and do not necessarily illustrate effective or ineffective management.

owner of the victorious team donated it to the New York Yacht club, it was decided that challengers from other countries should be allowed to compete for the trophy in a "friendly competition between foreign nations." The rules for these races were defined in a document called "The Deed of the Gift."

The first America's Cup challenge was held in 1870. Over the next 30 years, the American defenders successfully defended against teams from England, Scotland, Canada, and Ireland. At this time, participants were not limited in design, hence boats varied greatly in both size and power. However, since the European challengers were required by the rules to cross the stormy North Atlantic under their own sail power, their boats were often heavily built and slower than the Americans'. Races were often one-sided affairs, of little interest to spectators.

In 1920, the rules were changed to specify the use of J-class designs, enormous single-masted boats over 100 feet long, with masts 120 feet high and a crew of 40. While races became closer, ultimately, the results were the same. Between 1920 and 1937, the Americans made another four successful defenses. After a long break due to World War II, J-Class boats were ruled too expensive, and a new 12-meter class was created, with 65-foot long hulls, 90-foot masts, and a crew of 11. The rules were changed so that challengers' boats could be transported to the race site by ship rather than having to sail. As designs converged, racing became even tighter. Even so, between 1958 and 1980, the Americans defended successfully another eight times.

In 1983, the longest winning streak in sports history—132 years—ended when the revolutionary Australia II, with a radical and controversial "winged keel," defeated Liberty, under the helmsmanship of Dennis Conner. In 1987, however, Conner regained the cup in Perth with Stars & Stripes, racing for the San Diego Yacht Club. The next year, a team from New Zealand, exploiting a clause in "The Deed of Gift," challenged Conner with a huge boat nicknamed "The Big One." Without time to redesign, Conner defended successfully with a 60-foot ultralight catamaran, the first use of a double-hull in the America's Cup.

In 1992, a new yacht class was defined for the lighter winds of San Diego. The International America's Cup Class (IACC) required boats of 75 feet in length, with 110-foot masts and a crew of 16. By using advanced materials, boats became lighter for their size, and hence faster in the light winds. While America 3 eventually defeated the Italian challenger in the final, the 1992 races were enormously expensive. The American defender built five boats, the Italian challenger four. Both spent over $60 million. It was decided in the future to reduce expenses; each team would be limited to only two boats, with further limits on the use of sails and other equipment.

The 1995 cup races would follow a "round-robin" format. First, the boats would be divided into two groups: the defenders, from the country of the current cup holders, and the challengers, from all other nations. The racing would then be divided into three parts. In the first, which would start in January, the challengers race against each other for the right to enter the final (this was called the Louis Vuitton Cup). In the second, which would run simultaneously with the first, yachts from the host country race for the right to defend. Finally, in May, the winning challenger team would race against the winning defender team for the America's Cup. Boat designs would be allowed to evolve between each race, until the start of the final.

Exhibit 1 shows a picture from a recent America's Cup race. Typical time differences between first- and second-placed boats would usually be less than one minute.

THE DESIGN OF A RACING YACHT

The design of a modern day racing yacht comprises four essential elements—the hull, the keel, the mast, and the sails (see **Exhibit 2**). The objective of the design team is to produce a light boat with as low a drag factor as possible. The structure, however, must also have the strength and stability to cope with highly variable wind and sea conditions. To achieve this balance, teams rely heavily on the skills and experience of the lead designer to make many critical trade-offs during the design process.

The bulk of the initial design work focuses on the hull and keel, as these are on the critical path for the construction of the yacht. To develop these, designers have traditionally relied on what is referred to as the "tank and tunnel" process for getting feedback on performance. This process entails construction of a series of scaled-down physical prototypes, which are tested in a wind tunnel and a towing tank (a large swimming pool equipped with a winch at one end, which tows the prototype down the middle), providing data on the amount of drag generated by a particular design.

During the initial stages of a typical yacht development, around five to six physical prototypes are built at one-quarter scale (20 feet) and subject to testing in the wind tunnel and towing tank. Fabrication and testing of these prototypes takes several months and costs about $50,000 per prototype. Data on the performance of each of these designs are analyzed to assess their relative performance characteristics and used to project potential design enhancements. A further set of prototypes is then built, and the whole process repeated. This series of prototype iterations typically occurs three or four times prior to freezing the design for construction. As Peterson explained:

> The tank and tunnel method is a design process where experimentation occurs in bursts. Every couple of months, you get back the results of your experiments. As a result, there is a limit to the number of design iterations you can perform. A typical project can rarely afford more than 20 prototypes, due to time and money constraints. In each design cycle, you have to rely on big gains in performance.

THE USE OF SIMULATION IN DESIGN

The design of the critical surfaces on a modern day racing yacht is a complex activity. The presence of many interactions means it is not easy to predict the effect of even small changes in the structure. The system is "chaotic," and predicting its behavior is much like trying to predict the weather. While traditional "tank and tunnel" design methods rely on experienced designers and informed trial and error to overcome such complexity, the advent of cheap computer hardware and automated design tools have led to rapid advances in the possibility of simulating designs.

Modern day yacht design makes use of several tools to help automate the process. Among the most important are Finite Element Analysis (FEA), a tool that analyzes the structural characteristics of a design; Computational Fluid Dynamics programs (CFD), which help simulate the flow of water over the yacht's critical surfaces; and Velocity Prediction Programs (VPP), which predict how fast a particular design will be in a given set of wind and sea conditions.

CFD programs were originally developed for the aerospace industry, traditionally being used to model the flow of air over an aircraft's control surfaces. The software is "panel-based," the structure first being "broken up" into many small panels, each of which is represented by a set of mathematical equations. The program links these panels together to form a model of the complete design, then solves a set of equations governed by fluid mechanics theory to calculate the pressures and flows at the surface. While CFD had been around since the 1960s, its application to yacht design was a recent phenomenon as the teams began design work for the 1995 America's Cup. In its initial applications, it had met with only limited success, and opinions were mixed as to its usefulness.

Advantages of Simulation

The major advantages of simulation over traditional design methods fall into three main areas. It is cheaper and faster than constructing physical prototypes, generates more insight into why particular designs are better or worse than others, and avoids problems associated with "scaling up" the design from a physical prototype to the real world.

The primary advantage of simulation is in its speed and cost. While programs often require a significant amount of computing memory and processing power, once a basic design has been configured, design iterations can be run in a matter of hours, at little cost. The only limitation on how many iterations can be conducted relates to the amount of computer power available and, more important, the capacity of the design team to interpret results. In general, the bottleneck becomes a team's ability to generate and evaluate new configurations, not its ability to test them.

Another important advantage of simulation is that it establishes an understanding of the trade-offs involved with alternative design choices. Although tank and tunnel methods give a good indication of the overall performance of a design, they do not help the designer interpret why one design is performing better than another. CFD, by comparison, can show the pressure distributions and flows around a hull or keel which generate the drag produced by a given design.

A final advantage of simulation is that it avoids the problems of "scale-up." This occurs when the use of scaled-down models introduces distortions that affect the accuracy of test results. For example, certain types of drag, generated by the chaotic nature of a fluid flowing over a surface, are very sensitive to scale; hence, results from reduced-scale physical models are likely to be inaccurate. The use of simulation avoids such a bias.

Drawbacks of Simulation

While simulation has many advantages over tank and tunnel tests, these tools are, however, complementary. As Peterson emphasized, "Even with all the simulation in the world, no one is going to commit $3 million to a yacht without towing it down a tank first!" Physical prototypes are used extensively early in the design process to set the basic parameters of the hull and keel. Once these have been defined, simulation is used to help optimize their shape.

The importance of simulation is greatly increased once the hull and keel have been built. CFD can be used to substantially improve the performance of the yacht through the design of aerodynamic wings that attach to the bulb at the bottom of the keel (the lead weight that gives a yacht its stability). In the run-up to a major race program, extensive testing and refinement of these appendages occurs, driven by the results of simulating different designs. These changes can lead to substantial improvements in performance.

Ultimately, however, all of these tools are only as good as the designer in whose hands they are placed. The lead designer is responsible for putting together the initial concept, without which no amount of simulation will yield a good design. Also in charge of directing the experimentation strategy, the designer is the person who says "what to try next." The concept design and experimentation strategy together provide critical "stakes-in-the-ground" and a sense of direction—activities for which automated design tools provide little help. As Peterson noted:

> The CFD program can't design a yacht from scratch without conceptual input. It doesn't know what parameters it should be optimizing. Consider designing a golf ball to fly as far as possible off the tee. The computer won't tell you the ball should have dimples, but if you specify this as a design parameter, it will find the optimal dimple pattern and density for you.

TEAM NEW ZEALAND

During May 1993, general manager Peter Blake began putting together the team of people that would work together for over two years in an effort to win the America's Cup. The Team New Zealand syndicate comprised about 50 people, with activities split between team management, design and construction, and the crew, skippered by Olympic Gold medalist Russell Coutts (see **Exhibit 3**).

The budget for the syndicate, raised from corporate sponsors in New Zealand, was $20 million. While comparable to the budgets of other teams, Team New Zealand had decided to build two boats, rather than one, due to the experimental benefits this would give them during the testing period. Given that the full cost of a boat, mast, keel, and sail program was around $3 million to $4 million, it was clear from the start that the money for other resources would be severely limited. The team would need to be small, focused, and highly motivated, with everyone adopting multiple roles.

Blake's philosophy in running the team was to have all the critical people on board from the beginning. On May 24, 1993, the team assembled for the first time. Rather than dive straight into the detail of design and crew training, they spent the first three weeks working together with an external consultant to outline the mission for the team and a vision of how they would work together. Peterson described the process:

> We spent a lot of time going over why certain teams had won or lost in the past. What we found was that unsuccessful efforts were often driven by one or two personalities, be they designer-driven, skipper-driven, or owner-driven. Successful teams were truly "managed," not dominated by one voice. Hence, we wanted to run the syndicate in a democratic fashion. When we had differences of opinion on which direction to go, we'd put it to a vote. One of the most important outputs of the three weeks was the mission statement which described the way that things would run. Above all, we stressed open communication and dissemination of knowledge, even to the extreme of running classes on yacht design and weather forecasting for anyone who was interested.

With the three-week "vision thing" behind them, the staff at last assumed their more traditional roles. The crew began training, using the yachts that had been built for the last America's Cup, and the design team began work on the concepts for the new design.

The Design Process

Doug Peterson was appointed to lead the design team. An American by birth, Peterson had extensive experience with designing boats and racing yachts. Peterson had no formal design or engineering training, but had been designing boats for as long as he could remember: "This is what I have always done. I can remember when I was in high school, I would spend all my time designing boats on pieces of scrap paper instead of paying attention in class." About 30 years and thousands of designs later, he was considered to be one of the world's leading yacht designers. His latest achievement was the design of the America 3 boat, the America's Cup winner in 1992. Peterson was given responsibility for developing the overall design concept for the Team New Zealand boat, specifying test models, analyzing results, and developing construction plans.

As the design team planned to make extensive use of automated design and simulation tools, Peterson assembled a mix of experienced yacht designers and simulation experts. Among them, Dave Egan was recruited to run the design simulations. Egan's appointment brought to the team prior experience in simulating yacht designs and a working knowledge of the required computer hardware, having previously been a sales agent for Silicon Graphics.

The design was initially driven by Peterson, who defined the initial boat concept and specified an implementation plan. Peterson drew upon the knowledge he had accumulated with the America 3 team to put his first thoughts to paper. Given America 3 had built five boats, each of which was significantly different in design, he had a lot of experience to help him. During the design process, the America 3 team had conducted over 65 prototype tests in the wind tunnel alone.

Egan's first job was to code this concept design into a geometry model for the simulation program, providing a baseline for performance. With this accomplished, design iterations and performance simulations began in November 1993. The initial simulations focused primarily on the design of the hull, with relatively simple keel variations (see **Exhibit 4**). The team would have to commit to the hull design in May 1994 in order for construction to begin.

The Simulation Effort

Running CFD required substantial amounts of computer power. For example, to simulate the keel required coding 13,000 individual panels as part of the modeling program, creating data files of 6 to 8 gigabytes in size. While several syndicates were using similar analytical programs, the resources available to them and strategies they followed differed considerably.

Most syndicates had lined up large corporations to help with the task, allowing processing to be performed on the largest and latest supercomputers. Young America, for example, had over a million dollars of computer time available to them, through a partnership that included both Cray and Boeing. Boeing ran the design simulations on Cray supercomputers based in their headquarters in Seattle, using advanced CFD software developed for their aerospace needs. These machines were among the world's fastest computers, each costing several million dollars. Every few weeks, the Boeing engineers would run large batches of simulations and feed back their results to the Young America designers in San Diego. This allowed them to test a massive number of experimental designs.

The strategy adopted by Team New Zealand reflected the resource constraints presented by the budget. The team decided to use a small network of workstations that could be operated locally. Given the poor history CFD simulation had in yacht design, Egan was given less than $100K to cover personnel, hardware, and software. As he recalls:

> The early days of the project were a constant challenge to find resources. We were running around companies looking for computer time. At one, we managed to grab a 16 processor Challenge™ computer for a month prior to it being commissioned. The MIS guy never knew what happened! Then we gained access to a SunSparc2™ workstation. Soon, however, the rising number of design iterations we needed to explore began to exceed its capacity.

As luck would have it, during Christmas 1993, Jim Clark, the CEO of Silicon Graphics, was in New Zealand having his yacht refitted. A keen sailor, Clark had invited several members of the team aboard his yacht. Over dinner, as he learned of their predicament, he immediately offered the INDY™ workstation installed in his yacht for the team to use. As Egan explains:

> Making contact with Jim was extremely timely. Although we declined the offer of his waterproof INDY, he did put us in touch with the local SGI office. They gave us access to the spare cycles on their demonstration machines, a 4 processor Challenge™ server, and a couple of workstations.

The involvement of Silicon Graphics in the project grew with time. The company eventually became a sponsor of the team and lent a lot of computing equipment to the effort. This effectively increased the syndicate's simulation budget significantly. With a combination of workstations, the team could now simulate a new design every 2 or 3 hours. It gave the team immediate access to experimentation as the equipment was located a few feet from the dock. Egan emphasized the benefits of this approach compared with the tank and tunnel tests:

> Instead of relying on a few big leaps, we had the ability to continually design, test, and refine our ideas. The team would often hold informal discussions on design issues, sketch some schematics on the back of a beer mat, and ask me to run the numbers. Using traditional design methods would have meant waiting months for results, and by that time, our thinking would have evolved so much that the reason for the experiment would long since have been forgotten.
>
> We considered the crew our customers, in charge of what went into the design. They needed to drive the process. By having a computing strategy based upon local workstations, we had the ability to display results of simulations to them using flow-fill graphics. How we demonstrated the difference between two designs turned out to be a powerful marketing tool to help convince the crew of the benefits.

Team New Zealand's approach to simulation was extremely practical, heavily influenced by Peterson's experience. As he explained:

> Dave [Egan] was very realistic on the uses and limitations of CFD. In practice, if you start with a bad design, simulation won't get you anywhere near a good one. Some of the other syndicates let CFD drive their process. The Australians, for example, had some really deep simulation experts, and see where that got them.[1] At the end of the day, the real performance advantage is in the initial design. Everything else from there on in is just incremental improvement.

[1] The Australian boat sank in one of the early trials, while racing against Team New Zealand.

> Take the Velocity Prediction Program. Trying to work out how the sails will perform is an extremely unreliable science. There's so much variability in the air flow. I told them to tweak it until they got the answer I expected; then we looked at the coefficients to see if they looked reasonable. In the end, it doesn't matter. All you're looking at is the differences between alternative designs. No one really believes we can accurately predict the time we'll put up over the course in San Diego.

During the six months between November 1993 and May 1994, the team cycled through building physical prototypes for tank and tunnel testing three times, building 14 scaled-down models. The first set of prototypes provided a performance baseline for the initial concept, allowing the team to parameterize the Velocity Prediction Program and establish an estimate of the time around the course in San Diego. For the second and third set of prototypes, Peterson attempted to improve upon the initial design using a combination of experience and the flow-fill pictures generated by the CFD program. The improvements were significant, with the best prototype from the third set of tests bettering the time of the initial concept design by over two minutes. Egan described the situation as of early May:

> We were emerging with a robust design for the hull and keel. We had reduced the drag considerably over the concept design, but now, each new prototype was giving us less and less improvement. The third set of prototype tests, which we'd just got back, produced less than half the improvement of the second. There was a strong argument that the most improvement potential was now in the keel appendages, where a lot of enhancements can be made through the design and placement of the wings. To run those experiments, however, you have to put a real yacht in the water.

Testing of the actual boat in the water would be combined with CFD simulation of the keel. The two would have to be used together, since historically only about a third of the changes suggested by CFD resulted in "real" improvements to the design.

"TWO BOATS, OR NOT TWO BOATS—THAT IS THE QUESTION"

In late May 1994, the syndicate was faced with a major decision. Construction of the first yacht was planned to begin next month for an August delivery (boat construction took about two months). This would leave about four months for travel to San Diego, testing, and improvements before racing was to begin in January. However, the initial budget had provided money for two boats, and there were several theories on how to get the best value from the second one.

One option was to commit to building two yachts now for delivery in August. This way, the yachts could be used in combination to conduct test iterations on the keel wings. Another option was to build only one yacht now, use this to begin testing different keel wings, and meanwhile conduct another round of prototype testing on the basic hull and keel design. The second boat could then be built just prior to the start of the qualifying competition in January.

Building two boats now would allow Team New Zealand to put two boats in the water at the same time. Egan articulated the perceived logic behind a two-boat testing program:

> The two-boat testing philosophy is driven by the fact that the sea is a noisy environment in which to run experiments. If we build two yachts of similar design, we gain the ability to run better experiments. We can put two keels with different wing designs on each boat, race

them, and see how much difference there is. Then we can swap the keels and make sure the results hold for the other boat and crew. This way, there is no argument over whether the wind or sea conditions affected the results. The problem is especially relevant, given the improvements that come from changes to the keel wings are relatively small, in the order of two or three seconds over the whole course. Detecting these differences in noisy conditions is extremely difficult. Just a minor change in wind speed between two trials can easily swamp the effect of a design change.

In the past, teams using a two-boat testing program had shown that it was possible to run and verify the performance of a different keel wing design practically every 24 hours, particularly if the two boats were identical. During the day, while the crew were on the water, the simulation team would analyze hundreds of potential improvements to the keel appendages and select one or two that appeared most promising (**Exhibit 5** shows the results of a simulation run for a specific keel design). Overnight, the construction team would work on the new designs and have them ready to sail the next morning. When the crew arrived, they would take the boats racing to verify whether the design changes produced "real" improvements.

With only one boat, alternative keel designs had to be removed and fitted during the sailing day. If conditions changed, the crew would often have to sail each design a number of times to identify which was better. As a result, verifying the results of design changes was slower than with two boats. Therefore, some argued that the differences in improvement speed between one- and two-boat testing would soon add up.

Building only one boat now traded the benefits of rapid feedback inherent in a two-boat testing process in favor of another cycle of testing prior to committing to the second yacht. Proponents of this approach argued that although the improvement potential in the basic design of the hull and keel had diminished, another cycle of tank and tunnel tests was still attractive. At the same time, running experiments with different keel appendages, even with only one boat, would still produce significant design enhancements. In combination, these two activities would yield greater overall improvement to the design and in addition would give the team the flexibility of building the second boat later in the development cycle. Building two boats now, they argued, was a waste of money and opportunity, particularly if these were identical.

Team New Zealand was not alone in having a budget big enough for two boats. As they tapped the sailing grapevine, however, other syndicates were taking diverse approaches.

The Japanese syndicate had decided to stagger the construction of their boats, opting to conduct another round of prototype tests before committing to the second one.

The leading Australian syndicate was building two boats simultaneously, but each was of very different design.

None of the three American defenders had decided to build two boats, despite having budgets of similar size to that of the New Zealand team. They had spent the money on other items, including more prototypes and iterations for tank and tunnel testing.

Team New Zealand's decision boiled down to three basic options: building two identical boats now; building two different boats now, perhaps one following one of Peterson's more aggressive concepts that hadn't made it to the wind tunnel yet; and building one boat now and one boat after some additional testing.

EXHIBIT 1
America's Cup
Competition

EXHIBIT 2
Schematic of a
Recent Racing
Yacht

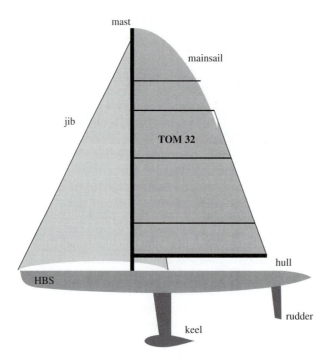

EXHIBIT 3
**Team New
Zealand
Syndicate: Key
Staff Members**

Syndicate Head:	Peter Blake
Yacht Club:	Royal New Zealand Yacht Squadron
Syndicate Budget:	Estimated $20 million
Team Sponsors:	ENZA (New Zealand Apple and Pear Board)
	Lion Nathan (Steinlager)
	Lotteries Commission
	Television New Zealand
	Toyota New Zealand

Management

Campaign Public Relations:	Alan Sefton
Campaign Business Manager:	Ross Blackman

Lead Crew

Skipper:	Russell Coutts
Navigator:	Tom Schnackenberg
Afterguard:	Brad Butterworth
	Rick Dodson
	Murray Jones

Design Team

Chief Designers	Doug Peterson
	Laurie Davidson
Computational Dynamicist	David Egan
Aero/hydro Dynamicist	Richard Karn
Performance Analyst	Peter Jackson
Structures/weather	David Alan-Williams

Construction

Construction Chief	Tim Gurr
Structural Experts	Wayne Smith
	Mike Drummond
	Chris Mitchell
	Neil Wilkinson

EXHIBIT 4
**Computer-
Generated
"Flow-Fill"
Picture of an
Early Design**

EXHIBIT 5
**Computer-
Generated
Results of Keel
Simulation**

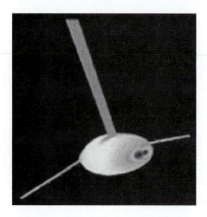

Article

Enlightened Experimentation: The New Imperative for Innovation

Experimentation lies at the heart of every company's ability to innovate. In other words, the systematic testing of ideas is what enables companies to create and refine their products. In fact, no product can be a product without having first been an idea that was shaped, to one degree or another, through the process of experimentation. Today, a major development project can require literally thousands of experiments, all with the same objective: to learn whether the product concept or proposed technical solution holds promise for addressing a new need or problem, then incorporating that information in the next round of tests so that the best product ultimately results.

In the past, testing was relatively expensive, so companies had to be parsimonious with the number of experimental iterations. Today, however, new technologies such as computer simulation, rapid prototyping, and combinatorial chemistry allow companies to create more learning more rapidly, and that knowledge, in turn, can be incorporated in more experiments at less expense. Indeed, new information-based technologies have driven down the marginal costs of experimentation, just as they have decreased the marginal costs in some production and distribution systems. Moreover, an experimental system that integrates new information-based technologies does more than lower costs; it also increases the opportunities for innovation. That is, some technologies can make existing experimental activities more efficient, while others introduce entirely new ways of discovering novel concepts and solutions.

Millennium Pharmaceuticals in Cambridge, Massachusetts, for instance, incorporates new technologies such as genomics, bioinformatics, and combinatorial chemistry in its technology platform for conducting experiments. The platform enables factory-like automation that can generate and test drug candidates in minutes or seconds, compared with the days or more that traditional methods require. Gaining information early on about, say, the toxicological profile of a drug candidate significantly improves Millennium's ability to predict the drug's success in clinical testing and, ultimately, in the marketplace. Unpromising candidates are eliminated before hundreds of millions of dollars are invested in their development. In addition to reducing the cost and time of traditional drug development, the new technologies also enhance Millennium's ability to innovate, according to Chief Technology Officer Michael Pavia. Specifically, the company has greater opportunities to experiment with more diverse potential drugs, including those that may initially seem improbable but might eventually lead to breakthrough discoveries.

This era of "enlightened experimentation" has thus far affected businesses with high costs of product development, such as the pharmaceutical, automotive, and software industries. By studying them, I have learned several valuable lessons that I believe have broad applicability to other industries. As the cost of computing continues to fall, making all sorts of complex calculations faster and cheaper, and as new technologies like combinatorial chemistry emerge, virtually all companies will discover that they have a greater capacity for rapid experimentation to investigate diverse concepts. Financial institutions, for example, now use computer simulations to test new financial instruments. In fact, the development of spreadsheet software has forever changed financial modeling; even novices can perform many sophisticated what-if experiments that were once prohibitively expensive.

A SYSTEM FOR EXPERIMENTATION

Understanding enlightened experimentation requires an appreciation of the process of innovation. Namely, product and technology innovations don't drop from the sky; they are nurtured in laboratories and development organizations, passing through a *system* for experimentation. All development organizations have such a system in place to help them narrow the number of ideas to pursue and then refine that group into what can become viable products. A critical stage of the process occurs when an idea or concept becomes a working artifact, or prototype, which can then be tested, discussed, shown to customers, and learned from.

Perhaps the most famous example of the experimental system at work comes from the laboratories of Thomas Alva Edison. When Edison noted that inventive genius is "99 percent perspiration and 1 percent inspiration," he was well aware of the importance of an organization's capability and capacity to experiment. That's why he designed his operations in Menlo Park, New Jersey, to allow for efficient and rapid experimental iterations.

Edison knew that the various components of a system for experimentation—including personnel, equipment, libraries, and so on—all function interdependently. As such, they need to be jointly optimized, for together they define the system's performance: its speed (the time needed to design, build, test, and analyze an experiment), cost, fidelity (the accuracy of the experiment and the conditions under which it is conducted), capacity (the number of experiments that can be performed in a given time period), and the learning gained (the amount of new information generated by the experiment and an organization's ability to benefit from it). Thus, for example, highly skilled machinists worked in close proximity to lab personnel at Menlo Park so they could quickly make improvements when researchers had new ideas or learned something new from previous experiments. This system led to landmark inventions, including the electric light-bulb, which required more than 1,000 complex experiments with filament materials and shapes, electromechanical regulators, and vacuum technologies.

Edison's objective of achieving great innovation through rapid and frequent experimentation is especially pertinent today as the costs (both financial and time) of experimentation plunge. Yet many companies mistakenly view new technologies solely in terms of cost cutting, overlooking their vast potential for innovation. Worse, companies with that limited view get bogged down in the confusion that occurs when they try to incorporate new technologies. For instance, computer simulation doesn't simply replace physical prototypes as a cost-saving measure; it introduces an entirely different way of experimenting that invites innovation. Just as the Internet offers enormous opportunities for innovation—far surpassing its use as a low-cost substitute for phone or catalog transactions—so does state-of-the-art experimentation. But realizing that potential requires companies to adopt a different mind-set.

Indeed, new technologies affect everything, from the development process itself, including the way an R&D organization is structured, to how new knowledge—and hence learning—is created. Thus, for companies to be more innovative, the challenges are managerial as well as technical, as these four rules for enlightened experimentation suggest:

1. Organize for rapid experimentation. The ability to experiment quickly is integral to innovation: as developers conceive of a multitude of diverse ideas, experiments can provide the rapid feedback necessary to shape those ideas by reinforcing, modifying, or complementing existing knowledge. Rapid experimentation, however, often requires the complete revamping of entrenched routines. When, for example, certain classes of experiments become an order of magnitude cheaper or faster, organizational incentives may suddenly become misaligned, and the activities and routines that were once successful might become hindrances. (See the sidebar "The Potential Pitfalls of New Technologies.")

Consider the major changes that BMW recently underwent. Only a few years ago, experimenting with novel design concepts—to make cars withstand crashes better, for instance—required expensive physical prototypes to be built. Because that process took months, it acted as a barrier to innovation because engineers could not get timely feedback on their ideas. Furthermore, data from crash tests arrived too late to significantly influence decisions in the early stages of product development. So BMW had to incorporate the information far downstream, incurring greater costs. Nevertheless, BMW's R&D organization, structured around this traditional system, developed award-winning automobiles, cementing the company's reputation as an industry leader. But its success also made change difficult.

Today, thanks to virtual experiments—crashes simulated by a high-performance computer rather than through physical prototypes—some of the information arrives very early, before BMW has made major resource decisions. The costs of experimentation (both financial and time) are therefore lower because BMW eliminates the creation of physical prototypes as well as the expense of potentially reworking bad designs after the company has committed itself to them. (Physical prototypes are still required much further downstream to verify the

The Essentials for Enlightened Experimentation

New technologies such as computer simulations not only make experimentation faster and cheaper, they also enable companies to be more innovative. But achieving that requires a thorough understanding of the link between experimentation and learning. Briefly stated, innovation requires the right R&D systems for performing experiments that will generate the information needed to develop and refine products quickly. The challenges are managerial as well as technical:

1) **Organize for rapid experimentation.**
   - Examine and, if necessary, revamp entrenched routines, organizational boundaries, and incentives to encourage rapid experimentation.
   - Consider using small development groups that contain key people (designers, test engineers, manufacturing engineers) with all the knowledge required to iterate rapidly.
   - Determine what experiments can be performed in parallel instead of sequentially. Parallel experiments are most effective when time matters most, cost is not an overriding factor, and developers expect to learn little that would guide them in planning the next round of experiments.

2) **Fail early and often, but avoid mistakes.**
   - Embrace failures that occur early in the development process and advance knowledge significantly.

- Don't forget the basics of experimentation. Well-designed tests have clear objectives (what do you anticipate learning?) and hypotheses (what do you expect to happen?). Also, mistakes often occur when you don't control variables that could diminish your ability to learn from the experiments. When variability can't be controlled, allow for multiple, repeated trials.

3) **Anticipate and exploit early information.**
   - Recognize the full value of front-loading: identifying problems upstream, where they are easier and cheaper to solve.
   - Acknowledge the trade-off between cost and fidelity. Experiments of lower fidelity (generally costing less) are best suited in the early exploratory stages of developing a product. High-fidelity experiments (typically more expensive) are best suited later to verifying the product.

4) **Combine new and traditional technologies.**
   - Do not assume that a new technology will necessarily replace an established one. Usually, new and traditional technologies are best used in concert.
   - Remember that new technologies emerge and evolve continually. Today's new technology might eventually replace its traditional counterpart, but it could then be challenged by tomorrow's new technology.

final designs and meet safety regulations.) In addition, the rapid feedback and the ability to see and manipulate high-quality computer images spur greater innovation: many design possibilities can be explored in "real time" yet virtually, in rapid iterations.

To study this new technology's impact on innovation, BMW performed the following experiment. Several designers, a simulation engineer, and a test engineer formed a team to improve the side-impact safety of cars. Primarily using computer simulations, the team developed and tested new ideas that resulted from their frequent brainstorming meetings.

Because all the knowledge required about safety, design, simulation, and testing resided within a small group, the team was able to iterate experiments and develop solutions rapidly. After each round of simulated crashes, the team analyzed the results and developed new ideas for the next round of experiments. As expected, the team benefited greatly from the rapid feedback: it took them only a few days to accept, refine, or reject new design solutions—something that had once taken months.

New technologies can slash the costs (both financial and time) of experimentation and dramatically increase a company's ability to develop innovative products. To reap those benefits, though, organizations must prepare themselves for the full effects of such technologies.

Computer simulations and rapid prototyping, for example, increase not only a company's capacity to conduct experiments but also the wealth of information generated by those tests. That, however, can easily overload an organization that lacks the capability to process information from each round of experiments quickly enough to incorporate it into the next round. In such cases, the result is waste, confusion, and frustration. In other words, without careful and thorough planning, a new technology might not only fail to deliver on its promise of lower cost, increased speed, and greater innovation, it could actually decrease the overall performance of an R&D organization, or at a minimum disrupt its operations.

Misaligned objectives are another common problem. Specifically, some managers do not fully appreciate the trade-off between response time and resource utilization. Consider what happens when companies establish central departments to oversee computing resources for performing simulations. Clearly, testing ideas and concepts virtually can provide developers with the rapid feedback they need to shape new products. At the same time, computers are costly, so people managing them as cost centers are evaluated by how much those resources are being used.

The busier a central computer is, however, the longer it takes for developers to get the feedback they need. In fact, the relationship between waiting time and utilization is not linear—queuing theory has shown that the waiting time typically increases gradually until a resource is utilized around 70 percent, and then the length of the delays surge. (See **Exhibit 1** on page 160, "Waiting for a Resource.") An organization trying to shave costs may become a victim of its own myopic objective. That is, an annual savings of perhaps a few hundred thousand dollars achieved through increasing utilization from 70 percent to 90 percent may lead to very long delays for dozens of development engineers waiting for critical feedback from their tests.

A huge negative consequence is that the excessive delays not only affect development schedules but also discourage people from experimenting, thus squelching their ability to innovate. So in the long term, running additional computer equipment at a lower utilization level might well be worth the investment. An alternative solution is to move those resources away from cost centers and under the control of developers, who have strong incentives for fast feedback.

As the trials accrued, the group members greatly increased their knowledge of the underlying mechanics, which enabled them to design previously unimaginable experiments. In fact, one test completely changed their knowledge about the complex relationship between material strength and safety. Specifically, BMW's engineers had assumed that the stronger the area next to the bottom of a car's pillars (the structures that connect the roof of an auto to its chassis), the better the vehicle would be able to withstand crashes. But one member of the development team insisted on verifying this assumption through an inexpensive computer simulation.

The results shocked the team: strengthening a particular area below one of the pillars substantially *decreased* the vehicle's crashworthiness. After more experiments and careful analysis, the engineers discovered that strengthening the lower part of the center pillar would make the pillar prone to folding higher up, above the strengthened area. Thus, the passenger compartment would be more penetrable at the part of the car closer to the mid-section, chest, and head of passengers. The solution was to weaken, not strengthen, the lower area. This counterintuitive knowledge—that purposely weakening a part of a car's structure could increase the vehicle's safety—has led BMW to reevaluate all the reinforced areas of its vehicles.

In summary, this small team increased the side-impact crash safety by about 30 percent. It is worth noting that two crash tests of physical prototypes at the end of the project confirmed the simulation results. It should also be noted that the physical prototypes cost a total of about $300,000, which was more than the cost of all 91 virtual crashes combined. Furthermore, the physical prototypes took longer to build, prepare, and test than the entire series of virtual crashes.

But to obtain the full benefits of simulation technologies, BMW had to undertake sweeping changes in process, organization, and attitude—changes that took several years to accomplish. Not only did the company have to reorganize the way different groups worked together; it also had to change habits that had worked so well in the old sequential development process.

Previously, for example, engineers were often loath to release less-than-perfect data. To some extent, it was in each group's interest to hold back and monitor the output from other groups. After all, the group that submitted its information to a central database first would quite likely have to make the most changes because it would have gotten the least feedback from other areas. So, for instance, the door development team at BMW was accustomed to—and rewarded for—releasing nearly flawless data (details about the material strength of a proposed door, for example), which could take many months to generate. The idea of releasing rough information very early, an integral part of a rapid and parallel experimentation process, was unthinkable—and not built into the incentive system. Yet a six-month delay while data were being perfected could derail a development program predicated on rapid iterations.

Thus, to encourage the early sharing of information, BMW's managers had to ensure that each group understood and appreciated the needs of other teams. The crash simulation group, for example, needed to make the door designers aware of the information it required in order to build rough models for early-stage crash simulations. That transfer of knowledge had a ripple effect, changing how the door designers worked because some of the requested information demanded that they pay close attention to the needs of other groups as well. They started to understand that withholding information as long as possible was counterproductive. By making these kinds of organizational changes, BMW in Germany significantly slashed development time and costs and boosted innovation.

2. Fail early and often, but avoid mistakes. Experimenting with many diverse—and sometimes seemingly absurd—ideas is crucial to innovation. When a novel concept fails in an experiment, the failure can expose important gaps in knowledge. Such experiments are particularly desirable when they are performed early on so that unfavorable options can be eliminated quickly and people can refocus their efforts on more promising alternatives. Building the capacity for rapid experimentation in early development means rethinking the role of failure in organizations. Positive failure requires having a thick skin, says David Kelley, founder of IDEO, a leading design firm in Palo Alto, California.

IDEO encourages its designers "to fail often to succeed sooner," and the company understands that more radical experiments frequently lead to more spectacular failures. Indeed, IDEO has developed numerous prototypes that have bordered on the ridiculous (and were later rejected), such as shoes with toy figurines on the shoelaces. At the same time,

IDEO's approach has led to a host of bestsellers, such as the Palm V handheld computer, which has made the company the subject of intense media interest, including a *Nightline* segment with Ted Koppel and coverage in *Serious Play,* a book by Michael Schrage, a codirector of the e-markets initiative at the MIT Media Lab, that describes the crucial importance of allowing innovators to play with prototypes.

Removing the stigma of failure, though, usually requires overcoming ingrained attitudes. People who fail in experiments are often viewed as incompetent, and that attitude can lead to counterproductive behavior. As Kelley points out, developers who are afraid of failing and looking bad to management will sometimes build expensive, sleek prototypes that they become committed to before they know any of the answers. In other words, the sleek prototype might look impressive, but it presents the false impression that the product is further along than it really is, and that perception subtly discourages people from changing the design even though better alternatives might exist. That's why IDEO advocates the development of cheap, rough prototypes that people are invited to criticize—a process that eventually leads to better products. "You have to have the guts to create a straw man," asserts Kelley.

To foster a culture in which people aren't afraid of failing, IDEO has created a playroom-like atmosphere. On Mondays, the different branches hold show-and-tells in which employees display and talk about their latest ideas and products. IDEO also maintains a giant "tech box" of hundreds of gadgets and curiosities that designers routinely rummage through, seeking inspiration among the switches, buttons, and various odd materials and objects. And brainstorming sessions, in which wild ideas are encouraged and participants defer judgment to avoid damping the discussion, are a staple of the different project groups.

3M is another company with a healthy attitude toward failure. 3M's product groups often have skunkworks teams that investigate the opportunities (or difficulties) that a potential product might pose. The teams, consisting primarily of technical people, including manufacturing engineers, face little repercussion if an idea flops—indeed, sometimes a failure is cause for celebration. When a team discovers that a potential product doesn't work, the group quickly disbands and its members move on to other projects.

Failures, however, should not be confused with mistakes. Mistakes produce little new or useful information and are therefore without value. A poorly planned or badly conducted experiment, for instance, might result in ambiguous data, forcing researchers to repeat the experiment. Another common mistake is repeating a prior failure or being unable to learn from that experience. Unfortunately, even the best organizations often lack the management systems necessary to carefully distinguish between failures and mistakes.

3. Anticipate and exploit early information. When important projects fail late in the game, the consequences can be devastating. In the pharmaceutical industry, for example, more than 80 percent of drug candidates are discontinued during the clinical development phases, where more than half of total project expenses can be incurred. Yet although companies are often forced to spend millions of dollars to correct problems in the later stages of product development, they generally underestimate the cost savings of early problem solving. Studies of software development, for instance, have shown that late-stage problems are more than 100 times as costly as early-stage ones. For other environments that involve large capital investments in production equipment, the increase in cost can be orders of magnitude higher.

In addition to financial costs, companies need to consider the value of time when those late-stage problems are on a project's critical path—as they often are. In pharmaceuticals,

In the 1990s, Toyota made a major push to accelerate its product development cycle. The objective was to shorten the time from the approval of a body style to the first retail sales, thereby increasing the likelihood that Toyota kept up with the rapidly changing tastes of consumers.

Toyota made a concerted effort to identify and solve design-related problems earlier in product development—a concept known as *front-loading*. To accomplish that, the company implemented a number of initiatives, such as involving more manufacturing engineers during the product-engineering stage, increasing the transfer of knowledge between projects, investing substantially in computer-aided design and engineering tools, and developing rapid-prototyping capabilities.

To measure the benefits of these initiatives—and to monitor the company's evolving capabilities for early problem solving—Toyota tracked problems over multiple development projects. (See **Exhibit 2** "Solving Problems Earlier.") The knowledge that a higher percentage of problems were being solved at earlier stages reassured Toyota's managers that they could aggressively reduce both development time and cost without risking product quality. In particular, between the first and third front-loading initiatives, Toyota slashed the cost (including the number of full physical prototypes needed) and time of development by between 30 percent and 40 percent.

It should be noted that in the early 1990s Toyota substantially reorganized its development activities, resulting in more effective communication and coordination between the different groups. This change most likely accounted for some of the performance improvements observed, particularly during the first front-loading initiatives.

shaving six months off drug development means effectively extending patent protection when the product hits the market. Similarly, an electronics company might easily find that six months account for a quarter of a product's life cycle and a third of all profits.

New technologies, then, can provide some of their greatest leverage by identifying and solving problems upstream—best described as *front-loaded development*. In the automotive industry, for example, "quick-and-dirty" crash simulations on a computer can help companies avoid potential safety problems downstream. Such simulations may not be as complete or as perfect as late-stage prototypes will be, but they can force organizational problem solving and communication at a time when many downstream groups are not participating directly in development. (See the sidebar "The Benefits of Front-Loaded Development.")

Several years ago, Chrysler (now DaimlerChrysler) discovered the power of three-dimensional computer models, known internally as digital mock-ups, for identifying certain problems in early development stages. When Chrysler developed the 1993 Concorde and Dodge Intrepid models, the process of decking—placing the powertrain and related components like the exhaust and suspension in the prototype automobile—took more than three weeks and required many attempts before the powertrain could be inserted successfully. By contrast, the early use of digital mock-ups in the 1998 Concorde and Intrepid models allowed the company to simulate decking to identify (and solve) numerous interference problems before the physical decking took place. Instead of taking weeks, decking was completed in 15 minutes because all obstruction problems had been resolved earlier— when it was relatively inexpensive and fast to do so.

Of course, it is neither pragmatic nor economically feasible for companies to obtain all the early information they would like. So IDEO follows the principle of three R's: rough, rapid, and right. The final R recognizes that early prototypes may be incomplete but can still get specific aspects of a product right. For example, to design a telephone receiver, an IDEO team carved dozens of pieces of foam and cradled them between their heads and shoulders to find the best possible shape for a handset. While incomplete as a telephone, the model focused on getting 100 percent of the shape right. Perhaps the main advantage of this approach is that it forces people to decide judiciously which factors can initially be rough and which must be right. With its three R's, IDEO has established a process that generates important information when it is most valuable: the early stages of development.

In addition to saving time and money, exploiting early information helps product developers keep up with customer preferences that might evolve over the course of a project. As many companies can attest, customers will often say about a finished product: "This is exactly what I asked you to develop, but it is not what I want." Leading software businesses typically show incomplete prototypes to customers in so-called beta tests, and through that process they often discover changes and problems when they are still fairly inexpensive to handle.

4. Combine new and traditional technologies. New technologies that are used in the innovation process itself are designed to help solve problems as part of an experimentation *system*. A company must therefore understand how to use and manage new and traditional technologies together so that they complement each other. In fact, research by Marco Iansiti of Harvard Business School has found that, in many industries, the ability to integrate technologies is crucial to developing superior products.

A new technology often reaches the same general performance of its traditional counterpart much more quickly and at a lower cost. But the new technology usually performs at only 70 percent to 80 percent of the established technology. For example, a new chemical synthesis process might be able to obtain a purity level that is just three-quarters that of a mature technique. Thus, by combining new and established technologies, organizations can avoid the performance gap while also enjoying the benefits of cheaper and faster experimentation. (See **Exhibit 3** "Combining the New with the Traditional.")

Indeed, the true potential of new technologies lies in a company's ability to reconfigure its processes and organization to use them in concert with traditional technologies. Eventually, a new technology can replace its traditional counterpart, but it then might be challenged by a newer technology that must be integrated. To understand this complex evolution, consider what has happened in the pharmaceutical industry.

In the late nineteenth century and for much of the twentieth century, drug development occurred through a process of systematic trial-and-error experiments. Scientists would start with little or no knowledge about a particular disease and try out numerous molecules, many from their company's chemical libraries, until they found one that happened to work. Drugs can be likened to keys that need to fit the locks of targets, such as the specific nerve cell receptors associated with central nervous diseases. Metaphorically, then, chemists were once blind, or at least semiblind, locksmiths who have had to make up thousands of different keys to find the one that matched. Doing so entailed synthesizing compounds, one at a time, each of which usually required several days at a cost from $5,000 to $10,000.

Typically, for each successful drug that makes it to market, a company investigates roughly 10,000 starting candidates. Of those, only 1,000 compounds make it to more extensive trials in vitro (that is, outside living organisms in settings such as test tubes), 20 of which are tested even more extensively in vivo (that is, in the body of a living organism such as a mouse), and ten of which make it to clinical trials with humans. The entire process represents a long and costly commitment.

But in the last ten years, new technologies have significantly increased the efficiency and speed at which companies can generate and screen chemical compounds. Researchers no longer need to painstakingly create one compound at a time. Instead, they can use combinatorial chemistry, quickly generating numerous variations simultaneously around a few building blocks, just as today's locksmiths can make thousands of keys from a dozen basic shapes, thereby reducing the cost of a compound from thousands of dollars to a few dollars or less.

In practice, however, combinatorial chemistry has disrupted well-established routines in laboratories. For one thing, the rapid synthesis of drugs has led to a new problem: how to screen those compounds quickly. Traditionally, potential drugs were tested in live animals—an activity fraught with logistical difficulties, high expense, and considerable statistical variation.

So laboratories developed test-tube-based screening methodologies that could be automated. Called high-throughput screening, this technology requires significant innovations in equipment (such as high-speed precision robotics) and in the screening process itself to let researchers conduct a series of biological tests, or assays, on members of a chemical library virtually simultaneously.

The large pharmaceutical corporations and academic chemistry departments initially greeted such "combichem" technologies (combinatorial chemistry and highthroughput screening) with skepticism. Among the reasons cited was that the purity of compounds generated via combichem was relatively poor compared to traditional synthetic chemistry. As a result, many advances in the technology were made by small biotechnology companies.

But as the technology matured, it caught the interest of large corporations like Eli Lilly, which in 1994 acquired Sphinx Pharmaceuticals, one of the start-ups developing combichem. Eli Lilly took a few years to transfer the new technologies to its drug discovery division, which used traditional synthesis. To overcome the internal resistance, senior management implemented various mechanisms to control how the new technologies were being adopted. For example, it temporarily limited the in-house screening available to chemists, leaving them no choice but to use some of the high-throughput screening capabilities at the Sphinx subsidiary and interact with the staff there.

Until now, pharmaceutical giants like Eli Lilly have used combinatorial chemistry primarily to optimize promising new drug candidates that resulted from an exhaustive search through chemical libraries and other traditional sources. But as combinatorial chemistry itself advances and achieves levels of purity and diversity comparable to the compounds in a library, companies will increasingly use it at the earlier phases of drug discovery. In fact, all major pharmaceutical companies have had to use combichem and traditional synthesis in concert, and the companies that are best able to manage the new and mature technologies together so that they fully complement each other will have the greatest opportunity to achieve the highest gains in productivity and innovation.

ENLIGHTENED IMPLICATIONS

New technologies reduce the cost and time of experimentation, allowing companies to be more innovative. Automotive companies, for example, are currently advancing the performance of sophisticated safety systems that measure a passenger's position, weight, and height to adjust the force and speed at which airbags deploy. The availability of fast and inexpensive simulation enables the massive and rapid experimentation necessary to develop such complex safety devices.

But it is important to note that the increased automation of routine experiments will not remove the human element in innovation. On the contrary, it will allow people to focus on areas where their value is greatest: generating novel ideas and concepts, learning from experiments, and ultimately making decisions that require judgment. For example, although Millennium's R&D facilities look more and more like factories, the value of knowledge workers has actually increased. Instead of carrying out routine laboratory experiments, they now focus on the early stages (determining which experiments to conduct, for instance) and making sense of the information generated by the experimentation.

The implications for industries are enormous. The electronic spreadsheet has already revolutionized financial problem solving by driving down the marginal cost of financial experimentation to nearly zero; even a small startup can perform complex cash-flow analyses on an inexpensive PC. Similarly, computer simulation and other technologies have enabled small businesses and individuals to rapidly experiment with novel designs of customized integrated circuits. The result has been a massive wave of innovation, ranging from smart toys to electronic devices. Previously, the high cost of integrated-circuit customization made such experimentation economical to only the largest companies.

Perhaps, though, this era of enlightened experimentation is still in its bare infancy. Indeed, the ultimate technology for rapid experimentation might turn out to be the Internet, which is already turning countless users into fervent innovators.

EXHIBIT 1
Waiting for a
Resource

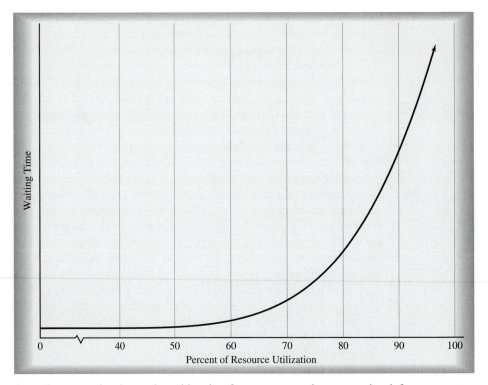

According to queuing theory, the waiting time for a resource such as a central mainframe computer increases gradually as more of the resource is used. But when the utilization passes 70 percent, delays increase dramatically.

EXHIBIT 2
Solving
Problems
Earlier

Source: Stefan Thomke and Takahiro Fujimoto, "The Effect of 'Front-Loading' Problem-Solving on Product Development Performance," *The Journal of Product Innovation Management,* Vol. 17, No. 2, March 2000.

As Toyota intensified its front-loading efforts, it was able to identify and solve problems much earlier in the development process.

In the early 1990s (see top graph), the first initiatives for front-loading began. Formal, systematic efforts to improve face-to-face communication and joint problem solving between the prototype shops and production engineers resulted in a higher relative percentage of problems found with the aid of first prototypes. Communication between different engineering sections (for instance, between body, engine, and electrical) also improved.

In the mid-1990s (see middle graph), the second front-loading initiatives called for three-dimensional computer-aided design, resulting in a significant increase of problem identification and solving prior to stage 3 (first prototypes).

In the ongoing third front-loading initiatives (see bottom graph), Toyota is using computer-aided engineering to identify functional problems earlier in the development process, and the company is transferring problem and solution information from previous projects to the front end of new projects. As a result, Toyota expects to solve at least 80 percent of all problems by stage 2—that is, before the first prototypes are made. And because the second-generation prototypes (stage 5) are now less important to overall problem solving, Toyota will be able to eliminate parts of that process, thereby further reducing time and cost without affecting product quality.

EXHIBIT 3
Combining the New with the Traditional

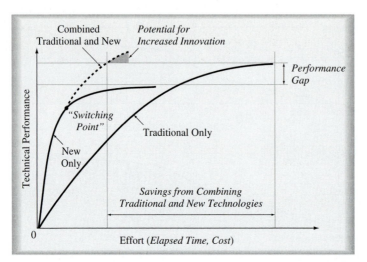

A new technology will reach perhaps just 70 percent to 80 percent of the performance of a traditional technology. A new computer model, for instance, might be able to represent real-world functionality that is just three-quarters that of an advanced prototype model. To avoid this performance gap—and potentially create new opportunities for innovation—companies can use the new and traditional technologies in concert. The optimal time for switching between the two occurs when the rates of improvement between the new and mature technologies are about the same—that is, when the slopes of the two curves are equal.

Case 1-6

Eli Lilly and Company: Drug Development Strategy

On a sunny morning in February 1995, Project Manager Bianca Sharma looked out her office window at the Indianapolis skyline and contemplated the critical decisions facing Eli Lilly's R&D team, which was racing to develop a new generation anti-migraine drug. In a few hours, she would present her business recommendations on product development options to Lilly's Project Team Advisory Committee.

Lilly's new drug candidate promised to be unlike any other market entrant; as such, it could be positioned as the first of a new product subclass. One approach for Sharma's team, therefore, might be to field the best possible compound, even if that meant a further delay in market entry since exploring additional compounds would take time. However, not only would every month's delay to market cost revenue, it would also enable prior entrants to consolidate their market positions.

The role of a new technology, "combinatorial chemistry," also might be factored into Sharma's recommendations. This new technology would still be a curiosity on the horizon had not two Lilly scientists seen its possibilities for speeding up the product development cycle. At the same time, the technology was untried as well as controversial, and Lilly, should it invest in it too early, could waste millions of dollars and months of research pursuing false leads. At a time of unprecedented market pressures, this was a huge risk.

Sharma knew that the stakes were high and her recommendations important to the choice the Project Team Advisory Committee would make. She once again turned to the data laid out on her desk.

THE PHARMACEUTICAL INDUSTRY IN THE MID-1990S

The worldwide pharmaceutical industry was one of the largest and most profitable of research and manufacturing businesses; by the mid-1990s, annual worldwide pharmaceutical sales were around $250 billion, with roughly 80 percent originating in the industrialized G7

Harvard Business School Case No. 9-698-010. Copyright 1997 President and Fellows of Harvard College. All rights reserved. For information: permissions@hbsp.harvard.edu.
This case was prepared by Stefan Thomke and Ashok Nimgade. HBS cases are developed solely for class discussion and do not necessarily illustrate effective or ineffective management.

nations. Top blockbuster drugs targeted diseases of particular concern to industrialized nations, such as depression, peptic ulcer disease, hypertension, and cholesterol-reduction. (See **Exhibit 1,** "U.S. Pharmaceutical Market by Therapeutic Category (1994).") These nations' aging populations were also expected to provide a boost to the pharmaceutical market.

Being first to market with a new class of therapeutic agents was increasingly crucial for a product to be commercially successful, however. Quite often, the first three drugs introduced within a new product class would together control over 80 percent of the market. At the same time, the process of drug discovery, development, and clinical approval was extremely effort-intensive and expensive. Large pharmaceutical companies spent up to 15–20 percent of sales in R&D. In the United States, as part of an extensive, highly regulated safety approval process, each drug had to pass three phases of clinical trials under the scrutiny of the U.S. Food and Drug Administration (FDA): Phase I, which tested clinical safety; Phase II, which assessed drug efficacy; and Phase III, which tested adverse effects from long-term use (see **Exhibit 2,** "Summary of Drug Development in the USA"). For each successful product the sponsoring drug firm typically spent more than $230 million, with the average time to market being 14.8 years[1] —over twice as long as it took the U.S. space program to get a man on the moon.

In addition, the time required for a pharmaceutical drug to be approved substantially decreased the effective term of its patent protection. Under current law, a patent's term expired 20 years from the time the patent application was filed. (Prior to 1995, patent protection extended 17 years after the patent was issued.) But even with whatever patent protection remained by the time a drug reached the market, seven out of ten products failed to return on a company's investment. Fortunately for these firms, sales of only a few products could provide exceptional returns. In the mid-1990s, 14 products had annual sales over $1 billion,[2] enabling profit margins of 15–20 percent. (See **Exhibit 3,**" Top 20 Prescription Drugs by Worldwide Sales (1994).")

Not surprisingly, because of long product development lead times and large marketing costs, combined with high risks, the pharmaceutical industry was dominated by large transnational companies, with the top 20 companies generating 47 percent of total sales.[3] Most major players were U.S. or European multinational pharmaceutical firms such as Merck & Co., Bristol-Myers-Squibb, Glaxo, and Eli Lilly; each had annual sales revenues running in the billions of dollars and employed several thousand employees worldwide. (See **Exhibit 4,** "Top 20 Firms Active in the Pharmaceutical Industry (1994).")

Meanwhile, drug makers worldwide were facing increased public pressure to reduce prices of most pharmaceuticals. Whereas prior emphasis had been placed on drug safety and efficacy, cost became an additional important factor in the 1990s. In the United States, the rapid growth of managed care organizations and the implementation of cost-containment practices—including price controls, volume discounts, and substitution of cheaper generic products in hospital formularies—had greatly increased competitive pressures. Top pharmaceutical firms also faced substantial loss of dollar market share to generic products because of patent expirations. Within a few months of a drug going off patent, leading firms were often forced to slash prices by 80 percent.

[1] FDA (1995), "From Test Tube to Patient: New Drug Development in the United States," *FDA Consumer,* Special Issue, January; J. DiMassi, R. Hansen, H. Grabowsky and L. Lasagna (1994), "Cost of Innovation in the Pharmaceutical Industry," *Journal of Health Economics,* vol. 10, pp. 107–142.

[2] "World Pharma Firm League," *Marketletter,* July 3, 1995.

[3] Ibid.

Although pharmaceuticals accounted for only about a tenth of all health care costs in the United States and in many cases reduced the need for more costly interventions like surgery, to consumers they represented a highly visible target. Pharmaceutical firms were often depicted as price-gougers, with retirees having to make substantial out-of-pocket payments for pills or AIDS patients spending thousands of dollars a year just for one drug. Given this environment, drug makers, in order to have their new, higher-priced products included in hospital formularies, had to demonstrate that these products would yield substantial therapeutic and cost benefits over existing ones. According to Martin Haslanger, Ph.D., executive director of Research Technology and president of Sphinx Pharmaceuticals, "The marketplace will only reward innovation. It is no longer rewarding to make incremental improvements."[4]

Drug makers confronted these market pressures in a variety of ways. At a strategic level, several firms responded by mergers that generated workforce reductions and other cost savings, while other firms invested heavily in, or acquired, innovative biotech companies in hopes of tapping new technologies. For all drug makers, speeding the drug development cycle became a priority—for every week's delay to market, millions of revenue might be lost. Moreover, since the R&D phase of product development was largely under the internal control of the individual company, it represented a powerful leverage point for controlling time and cost. Hence, in an attempt to shorten the drug development cycle, many pharmaceutical firms raced to incorporate emerging breakthrough technologies such as genetic engineering, combinatorial chemistry, and high-throughput screening.

ELI LILLY AND COMPANY

Eli Lilly and Company was founded in Indianapolis, Indiana, in 1876 by Colonel Eli Lilly. A pharmaceutical chemist and Civil War veteran, Colonel Lilly was frustrated by the poor quality of medicines and "sideshow hucksterism" of his time. Over ensuing decades, his company went from a family-run firm to a global corporation: in the mid-1990s, Lilly, operating in 150 countries, was one of the world's largest pharmaceutical companies, with over 25,000 employees and 1994 sales of $5.7 billion.

Through much of the twentieth century, Lilly was prominent in the traditional field of antibiotics. In the early 1980s, however, it made news by becoming the first marketer of a genetically engineered product when—through a collaboration with a biotechnology firm—it introduced human insulin. In the late 1980s, Lilly gained further public prominence by developing the innovative anti-depression drug fluoxetine (widely known by the brand name Prozac®).

By the 1990s, Lilly maintained major research divisions across a variety of treatment areas, including central nervous system disease, inflammatory disease, cardiovascular disease, cancer, and endocrinology (which dealt with hormonal diseases like diabetes and growth hormone deficiency). Its products ranged from the highly promising drug Zyprexa® for treating schizophrenia to Gemzar® for treating pancreatic cancer. For all its success, however, Lilly, like most other pharmaceutical firms, could not easily predict its next blockbuster. (See **Exhibit 5,** "Eli Lilly and Company: 1994 Financial Highlights.")

---

[4] K. Heine, "Sphinx Paves the Way to Discover," *Focus,* Eli Lilly, March 1995.

Nevertheless, Lilly had remained an industry leader through its 120-year history. By the early 1990s the company was expanding into allied businesses such as diagnostics and animal products. But it also faced high organizational costs and a dwindling product pipeline. An $11 billion drop in company stock value, from March 1991 to June 1993, signaled a loss of confidence in Lilly's competitiveness.

In 1993, under a newly appointed CEO, R. L. Tobias, Lilly sold its medical device and diagnostics unit in order to focus on vertically integrating drug discovery, development, production, and distribution. The new management slashed Lilly's workforce by 10 percent and acquired several key businesses and technologies that strengthened the core pharmaceutical business. The company also planned to restructure its research efforts to refill the product pipeline. As a result of these steps as well as several promising new products, Lilly's stock price substantially rose. (See **Exhibit 6,** "Eli Lilly and Company—Organization.")

INNOVATIONS IN THE NEW DRUG DEVELOPMENT PROCESS

Throughout history, drug discovery relied on the observations and experiments of naturalists and herbalists. Even in the 1990s, one-fourth of all medical compounds, including aspirin and the widely used heart drug digitalis, derived originally from plant extracts.

Synthetic chemistry, whose roots lay in the nineteenth century, marked the first modern revolution in drug development. It made possible the development of compounds never before seen in nature, including more powerful and potent variations of naturally occurring compounds (such as the cephalosporin antibiotics that were variations of the naturally occurring penicillin). Synthetic chemistry also aided in the patenting of drugs and as such helped spawn the multinational drug industry.

Through much of the twentieth century, however, drug discovery remained a labor-intensive process relying on inspiration, hard work, and luck. Metaphorically, drugs were molecular-sized "keys" that had to fit "locks" or targets (called receptors); chemists were the locksmiths. Indeed, they were effectively blind, or at least semi-blind, locksmiths, for they had to make up thousands of different keys to find the one that matched. Doing so entailed synthesizing compounds, one at a time, which typically required seven to ten days and $5,000–$10,000 per compound. For each drug reaching the market firms spent an average of 124 chemist-years on synthesizing starting compounds,[5] a critical path activity. The time spent on synthesis represented a place of high leverage for speeding up the drug development cycle.

Newly synthesized molecular keys were tested by biologists, typically using animals that served as models for a disease (for example, a mouse with a neurological problem similar to Parkinsonism). Most compounds would show no activity or be too toxic for further evaluation. A few, however, might show promise, and chemists would modify these "lead compounds" until a good clinical candidate emerged. Typically, for each successful drug that made it to market, a firm began with an average of 10,000 starting compounds. Of these, only 1000 would make it to more extensive *in vitro* trials (i.e., outside living organisms in settings such as a test tube), of which 20 would be tested even more extensively *in*

---

[5] R.G. Halliday, S.R. Walker, and C.E. Lumley, *Journal of Pharmaceutical Medicine,* 2 (1992): 139–154.

vivo (i.e., in the body of a living organism such as a mouse) before ten compounds made it to human clinical trials. The entire process represented a long and costly commitment, with the human trials closely monitored by the government.

The next major revolutions in drug development, *genetic engineering* and *rational drug discovery,* crystallized in the 1980s through a deeper understanding of biology—in particular, how drugs worked, and what receptors they targeted. Now drugs—Prozac being an early example—could be made by combining serendipity with working models of the human body.

With these revolutions, industry experts expected the R&D process to shift from a random screening approach toward a "rational" drug discovery process—a shift tantamount to replacing a shotgun with a viewfinder-equipped gun. Yet scientists still could not make accurate enough predictions about drug-receptor interactions, and drug discovery continued to remain a tedious, labor-intensive process, with hundreds or thousands of related compounds being generated and then examined. Although many drug firms had, over the decades, built "libraries" of hundreds of thousands of compounds, they had barely scratched the surface of the potential "molecular diversity" present on our planet.

Just as locksmiths could make thousands of differing keys based on just one template, so too could theoretical chemists envision creating hundreds of thousands or even millions of derivatives (or analogues) based around a relatively simple compound such as penicillin. Because of this staggering molecular diversity, drug makers tended to be uneasy, feeling that their particular drug on the market might by no means be the best, and that a rival firm would pluck out another, far better drug from the universe of related molecules—and it would eventually corner the market.

By the late 1980s, several biologists and chemists hoped that recent advances in synthetic chemistry, robotics, and information systems could tap this rich molecular diversity and allow for yet another major revolution in drug discovery: *combinatorial chemistry* (often shortened to "combichem") and its allied branch, *high-throughput screening.*

Combinatorial chemistry enabled a large collection or "library" of related chemical compounds to be quickly generated simultaneously. Instead of one compound being made at a time, variations were created around the backbone of a basic molecular structure. With just a few building blocks chemists could create a large, diverse set of molecules just as locksmiths could make thousands of keys from one template using just a dozen different shaped cuts (see **Exhibit 7,** "Principles of Combinatorial Chemistry"). With the molecule serotonin, for example, up to several millions of related molecules could be generated—a staggering feat to accomplish manually.

The human body, in essence, was a master of combinatorial chemistry (and high-throughput screening), churning out over a trillion different antibodies (specialized proteins that help neutralize bacteria, toxins, or other invaders) by shuffling around different molecular components. In the laboratory, however, combinatorial chemistry presented a major difficulty: many processes involved in drug synthesis were not routine and required individual adjustments by skilled chemists. Likewise, the vital step of screening presented a major challenge. Potential drug molecules were traditionally tested or "screened" in live animals—a venture fraught with logistical difficulties, high expense, and considerable statistical variation. Using traditional screens, drug makers could hardly manage to sift through their own historical libraries of compounds, let alone the unprecedented volumes of compounds generated by combinatorial chemistry.

Given this slow pace of screening, scientists would often jump on early leads and become invested in them at the expense of other promising new leads. The challenge, therefore, was to develop test-tube-based screening methodologies amenable to automation. As Stephen Kaldor, a Lilly scientist, explained, "We needed a system that allowed us to evaluate and prioritize our leads simultaneously, rather than letting the clock decide which molecules we would work up."[6]

High-throughput screening was aimed at solving this problem. Using this technology, high-speed robots would perform a series of biological tests or "assays" on all members of a chemical library virtually simultaneously. A simple biochemical response based on the fit between a potential drug and its receptor could be visualized simply—for instance, through a color change—and thus could be used to pick out compounds that showed the desired activity.

Obviously, the greater the number of compounds generated through combinatorial chemistry, the greater the demand placed on screening. Thus, generating a library of millions of compounds could outstrip the capacity of a screen capable of processing only a thousand compounds a week. One popular strategy chemists experimented with to get around this dilemma was restricting combinatorial diversity to representatives from major families of a compound's analogues. In essence, this was like examining major branches and sub-branches of a tree, rather than examining individual leaves.

For many traditional chemists in 1994, however, the larger issue centered around proving the merit of combinatorial chemistry. Although it looked promising in theory, it worked only for certain groups of compounds. Moreover, no new drug candidates had been uncovered by this new and untried technique.

COMBINATORIAL CHEMISTRY AT LILLY

The Technology Core group of the Research and Development Area of Lilly functioned as a separate division that supported the company's various research activities. In the early 1990s, this group recognized the potential promise of combinatorial chemistry and high-throughput screening and realized that other pharmaceutical firms were planning to acquire biotech firms with leading-edge expertise in these areas.

Under the direction of chemist Stephen Kaldor, Ph.D., Lilly started developing capabilities in combinatorial chemistry. Kaldor was charged with creating "libraries" or collections of compounds that could then be tested within the organization for therapeutic properties. In early March 1994, he gave a well-attended presentation on his team's work that helped disseminate knowledge of combinatorial chemistry through the organization.

In September 1994, as a vote of confidence in the new technology, Lilly acquired a financially strapped biotechnology firm named Sphinx Pharmaceuticals (of Durham-Research Triangle Park in North Carolina, and Cambridge, Massachusetts), which had leading expertise in combinatorial chemistry and high-throughput screening and boasted experts such as its vice president of research Michael Pavia, Ph.D. But it would be another year or more before Sphinx's capabilities could be integrated into Lilly's drug discovery division. At the same time, Kaldor's group made some remarkable progress. Normally, a Lilly chemist was able to synthesize one compound per week, and Lilly had a screening capacity of 50 compounds

[6] K. Heine, "Sphinx Paves the Way to Discover," *Focus,* Eli Lilly, March 1995.

per week. By the end of 1994, Kaldor's group, using combinatorial chemistry and high-throughput screening, increased the capacity to screen compounds for biological activity around eight-fold, and the capacity to synthesize new compounds by a factor of 120.

DRUG DISCOVERY FOR CENTRAL NERVOUS SYSTEM (CNS) DISEASES

In the mid-1990s, roughly one billion people, or one-fifth of the world's population, suffered from a neurological or psychiatric disorder at one point in their lifetime. World Bank estimates revealed that central nervous system (CNS) diseases accounted for roughly 10 percent of all lifetime years lost to disease. Even "less severe" psychiatric conditions—for instance, clinical depression, severe insomnia (sleeplessness), and migraine, each of which affected over 10 percent of the population—could take a severe toll on society. For instance, depression might predispose people to suicide, a point poignantly illustrated by the demise of the wife of Lilly CEO Randall Tobias. Because of similar tragedies, according to Tobias in a sobering journal interview, "we're spending over $1 billion a year in research and development. We don't know all the answers—and we need to keep going."[7]

Fortunately, modern medications had the potential to boost quality of life so dramatically that patients might end up taking medications regularly for years, with, for example, a depressive patient spending up to $25 a week for a daily Prozac regimen. This, of course, was a boon for drug makers in the small but growing CNS market, which had 1994 worldwide sales of $11.1 billion (80 percent originating in G7 nations).

Many CNS diseases were thought to result from imbalances of neurochemical agents (neurotransmitters) that transmitted signals between nerves. The number of active neurotransmitters normally present at any time was intricately controlled by biochemical mechanisms for production, storage, release, and rapid degradation of these agents. Scientists postulated that biochemical "machinery" dysfunctions leading to altered concentrations of certain neurotransmitters led to conditions ranging from panic disorder to obsessive compulsive disorder to depression.

Different neurotransmitters were known to activate different receptors just as different keys might open up different doorways. (See **Exhibit 8,** "Receptors and Neurotransmitters.") Not surprisingly, various classes of neurotransmitters, such as dopamine, norepinephrine, and serotonin, were associated with differing diseases. Serotonin, for example, was associated with a variety of conditions ranging from depression to insomnia to aggression to migraine. Its wide-ranging effects in the body were a consequence of at least a dozen known types of receptors (molecular "locks") in locations as varied as the digestive system and the nervous system where serotonin could act.

The serotonin family of molecules and receptors in the nervous system would play a large role in the fortunes of Lilly. Lilly's first billion dollar blockbuster anti-depressant drug, Prozac, launched in 1988, very *selectively* boosted levels of serotonin to exert its therapeutic effects. Prior anti-depressants, in contrast, had undesirable side-effects such as sedation, anxiety, and dry mouth because they non-selectively increased levels of several different neurotransmitters in addition to serotonin.

---

[7] "Lilly Rides a Mood Elevator," *BusinessWeek,* November 11, 1996, p. 63.

Prozac grew to become the world's fifth best-selling drug in 1994, its sales accounting for over one-fourth of Lilly's revenues. Leveraging on this success, Lilly's CNS research division grew to roughly one-third of all company research efforts. The aggressive emergence of other direct competitors to Prozac, which itself would come off patent in 2003, lent urgency to Lilly's CNS projects. Even if Lilly could not produce another blockbuster such as Prozac, it needed other solid hits.

Lilly turned once more to serotonin.

LILLY'S MIGRAINE PROJECT

I cannot describe the pain because it was so severe, but you might imagine how it would feel if someone hammered a sharp nail into your eye and out your temple. The pain affected the entire side of my head, even causing me to vomit. To curb the pain, my doctor gave me an injection which only put me to sleep.

—Description of a migraine sufferer[8]

"Migraine," a French word derived from the Greek *hemicrania,* referred to pain involving half the head at a time. Migraine afflicted 12 percent of the population, with a 3:1 preponderance in women; it was characterized by unilateral pulsating headaches often severe enough to restrict physical and mental activity. Historians of medicine speculated that visual disturbances experienced during migraines inspired Charles Dodgson (writing under the pseudonym Lewis Carroll) to describe various physical distortions his heroine Alice experienced in Wonderland.[9]

Traditional migraine therapies ranged from compresses to biofeedback to narcotic painkillers to tranquilizers. Some therapies dated back centuries: ancient Egyptians employed tight compresses around the scalp. Most therapeutic efforts focused on a theory, dating to the 1930s, that dilation of blood vessels in the lining of the brain caused migraine. It was only in the 1980s that scientists suspected that nerve inflammation involving the neurotransmitter serotonin played a role. By the early 1990s, two classes of therapies existed: those directed at prophylaxis (with expected 1996 worldwide sales of $200 million) and therapeutics directed at treating acute attacks (with expected 1996 worldwide sales of $1.5 billion).

Lilly scientists hoped to capitalize on their expertise in serotonin research to find a drug for acute attacks of migraine. The stakes were high. The only recent drug on the market targeted specifically at migraine was Glaxo-Wellcome's sumatriptan (Imitrex®). Imitrex, launched in 1992, was a mildly effective drug that acted by constricting blood vessels; it also had an adverse effect on the heart's vessels, thereby limiting its use in many patients. In addition, the effects of Imitrex were very short-lived for most patients. Yet Imitrex enjoyed almost 75 percent of the acute migraine market, with projected 1996 annual sales of $800 million (up from $250 million in 1993).

Many scientists, including those at Lilly, felt that the makers of Imitrex had followed the wrong path by trying to find a compound that constricted blood vessels (known as "vasoconstriction"). While Imitrex was believed to constrict blood vessels by mimicking serotonin, it affected a number of different serotonin subtypes, including the serotonin

[8] http://www.painclinic.com/treatment.htm, 1996.
[9] L.A. Rolak, "Literary Neurologic Syndromes: The Alice in Wonderland Syndrome," *Archives of Neurology*, 46 (1992): 353.

"1d" receptor. Several drug makers raced to develop therapies that targeted the "1d" subclass of serotonin receptors.

Lilly researchers, however, were not convinced that, of the variety of serotonin subtypes Imitrex was known to affect, the "1d" receptor was involved in anti-migraine activity. By 1991, Synaptic Pharmaceutical Corporation (Paramus, New Jersey), Lilly's collaborator, had found (cloned) a new serotonin receptor subtype, the serotonin "1f" receptor. Synaptic's scientists also demonstrated that Imitrex had affinity for the "1f" receptor. Lilly and Synaptic scientists theorized that it was the serotonin "1f" receptor that was specifically involved in migraine. In effect, they potentially held the biochemical anti-migraine lock (receptor) and now needed to find the right key.

This was no small task, for chemists could envision well over a million different variations of serotonin, any of which could prove the right key. The logical place to start looking, however, was in the 1000 or so serotonin-like compounds in Lilly's extensive decades-old collection of 250,000 compounds.

From 1991 to early 1994, spearheaded by senior chemists John Schaus, Ph.D., and James Audia, Ph.D., along with scientists David Nelson, Ph.D., and Lee Phebus, Ph.D., in Lilly's "Serotonin Working Group," researchers started out screening a few serotonin-like compounds weekly but later screened up to 20–30 compounds per week from Lilly's serotonin collection.[10] By March 1994, out of over 1000 previously synthesized serotonin-like compounds, one particularly good "lead" had been found. In addition, Lilly's experiments in which lab animals were administered these lead compounds showed further promise of the "1f" serotonin receptors as treatment targets for migraine without the need for inducing vasoconstriction.

But the work was not over yet. Schaus explained this "lead identification" stage of drug discovery: "In order to find a molecule that interacts with the target, you need to look in a systematic, iterative way. Some analogue of the initial, starting 'key' will work, but it is not likely to be potent or a good compound . . . at least it is a good starting point."

Using traditional methods of creating derivatives, researchers found a better compound, named LY329511. In the iterative process of drug discovery, this now became the current lead, against which further drug candidates would have to be tested. According to Schaus, LY329511 was:

> more than satisfactory with good affinity [for the receptor], activity, moderate selectivity [i.e., activity for that receptor alone], and oral activity, with moderate duration of effect . . . There was a lot of excitement about taking it into clinical trials. But we didn't know much about toxicology, and we hadn't explored other chemical modifications. We wanted to make another 100 derivatives—this might realistically take up to a year.

COMBINATORIAL CHEMISTRY AND LILLY'S MIGRAINE PROJECT

Fortunately, Schaus recalled Stephen Kaldor's March seminar on combinatorial chemistry. Both had obtained their chemistry Ph.D.s at Harvard, but at different times. Schaus, senior to Kaldor by several years, had originally attended the seminar because "Stephen is very bright. You want to follow what he's doing because it's sure to be interesting." Although

[10] This could be considered a "medium-throughput screen," and it contrasted favorably with technology available at the time of the discovery of Prozac, when only one compound could be screened per week in a screening process involving crude rat brain extracts.

Lilly's expertise in combinatorial chemistry still lagged behind that of specialized biotech firms, it was Kaldor whom he telephoned to say:

> I greatly enjoyed your presentation and feel it may pertain to one of our serotonin projects. We are under time pressure to get an anti-migraine compound into clinical trials and, fortunately, already have a good "hit." We have started to generate analogues of this lead compound but I am intrigued about using combinatorial chemistry to explore other leads. The last thing I want to do, however, is go down a path not well thought out and which will need a lot of fixing later on.

In mid-summer 1994, Schaus and Kaldor sat in the "Contemplative Garden" in the central courtyard of a large research building, an area where scientists often gathered for informal meetings, and discussed how they might collaborate. "I was delighted that John [Schaus] was willing to try our new technology for punching out analogues for his leads," Kaldor explained later. "But we were still working out bugs in our system; we were still interfacing extensive instrumentation and robotics with reproducible small-scale chemistry." The extent to which they should use combinatorial chemistry versus traditional chemistry to create new derivatives was difficult to decide. As an initial pilot effort, however, Kaldor agreed to make some 30–40 compounds, study the results, modify the search to make another 30–40 compounds, and continue in this iterative fashion. Traditional chemistry would be used at critical points.

The assay results on the first set of compounds showed that efforts should be focused on one subclass of derivatives. It was in the second batch of combichem compounds that they knew they had made a significant finding. A number of compounds showed significantly higher potency than LY329511. Detailed testing of these new compounds demonstrated that one of them, LY334370, was an improvement over LY329511. Importantly, it lacked the vasoconstricting adverse effects seen in the previous compound.

The company's philosophy of R&D management supported this ad hoc collaboration. As explained by Jim White, Ph.D., director of Neural Science Research, "There's a lot of serendipity in science. We can't lead science. Historically, Lilly didn't hire chemists to fill jobs. We left an open playing field in which Kaldor felt empowered to think." Lilly had created an R&D environment that attracted scientists from top universities; several Lilly scientists had studied under Nobel laureates.

But as word of this unusual collaboration spread through the company, even support from other superiors such as Ben Laguzza, Ph.D., director of Neuroscience Chemistry Research, and Richard DiMarchi, Ph.D., vice president of Endocrinology, could not shield the two scientists from criticism. According to Bill Heath, director of Target Validation and Screen Enablement:

> Schaus came under heavy criticism. People felt he was engaging in "voodoo science," and that the collaboration would divert valuable screening capacity. Schaus and Kaldor were gutsy, taking a big gamble. Even the concept of high-throughput screening was met with skepticism. Few at Lilly believed we could collapse three years of screening into three months or even less. It's very easy to stop something you don't believe in.

"Traditional chemists saw combinatorial chemistry as a threat to their jobs," according to Laguzza. Although going from traditional to combinatorial chemistry might be crudely likened to going from handcrafting to a production line, Kaldor noted that:

Combinatorial chemistry does not replace the wisdom or experience of conventional chemists. Instead, the tension centers around how much we "subjugate" traditional medicinal chemistry to have it supply us intermediates . . . much glory, after all, comes from the final product.

September 1994 witnessed indirect support for combinatorial chemistry in the form of Lilly's acquisition of Sphinx. Unfortunately, Sphinx's capabilities would not be able to be tapped for the migraine project since up to a year would be required to integrate its capabilities. (The two companies employed differing protocols for preparing materials for the screening process.)

The same month, however, also witnessed a broadside to the Kaldor-Schaus collaboration during a seminar Schaus presented on his research. The data on identifying potential anti-migraine serotonin compounds were well received until Schaus showed work involving combinatorial chemistry. Since combinatorial chemistry-generated compounds were only 80–90 percent pure (as opposed to almost 100 percent purity for conventional syntheses), several audience members questioned the scientific value of the combinatorial chemistry data. Could promising signs of activity in some of the combinatorial chemistry-generated compounds, after all, be simply due to impurities?

Fortunately, Schaus could present favorable comparisons of studies with the same compounds synthesized via both traditional and combinatorial approaches. But this did not spare him from further criticism along purely logistical lines. Some argued that he distracted the team's main efforts by testing an unproved technology. Others felt these experiments overloaded the company's biological screening assay, which was geared only for volumes generated by traditional approaches. But Schaus argued that "the benefits over the longer term of being able to synthesize many more compounds at once would far outweigh the extra time and effort over the short term."

As Lilly scientists drew battle lines over combinatorial chemistry, Lilly managers prepared to debate decision choices in bringing an anti-migraine compound to clinical trials.

DIFFICULT CHOICES: THE PROJECT TEAM ADVISORY COMMITTEE (PTAC) MEETING

Migraine Project Manager Bianca Sharma, who held an MBA as well as an advanced degree in biochemistry, looked forward with anticipation to the PTAC (pronounced "pee-tack") meeting, which would be dedicated primarily to the migraine project. The committee typically met for several hours each month and recommended whether (or how) compounds should go into clinical trials. The PTAC comprised some 20 high-level scientists and managers, including the president and VPs of Lilly Research Laboratories. Projects were voted on through an anonymous electronic scoring system, with the chairman, Dr. Douglas Morton, responsible for breaking deadlocks.

From the research scientist's viewpoint, the PTAC served primarily as a senior scientific peer review. For each project, it reviewed issues of safety as ascertained from animal studies, basic biology, and preclinical pharmacology (did the drug seem efficacious in animal models?) and chemistry (given constraints of time and money, had the company adequately surveyed all leads to field the best clinical candidate?). From the corporate strategist's viewpoint, however, PTAC also assessed market opportunities.

Representing the CNS business unit, Sharma's task was to present business recommendations on drug development options for the migraine project. Preparing for PTAC meetings, she had found, was an interdisciplinary effort that helped clarify issues of resource requirements and allocations. Sharma now mentally rehearsed what she felt were the three key business issues for her PTAC presentation:

Issue 1: Time to Market

In reviewing her spreadsheet model of market projections based on data from Marketing (see **Exhibit 9,** "Memo—Migraine Marketing Analysis"), Sharma realized that each month's delay to market would result not only in revenue losses, but also in opportunity costs from allowing prior serotonin-based entrants to consolidate their grasp on the market. Although time to market was of the essence, it appeared that Lilly's would most likely be the fourth or fifth serotonin-like compound to reach the market. But it would be the first serotonin 1f-based compound. For this reason, some strategists argued, it was critical to take the time required to field the best possible compound. But how much of a delay was tolerable?

Sharma recalled a discussion with senior corporate strategist Amy Velasquez who commented on the new competitive challenges: "In the old days we could hold back our lead compound. Not now; today's market is more competitive and calls for 'hustle.'" Velasquez added, "If we had a backup, we could put it on hold until we see anything that creates a hitch. Then the backup could be turned on quickly." Unfortunately, no backup existed now.

On the other hand, Martin Haslanger had made a theoretical argument for holding back:

> Sometimes it's almost better to be number two—a second fast-follower. The list of the top 100–200 best-selling drugs includes many good fast-followers. The chances of getting to market in first place can be near zero because of the long series of low probability steps involved in product development. For example, with Prozac, we went through some mine fields to get to the market first. We almost did not make it at many points. Then, when we faced rough patches, our competitors were able to play up their products, to our detriment.

Issue 2: Diversity of Leads

The second issue was intimately linked to the first. If Lilly were competing with unlimited time and resources on its side, it could take several similar leads simultaneously through the astronomically expensive clinical trials. But as Amy Velasquez had pointed out, "It is hard to justify two similar compounds racing down the track! The support infrastructure is enormous." Even if one lead were held back in favor of another, Haslanger noted certain intangible costs because, "the following group will lose a sense of urgency." Like other drug makers, therefore, Lilly simply had to send the best available compound candidate through the maze of clinical trials. And candidate LY334370, as Sharma recalled, was a significant improvement over the already promising LY329511.

Thus, diversity of leads was extremely important but would have to be explored earlier in the drug discovery process. Combinatorial chemistry could make its biggest impact here. Exploring further molecular diversity would also help broaden patent claims.

Issue 3: Traditional or Combinatorial Chemistry?

Combinatorial chemistry promised to dramatically boost the ability to create, and thus explore, related compounds. A Lilly chemist could now create orders of magnitude more compounds in a given time period. Yet many Lilly scientists viewed the new technology with considerable mistrust, as it still had many unresolved problems and had never before been used to get a compound to clinical trials.

With the above issues in mind, Sharma next reviewed predictions various corporate experts had made about the impact of combinatorial chemistry on clinical trial outcomes (see **Exhibit 10**, "Expert Estimates"). In September 1994, she had polled six experts within the firm for their estimates about how combichem could affect chances of getting a drug candidate through clinical trials. At the same time, she asked them how these chances might impact time to market. Two of the experts she polled, Drs. John Lee and Edward Pan, were senior scientists working closely with the incipient Kaldor-Schaus collaboration; another two, Drs. Beverly Bourell and John Wecker, were traditional chemists who had extensive experience with serotonin-based drugs and had raised their concerns in Schaus' presentation on his work with Kaldor. The final two were senior managers with scientific training—Dr. Clare Pimentel, a senior product manager from the Prozac program, and Ashley Peck, director of corporate marketing, who had worked closely with Lilly's R&D group for over 25 years. Sharma hoped that she could use the expert poll as an input to her projections but felt uneasy about the level of disagreement between the six experts on the various development options.

Then Sharma looked at her watch: the PTAC meeting was just two hours away.

GLOSSARY

Analogue: A structural variation of a parent molecule. Useful analogue compounds may exhibit fewer adverse effects or might be therapeutic in smaller doses.

Assay: A test to determine the properties of a chemical entity such as strength or purity or activity in a biological system.

Central Nervous System (CNS) Disease: Any disease primarily affecting behavior, movement, perception, or other components of the central nervous system. Examples include Alzheimer's disease, depression, and migraine.

Combinatorial Chemistry: A branch of synthetic chemistry developed to systematically generate large numbers of chemically diverse but related compounds. Combinatorial chemistry, thus, potentially allows drug makers to rapidly generate and explore thousands of compounds in just weeks in order to find promising compounds.

Compound: A distinct chemical entity formed by the union of two or more ingredients in a distinctive proportion. Drug compounds are formed from a distinctive proportion of differing chemical elements.

Library: A collection of differing compounds (analogous to a library of books), usually maintained for further study. Drug firms often maintain libraries of all compounds synthesized in the past by their scientists.

Molecular Diversity: The importance of molecular diversity—analogous to diversity found within the human race—stems from the fact that even minor changes in molecular structure can tremendously alter function. As a result, drug makers seek to adequately explore molecular diversity of a promising drug's analogues in order to field the best possible drug.

Neurotransmitter: A molecular agent capable of transmitting signals from one nerve to another (for instance, serotonin) by acting upon specific receptors.

Receptor: A specialized protein located on or within cells in the body capable of detecting specific environmental changes. Receptors in the nervous system, once activated by neurotransmitters, will often trigger specific responses within the body.

Screening: The process of systematically examining a collection of compounds to find those with the most promise for a given purpose (such as drug development). "High-throughput screening" refers to the ability to screen a large number of compounds in a short time period—a capability needed to successfully apply combinatorial chemistry.

Serotonin: A compound (chemically termed 5-hydroxytryptamine) widely distributed in the body. Serotonin serves as a neurotransmitter by acting at different receptors in the nervous system, and has been implicated with conditions and behaviors as diverse as depression, migraine, sleep, and aggression.

Serotonin Receptors: Specialized proteins in the body capable of detecting and responding to serotonin. Within the body, over a dozen different subclasses (for instance "1f" and "1d") of serotonin receptors exist at sites ranging from the blood stream to the intestines to the nervous system. Analogues of serotonin may act in differing ways at differing subclasses of serotonin receptors.

Synthetic Chemistry: The branch of chemistry dealing with the creation of compounds in the laboratory.

EXHIBIT 1
U.S.
Pharmaceutical
Market by
Therapeutic
Category
(1994)

Source: Lehman
Brothers Pharmaceuti-
cal Research, 1996.

Drug Category	1994 (US$ billions)	2000 Estimates (US$ billions)	% Change of Market Share
Cardiology	15.4 (18%)	13.1 (13%)	27)
Antibiotics	12.0 (14%)	8.1 (8%)	(42)
Gastrointestinal	11.1 (13%)	10.1 (10%)	(23)
Central Nervous System	6.8 (8%)	13.1 (13%)	62
Respiratory	5.1 (6%)	8.1 (8%)	33
Lipid Lowering	4.3 (5%)	5.0 (5%)	0
Cancer	4.3 (5%)	7.1 (7%)	40
Diabetes	3.4 (4%)	4.0 (4%)	0
Arthritis	3.4 (4%)	2.0 (2%)	(50)
Hematology	3.4 (4%)	7.1 (7%)	75
Imaging	2.6 (3%)	2.0 (2%)	(50)
Anti-viral	2.6 (2%)	3.0 (3%)	100
Thrombotics	2.6 (2%)	2.0 (2%)	0
Immunology	.86 (1%)	2.0 (2%)	100
Osteoporosis	.86 (1%)	4.0 (4%)	300
Other	8.6 (10%)	10.1 (10%)	0
Total	**$85.6 billion (100%)**	**$100.9 billion (100%)**	

EXHIBIT 2
Summary of Drug Development in the USA[a]

New drug development in the early 1990s was a costly affair with high failure rates. For each therapeutic drug entering the market, pharmaceutical firms invested more than $230 million (estimates go up to $359 million) and 14.8 years (up from 4.3 years in the 1970s). Estimated costs include out-of-pocket expenses, costs of failed projects, and opportunity costs. A brief outline of the drug development process follows:

Basic Research (About Two Years)
This phase typically started through the initial screening of plants, microorganisms, and other naturally occurring substances to find a "hit" or "lead" compound. In a painstaking iterative process, organic chemists would then make analogues or modifications of existing leads. Although this stage typically cost a firm $30–50 million, it represented a point of great leverage for speeding up a firm's drug development process. Only 40 out of an initial 10,000 compounds might make it to the next stage of pre-clinical testing.

Pre-Clinical (Biological) Screening (About Three Years)
Pre-clinical trials, which often overlapped the basic research phase, involved animal testing to assess drug safety and to gather data on biological effects (e.g., absorption, metabolism, and excretion). Only one in four drugs typically made it through this phase to enter human clinical testing as "Investigational New Drugs" (INDs).

Human Clinical Trials (About Six Years)
INDs faced the FDA's regulatory hurdles, the most stringent and time-consuming approval process for therapeutic drugs in the world. Total costs for conducting clinical trials topped $200 million, but with increasing proportions of this cost occurring with each of the three successive phases described below.

    Phase I Safety Trials (One Year)   In Phase I trials, researchers determined the highest tolerated doses, toxicities, and safe ranges in one or two dozen healthy volunteers. This phase also yielded invaluable information on absorption, metabolism, and excretion of the drug in humans.

    Phase II Efficacy Trials (Two Years)   Phase II tested the efficacy of drug candidates in up to several hundred volunteer patients based at test sites composed of participating hospitals. To ensure statistically relevant data, from this point onward, a portion of the volunteers received the drug while the others received placebos. Roughly one-third of all drug candidates survived Phases I and II.

    Phase III Long-Term Efficacy Trials (Three Years)   In the longest and most expensive phase of drug testing, researchers monitored drug use in thousands of volunteer patients for long-term safety, optimum dosage levels, and subtler adverse effects. Only about one-fourth of all drug candidates survived Phases I, II, and III, and moved on to the FDA review stage.

FDA Review (About Two to Three Years)
Despite a trend toward computer-assisted applications, the hundreds of thousands of pages submitted in the New Drug Application (NDA) to the FDA represented a tribute to the pharmaceutical industry's data-generating capacity. The NDA included data on each patient, as well as on the company's plans for producing and stocking the drug. The FDA committee took up to three years to review the NDA. Even after approval, however, post-marketing surveillance by the FDA continued. Only one-tenth of all drug candidates entering clinical trials ultimately reached the market.

[a] *Sources for this section:* J.A. DiMasi (1995), "New Drug Development: Cost, Risk, and Complexity," *Drug Information Journal*, May; FDA (1995), "From Test Tube to Patient: New Drug Development in the United States," *FDA Consumer*, Special Issue, January; Kenneth I. Kaitin, and Huub Houben (1995), "Worthwhile Persistence: The Process of New Drug Development," *Odyssey, The Glaxo-Wellcome Journal of Innovation in Healthcare*, June.

EXHIBIT 3   **Top 20 Prescription Drugs by Worldwide Sales (1994) (Dollars in Millions)**

Rank 1994	Rank 1993	Product Name	Product Type	Marketer	World Sales	% Change from 1993	U.S. Sales
1	1	Zantac	Ulcer therapy	Glaxo-Wellcome	3,663	12	2,280
2	2	Vasotec/Renitec	Hypertension treatment	Merck	2,185	6	975
3	4	Prilosec/Losec	Ulcer therapy	Astra & Merck	1,904	40	850
4	10	Zovirax	Herpes therapy	Glaxo-Wellcome	1,729	49	444
5	6	Prozac	Antidepressant	Eli Lilly	1,665	38	1,180
6	3	Capoten	Hypertension treatment	Bristol-Myers Squibb	1,500	2	581
7	5	Mevacor	Cholesterol reducer	Merck	1,345	3	1,115
8	8	Adalat line	Hypertension/angina	Bayer	1,300	8	120
9	9	Cipro/Ciproxin	Anti-infective	Bayer	1,300	8	712
10	16	Zocor	Cholestorol reducer	Merck	1,255	39	400
11	11	Voltaren	Anti-arthritic	Ciba	1,192	5	269
12	7	Procardia line	Hypertension/angina	Pfizer	1,177	(3)	1,177
13	12	Augmentin	Anti-infective	SmithKline Beecham	1,126	(3)	491
14	17	Sandimmune	Immunosuppressive	Sandoz	1,038	7	500
15	14	Cardizem line	Hypertension/angina	Hoechst Marion	933	2	812
16	18	Rocephin	Anti-infective	Hoffman-La Roche	930	4	413
17	20	Premarin	Estrogen replacement	Wyeth-Ayerst	853	14	723
18	23	Neupogen	Bioresponse modifier	Amgen	829	15	617
19	22	Pepcid/Pepcidine	Ulcer therapy	Merck	820	12	625
20	15	Ceclor	Anti-infective	Eli Lilly	812	(11)	394

Source: Derived from: "Top 100 drugs," *PharmaBusiness,* July 1995, p. 16; and "World Pharma Firm League," *Marketletter,* July 3, 1995.

EXHIBIT 4 Top 20 Firms Active in the Pharmaceutical Industry (1994) (Dollars in Millions, Unless Noted Otherwise)

Company[a]	Total Sales	R&D Expense	EBIT	Net Income	Return on Equity (%)	Return on Assets (%)	Employees (000s)
(1) Bayer, A.G.	28,023	2,050	2,430	1,271	11.9%	4.7%	146.7
(2) Ciba-Geigy	16,171	1,578	2,232	1,403	12.0	6.1	84.0
(3) Johnson & Johnson	15,734	1,278	2,867	2,006	28.2	12.8	81.5
(4) Merck & Co.	14,970	1,231	4,633	2,997	26.9	13.7	47.5
(5) Bristol-Myers Squibb	11,984	1,108	2,638	1,842	32.3	14.3	47.7
(6) Sandoz	11,639	1,199	NA	1,272	20.7	8.9	60.3
(7) Hoffman-La Roche	10,816	1,710	3,110	2,098	17.0	8.6	61.4
(8) SmithKline Beecham Plc	9,933	976	1,213	110	12.4	0.9	55.4
(9) Abbott Laboratories	9,156	964	2,228	1,517	37.5	17.8	49.5
(10) American Home Products Corp.	8,966	817	2,145	1,528	35.9	7.1	74.0
(11) Glaxo	8,484	1,287	2,826	1,955	25.2	16.1	47.4
(12) Pfizer Inc.	8,281	1,139	2,003	1,298	30.0	11.7	40.8
(13) Hoechst Celanese Corp.	7,794	313	(55)	186	5.9	2.3	29.2
(14) Tekeda Chemical Industries	7,778	677	1,124	518	7.7	4.5	11.0
(15) Eli Lilly and Company	5,712	897	1,828	1,286	22.1	8.2	24.9
(16) Sankyo Co. Ltd.	5,575	477	887	395	11.3	5.8	NA
(17) Schering-Plough	4,657	620	1,281	922	58.6	21.3	21.2
(18) Rhone-Poulenc Rorer	4,175	611	547	341	21.0	7.6	22.1
(19) Wellcome Plc—ADS	3,096	542	1,098	632	22.1	14.4	17.6
(20) Marion Merrell Dow Inc	3,060	462	632	438	20.5%	10.6%	9.4

Source: Standard & Poor's; Compustat, Global Vantage.

NA = not available.

[a] Some firms have substantial business activity outside pharmaceuticals, which is included in these figures.

EXHIBIT 5
Eli Lilly and Company—1994 Financial Highlights (Dollars in Millions, Except Per-Share Data)

Source: Eli Lilly and Company.

	1994	1993	% Change
Net sales	5,712	5,199	10
R&D expenses	839	755	11
Income from continuing operations	1,185	465	155
Net income	1,286	480	168
Earnings per share			
Income from continuing operations	4.10	1.58	159
Net income	4.45	1.63	173
As adjusted[a]			
Net income	1,398	1,336	5
Net income per share	4.84	4.54	7
Dividends paid per share	2.5	2.42	3
Capital expenditures	577	634	(9)
Income from continuing operations as a percent of shares	20.7%	8.9%	
Return on assets	11.8%	5.2%	
Return on shareholders' equity	25.9%	10.2%	

[a] For 1994, reflects the result of operations without the impact of acquisitions (including Sphinx) and product recall. For 1993, reflects results of operations without the impact of restructuring.

Eli Lilly and Company—Major Product Sales (Dollars in Millions)

Source: Eli Lilly and Company.

Drug	Category 1994 Sales	1994 Sales	% of Total Lilly sales	Launch Year
Prozac	Antidepressant	1,665	29	1988
Ceclor	Antibiotic	812	14	1979
Humulin	Diabetes	665	12	1980
Axid	Gastrointestinal	487	9	1988
Vancocin	Antibiotic	249	4	1958
Humatrope	Growth Hormone	226	4	1987
Keflex	Antibiotic	140	2	1971
Lorabid	Antibiotic	129	2	1992

EXHIBIT 6
Eli Lilly and Company—Organization

Source: Eli Lilly and Company.

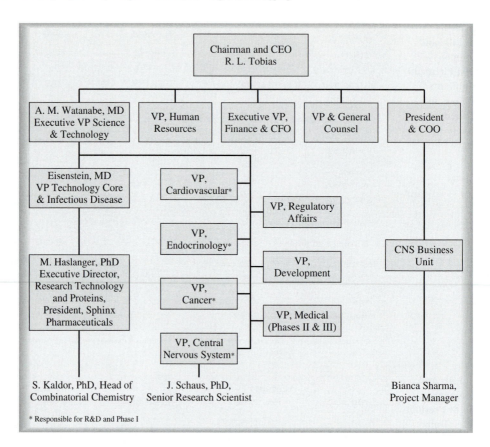

Chairman and CEO
R. L. Tobias

A. M. Watanabe, MD
Executive VP Science
& Technology

VP, Human
Resources

Executive VP,
Finance & CFO

VP & General
Counsel

President
& COO

Eisenstein, MD
VP Technology Core
& Infectious Disease

VP,
Cardiovascular*

VP,
Endocrinology*

VP, Regulatory
Affairs

VP,
Development

M. Haslanger, PhD
Executive Director,
Research Technology
and Proteins,
President, Sphinx
Pharmaceuticals

VP,
Cancer*

VP, Medical
(Phases II & III)

VP, Central
Nervous System*

CNS Business
Unit

S. Kaldor, PhD, Head of
Combinatorial Chemistry

J. Schaus, PhD,
Senior Research Scientist

Bianca Sharma,
Project Manager

* Responsible for R&D and Phase I

EXHIBIT 7
Principles of
Combinatorial
Chemistry

Combinatorial chemistry is an emerging technology for generating a large collection or "library" of related chemical compounds rapidly, instead of having to make one compound at a time. This allows for creating variations around the backbone of a basic molecular structure. With just a few building blocks chemists can create a large, diverse set of molecules just as locksmiths can create thousands of keys from one template using just a dozen different shaped cuts.

Two major combinatorial chemistry systems—"split-and-mix" and "parallel synthesis"—came into wide usage. In split-and-mix synthesis, illustrated below, chemists synthesize compounds on surfaces of small beads. In each successive step, different beads are recombined and partitioned into different vessels. To each vessel, the next building block is added, and the process continues until the desired number of compounds has been created. Sensitive detection techniques can take advantage of small built-in differences between the starting beads to fish out the more promising combinations.

In parallel synthesis, different compounds are synthesized in separate vessels arrayed into columns and rows. No remixing of compounds occurs. Although this method yields fewer compounds, it yields higher purity of compounds.

Combinatorial Chemistry (the "Split-and-Mix" Method)[a]

Round	Vessel 1	Vessel 2	Vessel 3	Number of Compounds
1	**A**	**B**	**C**	$3 (= 3^1)$
2	A**D**, B**D**, C**D**	A**E**, B**E**, C**E**	A**F**, B**F**, C**F**	$9 (= 3^2)$
	AD**G**, BD**G**, CD**G**	AD**H**, BD**H**, CD**H**	AD**I**, BD**I**, CD**I**	
	AE**G**, BE**G**, CE**G**	AE**H**, BE**H**, CE**H**	AE**I**, BE**I**, CE**I**	
3	AF**G**, BF**G**, CF**G**	AF**H**, BF**H**, CF**H**	AF**I**, BF**I**, CF**I**	$27 (= 3^3)$
. . .	. . .	. . .	. . .	. . .
K	. . .	. . .	. . .	$(= 3^K)$

The "split-and-mix" method works as follows (see table above): in **Round 1,** different polymer beads are reacted with compound A in vessel 1, B in vessel 2, and C in vessel 3. These beads are then mixed together and then split into three vessels. In **Round 2,** building block D is added to Vessel 1, E to Vessel 2, and F to Vessel 3. Once more, these compounds are mixed and split again. In **Round 3,** building block G is added to Vessel 1, H to Vessel 2, and I to Vessel 3. Note that newly added building blocks are bolded. With each consecutive round, the number of compounds increases by a factor of 3.

[a] S. Thomke, E. von Hippel and R. Franke, "Modes of Experimentation: An Innovation Process—and Competitive—Variable," *Research Policy* 27 (1998).

EXHIBIT 8
Receptors and Neurotransmitters (Simplified Illustration)

Source: Case authors.

(a) Receptors ("Locks") and Neurotransmitters

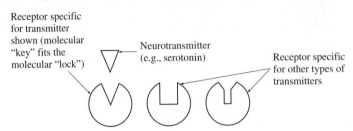

Receptor specific for transmitter shown (molecular "key" fits the molecular "lock")

Neurotransmitter (e.g., serotonin)

Receptor specific for other types of transmitters

(b) Transmitting Messages via Neurotransmitters

Neurotransmitters released from one nerve cell are recognized by certain receptors located on the surface of another nerve cell, which, in turn, may respond appropriately.

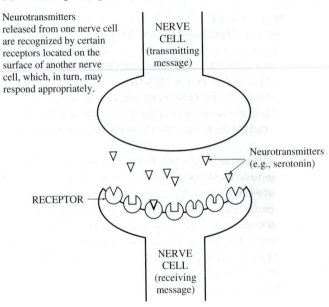

NERVE CELL (transmitting message)

Neurotransmitters (e.g., serotonin)

RECEPTOR

NERVE CELL (receiving message)

EXHIBIT 9 **Memo—Migraine Marketing Analysis**

MEMORANDUM
ATT'N: Bianca Sharma, Migraine Project Manager
FROM: Anh Thieu, Marketing
DATE: June 17, 1994

Here is some information excerpted from our marketing report on our migraine project:

Baseline projection: Based on current market data as well as prior experience, our projection is that our serotonin 1f-based compound will hit the market in 2001, and gradually build up market share by 2005 to its peak $300–500 million annual sales. (This is assuming that our product is indeed seen as more efficacious than 1d-based compounds.) Our models indicate that our drug could expect to remain at its peak levels for roughly another three years until competition would slowly erode market share to a negligible amount about two years before its patent expiration in 2012. (We discount revenue streams at 13 percent per annum.) Below are sundry items that went into our projection models:

- On average, each migraineur experiences 10–12 attacks per year, with a mean duration of 9–24 hours. The frequency of attacks is greatest in the age group of 35–45 years. Only 55 percent of migraineurs sought medical treatment, and of these, only half were correctly identified as migraine. Thus, we feel that patient education and physician education could considerably expand the market for migraine. In fact, based on Gallup polls, about 40 percent of non-consulters could be motivated to seek treatment. In this case, pharmaceutical firms can perhaps increase the total market size for new (serotonin-based) therapies by 3–4 times into a $3–4 billion market.

- Currently, two classes of migraine therapies exist: those directed at prophylaxis (which have expected 1996 worldwide sales of $200 million) and therapeutics directed at treating acute attacks (expected 1996 worldwide sales of $1.5 billion).

- Annual sales of our competitor Sumatriptan (Glaxo's Imitrex) since 1992 launch. (Note that only 10 percent of migraineurs are treated by sumatriptan)

Year	Sales ($ millions)	Sales Growth (%)
1992	100	
1993	250	175
1994	400	60
1995	525	40 (projected)
1996	800	50 (projected)

- In terms of migraineur preferences, 70 percent felt avoidance of cardiovascular adverse effects (such as those associated with sumatriptan) were important. Only 28 percent felt reduction in cost compared to sumatriptan was important.

With best regards, Anh

P.S.   I am also including below some information on our marketing experience with Prozac, in case you find it interesting.

Market Experience of Prozac—Market Share (in Percent)

Year	Prozac (%)	Zoloft (%)	Paxil (%)	Desyrel (%)	Pamelor (%)
1990	22.6	–	–	3.0	8.3
1991	18.9	–	–	2.5	9.6
1992	16.4	5.3	–	1.7	7.2
1993	14.7	10.0	4.3	1.1	2.3
1994	16.7	11.6	7.4	0.8	1.1

Source: J.R. Brinemeyer, et al., "Doctor's Orders," *New Rx Trends, September Industry Report,* November 7, 1995, Lehman Brothers.

Note: Prozac, Zoloft, and Paxil are from the new class of antidepressants ("Selective Serotonin Reuptake Inhibitors"); Desyrel and Pamelor are older antidepressants. Zoloft and Paxil were launched in 1992 and 1993, respectively.

EXHIBIT 10   Expert Estimates for Migraine Project

Participants
(all participants had first-hand knowledge of the Migraine Project):
Dr. John Lee, Senior Scientist, Combichem Group
Dr. Edward Pan, Senior Scientist, Combichem Group
Dr. Beverly Bourell, Senior Scientist, Central Nervous System
Dr. John Wecker, Senior Scientist, Central Nervous System
Dr. Clare Pimentel, Senior Prozac Product Manager
Mr. Ashley Peck, Director of Corporate Marketing

Scenario 1:
"If we bring our current lead migraine compound—'a bird in the hand'—to market with no further lead optimization, what do you feel is the chance of passing clinical trials?"

Expert	Months Delay	Chance of Passing Clinicals (%)
Lee	0	8
Pan	0	9
Bourell	0	12
Wecker	0	11
Pimentel	0	10
Peck	0	10
Average		**10**
Standard Deviation		1.4

Scenario 2:
"If we spend additional time seeking a better analogue of the current lead migraine compound using combinatorial chemistry, what do you feel is the chance of passing clinical trials? At what additional time to reach the market?"

Expert	Months Delay	Chance of Passing Clinicals (%)
Lee	7	15
Pan	6	14
Bourell	11	11
Wecker	12	11
Pimentel	8	10
Peck	10	11
Average	**9.0**	**12**
Standard Deviation	2.4	2.0

Scenario 3:
"If we go back to basic research and use combinatorial chemistry to try developing a new breakthrough migraine drug platform, what do you feel is the chance of passing clinical trials? At what additional time to reach the market?"

Expert	Months Delay	Chance of Passing Clinicals (%)
Lee	12	20
Pan	12	19
Bourell	26	13
Wecker	25	13
Pimentel	16	14
Peck	17	11
Average	**18.0**	**15**
Standard Deviation	6.2	3.6

EXHIBIT 11
Timeline

Source: Lilly migraine project dates: interviews conducted with Lilly personnel.

4000–2000 BC:	• Ancient Egyptians develop compresses around skull to stop migraines. (Procedure still used in 1990s)
1876	• Eli Lilly founded in Indianapolis, Indiana by Colonel Eli Lilly.
1970s	• Early research in Lilly on serotonin.
1988	• Prozac launched on market.
1991	• Serotonin "1f" receptor cloned by Lilly's collaborator, Synaptic Pharmaceutical Corporation. Rapid screening procedures utilizing Synaptic's technology allow 20–30 compounds to be screened weekly.
	• CNS group starts screening serotonin-like compounds from Lilly's historical library (total 250,000 compounds). During next three years over 1000 compounds will be screened.
1992	• Glaxo launches sumatriptin (Imitrex).
1994 March/April	• "Hot" lead compound found from the screen with good fit at the serotonin 1f receptor.
	• Kaldor gives combinatorial chemistry seminar to an in-house audience at Lilly that includes Schaus. This serves as a catalyst for Kaldor-Schaus collaboration.
March/June	• Improvements upon this lead made using traditional chemistry. Screening proceeds using an improved assay, which now tests 50 compounds per week.
September	• Sphinx acquired. Will take almost another year to integrate Sphinx's leading-edge technology in combichem and high-throughput screening.
December	• Schaus presents seminar on his research to other CNS research group leaders. Able to demonstrate that combichem can lead to pure, quantifiable results.
1995 February	• PTAC (Project Approval Committee) meets to discuss strategic choices in migraine project.
2001	• Projected launch, if approved, of Lilly's migraine product.
2003	• Patent protection of Prozac ends.

Module **Two**

Development Process Design and Improvement

Central to *Managing Product and Service Development*, and emphasized particularly in the material in this module, is the premise that every company's ability to create new products and services depends on a process of experimentation and learning that is integrated into its development organization and activities. In the previous module you learned what experimentation is, how it works, and, broadly, how it should be structured and organized. In this module, you will focus on the core aspects of development processes (their designs, operation, and management) and on how experimentation is integrated into them. You will also have the opportunity to "design" a development process yourself (as part of a team), giving you a feel for the uncertainties, complexities, and "stakes" involved in this activity.

A huge source of uncertainty (and complexity) in product development, of course, is determining what customers will want to purchase—ideally before huge sums are invested in a project! But it is by no means simple to figure out customers' wishes, and the more novel a potential product (or service) is—in itself or within a particular environment—the more difficult it is to discover "in advance" what the reaction will be.

Recall that in the Bank of America case, one rationale for running "live" (but brief) experiments in the branches was based on an inability to predict whether "new" services would be welcomed or rejected. Of course, these services were hardly new to customers; all were completely familiar, even routine, in other settings, where presumably they were welcomed. But it was not enough to know that customers "liked" TV monitors, copies of newspapers, and so on elsewhere; the issue was if bank customers would find these to be distracting, time-consuming, off-putting in *this* setting. What also mattered, crucially, was whether those services in the bank setting would increase sales of existing products. A lot was riding on free coffee!

This module begins with a case (on 3M) that introduces an interesting approach to using customers as sources for new product and service concepts, called lead users (it is detailed in the first module theme below). Another case (Bush Boake Allen) shows how customers can become involved in the actual design of products (for themselves), pushing innovation beyond the boundary of the supplier firm. That idea is explored in the fourth module theme. But a "classic" case on Dell also points to the uncertainty of customer wants (what trade-offs would customers be willing to make in laptop design) and the implications of Dell's decision for its entire process development structure. The stakes on something as seemingly minor as battery performance were enormous.

The Dell case and the subsequent in-class exercise dig deeply into development process design (explored in the second module theme in this note). Dell, as the situation makes clear, had a rather haphazard "approach" to product development (you saw something similar in the Apple case in the previous module). The discipline of a so-called stage gate process design worked wonders on Dell's development organization—as it has in numerous other organizations; it remains the most popular design today. But can "discipline" turn into "rigidity"? What happens to such "discipline" when there's a need to incorporate changes in technology, competitive moves, more specific customer information, and the like as development is ongoing? The nature of a measured, controlled stage gate process does not lend itself to such accommodation. But what would a "flexible" process look like? (You will find out for yourself in the exercise!) Is "flexibility" inherently a good thing, just as "rigidity" is presumably a bad one? These important questions are broached throughout the module.

Process design (including debates about "discipline" and "flexibility") takes on even greater salience when we return to a theme in the first module: how experimentation is being (potentially) transformed by new technologies like simulation. You learned how important it was that such technologies be *integrated* into a product development's organization, processes, and activities. If such integration did not happen, in fact, the potential of the technology to enhance innovation could actually threaten it. If the power is harnessed through new and improved processes, new opportunities for productivity, innovation, and value creation are possible.

But what does this "integration" look like? You got a glimpse in the Eli Lilly case in the previous module; but in the BMW case in this module, that glimpse becomes full-scale exploration of a multi-year attempt to overhaul a development organization such that the "power" could be effectively "harnessed." What is startling is not how *much* needed to change to maximize the value of new technologies for experimentation—but how much value could be created when those changes were made. The third module theme dives into this point.

At the end of this module, you should have the following "take-aways":

- Product (or service) development is not simply "drawing up specs" for a new offering and then "executing" upon them. Too often this leads to the flawlessly produced product or service that no one buys. Experimentation (including prototyping and managing the learning from these activities) removes many "unknowns," but even it is insufficient to create a "certainty" that what is produced is what will sell. While there never will be certainty in any product service development project, it's possible to eliminate a lot of uncertainties by having greater insight into what customers need and want or even use them as a source for new product and service concepts.

- Process design matters! There is not one, universally applicable, across-the-board approach. Labels like "rigid" and "flexible" aren't helpful for determining the most effective design given the challenges an organization faces when embarking on a product development project. You should realize that product development comprises integrated activities, each contingent upon the other. (This is particularly important to grasp as you turn to the final module, which explores the role of networks in product development.)

- Nowhere is this "contingency" more apparent that in integrating new technologies for experimentation into an organization's structure and activities. While this was a "take-away" from the first module, it should be even more sharply realized at the end of the second, for here you've witnessed a much broader view of how far-reaching the implications of new technologies are. These are not "swapped in" or substituted or piled on top of existing activities; to make maximum use of these potentially transforming applications, organizations have to rethink just about everything they currently do. The pay-off, of course, is huge when that happens.

MODULE STRUCTURE

There are four cases, one in-class exercise, and six readings in this module, and both product and service organizations, and their challenges, particularly vis-à-vis their customers, are covered. The situations you'll investigate range from how "lead user" customers can influence product development (at 3M), to how a firm's existing customers can actually participate in experimentation to influence the development of their *own* products (at Bush Boake Allen). Readings supplement each of these cases, amplifying the information and learning that come from classroom discussion. How process development is structured, and how experimentation best is integrated into it, is explored in the Dell and BMW cases, where the respective protagonists face superficially different problems but in fact must tackle them similarly: by considering the impact that *organization* has on process design and execution, in light of customer expectations. The "Internet Time" exercise (which also has a reading attached) adds the drama of speed to the process design, customer involvement, and organization—this is experimentation on steroids! See the **Exhibit** on page 201 for a synopsis of the cases.

THEMES

Four major themes help deepen your understanding of the material presented in this module.

Theme 1: New Approaches to Understanding User Needs

Having accurate information about users is clearly vital to any development project. Yet firms often bog down in their collecting, analyzing, and integrating of such data even though many market research methods are supposed to address these activities.[1] The problem is that understanding and integrating user needs is inherently complex: *which* users should companies study, *when* should they gather user need information from them, and *which* aspects should developers pay attention to? Also, traditional methods (such as focus groups) have not been very successful with products involving novelty.[2] And when

---

[1] For a reference text on market research methods in product development, see Glenn Urban and John Hauser, *Design and Marketing of New Products* (Prentice Hall, 1993).

[2] Dorothy Leonard-Barton, *Wellsprings of Knowledge* (HBS Press, 1995), and Gerald Zaltman, *How Customers Think* (HBS Press, 2003), describe other approaches that have successfully overcome the limitations of traditional methods.

FIGURE 2-1
The New
Products
Adoption
Curve

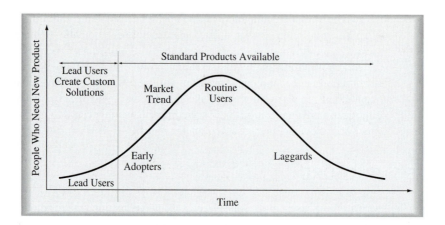

traditional customers have great influence on senior management, being too close to them can disrupt a firm's innovation capabilities.[3] Overall, while most managers agree that information about user needs should be integral to product development practice, how that actually happens is rarely so clear-cut.

One new method for understanding user needs is that of focusing on so-called lead users. It assumes that customers are not inevitably passive recipients of new products. Rather, lead users are often initially thought of—and even prototyped by these customers, not by manufacturers (see **Figure 2-1**).

Lead-users (who can be companies, organizations, or individuals) are often well ahead of market trends and tend to have needs that go far beyond those of the average user. With this perspective of "active" customers, the difficult job of creating breakthroughs from scratch is transformed into a systematic task of identifying lead users and learning from them.

Consider how an automobile manufacturer might apply the lead user approach. If the company wanted to design an innovative braking system, it might start by determining if any innovations had been developed by drivers with a strong need for better brakes—auto racers, for instance. The automaker wouldn't stop there, however. Next, it would look to a related but technologically advanced field where people had an even higher need to stop quickly—aerospace, for example. And, in fact, aerospace is where innovations such as ABS braking were first developed: military and commercial aircraft pilots have a very high incentive to stop their vehicles before the runway ends!

All processes designed to generate new ideas for products and services begin with information collected from users. What separates companies is the kind of information they collect and from whom they collect it. The traditional method relies on collecting information from users at the *center of their target market*. The emphasis is on a middle group of users, that is, eliminating "outliers." With this group in hand, marketing teams conduct focus groups and analyze sales data, reports from the field, customer complaints and requests, and so on. In other words, this is a reliance on the *past performance of existing products*. Then they rely on their own creative powers to brainstorm their way to new

[3] Clayton Christensen, *The Innovator's Dilemma* (HBS Press, 1997).

ideas. Teams that follow this approach assume it is the role of users to provide information about what they need, and that in-house developers then take that information to create new product ideas.

The lead user process represents a fundamentally different approach. It was designed to collect information about both needs and *solutions* from the leading edges of a company's target market and from markets that face similar problems in a more extreme form. Under the lead user approach, teams assume that savvy users outside the company have already generated innovations and that the team's job is to track down especially promising lead users and adapt their ideas to the business's needs. Such a radically different approach, of course, is not simply swallowed whole by people whose stakes in the traditional approach are high. Nor should any new approach be undertaken without challenge.

Thus, product concepts based on ideas from lead users still must be validated with traditional methods at the "belly" of the market where most of the sales potential falls. New approaches are not ipso facto "good," just as traditional ones are not inherently "bad." More subtle, however, is appreciating not only that the two can co-exist, but that development processes can be (re)designed to make this complementarity happen.

Theme 2: Structured Development Processes and Flexibility

How product development processes are both designed and executed results in either success or disaster: it's that important. While the causes of disaster are complex, it is often lack of structure that leads to poor coordination, ad hoc decision making, and weak risk management. The consequences are severe. As such, most firms have adopted *stage-gate* or *phased* development processes that are aimed at providing a clear, sequential model for coordinating and executing development tasks.[4] At each "gate," senior management provides input and (ideally) makes decisions that affect resources and schedule before proceeding to the next development stage.[5] In other words, the goal is to rationalize a development process and thereby guard against surprises.

Stage-gate processes come in many forms depending on the complexity of a project, and are used by most development organizations today. You will encounter versions of them in the situations highlighted in the module. A critical issue in assessing how effective these processes are is to distinguish between structure and rigidity, and between flexibility and "anything goes" (which is often confused with "autonomy"). That is, sequential stage-gate processes can be designed too rigidly—decisions are "frozen" at a particular gate, and making subsequent changes is discouraged, even forbidden, given the high costs of modification.

The economic cost of modifying a design arises from a change's impact on four factors: the product's development expense, its unit cost, its performance, and the development schedule. Changes in each of these factors can in turn be quantified and expressed in terms of cumulative profit impact. For example, suppose we determine that a program change will raise product cost by 3 percent and delay the schedule by two months. A sensitivity

---

[4] Robert Cooper, "A Process Model for Industrial New Product Development," *IEEE Transactions on Engineering Management EM-30,* 1983, explains the logic of stage-gate models.

[5] Examples of such stages: idea generation, preliminary assessment, concept, development, testing, trial and launch. Gates are "installed" between stages to ensure their satisfactory completion before proceeding to the next stage.

analysis determines that cost is worth $500,000 per percent and the schedule is worth $750,000 per month, representing a total economic cost of $3 million. The higher the economic cost of modifying a design as a response to a given change, the lower a firm's development flexibility.

But does the above definition (and calculation) restrict the *source* of flexibility? This is a challenge you will have to confront. Flexibility can stem from the choice of a particular design technology, as well as from other decisions designers and managers make early on. Academic research and many managers' experiences have shown, for example, that flexibility decreases as a development project nears completion, which can have a significant impact on product success.[6] Thus, when Ford decided to forgo a fourth passenger door on a new minivan—in spite of market research collected after development had begun indicating that customers wanted the door—it made a trade-off between potential revenue and a costly and late change to the body design. Having no structure (i.e., "anything goes") is not an option, but "too much" can pose major dilemmas when changes are clearly warranted. Therefore, understanding real customer needs is critical at the *outset* to ensure that stage-gate-type processes avoid the problem of rigidity.

Flexibility in process design, for its part, is critical to managing uncertainty in a rapidly changing external environment.[7] The source of uncertainty has many dimensions but ultimately results in unstable customer needs, which, in turn, affect the product or service under development. That product requirements are unstable is a fact known to practitioners and researchers. It has been shown that a significant part of these changes can be attributed to (1) the co-evolution of technical solutions in components that are part of a larger system; and (2) customers' inherent difficulty in accurately specifying their needs at the outset of a design project system.

Individual designs are often part of larger systems; the requirements placed on those designs derive from how they are to fit into these systems. As designers at the system and subsystem level engage in problem solving, they can alter interfaces within the system. Since these interfaces are in reality *the product requirements for subsystems*, the subsystems in turn are subject to changing requirements. This complicated interrelationship has been well documented by research on engineering problem solving and its related evolution of the technical solution path in the design of a number of aerospace systems.[8] The research showed that design engineers who were developing an aerospace subsystem conceived of and evaluated a number of design alternatives and selected the one judged best. The designers' preferences for these alternatives, however, changed frequently and quickly as the design evolved, and it would have been very difficult to conclusively determine the best alternative at the outset of the project. Moreover, these different alternatives required different subsystem components or interfaces to other system components—resulting in rapidly changing product requirements (or specifications) as the development project evolved.

---

[6] For studies in software development, see for example Barry Boehm (*Software Engineering Economics*, Prentice-Hall 1981).

[7] See also Marco Iansiti, *Technology Integration* (HBS Press, 1997).

[8] Thomas Allen, "Studies of the Problem-Solving Process in Engineering Design," *IEEE Transactions on Engineering Management EM-2*, 1966.

At the system level, requirements are driven by rapidly evolving customer needs, an additional source of instability. Indeed, familiarity with existing product attributes can interfere with an individual's ability to express needs for novel products.[9] In other words, it is hard for inexperienced customers to accurately describe what they want. Needs become more refined (or change) as the customer comes into direct contact with the product and starts to use it. This happens quite often in systems that involve human-machine interactions, resulting in responses such as the familiar "I'm really not sure what I want, but I'll know when I see it." For example, designers of applications software sometimes find that customers significantly revise requirements after they use their software for the first time, leading to very costly and time-consuming redesigns of an otherwise functional product.

At the same time, new approaches to figuring out user needs (and often actual product modifications) suggest that there are ways to understand—early on—both what customers want and how these can be realized. A calculated approach to experimentation is key.

Theme 3: The Integration of Experimentation Technologies into Development Processes

In previous cases you've been introduced to the changing economics of experimentation; technologies like computer simulation not only provide a greater capacity for experimentation itself but also make possible "blue-sky" ("what-if?") experiments that, up to now, have been prohibitively expensive. Experimentation is part of the larger development picture, however, and needs to be integrated into issues of process design—and must be considered at both the project and firm levels. In particular, large, complex development projects, often clouded by uncertainty, have relied heavily on both systematic and informal experimentation processes. To take advantage of new technologies, they must be (re)organized to enhance the *capacity* and *diversity* of experimentation that have now become available.

Suppose that a firm wishes to replace some physical experimentation methods being carried out in its labs with computer simulation methods. To do this, it must typically hire new people and reorganize the relationships between the various specialists who jointly carry out the experiments. In existing organizational arrangements created specifically for physical experimentation, the firm's routines might enable researchers to work with design engineers and model makers to design and build the experiments they wished to run. The procedures might also dictate that the completed experimental apparatus be transferred to experts at specialized test facilities who will actually run the experiments, collect the resulting data, and then supply that to the researcher for analysis. In contrast, experimentation via computer simulation would require quite different organizational routines. In some cases, a single researcher might be able to do the entire design-build-test-analyze experimental cycle in his or her own lab. In other situations, the routines might facilitate collaborative arrangements between the researcher and various types of experts, either within the firm or even outside its boundaries, who specialize in different aspects of computer simulation.

As might be expected (and as the case situations in this module make clear), existing processes, procedures, organizations, firms—people—rarely greet such impending changes with open arms. You will see various strategies that aim to overcome an array of roadblocks, and en route you will discover just how deeply existing approaches penetrate.

[9] Eric von Hippel, *The Sources of Innovation* (Oxford University Press, 1988), pages 102–106.

Many questions arise. How, when, and where are new technologies to be introduced? Are these to complement existing technologies? Replace them? Be integrated with them? And what about other, intersecting aspects of development—how are these arenas affected, and what modifications must be made there? Again, realizing that "development is a system" means that "development happens" beyond the confines of, say, a particular R&D organization. Introducing new ways of doing things in one area necessarily has impact elsewhere. And not everyone is happy at the prospect. The jobs of people trained in the old ways are threatened by new ways of doing things.

Morison's description of the U.S. Navy's fierce resistance toward then more modern weapons systems suggests that such "unhappiness" is not new:

> Military organizations are societies built around and upon the prevailing weapons systems. Intuitively and quite correctly the military man feels that a change in weapon portends a change in the arrangements of his society . . . Daily routines, habits of mind, social organization, physical accommodations, conventions, rituals, spiritual allegiances have been conditioned by the essential fact of the ship. What then happens to your society if the ship is displaced as the principal element by such a radically different weapon as the plane? The mores and structure of the society are immediately placed in jeopardy. They may, in fact, be wholly destroyed.[10]

Morison's depiction of "fierce resistance" was attached to the superimposition of something new and different: different and more advanced weapon systems. What's possible, and what is depicted in the situations you will be investigating in this module, is how organizations—people—can *participate* in these changes, manage the integration of new technologies, and be convinced that their work is enhanced by them. And that is particularly so if customers become even more involved—not only in determining what "should" be developed, but in the experimentation activities that determine it from the outset.

Theme 4: Involving Customers Directly in Product Development

You have already seen, in various case situations, the strengths and weaknesses of traditional approaches to customer research. You've understood the possibilities afforded by new technologies for experimentation—their ability to get preliminary "results" quickly and cheaply. Now you are able to appreciate that when these are introduced, the boundaries between existing elements in and beyond the firm are changed. (This topic is explored in terms of "networks" in the following module.) It's possible at this point to consider a different way of thinking about the organization of product development itself. What if, for instance, the customer "experimented"—but did so in ways that bonded the customer to the firm? What if a firm provided the *tools* of experimentation directly? The notion of enabling customers to "design their own" is neither radical nor new: toolkits have been around for decades, notably in custom-designed semiconductor chips.

Toolkits and other methods for bringing customers more intimately into the product development process early on have a twofold benefit. First, they eliminate the need to endlessly second-guess, or attempt to assess, what customers actually want and/or need. Customers themselves can "experiment" en route to discovering what they want and/or need. Second, customer-firm sharing in product development potentially generates tremendous value for both parties. But not without difficulty.

[10] Elting Morison, *Men, Machines, and Modern Times* (M.I.T. Press, 1966), pages 35–36.

FIGURE 2-2
Moving
Information
Between
Supplier and
Customers

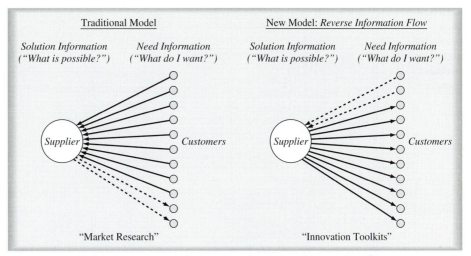

Explanation: Traditionally, "need" information is collected and moved from customers to suppliers via market research methods (left side). This process can be costly and time-consuming when needs are unique, complex, and fast changing. In the new model, the supplier's "solution" information is embodied in innovation toolkits that are moved to customers so that they can experiment and design their own products (right side).

Customers must be *easily* brought into the process; toolkits, for instance, have to be on the one hand user-friendly, and on the other sufficiently rich that customer experimentation is worth the effort and expense. Meanwhile, the offering must be robust enough to enable customers to conduct their own experiments, over and over. For their part, firms must be comfortable with sharing heretofore "crown jewel"-type information, rather than having it embedded in products they create themselves. They have to reconfigure their relationships with customers at a fundamental level, challenging notions of who controls what, when, where, how, and, why.

Despite these obstacles, companies are already going this route. Consider GE Plastics. In the late 1990s it set up a Web site from which registered customers could download "tools"—software, data sheets, and other knowledge and expertise the company made available. Only a few years later, more than a million people were annually accessing the site. Not only does this traffic dramatically reduce sales costs, it generates new customers, all while improving customer satisfaction. The company has even supplemented its toolkit offerings by running e-seminars that explain how the tools can be used.

Obviously, we've come a long way from focus groups and other traditional forms of market research aiming to pinpoint customer needs! In fact, the toolkit approach represents a massive change in information flow between company (supplier) and customer, as displayed in **Figure 2-2.**[11]

The implications of the shift suggested by Figure 2-2 are profound. Experimentation power is put into the hands of users, who thus become an integral part of a company's innovation efforts. The manufacturer can focus on developing better solution *platforms* that can

[11] For additional information, see Chapter 7 in Stefan Thomke, *Experimentation Matters* (HBS Press, 2003).

FIGURE 2-3
A New
Approach to
Developing
Custom
Products

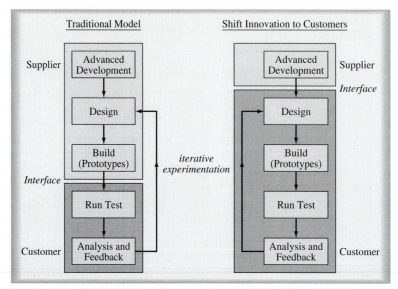

Explanation: Traditionally, suppliers have taken on most of the work—and responsibility—of product development. The result has been costly and time-consuming iterations between supplier and customer to reach a satisfactory solution. When the locus of experimentation is shifted to customers, a supplier provides the design tools so they can develop the application-specific part of a product on their own. This also shifts the location of the supplier-customer interface, and the iterative experimentation necessary for product development is now carried out by the customer only.

be customized (platforms are explored in the next module). The customer can experiment and get feedback more rapidly, control intellectual property on the application-specific part of a design, and, most important, find a solution that closely matches its needs. Note, however, that shifting product development activities to customers does not eliminate learning by experimentation—nor should it. What it does is make traditional product development better and faster—for two main reasons. First, a company can bypass the expensive and error-prone effort to understand customer needs in detail. Second, the trial-and-error cycles that inevitably occur during product development can progress much more quickly because the iterations will be performed solely by the customer (see **Figure 2-3**). [12]

DESCRIPTION OF CASES AND ARTICLES

The four module themes will be addressed in the various teaching cases and articles. The following summary of the material will prepare you for what you can expect to learn.

Innovation at 3M

3M's Medical-Surgical Markets Division has embarked on a so-called lead user (LU) research process in developing new products and services. Initially perceiving LU research

---

[12] For additional information, see the module article (page 383), "Customers as Innovators: A New Way to Create Value," *Harvard Business Review,* April 2002.

as a new methodology for overcoming the limitations of traditional customer needs during the very early stages of product development, the project team applies it to the field of surgical infection control and discovers not only new product concepts but also a promising new business strategy. The case emphasizes how user needs *and* solutions can be integrated into development processes and the ways in which different approaches (e.g., lead user research, deep exploration methods, focus groups, and so on) complement each other. The note "Understanding User Needs" describes these different approaches to researching user needs. The conceptual underpinnings and the impact of lead user research on management practice are described in the *Harvard Business Review* article "Creating Breakthroughs at 3M," which is one of the module articles.

Product Development at Dell Computer Corporation

At the time of this case (early to mid-1990s) Dell's product development process was run by autonomous teams, with relatively little senior management oversight. Investment decisions were not based on market and technical risk assessment, nor were development project bounds tightly established. After a major setback in the laptop market, Dell's senior management put a "stage-gate" process in place that introduced better structure and coordination. But was this new structure increasing rigidity? The new process was challenged when a development team had to make an important decision on a new battery technology: should they follow the process or make it more flexible? The case is a good primer on the widely used stage-gate process design and its advantages, but it also exposes the design's limitation—and helps to make the notion of "flexibility" in process design more precise. To fully understand how development flexibility can be managed, you will find that the *California Management Review* article "Agile Product Development: Managing Flexibility in Uncertain Environments" provides the motivation and a set of solutions to the challenges that uncertainty poses.

Process Design Exercise

This in-class, team-based exercise, based on the so-called browser war between Netscape and Microsoft, focuses on the "management" of a development project and how the dynamics of developing products in the fast-paced Internet environment are experienced as they evolve. The exercise introduces various realistic sources of uncertainty that have to be addressed through flexible processes, as first introduced in the Dell case. You and your team have to make decisions on organization, features, milestones, testing, and integration in a period of about 20 minutes and present your results to the rest of the class. The *Harvard Business Review* article "Developing Products on Internet Time" will show you how realistic the exercise can be, particularly in times of extreme uncertainty.

BMW AG: The Digital Car Project

In 1996, German automaker BMW began a "reengineering" effort seeking to slash development time in key areas with the ultimate goal of reducing its product development cycle in half. To achieve this seemingly impossible goal, three changes in the system—primarily involving increased computerization—were necessary: increased parallelization of development activities, elimination of as many process steps as possible, and quicker completion of the remaining steps. Because progress was slow, BMW executives increased urgency by using an actual car project for carrying out these reengineering efforts. Heralding the widening role of computers in BMW's new development process, the project is called the "digital car." But which "car" should this be? The next generation 7-series *platform* or a 3-series *derivative* (station wagon)? The choice of project would have implications for how BMW will manage change, including the integration of its new computer technology overall. The case study will also introduce you to the concept of "front-loaded development," which is now being adopted by leading companies. The module reading "The Effect of 'Front-Loading' Problem-Solving on Product Development Performance" will give you a deeper understanding of why BMW and other companies are so eager to fundamentally change their development systems.

Bush Boake Allen

Bush Boake Allen (BBA), a global supplier to companies like Nestlé in the $11 billion specialty flavor industry, faces slow growth and price erosion. Specialty flavors enhance the taste of nearly all processed foods and their development requires considerable customization and expertise—it's more art than science. However, companies asking for custom flavors neither pay for R&D nor commit to purchasing the flavors until *after* they have been developed. Given an acceptance rate of less than 10 percent, senior management has no choice but to focus on very large customers so that the expected volume can offset risk-adjusted R&D expenses. In 2000, BBA's CEO asked his people to develop a design "toolkit" through which smaller companies could customize flavors on their own, thus fundamentally changing the way specialty flavors are developed in the industry. While this new approach could provide BBA with new sources of growth, senior management struggled with how this toolkit technology should be used and the way it would profoundly affect their business model. Thus both the business potential and the possible organizational risks of pushing innovation "to" customers are explored. BBA's approach of shifting innovation activities to customers has already transformed other industries and the *Harvard Business Review* article "Customers as Innovators: A New Way to Create Value" will show you what is potentially at stake for companies like BBA.

EXHIBIT
Themes of
Cases in
Module

Module 2: Development Process Design and Improvement	
Innovation at 3M	• Designing the "voice of the customer" into development processes • Detailed analysis of lead user research and underlying theory • Methods class for students working on optional projects • Article: "Creating Breakthroughs at 3M" (*Harvard Business Review*) • Article: "Understanding User Needs"
Product Development at Dell Computer Corporation	• Introduction to stage-gate processes • Managing the transition from unstructured to structured development • Designing flexibility into phased development processes • Reading: "Agile Product Development: Managing Flexibility in Uncertain Environments" (*California Management Review*)
Developing Products on Internet Time: A Process Design Exercise	• Alternative models of developing new [software] products • Matching development processes with context • Hands-on process design exercise with team presentations • Reading: "Developing Products on Internet Time" (*Harvard Business Review*)
BMW AG: The Digital Car Project	• Revolutionizing automotive development through new technologies • (Re)designing processes for time to market • Managing projects as experiments and change agents • Reading: "The Effect of 'Front-Loading' Problem-Solving on Product Development Performance" (*Journal of Product Innovation Management*)
Bush Boake Allen	• Creating value through new development process paradigms • Design toolkits for customer innovation • New business models for capturing value • Reading: "Customers as Innovators: A New Way to Create Value" (*Harvard Business Review*)

Innovation at 3M Corporation

On the evening of October 23, 1997, Rita Shor, senior product specialist at 3M, looked across the conference room at her team from the Medical-Surgical Markets Division. She wondered when to draw to a close the intense ongoing debate on the nature of the team's recommendations to the Health Care Unit's senior management. A hand-picked group of talented individuals, the team had embarked on a new method for understanding customer needs called "lead user research." But this initiative to introduce leading-edge market research methods into 3M's legendary innovation process had now grown into a revolutionary series of recommendations that threatened to rip apart the division.

While senior management wanted the "lead user" team to execute a manageable project involving surgical draping material to protect surgery patients from infections, the team now wanted to rewrite the entire business unit's strategy statement to also include more proactive products or services that would permit the *upstream containment* of infectious agents such as germs. This went against the incrementalist approach that for so long had pervaded 3M. After all, as Mary Sonnack, division scientist and an internal 3M consultant on the new lead user methodology, noted, "3M gets so much revenue from incremental products . . . like a blue Post-it® Note instead of just a yellow one."

Outside the window, the late autumn breeze rippled through the tall Minnesota grass— a seasonal reminder that it had been a year since the group first embarked on the lead user process (see **Exhibit 1**). The method, including training, had called for less than six months dedicated to the entire process. But the lengthy commitment from participants as well as 3M senior management might just pay off if it took the Medical-Surgical Markets division from a stagnating business to a reinvigorated enterprise. Clearly, however, unless the team came up with successful product ideas and effective positioning, the new methodology for product innovation would die with the winter frost. And so might the entire business unit.

Harvard Business School Case No. 9-699-012. Copyright 1998 President and Fellows of Harvard College. All rights reserved. For information: permissions@hbsp.harvard.edu.

This case was prepared by Stefan Thomke and Ashok Nimgade. HBS cases are developed solely for class discussion and do not necessarily illustrate effective or ineffective management.

HISTORY OF 3M CORPORATION[1]

In 1902, on the banks of Lake Superior, five investors got together to excavate what they thought was high-quality corundum, a mineral almost as hard as diamond that manufacturers used for producing abrasives. What they dug up under the banner of the Minnesota Mining and Manufacturing Company, however, turned out low-grade and worthless. After filling one $20 order, the venture folded up its mining operations and turned instead to the sandpaper business. Here, disaster struck again: the abrasives they had imported from Spain refused to stick to the sandpaper.

Research and development (R&D) then at 3M, as the company became known, took place in a primitive laboratory so small the sole technician had to back out to let the boss in. The young technician figured out the problem after plunging some sandpaper into water and noting an oil slick. Follow-up investigations revealed that during shipment from Spain, an ocean storm had caused olive oil to leak into the abrasive material. This insight allowed for fixing the sandpaper problem while also establishing the emphasis on technology and innovativeness at 3M.

By 1916, survival assured, the company started paying stock dividends. The firm, now headquartered in St. Paul, Minnesota, initially stayed close to abrasives, developing the world's first waterproof sandpaper in the early 1920s. 3M technicians began bypassing purchasing agents in order to better understand product needs. Often, they walked into factories and workplaces and talked directly to workers, an unheard of practice that yielded unexpected dividends.

While visiting an auto-body shop in the 1920s, for instance, Richard Drew, a young lab assistant, heard a torrent of screams and curses. Workers had apparently just ruined a two-tone paint job when paint peeled away as they removed glued newspaper strips used as masking materials. Back in the lab, while working with a new and crinkly backing material for sandpaper, Drew came up with the idea that would provide the world with masking tape. To spend the long hours needed to perfect the new tape, however, he had ignored a direct order from the company head to put all his efforts into improving a preexisting product. Drew's success helped spawn the legend of the subversive 3M inventor and the 3M aphorism: "It's better to seek forgiveness than to ask for permission." It also helped inspire a "get-out-of-the-way" attitude on the part of management toward product developers. At the same time, Drew had opened up another "core technology" for 3M. A few years later, in fact, Drew went on to also invent Scotch® brand cellophane tape, which would help the company prosper through the Great Depression.

Over the decades, 3M enjoyed national and global growth as well as a reputation for remaining a "hothouse" of innovation. "We'll make any damn thing we can make money on," stated a past 3M president, Richard Carlton.[2] According to the International Directory of Company Histories: "Observers and outsiders frequently describe 3M in terms approaching awe. 3M earns such respect because of its improbable, almost defiantly non-corporate nature. The company is gigantic, yet it is as innovative and as full of growth potential as though it were a small venture."[3]

[1] Much of the information on 3M history comes from G. C. Nicholson, "Keeping Innovation Alive," *Research-Technology Management,* vol. 41 (3), May/June 1998, pp. 34–40 and 3M Annual Report, 1998.

[2] St. James Press, Chicago/London, 1988, vol. 1: 499–501.

[3] Ibid.

3M inventors did not share directly in product royalties; rather, the firm hoped that individual love for discovery would drive innovation. 3M sought to encourage innovation through a variety of means including awards for innovation as well as in-house grants for innovative projects. The company also allowed all staff to spend 15 percent of their time to explore new ideas outside of assigned responsibilities. Post-it Notes were developed on the 15 percent time scheme by 3M inventor Art Fry, who first used a weak adhesive to produce convenient hymnal markers for his music recitals.

3M also employed a "dual ladder" approach that allowed senior, technically inclined individuals with attractive career opportunities to advance, without having to switch to management. In addition, the company held internal showcases for products and ideas to help encourage inter-departmental cross-pollination or "bootlegging" of discoveries. As a result of these steps, 3M employees tended not to move to other companies.

The 3M model of expansion involved splintering off decentralized units based on new key product areas that were sufficiently different from prior key technologies. The first core technology from the 1920s had been adhesives and sandpaper. By the late 1990s, however, over 30 key technologies existed at 3M. Much market growth for 3M also came from finding new twists to existing product platforms: for instance, digital "Post-It Software Notes," or the use of 3M's Thinsulate®, first introduced in 1978 for apparel, in reducing sound in automobiles.

In the 1990s, 3M operated with four objectives: producing 30 percent of sales from products that did not exist four years earlier—an attempt to accelerate away from the incrementalism that had served as an engine for growth in the past few decades; greater than 10 percent annual growth in earnings per share; greater than 27 percent return on capital employed; and 20–25 percent return on equity. It also sought to change the mix of new products to emphasize products truly new to the world, instead of line extensions, which typically had provided two out of three new-product sales dollars.

To achieve high rates of innovation, 3M placed a heavy emphasis on R&D. In 1997, it employed 4,500 scientists, engineers, and technicians in the United States, and another 2,000 overseas. On average, 3M spent 6.5–7.0 cents of every sales dollar on laboratory-based R&D, which amounted to just over $1 billion in 1997—not including process engineering and quality control expenses. In 1997, 3M companies operated in more than 60 countries, and overseas businesses generated half of the firm's $15.07 billion in revenue and half of its $2.7 billion in operating income. 3M employed 75,000 workers, of whom 36,000 were outside the United States. (See **Exhibits 2 and 3**.)

The Medical Products Division, the first 3M division dedicated solely to health care, was founded in 1961. A decade later, the Health Care Group at 3M provided an umbrella for all health-related product divisions including the Medical-Surgical Markets Division. By 1997, 3M claimed over 10,000 health-related products ranging from surgical drapes to dental fillings to respirators to software. By 1994, Health Care sales topped $2 billion.[4]

Innovation at 3M in the 1990s

Product teams at 3M typically involved "skunkworks" teams primarily comprising technical individuals; teams also involved process engineers to help ensure that the particular product under development could be efficiently made. These engineers also provided teams with feedback about 3M's manufacturing capabilities. The entire team faced no risk if an

[4] 3M brochure entitled "3M Health Care," 1996.

idea flopped—indeed, there might even be a celebration. In case of failures, members of disbanded teams could go on to other projects. Although failures were often celebrated, each technical person's output over one or two years would be evaluated as a whole. The 3M mythology allowed for technical employees to take matters in their own hands—as exemplified by the Post-it Notes story.

Marketing input traditionally came from current customers and sales representatives. Product developers focused on finding new angles or twists on early trends. At the same time, few market researchers worked at 3M; only one market researcher served 900 engineers. Instead, the firm hired out for market research reports from smaller market research firms. To identify market needs and trends, 3M product developers in the Health Care unit, for instance, utilized several tools:

- Data from sales representatives with daily contact with physicians or registered nurses.
- Focus groups; for example, one business unit within the Medical-Surgical Division would gather some 30 nurses biannually from across the nation to obtain reactions to proposed products.
- Customer evaluations of currently marketed products.
- Site visits by 3M scientists and technologists to observe physicians and nurses at work, with the intent to identify unforeseen needs.
- Data on risk factors for diseases.

Several disadvantages to these methods had become apparent over the years. For one, hiring out for market research created too many interfaces between development teams and customers. Another major disadvantage was that the information obtained was not necessarily proprietary. Anyone, for example, could open up a medical textbook to find key risk factors for diseases. Attempts to seek more proprietary information through, say, focus groups provided virtually no clue about market needs some five to ten years down the road. While visiting customers provided an opportunity for Thomas Edison-type "innovations by serendipity," customers were somewhat blind about their own needs, and thus could not provide clues about developing revolutionary products.

Even these customer visits, although traditionally a part of 3M, had often become deemphasized during the past few decades of successful growth through incremental innovation. This often led to situations where, as Mary Sonnack pointed out: "Typically, one or two product developers or even marketers think of a product, then they throw it over the wall to the commercializers." As a result, thousands of 3M product concepts and inventions awaited markets and languished on drawing boards and R&D labs.

The Medical-Surgical Markets Division

Over the past century, a few medical pioneers, including Benjamin Lister and Florence Nightingale, had demonstrated that the cleanliness of healthcare providers and the hospital environment could reduce the rate of new infections in patients. Previously, patients died on account of the hospital nearly as much as because of what put them there in the first place. It took several decades, however, for the pendulum to swing from the medical establishment ridiculing such a stress on sanitation to mandating high standards of hygiene among health professionals. As a result, surgeons and attending staff now scrubbed with an almost ritualistic devotion using antiseptic detergents and donned sterile clothing and foot covers before entering operating rooms.

What was being operated upon was also antiseptically prepared or "prepped" for surgery. Thus, operating teams carefully established "sterile fields" on the skin around the pertinent area, freeing it from microbial contamination. A key part of this process involved use of surgical drapes, which served to isolate the "field of surgery" from all other potential sources of infection including the rest of the patient's body, the operating table, the anesthesiologist's equipment, and all members of the surgical team. But the diversity of the microbial world constantly challenged this artificial fortress. As a result, medical personnel had to remain vigilant about catheters and tubes along which agents of infections could migrate into the patient.

From mid-century on, surgical operating rooms became a product developer's dream-come-true. Product categories dedicated to preserving sterility included razors and clippers for shaving hair, presurgical soaps for scrubbing hands, sterile surgical gloves and masks, drapes, handwashes, antibiotics, lavages for washing away excess blood in a sterile fashion, sponges with or without handles, antiseptic solutions, and dressings.

The surgical drapes business unit within the Medical-Surgical Division focused largely on reducing infections from the skin through surgical drapes and surgical prepping. For 3M, the drape business represented one extension of Richard Drew's attempts to meet the needs of auto-body workshops. By the mid 1990s, 3M was highly penetrated in one niche of surgical drapes that brought the company over $100 million in yearly sales. But sales in the United States had limited growth remaining in these market niches. Overseas markets were limited by the high cost of 3M products when converted into local currencies.

Most surgical drape products were developed using the equivalent of one full-time product developer and generated about $1 million in sales each. Occasionally, a $1–20 million product would come along, but these big products were becoming fewer and fewer. Typically, it would take about two years to get a surgical drape product out from initial product conception to market. In the best case, this could be shortened to a year; in worse cases, it could take up to four years.

The surgical drapes section of the Medical-Surgical Markets Division had discovered the hard way that technological excellence by itself meant little. In the early 1990s, for instance, the division had spent three years developing a virus-proof gown that would let water vapor but not viruses pass through the fabric through microscopic pinholes. This manufacturing feat, however, came in just as managed care was taking hold. Although customers loved the fabric, the 10–15 percent price premium banished the product into a tiny niche in the European market.

By 1996, the business unit had gone almost a decade with only one successful product. Senior management charged Rita Shor with the mandate of developing a breakthrough product within the existing business strategy. She was assigned to the task not only because of her seniority, having been at the division 11 years, but also because she was thought of as being creative and a consensus builder.

LEAD USER RESEARCH AT 3M'S MEDICAL-SURGICAL MARKETS DIVISION

Shor realized, at the outset, that 3M's traditional methods for understanding customer and market needs would not suffice. Market research reports provided an abundance of data but contained little useful information for conceptualizing a breakthrough product. She recalled, however, an in-house lecture given a few weeks before by Mary Sonnack, who had become increasingly involved with new product development using a new methodology termed "lead user research" that she had studied at the Massachusetts Institute of Technology (MIT). Shor wondered if this might provide the key to a breakthrough product.

The premise of this novel methodology was that certain consumers experienced needs ahead of other consumers and that some of the former would seek to innovate on their own. By tapping the expertise of these so-called "lead users," manufacturers could find invaluable sources of innovation. Lead users had often already created innovations to solve their own leading-edge needs—familiar examples were white-out ("liquid paper"), invented by a secretary for correcting typographical mistakes, and the sports drink Gatorade, developed in Florida with invaluable input from athletes.

3M's experience with traditional market research had been disappointing; it had not led to the kinds of innovations senior management wanted for the marketplace. As Chuck Harstad, former vice president of the Commercial and Office Supply Division and now vice president of Corporate Marketing, recalled:

> At the end of the day, we didn't learn anything from our market research department. 3M had to find new ways to identify leading-edge customer needs and develop concepts for breakthrough products and services. Traditional market research methods couldn't deliver the goods. And product developers would not assume ownership for understanding customer needs because they considered that to be the responsibility of market researchers. So we ended up eliminating the market research department to learn about customer needs!

Sonnack, under mandate from Harstad to seek out newer and better customer-focused product development processes, thought that lead user research fit well with 3M's customer-focused philosophy (see **Exhibit 4**). In 1994, she began an unusual year-long stay at MIT to study with Professor Eric von Hippel, who had pioneered lead user research. For von Hippel, the collaboration represented a way to develop a step-by-step methodology for practitioners and seek further validation of lead user concepts. Since he had not charted out a "how-to" manual, he started this process with the help of Sonnack and Minnesota organizational psychologist Joan Churchill.

One of Sonnack's and Churchill's goals was to disseminate the lead user process throughout 3M. Support for the new methodology existed at high levels within the company. William Coyne, 3M's Head of Research and Development, for instance, was fairly critical of the strategic planning process because he felt that "traditional strategic planning does not leave enough room for innovation. And innovation cannot be planned ahead of time." This view did not go unchallenged within 3M's senior management and represented a radical departure from the incrementalist approach to innovation. "Strategic planning looks in the rearview mirror and cannot keep up with the rate of change in today's markets," added Coyne. "We need to understand leading-edge customer needs to change the basis of competition." Widespread adoption of the lead user process could help get 3M back to its roots of working more closely with customers and understanding such market needs.

Through one of Sonnack's in-house lectures, Shor first heard about the new methodology. In June of 1996, she telephoned Sonnack to say:

> Our business unit has been going nowhere. While we are number one in the surgical drapes market niche, and pull in over a hundred million in yearly sales, we are stagnating. We need to find new customer needs we haven't thought of before. If we don't bring in radically new ways of looking for products, upper management may have little choice but to sell off the business.

At the time, Sonnack's and Churchill's in-house consulting schedule was crowded. But Shor's degree of commitment appeared to match Sonnack's enthusiasm for the new methodology, and the two women agreed to meet. Were the Medical-Surgical Markets Division to focus product development based on the lead user method, it would became one of the first divisions at 3M to do so. During their preliminary meeting, Sonnack warned Shor about the need for high-level commitment from both team members and their management.

Selling the new approach to senior management would use much of Shor's time and efforts. At first, senior management had balked at such a large commitment. But Shor pointed out that an adequate human resources commitment to the new methodology might prove more cost-effective than having 10 to 15 people working disjointedly. She tactfully reminded management that far more human resources were often redeployed for attacking technical problems that developed later in the product development process: "3M can pour a hundred thousand dollars at the drop of a hat for a production problem late in the product development process, but it is not used to doing so for such an early stage." Finally, however, Shor obtained support from her senior management to assemble a product innovation team on the basis of creativity and enthusiasm from the Medical-Surgical Markets Division. In a few weeks she was able to assemble an impressive inter-disciplinary team.[5]

All team members were to commit half their time to the project. But as it turned out, several team members found that their managers still expected them to perform most of their traditional duties. As a result, much of the teamwork took place on Saturdays or outside the office at restaurants. The team sought in a disciplined manner to follow a project schedule with four stages prescribed by the lead user research methodology (see **Exhibit 4**).

Stage I: Project Planning

Stated goal in process manual: In this "homework" or scouting stage of the study, which typically lasted four to six weeks, teams identified the types of markets and new products of interest, and the desired level of innovation.

In September of 1996, as the first stage started, Sonnack and Churchill sat in on Shor's early lead user team meetings to focus the process. The two co-leaders probed the team with questions like, "What do you know about this market . . . what don't you know?" "How about reimbursement policies?" "How important is the skin itself as a source of infection?" The team met for four hours each week in a conference room lined with some 20 flip charts so that ideas could be jotted down quickly. Between meetings, team members would search the Internet, literature, and their people network for information on relevant topics. Through this process, the team built up an invaluable database of information. For instance, it learned that 30 percent of infections occurred from the patient's own skin—a figure that highlighted the need for good surgical drapes. Stage I took the team about six weeks.

---

[5] The Medical-Surgical Markets Division (MSMD) team included: Rita Shor, senior product specialist; Susan Hiestand, business manager with a marketing background; John Pournoor, research specialist and team co-leader; Matt Scholz, senior research specialist; Maurice Kuypers, market development supervisor; and Mark Johnson, process development specialist, Medical Products Resource Division.

Stage II: Trends/Needs Identification

Stated goal in process manual: The ultimate goal of this stage, which typically lasted five to six weeks, was to select a specific need-related trend(s) to focus upon for the remainder of the study. Typically a four-day team workshop kicked off this stage.

The 3M team started Stage II with a five-day workshop intended to make sense of all the information gathered in Stage I. Through the workshop, which marked the culmination of all weekly meetings thus far, the team developed the following parameters for a breakthrough product: It should conform to the body, prove more effective than current products, be easy to apply and remove.

The team, by now, had reached a stage where secondary literature could no longer add much of value. The second half of the workshop provided a turning point for the next phase of research: identifying appropriate expertise residing in experts at the leading edge of practice. The team undertook intensive group brainstorming about identifying appropriate experts to contact for more ideas and information from analogous areas of product development. Towards this end, workshop leaders encouraged participants to "step outside the box" because the most logical person might not prove the most appropriate expert. Through the rest of this stage, team members collected information from these identified experts.

Team members started talking over the telephone to a wide range of experts ranging from veterinary sciences to medics from the U.S. Mobile Army Surgical Hospital (MASH) unit in Bosnia. The MASH unit, discovered by team co-leader John Pournoor, had been considered a potential lead user because of its needs for portable, inexpensive, and flexible products. Product flexibility would ideally allow for low inventory; a prime consideration for a mobile medical unit. Hospitals, in contrast, could stock dozens of different product sizes and types. Interestingly, the MASH physicians did not fully realize their own need for manageable inventories since they focused on problems of communications, computerization, and telemedicine in the field; thus, they were not the lead users the team was looking for.

Although the MASH physicians would not be able to collaborate more intimately with the 3M Medical-Surgical Markets Division, this stage turned up other experts—from the theater make-up business to veterinary sciences to oceanographers—who would contribute to later stages. Stage II took the team about six weeks.

Stage III at 3M: Preliminary Concept Generation

Stated goal in process manual: In this stage, which typically lasted five to six weeks, lead user groups acquired a more precise understanding of market needs in the selected areas of focus. The teams began to generate preliminary concepts involving ideal attributes and features that would best meet customer needs.

By casting a wide net for product concepts, the division's business unit rapidly realized it knew precious little about the needs of customers outside the developed world. While sanitary conditions in the developed world had long since moved infectious disease down the roster of major killers (below causes such as cardiovascular disease and cancer), in the developing world infectious diseases were still major killers. If 3M hoped to find a breakthrough infection control product here, however, the team quickly realized it should visit several emerging market sites. The majority of new growth opportunities might lie here, even though disposable products were not popular or affordable.

Through December 1996 and January 1997, the team broke up into groups of two and traveled to hospitals in South America and Asia. Shor and Pournoor visited Malaysia, Korea, Indonesia and India. This was the first time the Medical-Surgical Markets Division had sent product developers, rather than marketers, to visit potential customers. It allowed the 3M team members to see how operating room personnel coped with infection challenges of extreme environments. According to Shor:

> While we saw some excellent, world-class hospitals in India, we also observed hospitals in which surgeons operated barefoot and even we visitors had to take off our shoes. For surgical field preparation, these teams used cloth (often with holes) that provided no resistance to fluids migrating to the wound itself! Sometimes, surgeons would use pieces of raincoat to cover over the patient's groin and other dirtier areas to keep microbes from migrating. Some surgeons used antibiotics wholesale, since these seemed cheaper to them than disposable drapes. . . . Often, only in side-conversations would surgeons reveal that surgical infection was a problem. We also quickly realized that many other nations did not care about labor-savings from our products. Labor was inexpensive and unlikely to be replaced or reduced. As a result, we realized we should not over-engineer our products for these markets.

The international fact-finding trips lengthened the expected duration of Stage III almost four-fold. While they yielded invaluable information about extreme environments and international market needs, they turned up no experts on lead use in terms of product efficacy.

With an eye toward bringing the project to a useful culmination, individual team members, under Sonnack's and Churchill's guidance, continued searching for appropriate lead users that might actually help develop product concepts. Team members continued talking with customers, academics, industry experts, as well as searching through refereed journals and the Internet. The team found no single lead user with the exact set of specifications that the proposed 3M breakthrough product or products would need. Instead, a variety of lead users were found with expertise about different relevant attributes.

Commenting on the often painstaking search for an appropriate expert, Pournoor felt, "It is like finding a partner for marriage." Some experts came from traditional backgrounds—for instance, an expert on infection control that consulted with the U.S. Center for Disease Control. Sometimes experts were found in the least likely places. During the premiere of the *Lion King* show in Minneapolis, for instance, a team member ended up chatting backstage with one of the make-up artists. As it turned out, the artist's husband, himself a make-up artist, had consulted with an orthopedic products firm. This make-up artist possessed specialized knowledge about the application of materials to the skin, which the team eventually felt would prove useful for developing breakthrough products. At the end, stage III took the team about six months—about four times as long as the process manual had recommended.

How to pool together the combined knowledge and talent of this diverse array of knowledge to develop product concepts would prove the challenge of the final project stage.

Stage IV at 3M: Final Concept Generation

Stated goal in process manual: In this stage, which typically lasts five to six weeks, lead user teams take preliminary concepts developed in Stage III toward completion and also seek to ensure that all possible solutions have been explored. This stage centers around a workshop with invited lead users.

In the summer of 1997, bad luck struck the team in the form of a change in senior management. Thus far, the team had kept upper management apprised of the team's progress because "that way, when you make recommendations and submit proposals, there are no surprises."[6] The new division manager, Sam Dunlop, was one of the rare managers to come with a traditional market research background. His vision was aligned with the old 3M strategy of incremental growth in high margin products. Dunlop had accepted the new post against his will, with the mandate to "stop the hemorrhage of profits and reconsolidate the division." He was close to retirement, and over the past few years none of the units he headed had thrived.

In an initial meeting with team leaders, Dunlop stated more than once, "We must not tax the current operating income!" Although he recognized the need for departing from traditional product development, the focus on finding "wild-eyed" lead users made him uncomfortable. His marketing training had stressed logic and quantifiable data, which could be collected and analyzed in a predictable, linear fashion. The lead user methodology, in contrast, collected qualitative data from people, with new questions leading to new concepts, which in turn started up a new cycle of questions that begged further answers. Where the process would ultimately lead was never known with full certainty at the project's start. As a temporary compromise, Dunlop reduced the lead user team by one member and made his opposition to the project quite clear.

Shor and her team had to sell the program starting from scratch, reminding the new managers about how inefficient the old ways of developing products had been. One tactic was to invite some of the business managers to join several team brainstorming sessions. This, according to Pournoor, "got them out of the box," and made them more receptive. Nonetheless, team members remained uncomfortably aware of the watchdogs of corporate profitability nipping at their ankles.

THE STAGE IV WORKSHOP: LEARNING FROM LEAD USERS

Even with the project's green light blinking anemically, the team finally decided to center the Stage IV workshop around the bold question, "Is there a revolutionary approach to infection control?" In deference to management's concern with the near-term bottom line, however, the team decided to focus specifically on product efficacy and cost. Rita Shor expressed the workshop goals to 11 3M personnel (see **Exhibit 5**) and 11 outside experts (see **Exhibit 6**) who had gathered on August 8 at a St. Paul hotel:

> By the end of the workshop, we want at least three product concepts that could dramatically improve microbial control in the surgical setting of today and tomorrow, with significant cost savings for surgeons in the United States and in the rest of the world. We seek breakthrough innovations that range from being so big as to render obsolete the current system, or, alternatively, so simple that they would use our existing technologies in new ways.

All assembled experts signed intellectual property rights to 3M, but received modest financial remuneration in the form of an honorarium. The workshop lasted two and a half days, a period, described by lead user team co-leader John Pournoor, a veteran of many product development focus groups, as "not too long and not too short." This length of time allowed for two to three iterations of concepts.

---

[6] "Teamwork with a Twist Helps 3M'ers Think Differently," *3M Stemwinder,* April 15, 1998.

In the introductory session, group members introduced themselves and discussed how their backgrounds might pertain to the task on hand. The group of experts, varying in age from 35 to 79, came from disciplines ranging from dermatology to make-up artistry to veterinarian sciences (see **Exhibit 6**). The workshop was divided into exercise sessions lasting several hours each. For each session, participants divided up into smaller groups of three to five individuals. Although groups constantly changed, "An element of competition among groups developed," according to Pournoor. "This reminded me of my old work at Boeing, where we'd have two different teams working in parallel on the same project."

Group members and facilitators faced at least four major challenges. The first arose from the lack of structure found in many corporate meetings. As a result, some groups tended to "flounder" during much of the exercise sessions. In a surprisingly large number of sessions, however, teams adhered to a strict schedule, which served to shepherd them toward solutions in the last few minutes.

A second challenge came from introverted and extroverted participants. Initially, for instance, the make-up artist, according to Pournoor, "felt intimidated by all the big words being thrown around, and I think he began to wonder what he was doing there. As time went on, however, his expertise and our needs converged. He contributed more and more." By contrast, the surgeon tended to squash all new ideas that arose early in the session. During a break, however, the veterinarian took him aside, saying, "Do you remember how during your training you were under someone's thumb? Well, that's what you're doing to us." After reflecting upon these words, the surgeon actually stayed up much of that night searching the Internet for new information, and thereafter went on to encourage other team members' contributions.

A third challenge came from finding ways to marry very creative ideas with technical feasibility. A rare nexus of lead user need and technological reality occurred following a period when the veterinarian stopped to reflect on his view of the ideal operating room:

> I—and probably most surgeons—want to focus on only one area on the operating table. I don't want to see anything except what I'm focused on, especially when I'm tired or under stress. With this in mind, could we create a material that we could quickly pull out of the wall or a box and place directly over the patient to create an infection barrier? Such a material should ideally draw the surgeon's attention to only the area being operated upon. This would prove valuable because time is of the essence, and surgery is a waltz that must be performed correctly every single time.

Subsequent brainstorming identified a preexisting material found in 3M's current line of products as possibly capable of bringing the veterinarian's needs to product reality. This exchange of ideas ended up forming the basis of one of the workshop's key product concept recommendations.

The fourth challenge lay in navigating a sea of facts. Here, an intricate interplay of questions and answers between experts from a diverse range of interrelated disciplines helped keep the entire product development process afloat. For example, one participant asked, "How do we make all these antimicrobial materials stick to the patient's body?" The make-up artist, heretofore in the background, pulled open his large binder of dozens of pre-fabricated/pre-made concoctions of skin-adhesive materials that 3M would have otherwise missed. By the end of the ensuing discussion, he ended up sketching a product concept for layering on materials onto surfaces with smooth contours that could be shown to the other participants.

In the course of several sessions, the invitees successfully rose to the challenges facing them and generated numerous product concepts. In the final session, the group met as a whole to rate and prioritize all concepts on the basis of commercial appeal and technical feasibility. Finally, team members agreed upon the next steps for refining the leading candidates (see **Exhibit 7**). The external experts ended up rating the workshops highly, from an A– to A+ largely because, in Shor's words, "They'd been in brainstorming sessions where everybody tossed out ideas, but this time, they got to turn the ideas into concrete concepts. . . ."[7] (See **Exhibit 8.**)

After the lead users and other invitees had left town, the product development team from the Medical-Surgical Markets Division met to decide upon its final recommendations to senior management. The team felt the following "metrics" should be used for ranking the product development concepts that had arisen from the recent workshop:

- Customer preference for the new products.
- Creation of new growth for the division, with the goal of double-digit annual growth. Creation of new businesses and industries that could change the basis of competition for the business unit.
- Boosted global presence of the division.
- Higher growth for the rest of 3M through, as much as possible, incorporation of proprietary 3M technology with patent protection.

The team ended up with three product recommendations that involved an "economy" line with a strong focus on cost, a "skin doctor" line, and an antimicrobial "armor" line (see **Exhibit 7**). The first two recommendations represented straightforward linear extensions of existing 3M product lines. The last, the team thought, represented a departure from past activities, and might thus open the door to new business opportunities. The team felt solidly confident in presenting these three recommendations to senior management, especially given the scope for synergy with 3M's existing activities and business unit strategy. For instance, all these proposed product lines could potentially boost sales from preexisting 3M products that helped reduce microbial contamination. As another example, the first proposal could also draw from a preexisting line of 3M drapes.

It was the fourth recommendation, however, that divided the team and formed the basis for a long, heated discussion among the team members.

THE FOURTH RECOMMENDATION: EVOLUTION OR REVOLUTION?

Over the past few months, the product development team had become increasingly aware of a gaping hole in medical knowledge involving infection containment. Discussions with lead users and associated experts indicated that the medical community still groped for ways to prevent infections and was easily swayed by any report that appeared credible. No health care company had yet stepped in to take leadership in the area of early intervention in the disease process. Thus a vacuum existed in which 3M could find a new growth area.

For the fourth recommendation, therefore, the product development team had begun thinking about re-writing the business unit's strategy statement to include *upstream containment*

---

[7] "Lead User Research Picks Up the Pace of 3M Innovation." *3M Stemwinder,* September 24, 1997.

of infections or, in other words, to keep infections from happening by precautionary up-stream measures. Entering the area of upstream containment, however, meant becoming adept at a new set of skills and knowledge. It meant, for example, being able to track early contamination and its possible consequences in a health care facility—not only detecting specific contaminants but also identifying and, depending on their risk-level, targeting individuals for interventions.

The new approach thus called for much more sophistication than the traditional industrial viewpoint, which held one patient just as deserving as the next of the latest surgical drape or the newest handwash. With the new approach, for instance, a malnourished patient might be targeted for nutritional interventions in addition to standard interventions, and diabetic patients might be identified for extra antibiotic coverage.

At 3M, such sophistication called for combining technologies from more than one core area or from areas in which 3M lacked depth. In particular, the product development team recognized the need to combine technologies from its Medical-Surgical division with diagnostics. But because the term "diagnostics" held a negative connotation at 3M—following the brief and unhappy acquisition of a small diagnostics company in the 1980s—the team diplomatically substituted the word "detection" in wording its recommendations.

The very need for diplomacy with phrasing of recommendations brought home the ramifications of a shift in direction. "While traditional product development team members at 3M face no immediate consequences for failures," according to Pournoor, the polymer chemist, "we were actually thinking about challenging the entire business strategy. We were crossing boundaries. . . . I think this resulted from using the lead user methodology, which, in addition to allowing us to gather and use information differently than before, also provided emotional support for change. Team members no longer felt like 'lone-rangers' as they might have under the traditional regime."

In the evening before the final recommendations were to be presented, the team met to resolve a deadlock over the fourth recommendation. Maurice Kuypers, the market development supervisor, sparked the debate by stating, "We don't want the lead user methodology to be viewed as a means for fomenting revolution. We already have three great product recommendations. If the team proceeds too quickly with the fourth recommendation, senior management may pull the plug on everything: the product recommendations as well as the lead user method itself."

Mark Johnson, the process development specialist, countered, "When I started with this method, I thought we were just going to develop new products. But now, talking with these lead user experts has shown me that what we were planning was not too effective anyway. We should seriously question our unit's business strategy."

Susan Hiestand, the business manager, chipped in: "Wasn't our mandate to find breakthroughs? We were warned that with the lead user method we will never be able to predict the final outcome or the path we will end up taking. Well, here we are with our breakthrough: It's not a product you can drop on your foot; it turns out to be a process or a service!"

"I think in the back of his mind," John Pournoor warned, "Dunlop would not mind seeing this process fail. Let's not give him any excuses for scrapping everything we've worked and sacrificed for, with our extra hours of hard work on this process. Let's focus on the first three recommendations, plant a few seeds about infection prevention, and draw the managers into making the intellectual leap themselves. Let them become the revolutionaries . . . or 'corporate visionaries.'"

Rita Shor looked at her watch. In less than an hour she would have to draw the discussion to a close and seek consensus. She recalled how in the final workshop, the sessions often floundered until very close to the end, when miraculously the group would arrive at consensus. But that—as invaluable to fostering creativity as it had proven—now seemed like playing a board game on a rainy day. Today's decisions would ripple through the very real world of business, with the future of a sizable business unit at stake.

EXHIBIT 1

Important Milestones

Source: Case interviews.

1902	Minnesota Mining and Manufacturing founded.
1948	3M Steri-Drape® Surgical Drape introduced.
1961	Medical Products Division, the first 3M division dedicated solely to health care, founded.
1993 May	Eric von Hippel at MIT contacts Mary Sonnack to see if 3M would help test lead user methodology. Sonnack would spend the entire next year to learn and help formalize the lead user methodology and initiate the involvement of psychologist Joan Churchill in the later part of the year.
1996 June	Rita Shor given task of finding breakthrough products for Medical-Surgical Markets Division. Shor approaches Mary Sonnack after hearing Sonnack lecture internally at 3M about lead user methodology.
September–October	Stage 1 of Medical-Surgical Markets Division lead user project starts. Shor's product development team meets with Mary Sonnack.
End of October	Stage 2 starts.
December	Stage 3 starts. The product development team decides to search internationally for breakthrough ideas on surgical draping.
1997 January–March	Medical-Surgical Markets Division team visits South America and Asia for breakthrough ideas on surgical draping.
April	Lead user meetings/workshops result in several concepts. Team starts search for appropriate lead users.
June–July	New management in Medical-Surgical Markets Division seeks justification for lead user process and wants accelerated outcome. The team convinces new management to maintain support. Stage 4 starts.
August	Large 2.5-day lead user workshop with 11 outside experts and 11 3M insiders.
October 27	Scheduled date for Medical-Surgical Markets Division team's presentation to management concerning recommendations generated from lead user process.
November	Medical-Surgical Markets Division management's deadline for resource allocation for product concepts generated from lead user process.

EXHIBIT 2
Selected 3M
Financial Data
(Dollars in
Millions,
Except Per-
Share Data)

Source:
3M Financial Reports.

	1995	1996	1997
Sales	**13,460**	**14,236**	**15,070**
Cost of goods sold	6,861	7,216	7,710
Gross profit	**6,599**	**7,020**	**7,360**
Selling, general, and administrative expenses	3,440	3,646	3,815
Depreciation, depletion, and amortization	859	883	870
Operating profit	**2,300**	**2,491**	**2,675**
Net income (after taxes)	**976**	**1,526**	**2,121**
Other data:			
EPS (primary)—excluding extra items and discontinued operations	3.11	3.63	5.14
Dividends per share	1.88	1.92	2.12
ROA (%)	9%	11%	16%
ROE (%)	19%	24%	36%
Market value	27,791	34,597	33,212
R&D expenses	883	947	

EXHIBIT 3
3M Revenue by
Classes of
Products/
Services
(Dollars in
Millions)

Source:
R. P. Curran,
"Minnesota Mining &
Manufacturing Co.—
Company Report,"
*Merrill Lynch Capital
Markets*, New York,
July 11, 1997.

	1995	1996	1997E	1998E
Tape products	$2,042	$2,096	$2,215	$2,370
Abrasive products	1,220	1,270	1,375	1,510
Automotive and chemical products	1,328	1,460	1,620	1,800
Connecting and insulating products	1,470	1,564	1,688	1,850
Consumer and office products	2,272	2,460	2,672	2,925
Health care products	2,221	2,356	2,545	2,775
Safety and personal care products	1,220	1,301	1,385	1,505
All other products	1,687	1,729	1,835	1,980
Total	**$13,460**	**$14,236**	**$15,335**	**$16,715**

EXHIBIT 4 Description of Lead User Research Methodology

The lead user method provides a means to unearth product development opportunities that are not immediately obvious by traditional methods. It allows for accurately forecasting market opportunities by tapping the expertise and experience base of "lead users," the individuals or firms that experience needs *ahead* of the market segment in which they operate. Lead users may lead in either the *target* or *analogous* markets. Some lead users may be involved with just one or more of the important *attributes* of the problems faced by users in the target market.

Ideally, lead user methods allow new product development to flow out of a sensitive understanding of product features that matter most to customers several years later. Specific benefits of lead user methods include: richer and more reliable information on the needs of emerging customer needs; better products and service concepts since these come out of better data on quality needs; and acceleration of the product and service development process.

These benefits, however, come only after substantial commitment of resources on the part of the sponsoring firm. Research indicates that three elements remain necessary for success in the lead user process: *supportive management,* use of a *cross-disciplinary team of highly skilled people,* and a clear *understanding of the principles of lead user research*.

Success of the study relies heavily on selecting a talented core team. Typically, the team consists of four to six people from marketing and technical departments, with one member serving as project leader. These team members typically spend 12 to 15 hours per week for the entire project on a lead user project. This high level of immersion fosters creative thought and sustains project momentum.

Lead user projects typically take five or six months, in which time the four to six people involved spend up to a third of their time on the project. In conducting a lead user study, four stages are involved, as described below, with typical time commitments provided in parentheses:

- *Stage I: Project Planning (up to four to six weeks)*. In this "homework" or scouting phase of the study, the team identifies the types of markets and new products of interest, and the desired level of innovation. For instance, does the company seek a "breakthrough" product or does it wish to merely extend current product or service lines? At the same time, the team identifies key business constraints. The team typically starts Stage I by informally interviewing industry experts, including customers, suppliers, and internal company managers, to get a feel for current trends and market needs. This lays the groundwork for developing strategies for future data collection and for helping focus on key market trends.

- *Stage II: Trends/Needs Identification (up to five to six weeks)*. The ultimate goal of this stage is to select a specific need-related trend(s) to focus upon for the remainder of the study. Typically a four-day team workshop kicks off this stage. In this workshop, members digest the information collected during Stage I to get a sense of the "conventional wisdom" relating to trends and market needs. Thereafter, the focus shifts to finding top experts, through querying experts, telephone "networking," scanning literature, and consulting with in-house colleagues. Thereafter, telephone interviews can start. Three or four weeks into Stage II, the team generally develops a good understanding of major trends and is now positioned for the vital task of "framing" the customer need that can be addressed by a new product or service. These initial ideas are reworked and refined throughout this stage.

- *Stage III: Preliminary Concept Generation (up to five to six weeks)*. In this stage, the group acquires a more precise understanding of the needs it has selected as the area of focus. The team begins to generate preliminary concepts involving ideal attributes and features that will best meet customer needs. The team also seeks to informally assess business potential for the product or service being conceptualized. The team continues interviewing lead user experts for technical knowledge that pertains to concept generation. Toward the end of Stage III, the team meets with key managers involved with implementing concepts after completion of the entire project to confirm that identified needs and initial concepts fit well with important business interests.

- *Stage IV: Final Concept Generation (up to five to six weeks)*. In this stage, the team takes the preliminary concept developed in Stage III toward completion. Participants in this stage seek to ensure that all possible solutions have been explored. Activity in Stage IV centers around a one- to two-day lead user workshop with invited lead users to improve and add to the preliminary concepts. Typically, 15 to 18 people attend this workshop, of which a third may come from the project team and from in-house technical or marketing divisions. In these workshops, subgroups comprised of in-house personnel as well as invited experts discuss independent parts of the problem to generate alternative product concepts. Thereafter, the entire group evaluates the concepts in terms of technical feasibility, market appeal, and management priorities. Finally, the entire group arrives at consensus on the most commercially promising concepts and develops recommendations for further steps to refine them.

EXHIBIT 4 (*continued*)

After the workshop, the team refines the preliminary concept on the basis of knowledge gained from the workshop. At a meeting with managers, the team presents the proposed products or services, covering design principles. The team comes prepared with solid evidence about why customers would be willing to pay for them. For any concept chosen for commercialization, at least one member of the lead user team should remain involved in further steps needed to take the concept to market. This helps fully leverage the vast body of knowledge captured through the lead user method.

While lead user methodology stresses qualitative probing of the right questions over the traditional focus on quantifiable questions, ongoing studies seek to compare performance of the new method with traditional methods.

Source: E. von Hippel, J. Churchill, M. Sonnack, *Breakthrough Products and Services with Lead User Research* (Cambridge, Mass. and Minneapolis, Minn.: Lead User Concepts, Inc., 1998, forthcoming Oxford University Press). For a detailed discussion and description of lead user research, see also S. Thomke and A. Nimgade, *Note on Lead User Research* (Harvard Business School Case No. 699–014).

EXHIBIT 5
3M Staff Participating in the Stage IV Workshop

Source: 3M.

Lead User Team Members:

- Rita Shor, Senior Product Specialist, Medical-Surgical Markets Division (MSMD) and lead user team co-leader
- Susan Hiestand, Business Manager, MSMD
- John Pournoor, Ph.D., Research Specialist, MSMD, and lead user team co-leader
- Matt Scholz, Senior Research Specialist, MSMD
- Maurice Kuypers, Market Development Supervisor, MSMD
- Mark Johnson, Process Development Specialist, MSMD

Lead User Team Consultants

- Joan Churchill, Ph.D., Clinical Psychologist
- Mary Sonnack, Division Scientist and Internal 3M Consultant

Other 3M Staff Members Involved

- *Microbiologist:* Joanne Bartkus, Ph.D., Clinical Studies
- *Business Development Manager:* German Chamorro, 3M Latin America
- *Synthetic Chemist:* John Dell, Ph.D., Senior Research Specialist
- *Organic Chemist:* Roger Olsen, R&D Manager
- *Marketing Manager:* Nicola Stevens
- *Product Designer:* Joy Packard

EXHIBIT 6
Outside
Experts
Participating
in the Stage IV
Workshop

Source: 3M.

Expertise on Advanced Methods for Understanding Bacteria

- *General surgeon and chemist (M.D., Ph.D.),* possessed considerable experience in minimally invasive surgery with very ill patients as well as epidemiological expertise. *Area of innovation:* understanding surgical contamination.
- *Dermatologist/surgeon (M.D.),* had worked on laser excision of skin cancer and possessed expertise on skin infection. *Area of innovation:* surgical wound healing.

Expertise on Methods for "Fast Track" to Market

- *Antimicrobial pharmacologist (Ph.D.),* had chaired the Food and Drug Administration's Antimicrobial Committee for pharmaceutical drugs and had worked with skin care and pharmaceutical products for 30 years. He had worked on a similar product focus group that had led "tortuously" to the anti-cold medication Nyquil. *Area of innovation:* antimicrobial agents.

Expertise on Advanced Agents to Kill Bacteria

- *Disease control expert (M.S.),* a water-purifying expert who had worked for the Centers for Disease Control (appearing here as a private consultant) and had a background in epidemiology and hospital staff-mediated infections. *Area of innovation:* expertise in controlling infections in wet environments as evinced by getting a flood-stricken hospital back in operation with antiseptic systems working within six days.
- *Antimicrobial chemist (Ph.D.),* with training in synthetic organic chemistry, held over 50 patents in better delivery of antiseptic solutions and had also researched synthetic materials used to make artificial skin. *Area of innovation:* delivery of antiseptic solutions.
- *Biologist (Ph.D.),* had started out researching meat industry infection but ended up appreciating the need for preventive medicine through "looking upstream" for the earlier sources of infection involving livestock. *Area of innovation:* study of the relationship between different microorganisms; development of light and reduced fat cheese.
- *Biochemical engineer (Ph.D.),* a university professor who worked in the areas of tissue engineering and sterilization. *Area of innovation:* tissue engineering and sterilization.

Expertise on Ease of Application to Skin

- *Broadway make-up artist,* had served as a consultant to an orthopedic products firm. *Area of innovation:* application of materials and cosmetics to the skin.
- *Veterinarian surgeon (D.V.M.),* explained his presence on the panel in terms of the extreme challenges infection control in animals poses since, in his words, animals "have hair, do not bathe, and carry no insurance!" Veterinarian input, thus, could help address an extreme end of the spectrum of human infection that was traditionally neglected. *Area of innovation:* surgical techniques and implant design, for which he had won the 1996 veterinarian "Practitioner of the Year" award.
- *"Creative health practitioner" (M.D.),* a psychiatrist with a B.S. in microbiology, also had a background in the assessment of performance of paint products. *Area of innovation:* assessment of chemical applications on hard surfaces.
- *Polymer chemist,* who had also studied acupuncture, in addition to polymers. *Area of innovation:* study of acupuncture, polymers, and rheology (the study of the flow of matter).

EXHIBIT 7
Excerpt from Memo on Product Recommendations

Source: 3M.

The abbreviated descriptions below are the lead user team's recommendations for three product lines for the Medical-Surgical Markets Division (MSMD). (Note that these are the leading contenders from the six concepts that came out of the final product development workshop.)

The "Economy" line. The MSMD should consider a line of surgical drapes using a combination of low-cost materials. Preexisting 3M adhesives and fastening devices may provide a variety of ways for sticking the materials to the body. A one-size-fits-all strategy and timesaving dispensing systems will boost product acceptance in the current cost-containment environment as well as in developing countries. (Impetus for this product line, in fact, came out of the divisional fact-finding trips to the developing world.) Following the veterinarian lead user's advice, these materials should allow focus on only the part of the body being operated upon. Being based on preexisting 3M technologies, this represents an incremental proposal.

The "Skin Doctor" line (See Exhibit 8). The MSMD should consider a line of hand-held devices resembling hand-held vacuums for antimicrobial protection. These devices would layer antimicrobial substances onto surfaces being operated upon. An advanced generation of the Skin Doctor could potentially operate in two modes: a vacuum mode, which could mop up surface liquids, in addition to the original layering mode. Impetus for this came from the lead user workshop. Being based on preexisting 3M technologies, this also represents an incremental proposal.

Antimicrobial "armor" line. Currently, 3M focuses on only surface infections and thus ignores other infection control markets that included blood borne, urinary tract, and respiratory infections. An armor product line would use 3M technologies to "armor" catheters and tubes from unwelcome microscopic visitors. This line would represent a breakthrough product because it is consistent with the current business strategy of reactive infection control but would provide the company entry into a new $2 billion market.

EXHIBIT 8
Drawing of the "Skin Doctor" Product Concept Generated During the Lead User Workshop

Source: 3M.

Article

Creating Breakthroughs at 3M

When senior managers think of product development, they all dream of the same thing: a steady stream of breakthrough products—the kind that will enable their companies to grow rapidly and maintain high margins. And managers set ambitious goals to that end, demanding, for example, that a high percentage of sales come from products that did not exist a few years ago. Unfortunately, the development groups at many companies don't deliver the goods. Instead of breakthroughs, they produce mainly line extensions and incremental improvements to existing products and services. And as the pace of change accelerates in today's markets, that's a recipe for decline, not growth.

Given the imperative to grow, why can't product developers come up with breakthroughs more regularly? They fail primarily for two reasons. First, companies face strong incentives to focus on the short term. Put simply, although new products and services may be essential for future growth and profit, companies must first survive today to be around tomorrow. That necessity tends to focus companies strongly on making incremental improvements to keep sales up and current customers—as well as Wall Street analysts—happy. Second, developers simply don't know *how* to achieve breakthroughs, because there is usually no effective system in place to guide them and support their efforts.

The latter is a problem even for a company like 3M, long known for its successful innovations. Traditionally, the company's management has fostered innovation by taking a get-out-of-the-way attitude toward product developers who, in turn, have worked according to the aphorism "It's better to seek forgiveness than to ask for permission." This relationship between managers and developers has resulted in the creation of a long line of profitable products, from waterproof sandpaper and Scotch tape in the 1920s to Post-it Notes and Thinsulate in the 1970s.

Reprinted by permission of *Harvard Business Review*. From "Creating Breakthroughs at 3M Corporation" by Eric von Hippel, Stefan Thomke, and Mary Sonnack, September–October 1999. Copyright © 1999 by the Harvard Business School Publishing Corporation: all rights reserved.

Eric von Hippel is a professor at the Massachusetts Institute of Technology's Sloan School of Management in Cambridge. Stefan Thomke is a professor at Harvard Business School in Boston. Mary Sonnack is a division scientist at 3M in St. Paul, Minnesota.

But by the mid-1990s, 3M's top managers were concerned that too much of the company's growth was coming from changes to existing products. Breakthroughs were fewer and farther between. The demands for—and the rewards from—incremental improvements spurred the company to focus on current products. To counter this trend, management set a bold objective: 30 percent of sales would come from products that had not existed four years earlier.

For the company to meet that goal, many people at 3M—senior managers, marketers, product developers, scientists—would have to change their approach to their work. Accordingly, some employees started becoming acquainted with a new method for developing breakthrough products: the *lead user process*. The process—which makes the generation of breakthrough strategies, products, and services systematic—is based on two major findings by innovation researchers.

First, the researchers found that many commercially important products are initially thought of and even prototyped by users rather than manufacturers. (See **Exhibit 1** "Users as Innovators.") Second, they discovered that such products tend to be developed by "lead users"—companies, organizations, or individuals that are well ahead of market trends and have needs that go far beyond those of the average user. Those discoveries transformed the difficult job of creating breakthroughs from scratch into a systematic task of identifying lead users—companies or people that have already developed elements of commercially attractive breakthroughs—and learning from them.

Consider how an automobile manufacturer would apply the lead user process. If the company wanted to design an innovative braking system, it might start by trying to find out if any innovations had been developed by groups with a strong need for better brakes, such as auto racing teams. The automaker wouldn't stop there, however. Next it would look to a related but technologically advanced field where people had an even greater need to stop quickly, such as aerospace. And, in fact, aerospace is where innovations such as antilock braking systems were first developed: military aircraft commands have a very high incentive to design ways to stop their very expensive vehicles before they run out of runway.

In September 1996, a product development team in 3M's Medical-Surgical Markets Division became one of the first groups in the company to test the merits of the lead user process. The team was charged with creating a breakthrough in the area of surgical drapes—the material that prevents infections from spreading during surgery. By November 1997, the team had come up with a proposal for three major new product lines as well as a new strategy that would take a revolutionary approach to treating infection. And the team may have done even more for 3M's long-term health: it persuaded senior managers that the lead user process could indeed systematize the company's development of breakthroughs.

But before we turn to that story, we must first explain how this process is different from other methods of product development.

LEARNING FROM LEAD USERS

All processes designed to generate ideas for products begin with information collected from users. What separates companies is the kind of information they collect and from whom they collect it.

Teams are usually taught to collect information from users at the center of their target market. They conduct focus groups and analyze sales data, reports from the field, customer complaints and requests, and so on. Then they rely on their own creative powers to brainstorm their way to new ideas. Teams that follow this method assume that the role of users is to provide information about what they need, and that the job of in-house developers is to use that information to create new product ideas.

The lead user process takes a fundamentally different approach. It was designed to collect information about both needs and solutions from the leading edges of a company's target market and from markets that face similar problems in a more extreme form. Development teams assume that savvy users outside the company have already generated innovations; their job is to track down especially promising lead users and adapt their ideas to the business's needs.

True lead users are rare. To track them down most efficiently, project teams use telephone interviews to network their way into contact with experts on the leading edge of the target market. Networking is effective because people with a serious interest in any topic tend to know of others who know even more about the topic than they do—people who are further up on the "pyramid of expertise."

Team members begin by briefly explaining their problem to individuals who have apparent expertise on the subject—for example, research professionals in a field, or people who have written about the topic. They then ask for a referral to someone who has even more relevant knowledge. It's usually not long before a team reaches lead users at the front of the target market. The next step is to continue networking until lead users are found in markets and fields that face similar problems but in different and often more extreme forms. Those people can help teams discover truly novel solutions to important needs that are emerging in the target market.

Consider how a team focused on medical imaging carried out its work. Its members knew that a major trend in this field was the development of capabilities to detect smaller and smaller features—very early-stage tumors, for instance. The team networked to the leading edge of the target market and identified a few radiologists who were working on the most challenging medical-imaging problems. They discovered that some lead users among those researchers had developed imaging innovations that were ahead of commercially available products.

Team members then asked the radiologists for the names of people in any field who were even further ahead in *any* important aspect of imaging. The radiologists identified, among others, specialists in pattern recognition and people working on images that show the fine detail in semiconductor chips.

Lead users in the area of pattern recognition proved especially valuable to the team. Specialists in the military had long worked on computerized pattern recognition methods because military reconnaissance experts had a strong need to answer questions such as, "Is that a rock lying under that tree, or is it the tip of a ballistic missile?" These lead users had developed ways to enhance the resolution of the best images they could get by adapting pattern recognition software.

Lead users often help project teams improve their understanding of the nature of the breakthrough they are seeking. For example, the medical-imaging team's initial goal was to develop new ways to create better high-resolution images. But their discovery of the military specialists' use of pattern recognition led them to a new goal: to find enhanced methods for recognizing medically significant patterns in images, whether by better image resolution or by other means. (See **Exhibit 2** "Networking to Lead Users.")

It is rare for a manufacturer to simply adopt a lead user innovation "as is." Instead, a new product concept that suits a manufacturer's needs and market is most often based on information gained from a number of lead users and in-house developers. Some information is transferred in the course of telephone interviews or through on-site visits. More information is transferred when the team hosts a workshop that includes several lead users who have a range of expertise, as well as a number of people from within the company—product developers, marketing specialists, and manufacturing people.

A lead user workshop typically lasts two or three days. During that time, the assembled group combines its individual insights and experiences to design product concepts that precisely fit the sponsoring company's needs. In the medical-imaging example, lead users with a variety of experiences were brought together: people on the leading edge of medical imaging, people who were ahead of the trend with ultra-high-resolution images, and experts on pattern recognition. Together they created a solution that best suited the needs of the medical-imaging market and represented a breakthrough for the company. Executives at 3M charted a similar course.

DIVING IN THE DEEP END

In 1996 Rita Shor, a senior product specialist in 3M's Medical-Surgical Markets Division, heard an in-house lecture on the lead user process. Shor had been charged with developing a breakthrough product for the division's surgical drapes unit, and she needed help. Traditional market research was providing abundant data but could not point developers toward a breakthrough.

Shor called Mary Sonnack at 3M. Sonnack—sponsored by Chuck Harstad, 3M's vice president of corporate marketing, and William Coyne, senior vice president of R&D—had spent the 1994–1995 academic year studying the lead user process with Eric von Hippel at MIT. Shor put the problem to Sonnack in stark terms: "Our business unit has been going nowhere. We're number one in the surgical drapes market, but we're stagnating. We need to identify new customer needs. If we don't bring in radically new ways of looking for products, management may have little choice but to sell off the business." After warning Shor about the high level of commitment that would be needed from team members and from senior management, Sonnack agreed to work with her.

Surgical drapes are thin adhesive-backed plastic films that are adhered to a patient's skin at the site of surgical incision, prior to surgery. Surgeons cut directly through these films during an operation. Drapes isolate the area being operated on from most potential sources of infection—the rest of the patient's body, the operating table, and the members of the surgical team. But the diversity of the microbial world constantly challenged this protective fortress, which couldn't cover, for example, catheters or tubes being inserted into the patient.

By the mid-1990s, surgical drapes were bringing 3M's Medical-Surgical Markets Division more than $100 million in annual sales. But the unit in charge of the draping business had not had a breakthrough product in almost a decade. Technological excellence was not

Step by Step Through the Process

The lead user process gets under way when a cross-disciplinary team is formed. Teams typically are composed of four to six people from marketing and technical departments; one member serves as project leader. Team members usually will spend 12 to 15 hours per week on the project for its duration. That high level of immersion fosters creative thought and sustains the project's momentum.

Lead user projects proceed through four phases. The length of each phase can vary quite a bit; the 3M team spent six months alone on phase 3, when it researched surgical conditions in developing countries through on-site visits. For planning purposes, a team should figure on four to six weeks for each phase and four to six months for the entire project.

Phase 1: Laying the foundation During this initial period, the team identifies the markets it wants to target and the type and level of innovations desired by key stakeholders within the company. If the team's ultimate recommendations are to be credibly received, these stakeholders must be on board early.

Phase 2: Determining the trends It's an axiom of the process that lead users are ahead of the trend. But what is the trend? To find out, the team must talk to experts in the field they are exploring—people who have a broad view of emerging technologies and leading-edge applications in the area being studied.

Phase 3: Identifying lead users The team now begins a networking process to identify and learn from users at the leading edge of the target market and related markets. The group's members gather information that will help them identify especially promising innovations and ideas that might contribute to the development of breakthrough products. Based on what they learn, teams also begin to shape preliminary product ideas and to assess the business potential of these concepts and how they fit with company interests.

Phase 4: Developing the breakthroughs The goal is to move the preliminary concepts toward completion. The team begins this phase by hosting a workshop with several lead users, a half-dozen in-house marketing and technical people, and the lead user team itself. Such workshops may last two or three days. During that time, the participants first work in small groups and then as a whole to design final concepts that precisely fit the company's needs.

After the workshop, the project team further hones the concepts, determines whether they fit the needs of target-market users, and eventually presents its recommendations to senior managers. By that point, its proposals will be supported by solid evidence that explains why customers would be willing to pay for the new products. Although the project team may now disband, at least one member should stay involved with any concepts that are chosen for commercialization. In that way, the rich body of knowledge that was collected during the process remains useful as the product or service families are developed and marketed.

the issue. In the early 1990s, the division had spent three years developing technologically advanced disposable surgical gowns. The gowns would safeguard surgeons and their patients from dangerous viruses such as HIV—and keep them more comfortable—by allowing water vapor but not viruses to pass through microscopic pinholes in the fabric. This technological and manufacturing feat, however, came to the market just as managed health care was taking hold in the United States. Surgeons loved the fabric, but insurers wouldn't pay for it, and sales were disappointing.

In short, the division saw little room for growth in existing markets; declining margins on existing products; and, because of the drapes' cost, few opportunities to penetrate less-developed countries. Under those circumstances, Shor convinced senior management to try the lead user process. A few weeks later, she and her project coleader, Susan Hiestand, had assembled a team of six people from the R&D, marketing, and manufacturing departments. They all agreed to commit half their time to the project until it was completed.

Lead user innovations generate some kind of competitive advantage. When this advantage is significant, innovating users won't want to share what they know with competing companies or with manufacturers that would sell their ideas to competitors. Yet, most lead users are quite willing to give detailed information to manufacturers, and are usually willing to do so for free. There are two basic reasons:

First, lead users with compelling information often are in other fields and industries and would feel no competitive effects from revealing what they've done. Those lead users are generally happy to share their knowledge.

Second, lead users develop innovations because they need to—not as a source of competitive advantage. In those cases, they may want to transfer their ideas to a willing supplier.

For example, in a lead user study devoted to improving credit-reporting services, a team found that at least two major users of such services had developed advanced, online credit-reporting processes. One of the users regarded the service it had developed as a significant source of competitive advantage and refused to discuss any details with the team. The other, however, welcomed the team with open arms and fully revealed its system. As one manager said, "We only developed this in the first place because we desperately needed it—we would be happy if you developed a similar service we could buy."

It is always good practice for lead-user project teams to tell interviewees up front that their company may have a commercial interest in the ideas being discussed. When someone hesitates to talk about his or her ideas, the interview comes to an end. That frees up team members to move on to find other lead users who don't have such concerns.

LOOKING FOR LEAD USERS

The team's initial goal was, in essence, "Find a better type of disposable surgical draping." That was admittedly not a very creative first directive, but the way the problem is framed at the outset is not critical to the project's success. Experts and lead users are never shy about suggesting better ideas, and the evolutionary improvement of goals is an expected and desirable part of the lead user process.

The group spent the first month and a half of the project learning more about the cause and prevention of infections by researching the literature and by interviewing experts in the field. The group then held a workshop with management in which they discussed all that they had learned and set parameters for acceptable types of breakthrough products. (This work constituted the first phase of the lead user process; see the sidebar on the previous page, "Step by Step Through the Process.")

For the next six weeks or so, team members focused on getting a better understanding of important trends in infection control. One cannot specify what the leading edge of a target market might be without first understanding the major trends in the heart of that market.

Much of the team's research at this early stage was directed at understanding what doctors in developed countries might need. But as the group's members asked more and more questions and talked to more and more experts, they realized they didn't know enough about the needs of surgeons and hospitals in developing countries, where infectious diseases are still major killers. The team broke up into pairs and traveled to hospitals in

Malaysia, Indonesia, Korea, and India. They learned how people in less than ideal environments attempt to keep infections from spreading in the operating room. They especially noted how some surgeons combat infection by using cheap antibiotics as a substitute for disposable drapes and other, more expensive measures.

As a result of their field observations, the team concluded that a crisis was germinating in the surgical wards of developing countries. Doctors' reliance on cheap antibiotics to prevent the spread of infection would not work in the long run—bacteria would become resistant to the drugs. The team also realized that even if 3M could radically cut the cost of surgical drapes, most hospitals in developing countries simply would not be able to afford them. Those insights led the team to redefine its goal: find a much cheaper and much more effective way to prevent infections from starting or spreading that does not depend on antibiotics—or even on surgical drapes.

The team members then networked their way into contact with innovators at the leading edge of the trend toward much cheaper, more effective infection control. As is usually the case, some of the most valuable lead users turned up in surprising places. For example, the team learned that specialists at some leading veterinary hospitals were able to keep infection rates very low despite facing difficult conditions and cost constraints. As one of the country's foremost veterinary surgeons explained to them, "Our patients are covered with hair, they don't bathe, and they don't have medical insurance, so the infection controls that we use can't cost much." Another surprising source of ideas was Hollywood. One of the team members learned that makeup artists are experts in applying to the skin materials that don't irritate and that are easy to remove when no longer needed. Those attributes are very important to the design of infection control materials that will be applied to the skin.

As a final step in the project, the team invited several lead users to a two-and-a-half-day workshop. (As the sidebar "Why Lead Users Will Talk to Your Company" makes clear, the lead users' reward for participating was purely intellectual; they all signed over to 3M any property rights that might result from the workshop.) The bold central question, which had come out of the team's research, was now this: "Can we find a revolutionary, low-cost approach to infection control?" The participants met for several hours at a time in small groups; the composition of the groups was then changed and the process continued. Some groups floundered for a while before pulling ideas together toward the end of their sessions. In others, extroverted people at first dominated the discussion; later, the introverts warmed up and began contributing. All the groups faced the challenge of navigating a sea of facts and trying to unite creative ideas with technical constraints.

In the end, the workshop generated concepts for six new product lines and a radical new general approach to infection control. The lead user team chose the three strongest product-line concepts to present to senior management. The first recommendation was for an economy line of surgical drapes. The drapes could be made with existing 3M technology and thus would not constitute a breakthrough product; nevertheless, they would be welcomed in the increasingly cost-conscious developed world.

The second recommendation was for a "skin doctor" line of handheld devices. These devices would eventually be able to do two things: layer antimicrobial substances onto a patient's skin during an operation and vacuum up blood and other liquids during surgery. The skin doctor line could be developed from existing 3M technology and would offer surgeons an important new infection prevention tool.

The third new product proposal was for an "armor" line that would coat catheters and tubes with antimicrobial protection. These products could also be created with existing 3M technology, and they promised to open up major new market opportunities for 3M. The company had previously focused solely on products designed to prevent surface infections; the armor line would allow it to enter the $2 billion market aimed at controlling blood-borne, urinary tract, and respiratory infections.

CHANGING STRATEGY

As a project team learns from lead users, the questions and answers it develops often point toward the need for strategic change. Indeed, that's what happened at 3M. Besides unearthing concepts for new product lines, the team had identified a revolutionary approach to infection control—but developing the competences, products, and services that would bring that approach to market would require the division to change its strategy.

Until this point, the division had focused on products that were, in a sense, one size fits all. Every patient, regardless of the circumstances that brought him or her there, would get the same degree of infection prevention from the same basic drapes.

In the course of their research, the team members learned that some people entered the hospital with a greater risk of contracting infection—because they suffered from malnutrition, for example, or because they were diabetic. Doctors thus wanted a way of treating individual patients according to their needs through "upstream" containment of infections. In other words, they wanted to treat people before surgery in order to reduce their likelihood of contracting disease during an operation.

Should 3M move in that direction? The members of the project team debated the wisdom of proposing a strategic change to senior managers. According to one team member, "In thinking about challenging the entire business strategy, we were crossing boundaries. I think the lead user methodology had pushed us in that direction. It allowed us to gather and use information in a different way than we had before, and it also provided emotional support for change. Based on extensive research, we were suggesting a major change—but as a team. We didn't feel like lone rangers."

But not everyone on the team wanted to make this last recommendation. One member feared that senior management might reject all the team's proposals if they made such a recommendation. In the end, the team decided to make the case for strategic change and successfully persuaded senior management to go along with it. As a result, implementation of the new strategy is well under way. 3M has established a "discovery center" service to develop and diffuse the new approach to infection control. And the product lines needed to deploy it are being developed. Details about the most revolutionary product lines are proprietary, and we can't reveal them here. But senior management believes the new strategy will produce very positive and far-reaching bottom-line results for the Medical-Surgical Markets group.

OPENING NEW AVENUES

3M has now successfully tested the lead user method in eight of its 55 divisions. Support among divisional managers who have tested the method has been strong. For example, Roger Lacey, head of the company's Telecom Systems Division and an innovative experimenter

Innovative product users often far outnumber an individual company's product developers. For instance, many people believe that user-developed software products, such as Apache's Web server software, are better than commercially developed products. That's less surprising when you consider that more than a half million Web sites use Apache software and that thousands of users participate in developing and supporting it. That is many times the number of people a commercial software developer like Microsoft can afford to dedicate to server software development and support.

And consider video game development. Sony recently set up a Web site to support hackers who are interested in exploring and developing new types of games that could be played on the Sony PlayStation. It quickly attracted 10,000 participants, a number that vastly exceeds the number of in-house and contract developers creating games for the PlayStation. It's likely that, taken individually, in-house developers are technically more skilled than most user-developers. But the user-developer community mobilized by Sony is diverse in its skills and interests. In a recent *New York Times* interview, Phil Harrison, Sony's vice president of third-party R&D, said he thinks several of them will come up with "some radically new forms of creativity that will break the conventions holding back the business today."

with the lead user process, says "the method brings cross-functional teams into close working relationships with leading-edge customers and other sources of expertise." Support among project teams also is strong. Developers at 3M regard lead user projects as creative, challenging work and will often adopt a project role on an informal basis before being officially assigned to a team.

William Coyne, 3M's senior vice president of R&D, believes the lead user process is the systematic approach to generating breakthroughs that had been missing at 3M. "Corporate management is very enthusiastic about the process, and the line of 3M people interested in learning the method from Mary Sonnack's group [3M's Lead User Process Center of Excellence] extends out her office door and around the block."

Does the lead user process always guarantee success? Of course not; nothing can. Things like inadequate corporate support and inadequately skilled teams can derail even the most promising project. Nor will the lead user process crowd out projects and processes aimed at developing incremental improvements. Obviously, incremental approaches still have major value. But by giving companies a systematic way of finding the people and organizations on the cutting edge—those who are so impatient and so much in need of the next big thing, they are willing to make it for themselves—the lead user method opens up new avenues. It takes teams and companies in directions they wouldn't have imagined during the day-to-day crush of business.

EXHIBIT 1

Users as Innovators

Research shows that many commercially important innovations are developed by product users rather than by the manufacturers that were first to bring them to market.

mfg | user
other

Computer Industry[a]

Systems reaching new performance high — 25% / 75%

Systems with radical structural innovations — 33% / 67%

Chemical Industry[b]

Chemical processes and process equipment — 30% / 70%

Pultrusion Machinery[c]

Major pultrusion-processing machinery innovations — 15% / 85%

Scientific Instruments[d]

First of type — 100%

Major functional improvements — 18% / 82%

Minor functional improvements — 30% / 70%

Semiconductor/Electronic Process Equipment[e]

First of type used commercially — 100%

Major functional improvements — 16%[1] / 21% / 63%

Minor functional improvements — 12%[2] / 29% / 59%

Electronic Assembly[b]

Wirestripping and connector attachment equipment — 11% / 33% / 56%[3]

Surface Chemistry Instruments[g]

New functional capability — 18% / 82%

Convenience or reliability improvement — 13% / 87%

Sensitivity or accuracy improvement — 48% / 52%

[a] Knight (1963)
[b] Freeman (1968)
[c] Lionetta (1977)
[d] Von Hippel (1976)
[e] Von Hippel (1977)
[f] Vander Werf (1982)
[g] Riggs and Von Hippel (1994)

[1] Developed by independent inventors and invention development companies.
[2] Developed by joint user-manufacturer innovation projects.
[3] Developed by connector suppliers.

EXHIBIT 2
Networking to
Lead Users

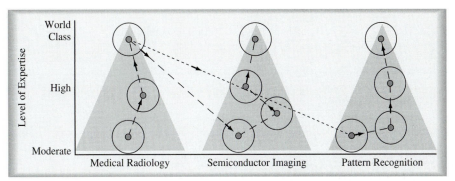

Project teams network their way up "pyramids of expertise" to identify lead users and experts, first in the target market and then in other key fields. The medical imaging team began by finding expert medical radiologists, who referred them to specialists in semiconductor imaging and pattern recognition. As a result of discussions with these lead users, the team's goal changed dramatically.

EXHIBIT 3
The Lead User
Curve

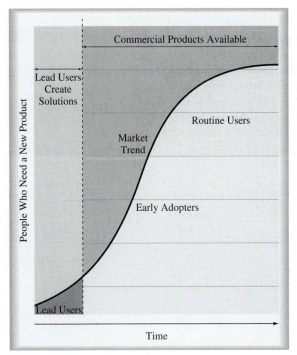

The curve illustrates the shape of a market trend. Lead users have needs that are well ahead of the trend; over time, more and more people feel the same need.

Note

Understanding User Needs

It is hard to imagine that paying attention to the wishes and desires of product users would be considered a novel idea. Even in the 1990s, however, there were many firms whose business decisions were driven strictly by internal criteria. In some instances—notably in emerging markets—an internally driven process may produce successful products. In most situations, however, investigating customer needs is critical to a project's successful outcome.

Evaluating customer needs is a subtle process, and even those companies with elaborate processes in place to gather customer input are not always successful. What happens? How can a "customer-focused" effort lead to bad results? The problem may lie in what information was accumulated, how it was gathered, how it was processed, and how it was translated into product requirements. Additionally, the timing of customer needs investigations is often as critical as their outcome. As time progresses, design flexibility will decrease. The identification of customer needs should thus be viewed as an integral part of the early stages of a development project, and should be performed while design options are still wide open. Narrowing product development options before customer requirements are explored may lead to product development disasters.

This note aims to synthesize concepts and methodologies developed by several practitioners and management academics. It seeks to provide a "how to" for the early stages of a product development project. It covers methods that are useful for gathering customer needs, and provides guidance for how these needs can be used effectively in a development project. The objective is to provide a practical, "hands-on" guide to characterizing the voice of the customer.

The note begins by discussing the nature of processes for investigating customer needs in different business contexts. It then describes a number of techniques for interviewing customers and accumulating needs information. It follows by discussing how this information should be organized and prioritized, and ends by focusing on how to translate customer needs into product requirements.

Harvard Business School Case No. 9-695-051. Copyright 1995 President and Fellows of Harvard College. All rights reserved. For information: permissions@hbsp.harvard.edu.

This case was prepared by Ellen Stein and Marco Iansiti. HBS cases are developed solely for class discussion and do not necessarily illustrate effective or ineffective management.

CUSTOMER NEEDS AND BUSINESS CONTEXT

Methods for gathering and analyzing customer needs information should reflect the "context" of the project.[1] There are two major dimensions for analyzing this context: the degree of newness of the product to the *firm,* and the degree of newness of the product to the *market.*

Newness to the Firm

There are few instances, if any, where a company should have absolutely no outside input to its design process. However, the more a given project involves issues that are new to the firm, the more critical is relying on outside information—from consultations with experts to focus groups with customers—to determine user needs and product specifications.

Microsoft, for example, felt that designing software for children would be substantially different from its previous experience. The company therefore spent more than 3000 person-hours talking with over 500 teachers, children's authors, and child psychologists, and conducted over 50 focus groups with children, parents, and teachers before developing its first software products for children.[2]

Newness to the Market

The degree of market newness will deeply influence the nature of effective methodologies for gathering customer needs. If newness is low and the product is well understood by customers, inquiries can be conducted easily and focused on specific areas of improvement. Customers will easily understand the product's context and quickly comprehend its possible evolution. Valuable information can therefore be gathered through highly specific and structured tools (for example, surveys and questionnaires).

When a product is new to the market, however, fewer existing users will be able to comprehend its potential, and they may find it difficult to visualize or verbalize how they might use it. In this case, investigative sessions should probe as broadly as possible. Rather than asking customers highly specific questions about product improvements, project members should focus on understanding the customer's needs and environment. In these types of situations, therefore, customer needs information should be gathered by flexible means (such as personal interviews with customers and observations of users in action). Lead user methods, described below, may also be quite useful. Team members should immerse themselves in the user's environment so they can themselves extrapolate what novel product features might or might not work.

In certain cases, the product may be so new that it will open up an unforeseen range of applications. In this case, there are few techniques left open for the development team apart from market experimentation—i.e., use intuition to develop the product, see what happens, redesign, and try again. Sony has done this effectively for a variety of consumer products, including the Walkman. It is unlikely, however, that a single product introduction will completely change the environment that surrounds it. New ways of using technologies tend to diffuse slowly; the usual time taken by something really new (such as the mouse pointing device or graphic user interfaces for computers) is still about 20 years and includes many product introductions (the mouse was invented in the mid-1960s).

Assessing firm or market newness is not always as simple as it sounds. The problem is that the newness of a product may be largely determined by the way it is developed.

---

[1] Dolan, *Managing the New Product Development Process.*

[2] One to One: Microsoft Products for Apple Macintosh Systems, Winter 1993.

Therefore, the methods for gathering customer needs may determine how new the final product will be, rather than the other way around. For example, if a development project began by sending customers a questionnaire with specific questions regarding possible improvements to the mouse for their current laptop computer, the project outcome would likely be a slightly improved mouse. Alternatively, if the project started with loosely structured sessions where users and their environment (e.g., airports or taxis) were observed, the project might result in a more substantial innovation, such as the track-ball configuration in the original Powerbook notebook computers. When in doubt, use the broadest means for customer needs identification first, and switch to more focused methods later.

COLLECTING NEEDS INFORMATION

Gathering "Typical" Customer Needs Data

Most product development projects will warrant interaction with "average" customers, most often through interviews or focus groups. In such settings, it is best to start conversations as broadly as possible to elicit overall impressions and images. Following are examples of the types of information that can be collected from customers:

- Role of the product in their lives and environment
- Images (scenes or emotions) related to the use of the product
- Specific needs
- Importance of each need

In determining the number of customers to approach, there is a trade-off between the cost of gathering the information and the thoroughness of the information collected. A more complex product or a wider range of targeted customers mandates more data collection to attain a level of confidence that customers' requirements are well understood (see **Figure 1** for the percentage of needs identified given the number of respondents). As a general guideline for interviews, 10 to 50 one-on-one interactions should be planned.[3] One way to

FIGURE 1
Data Gathering Efficiency— Interviews and Focus Groups[4]

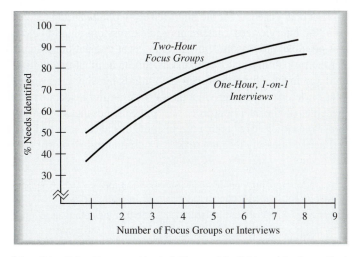

[3] See "Identifying Customer Needs," Chapter 3 in Ulrich and Eppinger, *Product Design and Development*.
[4] Adapted from Griffin and Hauser, "The Voice of the Customer."

know whether enough interviews have been conducted is to examine the information as it is gathered; when new information is redundant, the team can feel comfortable it has heard the voice of the majority of its customers and can stop interviewing.

There are a few common ways to gather customer information: questionnaires, interviews (in person or over the phone), focus groups, and observations of users in action. Regardless of the method, investigations should be aimed at exploration rather than at thesis-testing. The more surprises that turn up, the more successful the effort, since the purpose is to gain a broad understanding of the needs of future customers. Shoji Shiba characterizes this type of user needs research as "swimming in the fishbowl."[5] Traditional market research would dictate gathering data through observation of the "fishbowl" (i.e., the user's environment) from the outside. Shiba argues instead that gathering customer needs information is only successful if the interviewers become "swimmers" and totally immerse themselves with open minds in the "fishbowl" to gather their information.

Interviews may be more cost effective than focus groups for assessing user needs[6] (see Figure 1; note that interviews are shorter and involve only one person at a time). Because interviews can be conducted in the user's environment in many cases, they are also more natural representations of actual behavior than are focus groups conducted in a staged setting.

Ideally, more than one product development team member is involved in each interview and the participants are of different functional backgrounds. This provides more ears for capturing a greater number of customer comments. Moreover, more perspectives increase the likelihood that a greater variety of questions will be asked and that different interpretations of what the interviewee is saying will be proffered. This increases the probability that the results of the interview will be robust and that misunderstandings will not occur later in the process, particularly when user needs are translated into product requirements.

If one person is conducting the interview alone, he/she should use a tape recorder, if possible, because it is difficult (if not impossible) to collect all the points, especially the more subtle ones, made during an interview. Even with more than one interviewer, a tape recorder can capture points that come across only through tone of voice or offhand remarks not captured in notes. One of the most important guidelines to follow, particularly if a tape recorder is not being used, is for the interviewer(s) to *impartially* record the statements and emotions of the interviewees. Statements and expressions should be captured verbatim, or as close as possible, the reason being that the fewer translations a statement goes through, the higher the probability that it remains true to its original meaning. Interviewers should also record any images formed in their own minds by what interviewees said. Images are "the scenes or descriptions of product use or the emotion associated with the product's use that are generated in the interview process."[7] Some images that may be associated with mountain bikers, for example, are "taking the bike off of the car rack and riding it immediately" or "powering and finessing through rocks." These images are useful for forming pictures in

---

[5] Gary Burchill, "Concept Engineering: An Investigation of TIME vs. MARKET Orientation in Product Concept Development," Sloan School of Management Thesis, 1993.

[6] Griffin and Hauser, "The Voice of the Customer." Note that the data refer to a specific development project aimed at the design of a picnic cooler. More complex products would require more interviews or focus groups.

[7] Ibid.

the development team members' minds about the user environment so they can later ensure that their decisions support these images.

Each interview should yield a summary sheet that records the interviewee's name, position, and experience related to the product in question so that the comments can easily be put into context. For each question, *unedited* statements should be recorded, with interpretations performed at a later date.

Lead User Methods[8]

In some situations, customers will have a hard time removing themselves from the present in order to imagine what future products should look like. In such instances, the development team can conduct research with a special group of customers. This methodology, "lead user" analysis, is particularly useful if the degree of market newness in the project is high. Although the emphasis is on the product's customers or users, the methodology can be applied to other stakeholders as well. Lead users are defined as those who:[9]

- face needs that will be general in a market months or years before the bulk of the market encounters them; and
- are positioned to benefit significantly by obtaining a solution to those needs.

Unless a market is exceptionally small, trends and unfulfilled needs do not hit the entire market at the same time; there is always a subset of users that finds the current offering limiting before the majority of the population does. For example, marathon runners are more sensitive to shoe comfort than casual runners, because slightly uncomfortable shoes will cause injury if worn for long distances. Marathon runners can thus be considered "lead users" of running shoes.

Before lead users can be tapped for knowledge, they must be identified. The important question becomes "leaders of what?" It is important to identify *which* trend one wants to take advantage of in a new product. In the runner example, the trend is comfort. For a company providing test equipment to supercomputer design engineers, the trend could be processor speed; the lead users of test equipment would be those computer designers who were using the fastest computers.

Once lead users have been identified, their insights can be gleaned through interviews and focus groups. In some cases, lead users may even participate on a development team. Michael Jordan, for example, participated in several Nike basketball shoe development projects. If the potential rewards for finding an improvement over commercially available offerings are great enough, lead users may even make the effort to develop product improvements on their own. In those cases, developers will have a substantial part of their work already done for them. Makeshift personal computers, for example, were built in many hackers' garages before inexpensive commercial products became available. The design concept was there, ready for someone to commercialize it.

Not all markets have a population of lead users; in some instances, an early need may not exist. This will happen if the market is small enough to make the diffusion of information almost instantaneous, or if it is so mature that there is no moving trend for a user to lead in. In other situations, the rewards for developing solutions may not exist. For example, a

---

[8] Von Hippel, *The Sources of Innovation*.
[9] Ibid.

FIGURE 2 **A Simplified Product Value Matrix for a Car**[12]

Stakeholder

	Car Buyer	Car Dealer	Mechanic	Future Society
Purpose	Transportation of self, others, and cargo	Store, demonstrate, and sell car and service	Repair and maintain car	Dispose of remains of car
Physical	Opening door, seating position, using controls,	Storage space required, brochures to acompany	Means for diagnosing and repairing easily	Minimize interaction with waste created by car
Cognitive	Locating controls, knowing maintenance schedule	Knowledge of product, wrranties, financing, and its competitors	Knowledge of available tools for diagnosing and fixing	Knowledge of safe and sustainable environment
Aesthetics/ Emotion	Prestige, control of car, aesthetic form	Prestige and quality rating	Satisfaction of making fast, accurate diagnoses	Pride in re-use and recycling

CD-ROM user may not be entirely satisfied with the available encyclopedia offerings, but may also not feel that it is worth the effort to develop a better one.

Other Stakeholders: The Product Value Matrix

Ron Sears, president of the Design Consortium, stresses the importance of identifying *all* stakeholders, not just the end user. One way to do this is by using the Product Value Matrix[10] (PVM), which is designed "to map out the study, measurement, specification, and design of valued product interactions for everyone with a stake in a product."[11] In the example outlined in **Figure 2,** stakeholders are listed as column headers in the matrix, while the four "categories of human value" are listed as rows. These categories are:

- *Purpose*—rational, logical purpose for interacting with the product
- *Physical*—anthropometric, ergonomic interaction with the product
- *Cognitive*—learning, understanding, memory needed to interact with the product
- *Aesthetics-Emotion*—form, color, and emotion surrounding the product

Each cell of the matrix is filled with descriptive phrases corresponding to the stakeholder and category. For example, at the intersection of "emotion" and "car dealer" might lie the statement "wants to look knowledgeable in front of the customer." By identifying these needs, the development team will be able to judge more meaningfully whether it is creating an improved

[10] Product Value Analysis (PVA) and Product Value Matrix (PVM) are service marks of the Design Consortium, an association of consulting firms working in new product development.

[11] Innovation (prepublication draft, February 1992).

[12] Adapted from Ronald Sears, Michael Barry, and David Lieberman, "Product Value Analysis, Product Interactions Predict Profits," 1992.

product for the people who will interact with it. If the various groups of people and their wants are never researched, many desirable features may be left out of the product—not because they "lost" in a trade-off battle, but because they were never considered.

Product Value Analysis (PVA) pushes these concepts further by using the needs information organized in the PVM to compare products already on the market. This form of benchmarking is slightly different from the more standard version, where products are compared by performance-related specifications. For example, cars are often rated by the size and horsepower of their engines, cargo space, gas mileage, and so forth. The PVM might reveal, however, that the mechanic cares about how easy it is to get to the engine or how easy it is to diagnose mechanical problems with the car, while the driver might be concerned with how *usable*, rather than how *large*, the cargo space is or how well the car responds in snowy conditions. Using PVA, these more qualitative issues would serve as a basis of comparison among the various competitive products.

Assessing Customer Needs—An Example

A group of Harvard Business School students[13] with a variety of backgrounds worked in conjunction with Microsoft to design a "Personal Communicator for Kids." The team of six named their product "AESOP" and defined their mission as follows:

> To create a product that will apply commercial technologies existing today, but will envision a three-year window to introduction. The target age group of AESOP will be initially 7 to 15, which will later be refined to a more appropriate group, understanding the different needs and characteristics children have over this period of development. The product will combine computing and communications technologies in a cost-effective manner. It will be appropriate and appealing to children and their parents and will be portable, user friendly, and fun to use, while incorporating specific customer needs.

The team chose to use a combination of needs-assessment techniques to help them transform their mission into a physical model. The methodologies they chose were the following:

> Before delving into field analysis of end-user needs, the team first had to define the degree of newness to the market in order to determine the level of education that would need to be provided to the consumer, which would also help determine the nature of the questioning to pursue. The AESOP is unusual with regard to newness in that it is a combination of existing technologies and devices into a new offering that has no current, analogous, and unified product that encompasses all of the attributes that the AESOP will deliver. . . . As a result, the team's initial round of customer questioning, utilizing personal interviews, questionnaires, and focus groups with lead users, focused on general issues facing the user. Stakeholders used in the process include parents who will ultimately purchase the device for their child/children, the children themselves as end-users, teachers who have frequent contact with the age groups targeted, and distributors of the product who have experience with similar offerings. . . . After defining general concerns, needs, and likes/dislikes of the various constituencies, a more specific round of questioning followed and focused more on the applications of the AESOP itself. (See **Exhibit 1** for preliminary interview questions.)

---

[13] C. Fleming, M. Friend, S. Howe, T. Salah, S. Winoker, and T. Valkov, MBA '94.

After the personal interviews were conducted, more than 50 children in the target age group (12–15) were given a written questionnaire. This phase of the user needs assessment process was designed to uncover potential applications, physical characteristics, and product attributes that would be desirable to the selected population. (See **Exhibit 2** for a section of the sample questionnaire.)

The third step taken by the group in its search for user needs was a lead user analysis. According to the team,

> Defining such a group is more art than science, but the team felt that technologically sophisticated children would provide the best opportunity to learn about potentially desirable product characteristics. In a two-pronged approach, the team used an e-mail survey to selected MIT mail lists, which resulted in 30 respondents. Additionally, a group of 12 children, with an average age of 15, participated in a discussion and design session spanning two hours. This group regularly meets on Saturdays to discuss and research issues in the MIT "Schools of the Future" program. . . . All participants were asked not only to describe such a device, but to actually design and draw the AESOP. (See **Exhibit 3** for lead user sample drawings.)

The final stage of the user needs assessment came after the team tried, through brainstorming sessions, to combine all the knowledge they had gained through previously mentioned steps.

> Members created in text and sketches what they thought was the physical embodiment of the AESOP. Each team member then presented his or her personal vision and description of the product to the rest of the group. After copies were made of each sketch, the same group of lead users at MIT were re-approached to make final comments on the role and attributes of the AESOP, and then were asked to vote on each of the designs.

Not all product development efforts would undertake this many or similar kinds of steps. Another team in the same Harvard Business School course,[14] for example, was given the mission of developing an in-home fragrance delivery system that would incorporate a new ion spray technology. Although the team wanted to stay open-minded about the channel of distribution, pricing, and appearance for this product, they were not creating new markets or having to stretch customers' imaginations when trying to assess user needs. As a result, the type and extent of their research did not need to be as expansive as that executed by the AESOP group. As the air fragrance group explained,

> We plan to determine key customer needs by researching our target audiences through open-ended one-on-one surveys. As seen from the survey example, we intend to explore general usage occasions, pricing, unaided brand recognition and product types, perception of important features/benefits, scents, and a new product concept/price. We also will probe for strength of scent and expectations of product efficacy. (See **Exhibit 4** for a sample survey.)

The group felt that a single interaction with the end user would provide enough information to move on to the concept generation and selection stages of their project.

---

[14] P. Donohoe, D. Freytag, P. Gormley, M. Katz, and G. Spivak, MBA '94.

ORGANIZING CUSTOMER NEEDS DATA

Once the data collection has been completed (whether through interviews, questionnaires, observation, or other means), the information needs to be crystallized in a form that is usable internally by the development team.

Interpretation of Customer Needs

First, the set of customer statements should be "scrubbed," or made consistent and non-redundant, before being used further. Ambiguous statements should be clarified, if possible, or discarded if not understood. Duplicates should be removed, and multiple thoughts expressed in one statement should be separated. In the end, the group as a whole should have gone through each customer statement and produced a unique set of the clearest remarks possible.

An additional guideline for transforming customers' statements into user needs is to outline ranges of desired performances rather than discrete values.[15] Statements indicating that a feature should not be included at all if it does not achieve a specific goal are unnecessarily limiting at this early stage. For example, if the bicycle customer says that the location of the gear shifters is important and prefers to have them integrated into the handle grips, it is better to make the requirement "shifters should be as close as possible to the handle grips" than "shifters must be part of the handle grips." With the former statement the shifters may be moved to a location that is an improvement over the previous model, even if they cannot be integrated into the grips. Given the latter statement, the shifters might not be moved at all.

Forming the *Critical* List of Customer Needs

Further use of the stakeholder needs would be impossible if there were hundreds of customer requirements assembled in an unprioritized list. To make the set workable, the needs should be simplified, prioritized, and reduced to those that are vital to the success of the product.

The first step in narrowing the list of needs is to group those that are similar and to define a "summary need." For example, comments from mountain bike customers were translated into the following needs (among others):

- The rider shouldn't lose the feeling of control of the handlebars when going down a bumpy hill.
- I would like the bike to look sleek.
- The rider's wrists and hands shouldn't absorb so much of the bumpiness.
- The ride should feel smoother when going over rocks.

Needs 1, 3, and 4 could be grouped together and summarized by "The bike should buffer the roughness of the terrain from the rider."

It is important not to bias the design process or narrow the design options too quickly at this stage. Therefore, the list of needs should not include any implication of how these needs might be satisfied. For example, even if team members think that a shock-absorbing

---

[15] Center for Quality Management, Master Tool Book.

suspension system is the solution for this group of needs, it should be careful not to restrict the design space to that solution. Each decision will have an impact on other parts of the system (in this case the bike). At this point in the process, the interactions of the parts of the system have not yet been identified, meaning that one decision can have numerous unforeseen effects. When the interdependencies are later outlined, such a decision can be made with less risk.

It is best to focus on a relatively small number of basic needs; Ulrich and Eppinger, for example, suggest not going beyond 20.[16] If more than 20 exist, they suggest doing another round of grouping, yielding multiple tiers of needs. The "top" tier (i.e., that formed in the last round of grouping) should be used to determine product specifications, and the underlying detail should be kept for future reference either as an audit path tracing the certain customer needs (e.g., if future questions arise over what was meant by "buffer the roughness of the terrain") or as an aid in other parts of the development process (e.g., an advertisement announcing the new product could show the vibrations felt by the rider of an older model versus those experienced on the new version).

Prioritizing Customer Needs

Not all needs have the same impact on customer satisfaction and product success. After needs have been reduced to a manageable set of clear, unique summary statements, they still must be prioritized. Two basic types of information may be gathered to rank user needs: *relative importance* and *degree of importance*.

Relative Importance

The relative importance of user needs can be assessed through two basic methods: the development team and other company employees can use their own experience to rank the list, or customers can perform the ordering themselves. In situations where time or cost plays a critical role, the former method may have to suffice. The customer is the ultimate judge, however, and may serve as the best decision maker in this process.

If customers are consulted, there are various ways that the information can be gathered. The decision about which stakeholders to contact and in what quantity can be made in a manner similar to that used for the original data-seeking process. Unlike the prior case, however, this is not an open-ended exercise. Because the questions are more structured, this may be a perfect situation for a questionnaire—for example, a survey asking respondents to rank the order of importance of each of the needs. The number of needs should be limited, however, to those that are critical to the product and not obvious. If more than 30 or 40 needs are presented to users, they may find the task daunting and not return the survey. More elaborate methods for finding the relative ranking of needs are available through commercial marketing research firms.

Degree of Importance—The Kano Method[17]

The development team should learn the degree of importance of each need. Degree of importance refers to how pleased customers would be if a product had a certain feature or how angry they would be if it lacked it. The Kano method is useful for uncovering this information by recognizing that the degree of fulfillment of a customer requirement does not always

---

[16] Ulrich and Eppinger, *Product Design and Development.*

[17] Named for its creator, Professor Noriaki Kano.

FIGURE 3
A Kano Diagram

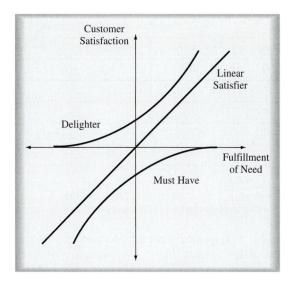

correlate with the level of customer satisfaction (or, in other words, the relationship between fulfillment and satisfaction is not always linear). **Figure 3** shows a Kano Diagram.

Kano developed five evocative labels to characterize customer needs: must have, linear satisfier, delighter, indifferent, and reverse.[18]

- *Must Have*—No matter how well the product meets that need, the customer simply accepts it as something that is expected. However, if the need is not met, the customer is very dissatisfied.

- *Linear Satisfier*—The better the product is at meeting the need, the better the customer likes it.

- *Delighter*—The delighter is not expected, so its absence does not cause dissatisfaction. If the need is met, however, it will increase customer satisfaction.

- *Indifferent Quality Element*—Produces neither satisfaction nor dissatisfaction in the consumer, regardless of whether it is met in the product.

- *Reverse Quality Element*—Creates dissatisfaction when fulfilled or satisfaction when not fulfilled. This implies that either the question on the survey was not written correctly, or that this trait is undesirable to the customer.

The Kano method is frequently implemented through a customer questionnaire. Two questions, one positive and one negative, are included for each customer need. For example, if a user need for a new mountain bike were that the rear tire be easy to change, one question would read: "If the rear tire is easy to change, how do you feel?" while the negative question would read: "If the rear tire is not easy to change, how do you feel?" For each question, the respondent is given five options: "I like it that way," "It must be that way," "I am neutral," "I can live with it that way," and "I dislike it that way." The responses are translated using a "two-dimensional table of evaluation" (see **Figure 4**).

---

[18] Clausing, *Total Quality Development*.

FIGURE 4
Kano Method Evaluation Table[19]

		Result of Negative Question				
		Like	Must Be	Neutral	Live With	Dislike
Result of Positive Question	Like	Q	D	D	D	L
	Must Be	R	I	I	I	M
	Neutral	R	I	I	I	M
	Live With	R	I	I	I	M
	Dislike	R	R	R	R	Q

I = Indifferent   M = Must Be
R = Reverse   L = Linear Satisfier
Q = Questionable Result   D = Delighter

The labels assigned by the respondents must be summarized for each user need before they can be used in the design process. Ideally, one summary label would be assigned to each need based on the responses. For example, if there is a dominant feeling among the respondents (e.g., 70 percent of them consider a particular need a must have), that label can be assigned to the need. However, if there is less harmony among the various respondents (e.g., 40 percent see it as must have, 35 percent as linear satisfier, 15 percent as indifferent, and 10 percent as reverse), assigning one label would misrepresent the level of agreement between customers. In this case, instead of simply attaching one label to the user need, it might be better to record the percentages for each label for those particular needs.

Once the labels have been summarized, they can be used to prioritize product requirements during the design process. In most development projects, trade-offs among product requirements take place. For example, if both "make the rear tire easy to change" and "make the bike light" are customer requirements, the team may be confused about whether to improve the ease of changing the rear tire if it would make the bicycle heavier. The decision might be easier to make if the development team knew that 60 percent of the respondents thought that lightness was a must have (note: the definition of "light" must be clarified), while only 20 percent of the respondents thought the ease of changing the rear tire was a must have. This information would indicate to the team that it should make the rear tire easier to change only if it did not negatively affect the weight of the bike.

The Kano Method—An Example

Another group of Harvard Business School students[20] used the Kano method to help create a product concept for a "Personal Communicator for the General Population." The group's charter was "to create a concept for an intuitive, truly useful, and inexpensive home communication product that not only adds value to the consumer, but opens up new software markets for [the company]." After conducting several stages of customer research that incorporated team brainstorming sessions, literature searches, home diary recordings, expanded brainstorming exercises, and customer interviews, the team felt it had a basic understanding of customer needs. From there, "designs were then bounded by technical,

---

[19] Adapted from Burchill, "Concept Engineering: An Investigation of TIME vs. MARKET Orientation in Product Concept Development."

[20] M. Bauer, T. Corn, S. Mertens, and M. Okuno, MBA '94.

infrastructural, and economic constraints. Certain applications were dropped based on technical and economic unfeasibility." To gain more specific insights into the desirability of product features under consideration, the team performed a Kano analysis (see **Exhibits 5a** and **Exhibit 5b**). With this feedback, the team was able to develop product concepts that were shown to customers in focus groups.

CONVERTING CUSTOMER NEEDS INTO PRODUCT REQUIREMENTS

Up to this point, stakeholder needs have been expressed in the stakeholders' terms. This is not a form that can be integrated directly into the design process, because it allows for a variety of interpretations. For example, given the customer attribute "I want a rear tire that is easy to put back on after being removed," one person might think of the bike store owner with numerous tools and substantial experience changing the tire indoors, while another might imagine a novice bike rider who is changing the tire on a hillside in the rain.

Needs may therefore be converted into product features, technical specifications, and product attributes (e.g., size, weight, appearance, and ergonomics) through a two-step process, sometimes known as quality function deployment (QFD).[21] The first step in QFD is to identify the set of product requirements or characteristics likely to affect stakeholder needs. The second step is to identify the actual relationship between each stakeholder need and product characteristic.

Identifying Product Requirements

There is no cookie cutter method for identifying the potential set of product requirements that may influence a customer's experience. One way to get started, however, is to involve the entire cross-functional team in a brainstorming session covering the following types of questions:[22]

- What is the function of the product?
- What is the state (e.g., size, appearance, ergonomics) of the product?
- What are the relevant costs (of manufacturing, service, sales, margins sought)?
- What is the buying experience?
- What is the field (i.e., service, sales, distribution) experience?

By answering these questions as a group, the development team may be able to identify which of the product's characteristics are particularly likely to impact customer needs. In the example of the mountain bike, some of its *functions* are to provide movement with a minimal amount of rider force, to provide braking capabilities, and to accommodate all terrain. Relevant issues of its *state* would include weight, corrosion resistance, and ergonomic comfort. The *buying experience* might be influenced by what components are on the bike, how knowledgeable the salesperson is, the sizes and colors available, and whether there is a warranty. *Field experience* might depend on how easily tires can be changed, how easily the bike can be cleaned, and the availability and price of parts.

---

[21] This description of QFD is highly simplified; a more comprehensive treatment may be found in Clausing, *Total Quality Development*.
[22] Ibid.

FIGURE 5

Product Requirement and Stakeholder Need Matrix

		Product Requirement				
		Wheel Tread	Shifter System	Fronter Fork Design	Frame Material	Seat Shape
Stakeholder Need	As light as possible	$X-$		X_0	XX_0	
	Buffer bumpiness from rider	$X+$		XX_0	XX_0	X_0
	Easy to change rear tire					
	Gear shifters rear handle grips		XX_0			

Correlation

$X-$ = slight negative $X+$ = slight positive X_0 = slight unknown
$XX-$ = strong negative $XX+$ = strong positive XX_0 = strong unknown

Displaying the Relationship Between Needs and Requirements

The link between each need and product characteristic can be displayed in a matrix with product requirements listed as column headers and user needs listed in rows. At the intersection of a product requirement and a user need, a note or symbol can be used to indicate the strength and type of relationship between the two (see **Figure 5** for a sample matrix). In situations where a requirement has no effect on the user need, the cell is left blank. By looking at the matrix, it is possible to judge whether important product requirements have been identified: a row (user need) with no marks indicates that none of the product requirements listed affect that need (e.g., the "easy to change rear tire" row in Figure 5). This, in turn, means that the list of requirements is incomplete because one critical customer need has not been addressed. A thorough listing of all requirements will be quite lengthy, even for a relatively simple product. It is therefore important to prioritize and focus attention on the characteristics that affect the most critical customer needs.

The team can now move forward with the confidence that it has done its best to discover which characteristics of the future product are most critical for success. Just in case, however, the team should make sure that the earliest product models and prototypes are put through severe peer and customer evaluations. Never underestimate the uncertainty and turbulence of the market!

REFERENCES

Bowen, H. K., K. B. Clark, C. A. Holloway, and S. C. Wheelwright (Eds.). *The Perpetual Enterprise Machine* (New York: Oxford University Press, 1994).

Clark, K. B., and T. Fujimoto. *Product Development Performance* (Boston, MA: HBS Press, 1991).

Clausing, D. *Total Quality Development* (New York: ASME Press, 1994).

Dolan, R. J. *Managing the New Product Development Process: Cases and Notes* (Reading, MA: Addison-Wesley, 1993).

Griffin, A., and J. R. Hauser. "The Voice of the Customer." *Marketing Science, 12* (1), Winter 1993.

Leonard-Barton, D. *Wellsprings of Knowledge* (Boston, MA: HBS Press, forthcoming).

Ulrich, K. T., and S. D. Eppinger. *Product Design and Development* (New York: McGraw-Hill, 1994).

Von Hippel, E. *The Sources of Innovation* (New York: Oxford University Press, 1988).

Wheelwright, S. C., and K. B. Clark. *Revolutionizing Product Development* (New York: The Free Press, 1992).

EXHIBIT 1
Preliminary
Interview
Questions

Microsoft Personal Communicator for Kids! — Managing Product Development Initial Questionnaire

Name of Interviewee: _____

Date of Interview: _____

Age: _____   Sex: _____

Interviewer: _____

Questions for Parents:
- What are your major concerns regarding your children?
- In terms of education? In terms of entertainment? In terms of safety?
- What do you think about during your workday?
- Do your children do their homework? What would help? Is it fun?
- How/when do you communicate with your children?
- How effective is your child's school?
- How much money would you spend to improve your child's education? Entertainment?

Questions for Kids:
- What electronic devices are really neat?
- Where do you spend most of your day?
- Walk me through a usual day.
- What do you like/dislike about school?
- Is school fun? Why or why not?
- What do you do for fun?
- What video games do you like? Why?
- How do you communicate with your parents/friends during the day?
- How do you like your teachers?
- How can they get better?
- Do you think/worry about your future? About what?

Questions for Teachers:
- Walk me through your school day.
- What are your concerns?
- What is fun in the classroom? What "works" on the kids?
- What tools would enhance the learning process?
- How should they be delivered? What content do they need to include?
- How do you communicate with students? (assignments, in class...)
- What is missing?

Notes from Interview:

EXHIBIT 2
Second Step
Questionnaire

Note: After you have put check marks in the appropriate places, please rank each item in each category from 1 to 10 in order of importance (1 being the best). For example, in the previous section you may not use the Yellow Pages often, so you may rank it a 10, but you really want to talk to your friends so that gets a 1! Only use each number once.

Product Attributes

This section tries to narrow the physical characteristics of the Personal Communicator for Kids! This area focuses on the function of the device and its appearance. Please put an "X" in the box that corresponds to your level of need or desire of the attribute, or lack thereof:

Personal Computer

Level of Interest	Low/ Don't Want		Moderate/ Don't Care		High/ Must Have!
Desk Top					
Lap Top					
Keyboard					
Mouse					
Pen-Based					
Color Screen					
Fast Speed					
Memory					
Windows					

Telephone

Level of Interest	Low/ Don't Want		Moderate/ Don't Care		High/ Must Have!
Portable					
Auto Dial					
Hold					
Call Waiting					
Conference					
Answering Machine					
Beepers					
Panic Button					
Other					

Video Game

Level of Interest	Low/ Don't Want		Moderate/ Don't Care		High/ Must Have!
Color Screen					
Lots of Games					
Gory Games					
Educational Games					
Portable					
2 Players					
Direction Arrows					
Joystick					
Cool Reputation					

EXHIBIT 3a
Lead User
Sample
Drawings

Show us how you want the machine to look:

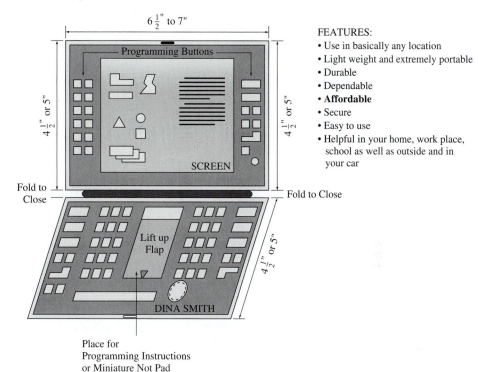

FEATURES:
• Use in basically any location
• Light weight and extremely portable
• Durable
• Dependable
• **Affordable**
• Secure
• Easy to use
• Helpful in your home, work place, school as well as outside and in your car

Place for
Programming Instructions
or Miniature Not Pad

EXHIBIT 3b
Lead User
Sample
Drawings

Show us how you want the machine to look:

2 boxes. Small one plugs into large and control it.

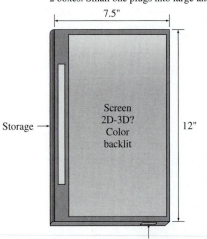

Storage →

Screen
2D-3D?
Color
backlit

7.5"

12"

Pen —

3"

5.5"

LITTLE UNIT
• Procesor
• Smaller storage than other one
• Can run by itself or run
  the other unit

Port to Plug
Little One in

BIG UNIT
• Processors to control itslelf
  but main brain in the little one
• Just an in/out (with storage)
• 1.5" thick
• Long batt life
  3 hrs.
• With low recharge time
• Physical tracing GPS
• Can plug in to chairs
  at school so you don't use
  bat. and modem in class

FEATURES OF BOTH UNITS:
• Voice recognition
• Pen based
• Must be water proof (and coke proof)
• Must be rugged enough to be droped
• Random security cheacks for correct voice pattern
• Voice-text messages
• Radio modem type communicator
• Confrencing
• Can talk
• 2D Projector on large one

EXHIBIT 4
**Customer
Survey for
Product with
Low Market
Newness**

Consumer Air Freshener Survey

Sex: M/F Age: _____   Occupation: _____

Questions: (circle one)

1) Have you bought or do you buy air freshener?   yes   no

2) What type(s) of air freshener?

aerosol spray   candles   solid   plug-in   stick-up   potpourri

3) What brand name(s)? _____

4) How often do you purchase air freshener for your home?

once/month   1/3 months   1/6 months   1/year   never

5) How often do you purchase air freshener for your office?

once/month   1/3 months   1/6 months   1/year   never

6) How strong do you like the scent in your air freshener?

strong   medium   light   minimal

7) What price do you typically pay for an air freshener?

$0.99 $1.99 $2.99 $3.99 $4.99 $5.99

8) How long do you expect it to last?

1-2 months   2-3 months   3-4 months   4-6 months   1 year

9) In what rooms do you use air freshener?

kitchen   living   dining   den   bedroom   bath   garage

10) What features or benefits do you look for in an air freshener?

_____

_____

11) What scents do you like?

_____

12) Would you be interested in an air freshener which had multiple changing scents?   yes   no

13) What price would you pay for such an air freshener?

$0.99 $1.99 $2.99 $3.99 $4.99 $5.99

THANK YOU VERY MUCH FOR YOUR TIME!!!!!!

EXHIBIT 5a   Kano Feature Survey

Product Features Questions

Please respond by circling the number that best matches how you feel after reading each statement.

1 – It must be that way	4 – I can live with it that way
2 – I like it that way	5 – I dislike it that way
3 – I am neutral	

Statement	Response				
Interaction with the device is through a keyboard.	1	2	3	4	5
The device interfaces with your home computer.	1	2	3	4	5
The device accepts handwritten input.	1	2	3	4	5
The product comes with a base station (recharging, interface with the phone jack, etc.) and the portable unit that contains the user interface.	1	2	3	4	5
Interaction with the device is not through a touch screen.	1	2	3	4	5
The product has a black-and-white screen.	1	2	3	4	5
The product is not water resistant.	1	2	3	4	5
Battery life is less than four hours.	1	2	3	4	5
The product does not accept voice commands.	1	2	3	4	5
The product has a built-in trackball.	1	2	3	4	5
The product does not have a built-in trackball.	1	2	3	4	5
The product primarily uses icons to communicate with the user.	1	2	3	4	5
The device does not interface with your home computer.	1	2	3	4	5
The portable unit is about the size of a large paperback book.	1	2	3	4	5
Interaction with the device is not through a keyboard.	1	2	3	4	5
The weight of the portable unit is between two and three pounds.	1	2	3	4	5
The product uses pull-down menus to communicate with the user.	1	2	3	4	5
Battery life is greater than four hours.	1	2	3	4	5
The device does not accept handwritten input.	1	2	3	4	5
The product is water resistant.	1	2	3	4	5
The portable unit fits in your pocket.	1	2	3	4	5
The device has a color screen.	1	2	3	4	5
The product comes as a single unit and a recharging stand.	1	2	3	4	5
The portable unit is about 9" wide by 12" long by 1.5" thick.	1	2	3	4	5
The portable unit weighs less than two pounds.	1	2	3	4	5
The product accepts voice commands.	1	2	3	4	5
Interaction with the device is through a touch screen.	1	2	3	4	5

EXHIBIT 5b   **Kano Feature Survey Results**

Product Features Kano Results

Feature	Reverse	Indiff.	Quest.	Must Have	Linear	Delighter
1. The device has a keyboard.	25.64%	33.33%	0%	7.69%	2.56%	30.77%
2. The device interfaces with your home computer.	0%	10.26%	0%	46.15%	15.38%	28.21%
3. The device accepts handwritten input.	0%	43.59%	0%	5.13%	10.26%	41.03%
4. The product comes with a base station and a portable unit that contains the user interface.	20.51%	48.72%	10.26%	0%	0%	20.51%
5. The device uses a touch screen.	10.26%	38.46%	2.56%	2.56%	10.26%	35.90%
6. The device has a color screen.	5.13%	30.77%	0%	25.64%	10.26%	28.21%
7. The device is water resistant.	0%	48.72%	2.56%	12.82%	10.26%	25.64%
8. Battery life is greater than four hours.	0%	5.13%	0%	66.67%	12.82%	15.38%
9. The device accepts voice commands.	2.56%	28.21%	2.56%	5.13%	17.95%	43.59%
10. The device uses a built-in trackball.	2.56%	58.97%	0%	5.13%	10.26%	23.08%
11. The device uses icons to communicate with the user (instead of menus).	2.56%	25.64%	30.77%	0%	2.56%	38.46%
12. The device fits into your pocket.	10.26%	33.33%	20.51%	15.38%	2.56%	17.95%
13. The device weighs less than two pounds.	5.13%	20.51%	2308%	7.69%	7.69%	35.90%

Product Development at Dell Computer Corporation

On an October afternoon in 1993, Mark Holliday, new head of Dell's Portable Division, laid down his papers and greeted key members of Dell's portable computer product development team now entering the conference room. The room occupied a corner of the firm's office park building on the outskirts of Austin, Texas.

Holliday had called the meeting in hopes the group could reach a consensus on recommendations for developing a new line of laptop computers. Dell did not currently market any portable computers. Its first line of portables, discontinued just a year earlier, had had technical problems—just the day before, in fact, the company announced a callback of some 17,000 units. Meanwhile, the lack of portables represented a gaping hole in the company's product line. Given the firm's sagging stock performance, the investment community was closely watching each and every move Dell made.

One way that Holliday and the product development team hoped to differentiate the new Dell line of laptops was through battery life. Batteries lasted less than three hours before needing recharging—a considerable inconvenience for executives trying to work on airline flights or on the road. But the new "lithium ion" (LiOn; pronounced "lee-on") technology being developed at Sony, one of Dell's manufacturing partners, promised to drastically extend laptop usage time without recharging. Unfortunately, since Sony was working to resolve some battery charging issues, LiOn technology was not yet qualified to be used in laptops.

A successful new line of portables, especially with cutting-edge LiOn technology, could catapult Dell back into the portable computer market. As a former engineer with prior computer industry experience on both coasts, Holliday realized, however, that premature commitment to an unproven technology could yield another fiasco for Dell in the laptop market. The discussion around this issue was sure to prove lively.

Harvard Business School Case No. 9-699-010. Copyright 1998 President and Fellows of Harvard College. All rights reserved. For information: permissions@hbsp.harvard.edu.

This case was prepared by Stefan Thomke, Vish V. Krishnan, and Ashok Nimgade. HBS cases are developed solely for class discussion and do not necessarily illustrate effective or ineffective management.

THE PERSONAL COMPUTER INDUSTRY[1]

Although the first digital computer was designed by Charles Babbage in the 1830s, the limitations of contemporary materials and manufacturing capabilities confined his vision primarily to the drawing board. Not until World War II did armies of engineers create factory-sized computers, such as the 50-foot Mark I at Harvard or the aptly named Colossus in London, capable of undertaking simple mathematical operations or breaking enemy codes.[2] Like dinosaurs, these early computers yielded way to more agile successors.

Technological breakthroughs over the decades allowed for dramatic size reductions with concomitant increases in computing power. Through the 1960s and 1970s, only government (especially defense) and big business could tap the power of computers. But as microchips replaced transistors and wiring, and manufacturing technologies improved, it appeared inevitable that the intersecting trends of miniaturization and lowered prices would ultimately place "microcomputers" at the disposal of individuals.

The microcomputer revolution started in the 1970s, with machines catering to hobbyists and "hackers." In July 1974, an electronic magazine promoted a printed circuit board that came with an instruction book for simulations. Known as the Mark 8 computer, over a thousand units were sold at $1,000 each, prompting the appearance of rival products. The market for similar machines grew to nearly 100,000 by 1977, thanks to several key developments: improved microprocessors, a standard operating system, increased availability of software, disk drives (which replaced cumbersome tape storage devices), and cheaper memory. Technology could now put more computing power on someone's desk than existed in the huge 50-foot machines of World War II.

Apple Computer and IBM

Through the late 1970s and 1980s, Apple Computer, a California-based firm, successfully commercialized an intuitively easy-to-use interface. Apple's engineers set the technological pace by cramming in as much new technology into products as possible, often working around the clock for days on end before a market launch. The firm drew on an entirely new cadre of users, primarily in the educational and hobbyist market. Business uses for the small computers, however, remained limited.

Initially, only a handful of larger firms like Texas Instruments and Zenith entered the business segment of the microcomputer market. To put matters in perspective, the Goliath-sized IBM's annual $1.5 billion R&D budget in the early 1980s alone loomed 50 percent larger than the entire microcomputer market. But IBM, and other giants such as Hewlett-Packard and DEC, which made business-oriented, closet-sized "mainframe" and "miniframe" computers, could no longer ignore the meteoric 30 percent annual growth of the microcomputer market.

To play catch-up, IBM rapidly leveraged off its traditional corporate base and strong direct sales and service organization. It outsourced hardware and software components to launch its IBM Personal Computer in 1981. Working with Microsoft, IBM created a new operating system that it made available to all personal computer manufacturers; this "open architecture" policy encouraged third parties to develop IBM-compatible software. Apple,

---

[1] Some of the information in this section derives from D. Narayandas and V. K. Rangan, "Dell Computer Corporation," Harvard Business School Case No. 596-058.

[2] *Encyclopedia Britannica,* 1991, Chicago: University of Chicago.

in the meantime, kept its technologically superior system proprietary. In a world of two incompatible operating systems, however, the IBM juggernaut eroded Apple market share. By 1983, IBM enjoyed 42 percent of the microcomputer market, with gross profits as high as 25 percent.

Enter the Clones

Even IBM could not meet the corporate demand for microcomputers that it had unleashed. During the 1980s, personal computer sales were to grow from ground level to $40 billion. Much of this growth came from manufacturers of IBM-compatible machines, termed "IBM clones." Most notable of these cloners was Texas-based Compaq, which in just five years joined IBM and Apple in the pantheon of the top three-selling retail brand names. Lacking a sales force, Compaq sold through recruited independent full-service retail dealers. (Some 5,000 computer stores had sprung up in the United States by the late 1980s, spurred by an explosion of hardware and software.)

By 1990, microcomputers accounted for 40 percent of all computers sold, and technological breakthroughs and competition helped drive down the costs of manufacturing the machines. For instance, the cost of processing a million instructions per minute fell from $75,000 in 1980 to $2,000 by 1991. The cost of storing a megabyte of information dropped from $250 in 1980 to $75 in 1991. Lower costs, increasing numbers of software applications, friendlier interfaces (including Microsoft's popular Windows operating system for IBM-compatible computers), and the entry of new manufacturers and distributors all boosted public demand. In 1993, personal computers sold faster than video cassette recorders and almost as fast as TVs.[3] The British journal *Economist* proclaimed that: "Once an icon of technological wizardry, personal computers have become a commodity. . . And customers are less willing to pay for service and hand-holding."[4]

THE HISTORY OF DELL[5]

In 1983, Michael Dell, a freshman at the University of Texas, Austin, started upgrading IBM-compatible personal computers and literally hawked them door-to-door to local businesses. With inventory piling up in his dorm room and crowding his roommate, Dell moved off-campus—and informed his parents of plans to drop out of school at the end of the year. To avoid parental fury, he agreed to return to his pre-med curriculum if business proved disappointing. But with $180,000 in personal computer sales during his very first month, Dell never returned.

He soon started buying and assembling components himself in order to sell computers under his own name directly to customers.[6] High growth rates and attractive margins allowed him to fund growth internally, and he began fielding orders for up to a hundred computers at a time from large oil companies and government agencies. Buyers wanted to meet directly with Dell, however, which created a dilemma: "We had to clean up our

---

[3] S. Lohr, "How Did Dell Computer Stumble?" *The New York Times,* May 28, 1993, Sec. D, p. 1.

[4] *The Economist,* November 2, 1991.

[5] Some of the information in this section derives from D. Narayandas and V. K. Rangan, "Dell Computer Corporation," Harvard Business School Case No. 596-058.

[6] A. Server, "Michael Dell Turns the PC World Inside Out," *Fortune,* September 8, 1997, pp. 76–80+.

workshop," Dell later confessed, "buy some suits and ties, and get ready for meeting America's largest corporations face-to-face."

Dell's seat-of-the-pants operations matched the needs of his computer-literate customers, who demanded quality at a reasonable price. In the years to come, Dell would start a 24-hour complaint hotline and offer a supply of backup replacement equipment. By upgrading IBM-compatibles with the latest microprocessors and peripheral technologies at low costs, Dell's company grew to $6 million by 1985. That year, the firm introduced its own brand of personal computers and ended with $70 million in sales.

By 1990, Dell Computers fielded a broad line of personal computers, winning several trade magazine awards for products and services. Michael Dell himself gained the distinction of becoming the wealthiest person in Texas.

The Dell Business Model

Dell Computer used the same principle to sell computers as Michael Dell had devised during his college venture: eliminate the middleman. The company focused on selling customized products directly via mail to savvy customers. Large clients, which included Fortune 500 firms, government agencies, and universities, generally demanded reliability and compatibility with existing computers. Competitors in this arena included resellers of leading brands such as IBM, Compaq, and Hewlett-Packard. For clients from small to medium businesses, Dell's primary competitors were mail order firms such as Gateway 2000.

Dell serviced its customers with combinations of home-based telephone representatives and field-based representatives. By tracking historical sales records on line, Dell could assess purchase patterns to better respond to customer needs. With direct marketing, in Michael Dell's words, "you actually get to have a relationship with the customer. And that creates valuable information, which, in turn, allows us to leverage our relationships with both suppliers and customers."[7]

Dell assured product quality by extensively pre-testing all the configuration options it offered. Once customers called in orders, customized configuration details were sent on "spec sheets" to the appropriate assembly line (an assembly line in Austin for U.S. customers, and a plant in Ireland for European customers). Assembly proceeded in a manner similar to that for automobiles. It started with a chassis upon which an appropriate motherboard, memory, microprocessor, video card, and other peripherals were installed and then wired. Next, the appropriate software was loaded, and the entire machine was sent to the "burn in" area for four to eight hours of testing. Quality checking occurred at several points along the line. Finally, the machine would be packaged along with manuals and shipped, typically in three to five days after order receipt (a week longer for orders over 100 machines).

A 24-hour telephone support system comprising well-trained technical representatives provided the first post-shipment level of support. This team was able to help Dell's computer-savvy customers diagnose and solve problems themselves 91 percent of the time.[8] A room in Austin the size of a football field, with 760 cubbyholes with telephones, housed this team within the heart of Dell's sales representatives.[9]

---

[7] J. Magretta, "The Power of Virtual Integration: An Interview with Dell Computer's Michael Dell," *Harvard Business Review,* March–April 1998, pp. 73–84.

[8] *BusinessWeek,* July 1, 1991.

[9] S. Lohr, "How Did Dell Computer Stumble?" *The New York Times,* May 28, 1993, p. D1.

Dell maintained a month's worth of component inventory, but its suppliers generally carried supplemental buffer stock that could be immediately shipped. Outsourcing provided several advantages, according to Michael Dell: "There are fewer things to manage, fewer things to go wrong. You don't have the drag effect of taking 50,000 people with you."[10] Smaller inventory also allowed new technologies to be adopted quicker, and product development cycles to move faster.

By creating close, coordinated relationships with its suppliers, vendors, and third-party maintenance providers, Dell created the illusion that its customers were dealing with just one large, well-run company. "The supplier effectively becomes our partner," according to Michael Dell.[11] "The rule we follow is to have as few partners as possible. And they will last as long as they maintain their leadership in technology and quality." This relationship also provided Dell with a front-row seat to new technologies its suppliers developed.

Dell Computer Stumbles

By 1990, Dell's success had spawned imitators such as Gateway 2000 and CompuAdd, which also enjoyed low overhead through mail order sales. IBM and Compaq also announced plans for entering the direct mail order business. Compaq, at the same time, sparked off a price war by announcing a 30 percent cut in its prices.

Meanwhile, feeling the pinch of competition, Dell had expanded into the retail market to attract smaller customers who preferred shopping in showrooms. The new markets spurred Dell's annual sales from $890 million in 1991 to more than $2 billion a year later, overshooting the company's 1992 sales target by half a billion dollars.

The rapid pace caught Dell in a cash crunch. In 1993, after 14 consecutive quarters with rising profits, the firm reported that its profits had been slashed to $10 million, half of what it had projected. Dell stock plunged $7 a share, to $25, on the day of this announcement.[12] Industry observers began speculating about the end of the Dell miracle. Michael Dell, they feared, had lost his legendary attention to detail and his ability to take cues from direct contact with customers and engineers. At any rate, several weaknesses had started to show in the company.

The first problem was that retail selling proved contrary to the spartanism of Dell's traditional direct model. Dell lost the advantage of being able to turn over inventory 12 times a year—twice as fast as its competitors—making it increasingly hard to find a premium in this market. Gateway, in the meantime, stuck to the direct model, growing from $275 million sales in 1990 to $914 million in 1992, with a promise of yet more growth to come.

The second problem involved the lack of senior management capable of guiding the firm toward maturity. Michael Dell became aware of this and hired several senior executives from larger firms such as Motorola to handle Dell's expanding operations.[13]

A third problem involved the lack of structure in Dell's product development process, symbolized, as some thought, by Dell's disastrous foray into the portable computer market.

---

[10] J. Magretta, "The Power of Virtual Integration: An Interview with Dell Computer's Michael Dell," *Harvard Business Review,* March–April 1998, pp. 73–84.

[11] Ibid.

[12] S. Lohr, S., "How Did Dell Computer Stumble?" *The New York Times,* May 28, 1993, p. D1.

[13] A. Server, "Michael Dell Turns the PC World Inside Out," *Fortune,* September 8, 1997, pp. 76–80+.

Product Development at Dell

In accordance with its strategy of commoditization, Dell's R&D budget was smaller than most other large computer firms. This also went hand-in-hand with Michael Dell's philosophy of spartanism that permeated the entire organization. A modest one-story converted industrial warehouse with fluorescent lights and cubicles housed Dell's management and product development professionals.

In this setting, product development at Dell in the early nineties had remained an informal process, run by autonomous teams that often centered around experienced developers. While such an approach delivered several successful products, the results were neither consistent nor predictable. The informality of the process meant that risks were not assessed rigorously in making project investment decisions, nor were the project bounds tightly established. Project execution experienced enormous variability depending on the project leader in charge. In many projects, team members did not all share the same vision of the project's objectives. Designed products were frequently "thrown over the wall" to manufacturing, and in some cases quality issues were addressed too late in the development process.

Some experienced managers began advocating a more structured approach. But engineers, used to a free-wheeling approach, decried formality, which they felt had the potential to lock out creativity. But after one computer project had to be canceled following an investment of several million dollars, Dell's senior management realized the need for a more structured approach adapted to the increasingly rapid product development cycles in the computer industry.

With input from industrial and academic consultants, Dell management started in early 1993 to organize product development around "core teams" of development professionals from several different functions. These teams, led by nominated core team leaders, were to take charge of the product's success from start to finish. Thus, through daily contact between different core team members, and through phase reviews, core teams hoped to avoid the pitfalls of the previous era. At phase reviews, typically slated for every three months, development work was to be reviewed, technical and market risks assessed, and funding for the next phase approved. The new process had the following phases (see **Exhibit 4**):

1. *Profile Phase:* The product development team arrived at a product and market definition, resulting in a two to three page "product features guide."

2. *Planning Phase:* Product team members developed a detailed business case for the product, which senior executives subsequently scrutinized for underlying assumptions and financial impact. This ensures that product developers paid enough attention to business issues before investing in the subsequent expensive phases.

3. *Implementation Phase:* The product development team designed, built and tested functional prototypes of the proposed product. This phase also marked the commencement of the development of instruction manuals and service plans. At the end of this phase, orders for long lead time tooling were placed with suppliers, resulting in a major financial commitment to Dell.

4. *Qualification Phase:* The product development team built production prototypes of the proposed product. Prototypes were distributed to key customers to obtain their feedback on potential product improvements. Salesforce training also began during this phase.

5. *Launch Phase:* The entire customer buying experience, from opening the packed finished product to running various software applications, was exhaustively tested. Production was ramped up and early customer shipments were made toward the end of the launch phase.

6. *Acceptance Phase:* The team collected customer feedback about the product for up to three months after launch. The phase was completed with an acceptance report that compared the results achieved with planned objectives and included a summary of lessons learned in the spirit of continuous improvement.

Through much of 1993, however, informality prevailed while the new process was being put in place, and core teams often approached the new process in spirit only.

THE PORTABLE COMPUTER INDUSTRY[14]

For several years, technological and pricing breakthroughs promised to free personal computers from the desktop. Although Osborne marketed the first portable computers in 1981, the machines remained only a small market presence throughout the 1980s. Most weighed over 20 pounds and were derogatorily termed "luggables." Many suffered from severe quality problems because manufacturers viewed the computers as "shrunken desktops."

Nevertheless, by the end of the decade, the quality of portability itself gave these machines gross margins that were typically 3 percent to 5 percent above desktops. When several leading computer firms entered the portable field, it was predicted that the market would soon soar. Such predictions forced firms like Dell to determine the appropriate product balance among desktops, portables, and servers (microprocessor systems that created local networks between different computers and communication devices).

Portable computer development relied on several technological breakthroughs: flat liquid crystal display screens developed in Japan that took substantially less space than traditional cathode ray tubes; compact hard drive disks that consumed less energy; and improved battery technology, which allowed over an hour of operations before needing to be recharged.

Manufacturing portables involved less hardware customization than desktops. Laptops, however, often enjoyed more feature differentiation than desktops. Overall, higher workmanship and quality went into these machines given the harsher range of conditions they would face in use. Portables underwent a commensurately challenging array of tests including exposure to shock, vibration, drops, and accelerations.

In 1993, portables were classified as laptops if they weighed between 4.5 and 8 pounds, and subnotebooks if they weighed under 4 pounds.

DELL'S LATITUDE DEVELOPMENT PROJECT

Early Setback in Portable Computers

In 1991, Dell came out with its first line of portable computers. At Dell's assembly line, the chassis with display and motherboard came prepackaged from outside vendors; only the microprocessor, hard disk drive, and memory were added in the assembly line, followed by

---

[14] Some of the information in this section derives from D. Narayandas and V. K. Rangan, "Dell Computer Corporation," Harvard Business School Case No. 596-058.

software. Through software and communications capabilities, it was possible to create significant personalization. And personalization remained Dell's forte.

In 1992, with portables accounting for 17 percent of Dell's sales, rumors circulated about quality problems, ranging from faulty battery packs to unreliable screens to frequent power failures to broken hinges. Dell's notebooks, based on older 386 microprocessors, were consequently slower than the 486-based machines fielded by rivals. Even Dell's commodity-like prices could not draw sufficient buyers, many of whom wanted machines that would keep them competitive in the business arena.

Early in the 1993, in what was shaping into the company's *annus horribilis,* Dell canceled a new line of laptops under development, since these were deemed too slow and expensive. A subsequent write-off of $20 million in associated expenses sparked a reorganization of the portables division. When questioned by a reporter about the portables, Michael Dell replied, "One plane is late and these guys claim the whole airline is going down the tube. . . . These guys are babies."[15]

Michael Dell had a point, for the desktops division had racked up unit volume increases of 155 percent over the previous year. By May, however, notebook sales had slipped to just 6 percent of Dell sales, at a time when the company had envisioned portables to account for 20–25 percent of sales. Dell's portable division, one Dell official admitted, suffered from "significant underinvestment" and a "shrunken desktop mentality."[16] Rivals, in the meantime, reported strong portable sales: a Compaq notebook with the more advanced 486 microprocessor, for instance, broke a market launch record for all Compaq products.[17]

In a vote of confidence, however, Bill Gates, chairman of Microsoft and himself a Dell desktop user, stated, "Dell is a super-solid company. They'll get on top of the situation."[18] But Dell went on to post a $75.7 million second-quarter loss. Company officials blamed years of explosive growth, which they claimed strained company performance ranging from inventory management to product forecasting.

Unintentionally rubbing salt in the wound, three owners of Dell portables returned their machines during the fall because they had noted smoke or melted spots on the plastic housing. Investigating engineers found a weakness in an electronic circuitry component: under physical stresses such as jiggling the power cord and AC adapter, the component could sometimes crack.[19] In October 1993, Dell recalled 17,000 notebooks. The company's direct relationship with customers, it turned out, had facilitated tracking down the owners.

Commenting on Dell's woes, industry analyst Steve Ablondi noted, "This industry moves so fast that you can get thrown off the merry-go-round on one side and still get back on the other side. . . . so Dell can come back from the dead in the portable business."[20] When Dell announced plans for launching a new line of notebooks in 1993, named the "Latitude" series, Michael Dell himself acknowledged that "it's very, very important for us to get this right."

---

[15] S. Lohr, "How Did Dell Computer Stumble?" *The New York Times,* May 28, 1993, p. D1.

[16] S. Lohr, "Dell's Second Stab at Portables," *The New York Times,* February 22, 1994, p. D1.

[17] T. Hayes, "Dell's Profit and Stock Plummet," *The New York Times,* May 26, 1993, p. D1.

[18] S. Lohr, "How Did Dell Computer Stumble?" *The New York Times,* May 28, 1993, p. D1.

[19] K. Jones, "Dell Recalls Thousands of Notebook Computers," *The New York Times,* October 9, 1993, Sec. 1, p. 47.

[20] S. Lohr, "Dell's Second Stab at Portables," *The New York Times,* February 22, 1994, p. D1.

The Next Generation: Choosing Which Features to Emphasize

To prepare for the challenges ahead, Dell reorganized its portable division. In spring 1993, Mark Holliday, the division's new head, immediately formed a core team that was charged with developing a new portable product to be launched in late fall 1994. The nucleus of the team included Robert Parker and Harry Longbaugh, electrical engineers; Pearl Taylor, a mechanical engineer; Ann Oakley, an industrial designer; and Bill Cody, a software engineer. Henry McCarty, the product marketer, headed the team, which reported to Holliday. Holliday, in turn, reported directly to Michael Dell (see **Exhibit 5**).

Part of the reason for the reorganization was to speed decision-making in an industry with ever-shortening product development cycles. By 1993, it took Dell 18 months to take an idea to production, of which some 14 months were involved with development. Once specification data were available, the process of tooling took four to five months. Product life cycles, by way of comparison, lasted roughly three years. The team expected to spend $10 million on the product development effort that would hopefully resuscitate Dell's portable computer line.

The first task the team faced involved taking stock of the situation. Within Dell there was great controversy about the future of the portables market—about its growth, pricing and marketing strategy, and resources needed to implement a successful strategy. Within the team there was some debate about whether to enter the subnotebook market rather than just focus on notebooks.

Which features to emphasize formed a large question. Some features engineers had to think about were not immediately obvious to customers—for instance, safety, microchip specifications, and component supply. While product developers thought along 10 or more dimensions, individual customers only thought along two or three. With this in mind, McCarty, the product marketer, and some of the engineers on the team talked with customers, strategized about incorporating new technologies, and even started lining up suppliers.[21]

In the summer of 1993, early in the "Profile Phase," a discussion panel comprising all team members debated which features to highlight in a new line of laptops. Market research indicated that several features rated high in the minds of laptop consumers: price, microprocessor choice, battery life, screen resolution, reliability, weight, and size (see **Exhibit 6**). Dell considered emphasizing battery life—a feature that ranked only behind price and microprocessor choice.

Battery Life as a Value-Adding Feature

The consideration to highlight battery life grew out of a serendipitous encounter in January 1993 in Tokyo. Michael Dell recounted how after a meeting with one of Dell's primary manufacturing partners, Sony, someone ran up to him saying:

> "Oh, Mr. Dell, please wait one minute. I'm from Sony's power technology company. We have a new power-system technology we want to explain to you." And I remember thinking, Is this guy going to try to sell me a power plant? He starts showing me chart after chart about the performance of lithium ion batteries. "This is wonderful," I tell him. "And if it's true, we're going to put this in every notebook computer we make."[22]

---

[21] Ibid.

[22] J. Magretta, "The Power of Virtual Integration: An Interview with Dell Computer's Michael Dell," *Harvard Business Review*, March–April 1998, pp. 73–84.

According to a senior manager at Dell, "Michael has a great memory for these types of details, and he filed it away." When the company sought to reenter the laptop market, Michael Dell pulled out this piece of information for his engineers to contemplate.

At the time, most portable computers used nickel metal hydride (NiHi) rechargeable batteries (see **Exhibit 7**). Under optimal conditions, NiHi batteries typically provided less than three hours of power at normal usage. But these batteries suffered from an annoying tendency to recharge only a fraction of their full capacity unless properly managed—a problem referred to as "battery memory." Furthermore, if not properly disposed of, they could release heavy metal toxins into the environment.

In contrast, lithium ion (LiOn), the technology the Sony engineer had mentioned to Michael Dell, suffered from neither of these deficiencies and promised longer recharge lives. LiOn was just starting to be used in camcorders. Thus far, however, no one had figured out how to power larger devices like computers using LiOn technology, especially given the tendency of lithium in larger batteries to separate and even explode. Some battery developers had even given up on the quest, following minor calamities in their laboratories. An unknown number of companies, however, remained in the race for lithium ion technology. Toshiba was known to have a good start, but conceivably Sony engineers might be ahead.

It remained unclear if customers were as excited about new developments in batteries. Focus groups showed that new customers would not necessarily view portables with LiOn as better than portables with traditional batteries. But Michael Dell did not worry about this. As he pointed out, "The customer doesn't come to you and say, 'Boy, I really like lithium ion batteries. I can't wait to get my hands on some lithium ion.' The customer says, 'I want a notebook computer that lasts the whole day. I don't want it to run out when I'm on the plane.'"[23] Furthermore, among experienced customers—Dell's traditional customer base—battery life proved more important.

Thus, the product development team began viewing the LiOn battery as a tangible feature mirroring the new Latitude computers' overall quality. The new technology could potentially boost the entire product line's market size by anchoring product image in a business with sales cycles of only six to nine months. In the worldwide portable computer market, with annual sales of 11 million units, Dell's management believed that a good Dell product might recapture its old market share of 2.5 percent, and a superb product might even gain 3 percent.

The Next Generation: Which Battery?

A new battery technology was not the only computer powering option available to the product development team. Another possibility for doubling battery time could come from allowing users to eject the disk drive and replacing it with a second battery—a strategy that, in Shakespeare's words, "gives to every power a double power." Essentially, Dell could choose between better fuel or a bigger gas tank—two tanks, in fact. The product development team agreed with Henry McCarty, however, that the dual battery option alone would not make customers perceive the Latitude line as leading technologically.[24]

---

[23] Ibid.

[24] In addition to addressing the issue of power supply, Dell engineers also were working on power management tools that let users determine power demand. For instance, maneuvers such as dimming the screen or shutting down nonessential programs could lower energy usage.

Thus, at the end of the Profile Phase where a decision had to be made, Holliday and his team entertained only a few realistic development options:

(a) *Continue with a proven battery technology (NiHi):* Dell could continue placing traditional batteries into its Latitude notebooks. McCarty and Taylor, the mechanical engineer, favored this option. This would take less space than the LiOn battery and thus allow for packing in some other feature such as communications control or memory management accessories. All members of Dell's portables division agreed about the viability of this proven option, which would involve no delays and deliver a good Dell product. On the other hand, this option would provide limited product differentiation in an increasingly competitive market.

(b) *Go with the new battery technology (LiOn):* Dell could incorporate new Lithium ion batteries into the notebooks. Parker and Longbaugh, both electrical engineers, championed this option. This option would mean incorporating an unproven and more expensive technology, which would also take up more space than conventional batteries. The new batteries were thicker than traditional batteries, requiring 40 cubic-mm more space—valuable space that could be used for other features. Because of uncertainty over the new technology, other leading manufacturers, such as Compaq, had decided to delay using LiOn technology. Sony (which currently turned out 100,000 rechargeable plain lithium batteries a month for cellular telephones[25]) had yet to complete testing and ramping up production capabilities for LiOn. In fact, if Dell committed to the batteries, it would most likely end up using all of Sony's production for the next few years.

(c) *Defer commitment to either battery technology:* Dell could continue to pursue the laptop development without committing to either battery technology at the current phase review. Buying just two or three months would not pose a major problem, but defering the decision until the qualification phase review, or another nine months—the time McCarty estimated it would take for Sony to provide conclusive test data—was another matter. The Dell team could potentially defer commitment until this point using either one of the following two approaches:

- The team could "overdesign" the battery space and the rest of the product to accommodate either battery. This implied that the mechanical engineering and industrial design groups would design the product to ensure that the thicker LiOn battery would fit as well. In addition—and Parker felt this was the harder requirement—the battery charging circuitry and software would have to remain compatible with either system. McCarty felt that the resulting bulkier product would be less attractive to the customer, and the variable cost of over-designing could be as large as 2 percent of margins on each unit.

- Alternatively, the team could follow a "dual path" approach in which two different products are developed independently—one using LiOn and the other using NiHi battery technology. The fixed cost of duplicating engineering activities and tooling meant an additional expense of $2.5 million. These costs stemmed from performing parallel electrical configuration and battery management software tooling, among other engineering tasks. These estimates, of course, did not include the potential demoralization of

---

[25] "Recharged: the Battery Market," *Economist,* May 2, 1992, pp. 323: 82.

engineers that would result from discarding half the craftsmanship in the final product and the opportunity cost of pulling developers away from other projects.

The October Meeting

As he called the meeting to order, Holliday indicated that he would encourage divergent viewpoints on the various options.

Taylor, the mechanical engineer, sparked the discussion: "We really can't afford the risk of delivering one failed product on top of another," she pointed out. "For this round, let's stick to NiHi and get a reliable product out the door. Let's not defer our decision: It runs counter to our new product development process which requires us to commit now. I mean, too much informality and delayed commitment in the past led us to scrap a $20 million product development project midstream. Isn't that why we reorganized the portables division and installed the new development process?"

Parker, the electrical engineer, interjected: "I think we need to get LiOn in our product somehow. That's what will hit our users between the eyes and add value to the entire line. And just think that a successful product could use all of Sony's new batteries and could lock out our competitors from LiOn technology. We could get a strong technical edge on the market."

"That's playing with fire!" McCarty, the marketer and team leader, responded. "I see so many question marks about Sony's supply capabilities that a small LiOn supply could choke our own ability to deliver portables. Remember that we want to use the new technology to build market share? So even if we boost product price to make up for smaller quantity, we may not meet our sales objectives. And let's not ignore the technical risks that make me feel uncomfortable."

"That's why we bother examining all branches of the decision tree," Holliday quietly reminded everyone and thought of the recent analysis that McCarty had prepared for him (see **Exhibit 8**).

"I think deferring our decision is the way to go," said Oakley, the industrial designer. "Worst case, if the LiOn option looks bad, we'd revert to NiHi and lose some valuable internal space that could have supported other features. I know there are other costs, too, but staying flexible isn't a straight gamble; it's just half a gamble."

Longbaugh, the other electrical engineer, threw up his hands. "Listen, you don't rob a stagecoach by perching on the fence. Let's make up our minds one way or the other now. Dell has always had a strong culture of commitment and this doesn't seem right. I, for one, think LiOn is a really neat technology. I suggest we go straight to LiOn, keeping in mind that if it does flop, we could still develop a product with our proven battery technology."

Cody, the software engineer, slipped in the last words before a break in the meeting: "True, but if it fails, think of the substantial rework needed—we've estimated the rework to require 70 percent of the original schedule and 30 percent of the $10 million development cost. And Henry [McCarty] thinks that the resulting late market entry would likely halve projected unit sales. And any technical fiasco could severely tarnish our reputation, and lead to spillover effects in our desktop business. Let's not fan a brush fire!"

* * *

Looking out the conference room windows at the sun setting over the Texan landscape, Holliday reflected on how Dell had helped catalyze Austin's booming high-tech economy.

Dell had flourished in the Texas Hill Country, relying on its unique model of making and selling computers. Now Wall Street and the business world scrutinized its every move. *The New York Times* had noted, "In the fast-paced personal computer industry, the real test of a company's mettle is not if it slips, but whether it can recover quickly. . . . Unless Dell comes back with a strong portable business, the company risks being relegated to second-rate status in the personal computer industry."[26]

Yet after suffering from the prior setback, Holliday personally felt that his product development team had nothing more to lose—not in terms of revenue nor even worker morale. Once again, Holliday watched his colleagues enter the conference room and seat themselves around the table. He then called the meeting back to order. It was time to make a decision.

[26] S. Lohr, "Dell's Second Stab at Portables," *The New York Times,* February 22, 1994, p. D1.

EXHIBIT 1
Timeline

1984	Michael Dell founds Dell Computer Corporation.
1985	Dell offers first personal computer of its own design.
1987	International expansion begins, with opening of subsidiary in the United Kingdom. Manufacturing will start there in 1990.
1988	Dell goes public.
1991	Dell introduces its first notebook computer.
1992	The company joins ranks of Fortune 500.
1993 January	Michael Dell first hears about Sony's lithium ion battery technology in Tokyo.
March	Amid great uncertainty at Dell about fate of its laptop line, Dell reorganizes its portable division.
May	After 14 consecutive quarters with rising stock profits, the firm reports that its profits had been slashed to $10 million, half of projected profits. Dell's stock plunged $7 a share to $25 on the day of this announcement.
August	Market decisions are made about new laptop computer line.
October	Dell recalls 17,000 discontinued notebooks after three machines were returned by owners reporting such technical problems as smoke or melted spots.

EXHIBIT 2
Portable
Computer
Market Data

(a) Portable Computer Market Size (Millions of Units)

	World	United States
1992	4.3	2.2
1993	6.2	2.9
1994*	7.4	3.2
1995*	8.9	3.7

* IDC Projections for Laptop Market

Source: Computer Industry Forecasts and New Games—Strategic Competition in the PC Revolution by John Steffens (Pergamon Press, 1994) in D. Narayandas and V. K. Rangan, "Dell Computer Corporation," Harvard Business School Case No. 596-058, Rev. March 11, 1996.

(b) Personal Computer Market Size (Millions of Units) by Vendor

	1987	1989	1991	1992	1993
IBM	28.0	16.9	14.1	11.7	14.0
Compaq	7.5	4.4	4.1	5.7	9.6
Apple	14.0	10.7	13.8	13.2	13.9
Dell	—	0.9	1.6	3.7	5.4
AST/Tandy	2.0	1.7	2.7	2.7	3.6
Gateway	—	0.2	2.5	3.6	4.4
Packard Bell	—	3.3	4.7	5.3	6.7
HP	—	NA	NA	NA	NA
DEC	—	NA	NA	NA	NA
Others	40.0	61.9	56.5	54.1	42.4

Source: BIS Strategic Decisions, Inc. (in D. Narayandas and V. K. Rangan, "Dell Computer Corporation," Harvard Business School Case No. 596-058).

(c) U.S. Personal Computer Market Growth

	1988	1990	1992	Projected 1994	Projected 1996
Desktops					
Sales (billion $)	20.05	20.78	22.52	25.06	33.0
Units (000s)	8,100	8,750	9,835	11,802	13,100
Portables					
Sales (billion $)	3.28	3.87	4.75	8.48	11.6
Units (000s)	1,130	1,540	2,150	3,800	5,400
Servers					
Sales (billion $)	1.64	2.97	5.47	8.11	12.5
Units (000s)	195	338	457	739	1,250

EXHIBIT 3
Dell Computer Corporation—Selected Sales and Financial Data

Source: D. Narayandas and V. K. Rangan, "Dell Computer Corporation," Harvard Business School Case No. 596-058.

(a) Sales by Products and Segments (1991–1993)

	1991	1992	1993
Net Sales ($M)	$890	$2,014	$2,873
Products			
Desktops	90%	88%	94%
Laptops	10%	12%	2%
Servers			4%
Market Segment Sales			
Relationship	59%	61%	64%
Transaction	41%	39%	36%
Markets			
U.S.	72.8%	72.5%	70.9%
Europe	27.2%	27.5%	27.2%
Asia			1.9%

Source: Dell Financial Reports

(b) Selected Financial Data (Dollars in Millions, Except Per-Share Data)

	1991	1992
Net sales	890	2,014
Cost of goods sold	594	1,545
Gross profit	296	469
Selling, general and administrative expense	214	310
Depreciation, depletion and amortization	14	20
Operating profit	69	139
Net income (after taxes)	51	102
Other data:		
EPS (Primary)—excluding extra items and discounted operations	0.18	0.32
Dividends per share	0	0
ROA (%)	9%	11%
ROE (%)	19%	28%
Market value	761	1,705
R&D expenses	42	49

EXHIBIT 4
Dell's New
18-Month
Development
Process

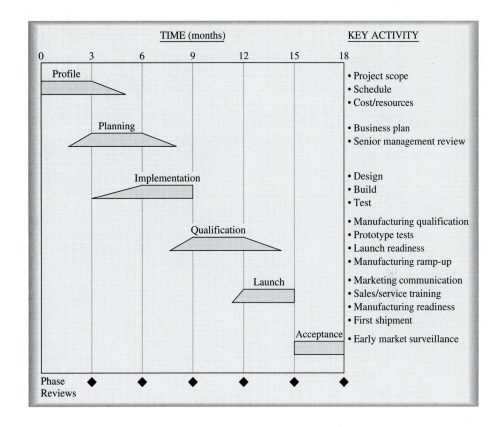

TIME (months)   KEY ACTIVITY

0   3   6   9   12   15   18

Profile
- Project scope
- Schedule
- Cost/resources

Planning
- Business plan
- Senior management review

Implementation
- Design
- Build
- Test

Qualification
- Manufacturing qualification
- Prototype tests
- Launch readiness
- Manufacturing ramp-up

Launch
- Marketing communication
- Sales/service training
- Manufacturing readiness
- First shipment

Acceptance
- Early market surveillance

Phase Reviews

EXHIBIT 5 **Dell's Organizational Structure and the Notebook Development Team (1993)**

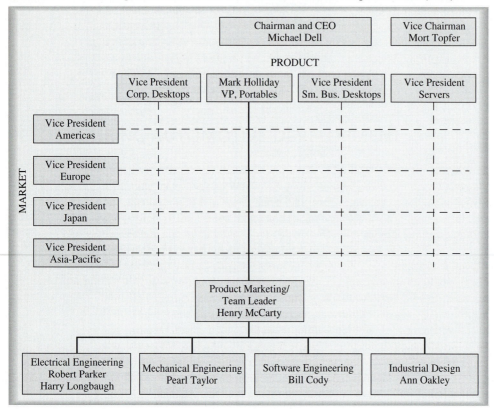

EXHIBIT 6 **Marketing Memo**

MEMO: PERSONAL COMPUTER MARKET
ATTENTION: Henry McCarty
FROM: Gordon Lillie, Marketing
DATE: August 15, 1993

Here is the summary market information you requested: we think Dell may capture 2.5% of the market with a good product, but even up to 3% with a superb product. If our gross margins average a fourth of our average price of $2400 over the life of the product, then expected margins over the three-year product cycle would be close to a half-billion dollars. Our models lead us to believe that each month's delay in product development would lead to a loss of about 4% of sales.

Market research shows that most laptop users already have considerable experience with desktops, and that new consumers are more likely to buy a desktop rather than a laptop. But portables are increasingly bought as the primary computer. In 1992, a fourth of portables were bought for this purpose by business customers of all sizes. At the same time, portables were also being purchased to replace desktops. (IDC Customer Directions and Buying Behavior, Year-End Surveys.)

P.S. I am also including marketing information about market size and product features that went into our deliberations.

Top 10 Notebook Evaluation Criteria for Actual Business Customer Purchases

Criterion	Incidence %
Price	54
Microprocessor	35
Battery life	27
Screen resolution	15
Reliability	11
Weight	9
Hard drive storage	6
Durability	3
Compatibility	3
Speed	1

Source: IDC Customer Directions and Buying Behavior, Year-End Surveys.

Top Six Leading Brands for Portables Among 1993 Business Customers

Brand	Purchases
IBM	34%
Compaq	51%
Toshiba	32%
Dell	7%
NEC	8%
Gateway	2%

Source: IDC Customer Directions and Buying Behavior, Year-End Surveys.

EXHIBIT 7
Battery Technology

Source: Dell Marketing Division.

"Life is a search after power."

—*Ralph Waldo Emerson*

Batteries are energy storage devices that convert chemical energy into electrical energy in order to power attached devices. The first operable battery dates back to 1800, when Italian physicist Alessandro Volta devised the "voltaic pile," a simple arrangement of zinc and silver plates and salt water. Like most batteries to follow, this exploited the different electron-attracting properties of two different metals to deliver sustainable currents. But almost a century of further developments would be needed for the first commercial applications of batteries.

Battery technology remained a slow-moving field through much of the twentieth century. Development of rechargeable batteries, however, helped power the automobile revolution, and decades later opened up use of small portable devices such as portable computers. In the early 1990s, computer batteries in widespread use were of the rechargeable nickel metal hydride (NiHi) and nickel-cadmium (NiCad) types. These batteries suffered from two major deficiencies, however: First, they would only recharge up to the point where they had been discharged. Users could take care of this annoying "memory effect" by occasionally allowing fully charged batteries to discharge all the way. Second, the NiCad batteries contained heavy metals that posed environmental health hazards if improperly disposed. (A serious consideration, given that if all the nickel-cadmium batteries produced each year in the Western World were lined up side by side, they would circle the Earth four times.)[a]

These two deficiencies, combined with the short times between recharges, conspired to make battery technology a bottleneck for growth of the portable computer industry. By the early 1990s, manufacturers in Japan (which produced half the world's NiCad batteries), Europe, and the USA raced to develop better products for the $800 million portable computer battery industry[b] One promising innovation came from lithium ion technology. Plain lithium had already found prior use in the non-rechargeable button-sized batteries that powered watches and cameras for up to years. Chemical innovations now allowed for building lithium ion batteries without size limitations that could be recharged safely. These toxin-free batteries could pack perhaps three times more energy as NiHi battery of the same size and possessed no memory effect. Furthermore, these could be recharged even more rapidly.

But lithium in larger batteries had a worrisome tendency to separate and pose an explosion hazard. Some battery developers had even given up on the quest, following minor calamities in their laboratories. An unknown number of companies, however, remained in the race for lithium ion technology.

A final hurdle for all new battery technologies involved testing. Actually, this was often not much of a hurdle at all given that little standardization existed for testing conditions. Manufacturers, thus, could claim long battery lives based on tests run under low power demand, thus creating a spate of "lies, damn lies, and battery lies." But scrupulous battery manufacturers often hired independent battery testing outfits to conduct two types of tests: "sprint tests," which ran systems at maximal power demand, and "steeplechase" tests, which, mimicked the more typical patterns of intermittent use.

---

[a] F. E. Katrak, and I.S. Servi, "Battle of the Nickel Links," *Electronic Engineering Times,* February 4, 1991, p. 52.

[b] P. J. Barry, "Valence Technology, Inc.—Company Report," C.J. Lawrence, Inc., 1993.

EXHIBIT 8   McCarty's Data on the Different Development Options

Estimates

Forecasted market size (1995–97)	= 11 million units per year
Potential Dell market share (good product, e.g. NiHi)	= 2.5% (or 825,000 units over 3 years)
Potential Dell market share (superb product, e.g. LiOn)	= 3.0% (or 990,000 units over 3 years)
Average price per unit over life of product	= $2400
Average gross margin per unit over life of product	= $600
Expected product life	= 3 years
Cost of each month delay in development schedule	= 4% of unit sales
Expected length of development schedule	= 18 months (incl. acceptance phase)
Expected cost of development effort	= $10 million

Option 1: Continue with a proven battery technology (NiHi)
- Confidence = 100% (likelihood that it works as expected)
- Net margin = 825,000 units × $600/unit − $10 m
    = $485 m

Option 2: Go with the new battery technology (LiOn)
- Confidence = 60% (likelihood that it works as expected); risky!!!
- Net margin (if LiOn works) = 990,000 units × $600/unit − $10 m = $584 m
- Net margin (if LiOn fails) = (825,000 units × 0.5) × $600/unit − ($10 + 0.3 × $10) = $234.5 m
- If LiOn fails at launch, a switch to NiHi would require substantial rework (70% of original schedule and 30% of cost). Because competitors would have an established product on the market before them, Dell would lose about 50% of projected units sold.
- If LiOn causes a failure, there could be spillover effects into the desktop business. Dell's reputation for quality could be tarnished.

Option 3: Defer commitment until qualification phase review (dual development *or* overdesign)
- If dual development paths[a]: Estimated additional fixed cost = $2.5 million
- If product is overdesigned[b]: Estimated additional variable cost = 0.5% of revenue (2% of margin)
- Gross margin (if LiOn works): = 990,000 units × $600/unit = $594 m (before additional cost)
- Gross margin (if LiOn fails): = 825,000 units × $600/unit = $495 m (before additional cost)
- The analysis assumes that Sony will give us enough information at the end of the qualification phase to determine with full certainty if LiOn will work or fail. If it fails, Dell can drop it and revert to option 1.

[a] These are the actual project costs incurred. They include additional designers and engineers, material and tooling costs, etc. if we follow a dual path until the qualification phase review. The costs do not include the product opportunities we would forego if we had to pull people away from other projects.

[b] Because of the LiOn battery's different dimensions and properties, we would have to "overdesign" the computer case, the charging circuitry, and battery management software to accomodate either battery technology, which would add about $12 cost per unit.

Article

Agile Product Development: Managing Development Flexibility in Uncertain Environments

Many companies appreciate the importance of agility in executing business processes. While academic research has established a linkage between flexibility and firm competitiveness, thus far it has focused primarily on manufacturing and strategic flexibility.[1] But another business process has a clear and compelling need for flexibility as well: product

[1] There are many research and managerial publications that focus on manufacturing flexibility. See, for example, S. Beckman, "Manufacturing Flexibility: The Next Source of Competitive Advantage," in P. E. Moody, ed., *Strategic Manufacturing* (Homewood, IL: Dow-Jones Irwin, 1990); M. Cusumano, "Shifting Economies: From Craft Production to Flexible Systems and Software Factories," *Research Policy*, 21/5 (October 1992): 453–480; X. De Groote, "The Flexibility of Production Processes: A General Framework," *Management Science*, 40/7 (July 1994): 933–945; R. Jaikumar, "From Filing and Fitting to Flexible Manufacturing: A Study in the Evolution of Process Control," Harvard Business School Working Paper No. 88-045, 1988; W. Jordan and S. Graves, "Principles on the Benefits of Manufacturing Process Flexibility," *Management Science*, 41/4 (April 1995): 577–594; K. Stecke, "Flexible Manufacturing Systems: Design and Operating Problems and Solutions," in W. K. Hodson, ed., *Maynard's Industrial Engineering Handbook*, 4th Edition (New York, NY: McGraw Hill, 1992); D. Upton, "Flexibility as Process Mobility: The Management of Plant Capabilities for Quick Response Manufacturing," *Journal of Operations Management*, 12 (1995); D. Upton, "Process Range in Manufacturing: An Empirical Study of Flexibility," *Management Science*, 43/8 (August 1997): 1079–1092; D. Upton, "The Management of Manufacturing Flexibility," *California Management Review*, 36/2 (Winter 1994): 72–89.

The authors would like to thank Steven Wheelwright and two anonymous reviewers for their very thoughtful feedback. Stefan Thomke would also like to acknowledge discussions with David Bell, Marco Iansiti, Gary Pisano, David Upton, and Eric von Hippel. The financial support of the Harvard Business School Division of Research is gratefully acknowledged.

development.[2] This article examines what development flexibility is, how it can be quantified, how it enhances performance, and how it can be introduced into an organization.

DEVELOPMENT FLEXIBILITY

Although the term "flexibility" is used in many contexts, here we propose the following operational definition:

> Development flexibility can be expressed as a function of the incremental economic cost of modifying a product as a response to changes that are *external* (e.g., a change in customer needs) or *internal* (e.g., discovering a better technical solution) to the development process. The higher the economic cost of modifying a product, the lower the development flexibility.

The economic cost of modifying a product arises from a change's impact on four factors: the product's development expense, its unit cost, its performance, and the development schedule. Changes in each of these factors can in turn be quantified and expressed in terms of cumulative profit impact. For example, suppose that a program change will raise product cost by 3 percent and delay the schedule by two months. If a sensitivity analysis determines that the cost is worth $500,000 per percent and the schedule is worth $750,000 per month, then this change has a total economic cost of $3.0 million.[3] The higher the economic cost of modifying a product as a response to a given change, the lower a firm's development flexibility.

Note, however, that our definition does not restrict the *source* of flexibility. Flexibility can stem from the choice of a particular design technology, but it can come from other choices that designers and managers make as well. Academic research and many managers' experiences have shown, for example, that flexibility decreases as a development project nears completion, which can have a significant impact on product success.[4] Thus, when Ford decided to forgo a fourth passenger door in its new minivan—in spite of market research that indicated a change in customer preference for the door—it made a trade-off between potential revenue and a costly and late change to the body design. As a result, many customers switched to a competitor that met their need for a fourth door.[5]

---

[2] For example, see S. Wheelwright and K. Clark, *Revolutionizing Product Development* (New York, NY: The Free Press, 1992), p. 183; K. Eisenhardt and B. Tabrizi, "Accelerating Adaptive Processes: Product Innovation in the Global Computer Industry," *Administrative Science Quarterly*, 40/1 (March 1995): 84–110; M. Iansiti, "Shooting the Rapids: Managing Product Development in Turbulent Environments," *California Management Review*, 38/1 (Fall 1995): 37–58; S. Thomke, "The Role of Flexibility in the Development of New Products: An Empirical Study," *Research Policy*, 26/1 (March 1997): 105–119; M. Iansiti and A. MacCormack, "Developing Products on Internet Time," *Harvard Business Review*, 75/5 (September/October 1997): 108–117.

[3] The technique for doing this is a simple financial sensitivity analysis, which is described in: P. Smith and D. Reinertsen, *Developing Products in Half the Time: New Rules, New Tools* (New York, NY: John Wiley & Sons, 1998); D. Reinertsen, *Managing the Design Factory: A Product Developer's Toolkit* (New York, NY: The Free Press, 1997), Chapter 2.

[4] For evidence from software development, see, for example, B. Boehm, *Software Engineering Economics* (Englewood Cliffs, NJ: Prentice Hall, 1981).

[5] "An Embarrassment of Minivans, *BusinessWeek,* March 11, 1996, pp. 30–3l.

Changes occur for many reasons, some of which are difficult to predict or anticipate. Consider the following incident that a development manager described to us:

> His design firm was asked to develop a single integrated circuit (IC) that would combine the functions of multiple ICs on a personal computer. These ICs usually execute support functions for the central processing unit (CPU), such as controlling external and internal devices. A critical feature in the design was the exact CPU clock frequency, because it determined the speed at which the design had to operate. Late in the design process, the manufacturer of CPUs (Intel Corporation) introduced an improved microprocessor that ran at a 50 percent higher clock rate. This technology shift caught the design firm by surprise since it expected no changes in clock speed during the development project. The lack of flexibility led to a complete redesign, which eventually added 15 percent to their total development time.

Quantifying Development Flexibility

As the above suggests, while the term flexibility is often used qualitatively, there is value in trying to express development flexibility in more precise, quantitative terms. To do so, we propose a construct that we call the "Flexibility Index" of a design. It measures how well a design responds to a specific change.

As shown in **Figure 1,** the need for change arises from a change in a perturbing variable. A change in a development project should be made when the economic cost of making this change is less than the economic benefit of making the change. *Thus a project can be considered flexible if the economic cost of a change is low in relation to the change in the perturbing variable.* Projects in which this economic cost is high can be viewed as inflexible.

Flexibility can be expressed in terms of a "Flexibility Index," which is the ratio between the percent change in a perturbing variable and the percent change in projected life cycle

FIGURE 1
The Flexibility Index

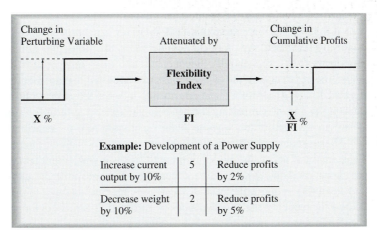

Note: In this illustration, the relationship between change and the flexibility index (FI) is shown to be linear. In reality, we suspect the relationship to be of a more complex functional form—for example, piecewise linear, consisting of linear sections and discontinuities. In a practical setting, however, a good starting point would be an average FI value over a range of interest. Furthermore, the change in cumulative profits only considers the economic cost of the change. This should be compared with the economic benefit of the change to determine whether making the change is a good business decision.

profits. For example, consider a power supply that was designed to weigh 10 pounds and to provide 10 amps of output current. If a change in market requirements demanded 11 amps (a 10 percent change), it would be necessary to assess how this change will alter projected life-cycle profits. If the cost of making this change was 2 percent of project profits, then the ratio between these two variables would be 10:2 giving a Flexibility Index of 5. Similarly, if a change in market requirements demanded a 1 pound lighter power supply, it would be necessary to assess the cost of making this 10 percent weight reduction. Suppose that such a change would delay the project and add costs leading to a 5 percent reduction in project profits. The Flexibility Index with regard to weight reduction would be 2, less than half the Flexibility Index for a change in output current. This means that the design is less tolerant of a need to reduce weight. Generally, the higher the Flexibility Index, the less economic cost is incurred to change a particular product attribute.

The Flexibility Index is attribute-specific. It is possible to change the current output of this power supply with lower economic cost than changing its weight. Thus, development projects do not have some vague, general property of flexibility, but rather are able to respond to changes in specific perturbing variables with reduced economic costs. *This attribute-specific property is important, because managers should only invest in flexibility on attributes where the likelihood of future changes makes this flexibility potentially valuable.* For example, personal computer designers can easily anticipate that their designs will have to accommodate larger disk drives. It is wise to design the product to make this change easy to do. In contrast, it is very unlikely that a personal computer will need two or three keyboards attached to it at the same time. To leave flexibility on this attribute would be wasteful.

The New Need for Flexibility

If development flexibility has so far not been explicitly managed, why should managers do so now? They should, quite simply, because the product development environment is shifting in such a way that makes development flexibility increasingly important.

Two primary forces lie behind this shift. First, for many projects, product complexity has dramatically increased. As products acquire more functions, the difficulty of forecasting requirements rises exponentially. Second, the rate of change in most markets is also increasing, thereby reducing the effectiveness of traditional management approaches to forecasting the future. As a result, managers need to redefine the problem from one of improving forecasting to one of eliminating the need for accurate long-term forecasts.

There are two important ways to reduce exposure to the consequences of forecasting errors. The most obvious is to shorten development cycles. This acts to reduce the number of changes that will occur during development. This is an important benefit of rapid product development, and one that has already been emphasized in the literature.[6] In contrast, the use of flexibility reduces the cost of those changes that do have to be made, and thus is a method for reducing the consequences of forecasting errors—a theme that has received little attention up to now.

---

[6] For example, see p. 69 in P. Smith and D. Reinertsen, *Developing Products in Half the Time: New Rules, New Tools* (New York, NY: John Wiley & Sons, 1998).

Development Flexibility as an Alternative to Accurate Forecasting

Flexibility is a powerful method of controlling development risk. Traditionally, risk-reduction efforts have emphasized acquiring information about the future so as to increase the probability that the firm makes a correct choice. However, acquiring accurate information about the future becomes difficult or impossible when markets have many degrees of freedom and when the rate of change is high.

Development flexibility provides a powerful alternative to forecasting the future. By choosing design technologies and management strategies that decrease the "turning radius" of the firm, managers become less reliant on accurate long-term forecasting. Consider the example of the original IBM Personal Computer.

During the design of the PC, there were two viable design solutions for long-term storage. The Radio Shack TRS-80 successfully offered a cassette recorder, while the Apple II used a floppy disk drive. Both technologies were accepted in the marketplace, and it was unclear if either would become dominant. IBM could have performed market research to resolve this risk, but generating consumer preference data that could be relied upon was unlikely. Instead, IBM's PC offered both a cassette port (a socket that a cassette player could plug into) and a floppy drive. This is an example of a management choice, in this case regarding the architecture and feature set of the product, that made the product more flexible. Such flexibility made the product more tolerant of changes in the marketplace. The IBM Personal Computer was positioned such that it would *not* have to react to a change in consumer preference. As the market developed, consumers expressed a clear preference for the easier-to-use floppy disks and the cassette port was eliminated in IBM's next product, the IBM PC-XT.[7]

Thoughtful choices regarding development flexibility are critical, since without such flexibility the firm is forced to invest in the more difficult risk-management strategy of accurately forecasting a potentially unknowable future. The lower the development flexibility, the greater the economic incentive to invest in such forecasts. This is important because such investments may provide a small return in markets that move rapidly. One could argue that in the IBM Personal Computer situation, it was cheaper to pay the cost of the extra components for a cassette port than to forecast with high certainty the true needs of the marketplace and to bear the consequences of an incorrect forecast.

The Main Problem: Unstable Customer Needs

That product requirements are unstable is a fact known to practitioners and well documented in academic literature.[8] One of the authors has worked with hundreds of product developers and has yet to find a single project in which the requirements remained stable throughout the design. Surveying more than 200 product developers over the past five years, he found that fewer than 5 percent had a complete specification before beginning product design. On average, only 58 percent of requirements were specified before design

---

[7] This classic example of architectural flexibility appears in an article by D. Reinertsen ("Blitzkrieg Product Development: Cut Development Times in Half," *Electronic Business*, January 15, 1985), which advises that designers "stay flexible on unresolved issues. If you cannot resolve an issue, structure the design flexibly enough to go either way."

[8] E. von Hippel, "Adapting Market Research to the Rapid Evolution of Needs for New Products and Service," Working Paper No. 3374-92-BPS, MIT Sloan School of Management, 1992.

activities began. The inevitable result is changes. Academic research in the area of technological innovation has shown that a significant part of these changes can be attributed to:

- the co-evolution of technical solutions in components that are part of a larger system; and
- customers' inherent difficulty in accurately specifying their needs at the outset of a design project system.

Individual designs are often part of larger systems, and their requirements are derived from their role in such systems. As designers at the system and subsystem level engage in problem solving, they can alter interfaces within the system. Since these interfaces are in reality the product requirements for subsystems, these subsystems in turn are subject to changing requirements. These findings have been supported by Allen, who studied engineering problem solving and its related evolution of the technical solution path in the design of a number of aerospace systems.[9] He found that design engineers who were developing an aerospace subsystem conceived of and evaluated a number of design alternatives and eventually selected the one judged best. The designers' preferences for these alternatives, however, changed frequently and quickly as the design evolved, and it would have been very difficult to conclusively determine the best alternative at the outset of the project. Moreover, these different alternatives required different subsystem components or interfaces to other system components—resulting in rapidly changing product requirements (or specifications) as the development project evolved.

In many areas of product development, the increasing speed of technology development and its related technological obsolescence have further increased the instability of component requirements. For example, a designer of a personal computer may find that the chosen central processing unit (CPU) becomes obsolete before development is complete—resulting in costly and time-consuming design changes if the Flexibility Index relative to this product attribute is low.

At the system level, requirements are driven by rapidly evolving customer needs, an additional source of instability. Academic research has shown that familiarity with existing product attributes can interfere with an individual's ability to express needs for novel products.[10] In other words, it is hard for inexperienced customers to accurately describe their needs. Needs become more refined (or change) as the customer comes in direct contact with the product and starts to use it. This happens quite often in systems that involve human-machine interactions, resulting in responses such as the familiar "I'm really not sure what I want, but I'll know when I see it." For example, designers of applications software sometimes find that customers significantly revise requirements after they use their software for the first time, leading to very costly and time-consuming redesigns of an otherwise functional product.

Benefits of Development Flexibility

Development flexibility should be viewed as a parameter in an economic trade-off. A PC motherboard, for instance, can be designed to work at a certain clock frequency. If the clock frequency of the CPU increases, a costly redesign may be needed. Alternatively, the same

---

[9] T. Allen, "Studies of the Problem-Solving Process in Engineering Design," *IEEE Transactions on Engineering Management,* 2 (1966).

[10] E. von Hippel, *The Sources of Innovation* (New York, NY: Oxford University Press, 1988).

motherboard could be designed to operate at the higher frequency from the very beginning of the design process. The choice to design for the higher frequency would add unit cost to the design since it alters the layout and component choices for the motherboard. Yet this extra cost may be paid back handsomely if the market shifts more quickly than expected to higher-frequency motherboards. Again, the investment in raising the Flexibility Index with regard to CPU clock frequency is only worthwhile when its benefits exceed its costs.

Such investments to raise the Flexibility Index of the design with respect to certain attributes can be viewed as an insurance policy on the design. For example, if there was a 10 percent chance that the motherboard market was going to shift, and the shift would cost $2 million in profit before tax, a "fair" price to pay to raise flexibility on this attribute would be $200,000.

The benefits of flexibility vary with the competitive environment. In slow-moving and in easily predictable environments, there may be little value in investing in flexibility. In fast-moving and "turbulent" environments, however, flexibility can have large benefits. It is in such environments where the ability to accommodate evolving customer needs and technologies is of exceptional benefit. The benefit of such high design flexibility can be derived from the ability:

- to pursue a more efficient development strategy that can tolerate a higher risk of design changes;
- to make (late) product changes that lead to better design solutions with respect to customer needs and technologies; and
- to avoid the need for product changes entirely because design commitments can be made very late.[11]

As noted earlier, if flexibility is low (i.e., the economic cost of modifying a product is high), designers are more likely to engage in expensive and time-consuming information-gathering activities (such as forecasting and market research) aimed at minimizing the risk of design changes. For instance, designers would be more likely to invest effort in the careful understanding, specification, and documentation of design requirements. In contrast, when flexibility is high, designers are more likely to modify their products as more information becomes available, say with the aid of an early prototype that is used to generate customer feedback. Such an approach not only would lead to higher conformance to customer requirements, but could also have a significant impact on development cost and time. A large investment in early specification may provide little return if requirements were either hard to forecast or unstable.

With respect to making late product changes, consider some findings in a study of new product and process development. Using a controlled experiment, Boehm and his colleagues compared a prototype-driven approach (i.e., using a prototype to get customer feedback and change the design to incorporate new information) to the more traditional specification-driven approach (i.e., "freezing" the design after specification is complete) in

---

[11] See Iansiti, op. cit.; Iansiti and MacCormack, op. cit. They refer to the ability to delay decisions regarding a product's architecture as "the flexible approach" as opposed to their description of the traditional approach where a concept is frozen relatively early.

the development of applications software.[12] They found that prototyping—a process that allowed changes late in the design process as a result of new information from customers—resulted in products that not only were judged superior from a customer perspective, but also were developed with fewer design resources. Other studies of product and process development have resulted in similar findings: the ability to make changes close to product or process introduction was positively associated with higher customer quality and firm performance.[13]

With respect to avoiding product changes, the ultimate level of flexibility is achieved when the need for change itself has been eliminated. One possibility is to sequence design choices such that certain decisions are deferred until late in the development process when better information is available. For example, a daily newspaper makes content decisions at a time horizon that ranges from weeks to hours. Special sections are planned weeks in advance and even printed in advance. Advertisements are planned and prepared days in advance. However, the content of the front page and certain other pages is decided just hours before press time. Instead of bearing the cost of expensive changes, the "product requirements" are progressively frozen. Each section of the paper has its own timetable. Such a strategy means recognizing that a product requirement is not a single monolithic entity that is either "frozen" or "liquid," but rather a more complex structure that can be both "frozen" and "liquid" at the same time. This provides the ability to enjoy the benefits of late commitment while gaining the advantages of early commitment.

A manager could also avoid change by anticipating the areas in which the change will occur and leave adequate margin for these changes if they materialize. The backplane of an electronic system, for instance, can be designed to run at a higher frequency than actually needed. If a need to use higher speed components emerges, they can be adopted without costly redesign. Since this extra margin is not free, the Flexibility Index should be raised only in areas where it is really needed.

EMPIRICAL FOUNDATION: RESEARCH ON FLEXIBLE TECHNOLOGIES

To support our contention that flexibility in product development is important, we studied several hundred development projects as part of an empirical investigation.[14] The study concentrated on the integrated circuit (IC) design industry, a field chosen in part due to its emphasis on fierce competition and rapid change and in part due to its overall economic significance.

---

[12] B. Boehm, T. Gray, and T. Seewaldt, "Prototyping Versus Specifying: A Multi-project Experiment," *IEEE Transactions on Software Engineering,* 10/3 (May 1984): 290–303.

[13] For example, see J. Kluge, L. Stein, E. Krubasik, I. Beyer, D. Düsedau and W. Huhn, *Wachstum durch Verzicht* (Stuttgart, Germany: Schäffer-Poeschel, 1994).

[14] The results of this 1994 study have been reported in more detail in S. Thomke, "The Role of Flexibility in the Development of New Products: An Empirical Study," *Research Policy,* 26/1 (March 1997).

The study focused on integrated systems development projects that used one of the following two technologies:

- application-specific integrated circuits (ASICs), where the cost and time of making design changes to a prototype are high (*low flexibility*); and
- electrically programmable logic devices (EPLDs), where the cost and time of making design changes to a prototype is low (*high flexibility*).[15]

While ASIC technology has been available to designers for more than a decade, modern EPLDs are relatively new—they were invented in the late 1980s and have dramatically improved since then. While it is clear that technology choices are not the only way to increase development flexibility, they are one of the most important strategies available to management. In fact, we found significant differences between these two design technologies, specifically with respect to development efficiency and the ability to make late design changes. *First,* projects using flexible design technologies outperformed projects using inflexible technologies by a factor of 2.2 (in person-months), and over 23 percent of that difference can be attributed to differences in managing the risk of design changes. High flexibility enabled developers to tolerate fast-moving and turbulent environments, whereas low flexibility resulted in significantly higher resource investments that were aimed at minimizing the probability of design changes. *Second,* projects using flexible design technologies also were able to make more frequent prototype changes in the development process, which suggests a possibly higher degree of customer interaction throughout the development process and better conformance to the customer's final product requirements.

Research Methodology

A mail questionnaire was used to learn about the impact of flexibility on the development of integrated circuits. The questionnaire was sent to 1000 system designers that were selected from the subscriber database of a leading technical industry journal. The questionnaire was sent to two groups (500 EPLD designers and 500 ASIC designers) that were randomly chosen from a large pool of designers that qualified for the survey.[16] The responses left us with information on 391 development projects that were evenly divided between ASIC and EPLD technologies. A comparison of the respondents' length of design experience resulted in no significant difference between the groups—both had been designing systems with integrated circuits for an average of ten years. The study also included measures of project complexity which allowed us to compare development projects of comparable complexity.[17]

[15] The cost to build (and to modify) a prototype is commonly referred to as nonrecurring engineering (NRE) costs. As a general rule, NRE costs of ASICs can exceed $10,000 while the cost of a single EPLD varies but can fall under $100. Furthermore, it can sometimes take several weeks to get an ASIC prototype, while EPLD prototypes can be programmed in-house and are available within hours. A very well known EPLD technology are field-programmable gate arrays (FPGAs).

[16] Selected participants work either in system design or design and development engineering. They design a large variety of end products, ranging from communications systems to medical electronic equipment, and they are employed in companies all over the United States.

[17] In order to control for complexity, the sample sizes had to be reduced to n=51 (EPLDs) and n=38 (ASICs). The statistical methods employed accounted for these differences.

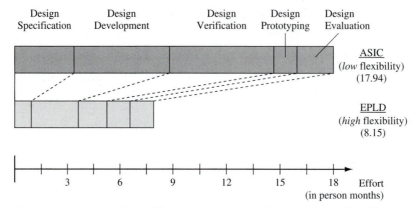

FIGURE 2
Distribution of Development Effort

Note: Data are from projects with comparable complexity. Project complexity was approximated with the aid of six different measures such as design size, novelty, experience, etc.

Results

Earlier it was proposed that flexibility has a strong impact on development strategy and performance. Thus, in the case of a low-flexibility technology (ASIC), a design strategy that minimizes the risk of prototype changes (for example, by focusing much effort on understanding, specifying and documenting design requirements) would be expected. In contrast, a high-flexibility technology (EPLD) enables designers to accept higher levels of risk because changes can be made at low cost and less time as development projects and the related requirements evolve.

Since a strategy of high risk makes smaller investments in activities aimed at minimizing the risk of design changes, and as the penalty for these changes is relatively low if they occur, one would expect higher flexibility to result in higher development efficiency. Similarly, as design requirements and technical solution approaches evolve during the development process, it would further be expected that the ability to incorporate late changes enables the designer to achieve a higher degree of design performance and conformance to customer needs.

The analysis of the project performance data shows that EPLD designers needed an average effort of 8.15 person-months to complete their projects, while ASIC designers needed 17.94 person-months (see **Figure 2;** projects were of comparable complexity).[18]

Much of this difference can be attributed to the higher flexibility of EPLDs. If one considers that development effort correlates highly with time-to-market (quite often, these projects are completed by one- to two-member teams), and that product life cycles in this industry are

---

[18] As the measured variables can be influenced by design complexity and ASIC designs are on average more complex than EPLD designs, two subsamples were extracted and compared along several complexity measures. A comparison between EPLD and ASIC design projects that are in the two subsamples shows no significant difference for the first five measures. (Only the sixth variable showed a difference significant at 5 percent which would provide some weak support of higher EPLD complexity.) Thus it is reasonable to assume that projects from both subsamples are of similar complexity and that an objective comparison of project performance can be conducted. Results of the study were compared using these subsamples only.

very short, then a difference of such magnitude represents a significant competitive advantage for a firm.

A statistical analysis of design effort shows that the overall performance difference came primarily from a project's earlier phases: design specification, development, and verification. EPLD designers required significantly fewer resources than ASIC designers in all of these three phases, while no significant differences were found for design prototyping and evaluation.

Design specification—where information on customer needs is gathered and specifications are determined—accounted for 23.4 percent of the total design performance difference. EPLD designers invested by a factor of 3.1 less effort in specification than their ASIC counterparts. This difference, in fact, is a rational response to the different expected cost and time of making prototype changes. EPLD designers, who face low cost and less time for making changes, spend less time on developing a clear and precise understanding of customer requirements and definition of specifications, several of which are likely to be modified as the design evolves anyway. In contrast, ASIC designers have an incentive to spend considerably more time up front to clearly understand, specify, and document requirements, since any prototype changes could prove expensive and jeopardize the financial success of the project.

In sum, these differences suggest different approaches to managing the risk of changes. EPLD technology (*high* flexibility) enabled designers to tolerate higher levels of risk whereas ASIC technology (*low* flexibility) resulted in higher resource investments aimed at minimizing the risk of change. Significantly, the EPLD designers were able to defer the resolution of certain requirements to a later stage of the development, when these could be defined more efficiently and where they would be less likely to change.

Another 28 percent of the total performance difference can be attributed to *design development*. ASIC designers spent significantly more effort on development than did EPLD designers. Interviews showed that much of the additional effort ASIC designers invested was driven by their expectations of the high cost and time to make changes during prototype testing. First, ASICs were more carefully designed so as to reduce the likelihood of running into problems during prototype testing. Second, as a means of minimizing the risk of failure, ASIC manufacturers required thorough design documentation, which in turn requires additional preparation time on the designer's part. In contrast, EPLD designers could come up with a design solution and quickly move to an experimental trial (via simulation or prototype testing) as a means of getting rapid feedback.

Finally, *design verification* accounts for 43.2 percent of the total performance difference. ASIC designers spent significantly more effort on verification than did EPLD designers—primarily because ASIC designers stayed longer with computer simulation; the high cost and increased time of prototype changes makes prototype testing less attractive. However, sometimes prototype testing can become more efficient than simulation, usually after having performed some degree of initial simulation testing. But because of the high cost and increased time in making prototype changes, ASIC designers try to stay with simulation as long as possible, thus forgoing some of the efficiency benefits that switching to prototype testing can provide.[19] Interestingly, less simulation did not lead to significantly

[19] For a detailed explanation, see S. Thomke, "Managing Experimentation in the Design of New Products," *Management Science*, 44/6 (June 1998).

FIGURE 3
**Comparing
Prototype
Changes
Between
Development
Projects**

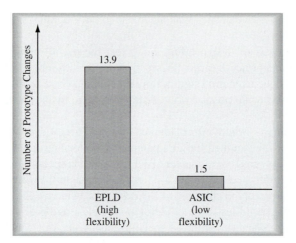

Note: Data are from designs of comparable complexity. Prototype changes were defined as "changes that were made to any part of the physical design prototype and that were subsequently verified by the designer."

higher EPLD effort during *design evaluation*—the phase where most prototype testing occurs.

Earlier it was also proposed that, in addition to better development performance, higher flexibility enables designers to incorporate the most current design requirements and user needs as these co-evolve with the development process. The study, however, provided only an indirect measure of the extent to which the most current requirements were possibly incorporated. Designers were asked to provide the number of design changes that were made in the physical prototype (the last phase of the design process). Since a significant percentage of these changes were due to new or modified product requirements, the higher number of changes indicates that the development team was able to respond to a larger number of often very late change requests. This suggests a higher degree of conformance to the customer's ultimate requirements. In contrast, fewer changes indicate that more requirements were frozen early and were not allowed to change, in spite of a change in needs or the availability of information pointing towards a more optimal design solution.

The variable "number of prototype changes" **(Figure 3)** shows that, on average, EPLD designers made 13.9 prototype changes before the product was complete while ASIC designers made 1.5 prototype changes. Thus, assuming that some of these late changes were due to information not available prior or during design specification, the data provides some indirect evidence that EPLD designs were also more current with respect to user requirements, leading to better development solutions.

Why would firms select ASIC technology if EPLD technology was technically feasible and allowed developers to be more flexible? A number of alternative explanations were discovered during the study.

First, designers choose to stay with ASIC technologies because at large-volume production, lower variable cost for ASICs would provide significant savings that are "traded against" a more inefficient, slower, and less flexible development process. The data from the two subsamples supports our notion that development flexibility can be viewed as an economic trade-off: on average, EPLD designers eventually produced 1581 units whereas ASIC designers had average production volumes of 113,232 units. However, the economics of the underlying trade-off are changing: the variable cost of EPLDs is decreasing rapidly, the monetary value of shorter development time is increasing, and some firms have started to specialize on technologies and services that combine flexible EPLD-based development with ASIC-like production costs. The result is a gradual migration away from traditional ASIC design technology where EPLDs are feasible alternatives (i.e., at designs of low to medium complexity), even if larger production volumes are required.

Second, we were told in interviews that ASIC designers are reluctant to switch to a technology they often consider "inferior." Doing so requires them to make an investment in acquiring different skills and, if they became EPLD designers, offers a career track with lower pay, less peer recognition, and fewer opportunities to grow (e.g., moving into high-end design projects). Nonetheless, market forces are pushing towards a proliferation of the more flexible EPLD technology, particularly for designs of low to medium complexity, for many of the reasons that are described in this article.

APPROACHES TO INCREASING DEVELOPMENT FLEXIBILITY

There are three broad strategies for increasing development flexibility. The first and most obvious was implied in the previous section: adopting technologies that are inherently flexible. The second involves structuring management processes to increase development flexibility. Indeed, managers can only fully exploit the power of flexible technologies when they tailor their management process to exploit them. The third and most subtle strategy is to exploit product architecture as a tool to increase development flexibility.

Adopt Flexible Technologies

The first broad strategy is using flexible technology, because the chosen product and process technology will affect the economic cost of making changes in the product. For example, the recent emergence of computer-aided design and engineering tools, combined with rapid prototyping technologies, has reduced the cost and time of product changes significantly. Complex three-dimensional objects used to require days or weeks of work in a machine shop to fabricate. Many such shapes can now be made rapidly—in a few hours—by using computer-controlled machining equipment and/or equipment for creating objects via "three-dimensional printing."[20] Similarly, designers can now create and change physical prototypes of complex electronic circuitry at their desks or lab benches in minutes by using the flexible EPLD technology just described in the previous section.

A key attribute of these new technologies is that they lower iteration cost. Many traditional businesses treat the cost of each iteration on their design as a fixed and unchangeable charge. In fact, the fixed cost of iterations in the process depends on the design of the process itself. Just as word-processors change the cost of iterations on documents, changes in design technology and processes reduce the economic cost of design iterations. For example, investing in an automated testing facility to permit round-the-clock testing can

[20] For a description of this technology, see E. Sachs et al., "CAD-Casting: Direct Fabrication of Ceramic Shells and Cores by Three Dimensional Printing," *Manufacturing Review,* 5/2 (June 1992).

lower the duration of the testing process and its associated economic costs. When the choice is made to lower the cost of doing iterations on the design, the Flexibility Index for many types of design changes is raised.

If high flexibility can provide such significant R&D performance improvements, why are some firms slower than others in adopting technologies and concepts that lead to higher degrees of flexibility? Very often, flexibility gains require investments in technology, skills, and knowledge. However, firms are better at assessing the investment cost of achieving flexibility than they are at assessing the economic value of flexibility. As shown in the empirical study, the switch to the more flexible EPLD technology requires investments in new design and simulation tools as well as the skills to test and "debug" complex hardware prototypes. In general, firms find it difficult to change routines and knowledge that are deeply embedded in the organization,[21] and adopting more flexible technologies is no exception. Thus, managers not only must understand the costs and benefits of more flexible technologies, but also how to tackle obstacles in the way to an effective adoption.

Modify Management Processes

A second general strategy for creating development flexibility is to modify management processes to maximize flexibility. This can be done in a variety of ways.

Progressively Lock Down Requirements

Many companies are stuck because they use a model of development in which all requirements must be defined before any design work can begin. They argue that you cannot begin to design until you know what you will be designing. This forces them to specify items for which accurate information is not yet available, and it exposes them to making changes when accurate information does become available. However, there is an alternative model of development that locks down requirements progressively. In this model, firms are less vulnerable to change because they defer commitment on the most uncertain items. In effect, firms are making specification decisions at a shorter time horizon, where the decisions can be made both more efficiently and where they are more likely to remain stable.

Consider the example of developing a new telephone. A traditional approach might require full electronic and mechanical specification before any design activities could begin. However, the tools exist today to do photo-realistic models of different enclosure concepts before committing to a single approach. Furthermore, it is possible to take the computer files from such images and rapidly produce physical models. This enables direct feedback from users well before the specification is finalized. As long as the design process assumes that 100 percent of the product will be specified before any of it is designed, it is not possible to take advantage of these new tools. Such an approach lowers the Flexibility Index associated with changes in physical packaging.

---

[21] For example, see M. T. Hannan and J. Freeman, "Structural Inertia and Organizational Change," *American Sociological Review,* 49 (1984); R. Henderson and K. Clark, "Architectural Innovation: The Reconfiguration of Existing Product Technologies and the Failure of Established Firms," *Administrative Science Quarterly,* 35/1 (March 1990): 9–30; M. Tushman and P. Anderson, "Technological Discontinuities and Organizational Environments," *Administrative Science Quarterly,* 31/3 (September 1986): 439–465.

Keep Multiple Back-Up Approaches Viable Even After Concept Selection

In most companies, once a design concept is selected everyone must support it or risk not being a team player. A healthier approach is to recognize that the moment a preferred concept is selected, it is human nature to devalue other competing concepts. While this builds psychological commitment to the chosen concept, it leaves no options open if the dominant concept fails. It is better to keep at least one back-up approach alive in case the primary concept has unexpected problems. For example, if you were designing a medical product that required bioactivity tests on its materials, you might qualify both the materials you had chosen and the back-up materials. This way, if you had to switch to a back-up material, you will have eliminated some of the time required to adopt it. This approach is particularly useful for materials and design approaches that have long testing cycles.

Provide a Sound Framework for Making Trade-off Decisions

Much decision-making delay arises because people working on programs do not have appropriate tools to make trade-off decisions. The longer it takes to make a decision, the higher the cost of change and the lower the flexibility. Development flexibility can be increased by providing decision support tools that facilitate rapid and correct decisions. Such tools have been used by practitioners for years and are described in the product development literature.[22]

For example, consider the issue of optimizing the cost of early production units. Many companies try to achieve low unit costs on their initial production units. A straightforward path to doing this is to invest in production approaches with high fixed costs and low variable costs. For example, castings can be used instead of weldments, hard tooling can be used instead of soft tooling, and ASICs can be used instead of EPLDs. Most often these low–variable cost approaches have long lead times associated with them, forcing early commitment to a particular course of action. Unfortunately, the combination of early commitment and high fixed cost is particularly dangerous. It dramatically lowers the Flexibility Index of the design.

Instead, managers should carefully examine whether initial production units can be produced with less cost-effective but more flexible approaches. If so, the cost of making changes in the design can be lowered. In fact, with good decision tools the cost of design changes can be quantified and compared to the cost of expensive initial production units. This shifts the debate to a fact-based arena where it is likely to generate better decisions. Furthermore, a much higher buy-in is likely from all parties involved because they will understand the reasons for the decision.

Measure and Improve Reaction Time

One consequence of providing the right decision tools is that managers will begin to focus on measuring the right development process parameters. Since late changes usually cost more money, process and decision-making delays reduce process flexibility. When managers try to measure and improve reaction time, they raise flexibility.

One medical products company found that it could reduce tooling delays simply by measuring the tooling shop on the basis of percent delivery to customer-required schedule rather than cost per tool. In this case, the firm discovered that the primary economic cost associated with tooling iterations was the time that it added to a program's critical path. By knowing the

---

[22] For example. see Reinertsen and Smith. op. cit.; Wheelwright and Clark, op. cit.

value of these delays, the correct metrics could be applied to the tooling shop. With metrics encouraging fast-responsiveness from the tooling shop, iterations could be done faster and with lower economic cost. This raised the Flexibility Index associated with tooling changes.

Make Piecewise Commitments versus Binary Choices

The cost of change can be reduced by making piecewise commitments rather than binary choices. For example, the traditional approach to manufacturing release is to consider a part either unreleased or released. This can be called a binary choice. In contrast, multiple release levels for a drawing can be established, each of which conveys different information. A drawing can be released for purposes of buying material even though it may not be released for purposes of tool design or tool machining. For example, on the Boeing 777 program, part drawings often had six or more release levels, each of which permitted certain downstream activities. Such multiple release levels increase flexibility because they provide a controlled process to make late decisions on certain design features. In contrast, the normal one-release approach requires all decisions to be made at the same time, which means that the entire part must be frozen at procurement lead-time of the part. This raises the cost of change very early in the program.

Unfortunately, most development processes are generally structured around such binary choices. The specification is 0 percent approved until a key management checkpoint, at which it becomes 100 percent approved. Such procedures prevent beginning any design work without an approved specification. A better approach is to allow individual chunks of the specification to be progressively approved, as described earlier in this article. Then design issues can be resolved without raising unnecessary barriers to change. This increases the Flexibility Index with respect to many requirements changes.

Structure Design Tasks

Flexibility can also be increased by the way design tasks are structured. Development projects are typically partitioned into smaller tasks, and the boundaries between these tasks can affect development flexibility due to the associated interdependencies among tasks. For example, if two very interdependent tasks are geographically separated but require much personal interaction, any changes to one of the tasks can result in costly and time-consuming changes in the other tasks as well. On the other hand, if both tasks were co-located, changes could be dealt with much more effectively. Unfortunately, firms do not pay enough attention to task interdependence. As von Hippel noted:

> If improvements to innovation task partitioning can yield major benefits to firms, we then have much to learn about it. Firms I have interviewed to date appear not to think about task problem-solving interdependence as an input to partitioning decisions at all, at least not explicitly. Instead, some appear to make such decisions primarily on the basis of assumed economies of specialization (e.g., "All electrical design work will be done by group A"; "All marketing research studies will be done by group M."). Other firms appear to simply follow some traditional pattern of innovation task partitioning without analysis (e.g., "We have always designed aircraft bodies by dividing them into a series of cylindrical sections and assigning each section to a different task group. No one now at the company has thought about why we do this or whether it currently makes sense from any point of view. It is just the way we do it.").[23]

[23] E. von Hippel, "Task Partitioning: An Innovation Process Variable," *Research Policy,* 19/5 (October 1990):407–418.

FIGURE 4
**Increasing
Flexibility by
Effective Task
Partitioning**

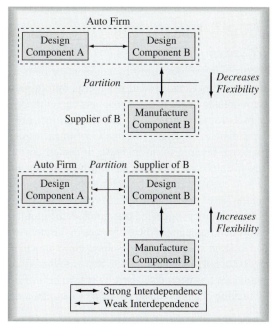

Note: Redrawn with modifications from E. A. von Hippel, "Task Partitioning: An Innovation Process Variable," *Research Policy 19* (1990): 407–418.

Thus, carefully selecting the boundaries between system components and design tasks (so as to minimize total system interdependencies) can have a significant impact on design flexibility and its associated development strategy. Consider the example of an auto firm and one of its suppliers as depicted in **Figure 4.**[24] The interdependence between two of the auto firm's design tasks (components A and B) is weak, but the design and the manufacture of component B have a high problem-solving interdependence. Traditionally, the firm would keep the design of component B in-house but would outsource the manufacture of B to a supplier. Because of the high interdependence between design and manufacture, it becomes very difficult to manage an often geographically separated interface that would experience a high degree of interaction during times of rapid change. On the other hand, moving the design and manufacture to B (such as in modular procurement) internalizes the design–manufacture interface to the supplier, which, in most cases, can be managed more effectively.

Since task boundaries are usually selected in the earlier phases of a development project but play such an important role in the ability to react to rapid change, managers are well advised to plan the division of activities with great care or at least build in sufficient flexibility to allow changes in partitioning as a project evolves.

Leverage Design Architecture

A third general strategy for increasing flexibility is to attack the problem at an architectural level. In general, few managers appreciate the enormous leverage that can be obtained

[24] Ibid.

using this approach. Too often, architecture is left as a technical decision, which fails to exploit its potential to improve business performance.

Use Modular Product Structures

Modular product structures increase flexibility by aggregating certain functions together and isolating them from other functions. How this aggregation, or partitioning, is done is quite important because it creates interdependencies between components. The economic cost of making changes to a product, particularly later in a project, are strongly influenced by these design interdependencies. A change in one component can cause a sequence of changes in other components, leading to an increase in design cost and time. Thus, the Flexibility Index of a design can be increased by developing a design architecture that minimizes interdependence between its individual components. This approach is not novel and has been proposed by a number of researchers who have studied the design and innovation process. In his 1964 book, Alexander suggested that good architectural designs are made of subsystems that can be adjusted independently to changes in the environment.[25] As a result, he noted, the speed of adaptation is a function of subsystem interdependencies: if they are too strong, a system may be unable to adapt at a rate that is higher than the rate of change. More recently, interdependence has been discussed by researchers of design structure who proposed that the cost of making changes can be reduced by a modular design architecture.[26]

Isolate Volatility in the Design

In practice, modularity alone is not enough to create flexibility; it matters greatly how you partition functionality within the design. By partitioning well, you can isolate the influence of a perturbing variable to a small portion of the design. This will raise the Flexibility Index with respect to this perturbing variable.

The traditional literature on partitioning of designs emphasizes certain classic heuristics such as aggregating common functions or partitioning the design to reduce communications between modules. We propose that there is another powerful strategy for partitioning a design—to segregate volatility within the structure. For example, a large telecommunications switch design contains a lot of software. There is both mission-critical real-time call-processing software and less-critical management information reports. The call-processing software must be highly reliable and does not change frequently. In contrast, almost every customer wants slightly different management information. A good software design on such a project will partition MIS functions into a distinct module that is loosely coupled to the rest of the software. This permits the switch designer to respond to customer requests for different reports without tampering with the vital call-processing software.

---

[25] C. Alexander, *Notes on the Synthesis of Form* (Cambridge, MA: Harvard University Press 1964).

[26] For example, see M. Meyer and J. Utterback, "The Product Family and the Dynamics of Core Capability," *Sloan Management Review,* 34/3 (Spring 1993): 29–47; K. Ulrich, "The Role of Product Architecture in the Manufacturing Firm," *Research Policy,* 24/3 (May 1995): 419–440; C. Baldwin and K. Clark, *Design Rules: The Power of Modularity* (Cambridge. MA: MIT Press. forthcoming 1999); C. Baldwin and K. Clark. "Managing in an Age of Modularity," *Harvard Business Review,* 75/5 (September/October 1997): 84–93 ; K. Ulrich and S. Eppinger, *Product Design and Development* (New York, NY: McGraw-Hill. 1995); R. Sanchez and J. Mahoney. "Modularity, Flexibility, and Knowledge Management in Product and Organization Design," *Strategic Management Journal,* 17 (Winter 1996): 63–76.

Although a software design is modular with low interdependencies between modules, if the MIS functions appear in all the modules, then a change in such reports will cause high change costs.

A special case of the general strategy of isolating volatility is to displace it outside the system boundary. This can be done by taking the most variable portion of the functionality and moving it outside the system boundary. This is a common strategy among companies doing "mass customization." For example, a manufacturer of window shades designs the pole such that the shades are adjustable. The plasticized fabric can be ripped to size for a variety of window widths. Because the product's customization can be done by the customer, there is no need to respond to changes in the width of shades or metric versus English requirements. Application software companies use a similar strategy when they let users customize menus or record macro operations. Shifting the burden of customization onto the user effectively insulates the design from many perturbing variables and therefore raises its Flexibility Index.[27]

Reduce Coupling Between Modules

Another architectural strategy is to reduce the coupling between modules within the system. Lower coupling, or interdependency, will lead to more flexibility. Consider the design of popular personal computer operating systems such as Microsoft Windows. These operating systems use many files that are shared between applications. Such a structure cross-couples application programs that share these modules. The effect on the system user is that loading a new program has the potential to update shared modules being used by many other programs. This creates the result that loading a new application program can irretrievably damage other apparently unrelated programs. Every user of Windows has probably had the experience where loading a new program "broke" other programs that had been previously working perfectly.

A key technique for reducing coupling within the design is to increase the design margins in the interfaces within the architecture. This enables us to buffer changes that originate in one module from another module. The essence in achieving this sort of architectural robustness lies in what sort of design margins are allocated to system interfaces. *Again, it is not modularity itself that produces robustness, but rather modules that are loosely coupled to one another.*

A robust architecture will carefully provide higher design margins in the interfaces that exist around volatile and risky system components. For example, if you design a power supply for exactly the amount of power required by the system, any increase in the power requirements may force a change in the system. If you allow extra margin you can absorb a change with much less design change, thus increasing the Flexibility Index of the design.

CONCLUSIONS

Development flexibility is a measurable attribute of a development process and one that can be proactively managed. There are three major strategies for improving development flexibility. First, managers can explicitly choose flexible development technologies. Second,

---

[27] This strategy is also discussed in E. von Hippel, "Economics of Product Development by Users: The Impact of 'Sticky' Local Information," *Management Science,* 44/5 (May 1998).

FIGURE 5
**Approaches to
Increasing
Development
Flexibility**

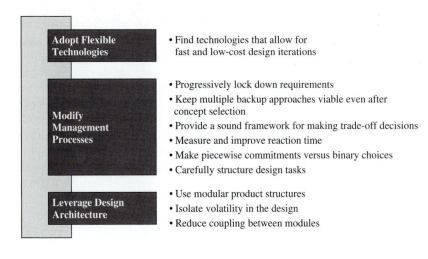

**Adopt Flexible
Technologies**

- Find technologies that allow for
  fast and low-cost design iterations

**Modify
Management
Processes**

- Progressively lock down requirements
- Keep multiple backup approaches viable even after
  concept selection
- Provide a sound framework for making trade-off decisions
- Measure and improve reaction time
- Make piecewise commitments versus binary choices
- Carefully structure design tasks

**Leverage Design
Architecture**

- Use modular product structures
- Isolate volatility in the design
- Reduce coupling between modules

managers can exploit management approaches that lower the cost of change in the process. Third, managers can make product architectural choices that allow the product to easily accommodate change. **Figure 5** provides some specific suggestions that managers can use to position their company to succeed in markets that are accelerating and becoming more turbulent. Development flexibility should be more than an accidental attribute of a development process—it should be a capability that is explicitly managed.

Developing Products on Internet Time: A Process Design Exercise

Your team has started a company that plans to develop an Internet-based game. The game would be aimed at high school and college students and would allow them to play with and against each other over the Net. The software would allow them to build cities in cyberspace, trade with each other, wage war, and engage in a variety of other activities. Its tentative name is **CitiNet.**

You have also learned that another company, **NettGames,** has just started to develop a similar game and there are some significant first-mover advantages. Analysts believe that the first game will capture over 80 percent of the market because of significant network effects.

You estimate that it will take six months to develop CitiNet, which should be sufficient to beat NettGames to market. Your team's task is to:

- **Release** your product to market on time.
- **Organize** your team (roles and responsibilities).
- Select **features.**
- Create a complete **development schedule,** including:
  1. Sequence of feature development activities
  2. Milestones or phase reviews
  3. Number, dates, and content of beta releases

To simplify your task, marketing and product development have come up with the six potential features and their development time estimates shown in **Exhibit 1.** Only one team member can work on one feature at a given point in time.

Harvard Business School Case No. 9-600-121. Copyright 2000 President and Fellows of Harvard College. All rights reserved. For information: permissions@hbsp.harvard.edu.

This exercise was prepared by Stefan Thomke. HBS exercises are developed solely for class discussion and do not necessarily illustrate effective or ineffective management.

You will have 30 minutes (5 minutes per expected month of schedule) of class time to prepare a development plan that includes (a) the team's roles and responsibilities, (b) selected features, and (c) a development schedule. Some teams will be asked to present plans at the end of the exercise.

EXHIBIT 1
**Six Potential
Features and
Development
Time Estimates
(e.g., It would
take one team
member two
months to
develop 3D
graphics.)**

Feature	Estimated Time Requirement (Months)
Multi-player (> 5)	3
3D graphics	2
Sound	1
Keeps highest scores on main server	1
Integrated chat/instant messaging	2
Works on Windows *and* Mac	5
Also: Managing each beta release	**0.5**
Also: Managing testing/feature integration	**3**

Note: You may develop some features in parallel, but experience has shown that more overlap increases rework and coordination cost.

Article

Developing Products
on Internet Time

The rise of the World Wide Web has provided one of the most challenging environments for product development in recent history. The market needs that a product is meant to satisfy and the technologies required to satisfy them can change radically—even as the product is under development. In response to such factors, companies have had to modify the traditional product-development process in which design implementation begins only once a product's concept has been determined in its entirety. Instead, they have pioneered a *flexible* product-development process that allows designers to continue to define and shape products even after implementation has begun. This innovation enables Internet companies to incorporate rapidly changing customer requirements and evolving technologies into their designs until the last possible moment before a product is introduced to the market.

Flexible product development has been most fully realized in the Internet environment because of the turbulence found there, but the foundations for it exist in a wide range of industries where the need for responsiveness is paramount. Product developers in industries from computer workstations to banking increasingly face dynamic and unpredictable environments characterized by rapidly evolving technologies, changing customer tastes, and sweeping regulatory changes. In these industries, companies that have begun to adopt more flexible product-development approaches are setting new competitive standards.

What's involved in increasing the flexibility of the product development process? Many of the companies we studied have adopted a coherent set of mechanisms that allow product developers to generate and respond to new information about what customers want and about how technology has evolved over the course of a project. These mechanisms not only

Marco Iansiti is a professor at the Harvard Business School in Boston, Massachusetts, where his research focuses on the factors that influence R&D performance. He is the author of *Technology Integration: Making Critical Choices in a Dynamic World*. His last article for HBR was "Technology Integration: Turning Great Research into Great Products" (May–June 1997). Alan MacCormack is an associate professor at the Harvard Business School. His research explores how companies manage product development in rapidly changing business environments.

enable a continuous flow of information about customer needs and new technologies, but also reduce both the cost and the time it takes to integrate that information into the evolving product design. They allow designers continually *to sense* customer needs, *to test* alternative technical solutions, and *to integrate* the acquired knowledge into a coherent product design. This flexible process continues iteratively throughout the development process.

The traditional development processes that many companies use are highly structured. A future product is designed, developed, transferred to production, and rolled out to the market in clearly articulated, sequential phases. Such processes usually begin with the identification of users' needs and an assessment of the various technological possibilities. Then a detailed set of product specifications is created and, once approved by senior management, is set in stone. At that point, attention shifts to implementation as a functionally integrated team translates the concept into reality. If the up-front work has been done correctly, inherently expensive changes to the product's specifications are kept to a minimum. Indeed, the number of engineering changes is often used as a measure of a project's effectiveness: many changes signify an inferior effort.

In contrast, flexible product development delays until as late as possible any commitment to a final design configuration. The concept development phase and the implementation phase thus overlap instead of following each other sequentially. By accepting the need for and reducing the cost of changes, companies are able to respond to new information that arises during the course of a product's development. Systemic changes in a project's definition and basic direction are managed proactively; designers begin this process with no precise idea of how it will end. (See **Exhibit 1,** "Two Approaches to Product Development.")

When technology, product features, and competitive conditions are predictable or evolve slowly, a traditional development process works well. But in turbulent business environments, a sequential approach to product development is more than inefficient; it risks creating an obsolete product—one that fails to address customer needs and to make use of the latest technologies. When new competitors and technologies are likely to appear overnight, when standards and regulations are in flux, and when a company's entire customer base can easily switch to other suppliers, businesses don't need a development process that resists change—they need one that embraces it.

A FLEXIBLE PROCESS AT WORK

Not every company interested in developing a flexible product-development process would have to go to the extremes that Netscape did. But by looking at Netscape's experiences, we can see how a highly flexible process works. Founded in 1994, the company pioneered the easy-to-use Web browser: a software interface that provides access to the World Wide Web. The Web browser has transformed the Internet from a communications channel for scientists and technicians into a network connecting millions of ordinary users across time and space—and thus into an industry in its own right.

But Netscape faced no easy task in developing its Web browser, Navigator. In the rapidly evolving Internet industry, many alternative technologies and applications compete for attention, and product development is a project manager's nightmare. The major challenge in the development of a Web browser is the level of technical complexity involved: a typical program rivals a traditional word processing or spreadsheet application in size, and it must work seamlessly with myriad different hardware and software platforms. The level of uncertainty is so high that even the most basic decisions about a product must be continually revised as new information arises. And the fact that industry giant Microsoft, which had already developed its own flexible product-development process, was readying a product to compete with Navigator only added to the complexity and urgency of Netscape's development effort.

Netscape introduced Navigator 2.0 to the market in January of 1996 and immediately thereafter began to develop the next version of the Web browser, Navigator 3.0, which was to be released in August of the same year. (See **Exhibit 2**, "The Development of Navigator 3.0: A Timeline.") The Netscape development group—which included staff from engineering, marketing, and customer support—produced the first prototype quickly. By February 14, just six weeks into the project, it had put a Beta 0 version of the program up on the company's internal project Web site for testing by the development staff. Although many of the intended functions were not yet available, the prototype captured enough of the essence of the new product to generate meaningful feedback from members of the development group. On February 22, less than two weeks later, the team posted an updated version, Beta 1, again for internal development staff only. In early March, with major bugs in the product worked out, the first public release, Beta 2, appeared on Netscape's Internet Web site. Additional public releases followed thereafter every few weeks until the official release date in August, with gradual refinements appearing in each beta iteration.

The sequence of beta versions was extremely useful to Netscape because it enabled the development team to react both to feedback from users and to changes in the marketplace while the team was still working on the Web browser's design. Beta users by and large are more sophisticated than Netscape's broader customer base and therefore are a valuable source of information. Most useful among them are developers from other Internet software companies, who tend to be extremely vocal customers. Because many of these customers use the Navigator browser as part of the environment in which their own products operate, they are often the first to find the more complicated bugs—bugs that are revealed only when the product is stretched to the limits of its performance in complex applications.

Getting input from users was one way in which the Navigator team generated new information during the course of the project. During the seven-month development cycle, however, the team also paid careful attention to competing products. As the largest and most powerful software developer in the industry, Microsoft was considered a very serious threat to Netscape's then-dominant position in the browser market. The software giant had just undertaken a dramatic—and very public—switch in strategy, refocusing its formidable talents squarely on the Internet. As a result, Netscape continually monitored the latest beta versions of Microsoft's competing product, Explorer, to compare features and formats. Based on the information that it gathered, the Netscape team would often add format or feature changes to the current beta version of its own product.

In order to respond to the constant stream of new information being brought into the development process, the team carried out extensive experimentation and testing. Subgroups working on individual features went through numerous design-build-test cycles, gradually adding functionality to the product. As features were completed, the team integrated them into the evolving product, then conducted tests to ensure that the new feature did not produce unwanted interactions with other parts of the system. These so-called system builds occurred with increasing frequency as the project progressed; they were performed at least daily in the run-up to the official release.

To facilitate the integration of the vast amounts of information generated during the project, Netscape set up a project Web site on its intranet. The site contained the product's development schedule and specifications, each of which was updated as target dates changed or new features were added. In addition, it contained bulletin boards through which team members could monitor the evolution of various parts of the design, noting the completion of specific features and logging problems in the existing version. Once Navigator moved to public beta testing, these intranet features became especially valuable because an increasing amount of information then had to be received, classified, and processed.

Netscape built into its product-development process considerable flexibility to respond to changes in market demands and technology. And what is already true of companies in the Internet industry is becoming true of companies elsewhere. Our research on the computer-workstation-and-server industry has shown that there, too, a more flexible process is associated with greater performance. In this environment, companies with a faster response time, as measured from the construction of the first physical prototype to commercial shipping, clearly outperform those with slower response times. The use of sophisticated simulation tools allows teams to work with a virtual prototype for much of the project—in effect, creating a significant overlap between the concept and the design implementation phases.

According to Allen Ward and his colleagues in "The Second Toyota Paradox: How Delaying Decisions Can Make Better Cars Faster" (*Sloan Management Review,* Spring 1995), there also is evidence that a more flexible model has emerged in the automotive industry. Toyota's development process allows it to delay many design decisions until later in the development cycle. The development team creates several sets of design options and, finally, through a process of elimination, selects only one for implementation. As a result, Toyota can respond to changing market conditions at a later stage than many of its competitors.

THE FOUNDATIONS OF A FLEXIBLE PROCESS

How should companies create a flexible development process? The experiences of leading companies suggest that senior managers first must understand what gives the process its flexibility. Product development flexibility is rooted in the ability to manage jointly the evolution of a product and its application context. The goal is to capture a rich understanding of customer needs and alternative technical solutions as a project progresses, then to integrate that knowledge into the evolving product design. The faster a project can integrate that information, the faster that project can respond to changes in the product's environment.

The value of flexible product development, however, is only as good as the quality of the process it uses to generate information about the interaction between technical choices and market requirements. Unlike traditional development projects, which rely on periodic bursts of input on users' needs, projects in turbulent business environments require continual feedback. To acquire and use this information, the development process must be able to sense customer needs, to test alternative technical solutions, and to integrate the knowledge gained of both markets and technologies into a coherent product. (See **Exhibit 3,** "The Structure of a Flexible Product-Development Process.")

As we describe how leading companies have achieved a more flexible development process, many of the examples we cite come from our work with several software companies that have recently launched Internet products or services. But bear in mind that this is not the only industry in which these lessons apply. We also describe specific practices from other, more traditional industries to illustrate that the approaches used are not unique to the Internet. In fact, they represent cutting-edge practice across a range of environments where change is—or is becoming—the norm.

Sensing the Market

The first element of a flexible process is sensing the needs of customers and the market. Flexible projects establish mechanisms for getting continual feedback from the market on how the evolving design meets customers' requirements. They do so by creating intensive links with the customer base—links that range from broad experimentation with many customers to selective experiences with a few lead users. Furthermore, these customers do not have to be external to the company: leading companies make extensive use of internal staff and resources to provide a test bed for evolving new products.

Gaining continual feedback from customers was particularly critical at Netscape because of its dramatic head-to-head race with Microsoft. Netscape's broad-based release of multiple beta versions to its entire customer base allowed users to play a significant role in the evolving product design. At the same time, it allowed Netscape to test an extremely complex technical product. Although not all Netscape's customers actually experimented with beta versions, the Web browser's most advanced users had to because they themselves were creating products that needed to work seamlessly with the Navigator release. And their feedback clearly had an impact: a significant portion of the new code, features, and technology that were integrated into the new release was developed only after the first beta version went public.

Microsoft, Netscape's chief rival, was slow to recognize the opportunities offered by the World Wide Web. Not until the end of 1995 did the company begin to focus on developing Internet products. Yet when Bill Gates and the rest of the senior management team finally acknowledged the need for a strategic shift, Microsoft's development expertise was unleashed with astonishing speed. In the six months from the end of 1995 to the middle of 1996, the company went from having no presence in the critical browser market to offering a product that several industry experts claimed was comparable to or better that Netscape's Navigator.

Microsoft was able to react quickly because its existing product-development process had been founded on the rapid iteration of prototypes, early beta releases, and a flexible approach to product architecture and specification. (For a detailed account of Microsoft's development process, see Michael A. Cusumano and Richard W. Selby, *Microsoft Secrets* [Free Press, 1995].) The process that Microsoft followed in developing its Internet Explorer was similar to Netscape's but was more internally oriented. With more than 18,000 employees to Netscape's 1,000 at the time, Microsoft could test successive Explorer beta versions extensively just by putting them up on its own intranet. "Everyone around Microsoft is encouraged to play with it," explained a Microsoft program manager. "Internal testing means that we release it to thousands of people who really hammer away at it. We use the product much more heavily than the average Web user." Microsoft combined broad internal testing by employees with carefully staged external beta releases, using only two or three in contrast to Netscape's six or seven. The company thus limited the risk that imperfections in early releases might damage its reputation.

A similar flexible philosophy can be used in the development of services. Consider Yahoo!. Founded in 1995, the company offers search, directory, and programming services for navigating the World Wide Web. As a service provider, the company believes that before a new offering is released to the outside world, it needs to be more robust than the typical Internet software beta. The market risk of broad, public testing is too high: users who try a new service once and have an unsatisfactory experience with it either are unlikely to return or, worse, may defect to competitors. Furthermore, Yahoo! assumes that competing companies will copy the innovative features of a new service once it has been released. These factors suggest delaying external testing to late in the development cycle.

For these reasons, Yahoo! puts early versions of new services online for internal use only. Given its development team's technical skills and breadth of experience, these trials expose any major technical flaws in the service and provide additional suggestions for improving functionality. Only then does Yahoo! begin a "soft release" of the offering: the service is put up on Yahoo!'s Web site but without any links to highly frequented parts of the site. As a result, only the more technically aggressive users are likely to find and use the service at this stage. Yahoo! also asks some of the 30,000 users, who have volunteered to be beta testers, to try the new service—thus exposing the service to rigorous external testing without revealing it to unsophisticated users who might be frustrated by a slow, incomplete, or error-ridden version.

The Netscape, Yahoo!, and Microsoft examples illustrate several approaches to sensing customer and market needs: broad consumer testing, broad internal testing, and testing by lead users. Companies adopting a flexible development approach should consider the merits of each, as well as the potential for using a balanced combination of all. It is important to emphasize, however, that these techniques are not unique to the Internet. Advances in information technology now allow companies to sense customer needs in ways not possible a few years ago. Leading companies in many industries have begun to use these new capabilities.

Fiat, for example, used a broad, external testing approach, not unlike Netscape's, to evaluate several automobile concepts. A link on the company's Web site directed customers to a page aimed at evaluating users' needs for the next generation of the Fiat Punto, its highest-volume car, which sells about 600,000 units per year. Customers were asked to fill out a survey indicating their preferences in automobile design. They could prioritize the following five considerations: style, comfort, performance, price, and safety. Then they were asked to describe what they hated most in a car and to suggest ideas for new features. Next the software allowed customers to design a car themselves. They could select from a variety of body styles, wheel designs, and styles for the front and rear of the automobile. They also could examine different types of headlights, details, and features. In this way, users could experiment with different designs and see the results immediately on the screen. The software captured the final results; in addition, it traced the sequence that customers went through in evaluating and selecting options. This information told designers much about the logic customers used to evaluate features, styles, and characteristics in order to arrive at a given design solution.

Fiat received more than 3,000 surveys in a three-month period, each comprising about ten pages of detailed information. The ideas suggested ranged from clever (an umbrella holder inside the car) to significant (a single bench front seat). Fiat used the information to inform a variety of styling and concept decisions for the next-generation Punto. And the total cost of the exercise was only $35,000, about the cost of running a few focus groups. Moreover, Fiat executives claimed that the surveys provided them with precisely the data they needed. The profile of the survey's participants—trend-setting individuals with high incomes, who are 31 to 40 years old and frequent car buyers—was the target segment most useful to Fiat.

General Motors' Electro-Motive division has adopted a similar philosophy in its new virtual-product-development process. That process allows engineers to give customers digital tours of next-generation locomotives even as their development proceeds. Although the GM system is still evolving, the aim is to move to an all-digital environment in which the product moves electronically through concept design, analysis, prototyping, and manufacture, and along the way makes several stops on the customer's desktop for feedback.

Testing Technical Solutions

Sensing customer and market needs as a project progresses is one element of a flexible development process. If companies are going to allow a product's design to evolve well into the design implementation phase, however, they also must adopt mechanisms that lower the cost of changes, speed their implementation, and test their impact on the overall system. Such mechanisms allow companies to evaluate and test alternative technical solutions at a rapid rate: the second element of a flexible development process.

Early prototypes and tests of alternative technologies are critical to establishing the direction of a project. Consider NetDynamics, a company that develops sophisticated tools for linking Web servers to large databases. The single most important technical decision confronting NetDynamics during the development of its second product release was the early choice of language in its product. Either the company could develop a proprietary language, or it could use Java. At that time, in early 1996, the Java programming language had received a lot of publicity, but it was still highly unstable, relatively immature, and little understood. "We knew Java was going to be big," recalled chief engineer Yarden Malka, "but it was still only available as a Beta 1 version. This meant that the development tools that went along with it were either terribly buggy or nonexistent. If we chose it, we knew we also had to develop many of our own tools."

NetDynamics' commitment to an open platform tended to favor Java. If there was a standard—either existing or emerging—it should be used, and Java appeared to be that standard. To make the decision, however, NetDynamics' engineers spent considerable time experimenting with various options, trying to become as comfortable as possible with the benefits and risks of each language. They began by developing simple prototypes and gradually migrated to more complex programs, attempting to gauge the advantages each would give the user. This "user-centric" approach to prototyping and experimentation was critical to the final choice and stands in stark contrast to the approach often adopted by high-tech companies in which technologies often are evaluated purely on the basis of the advantages they give the design team.

As a project progresses, the design team must have the capacity to evaluate and test alternative design solutions quickly and cheaply. Yahoo! can easily do just that because of the way it has elected to provide its Internet service. The company meets its processing needs with many inexpensive computers instead of a few large (and expensive) servers. The small investment required for each machine allows Yahoo! to scale up its capacity smoothly to meet new demand. It also means that Yahoo! can easily run experiments to test different design options. According to Farzad Nazem, the vice president of engineering, "Our Web site setup works just like a spigot valve. If we want to test out a new product or feature on several thousand users, we promote it on the home page of only a few machines. As users access the service and we reach the required volume, we can turn off the promotion on each machine. We can also conduct comparative experiments by running multiple versions of the same service on different computers in the network, then track the results to see which version attracts more customers."

To reduce the cost of testing alternative design choices, companies outside the software industry increasingly have invested in new technologies for virtual design. By designing and testing product designs through simulation, for example, companies achieve the flexibility to respond to new information and to resolve uncertainties by quickly exploring alternatives. Computer-aided design software also has dramatically reduced the cost of design changes, while at the same time speeding up experimentation. At Boeing, for example, the all-digital development of the 777 aircraft made use of a computer-generated "human" who would climb inside the three-dimensional design on-screen to show how difficult maintenance access would be for a live mechanic. Such computer modeling allowed engineers to spot design errors—say, a navigation light that would have been difficult to service—that otherwise would have remained undiscovered until a person negotiated a physical prototype. By avoiding the time and cost associated with building physical prototypes at several stages, Boeing's development process has acquired the flexibility to evaluate a wider range of design options than was previously possible.

Integrating Customer Needs with Technical Solutions

It's no good knowing what customers want in a product under development if the development team can't integrate that information with the available technical solutions. As a result, all the organizations we discuss have established dynamic integration mechanisms. Some of them are based on well-understood concepts, such as using dedicated teams—an approach adopted by Netscape, NetDynamics, and Microsoft. Others are less traditional. All three companies, for example, use their intranets to integrate tasks, synchronize design changes, and capture customer information as projects evolve. Thus project teams are able to keep track of the evolving relationships among tasks, schedules, and design changes in a dynamic way. Such integrating mechanisms are essential for managing a flexible process, given the many rounds of experimentation and the wide range of information generated. Without a way of capturing and integrating knowledge, the development process can quickly dissolve into chaos, with ad hoc design changes creating masses of rework because of unanticipated interactions with other components in the system.

In the Internet world, integrating mechanisms are dictated by the nature of the product—software. Each of the projects we describe adopted sophisticated design-integration tools to hold the master version of the emerging product. As team members went to work on individual components, they checked out the code for that part of the system. Once finished, they had to run a series of tests to ensure that the component did not create problematic interactions with the rest of the system. Only then could they check in the new component. At the end of each day, when all the new components had been checked in, engineers ran the program. Any problems that occurred had to be corrected before new code could be permanently integrated.

Similar approaches are found in projects outside the Internet world where new information systems allow companies to share knowledge more effectively. At Silicon Graphics, a leading manufacturer of workstations and servers, a new product-introduction process makes extensive use of the company's intranet to coordinate development activities. Managers and engineers throughout the world, who respond daily to the problems of current customers, provide input during the concept-generation stage. In addition, lead users in target application segments (referred to as "lighthouse" customers) are linked directly to the development teams, allowing the teams to get fast and effective guidance on critical decisions as the project evolves. The intranet also is used to integrate design tasks on a daily basis. Project engineers work from a shared body of software that simulates the hardware design. As with the Internet projects, when team members want to make a change, they check out the relevant code, make the desired design improvements, test it for errors and unanticipated interactions, then check it back in.

Such approaches are not limited to high-technology products. Booz Allen & Hamilton, a management consulting firm, approaches the problem of integrating a diverse and geographically dispersed knowledge base by using its intranet. The intranet allows consulting staff quickly to locate and contact industry experts with specific skills and to identify previous studies that are relevant to current projects. In this way, the collective experience of the organization is available to all employees online. The intranet also allows the company to develop its intellectual capital. In management consulting, new-product development consists of developing new frameworks, industry best practices, performance benchmarks, and other information that can be applied across projects. By having these products online during development and thereafter, Booz Allen can integrate new information and experiences into its knowledge base.

Integrating within the company, however, is not always sufficient. In some cases, the ability to integrate knowledge across networks of organizations may also be important. For Internet software companies, given the novelty and complexity inherent in their products and the rapidity of their development cycles, no single organization can research, make, and market products alone. Instead, they take advantage of technical possibilities that are beyond the boundaries of any individual company; those technologies can then be integrated into their own core products. (Internet users will be familiar with Java applets and Web browser plug-ins.) Doing so, however, means that just as the technologies must be seamlessly integrated into a product, so must the organization accommodate a changing cast of players. The companies we describe have built alliances with third-party developers, engaged in joint development projects, and worked hard to foster open product architectures and modular designs. And such arrangements are not peculiar to software. Workstation manufacturers such as Sun, Hewlett-Packard, and Silicon Graphics frequently engage in joint development efforts with other hardware companies (such as Siemens, Intel, Fujitsu, Toshiba, and NEC) to leverage the performance of their systems.

PUTTING FLEXIBILITY TO THE TEST

In combination, the foundations of a flexible product-development process allow a company to respond to changes in markets and technologies *during* the development cycle. We found a striking example of how that is done in a setting that is about as far from the typical high-tech world as one can get: the America's Cup. In 1995, a small team from New Zealand dominated the races from start to finish. Team New Zealand's effort shows how the mechanisms we have described can be combined to dramatic effect in a flexible process.

Team New Zealand recruited Doug Peterson, who had been on the winning America's Cup team in 1992, as its lead designer. It also recruited an experienced simulation team to make use of advanced design software. Although Peterson's extensive experience drove the initial concept design, once the team's yachts were constructed the emphasis shifted to evaluating design changes through thousands of computer-simulated design iterations. The simulations were run on a small network of workstations located a few feet from the dock. To ensure rapid feedback on the performance of design changes, the team built two boats. Each day, one of them was fitted with a design change for evaluation; then the two boats raced each other to gauge the impact of the change.

Team New Zealand's flexible process sensed "market needs" through the two-boat testing program, which generated feedback each day on how the evolving design fit the racing environment. It tested alternative designs through a simulation program that was directed by one of the world's most experienced yacht designers. And it integrated knowledge by making the resulting information available locally. The crew, design team, and management were therefore able to make suggestions for the design, to see the impact of potential changes, and to know what to expect when those changes were tested on the water.

The U.S. boat that Team New Zealand faced in the final race had been designed on the latest supercomputers with the support of large, well-heeled corporations. Although the U.S. team could test a massive number of experimental designs, the computers were located hundreds of miles from the dock. As a result, there were significant delays between detailing a design and getting feedback on results. Furthermore, the team had only one boat on which to test design changes; given the varying sea and wind conditions, it took far longer than its rival to verify the impact of a change.

Team New Zealand's approach had better mechanisms than its U.S. rival for sensing, testing, and integrating what it had learned. Its flexible process produced a yacht of superior design, which many observers believed to be a full generation ahead of its competitors' boats. As Paul Cayard, skipper of Team New Zealand's opponent in the final race, remarked, "I've been in some uphill battles in my life. But I've never been in a race where I felt I had so little control over the outcome. It's the largest discrepancy in boat speed I've ever seen."

We have seen a similar pattern throughout many environments we have studied. Organizations that have adopted a flexible product-development process have begun to transform the very industries that forced them to adopt it. They have implemented strategies that companies clinging to traditional approaches cannot follow. Competitors without flexible development processes will almost certainly find their industries growing more and more turbulent in appearance. And in such an environment, their products and services will always seem to be one step behind those of their more flexible rivals.

EXHIBIT 1
Two Approaches to Product Development

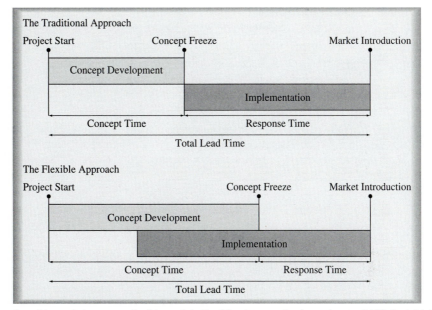

Speed is a subtle concept in this model. *Total lead time*—the time taken to fulfill the initial objectives of the project—is clearly important; but *concept time* and *response time* are critical measures themselves. Concept time is the window of opportunity for including new information and for optimizing the match between the technology and its application context. Response time is the period during which the window is closed, the product's architecture is frozen, and the project is unable to react to new information. Although the total lead time is the same for both processes above, the flexible process has a shorter response time and is therefore preferable in rapidly changing environments.

EXHIBIT 2
The Development of Navigator 3.0: A Timeline

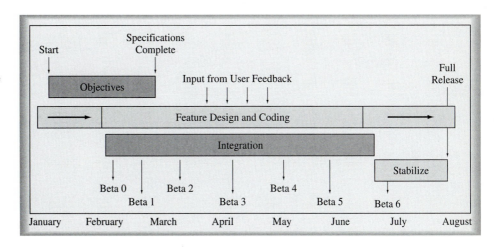

EXHIBIT 3
The Structure of a Flexible Product-Development Process

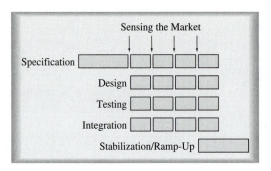

BMW AG: The Digital Car Project

"Looks great," thought Chris Bangle as he walked by a picture of the new BMW 3-Series, which was about one year away from its scheduled 1998 launch in Germany. Bangle, a former Wisconsin native, who became the company's director of worldwide design at age 35, glanced at his watch. In just 30 minutes, he would meet with other senior managers about project recommendations that might revolutionize the way cars had been designed over the past eight decades at BMW. The meeting was in the inner sanctum of BMW's research and engineering building, the *Forschungs-und Ingenieurszentrum,* known locally as the *"FIZ"* (pronounced "fits"). Built in 1987, this massive building centralized the work of 40 facilities previously scattered through Munich. All work from product concept to pilot production occurred in the *FIZ.* But only a privileged few out of the 5000 who worked in the building had ever visited this corner of the company where the meeting was to be held.

Bangle pulled out his card key that would let him pass through a sleek space-age security system that resembled an oval chamber. After negotiating a push card entry system, a set of doors slid close behind him and another set opened up to reveal the styling area—a world of future visions, inhabited by many life-size clay models of cars under development that would eventually come to life on roads of the next millennium.

BMW had weathered several storms over the past century, almost spluttering out of business thrice. On one humbling occasion in the firm's early history, it survived by using its machinery to manufacture cooking pots and pans. Now BMW rode high, outperforming many other European auto manufacturers. It had become one of the few European companies consistently making both cars and profits. Yet, BMW had one of the slower product development cycles when compared to its international competitors—a problem if it wanted to retain its technological leadership and cater to fickle customer tastes.

Thus far, BMW's cars had been designed along the lines of fine Bavarian craftsmanship that stretched back for centuries. Designing BMW cars had involved months and sometimes

Harvard Business School Case No. 9-699-044. Copyright 1998 President and Fellows of Harvard College. All rights reserved. For information: permissions@hbsp.harvard.edu.

This case was prepared by Stefan Thomke and Ashok Nimgade. HBS cases are developed solely for class discussion and do not necessarily illustrate effective or ineffective management.

years of painstaking iterations between hand-drawings and hand-built clay models. This process was especially belabored during the creation of a new car platform, which for a given series was launched only every seven or eight years, as compared with derivative, incremental models that were released every year or so.

Bangle wondered if today's meeting would help decide about doing away with this almost entirely, and begin work from computer models only as required by the new development system that called for a 50 percent time reduction. He was sure that many middle managers would cringe at the thought. But the decision that had to be made was one of managing organizational change: how should BMW roll out its new and unproven development system?

Many in the top brass pondered privately about whether BMW was ready for change. Its current success, after all, might prove a potent roadblock to change. Bangle's colleague, Dr. Hans Rathgeber, the head of body development, had pointed out that BMW was "blessed with very good products, but—because change comes easier when a company is on its knees—cursed by lacking a crisis!" The day's crisis, thus, was that there was no crisis. Perhaps too many BMW engineers and managers worked with a business-as-usual mentality.

Just a few months ago several of the BMW designers had sat through a pre-screening featuring their 7-Series flagship car in the major motion picture, *Tomorrow Never Dies.* Several had watched proudly, as British Intelligence senior product developer "Q" stated to secret agent James Bond: *"Here's the insurance damage waiver for your beautiful new car. . . . Your new BMW 750, with all the usual refinements. . . ."* And many had suffered along with their silver 750iL through a rain of blows from a sledgehammer, several machine gun volleys that had blown out the windshield, and a plummeting fall several stories before a crash-landing into a car-rental agency. Some designers had winced to see the rapid destruction of the beautiful contours of a car that had represented several years of toil under BMW's old product development plan involving thousands of people from product conception to market release.

Today, Bangle, like all senior BMW managers remained aware that a mistake anywhere along the long chain of critical points in product development for the new models might cause ruination of a much slower but equally painful kind: market erosion. One did not even need to look much further beyond this part of Germany—described as the "silicon valley of the automobile industry"—to find worldwide competition. Just 150 miles up the *Autobahn,* plans were afoot at Daimler-Benz, BMW's best competitor, to launch a sleek new Mercedes-Benz S-Series model that might hammer away at the 7-Series car.

HISTORY OF BMW

In 1916, Gustav Otto founded Bayerische Motoren Werke (translated as Bavarian Motor Works), better known worldwide by its acronym BMW, to manufacture aircraft engines (see **Exhibit 1** for historical milestones). In 1923, with the Treaty of Versailles banning Germany from producing aircraft, BMW lowered its sights to the ground. In just six years, one of its motorcycles would set a world speed record of 134 mph.

By the 1930s, however, it became apparent that the more sedate automobiles would replace motorcycles as the preeminent mode of transportation. To establish itself quickly in this market, BMW bought the license for a small British Austin model. Over the next few decades, BMW drew on its expertise in high-performance engines and aerodynamic design to manufacture world-class automobiles. The legendary BMW 328 sports car, which debuted in 1936, won numerous international race events, helping set the pace for BMW for ensuing decades as a prominent manufacturer of sporty roadsters. (It remains a tribute to BMW craftsmanship that over 200 of the 462 BMW 328 automobiles made still lived on in the mid-1990s.)

For all its engineering triumphs, however, BMW remained a niche player in the developing automobile industry. In 1951, when the firm started car production in Munich, it made egregious marketing errors. First, it produced prestige limousines that, in the post-war economy sold just 19,000 units over 14 years. The company only compounded the losses from this model through a tiny three-wheel "bubble-car" that reached the market just when an economic upturn boosted the demand for more comfortable transportation.[1]

In 1959, the company's weak financial position almost led to a takeover by its traditional rival Mercedes-Benz in Stuttgart. This was the third time the company's very existence was threatened. (The other two times had followed the world wars.) Only a $1 million investment by Herbert Quandt, one of Germany's wealthiest and most reclusive industrialists, who had slowly developed a majority shareholder position, rescued the firm. (The Quandt family in the mid-1990s still held some 60 percent of the company stock). In the 1960s, BMW found its stride when it combined its high performance sports car engineering with the comfort of luxurious cars. This winning combination in just a little over two decades took the firm from sixty-ninth to eleventh place among Germany's top corporations. Financial turnover in this period rose almost tenfold and the workforce sevenfold.

By the 1970s, BMW exported two-thirds of all its cars and three-fourths of all its motorcycles and had established subsidiaries on six continents. Its status as a manufacturer of dream cars was cemented through use of its cars in major motion pictures. BMW returned to its aerial heritage temporarily in the 1940s, when it helped develop rockets, and more permanently in the 1990s, through a jet engine manufacturing collaboration with Rolls Royce. Through all these decades, however, it retained its white-and-blue propeller logo that reflected its roots in the aircraft industry.

In 1996, BMW employed more than 116,000 persons worldwide and sold its products in 140 nations ranging from the United States to the Fiji Islands. It had a turnover of DM 52.3 billion in 1996, its best year in its history thus far (see **Exhibit 2** for selected financials and operating data). By the end of June 1997, BMW's deliveries of new cars rose 10 percent over the past year worldwide, with 62,000 units in the United States alone.[2] Despite its impressive growth over the past few decades, BMW in the mid-1990s had a world market share of only 1.5 percent. BMW viewed itself as a "manufacturer of unique automobiles for a clearly defined, exclusive, and demanding clientele all over the world."[3] To expand into other niches, without diluting its solid brand name, the company acquired the British Rover Group in the 1990s.

Although sports and luxury cars remained BMW's flagship products, it also made sedans and models for the broader markets. In the 1990s, BMW made several major series

---

[1] J. Dornberg, "Life in the Fast Lane: Bavarian Motor Works," *International Management,* V. 48(5), June 1993.

[2] BMW AG *Presse,* September 1997.

[3] W. Reitzle, "How to Shape a World Brand." Speech at Harvard Business School, November 16, 1995.

of automobiles, which, following European tradition, were numbered rather than named (see **Exhibit 3** for pictures of 7, 5, and 3-Series models):

- The *7-Series,* the company's luxury limousines (1996 sales totaled about 51,000 cars). Competitors included the Mercedes-Benz S-class, the Audi A8, Toyota's Lexus LS400, and GM's Cadillac Seville.
- The *5-Series,* consisting of BMW's "core" middle-range luxury performance cars (1996 sales totaled about 190,000 cars). Competitors included the Mercedes-Benz E-class, the Audi A6, Toyota's Lexus GS300, Ford's Lincoln LS6, and Chrysler's 300M.
- The *3-Series* sports sedans (1996 sales totaled about 400,000 cars). Competitors included the Mercedes C-class and the Audi A4.
- The low-volume *8-Series* sports coupes.
- The roadster series (e.g., Z3) and the new "Sport Activity Vehicle" (SAV) X5 (to be launched in 1999)—both manufactured in BMW's Spartanburg, South Carolina plant.

BMW also made a line of motorcycles. Introduction of many technological innovations such as side airbags generally started with the 7-Series, since this was the most expensive line and could absorb the costs of early innovation. From here, innovations trickled down to the 5-Series and 3-Series cars. All segments were viewed by automotive executives to be very competitive, with more automotive products and firms entering in the next few years.

AUTOMOTIVE COMPETITION IN THE 1990s

According to BMW Executive Chairman, Bernd Pischetsrieder, "When historians look back on the motor industry in 50 years' time, they will say that the mid-1990s was a period of fundamental change." This time period had seen development of a consumer's market. In 1996, the European market sported some 50 car brand names, with about 300 different base models and virtually thousands of derivatives. The European market production capacity of 20 million overwhelmed the total yearly sales of 14 million.

"We've entered the biggest buyer's market in history," commented Ford's chairman, Alex Trotman, ". . . the customer revolution." Customers demanded more choices while wanting to pay less. This had led to a rise in second-hand and almost new car sales along with an upsurge in generous financing schemes for new car purchases. Car manufacturers had to respond with acceleration of new model development and an increase in model variations. To worsen matters, Japanese, Korean, and U.S. automakers waited in the wings for lifting of all European Market barriers by 1999. Ford's Trotman admitted that "I keep a collection of old bonnet ornaments from defunct auto companies in my office. They serve as a reminder that the world doesn't owe anyone a living, and doesn't owe any company its business."[4]

As a response to these rapidly changing markets, automakers all over the world placed an increased emphasis on speeding up development as a competitive weapon. The Japanese had led the way, aiming to reduce their traditional 50-month development lead times by over 30 percent, even though they were not known for technological advancement so much as for producing reliable cars. In the United States, auto firms such as Chrysler were trying

---

[4] A. Lorenz, "Cars on a Collision Course," *Management Today,* August 1996, pp. 66+.

to achieve a similar feat. In recent years, intense pressures from international competition to reduce product development time had also reached Europe and BMW.

The whims of customers in the mid and upper luxury car market made the competitive environment even harder to predict. In the early 1990s, German luxury carmakers found that "cost-be-damned" overengineering might not be rewarded. Consumers, for instance, found the $127,800 Mercedes S-Series model of 1991 too large and unwieldy. Mercedes-Benz had designed this car for tastes of the early 1980s, but partly because of its long product development cycle it floundered on the quicksand of consumer taste.[5] Japanese carmakers were quick to strip away market share from these overpriced models and break into the coterie of car manufacturers that included well-known firms such as Mercedes, BMW, and Jaguar. Japanese luxury cars had started to win international automotive awards, but, as the following passage from 1996 illustrates, the pendulum of consumer taste was reversing course:

> Toyota's Lexus LS400 was the epitome of vehicular correctness. [It] was so quiet and smooth that it was more like an appliance—a horizontal elevator. The Lexus had its 15 minutes of fame. Then the yen gained strength, as did the tastes of affluent American car buyers. Suddenly, as fast as you could say, ". . . start your engines!" Mercedes-Benz and BMW roar to the front of the line for speed, power, and status. . . . These high-end German cars are not transportation for the timid. With their top-gun cockpits, super firm seats, and beefy controls, they demand driver involvement.[6]

The shift in market trends, however, favored BMW disproportionately. Its appeal to younger, affluent buyers interested in performance, handling, and physical activity, and the sheer fun of driving boosted sales to the point where, for the first time in history, BMW unit sales surpassed that of Mercedes-Benz, its longtime rival.

The competition between BMW and Mercedes-Benz, while spurring both companies to higher levels of excellence, could at times prove personalized and acerbic. The head of sales at Mercedes-Benz, Dieter Zetsche, admitted, "with our emphasis on comfort, safety, and longevity, we were becoming like Rolls-Royce"—overpriced and technologically outdated, "we didn't realize that the world had changed." Much soul-searching at Mercedes-Benz led to plans for radical changes in the Mercedes lines, including the very successful E-Series and a new and radically redesigned S-Series model to be launched in 1998 that industry observers perceived as a serious threat to BMW's current 7-Series model.[7]

PRODUCT DESIGN AND ENGINEERING AT BMW

> A successful design is not characterized by the ability to create a brief sensation, but by the influence it exerts on subsequent designs in the years that follow.
>
> —*Chris Bangle, Director of Worldwide Design*

Automobile development in the 1990s entailed literally thousands of steps involving 20,000 to 30,000 components from screws to lamps to upholstery that had to be coordinated to

---

[5] R. Serafin, "Mercedes-Benz of '90s Includes Price in Its Pitch." *Advertising Age*, November 1, 1993.

[6] A. Taylor III, "Speed! Power! Status!" *Fortune*, June 10, 1996, pp 46+.

[7] Ibid.

produce a final product. This five-year process relied on the work of thousands of designers, skilled craftsmen, and engineers, as well as numerous specialized outside vendors. To simplify matters, however, an automobile can be thought of as having two major components: the "package" and the "skin." The term "package" refers to the components involved in propelling the automobile. This basically involved whatever is under the hood in addition, of course, to wheels, axles, steering, climate control, and exhaust. The skin refers to what the buyer first sees in the showroom: the exterior, the seating, and the layout of the dashboard. In the initial phases of car development, design of the package and skin could proceed in parallel, with ongoing communications and "negotiations" between engineers and designers managing both processes. The centralization of car development at BMW through placing everyone in the FIZ building had smoothened this process of communications—and had led to similar initiatives at other car manufacturers.

BMW viewed design as the link between its past and future. Thus, BMW designers sought to retain a familiar resemblance between all its models. Consistent design features included the dual circular headlights and the "double kidney" grille in the front of the car. Traditionally, design for a proposed model started with manual renderings on paper using traditional artistic media ranging from watercolor to pencil to charcoal. In this brainstorming ("Design Concept") phase the company explicitly sought through a competitive process a large variety of concepts (which typically fell into four self-explanatory directions labeled "revolutionary," "evolutionary," "aerodynamic," and "classic") from in-house designers and sometimes external industrial designers.

Next the firm worked toward a "refinement" of its design choices by whittling down the choices. To this end, the design department made small (1:2.5) clay models of several favored initial concepts. Finally, based on feedback from senior management, the department made a few life-size models of leading contenders. These clay models were milled with computer-guidance so precisely that, once painted, an inexperienced observer could not tell a finished 1:1 clay model apart from a real car.

These clay models also served to create an "excitement" among personnel involved with auto development; in the words of Peter Ratz, a manager responsible for the technology interface between design and engineering, "nothing takes the place of seeing the real thing." Typically, it took about 12 weeks to go from initial concept to a finalized clay model, a process that was repeated at least four to five times with intermediate clay models before arriving at a final design concept. Each 1:1 clay model cost upwards of $150,000 and could be produced in about a month, but in as little as two weeks for all-stops-out emergencies.

Once the design was frozen, a scanning device would capture the geometry of the final clay model digitally—a process that generally took over a day and could be done over the weekend. Once captured digitally, however, the design models could be made available to engineering in the form of computer-aided design (CAD) models. The computer models also sped up refinements in the design process itself. For instance, if a designer ground down one curve or lay on more clay to build up another curve, computer guidance could ensure that corresponding changes on the other side of the car would match to within half a millimeter or so.

Recent advances in computer-aided styling (CAS) were aimed at making the power of computers available to designers up to the early brainstorming phases. CAS allowed for work at resolutions of one-hundredths of millimeters—an order of resolution greater than engineers traditionally worried about. The ability of CAS to accurately predict the course of lines of reflection also helped convince skeptics about its potential utility. In addition, a major advantage to working digitally from the very beginning was in allowing for direct data links to computer-aided design (CAD), allowing for parallel development with engineering. Working with clay models, in contrast, required laser scanners to "digitize" information about the clay models. This process of data conversion usually necessitated time-consuming fine corrections by hand.

But even with all the potential advantages of CAS, BMW prided itself on its *hand-craftsmanship*. In fact, Bangle himself noted that "cars are not machine-produced, they are machine-reproduced—a human hand makes every surface." Not surprisingly, BMW's designers, generally came from art schools or industrial design schools, and its model-makers were skilled craftsmen who perfected their trade through many years of apprenticeships. Working alongside them were over a dozen "color and trim" craftsmen and designers (including fashion designers). Working with physical models was an integral part of their training and often defined the emotional experience of a designer (see **Exhibit 4** for designers at work). Thomas Platt, general manager of advanced design, underscored the emotional side of using physical models by pointing out "that computers are an indispensable tool for simultaneous thinking and working but there will be a point where you want to touch what you love."

BMW designers prided themselves on the emotions that good design would create: the way light sparkled off the surfaces of their cars, and the way the lines of contour flowed. Three properties with enough mystery for a café full of artists guided car design at BMW: *Flächengenauigkeit,* the precision of the surface; *Flächenspannung,* the surface "stress"; and *Reflektionslinien,* the lines of reflection. The BMW design philosophy held that the contour lines should never be interrupted, even when running across transition points (such as from body to door). Furthermore, the company prided itself on the number of distinctive curves the side of a car possessed when viewed in cross-section (see **Exhibit 5** for a comparison with other cars).

While many automakers had just one or two design surfaces running down the side of a car, interrupted by a metal strip, BMW sought to create a subtle interplay of multiple surfaces that could not be easily created on a digital computer. "While all car makers use the very same sheet metal, and while anyone can bend sheet metal," Ratz, a manager and design engineer with 13 years' experience at BMW, could claim with some pride, "*we* practice the *artful* deformation of sheet metal." All these elements created what the firm felt was the finest expression of human artistry. A customer, thus, paid for a BMW not just with the wallet but also with a commitment that came from the heart.

After exterior design was complete, the CAD data moved to Andreas Weber's group in body engineering. His group bore responsibility for making the exterior design functional and manufacturable. It made the surfaces "more precise" by filling in gaps in design. For example, Weber's group would figure out where the screws should go into the taillight that had been designed, or if the design affected the door functioning. The group, like other BMW engineers, operated at the level of fractions of millimeters to ensure that the final assembled product would function with silky precision.

Weber also worked with many other groups within body engineering to ensure that the design concept chosen could achieve its desired functionality such as crashworthiness and vehicle dynamics. For example, the design data was handed over to Dr. Holzner's group, who would perform crash simulations to get early feedback on potential safety problems—months before data from the first prototype crash was available. One of engineering's evolving objectives, though not stated explicitly, was to identify and solve functional and manufacturing problems as early as possible (a concept know as "front-loading"). Once design commitments were made, changes such as tooling could cost millions of dollars and often led to significant delays in the development schedule.

Because making a car involves dozens of functional teams working together on thousands of components that must ultimately fit together, at some point the model design had to be "frozen." Otherwise, engineers and designers would forever chase moving targets. Another reason for freezes stemmed from high tooling costs; single stamps or die could cost between $20-$30 million each. In BMW's current development plan, the firm froze the package about 50 percent of total schedule and the design itself just two or three months after that. Occasionally, BMW's pride in incorporating the latest technological breakthroughs into its new models would lead senior management to override these freezes.

Through the millions of man hours of work involved for each new car model, Dr. Reitzle, head of products and markets, stressed the importance of remembering the ultimate goal of car development: "The thrill of BMW is based on characteristics such as *dynamism* and *performance, esthetic style* and *emotion,* as well as *innovation* and *perfection to the last detail.* The harmony of the overall concept has always been BMW's guiding factor and target."[8]

THE EVOLUTION OF PRODUCT DEVELOPMENT AT BMW

Since the 1970s, two generations of product development regimes could be delineated at BMW based on total development lead time, the entire time it took from initial concept development to market launch, and the number of major prototyping cycles. BMW developed all 3-, 5-, and 7-Series models using these processes (see **Exhibit 6** for average development times in the automotive industry):

- *The old process:* This system of product development dominated in the 1970s and 1980s (see **Exhibit 7a**). But because of the long lag times, the last car developed under this 72-month-long process was launched in the mid-1990s. The plan allowed for three major prototyping cycles with each cycle involving a generation of dozens of physical prototypes with increasing degrees of fidelity. A high-quality physical prototype could exceed one million dollars and often required months of superb craftsmanship by BMW's many prototype builders. During each prototyping cycle, functional and manufacturing problems could be identified via testing and solved while an increasing number of design and financial commitments were made to suppliers and manufacturing. For example, a critical variable during design engineering—the time from concept freeze to market launch—were the relatively long lead times it took suppliers to manufacture dies for pressing sheet metal during production. While the early release of design specifications to suppliers could speed up development, it had to be balanced against the very high cost of making design changes to such dies. The last cars developed under this development process belonged to the current 5-Series, which won not only numerous international awards but also commercial success.

---

[8] W. Reitzle, "How to Shape a World Brand." Speech at Harvard Business School, November 16, 1995.

- *The current process:* This system, which took root in the early 1990s, entailed a 60-month-long process (see **Exhibit 7b**). The plan allowed for only two major prototyping cycles but for the first time started to take advantage of rapidly emerging computer simulation methods to identify potential design problems earlier in the development schedule ("front-loading"). For example, a vehicle's crashworthiness could be simulated and improved well before the results from the first actual prototype crash test became available—a milestone that came relatively late under the old development plan. However, much of the potential of computer-aided technologies remained untapped in the current process, which was modeled after the old hardware-driven process. The first cars emerging from this process belonged to the new 3-Series, scheduled to be launched in 1998, and were already receiving very positive reviews from automotive journalists around the world.

Through the past few decades, BMW generally came out with new platforms every seven to eight years, but with only incremental or derivative model changes from year to year (for instance, converting a sedan to a station wagon by primarily modifying the rear end of the vehicle). Some industry observers likened the emergence of a new platform to "punctuated evolution," whereby the fossil records remained fairly constant for long periods of time only to be disrupted by dramatic evolutionary changes over short periods of geologic time.

Contributing to the long spans of time between platform changes was the meticulous handcraftsmanship that went into BMW products—a process that relied far less on outsourcing than at other firms. Compared to other firms, the company had higher fixed costs because of its significantly smaller volumes per model. Thus, BMW traditionally sought to squeeze sales from each model for a longer time than many other carmakers. This strategy, however, hinged on the ability to develop cars whose lives outlasted competitors' products. With competition increasing the rate and quality at which "fresh" models were introduced, designing products with seven- to eight-year life cycles was becoming a very difficult—if not impossible—challenge indeed.

In recent years, BMW started to feel the pressure of the changing market dynamics in all its product segments: sales volumes were getting smaller for each model because changing customer demands required increasingly differentiated markets. When BMW surveyed the international arena, it found, not surprisingly, that its current five-year development plan lagged behind other industrial competitors in Japan and the United States. While the Japanese tended to make fewer changes between consecutive models, their new strategy also emphasized the leverage of shorter development times to allow them to cover more market niches and market whims. To be more aggressive in all of its market segments, BMW had no choice but to substantially increase the productivity of its development pipeline.

In surveying the market, BMW found that *engineering lead time,* the time required from concept freeze to product launch, had remained remarkably constant at 40 months from the 1970s through the early 1990s among many other European and U.S. firms. Forty months appeared like an impenetrable barrier as the four-minute mile had been for runners for decades. To work around this barrier, some car manufacturers tried to overlap the planning with engineering phase. Many competitors had also started adopting the practice of reducing the complexity of their newer models by creating derivatives of platforms. Starting in the early 1990s, top managers from BMW made a series of benchmarking visits to leading companies from other industries worldwide. These included visits to Canada to Bombardier, the manufacturer of jet skis, boats, and airplanes and to France to Dassault, which had pioneered the widely used three-dimensional computer-aided design (CAD) system CATIA. By the mid-1990s, however, no matter which way they looked, BMW's senior managers found that change was in the air not only in the automobile industry, but in many other manufacturing industries as well. In short, the time was ripe to create a faster, third generation system for automobile development.

REENGINEERING AUTOMOTIVE DEVELOPMENT

In the mid-90s, senior management approved a bold target for slashing product development time by 50 percent percent. A more modest goal, such as 20 percent or even 30 percent, management felt, would have had BMW chasing a moving target. After all, leading competitors in the United States and Japan were reported to aim at total development times between 30 and 40 months.[9] In the race to develop cars faster, this ambitious target should take BMW from the tail end of the pack to the front end.

Shortly after this decision, senior management assembled a reengineering task force to examine how to reduce lead time and cost for product development. The task force concluded that rather than think about some grand development plan for process planning, the firm should focus on streamlining key engineering processes. The task force identified five key process areas—body, climate control, fuel supply, test engines (power train), and acoustics—that accounted for about 90 percent of the critical processes in the product development timeline. Thus was launched a "reengineering" effort focusing on these areas and that would also entail needed organizational changes.

Senior management next sought to recruit involvement of functional managers in these identified five areas by asking them to contemplate the hypothetical scenario, "what would have to happen to all of our products/processes if we were to cut product development time in half?" To ultimately achieve the daunting new product development cycle (see **Exhibit 8** for a rough plan), three changes in BMW's car development system would have to take place: increased parallelization of design tasks, elimination of some design iterations such as physical prototyping, and quicker completion of the remaining design iterations. These changes would entail increased coordination of efforts of in-house engineers and craftsmen as well as outside suppliers. Helping BMW was that it had been the first major automaker to place all employees—numbering some 5000—involved with product development together in one research and engineering center.

1. *Increased parallelization of design tasks:* The challenge here was to allow development of various components of product development to proceed in parallel. This entailed coordinated teamwork, with each team passing on information on the component it worked on to other teams in a timely manner. Parallel processes required the coordination of efforts made possible by computerization of design. Through computer simulations, "virtual cars" that existed only in computer memory and not in the real world could be tested in parallel with ongoing design activities. The world of virtual reality

[9] Julie Edelson Halpert, "Kicking Digital Tires on Cars of Tomorrow," *The New York Times,* Dec. 5, 1997.

also provided a logical venue for coordinating the efforts of different functional divisions of a company such as between design and design engineering. But this meant not only reorganizing the way different groups worked together but also the difficulty of changing habits that had worked so well in their old sequential development plan.

Experience at BMW had shown that engineers were often loath to release less than perfect data. To some extent, it was in each group's interest to hold back and monitor other groups' output. The earliest group to submit its data to a central database, after all, would quite likely have to make the most changes since it would have enjoyed the least amount of feedback from other areas. But delay on part of only one team could derail the entire schedule, just as delay by an obsessive sauce chef could spoil an entire banquet. For example, BMW's crash simulation group found its reengineering efforts stymied because the sideframe designers hesitated to release design data. It turned out that the door subgroup only wanted to release perfect data, as it had been accustomed to in the days of sequential development. Only after convincing the door subgroup that its early, rough data would suffice did the crash simulation group get the needed design data but with a six-month delay. But in the new development process, a six-month delay could derail the entire development program. Crash simulation and design engineers both learned that an appreciation and understanding of each other's needs and activities had to be patiently built over time. It was not at all clear that many of the other areas had learned the same lesson.

2. *Elimination of some design iterations:* A process as complex as developing a new car model, provides opportunities for pruning unnecessary design iterations. For instance, the widespread use of computer-aided testing for functionality and manufacturability helped to substantially decrease the number of physical prototypes needed in the past. Interestingly, while the number of prototype-driven design iterations would decrease, the total number of iterations would increase substantially if one counted the thousands of additional low-cost and quick iterations that would be carried out using computers only. But would only one generation of prototypes before market launch—as the new plan called for—be sufficient to identify all potential design problems? Even though many auto firms were trying to achieve one prototype generation only, BMW did not know if any of the firms actually succeeded at it.

3. *Quicker completion of the remaining design iterations:* Every remaining design step from prototype development to tooling simulation would have to be sped up. In many cases, this could be achieved at the tactical level through setting more stringent deadlines. For example, traditionally the engineering group released data for tools manufacturing in about ten months; the goal now became six months. In many cases, the process of shortening steps involved proactively searching for problems that might arise downstream. Would a late design change involving a taillight, for instance, cause a tooling headache several months hence? But most of all, computer simulation itself allowed engineers to iterate more quickly. For example, design-build-test cycles of a new safety concept could be carried out via crash simulation in a matter of days or weeks as opposed the many months it had taken to design, build and crash prototype vehicles.

Top managers concurred that without the direct involvement and support of functional managers, the reengineering effort had little chance of success. A friendly rivalry developed between different areas to see which team could come up with the best development process. According to Dr. Rathgeber, the head of body development, "We were ready to adopt anything that would make us faster as long as it was not at the expense of quality." It was Rathgeber's reengineering team, which had been meeting weekly, that came up with the plan eventually selected by senior management.[10]

After acceptance of the new plan, senior management charged the other four development areas to follow and work on the many details and methods development required to make the plan work. The new development system—code-named "Digital Car"—heralded the widening role of computers in car development at BMW—a development that could potentially cast many departments in turmoil.

THE DIGITAL CAR PROJECT

Although much thought had gone into the digital car task force proposals, most middle managers and engineers found it hard to break away from daily business to press for reengineering changes and start investing in the building of necessary functional capabilities (such as training and new methods development involving computer-aided technologies). Functional managers, in particular, were simply too busy with the daily demands of development work necessary to bring the next BMW models to life. Thus a year went by without much progress on implementing the new development system.

Senior management understood how frustrated engineers and designers must feel with the company struggling toward slashing development time by half while simultaneously attending to routine matters. But this did not concern them at the moment, given the mandate to boost productivity and efficiency. A Paris luncheon during a benchmarking visit to Dassault—the corporate jet manufacturer that had also developed the CAD system named "CATIA" used by BMW—provided an informal venue for several top-ranking executives to discuss BMW's future direction. The key role that computer-aided styling, design, and engineering would play in the company's future plans, however, could equally well have justified this venue. In any case, the Dassault meeting would prove to jump-start BMW's quest for change.

At the Dassault luncheon, fueled by fine French wines, several executives boldly proposed testing feasibility of the new development system on a real development project. This project, they concurred, should entail so much risk and suffering that no cautious manager would ever block it. After much heated discussion, some executives proposed using the latest and revolutionary 7-Series platform that was already one year into development using BMW's current five-year process. The project would serve as a psychological Rubicon—once crossed, there would be no turning back for managers and engineers.

Other executives favored a much more cautious approach that emphasized the need to carefully build new development capabilities before betting the company's future on an unproven process. They argued that 7-Series project management had already invested a year of time and effort into incrementally improving a proven system of development that

---

[10] This team was led by Dr. Rathgeber and represented several groups including package design (Pregl), in-house consulting (Osada, Dr. Grote, and later Stuhec), exterior design technology (Ratz), exterior design engineering (Weber), body stamping (Dr. Pfrang), tool design engineering (Bölsterl), body structure design engineering (Lüdke) and CAE (Dr. Finsterhölzl), prototyping (Baumann), prototype testing (Martin), and manufacturing planning and engineering (Dr. Mayer, Drasch).

had produced some of the world's finest cars. Furthermore, failure of the overly ambitious Digital Car development system might reflect unfairly upon any BMW division involved. As an alternative, they proposed to use a new derivative model—the 3-Series Touring station wagon—as a pilot project to manage and drive organizational change. The derivative project was based on the nearly completed 3-Series platform, involved little technical risk, and could be used as a learning laboratory. Problems with the new and unproven process could be limited to the Touring station wagon and thus would not put the entire company at risk.

After much debate, the executive group decided to make the final project decision the topic of a larger senior management meeting after their return from Paris. Dr. Rathgeber later pointed out the high stakes involved in reducing development time by half: "Developing a new product with a new process is dangerous. We didn't know how to develop a car in such a short time, but many felt that the longer we waited, the longer people would find reasons not to do it!"

In the back of their minds, however, many BMW managers wondered how long it would take to build up capabilities for digitizing automobile development. Would just a couple of years suffice? Even the swift-moving Japanese car manufacturers, after all, had built up critical capabilities gradually over the past decade. The challenge, after all, was not the procurement and installation of state-of-the-art computer hardware and software but the patient development of new capabilities and changes to processes and organization in order to leverage the opportunities that new technologies would offer. Would applying intense pressure within the firm, however, make up for lost time or simply demoralize developers?

Aware of the latest senior management discussions at the Paris meeting, Chris Bangle reminded himself that BMW's loyal customers did not care about the company's processes as long as it produced attractive and exciting high-performance cars. As Bangle walked to the senior management meeting in the inner sanctum of BMW's research and engineering center, he took another look at the latest design sketches of the next generation 7-Series sedan and 3-Series Touring station wagon.

EXHIBIT 1
Historical
Milestones

Source: BMW AG.

Automotive History	
1885	First automobiles powered by internal combustion engines developed in Germany by engineer Karl Benz (followed in 1886 by compatriot Gottlieb Daimler).
1916	Bayerische Motoren Werke (BMW) founded to manufacture aircraft engines.
1923	Treaty of Versailles leads BMW into manufacturing ground-based transportation, starting with motorcycles.
1959	BMW's weak financial position, after several marketing errors, almost leads to a takeover by its traditional rival Mercedes. German industrialist Herbert Quandt rescues firm with personal investment.
Early 90s	Entry of the Japanese (such as Lexus) as serious contenders in the luxury car market.
1995	For the first time ever, BMW's unit sales overtake Mercedes.
Reengineering Project	
Mid-90s	Decision to reengineer current 60-month development process because of changes in competitive landscape. Task force identifies five key process areas (body, climate control, fuel supply, engines, accoustics) that account for 90 percent of critical path activities.
1997	Dassault visit in Paris: decision made to use real project to drive changes towards a new 50 percent faster development plan. Project code-named "Digital Car." Decision point: should a derivative (3-Series Touring station wagon) or platform project (7-Series sedan) be selected for the new "Digital Car" development system?

EXHIBIT 2
BMW Selected Financials and Operating Data

Source: BMW Annual Report 1996.

	1995	1996
Production (units)		
Automobiles—BMW	595,056	639,433
Automobiles—Rover Group	503,526	504,125
Motorcycles	52,653	48,950
Workforce	115,763	116,112
Income Statement (million DM)		
Net Sales	**46,144**	**52,265**
Automobiles	33,547	37,966
Motorcycles	731	744
Leasing	5,044	6,054
Other (spare parts, accessories, etc.)	6,822	7,501
Germany	13,862	14,621
United Kingdom	8,242	8,930
Rest of Europe	10,088	12,218
United States	6,177	8,228
Asia	5,291	5,574
Other markets	2,484	2,694
Increase in inventories and own work capitalized	1,189	696
Total Value of Production	**47,333**	**52,961**
Other operating income	1,814	2,078
Net income from investments	91	69
Net interest income	220	204
Total Revenues	**49,458**	**55,312**
Material costs	27,397	31,057
Personnel costs	8,846	9,844
Depreciation on intangible and tangible fixed assets	2,877	3,002
Other operating expenses (administration, distribution, warranty, etc.)	8,444	9,248
Interest expense from lease financing	527	501
Net Income Before Taxes	**1,367**	**1,660**
Taxes	675	840
Net Income	**692**	**820**

EXHIBIT 3
Major BMW Models (3-, 5-, and 7-Series) in the Late 1990s

Source: BMW AG.

BMW 7-Series

BMW 5-Series

New BMW 3-Series

**EXHIBIT 4
BMW
Designers and
Craftsmen
Using Manual
Renderings,
CAS, and Clay
Models**

Source: BMW AG.

Designer preparing hand sketches for brainstorming design concepts.

Designers using computer-aided styling (CAS) for group brainstorming.

Craftsman working on clay model of concept car.

Designers and craftsmen making refinements to clay model of concept car.

EXHIBIT 5
**Comparison of
Exterior
Designs**

Source: BMW AG.

Compact Car (about $13,000)

BMW 3-Series (about $27,000)

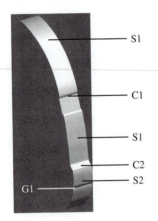

— S1

— C1

— S1

— C2
— S2

G1 —

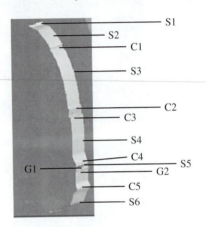

— S1
— S2
— C1

— S3

— C2
— C3

— S4
— C4
— S5
— G2
— C5
— S6

G1 —

Legend: **S:** basic surface
C: character element
G: gap

Number of design elements ("design complexity"):

• **Basic design surfaces**	2 (Sx)	6 (Sx)
• **Additional elements**	3 (Cx + Gx)	7 (Cx + Gx)
TOTAL	5	13

EXHIBIT 6
Research on Global Automotive Development Performance

Source: K. Clark and T. Fujimoto, *Product Development Performance*, Harvard Business School Press, 1991; D. Ellison, *Dynamic Capabilities in New Product Development: The Case of the World Auto Industry*, Unpublished Ph.D. Thesis, Harvard University, 1996.

**Average Automotive Development Times
(in months; not adjusted for product complexity)**

	Japan	United States	Europe
Late 1980s			
Total Lead Time (months)			
Planning	43	62	61
Engineering	14	23	20
Planning/Engineering Overlap	30	40	42
	1	1	1
Early 1990s			
Total Lead Time (months)			
Planning	51	55	58
Engineering	18	19	23
Planning/Engineering Overlap	32	40	42
	−1	4	6

Definitions:

Total lead time: months from the start of concept development to market introduction.

Planning lead time: months from the start of concept development to formal product approval.

Engineering lead time: months from the start of detailed design engineering to market introduction.

EXHIBIT 7a   **Old Development Schedule—Selected Activities (1970s to Late 1980s)**

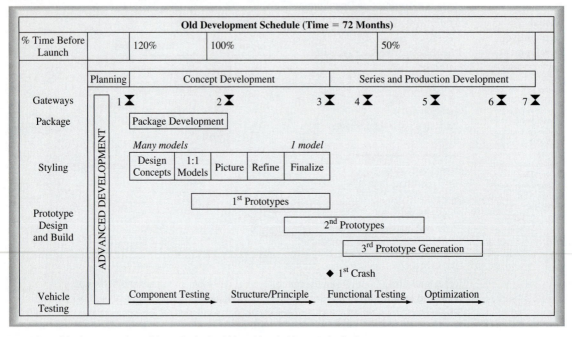

Note: Advanced development runs in parallel to project level activities and is typical in automotive development.

Source: BMW AG.

EXHIBIT 7b **Current Development Schedule—Selected Activities (Early to Mid-1990s)**

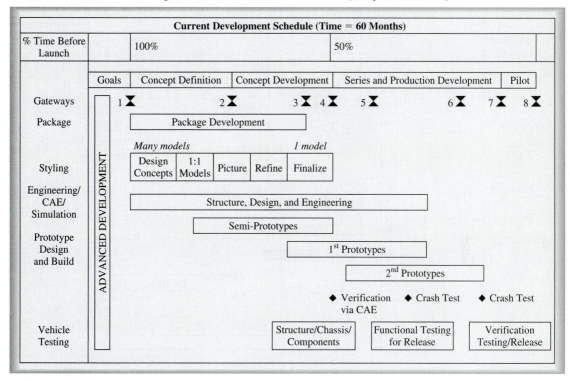

Note: Advanced development runs in parallel to project level activities and is typical in automotive development.

Source: BMW AG.

EXHIBIT 8 New "Front-Loaded" Development Schedule—Selected Activities

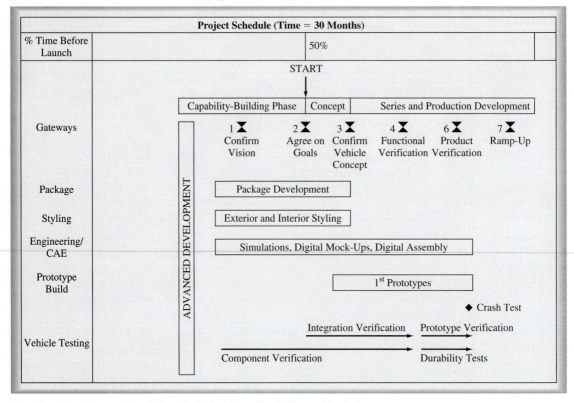

Note: Advanced development runs in parallel to project level activities and is typical in automotive development.

Source: BMW AG.

Article

The Effect of "Front-Loading" Problem-Solving on Product Development Performance

In recent years, there has been a growing interest in the link between problem-solving capabilities and product development performance. In this article, the authors apply a problem-solving perspective to the management of product development and suggest how shifting the identification and solving of problems—a concept that they define as front-loading—can reduce development time and cost and thus free up resources to be more innovative in the marketplace.

The authors develop a framework of front-loading problem-solving and present related examples and case evidence from development practice. These examples include Boeing's and Chrysler's experience with the use of "digital mock-ups" to identify interference problems that are very costly to solve if identified further downstream—sometimes as late as during or after first full-scale assembly.

In the article, the authors propose that front-loading can be achieved using a number of different approaches, two of which are discussed in detail: (1) project-to-project knowledge transfer—leveraging previous projects by transferring problem and solution-specific information to new projects; and (2) rapid problem-solving—leveraging advanced technologies and methods to increase the overall rate at which development problems are identified and solved. Methods for improving *project-to-project knowledge transfer* include the effective use of "postmortems," which are records of post-project learning and thus can be instrumental

Address correspondence to Takahiro Fujimoto, University of Tokyo, Faculty of Economics, Tokyo 113, Japan or Stefan Thomke, Harvard Business School, Morgan Hall T63, Boston, MA 02163.

in carrying forward the knowledge from current and past projects. As the article suggests, *rapid problem-solving* can be achieved by optimally combining new technologies (such as computer simulation) that allow for faster problem-solving cycles with traditional technologies (such as late stage prototypes), which usually provide higher fidelity.

A field study of front-loading at Toyota Motor Corporation shows how a systematic effort to front-load its development process has, in effect, shifted problem-identification and problem-solving to earlier stages of product development. They conclude the article with a discussion of other approaches to front-load problem-solving in product development and propose how a problem-solving perspective can help managers to build capabilities for higher development performance.

"Managing the problem solving curve is vital to our company's survival and front-loading is one of the main arenas of our current capability-building."

—*Managing director at a leading automotive firm (1998)*

INTRODUCTION

The link between problem-solving capabilities and superior product development performance has become the subject of a growing body of research in recent years [8,24,25,36,38,44,46]. For example, shorter development times—an important dimension of development performance—have been associated with overlapping problem-solving activities [8,21,22,35]. In this article, we propose a direct link between *early* problem-solving and development performance and discuss different approaches that firms can use to improve their development processes.

To understand how problem-solving and performance are related, we adopt a problem-solving perspective that increasingly is recognized by researchers as being fundamental to product development. Managers of development projects usually are very concerned about the identification of problems, because solving them becomes, on average, increasingly expensive and time-consuming as projects progress and financial commitments are made. With the recent emergence of new technologies and methods—such as computer-aided engineering (CAE) and rapid prototyping—that aid in the acceleration of problem-solving, it is not surprising that some practitioners have initiated concentrated efforts to reengineer their development processes to move (or "load") their problem identification and solution backward in time (to the "front" of the process).[1] In this article, we provide a conceptual framework and some evidence from development practice to describe the basic principle behind "front-loading."

We base our discussion on a problem-solving perspective of product development. We describe and analyze a product development project as a bundle of interdependent problem-solving cycles that include modeling and testing via computers or physical prototypes as core activities. Using this perspective, we define front-loading problem-solving as *a strategy that seeks to improve development performance by shifting the identification and solving of [design] problems to earlier phases of a product development process.* While we present

---

[1] For example, the automotive firm BMW recently initiated a large-scale reengineering program that aims to reduce development time of new models by 50 percent. New technologies such as "digital mock-ups" and advanced computer simulation play an integral role in these efforts [40].

examples of front-loading from different industries, we primarily report on findings from the automotive sector, where the methodology currently is being applied to the reengineering and shortening of product development. Our evidence is mostly case-based, but we feel it points toward the emergence of an important capability for improving development practice.

The article proceeds as follows. We start with a very brief discussion of development lead time. We then describe our problem-solving perspective of product development and apply it to automotive development, where much of our empirical evidence was collected. In the next sections we explain the basic principle behind front-loading, including several examples from current practice, which is followed by a field study of front-loading at Toyota Motor Corporation. We conclude the article with a discussion of other applications that may result from front-loading, such as its role in the building of development capabilities.

PRODUCT DEVELOPMENT LEAD TIME

The performance of development processes generally can be measured along multiple dimensions such as lead time, productivity, and product quality [9]. Development lead time is a measure of how quickly a firm can move a product from concept to market, whereas productivity relates to the level of resources (e.g., engineering hours, material, equipment) required to accomplish the same objective. The output of a process, however, is a product, and its complexity and the extent to which it conforms to customer expectations drive product quality. These three performance dimensions are closely related—any attempts to change one variable can have consequences for the other two in ways that sometimes are difficult to predict.

In the remainder of the article, we primarily focus on lead time. The extensive literature on product development speed reports on a number of different approaches or characteristics associated with shorter development times, including the level of human resources [6], overlapping tasks [7,8,21,29,35], cross-functional teams, and pre-development work [9,10,46], and the utilization of carry-over parts and platforms [9,12,26,31]. Discussions of the different factors and strategies to reduce development time can be found in Crawford [11], Griffin [16]; Table 2, Gupta and Wilemon [17], Smith and Reinertsen [34], Wheelwright and Clark [46], and others. The objective of this article is not to add another factor or approach to the myriad of studies already published on development time. Instead, we propose that both academics and practitioners can benefit from examining product development processes and its link to performance through the lens of problem-solving. More specifically, we discuss different approaches for early problem-solving—grouped under the concept of "front-loading"—and examine how they can affect development performance.

A PROBLEM-SOLVING PERSPECTIVE OF PRODUCT DEVELOPMENT

Whereas the early innovation and R&D management literature views problem-solving as a fundamental design activity [4,23,32,33], only in recent years has problem-solving been discussed and explicitly adopted in the product development literature [8,14,24,36,38,41,46]. In this article, we view problem-solving as an iterative process, driven by trial-and-error experiments that are guided by knowledge of underlying relationships between cause and effect (**Figure 1**).

FIGURE 1 Product Development as a Process of Repeated Problem-Solving [9]

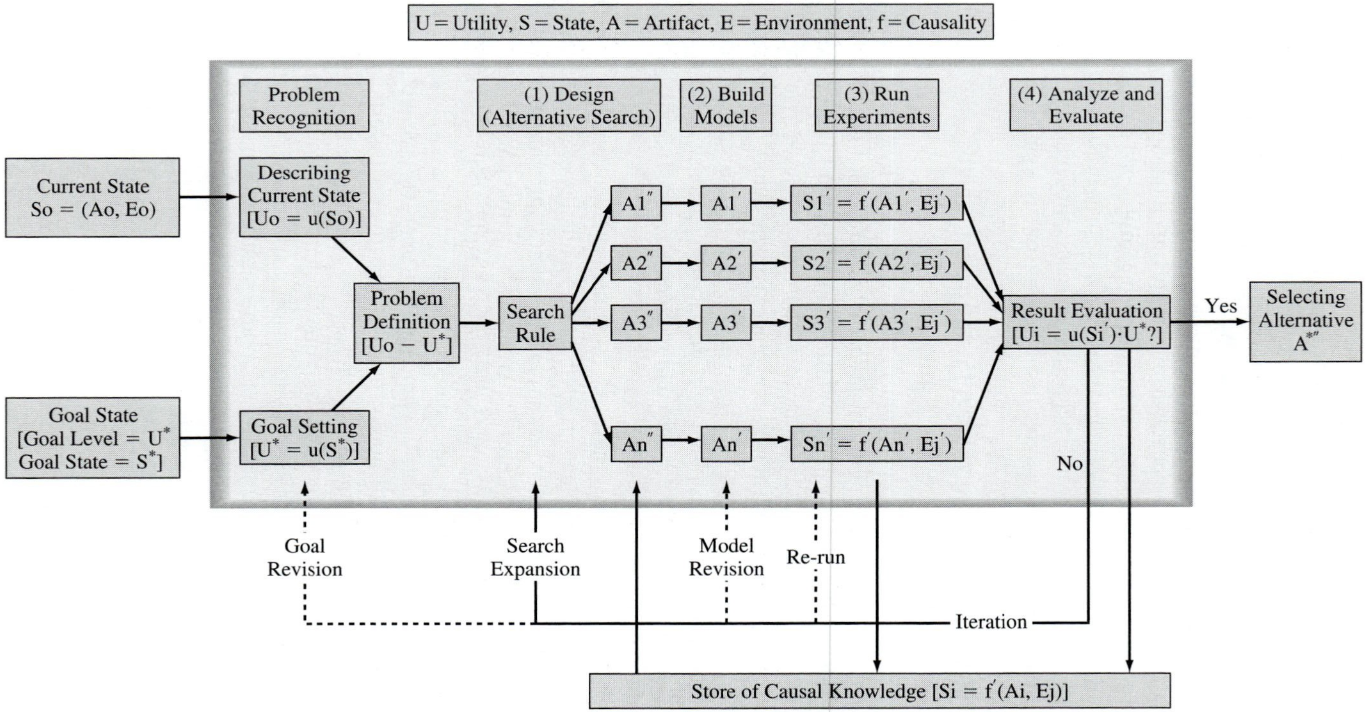

U = Utility, S = State, A = Artifact, E = Environment, f = Causality

Problem-solving starts with problem recognition and goal definition and continues with an iterative process of experimental search through alternatives that are designed and built during step 1 (design) and step 2 (build models) of a four-step problem-solving cycle.[2] These alternatives may or may not include the best possible solutions—one has no way of knowing. The alternatives are tested against an array of requirements and constraints during step 3 (run experiments). Test outcomes are analyzed during step 4 (analyze and evaluate) and used to revise and refine the solutions under development, and progress is made in this way toward an acceptable result. For example, one might (step 1) conceive of and design a new, more rapidly deploying airbag for a car; (step 2) build a prototype of key elements of that airbag as well as any special apparatus needed to test its speed of deployment; (step 3) run the experiment to determine actual deployment speed; and (step 4) analyze the result. If the results of a first experiment are satisfactory, one stops after step 4. However, if, as is usually the case, analysis shows that the results of the initial test(s) are not satisfactory, one may elect to modify one's experiment and "iterate" (or try) again.

Modifications may involve the experimental design, experimental conditions, fidelity of the experimental setup, or even the nature of the desired solution. The new information provided by a problem-solving cycle to a designer are those aspects of the outcome that he or she did not (was not able to) know or foresee or predict in advance—the "problem" or "error" [3,28].

Applying the problem-solving perspective to automotive development (**Figure 2**), one finds that it consists of a bundle of numerous *problem-solving cycles,* each of which consists of design, build, run, and analysis activities. Problem-solving cycles can be small, involving only a single designer (such as individual simulation experiments) or they can be very large, involving several development groups (such as major prototyping cycles). As projects progress, cycles tend to include models of increasing completeness, or fidelity, (e.g., thought experiments, computer simulations, physical prototypes, pilot vehicles, etc.) for testing the effect of design decisions on functionality, geometric fit, and manufacturability [14]. Sometimes a model is incomplete because one cannot economically incorporate all respects of "reality" (i.e., the *full-fidelity* model being used under *real* conditions) or simply does not know them. Other times, it is economical to build incomplete models in order to reduce investments in aspects of "reality" that are irrelevant to the problem being solved. Thus, a model of an airplane tested in wind tunnel experiments has no internal design details—these are both costly to model and mostly irrelevant to the aerodynamics problem being solved. Problem-solving cycles can be structured in hierarchical form: they are iterated to complete a *task* that creates a solution for each component; tasks then are integrated into major *stages* of development such as product engineering and process engineering.

---

[2] Similar building blocks to analyze the design and development process were used in earlier research. Simon [33] examined design as series of "generator-test cycles." Clark and Fujimoto [8] and Wheelwright and Clark ([46]; Chapters 9 and 10) used "design-build-test" cycles as a framework for problem-solving in product development. Thomke [36] modified the blocks to include "run" and "analyze" as two explicit steps that conceptually separate the execution of an experiment and the learning that takes place during analysis.

FIGURE 2
Automotive Development as Problem-Solving Cycles and Stages

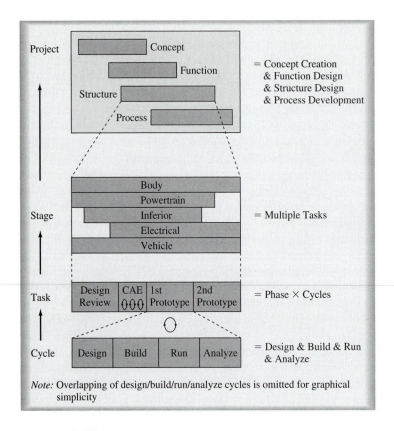

Project — Concept — Function — Structure — Process
= Concept Creation & Function Design & Structure Design & Process Development

Stage — Body — Powertrain — Inferior — Electrical — Vehicle
= Multiple Tasks

Task — Design Review | CAE 000 | 1st Prototype | 2nd Prototype
= Phase × Cycles

Cycle — Design | Build | Run | Analyze
= Design & Build & Run & Analyze

Note: Overlapping of design/build/run/analyze cycles is omitted for graphical simplicity

EARLY PROBLEM-SOLVING THROUGH "FRONT-LOADING"

An important part of an effective development strategy is the timing and fidelity of test models [39,46]. The information generated from these models plays an integral role in the identification and solution of design and manufacturing problems. If models are built and tested very late in a development process, the cost and time required to solve identified problems can be very large. Thus, it is not surprising that the benefits of early problem identification and solving can be quite remarkable and provide an area of great leverage for improving product development performance. For example, a study of several large software projects showed the relative cost of correcting software errors (or making software changes) to go up significantly as a function of the phase in which the corrections or changes were made [5]. It was found that a software requirements error corrected during the early specification phase consisted merely of updating the requirement specifications. A correction in the (very late) maintenance phase, however, involved a much larger inventory of specifications, code, user and maintenance manuals, training material, and, of course, revalidation. On average, the study found a change in the maintenance phase to be roughly 100 times more costly than in the specification phase, not counting any indirect operational problems in the field. Whereas considerable progress to make development processes more flexible has been made in recent years [18,37], late engineering changes as a response to identified design problems still can be very costly and time consuming. This is particularly true in automotive development where late design changes can cost millions of dollars and take weeks or months to be carried out—partially due to increasing tooling commitments.

Definition of Front-Loading Problem-Solving

We define front-loading problem-solving as *a strategy that seeks to improve development performance by shifting the identification and solving of [design] problems to earlier phases of a product development process.* We propose that effective front-loading can be achieved using a number of different approaches, two of which will be presented in detail. These two approaches have been proven to be very important but, in our opinion, have not received the kind of academic attention they merit.

The first approach, *project-to-project knowledge transfer,* involves the effective transfer of problem- and solution-specific information between development projects to reduce the total number of problems to be solved from the onset of development activities. For example, postmortem reports prepared by software developers after a project is complete usually include detailed information on problems (or "bugs") that can be reviewed by teams prior to the start of a new project.

The second approach, *rapid problem-solving,* leverages advanced technologies and methods to increase the overall rate at which development problems are identified and solved. Consider, for example, that building prototype vehicles that can be used in a crash test can take many months and thus limits the rate at which crashworthiness-related problems can be identified. However, the availability of lower cost and faster computer-aided engineering (CAE) tools permit higher rates of problem-solving, particularly at the early phases of product development. Combined with traditional hardware tests, these advanced technologies permit significantly faster and more frequent problem-solving cycles.

Front-Loading Problem-Solving: A Taxonomy and a Conceptual Framework

To solve a problem, problem- and solution-related information must be created, made available, and recognized by the problem-solver. Studies of the problem identification process show that such information can become available to a developer in two ways: (1) it already exists as very similar problems were identified and solved in prior development projects; and (2) it is created as part of repeated problem-solving during the development process [43].

With respect to problems involving information that already exists, a process should be in place that allows problem identification and solving at the start of the project. However, firms often neglect project-to-project learning and information transfer, resulting in the "rediscovery" of old problems in new projects. Or developers are simply unable to cope with the complexities of large development projects: the information generally is available to them but they are unable to predict the often subtle chain of cause and effect that leads to a design problem. In their study of 27 field problems that affected two novel process machines, von Hippel and Tyre [43] found that 15 of 22 problems identified after the machines were installed in the field involved information that existed prior to the installation. In 10 of the 15 problems, the problem-specific information was not transferred between designers; in the remaining five problems, the designers had the information but were unable to use it effectively.

With respect to problems involving information that is created as part of the problem-solving process, it is desirable to create such information as early as possible. One could, for example, increase early problem-solving capacity by shifting ample design resources and increased testing budgets to the very early stages of a new development project. However, development practice often looks different: resources are ramped up slowly as a project unfolds, and thus problem-solving activities and the related generation of information ramp up slowly as well. Hence, observed patterns of problem identification often are shifted downstream ("end-loaded"). The objective of this article is to present the concept of front-loading as a way to reverse this effect and to shift problem-identification and problem-solving upstream.

To conceptualize front-loading with the aid of a framework, consider a product development process where problems are identified and solved in an iterative fashion, following the design-build-run-analyze (d-b-r-a) cycles described earlier (**Figure 3**). Suppose that we develop in an environment where problems are identified via high-fidelity (h-f) prototype testing only and no problem or solution-specific information is being transferred between projects (Figure 3; case a). Problems are identified and solved at a constant rate r_{h-f} that depends on the speed at which a d-b-r-a cycle can be completed.[3] Total development time T can only be shortened if the problem-solving rate r_{h-f} is increased by carrying out d-b-r-a cycles more rapidly. These cycles can be *compressed* by restructuring prototype build and test processes (e.g., by adding capacity to bottleneck operations) or through a change in the explicit or implicit incentive structure such that early problem-solving is emphasized.

FIGURE 3
Problem-Solving Cycles with (a) a Single High-Fidelity (*h-f*) Mode and No Project-to-Project Knowledge Transfer; and (b) Two Modes (*l-f* and *h-f*) with Knowledge Transfer (for Simplicity, Trajectories Are Shown to Be Linear)

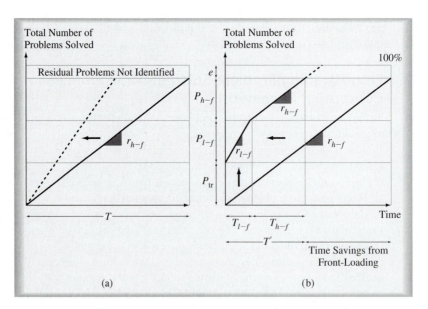

[3] To keep the framework at a conceptual level, we are using a linear approximation of problem-solving rates. Thomke [36] showed that this rate is more likely to experience diminishing returns and thus follow a nonlinear trajectory.

However, if a second class of test prototypes (e.g., "Virtual" prototypes generated by a computer) of lower fidelity (*l-f*) but a higher problem-solving rate r_{l-f} was available and knowledge could be transferred between projects (Figure 3; case b), developers would be able to use the following two approaches to shift their problem-solving trajectory:

- Increase the initial number of development problems solved, or "avoided," by more effective project-to-project transfer of problem and solution-specific information (p_{tr}).
- Use the lower-fidelity prototype to solve development problems that it can identify (p_{l-f}) more rapidly and then *switch* to the slower, higher fidelity prototype for the remaining problems (p_{h-f}).

The combined benefit will be a shorter total development time *T* as shown in Figure 3, case b. In general, management could extend the same logic to determine an optimal number of prototypes *n*, each with a different fidelity, such that total development time and cost is minimized. The price one would pay for a large *n* is the cost of repeated testing via multiple prototypes and the benefit would be the availability of early information. (For a formal treatment of this important tension, see Thomke and Bell [39]). The opportunities that advanced technologies, such as computer simulation, three-dimensional computer-aided design (CAD), and rapid prototyping, can provide now become quite apparent: even though they sometimes are of lower fidelity than full physical prototypes, they can identify a significant percentage of total development problems at a rate significantly higher than conventional high-fidelity prototypes. Combined with traditional hard-ware prototyping, we suggest that these technologies can result in remarkable development time reductions through earlier and more rapid problem-solving.

MANAGING FRONT-LOADING: EVIDENCE FROM INDUSTRIAL PRACTICE

In the previous section, we used a problem-solving perspective to identify two general approaches to the management of front-loading activities—activities that would result in a shift of problem-identification and problem-solving to earlier phases of product development. The first approach (project-to-project knowledge transfer) involves the transfer of problem- and solution-specific information between development projects to reduce the total number of problems to be solved from the onset of development activities. The second approach (rapid problem-solving) leverages advanced technologies and methods to increase the overall rate at which development problems are identified and solved. As Figure 3 shows, each of these approaches can result in an upstream shift of problem-solving, and thus their combination enable firms to reduce development time and cost significantly. We now present examples from development practice that demonstrate the benefits of both approaches.

Project-to-Project Knowledge Transfer

Studies of problem-solving have shown that firms often find old problems in new development projects. For example, in their study of the development of front and rear auto body closures (i.e., hoods, trunk lids, and lift gates), Watkins and Clark [45] found that design problems often were repeated between consecutive projects. (As an example, they presented one problem that showed up repeatedly over three sequential projects.) As discussed earlier, von Hippel and Tyre [43] observed a similar pattern and found that not only was there a lack of problem-specific information being transferred, but designers sometimes were unable to use the transferred information effectively. Thus, it appears that more effective transfer of knowledge between projects can improve development performance [2, 12]. This observation is shared by Adler [1], who studied different coordination mechanisms and interdependence issues in the design and manufacturing of printed circuit boards for electronic components and hydraulic tubing for aircraft. Among three different phases of coordination, he found pre-project [coordination] activities to have a key role in capturing the learning from previous projects and in the acceleration of new product development. In this article, we are particularly interested in one kind of pre-project coordination mechanism: the transfer of problem- and solution-specific information that can reduce the overall number of problems for a new project, as shown in Figure 3.

As an example of effective transfer practice, consider the use of "postmortems" in the development of computer software. Good postmortems are detailed records of a project's history and include, among other things, information on specific product and process problems discovered at various stages of software development. Cusumano and Selby [13] reported that much of the learning between projects at Microsoft can be attributed to its systematic use of such postmortem reports. In their research, they found that development teams generally take three to six months to prepare a postmortem, which can be between less than 10 to more than 100 pages long. In addition to accounting for people, product, and scheduling issues, the postmortems also contain detailed information on number of problems [bugs] identified, problem severity, and record of finding and solving problems. Preparing, discussing, and reviewing these postmortem reports, particularly before and/or at the beginning of a new project, has proven to be instrumental in carrying forward the knowledge from current and past projects. In their many years of using postmortems, Microsoft also discovered that transferring information on problems alone is very helpful but not sufficient; they needed to understand why a problem occurred and what solutions are possible [13]. Equipped with such information, developers can move more quickly toward the early identification and solution of problems that seemed novel at first but were experienced in different forms during past projects.

Postmortems are a very good example of effective transfer mechanism when the information being transferred can be economically encoded; however, that may not always be the case. In a study of 229 project members of 25 Japanese automobile projects, Aoshima [2] found that effective knowledge transfer mechanisms were also a function of the kind of knowledge being transferred. When information can be easily encoded, such as component-level data, he found that it was more effective to use archival-based mechanisms (documents, drawings). However, if the knowledge is "sticky" [42] or very costly to encode and transfer, such as tacit knowledge about the integration of components, firms performed better if they relied on face-to-face communication, people transfers, and other mechanisms that allow for effective transfer of such tacit knowledge between projects.

Rapid Problem-Solving Using Advanced Technologies and Methods

In this second approach, we are primarily concerned with the rate at which new problems are being solved. To gain deeper insights into the kinds of technologies and methods that are available to accelerate problem-solving, we divide problems into two categories—fit and function.

When different parts and/or subsystems occupy the same coordinates in three-dimensional geometric space, they interfere with each other, that is, they do not fit. Such problems are known as "interference" problems and are very common during the geometric integration of a complex product. Problems of fit are different than problems of function, where developers are concerned with the actual performance of a product (such as the fuel consumption or aerodynamics of an airplane). With the emergence of advanced computer technologies, many companies have been able to complement traditional hardware-based models with so-called "virtual" approaches utilizing computer models.[4] However, as we will see, the technologies and process changes chosen depend on the problems being solved.

Early Identification of Problems of Fit Through Digital Mock-Ups

Designers often are unaware that their designs interfere in space, and the traditional approach of mapping three-dimensional designs onto separate two-dimensional drawings provides very limited help in the identification of such interference problems. Complex products can involve thousands or hundreds of thousands of parts that could potentially interfere in three-dimensional space—designed by engineers who often do not even know each other.

When Boeing developed its new 777 aircraft, they also designed a new process for problem identification and correction [30].[5] Experience had taught them that their prior use of increasingly refined physical prototypes (also known as mock-ups) detected most design problems—but not all of them—and many of them very late in the development process. Developers were particularly concerned with interference problems, as the account of one Boeing chief engineer tells us:

> You have five thousand engineers designing the airplane. It's very difficult for those engineers to coordinate with two-dimensional pieces of paper, or for a designer who is designing an air-conditioning duct to walk over to somebody who is in Structures and say, "Now, here's my duct—how does it match with your structure?" Very difficult with two-dimensional pictures. So we ended up using the [physical] mock-up and, quite honestly, also using the final assembly line to finish up the integration. And it's very costly. You end up with an airplane that's very difficult to build. The first time that parts come together is on the assembly line. And they don't fit. So we have a tremendous cost on the first few airplanes of reworking to make sure that all the parts fit together. (Sabbagh [30])

Boeing's management wanted a process that allowed them to "front-load" [our words] interference problem-identification and correction to earlier points of the 777 development. They took advantage of the three-dimensional CAD system CATIA® and coupled it with an in-house software that enabled engineers to assemble and test "digital mock-ups" for interference problems. Similar to physical mock-ups that are built to detect problems of fit,

---

[4] Adler [1] made a similar observation. He found that computer-aided technologies (CAD/CAM) not only helped organizations to avoid errors that would normally result in costly engineering change orders, but also allowed them to process these changes or "problem solutions" more rapidly.

[5] The description of Boeing's development practice is based on Sabbagh's [30] detailed account of the 777 aircraft project.

FIGURE 4
Illustration of
"Virtual"
Decking Where
Interference
Problems are
Identified and
Solved with the
Aid of Digital
Mock-Ups
Before Physical
Assembly
Takes Place

"digital mock-ups" allow a virtual assembly of a product that can be checked automatically for interferences. While these automatic interference checks could be performed many times throughout the development process, they also changed the way people interacted with each other. Designers were more likely to change their designs early and relied on others to track these changes using the new computer technology. To add discipline and structure to the problem-solving process, Boeing instituted a process that was divided into alternating periods of design and stabilization. During the design period, engineers were allowed to make changes. During the stabilize period, software checked for interference problems that had to be resolved before proceeding to the next design period. The resolution of interference problems was no trivial task as shown by an early interference test of 20 pieces of the 777 flap (wing section): the software made 207,601 checks that resulted in 251 interference problems—problems that would have been very costly and time-consuming to correct during final assembly.[6]

Other firms currently are experiencing similar benefits from using advanced technology to front-load problem-solving. Chrysler Corporation discovered that the use of three-dimensional CAD mock-ups (internally known as digital mock-ups) could help them to identify interference problems at much earlier stages of automotive development. Consider, for example, their experience with "decking"—a process where the powertrain and its related components (e.g., exhaust, suspension) are assembled into the upper body of an automobile for the first time (**Figure 4**). When Chrysler developed the 1993 Concorde and Dodge Intrepid models, decking took more than three weeks and required many attempts before the powertrain could be inserted successfully. In contrast, the early use of digital mock-ups in their 1998 Concorde/Intrepid models allowed them to simulate decking and to identify

---

[6] We also should note that the use of interference testing via three-dimensional CAD led to unusual but very productive interactions between design engineers. For example, Alan Mulally, director of engineering on the 777, reported on an incident where he saw a senior structures engineer going up and down the building looking for a hydraulic designer. The engineer wanted to put a bracket on his floor beam, and he and the hydraulic designer had not come to an agreement on the location and the size of the bracket and whether it was going to create an interference. Extremely mad, the engineer stopped Mulally and asked "what they [the hydraulic designers] looked like. Do they have tubes in their pockets? Do they have tubes coming out of their heads?" (Sabbagh [30]). The unusual interaction arose because interference testing via three-dimensional CAD forced designers to interact and solve integration problems early.

(and solve) numerous interference problems before physical decking took place for the first time. Instead of more than three weeks in the 1993 models, Chrysler now could success-fully complete the physical decking process in 15 minutes, because all decking problems had already been solved. Thus, by combining new design technology with a different development process, Boeing and Chrysler were able to front-load problem-solving to phases where problems could be identified and solved at much lower cost and time.

Early Identification of Problems of Function Through Advanced Simulation

Consider the rapid proliferation of computer simulation in product development and its impact on the early and rapid identification and solving of functional problems. Until rela-tively recently, "virtual" experimentation was limited to what could be done using thought experiments and/or calculations that could be done essentially by hand. Experiments that were difficult or impossible to execute by these means were performed using some sort of physical apparatus. However, the rapid improvement of general purpose computers has made it economically possible and desirable to carry out more and more problem-solving via computer simulation.

The advantages of substituting computer models (i.e., simulation) for real physical objects can be very significant. For example, testing automobile structures via real car crashes is expensive and time consuming. In contrast, once set up, a virtual car crash can be run again and again under varying conditions at very little additional cost per run. Further, consider that a real car crash happens very quickly—so quickly that an engineer's ability to observe details is typically impaired, even given high-speed cameras and well-instrumented cars and crash dummies. In contrast, one can instruct a computer to enact a virtual car crash as slowly as one likes and can zoom in on any structural element of the car (or minute sec-tion of a structural element) that is of interest and observe the forces acting on it and its response to those forces during the simulated crash. Thus, if computer simulation is accurate—and there are several areas where its model fidelity is still evolving—it may not only decrease the cost and time of an experimental cycle but also can increase depth and quality of the analysis.

In recent research on automotive development, Thomke [38] found that computer simu-lation is already having an important impact in the design for crashworthiness and is rapidly changing other important areas as well. His research showed that by speeding up and simultaneously reducing the cost of design iterations, developers were able to increase the frequency of problem-solving cycles while reducing the total time and money spent on the development process. Close examination of an advanced development project (at BMW in Germany) that involved 91 design iterations via crash simulation showed that developers were able to improve side-impact crashworthiness by about 30 percent—an accomplish-ment that would have been unlikely with a few lengthy problem-solving cycles using phys-ical prototypes only.

Because of the importance of automotive crashworthiness, the improvements from crash simulation were verified with two physical prototypes that were built after the 91 iterations were completed. Interestingly, building, crashing, and analyzing the two prototypes cost hundreds of thousands of dollars (as opposed to a few thousand dollars for a simulated crash) and took longer than the entire advanced development project that was studied (**Table 1**).

TABLE 1 Approximate Lead Times and Cost for Design Iterations Using Computer Simulation and/or Physical Prototypes in an Advanced Development Project at BMW AG, Germany

Problem-Solving Step	Simulation[a] (per iteration)	Physical Prototype (per iteration)
(1) Design	*Technical Meeting* • <0.5 days	*Planning and Piece Part Design* • >2 weeks (involves many meetings)

(2) Build	*Data Preparation and Meshing*
	• Small change: <0.5 days
	• Significant change: 1 week
	• Entire automobile: 6 weeks
		Design and Construction
		• Using existing model: 3 months
		  (at $150,000 per prototype)[b]
		• New model: >6 months (at $600,000 per
		  prototype)

(3) Run	*Crash Simulation* • 1 day (varies with computer hardware) @ $250/day	*Crash Physical Prototype* • 1 week (includes preparation of test area)
(4) Analyze	*Post-Processing and Analysis* • <0.5 days	*Data Preparation and Analysis* • 1 day (crash sensor data only) • 1–3 weeks (data, crash films, and analysis of physical parts)
Total time	About 2.5 days to 6.3 weeks	About 3.8 months to >7 months
Typical cost (including effort)	About <$5,000	*About >$30,000*

[a] Prior to starting simulation, there is a one-time fixed investment necessary to build a basic model that is used during simulation. This one-time investment is approximately $100,000 and 2 months, but is not reincurred during design iterations.

[b] Prototype build cost and time are a function of the magnitude and number of modifications, but even modest changes can drive up cost and time very quickly. From reference [38].

Of course, not all crash safety tests can be conducted via simulation because of the complex dynamics necessary to construct very accurate models that would identify all functional problems (examples of tests that are very difficult to model are rollover crashes or crash-related fire hazards). However, identifying and solving a significant percentage of all crash-related design problems more quickly with simulation and then switching to prototype testing later can be a very economical strategy for reasons than we described earlier and is shown in **Figure 5.**

Thus, being able to test for functionality with the aid of computer simulation is having an important impact on automotive development processes. CAE now affects most areas of product functionality, including acoustics, vibration, aerodynamics, and thermodynamics, and currently is being applied to complex metal-forming processes such as stamping. Developers can test for functionality very early in the process—as early as styling—and receive feedback on functional problems before significant development commitments are made. For example, it is well known that exterior styling and aerodynamic flows are highly interdependent, particularly at high velocities. With computational fluid dynamic (CFD) simulations, stylists now can have their concepts evaluated for aerodynamic problems in a matter of days and can make the necessary changes in a matter of hours.

Finally, we should point out that faster and less costly problem-solving via simulation can open new possibilities for learning and design innovation. The 30 percent improvement

FIGURE 5
**Combining
Prototype
Crashes with
Simulation
Can Result in
Faster
Development
and Discoveries
of Novel Design
Solutions**

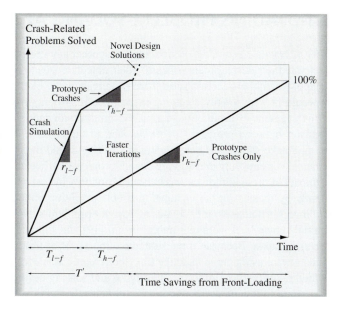

in crashworthiness reported earlier was the direct result of technical innovations that resulted from problems identified with the aid of simulation. Because of the economies of running and the difficulties of analyzing many physical crashes with traditional methods, it would have been very unlikely that some of these novel discoveries had been identified during development. Consider the following example [38] in a study of a design team's problem-solving and learning process:

> In the analysis of prototype crashes of earlier development projects, test engineers repeatedly found that a small section next to the bottom of the center B-pillar "folded" after a side-impact crash. Extensive testing experience suggested that such "folding" can result in increased crash barrier penetration and, as a result, in a higher degree of passenger injury. Based on the knowledge and understanding of the underlying crash dynamics, it was commonly assumed that adding metal would strengthen the "folded" area and thus provide a higher resistance to a penetrating crash object. As prototype crashes had been costly and difficult to evaluate, engineers felt that it was neither necessary nor cost-effective to verify that assumption. However, since simulation was quick, inexpensive, and easy to evaluate, one development team member insisted on a verification test. The entire team was very surprised to find out that strengthening the "folded" area decreased crashworthiness significantly and initially none of the team members had a plausible explanation. However, after careful analysis of the crash data and a detailed study of the underlying crash physics, they learned that an unanticipated secondary and negative effect—the interaction between the "folded" area and the B-pillar—in fact dominated the primary positive effect that they had anticipated. Equipped with this new knowledge, the team conducted a critical reevaluation of all other enforced areas in the automotive body which led to the improvement of the design for all automobiles currently under development. [38], pp. 67–68]

This suggests that simulation, combined with traditional technologies such as physical prototypes, has the potential to move learning and product performance beyond current levels while cutting both development cost and time.

FIELD STUDY: FRONT-LOADING PROBLEM-SOLVING AT TOYOTA

In the early 1990s, Toyota Motor Corporation, like most other automotive firms, intensified efforts to accelerate their development process. Their objective was to reduce the time between styling approval and production start, thereby increasing the likelihood that a chosen auto concept would fit with rapidly changing market needs. Among many initiatives such as increased involvement of production during the product concept stage and increased knowledge transfer between projects, Toyota decided to target some development areas where they would make significant investments in CAD/CAE and rapid prototyping capabilities as a means of identifying and solving design problems earlier in their development process. The impact of these initiatives was measured not only in cost and time savings, but more importantly by measuring the changes in problem-solving patterns over time. The data presented in this article are our estimates of Toyota's problem-solving patterns and are based on material shown by Toyota in a public forum [19] and follow-up interviews with Toyota managers in Japan. Because of the strategic importance of front-loading to Toyota, no additional data were available to us at the time the research was conducted.

The front-loading initiatives[7] aimed at identifying and solving design-related problems earlier in the process following styling approval. In their efforts to manage front-loading, Toyota used both of the approaches we suggested earlier: (1) more effective transfer of problem- and solution-specific knowledge between development projects; and (2) early use of advanced technologies such as CAD and CAE. To measure the initiatives' impact, data on problems were collected and tracked over multiple development projects, but each time the intensity of front-loading was increased—more project-to-project knowledge transfer, CAD, and CAE, and even earlier involvement of production engineering in design decisions (**Figure 6**).

The internal study focused primarily on problems that would be particularly costly and time consuming to solve as they were close to production start and would involve changes such as the modification of production tools. The findings were consistent with expectations: problems were, in fact, identified and solved much earlier in the development process. More specifically, the following observations were made during each round of increasing front-loading activities:

- *Conventional process (prior to 1980s)*: As many as a half of the problems remained unsolved at the S5 point, when pilot runs start.
- *Preceding front-loading activities (1980s)*: The communication between prototype shops and production engineering did exist, but it was rather informal and unsystematic. Simultaneous engineering between body engineering and die shops, as well as engines and suspensions, increased, but simultaneous engineering activities among other engineering sections was still lagging behind. As a result, the simultaneous engineering between body and die tended to result in localized problem-solving on body design, but no improvements were made on other components (such as gas tanks, wire harness and connectors, exhaust pipes, clips and bolts).

---

[7] Because the term "front-loading" was unknown to them at the time the initiatives were started, Toyota—in the absence of a more suitable term—referred to their internal front-loading activities as simultaneous engineering.

FIGURE 6
Problem-Solving Trajectories as a Function of Development Stages and Front-Loading (FL) Intensity (Increasing From "Conventional" to "Third FL Initiative")

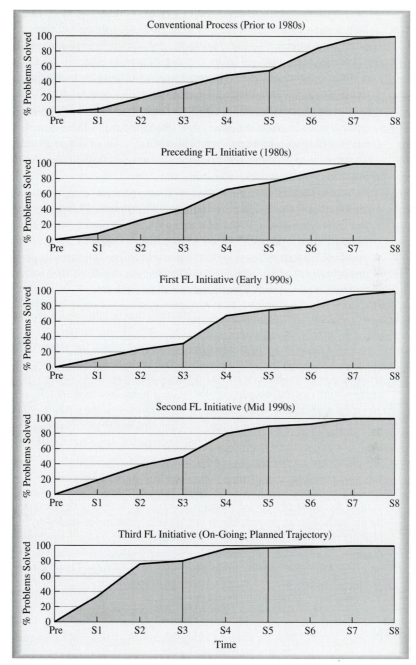

- *First front-loading initiatives (early 1990s)*: Formal and systematic efforts to improve face-to-face communication and joint problem-solving between prototype shops and production engineers were made (e.g., formal visits to prototype shops by production engineers). This resulted in an increase of problems identified and solved between the S3 and S4 stages of the development process (Figure 6), increasing the relative percentage of problems found with the aid of first prototypes. Communication between different engineering sections (e.g., between body, engine, and electrical) also were improved.
- *Second front-loading initiative (mid 1990s)*: Move to three-dimensional CAD to identify interference problems ("problems of fit"). As shown in Figure 6, this resulted in an increase of problem identification and solving prior to development stage S3 (first prototypes).
- *Third front-loading initiative (still ongoing)*: Move to CAE to identify functional problems earlier in the development process. The transfer of problem and solution information from previous projects to the front end of new projects plays an important role in this initiative as well. As a result, Toyota expects to solve about 80 percent of all problems by stage S2 or prior to the first prototypes. The second-generation engineering prototype (S5) only makes a small contribution to solving the total number of problems and thus may be partly eliminated to reduce lead time.

To verify that early problem identification and solving did lead to efficiency and lead time improvements, Toyota examined development cost, number of full physical prototypes built, and lead time over the same periods during which the front-loading initiatives were launched. They found the improvements to be remarkable: Time, cost, and prototype reductions between the first and third front-loading initiatives were reported by Toyota to be in the vicinity of 30–40 percent. We should note, however, that Toyota also underwent a major reorganization of its development activities in the early 1990s, which resulted in more effective communication and coordination between different areas [12].

Although the data presented did not undergo the same rigor as if we had collected all of it ourselves and thus do not permit us to examine the causal relationship between specific front-loading activities and performance, the data nonetheless present interesting field support for front-loading as an important methodology to improving development performance. According to Toyota managers, many of the recent development process improvements were due to project-to-project knowledge transfer (aided by the increased use of product platforms) and the effective and early use of computer and rapid prototyping technologies. Toyota managers are now applying the lessons learned from these initiatives to other development areas, with the objective of identifying many potential engineering and production problems as early as the concept phase.

DISCUSSION

This article introduces the concept of front-loading problem-solving, which we define as a strategy that seeks to increase development performance by shifting the identification and solving of [design] problems to earlier phases of a product development process. We started our discussion by describing product development as a bundle of problem-solving cycles. Using this view, we proposed that faster product development can be achieved with an earlier generation of problem- and solution-related information, particularly if it involves critical path activities. Such information may be obtained from previous projects or other repositories of developmental knowledge if it already exists, or with new problem-solving cycles if the information has to be generated. With the aid of a conceptual framework and field observations, we examined two approaches to shifting problem-solving trajectories upstream:

- *Project-to-project knowledge transfer:* increase the initial number of problems solved (or avoided) by more effective project-to-project transfer of problem and solution-specific information;
- *Rapid problem-solving:* leverage advanced technologies (such as CAD and CAE) or other methods to increase the overall rate of development problems identified and solved.

These approaches were described in detail and supported with examples and empirical observations from development practice.

Other Approaches to Front-Loading Problem-Solving

Although we presented two approaches to front-loading, it is important to note that other approaches can also lead to upstream shifts in problem-solving. Complementary methodologies already reported in the literature and mentioned earlier in the article include the overlapping and optimal partitioning of development tasks to reduce development lead time. For example, *rapid problem-solving* focuses on the more rapid and efficient completion of a given development task through faster problem-solving cycles. In contrast, the overlapping or concurrent completion of individual tasks can lead to early problem-solving by starting downstream problem-solving earlier than in a sequential development process (see **Figure 7** for a comparison of different approaches).

As suggested by Figure 7, a problem-solving perspective of product development can help in understanding how different approaches to improving development performance complement each other. Similarly, seemingly unrelated approaches from other research can be examined in terms of their impact on the upstream shift of problem-solving activities. A recent research example illustrates how a well-known managerial problem—the structure of explicit and implicit contracts and reward systems—can be examined in the context of changes in problem-solving patterns. A study by Garel and Midler [15] on contractual relationships between European automotive firms and their suppliers showed that contracts can affect a firm's problem-solving patterns. Under traditional contracting, suppliers could charge any design changes due to problems discovered in the late tool production phase to the automotive customer, irrespective of who originated the change. According to Garel and Midler, these late and costly tool changes generated an average of 20 percent in additional revenues for suppliers. Not surprisingly, the same suppliers had little incentive to cooperate with their customer or invest in technologies or methods that would result in early problem-solving. The researchers then compared these traditional contracts with a recent project where the contract had provisions that would penalize suppliers for tool changes late in the design process. As a result, the suppliers became very active in exchanging problem and solution-specific information with the customer as early as possible and, as the results showed, focused on decreasing late and costly tooling changes. In their comparison, Garel and Midler found a remarkable cost difference: not only was the new contract more

FIGURE 7
Summary of Complementary Approaches That Can Lead to an Upstream Shift of Problem-Solving and, as a Result, Increased Development Performance

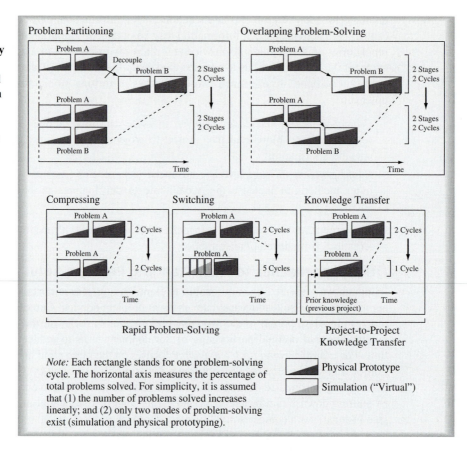

Problem Partitioning

Overlapping Problem-Solving

Compressing

Switching

Knowledge Transfer

Rapid Problem-Solving

Project-to-Project Knowledge Transfer

Note: Each rectangle stands for one problem-solving cycle. The horizontal axis measures the percentage of total problems solved. For simplicity, it is assumed that (1) the number of problems solved increases linearly; and (2) only two modes of problem-solving exist (simulation and physical prototyping).

Physical Prototype

Simulation ("Virtual")

cost effective for both parties involved but also resulted in significant differences in the timing of problem-solving. Under the traditional contract, 49 percent of estimated tooling costs were due to post-design freeze tooling changes, compared to only 15 percent under the revised contract. This suggests that other approaches, such as the change in contracting described, can lead to important changes in problem-solving patterns for firms and thus provide opportunities for further research undertakings.

Role of Front-Loading Problem-Solving in Building Development Capabilities

It is important to understand the role that front-loading problem-solving can play in building organizational capabilities for increased development performance, or as Nelson [27] states with respect to core capabilities: "At any time the practiced routines that are built into an organization define a set of things the organization is *capable* of doing confidently. If the lower-order routines for doing various tasks are absent, or if they exist but there is no practiced higher-order routine for invoking them in the particular combination needed to accomplish a particular job, then the capability to do that job lies outside the organization's extant *core capabilities*." But how can a firm measure the presence and/or any improvements of such lower- and higher-order routines? Certainly, one possibility is a focus on indirect measures such as time, resources, and product quality. Organizations with superior development capabilities should do well along all of these dimensions. But like a plant manager who may have difficulty in improving the hundreds or more manufacturing routines by focusing on aggregated plant level variables only, development managers can benefit from more direct measures of changes in capabilities. We propose that the systematic measurement of problem-solving; as described in the Toyota data, can provide a more direct focus on capability building.

As an example, consider that many automotive firms currently are trying to reduce development times by aggressively substituting physical prototypes with computer models. (An example would be the elimination of second-generation hardware prototypes.) However, without an explicit understanding of their problem-solving capabilities, firms do not know if they have all the lower- and higher-order routines in place that would allow them to reduce time without sacrifices in product quality, as measured by the number of unidentified problems after releasing a product to market. In contrast, the management of problem-solving trajectories (as shown in Figure 6) that we propose in this article may help firms to measure more directly changes in their capabilities over time, using some of the approaches that we described. (Using the automotive example once more, second-generation hardware prototypes ought to be eliminated after—and not before—changes in development capabilities have been measured and validated through changes in problem-solving trajectories.) Shifting problem-identification and problem-solving to earlier phases in development thus can be an explicit objective, whereas faster development will be an indirect benefit of having solved more problems at these earlier stages.

We would like to thank the many colleagues who contributed to the ideas expressed in this article through private conversations, seminars, and feedback on earlier drafts of this paper. The financial support of the Harvard Business School Division of Research and Tokyo University's Division of Economics are gratefully acknowledged.

REFERENCES

1. Adler, P. "Interdepartmental interdependence and coordination: The case of the design/manufacturing interface." *Organization Science* 6 (1995).

2. Aoshima, Y. "Knowledge Transfer Across Generations: The Impact on Product Development Performance in the Automobile Industry." Unpublished Ph.D. Dissertation. Massachusetts Institute of Technology, 1996.

3. Argyris, C. *Reasoning, Learning and Action,* San Francisco: Jossey-Bass Publishers, 1982.

4. Allen, T. J. "Studies of the problem-solving process in engineering design. *IEEE Transactions on Engineering Management* EM-13:72–83 (1966).

5. Boehm, B. *Software Engineering Economics,* Englewood Cliffs: Prentice Hall, 1981.

6. Brooks, F. P. *The Mythical Man-Month.* Reading, MA: Addison-Wesley, 1982.

7. Brown, S. and Eisenhardt, K. "Product development: Past research, present findings, and future directions." *Academy of Management Review* 20:343–378 (1995).

8. Clark, K. and Fujimoto, T. "Lead time in automobile development: Explaining the Japanese advantage." *Journal of Technology and Engineering Management* 6:25–58 (1989).

9. Clark, K. and Fujimoto, T. *Product Development Performance.* Boston: Harvard Business School Press, 1991.

10. Cooper, Robert and Kleinschmidt, E. "Determinants of timeliness in product development." *Journal of Product Innovation Management* 11:381–396 (1994).

11. Crawford, M. "The hidden cost of accelerated product development." *Journal of Product Innovation Management* 9:188–199 (1992).

12. Cusumano, M. and Nobeoka, K. *Thinking Beyond Lean: How Multi-Project Management is Transforming Product Development at Toyota and Other Companies.* New York: The Free Press, 1998.

13. Cusumano, M. and Selby, R. *Microsoft Secrets.* New York: The Free Press, 1995.

14. Fujimoto, T. "Organizing for Effective Product-Development: The Case of the Global Automobile Industry." Unpublished Dissertation. Harvard Business School, 1989.

15. Garel, G. and Midler, C. "An analysis of co-development performance in automotive development processes: A case study testing a win-win hypothesis." 5th EIASM International Product Development Conference, Como, Italy, 1998.

16. Griffin, Abbie. "Modeling and measuring product development cycle time across industries." *Journal of Engineering and Technology Management* 14:1–24 (1997).

17. Gupta, A. and Wilemon, D. "Accelerating the development of technology-based new products." *California Management Review* 32:24–44 (1990).

18. Iansiti, M. *Technology Integration: Making Critical Choices in a Turbulent World.* Boston: Harvard Business School Press, 1997.

19. Jagawa, T. "Frontloading: Shortening development time at Toyota through intensive upfront effort." *IBEC 95,* Detroit, Michigan, 1995.

20. Kamien, M. I. and Schwartz, N. L. *Market Structure and Innovation.* Cambridge: Cambridge University Press, 1982.

21. Krishnan, V., Eppinger, S., and Whitney, D. "A model-based framework to overlap product development activities." *Management Science* 43 (1997).

22. Liker, Jeffrey, Fleischer, Mitchell, Nagamachi, Mitsuo, and Zonnevylle, Michael. "Designers and their machines: CAD use and support in the US and Japan." *Communications of the ACM* 35 (1992).

23. Marples, D. L. "The decision of engineering design." *IRE Transactions on Engineering Management* 2:55–71 (1961).

24. McDonough, Edward, III, and Barczak, Gloria. "The effects of cognitive problem-solving orientation and technological familiarity on faster new product development." *Journal of Product Innovation Management* 9:44–52 (1992).

25. Meyer, C. *Fast Cycle Time.* New York: The Free Press, 1993.

26. Meyer, M. H. and Lehnerd, A. *The Power of Product Platforms.* New York: The Free Press, 1997.

27. Nelson, R. "Why do firms differ, and how does it matter." In: *Fundamental Issues in Strategies.* R. Rummelt, D. Schendel, and D. Teece (eds.). Boston: Harvard Business School Press, 1994.

28. Petroski, H. *To Engineer Is Human.* New York: Vintage Books, 1992.

29. Pisano, G. *The Development Factory.* Boston: Harvard Business School Press, 1996.

30. Sabbagh, K. *Twenty-First Century Jet: The Making and Marketing of the Boeing 777.* New York: Scribner, 1996.

31. Scott-Morton, M. "Computer-Driven Visual Display Devices." Unpublished Doctoral Dissertation. Harvard Business School, 1967.

32. Senge, P. *The Fifth Discipline: The Art and Practice of the Learning Organization.* New York: Doubleday, 1990.

33. Simon, H. A. *The Sciences of the Artificial.* Cambridge: MIT Press, 1969.

34. Smith, P. and Reinertsen, D. *Developing Products in Half the Time: New Rules, New Tools.* New York: Van Nostrand Reinhold, 1998.

35. Terwiesch, C. and Loch, C. "Measuring the effectiveness of overlapping development activities." Working Paper No. 98/45/TM, INSEAD, *Management Science* (1998).

36. Thomke, S. "Managing experimentation in the design of new products." *Management Science* 44:743–762 (1998).

37. Thomke, S. "The role of flexibility in the development of new products: an empirical study." *Research Policy* 26:105–119 (1997).

38. Thomke, S. "Simulation, learning and R&D performance: Evidence from automotive development." *Research Policy* 27:55–74 (1998).

39. Thomke, S. and Bell, D. "Optimal testing in product development." Harvard Business School Working Paper No. 99-053 (1998).

40. Thomke, S. and Nimgade, A. "BMW AG: The Digital Auto Project (A)." Harvard Business School Case Study No. 699-044 (1998).

41. Verganti, Robert. "Leveraging on systemic learning to manage the early phase of product innovation projects." *R&D Management* (1997).

42. von Hippel, E. "'Sticky' information and the locus of problem-solving: Implications for innovation." *Management Science* 40:429–439 (1994).

43. von Hippel, E. and Tyre, M. "How 'learning by doing' is done: Problem identification in novel process equipment." *Research Policy* 19:1–12 (1994).

44. von Hippel, E. "Task partitioning: An innovation process variable." *Research Policy* 19:407–418 (1990).

45. Watkins, M. and Clark, K. "Strategies for managing a project portfolio." Working Paper, Harvard Business School (1994).

46. Wheelwright, S. and Clark, K. *Revolutionizing Product Development.* New York: The Free Press, 1992.

Case **2-5**

Bush Boake Allen

"I'll have tea, with milk and no sugar, please," said Julian Boyden, chief executive officer of Bush Boake Allen (BBA), to the waiter serving him and John Wright, vice president of commerce and technology and a fellow British expatriate. With nearly six decades of experience at BBA between them, the two were veterans of the flavor and fragrance industry. Over lunch, Boyden and Wright had been discussing whether BBA should boost customer participation in flavor development through an Internet-based toolkit that relied on a half-million dollar prototyping machine. It was late spring in 2000, and sunlight streamed through the windows of the cozy Saddle River Inn restaurant. This part of New Jersey lived up to its "Garden State" name and lay close to what industry insiders called "The Silicon Valley of the flavor and fragrance industry." BBA had played no small role in helping maintain this reputation.

Nearly all processed foods had "flavor" added to them because manufacturing techniques weakened the "real" flavors involved. A small quantity of, say, natural beef flavor added to a recipe for canned beef stew made the resulting product taste "more like" beef stew to the consumer. But exactly what beef was "supposed" to taste like was not clear—to beef stew manufacturers, to consumers of beef stew, or even to flavor development companies focused on creating beef flavors. There was no one, universal, standard. As such, flavor development itself was considered more art than science. Many "flavorists" had methodological idiosyncrasies and biases they drew upon when developing a flavor. This would likely never change, despite breakthroughs in chemistry and robotics. The human nose and tongue appreciated nuances of flavor too subtle for human ingenuity to replicate.

Most of the risk of flavor development was borne by flavor development companies like BBA, who paid for all R&D expenses and collected revenue only after a client was fully satisfied *and* consumers eventually bought its end products. If clients themselves were able to participate in the development effort, Wright and Boyden reasoned, that might boost the

Professor Stefan Thomke and Research Associate Ashok Nimgrade prepared this case. HBS cases are developed solely as the basis for class discussion. Cases are not intended to serve as endorsements, sources of primary data, or illustrations of effective or ineffective management.

effective rate of flavor acceptance, which hovered around 5 percent to 10 percent. Thus, even if the new toolkit made little impact on the cost and speed of development, the system might positively affect customer relations. But how far to place control in the hands of clients remained a puzzle. A pilot machine for prototyping flavor samples was already in place in Rotterdam, the Netherlands, and would hopefully help answer some of the questions. Yet even if the new way of developing flavors would prove feasible, uncertainty remained about how much, if at all, to charge customers.

In an hour Boyden would host a teleconference with executives from BBA's many international offices to assess support for the new project. Initial feedback had thus far been mixed. But Boyden himself was no stranger to opposition. Early in his career he raised eyebrows while working as an analyst for a chemical company when he recommended closing the firm's Malaysian fertilizer operation. His report collected dust. Through a twist of fate, Boyden was later assigned to head the very same operation. The first thing he did was to lay off 80 percent of the entrenched personnel in favor of outsourcing. In a shock, headquarters telephoned him. "You read my recommendations that we not buy the place," Boyden responded. "What else did you expect me to do?" Back came the slow reply: "Uh, oh . . . you're the chap who wrote that report . . . "

THE SCENT OF SUCCESS

"Bush Boake's invisibility is nearly rivaled by its ubiquity," was how one newspaper described the firm.[1] In an $11 billion industry dominated by trade secrets and not patents, this cloak of invisibility had thus far suited all players well. BBA could trace its roots to the 1966 merger of three British companies, the oldest of which, Stafford Allen Ltd., had started in the 1830s, as a seasoning and distillery company. Each had a strong overseas presence, especially in British Commonwealth nations and the United States. In 1982, Union Camp (which later merged with International Paper Company) acquired BBA. After its initial public offering in 1994, BBA shifted its headquarters to the Garden State (see **Exhibit 1** for financials).

Key to the company's strategy was maintaining a decentralized structure, which allowed local managers to make decisions swiftly and respond to regional needs while providing the flexibility to service large customers such as Nestle and Unilever. To further strengthen and extend its international presence, BBA launched a "Gaps in Maps" strategy in the 1980s. Lasting two decades, the effort established new manufacturing sites in Thailand, China, Turkey, and Mexico, among other countries, based on the goal of supplying consistent, locally produced ingredients and gaining a better understanding of local preferences (see **Exhibit 2**).

By 2000, BBA operated as a public company in 38 countries on six continents and had nearly two thousand employees. Flavors and fragrances accounted for about 80 percent of its half-billion dollar annual revenues, and aroma chemicals for the remainder. The Americas accounted for 35 percent of sales, Europe for 33 percent, and Pacific Asia for 16 percent (see **Exhibit 3**). The importance of the international sector was indicated by BBA's near double-digit growth in India, the world's fastest growing flavor market. To ensure its

---

[1] Moritz, S., "Hidden Products, Modest Gains: Bush Boake Posts 4% Earnings Rise," *The Record,* Northern New Jersey, May 8, 1997.

international prominence, the company pumped some $25 million annually into research and development, not only at its three main technical facilities in New Jersey, London, and India, but in 36 other labs worldwide.

Although BBA encouraged regional autonomy, it exercised strong central financial control, with international managers having to provide monthly basis reports to headquarters and file for capital expenditure endorsements. International offices also coordinated efforts, partly through a common computer system, to share information on large multinational corporations and other key clients. Boyden traveled frequently to different regions of the globe to keep in touch with his firm's many locations.

In 1999, BBA's 10 largest customers represented one-fourth of total net sales. While most customers did not buy all their flavors from a single source, they traditionally used only a few "select suppliers." Also, in exchange for a guaranteed amount of yearly spending, customers could extract rebates from these select suppliers.

BBA purchased its raw materials from varied sources worldwide to ensure an uninterrupted supply. No one source accounted for more than 4 percent of the company's raw material requirements in 1999.

BBA's sales force operated from four offices in the United States and 50 offices worldwide. In North America, for instance, the firm employed six marketers and 12 sales representatives; each salesperson handled some three major customers—each generating annual revenues of $3 to $5 million, typically through a dozen or so flavors—as well as several minor customers. A large customer might have as many as six to eight divisions that a salesperson would have to work with. Sales representatives were responsible for maintaining an open line of communications with customers. This entailed not only obtaining product specifications from clients but also actively managing the customer interaction with R&D during flavor development, including keeping clients informed about new "base" flavors coming out BBA's research labs. For their work, salespeople could potentially earn some of the highest salaries in the company thanks to bonuses and commissions.

BBA's earnings and revenues modestly increased every year during the 1990s, a period when several competitors had floundered. "This company is a steady grower," according to Arthur Weise, a New York-based investment analyst. "The only double-digit growth we would have expected to see is if they had a revolutionary flavor that would help drive up sales dramatically . . . It's been primarily a value investment. It's a stable business not subject to great changes because they are providing things for food. You'll always need food . . ."[2]

Given the industry's business model, which transferred most flavor development risk onto the flavor makers, BBA sought to appear "solid and trustworthy," according to Theresa Gordon-Wright, international marketing manager. Flavor makers, for instance, provided investment firms with deliberately staid annual reports. Not surprisingly, the shareholder meetings themselves were generally sparsely attended. As one witness from the press described the 1997 BBA annual meeting, "The 40 attendee—nearly all of them company officials—couldn't even fill the small Woodcliff Lake hotel ballroom, or muster a single question from a shareholder. The meeting adjourned in under 20 minutes, leaving a relatively undisturbed table full of bagels and cinnamon buns for the support staff to claim."[3]

[2] Ibid.
[3] Ibid.

But according to Gordon-Wright, "We are thinking about changing the way we have operated in this traditionally low-key industry."

Some of these changes were being spearheaded by Boyden, who actually started as a chemist in the detergent industry, then switched to management by getting an MBA in the early 1970s. BBA's parent company hired him as a senior manager to "bring a breath of fresh air" into what had been a traditionally run company. In a manner unusual for a manager, Boyden spent a considerable time in his early days learning about the mundane aspects of the flavor industry by working several hours a week in the confectionery lab. "From the outset," said Gordon-Wright, "it was clear that he was very smart . . . and he stood out as the clear choice for company leadership . . . "

In 1989, Boyden assumed company leadership, eventually becoming president, CEO, and chairman of the board (see **Exhibit 4** for BBA's organizational chart). Like Boyden, several of the company leaders came from the British working and middle class, and rose through the ranks. Partly for these reasons, according to Wright, they remained "blind to the distinctions between the governed and the governors . . . fostering a collegial, parliamentary type of debate and discussion that allowed the freedom to experiment, at least in the stages before the entire company committed to one direction." American manager Debbie Johns, vice president of marketing, found her 16 years with the company far "more open" than her time at her previous job, thanks in part to Boyden's open-door policy, which she found "surprisingly democratic for a manager of British origin."

BBA went public in 1994, emphasizing the development of new products, improving the company's product mix, expanding into high-growth markets, and increasing margins.[4] Some new measures to improve productivity, embedded in a seven-year $240 million capital investment program, included automating certain processes and launching a new technical and sales "creativity center" near Rotterdam. The firm also reduced headcount and improved productivity, changes that allowed it to increase its sales and earnings to above industry averages.

By the year 2000, the company was debating ways to use e-commerce capabilities to leverage creativity through establishing virtual teams of flavorists and managers internationally. "After surviving for many years in the middle of the flavor and fragrance pack," one industry observer declared, "Bush Boake Allen is finally ready to play with the big boys."[5]

THE FLAVOR AND FRAGRANCE INDUSTRY

Who could not be interested in this industry? I can't imagine a more interesting line of work. It's about food, flavors, and physical attraction from drosophila to moths to humans. It's about everything that makes the world go around! But scents are subtle . . . with ingredients that may work in parts per billion concentrations we can certainly concoct a nearly infinite variety of flavors and scents.

—*Julian Boyden, CEO, Bush Boake Allen*

[4] *Chemical Market Reporter,* "Bush Boake Allen Aims for the F&F Big League: Bush Boake Allen's Sales May Reach $500 Mil in 1997," August 11, 1999, p. 5.

[5] *Hoover's Online Overview,* 2000.

BBA operated in a field of over 300 competitors worldwide. Only a tenth of these, however, had significant multinational operations. Leading the industry was the U.S. firm International Flavors and Fragrances (IFF), at three times the size of BBA, followed by the Swiss firm Givaudan Roure. The top nine global companies accounted for over three-fourths of this $11 billion world market (see **Exhibit 5**). Although BBA enjoyed membership in this elite club, it held only about 4.7 percent world market share in 1999.

The worldwide flavor and fragrance industry was split about evenly between flavors and fragrances. The three dominating regions in order of decreasing market share were North America, Western Europe, and Asian Pacific. In the setting of a worldwide annual growth rate in the late 1990s of 3.2 percent for flavors and of 2.5 percent for fragrances, an industry journal noted, "One thing is sure: flavor and fragrance companies can still grow but just not as fast as they would like."[6]

In India, whose 8 percent to 9 percent annual growth led the world, BBA enjoyed a 30 percent market share by capitalizing on relationships established since British colonial times. According to Bruce Edwards, vice president of International, "The average candy consumption in the United States is 20 kg/year per person; in India it is 20 g/year. In fact, there are kids in places like India or even Russia who have yet to taste their first candy. So the third world is a burgeoning market!"

But to grow in such markets took great effort; simply producing basic flavors and arranging for distribution proved challenging. "In India, they're still struggling with issues such as not having uninterrupted electricity," Gordon-Wright pointed out. "In Pakistan, it's hard weaning Pakistanis off old flavors and onto new flavors. They're the only ones left using some of our older flavors! Even in Eastern Europe, where flavor development was done traditionally by the government, you end up doing product demos right on corners of their desks!" To add to the challenge, competitors also sought footholds in markets like India, often luring away local managers trained by BBA.

All flavors produced worldwide were subject to regulation by equivalents of the U.S. Food and Drug Administration, and other state and local regulatory agencies. In some countries, one also needed to register all samples with the government—just because two or three ingredients were safe did not mean that combining them would prove safe. Complying with these regulations, however, had not been problematic and had not impacted the company's earnings or competitive position.

In a setting where reverse engineering using even the latest technology was difficult, most companies relied on trade secrets to protect intellectual property. Only on occasion would a firm patent a flavor. "The entire industry is based on trust," said Gordon-Wright. "If we develop a brand new flavor for a client, we don't turn around and sell a small modification of it to the client's competitor."

But things were changing rapidly. Players in the flavor and fragrance industry already faced cost pressure and high risk given the prevailing business model. Moreover, by using new technologies some large clients themselves were able to analyze flavors within days; not only would chemical formulations be revealed but production cost data could also be gathered. As a result, the erosion of flavor prices was accelerating. In Boyden's terse assessment: "The days of attractive and stable margins are over unless we change our business model."

---

[6] *Chemical Market Reporter,* "F&F Financial Results Show There's Growth in Industry," January 26, 1998, p. 17.

THE ART OF FLAVOR DEVELOPMENT

Taking a flavor from nature was a complex task. One could, in theory, smash a strawberry in a beaker and summon the power of such modern analytical techniques as nuclear magnetic resonance, chromatography, and mass spectrometry to identify all components present (see **Exhibit 6**). Thereafter, one should be able to add back all these components in their respective quantities to re-create the flavor of a strawberry. But such a reductionist scheme quickly invited complexity. Within a strawberry, one may find 200 to 500 components in varying concentrations. Not surprisingly, some of the ingredients identified prove incidental and some even detrimental to the flavor, while trace elements might make a world of difference. As a result, scientific shortcuts quickly become complex, lengthy, and expensive.

But even if one decided to recreate a flavor sparing no expense, could the flavor of strawberry be exactly reproduced? Unfortunately not. Because of enormous variations in freshness, sweetness, ripeness, texture, size of seeds, and so on, no one, true "strawberry reality" existed.

Therefore the onus fell upon the flavorist. Different flavorists might use a slightly different blend of ingredients based on their personal recollection of a strawberry. A superb flavorist might even reach back to his or her very first childhood memory of savoring a strawberry—a pristine remembrance, unsullied by all subsequent psychological associations of adulthood—to create a flavor. The difference between excellent and good flavorists boiled down to imagination and creativity: imagination for recreating a flavor in the "mind's nose," and creativity for blending ingredients in innovative ways.

Working in their labs filled with hundreds of bottled ingredients bearing labels like "strawberry-aldehyde" or "gamma-deca-lactone," flavorists needed self-confidence to present their reality as the best one. Reaching this stage took time and experience. It took three to five years of training to learn how to choose the three-to-15 ingredients that could recreate primary flavor characteristics, but it might take 10 years to become a virtuoso. Despite a worldwide shortage of flavorists, theirs was a risky career, because only after several years of training could they tell if one was good enough to continue. Flavorists also needed to deal with any of their flavors being rejected. In this setting, according to John Wright, "Unless you're slightly arrogant, you're in bad shape."

But along with self-confidence often came eccentricities and quirks. Some experienced flavorists mixed up formulae in sloppy batches while others obsessively measured items and recorded formulae in meaningless levels of accuracy well beyond the capability of production. One of Wright's early teachers, for instance, was a rigid contrarian, quick to denigrate anyone's opinion about a flavor. Apprentices learned to present their concoctions with the preface, "I think this is rubbish, but I brought it anyway . . ."

At the same time, flavorists faced substantial pressures. Turnaround times might vary from as little as one day for a cheese snack product to three weeks for an entirely new mushroom product to as much as 40 days for a mint-flavored pharmaceutical product. Furthermore, clients often expected BBA to get the flavor right the first time, or at the most, after two or three iterations of client feedback. A shopper in a supermarket, after all, might never buy a particular dessert again if it tasted more like black pudding than chocolate.

Although analytical training only gave the flavorist perhaps 20 percent of the tools necessary for creating a flavor—the rest coming from experience—it provided a common basis for developing flavors. Scientific training, for instance, led to an understanding that part of the strawberry's charm came from having sulfur as an integral ingredient or that the quality of creaminess could come from addition of delta-deca-lactones.

Usually the initial idea for a client's flavor would come from the client; sometimes, however, BBA itself might propose a new base flavor coming out of its R&D labs. New flavors were either line extensions or radical new ideas. The client would detail several parameters such as the "flavor profile application" (how the flavor should taste in the final application), price, regulatory issues, storage conditions, and even temperature of the final product. The trickiest problem, however, involved the language of flavor itself.

The course of a typical project might run as follows. A customer would request a "meaty" flavor for a haggis-substitute soy product it was developing, with the sample flavor to be delivered in seven days. Marketing, management and flavorists would then decide about the client's needs. The flavorists would then work hard to ship out a sample in six days. Thereafter, it might take a frustrating three weeks for the salespeople to get the following feedback from the client: "It's good, but we need it less smoky and more gutsy." This might lead to another frenzied couple of days of adjusting the flavor. Another few weeks might pass before the salespeople brought back further word from the client: "The competition has a better flavor so far. But we'll look at another sample from you."

The entire process could ping pong salespeople back-and-forth for several iterations, sometimes with no end in sight. "We're tailor-making our products . . . not churning out Ford cars," said Wright. On average, about 15 percent (ranging from 7 percent to 40 percent) of all development requests would eventually be accepted by a client for market evaluation. Even if the client liked the flavor, however, the final decision to source the flavor was based upon taste tests with end consumers. In fact, only 25 percent to 50 percent of flavors accepted for market evaluation would successfully make it to market and generate revenue. As Bruce Edwards noted, "It's an iterative process . . . The bigger the company the more laborious the process of waiting . . . but by the end, between steps 'a' and 'z' we've already given our customers a sense of ownership."

BBA, like its competitors, paid for all the R&D expenses which could amount to as little as $1,000 for tweaking an existing flavor to as much as $100,000–$300,000 for an entirely new family of flavors. Flavor development would involve many different functions, including sales, marketing, analytical and synthetic chemists, flavorists, regulatory, and quality control. The odds of getting a flavor accepted were somewhat higher with large customers because the firm usually put in more effort. Usually, BBA would find itself competing against at least one other flavor company. But things were not all bleak. Flavor companies did control all flavors they concocted. Furthermore, scale-up costs were minimal, and margins on the order of 40 percent for accepted flavors were attractive.

This, then, was the way of the traditional order, in which, according to Edwards, "The flavorists can be virtuosos, with the rest of us playing a supporting role." But clouds on the horizon were starting to signal that "our industry is coming onto more hard-nosed days now."

PROJECT MERCURY

According to Berto van der Manden, Managing Director of BBA's Rotterdam facility, "Even just five years ago, flavors were a mystery to many of our clients; today, they undergo very serious economic scrutiny. Now flavor costs matter because of cost pressures in the supermarkets." Partly because of these pressures, BBA had started automating certain parts of its operation.

The natural place to begin making changes was in the tedious but complex process of dispensing, weighing, and adding ingredients to batches of flavors or fragrances. At several key facilities a few years earlier, BBA had begun to automate the process of compounding orders for delivery to customers using robotic carousels that could dispense measured amounts of ingredients. Now senior management shifted its attention further upstream to flavor development itself.

The logical place to start in this complex process was with secondary flavor characteristics. A fundamental block to this process, however, lay in semantics. A client's use of terms like "peely" or "juicy" might differ from BBA's understanding of the flavor. While everyone knew how to describe primary flavor characteristics (e.g., "strawberry" or "vanilla"), vast discrepancies existed between individuals about how to describe secondary flavor characteristics (e.g., "fruitiness," "green tones," "rosy-ness"). A vocabulary to match that of oenophiles was developing, one often as imprecise as it was vast.

BBA itself lacked internal precision involving flavors. "Strawberry" in Amsterdam was not the same as "strawberry" in India or Australia. This was not only because of regional preferences, but also because of regional agency approvals for flavors and flavor ingredients. Even religious differences mattered: in some nations, even trace quantities of alcohol would prove unacceptable. Furthermore, with so many flavor variants possible, it would be hard to decide which flavors to standardize. The U.K. office alone had some 2,000 different strawberry flavors among its collection of 26,000 flavors.

Nevertheless, management felt it was important to bridge the semantic gap because the future promised only more new compounds. The challenge, Boyden noted, had become "how to translate the ephemeral into the concrete, and the concrete into revenue." Through BBA's participation in the Innovation Lab at the Massachusetts Institute of Technology, the idea crystallized in 1998 to use the Internet for allowing customers to develop flavors remotely. This would be facilitated through a modified online automatic ingredient pouring machines for helping facilitate flavor creation. The modified machine would quickly become known in the New Jersey offices as "the Spider" (see **Exhibit 7**). The machine hardly resembled a spider; the name, in fact, derived from conceptual reasons from the so-called "spidergrams"—spiderweb-like diagrams that flavorists used to graphically illustrate the varying quantities of different ingredients involved in a flavor (see **Exhibits 8A** to **8E**).

The amount of user involvement in the new system could vary from as little as placing labeled sample bottles in the machine to manipulating the software to develop a new flavor. To simplify matters initially, however, management decided that software users would only be allowed to utilize the machine for developing secondary flavor characteristics, that is, for merely "tweaking" these basic flavors already created by BBA's flavorists. The company, in fact, planned to set up the software so that users could alter any given ingredient by only a certain amount—flavorists feared that a heavy-handed approach on part of a user could lose the flavor's recognizability. How much users should eventually control the development of their flavors, however, remained an open question.

The entire project went by the official name of "Project Mercury"—so named by Ian Goddard, Director of Corporate Engineering—to indicate that the project would facilitate communication between BBA and its clients, just as Mercury served as the messenger of Greek gods. Project Mercury, the team hoped, would allow more data about customer preferences to be captured or at least improve the BBA's's responsiveness to customer requests for samples. For instance, was a certain client enamored of "green tones" in all their strawberry flavors? At the same time, it would allow the cost of ingredients to be calculated and even facilitate cost reduction to meet a client's budgetary goals.

The new system could also help manage raw ingredient inventory by keeping tabs on how much of each ingredient was remaining. Since the starting ingredients themselves were proprietary and difficult to reverse-engineer, management did not worry too much about ownership should clients be allowed to produce flavor samples internally. BBA's lawyers remained confident that regardless of the amount of customer input into a new flavor, the company would still control the final formula.

BBA's revamped technical and creative center in Rotterdam was the site chosen for the prototype machine. The new facility's proximity to the airport would also make its output readily accessible to most points in Western Europe.[7] The R&D labs were still being set up when Managing Director Berto van der Manden received a surprise phone call from Boyden stating: "We have a special new flavor-development system; we need to try it out at Rotterdam . . . " That was the first van der Manden had heard of Project Mercury.

The Rotterdam facility shuffled around its floor space, eventually dedicating a ground-level 40-foot long room for the prototype Spider. The computer interface required only a desktop. To meet the goal of having the system operating smoothly by the summer of 2000, technologist Arjan Speijar worked solely on the project, loading up all the ingredients, and wrestling with unexpected problems such as the magnetically-driven valve releases being too sticky to dispense properly. It would take several further months of internal testing, however, before the Spider prototype could be used with customers. Van der Manden, with a background in food technology, was delighted, viewing the new system not only as a time saver for his four flavorists, but also as an opportunity for their Benelux clients. Initial plans, however, were to continue sending samples to European clients the traditional way, through overnight express delivery.

In the meantime the Rotterdam office proudly showed the prototype system to clients that visited the facility, with the hopes of finding one or two enthusiasts with whom to pilot the machine. According to Speijar, "Our customers say, 'wow, we've never seen anything like this!'" They might be baffled, however, if they had been asked how much they would be willing to pay for using it.

While management believed it would be technically possible to locate a prototyping machine at each client's site, the cost might be nearly $500,000 for the larger models—and flavor clients did not currently pay for any of BBA's R&D expenses. Also, customer volume was a consideration. Wright himself was cautious: "If a client did only two or three samples a day, then it might not be worth having a dedicated system at their site." On the other hand, large customers abounded through the world. "Off the top of my head, I can think of 10 possible customers in the United States alone definitely large enough to merit having a Spider system," Debbie Johns noted.

Managers debated about whether to have centralized systems located in key locations such as Singapore, Australia, and several throughout Asia, Europe, and the Americas. Clients could play with ingredients over the Internet to create new blends. Under this scenario,

---

[7] *Chemical Market Reporter,* "Bush Boake Allen Inc. Is Building a Technical Center in the Netherlands to Develop Flavor Technology," February 15, 1999, p. 19.

mixed samples could be express mailed or even delivered within hours by couriers to clients. Another possibility was to have portable Spider systems that could be taken around in semi-trucks, which could be parked temporarily at a client's site for as long as needed. This practice was already prevalent in some industries—for instance, large radiological imaging machines for hospitals.

RELEASING THE SPIDER

Yet another concern facing management was internal acceptance. Senior management at New Jersey had already taken pains to explain to flavorists that the Spider was not meant to replace them—instead, it would allow flavorists to work in their area of greatest value. Flavorists were encouraged to start using the Spider as a tool for their own work in flavor concoction and as a means to experiment more rapidly.

In terms of upper level support, R&D management in the United States and Europe was very supportive from the beginning. But how marketing and other overseas branches would view Project Mercury remained to be seen. While Project Mercury was never kept a secret from all other branches, it was not brought up in the regular business of running the company. Boyden filled in the managers one by one.

One key individual would be Bruce Edwards, the head of BBA's fastest growing markets, the International Division. Both Edwards and Boyden were, in the words of their U.K. production manager, "London laddies who made good." Both retained their roots, often walking the plant floors to chat with old timers and new hires. At one point Edwards left the company, but Boyden re-hired him. There was little in Edwards's background to suggest his success. Without a managerial or technical background, Edwards claimed, "I literally walked off the street in 1968 after high school and asked for a job . . . my father said it was about time I started buying my own shoes." Now Edwards spent half his time from Delhi to Dubai growing his division on his "patch of the earth covering some 3.5 billion people" successfully for well over a decade. But he was cautious:

> The first time I heard of the Spider, we were waiting for a cab together and Boyden said, "what about this as an idea . . . " After listening, I said, "I think it's a fine idea." It's a great idea to use the Spider for flavor production. We do need faster compounding. If we can feed in a formula at one end and out pops the compound, that's great! From an ownership point of view, where the machine is kept entirely centrally with us, I'm 100 percent behind Mercury. But for outside uses I have reservations . . .

A more formal internal "release" occurred in the spring of 2000 during a companywide teleconference on e-commerce opportunities involving 10 high level BBA managers, a few key central managers, and two representatives from Information Technology. Fred Stults, vice president of R&D, summarized a sentiment shared by the project champions involved in the teleconference: "Mercury should help the customers feel they are driving the creative function. At the very least, it should allow our flavorists to experiment faster."

At least one participant voiced concerns that the machine might prove to be "too costly." The rebuttal came back: "Only if implemented incorrectly." More ominous was silence on part of some of the international managers. "It was a disbelief that it would ever work expressed only indirectly through a lack of enthusiasm. . . ," Stults said. "Some managers were saying, in essence, 'I'll do what I have to do . . . and no more.'" Edwards volunteered to speak on behalf of his concerned colleagues. Although he recalled feeling "sick as a dog" on the day of the teleconference, he held forth. "I suppose I'm naturally cautious," he began, "we're being first in a new arena, but I'd rather be third or fourth." Speaking from the viewpoint of the international market pointed, he pointed out:

> We have a lot of old clients in places like Dubai who like to be dealt with the old-fashioned way. In India, the priority is on distribution costs (the most important factor), then on production cost. Flavor, let alone the nuances of flavor, is not a priority. They don't care about flavor so long as it is in the ballpark. In India, with less production skills, customers want reproducibility on the factory floor, not flavor nuances à la Mercury. They're focused a hundred times more on whether they can get the product to all four corners of the country than on whether the flavor is good!

But the bulk of discussion involved developed markets. Here Zoe Gleisner, International Finance Manager, stated: "We can put a box on the customer's desk, but they have to learn about the ingredients in our palette to make a decent flavor. Customers may not admit that they can't do it. If they do three trials and it flops, they won't use it . . . then they'll blame Bush Boake Allen." Edwards concurred:

> Our industry has made our customers lazy! Our competitors have a team of salespeople virtually camped on the lawn of our most important customers. So even if we give one of our largest clients a machine, our traditional competitors will still probably give samples faster. On top of that, I don't know if we have customers clever enough to do it; but we'll have customers who think they're clever enough to do it. If the customer feels that making flavors is easy, they'll devalue the worth of our flavorists. Promoting client-based machines might be like the turkeys voting for Thanksgiving or Christmas.

Another marketing manager added:

> There may be five different flavorists employed by a large customer, each with different philosophies and needs. Computer nerds play with the machine, exhausting the ingredients quickly, and losing interest in the "new toy." Others may have a hard time with the new system: overriding whatever services we provide. Probably most might require more hand-holding than we suspect, and not just for computer-related reasons. If no BBA person is around the Spider, the customer may work with an ingredient without understanding that the ingredient might work in a high fat but not a low fat ice cream.

Near the conclusion of the teleconference, one international manager asked, "Is anyone else working along the same lines?" No one knew of any such case. But as no clear answer existed, this question was open to discussion. John Wright warned, "It's a very competitive industry. If we don't reinvent the industry, someone else will!"

Shortly thereafter, in May, at the annual BBA international sales conference in New Jersey with some 100 people in attendance, Wright made a formal presentation to the rank and file about Project Mercury. Afterwards, for the fun of it, the crowd in the auditorium voted on how much to adjust various secondary flavor parameters over the Internet toolkit to improve upon a popular and already optimized BBA raspberry flavor. The modification was created and then brought back into the room alongside the original in unlabelled containers. In a blind taste test between the standard flavor and the modified flavor, the original flavor won by a margin of three-to-one.

The next day found Boyden and Wright at the Saddle River Inn at end of a business luncheon involving senior level international office marketers. Over tea, when only Boyden and Wright remained, discussion turned to Project Mercury, and Boyden summed up his thoughts: "There are three key issues: Does it work conceptually? I think we can answer that with a 'yes.' Does it work practically? I think the answer to that may also become a 'yes.' Finally, can it make money? We still need to find out about that."

The following themes dominated their subsequent discussion. Should the Spider system only be used by BBA's R&D group or be placed in the hands of customers as well? If customers were to be involved, how much control over flavor development should be given to international managers and customers? And which customers should be approached and how much should they pay to take advantage of the new Spider technology?

In particular, Boyden and Wright were discussing three strategic proposals that senior management was considering and would be discussed shortly in a teleconference with international executives. The first proposal—strongly favored by international division and marketing—would keep the Spider technology in-house. Management efforts would focus on leveraging the system to link BBA development centers around the world and provide them with rapid flavor development capabilities. Customers would still go through traditional sales channels but get samples more quickly, thereby increasing service quality. No customer would have direct access to the Spider technology. The proposal was a good fit with BBA's "Gaps in Maps" strategy and would significantly boost the efficiency of an organization marked by two decades of decentralization.

The second strategic proposal involved physically placing the flavor prototyping machine with some large customers and allowing them to design their own flavors via Spider technology. These customers would have full control over their flavor development process and BBA would only support them on a per-need basis. Because customers would have to go through BBA's Web site to access the Spider flavor design tools, the company could closely monitor outside development activities. Moreover, only BBA's R&D would know how to translate design parameters (such as "fruity," "cheesy," and "creamy") into chemical formulations that would be needed to make prototype samples—know-how that was difficult for competitors to imitate. It was still unclear, however, which customers should be signed up and how the cost and maintenance of the prototyping machine would be divided between BBA and those customers. This proposal implied that sales and R&D increasingly would focus on smaller and less profitable customers, who would not have access to the Spider technology.

The third, and most radical proposal would abandon the current business model altogether. The Spider technology would be available to anyone, anywhere, who needed flavors, and BBA would yield 100 percent control to customers. The company could establish sample prototyping centers around the world using the $500,000 machine, putting flavor samples within a 24-hour shipping distance to any customer. New customers would be able to design flavors using the Spider flavor design tools through BBA's Web site and automatically receive sample shipments from the nearest prototyping center. Marketing's role in this proposal was still unclear and there were numerous unresolved issues around how it would affect BBA's current business model.

"Over the last six years, the combined market valuation of BBA and IFF has substantially declined," Boyden concluded as he leafed through the assortment of teas. "If you compare this change to the general rise in the stock market, our industry has been very successful at destroying shareholder value but not at creating sufficient new opportunities for growth and profitability."

EXHIBIT 1
Selected BBA
Financial Data
(dollars in
millions, except
per share data)

Source: Bush Boake
Allen Financial
Reports.

	1999	1998	1997
Sales	**499.0**	**485.4**	**490.6**
Cost of goods sold	330.0	311.0	316.1
Selling and administrative expenses	98.0	92.2	98.1
Research and development expenses	25.4	25.2	23.6
Income from operations	**45.6**	**56.8**	**52.7**
Interest expenses	2.3	3.3	3.1
Other (income) expense, net	4.3	2.8	3.4
Income before income taxes	**39.0**	**50.7**	**46.3**
Income taxes	15.0	17.0	15.3
Net income	**24.0**	**33.7**	**31.0**
Other Data:			
EPS (primary)—excluding extra items and discontinued operations	1.24	1.75	1.61
Cash Dividends Per Share	0	0	0
ROA (%)	5%	7%	7%
ROE (%)	7%	11%	11%
Market Value	474	680	504

EXHIBIT 2
BBA's International Centers as a result of the "Gaps in the Map" Strategy

Source: Bush Boake Allen.

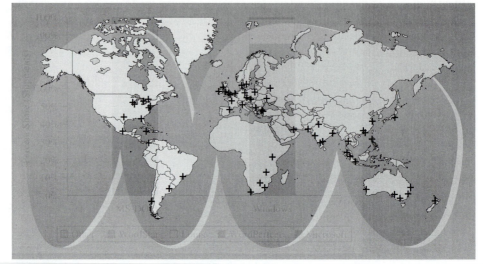

Major Sites
• Montvale
• Dallas
• London
• Chennai
• Singapore

Minor Sites
• Mexico
• Chile
• Argentina
• Germany
• Holland
• Sweden
• Turkey
• Dubai
• Philippines
• Japan
• China
• Australia
• New Zealand

EXHIBIT 3
BBA Sales in 1999 by Region

Source: Dun & Bradstreet, USA Data Market Research.

	$ Million	% of Total
US	192.5	35
Europe	185.1	33
Asia/Pacific	88.4	16
Other regions	88.7	16
Adjustments	(55.7)	—
Total	**$499**	**100**

EXHIBIT 4   Organization of Bush Boake Allen Inc.

J. W. Boyden*
Chairman,
President & CEO

P. C. Mathew*
VP Aroma &
Terpene Chemicals
- P. A. Thorburn*
  VP Global Sales/
  Marketing
- T. Fore
  Director
  Operations A&T
- D. Flowers
  Division
  Controller
- M Britten-Kelly
  Technical
  Director

J. H. Dunsdon*
Exec. VP
Flavors & Fragrances
- R. B. Cavalli
  VP Flavors
  Americas
- J. Thompson
  VP Fragrances
  Americas
- K. Gibson
  VP/GM Seasonings
  Americas
- A. Muller
  VP Latin America/
  Caribbean
- S. Goldberg
  Human
  Resources
  Manager
- R. Holewinski
  Controller
  Americas
- T. J. Dunlea
  VP Materials
  Management

J. R. Wright*
VP Commercial
& Technical
- J. Kirven
  VP
  Information
  Resources
- I. Goddard
  Director
  Corporate
  Engineering
- D. Carroll
  Director
  QA Regulatory
  Affairs
- F. Stults
  VP R&D
  Flavors &
  Fragrances

R. Landis*
VP Human Resources
& Safety
- J. Hollyhead
  Corporate
  Safety & Health
  Director
- D. J. Owen
  Global HR &
  Safety
  Manager

F. W. Brown*
VP Finance
- C. Weller
  VP Corporate
  Treasurer
- K. McHugh
  VP Corporate
  Controller
- A. Kelsey
  Director, Tax &
  Asst. Secretary

D. M. Meany*
VP General Counsel
& Secretary
- B. Batten
  Paralegal

Chia Siang Ee*
VP Asia
Pacific
- G. Cadwallader
  Reg GM
  Flavors
  Asia Pacific
- D. Chan
  Reg GM Frag
  Asia Pacific
  MD Greater China
- C. R. Pickford
  MD Australia
  Reg GM NPD
- T. Saito
  Managing Director
  Japan
- F. Ancheta
  Managing Director
  Phillipines
- A. Koh
  GM Finance
  Asia Pacific
- Wan Fook Keong
  GM
  Human Resources
  Asia Pacific
- W. Lee
  Managing Director
  Malaysia
- C. Lim
  GM
  Purchasing
  Asia Pacific

B. J. Edwards*
VP International
- O. Ryder
  Managing Director
  South Africa
- A. Bewoor
  Managing Director
  India
- G. Pietzsch
  VP Eastern
  Europe
- M. Potterton
  GM Turkey
- P. Gould
  GM Dubai
- Z. Gleisner
  Finance &
  Administration
  Manager
- T. Gordon-Wright
  Regional
  Marketing
  Manager

C. W. Colesanti*
VP Western
Europe
- N. Sheehan
  European Director
  Sweet
- J. Kowalewski
  European Director
  Fragrances
- R. Kristensson
  European Director
  Savoury
  MD-Sweden
- A. McFarlane
  European
  Marketing
  Manager
- R. Wood
  European
  Human Resources
  Manager
- Vacant
  Regional
  Controller

EXHIBIT 5
Top Nine Firms in the Flavor Business (by annual sales)

Source: OneSource Global Business.

	Sales 1999 (US$ Million)	Employees	Ownership
International Flavors & Fragrances, Inc.	1,439	4,680	Public/US
Givaudan Roure Corp.	1,300	5,000	Public/Swiss
Quest International Fragrances Co.	820	3,000	Public/UK
Firmenich SA	794	3,300	Private/Swiss
Haarman & Reimer GmbH	701	3,800	Public/German
Takasago International Corp.	784	987	Public/Japan
Bush Boake Allen, Inc.	499	1,978	Public/US
Universal Flavor Corp.	360	1,325	Public/US
Dragoco Gerberding & Co AG	286	1,848	Public/German

EXHIBIT 6
Description
of Flavor
Development

Creating a flavor at the turn of the millennium involved three major steps. The first step, "Extraction," involved grinding up the source material with the goal of extracting fluids for chemical analysis. This step might need to be repeated as many as ten times under different conditions. For example, to create a strawberry flavor, the lab might puree a strawberry and use the extracted juices for analysis. Strawberries from different stages of freshness might be analyzed separately.

In the second step, food chemists would actually analyze subtler components of the source material. For instance, they would sample the air around a strawberry for presence of trace compounds that also enhanced the flavor. This step also required repetition under different conditions—for instance, under different stages of ripeness. Ultimately, some 200 to 500 chemical ingredients might be discovered in a strawberry.

In the third step, the flavorists would select the most important components to create a manageable palette of 10 to 15 ingredients to recreate the primary flavor characteristics. But even just 15 components to play with posed a large challenge. If each of these 15 components had, for example, only four levels of concentration, the flavorists would have 415 or over one billion potential flavors to choose from! Flavorists therefore relied on pattern recognition as well as imagination. In producing a flavor, they often reached back into their childhood memories (recall that the sense of smell ties into the limbic system of the brain, one of the most primitive parts of the brain, which happened to be involved with memory). Experienced flavorists would worry if, after the first few trials, they were not in the ballpark.

Because the above steps used essentially destructive technologies, flavorists had to use technology again later to help maintain product freshness. It would really take a lifetime to get the flavor right, and even then, different flavorists would come up with different approaches, although their primary ingredients would most likely overlap substantially. If customers were not in a great hurry (e.g. pharmaceutical firms with product cycles stretching out into several years), then flavorists could experiment with up to 40 real trials. These trials could occur as quickly as 5 to 6 per a day or as slowly as one trial a day.

After the basic flavor had been concocted, flavorists work on the fourth step of secondary characteristics that added extra character. These might be likened to the staged process of making tea. First one pours the tea; then to make the drink recognizable to anyone in the British Commonwealth one adds the secondary flavors of milk and then sugar. In the strawberry example, did the client want the strawberry flavor to be "green," "leafy," "stewed," "jammy," or "woody"? The flavorist had to reduce these terms to more definable flavor characteristics.

The fifth step and final step tested the flavor through the "applications trial," i.e., in the customer's end product. For example, the strawberry flavor concocted through the above steps might now be baked in a pilot kitchen by the client's "applicationists" into a strawberry shortcake. Flavorists remained all too aware about the need to work side by side with the client's applicationists. For instance, a client's applicationist might understandably undercook the strawberry shortcake on a late Friday afternoon, torpedoing all chances of the flavor being accepted. Working side by side also decreased communication glitches. To test the application, it might take just half an hour to test a beverage, but up to a day for a baked product. After the applications team tested out an application, sometimes on fortunate staff members in the vicinity, the final product would be tested on the client's end consumer.

EXHIBIT 7
The "Flavor Prototyping" machine in Rotterdam, the Netherlands

Source: Bush Boake Allen.

Objective: A machine which can be installed in a remote facility, capable of producing a variety of liquid "prototype" samples very simply with minimum technical support.

Selected Machine Specifications:
- Manufacturer: Fricke Abfülltechnik GmbH (Germany)
- 500 ingredients possible
- Minimum pour 20 to 80 milligrams
- Average number of ingredients per sample: 20
- Current sample size: 200 grams
- Accuracy 5 milligrams (1/5 of a drop)
- Speed: 3 samples per hour
- Can run unattended (up to 38 samples)
- Can be operated by remote control

Uses proprietary software to control formulations

EXHIBIT 8A
The "Spider"
in Action:
Step [1]

Source: Bush Boake
Allen.

- Example: User designs strawberry flavor for dairy product using the Internet-based Spider toolkit.
- Customer begins by selecting end product in which flavor will be used.

**EXHIBIT 8B
The "Spider"
in Action:
Step [2]**

Source: Bush Boake
Allen.

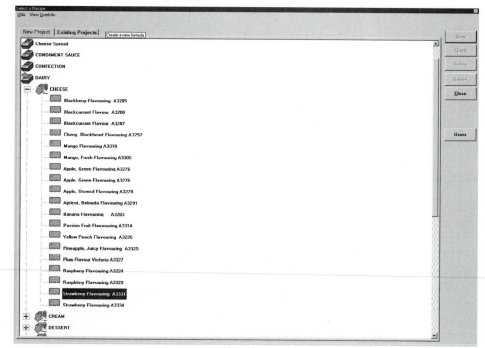

- User selects cheese as end product.
- Spider toolkit offers portfolio of base flavors (blackberry, cherry, mango, etc.) on which new flavor will be built.
- User selects strawberry flavoring A3331 as desired base flavor.

EXHIBIT 8C
The "Spider"
in Action:
Step [3]

Source: Bush Boake
Allen.

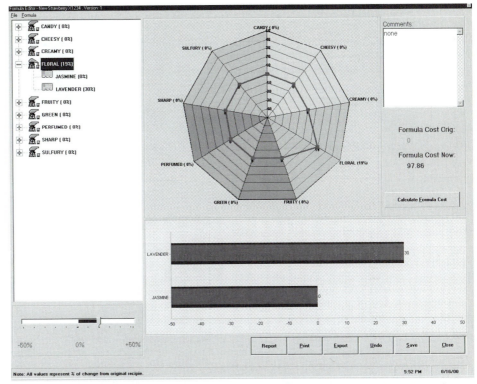

- User utilizes Spider toolkit to redesign base flavor by making adjustments to flavor dimensions.
- To increase the "floral" dimension of strawberry, the customer increases lavender — one of the two floral subdimensions — to 30%.
- The cost of the new flavor formula is adjusted accordingly.

EXHIBIT 8D
The "Spider"
in Action:
Step [4]

Source: Bush Boake
Allen.

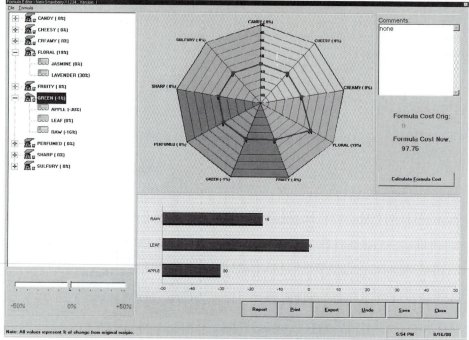

- User lowers the "green" dimension of strawberry by decreasing apple and raw (two subdimensions of green).
- Steps [3] and [4] are repeated with other dimensions on the Spider toolkit until user is ready for testing prototype samples.

EXHIBIT 8E
The "Spider"
in Action:
Step [5]

Source: Bush Boake
Allen.

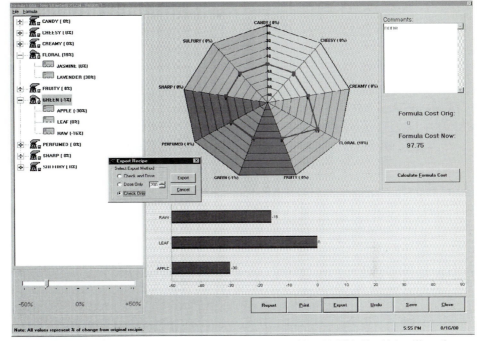

- User is finished and sends flavor design to prototyping machine (Exhibit 7) which will produce a flavor sample.
- Spider toolkit checks feasibility of new flavor and translates it into chemical formulation.
- After evaluating flavor sample, the user will revisit file and iterate through steps [3] and [4] until satisfied with the final design.

Article

Customers as Innovators: A New Way to Create Value

"Listen carefully to what your customers want and then respond with new products that meet or exceed their needs." That mantra has dominated many a business, and it has undoubtedly led to great products and has even shaped entire industries. But slavishly obeying that conventional wisdom can also threaten a company's ability to compete.

The difficulty is that fully understanding customers' needs is often a costly and inexact process. Even when customers know precisely what they want, they often cannot transfer that information to manufacturers clearly or completely. Today, as the pace of change in many markets accelerates and as some industries move toward serving "markets of one," the cost of understanding and responding to customers' needs can easily spiral out of control.

In the course of studying product innovation across many industries, we have discovered that a number of companies have adopted an intriguing approach, which at first seems counterintuitive. Essentially, these companies have abandoned their efforts to understand exactly what products their customers want and have instead equipped them with tools to design and develop their own products, ranging from minor modifications to major new innovations. The user-friendly tools, often integrated into a package we call a "toolkit for customer innovation," deploy new technologies like computer simulation and rapid prototyping to make product development faster and less expensive.[1]

A variety of industries use this approach. Bush Boake Allen (BBA), a global supplier of specialty flavors to companies like Nestlé, has built a toolkit that enables its customers to develop their own flavors, which BBA then manufactures. In the materials field, GE provides customers with Web-based tools for designing better plastic products. In software, a number of companies let people add custom-designed modules to their standard products and then commercialize the best of those components. Open-source software allows users to design, build, distribute, and support their own programs—no manufacturer required. Indeed, the trend toward customers as innovators has the power to completely transform industries. In the semiconductor business, it has led to a custom-chip market that has grown to more than $15 billion.

[1] Stefan Thomke, "Enlightened Experimentation: The New Imperative for Innovation," *HBR*, February 2001.

Tapping into customer innovation can certainly generate tremendous value, but capturing that value is hardly a simple or straightforward process. Not only must companies develop the right toolkit, they must also revamp their business models as well as their management mindsets. When companies relinquish a fundamental task—such as designing a new product—to customers, the two parties must redefine their relationship, and this change can be risky. With custom computer chips, for instance, companies traditionally captured value by both designing and manufacturing innovative products. Now, with customers taking over more of the design task, companies must focus more intently on providing the best custom manufacturing. In other words, the location where value is both created and captured changes, and companies must reconfigure their business models accordingly. In this article, we offer some basic principles and lessons for industries undergoing such a transformation.

A COSTLY PROBLEM—AND A RADICAL SOLUTION

In a nutshell, product development is often difficult because the "need" information (what the customer wants) resides with the customer, and the "solution" information (how to satisfy those needs) lies with the manufacturer. Traditionally, the onus has been on manufacturers to collect the need information through various means, including market research and information gathered from the field. The process can be costly and time-consuming because customer needs are often complex, subtle, and fast changing. Frequently, customers don't fully understand their needs until they try out prototypes to explore exactly what does, and doesn't, work (referred to as "learning by doing").

Not surprisingly, traditional product development is a drawn-out process of trial and error, often ping-ponging between manufacturer and customer. First, the manufacturer develops a prototype based on information from customers that is incomplete and only partially correct. The customer then tries out the product, finds flaws, and requests corrections. The cycle repeats until a satisfactory solution is reached, often requiring many costly and time-consuming iterations.

To appreciate the extent of the difficulty, consider product development at BBA (now International Flavors and Fragrances). In this industry, specialty flavors are created to bolster and enhance the taste of nearly all processed foods because manufacturing techniques weaken the real flavors. The development of those added flavors requires a high degree of customization and expertise, and the practice remains more an art than a science.

A traditional product development project at BBA might progress in the following way: A customer requests a meaty flavor for a soy product, and the sample must be delivered within a week. BBA marketing professionals and flavorists jump into action, and the sample is shipped in six days. A frustrating three weeks ensue until the client responds with, "It's good, but we need it less smoky and more gutsy." The client knows precisely what that means, but BBA flavorists find the request difficult to interpret. The result is more frenzied activity as BBA struggles to adjust the flavor in a couple days. Depending on the product, BBA and the client could go back and forth for several more iterations. This represents a huge problem because clients often expect BBA to get the flavor right the first time, or within two or three iterations.

To make matters worse, BBA bears most of the development risk. The company collects revenue only after both the client and consumers are fully satisfied. R&D expenses could be just $1,000 for tweaking an existing flavor, but they could go as high as $300,000 for an entirely new family of flavors that require not only chemists and flavorists but also sales, marketing, regulatory, and quality control expertise. On average, the client eventually accepts only 15 percent of all new flavors for full market evaluation, and only 5 to 10 percent make their way to the marketplace. Meanwhile, margins in the flavor industry have been falling because of increased competition and cost pressures from customers.

In response, BBA's CEO Julian Boyden and vice president of technology John Wright investigated the option of shifting more innovation activities to customers. The company developed an Internet-based tool containing a large database of flavor profiles. A customer can select and manipulate that information on a computer screen and send his new design directly to an automated machine (perhaps located at the customer site) that will manufacture a sample within minutes. After tasting the sample, the customer can make any adjustments that are needed. If the flavor is too salty, for instance, he can easily tweak that parameter on the profile and have the machine immediately produce another sample.

It is important to note that outsourcing product development to customers does not eliminate learning by doing—nor should it. What it does is make traditional product development better and faster, for two reasons. First, a company can bypass the expensive and error-prone effort to understand customer needs in detail. Second, the trial-and-error cycles that inevitably occur during product development can progress much more quickly because the iterations will be performed solely by the customer. (For a basic illustration of the customers-as-innovators approach, see **Exhibit 1**, "A New Approach to Developing Custom Products.")

But developing the right toolkit for customers is hardly a simple matter.[2] Specifically, toolkits must provide four important capabilities. First and most important, they must enable people to complete a series of design cycles followed by learning by doing. Computer simulation, for example, allows customers to quickly try out ideas and design alternatives without having to manufacture the actual products. When the simulation technology lacks the desired accuracy, it can be supplemented with rapid prototyping methods. Second, toolkits must be user-friendly. They should not require customers to learn an entirely new design language. (Flavorists, for example, think in terms of formulations and chemical compounds, whereas customers think of tastes such as smoky, sweet, fresh, and so on.) Third, they must contain libraries of useful components and modules that have been pretested and debugged. These save customers from having to reinvent the wheel. Instead, people can focus their efforts on the truly novel elements of their design. Fourth, toolkits must contain information about the capabilities and limitations of the production process that will be used to manufacture the product. This will ensure that a customer's design will in fact be producible.

AN INDUSTRY TRANSFORMED

To understand the major impact that the customers-as-innovators approach can have, consider the history of the custom computer chip industry. The story holds several profound lessons about how the right toolkit can turn a market on its ear.

[2] Eric von Hippel, "Perspective: User Toolkits for Innovation," *Journal of Product Innovation Management*, July 2001.

When Customer Innovation Makes Sense

From our research, we have identified three major signs that your industry may soon migrate to a customers-as-innovators approach:

1. Your market segments are shrinking, and customers are increasingly asking for customized products. As you try to respond to those demands, your costs increase, and it is difficult to pass those costs on to customers.

2. You and your customers need many iterations before you find a solution. Some customers complain that you have gotten the product wrong or that you are responding too slowly. You are tempted to restrict the degree to which your products can be customized, and your smaller customers must make do with standard products or find a better solution elsewhere. As a result, customer loyalty starts to erode.

3. You or your competitors use high-quality computer-based simulation and rapid-prototyping tools internally to develop new products. You also have computer-adjustable production processes that can manufacture custom products. (These technologies could form the foundation of a toolkit that customers could use to develop their own designs.)

During the late 1970s, suppliers of custom chips experienced the same types of market dynamics that BBA has more recently encountered. (See the feature box "When Customer Innovation Makes Sense.") At the time, a typical user of custom semiconductors, such as a toy manufacturer that needed circuitry to operate its robotic dog, might have hired a chip company to develop a custom design. Because that process was complicated and costly, the chip company could afford to undertake projects only for high-volume customers.

Then a handful of start-ups turned everything upside down. Companies like LSI Logic Corporation and VLSI Technology provided both large and small customers with do-it-yourself tools that enabled them to design their own specialized chips. Customers could benefit by getting what they wanted through their own experimentation, and the fledgling chip companies could profit by manufacturing those customer designs. The win-win solution was right on the money. Between the 1980s and today, the market for such custom integrated circuits has soared from virtually nothing to more than $15 billion, with the number of customers growing from a handful of high-volume buyers to hundreds of thousands of companies with very diverse end-user applications.

A key to that $15 billion market is the toolkit technology. In principle, outsourcing custom design to customers can help slash development times and costs, but customers are not experts in a supplier's business. So how could customers be expected to create custom designs that can be produced on a manufacturer's sophisticated process equipment? The answer to that was found in a major shift that had been taking place in the semiconductor industry.

Traditionally, specialized information used by a manufacturer to design and build custom products has been locked in the minds of the company's development engineers. This knowledge accumulates over decades of experience. In recent years, companies have been able to incorporate a considerable amount of this human expertise into computer-based tools. These CAD/CAM programs have grown increasingly sophisticated, and many now contain libraries of tested and debugged modules that people can simply plug into a new design. The most effective tools also enable rapid testing through computer simulation and provide links to automated equipment that can build prototypes quickly. This leading-edge technology, which manufacturers had been using internally, has become the basic building block for customer toolkits.

When LSI was founded in 1981, R&D engineers at large semiconductor companies were already using many elements of the customer toolkit, but there was no integrated system that less-skilled customers would be comfortable with. So LSI bought some of the pieces, made them customer-friendly by adding graphical user interfaces, and integrated them. The result was a packaged toolkit that let customers design their own chips with little support from LSI.

The brilliant insight that made possible a toolkit for less-skilled customers was that the design of the chip's fundamental elements, such as its transistors, could be standardized and could incorporate the manufacturer's solution information of how semiconductors are fabricated. Then, all the information the customer needed about how the chip would function could be concentrated within the electrical wiring that connects those fundamental elements. In other words, this new type of chip, called a "gate array," had a novel architecture created specifically to separate the manufacturer's solution information from the customer's need information. As a result, all customers had to do was use a toolkit that could interconnect a gate array based on their specific needs. For its part, LSI had to rethink how to make its production processes more flexible so that it could manufacture the custom chips at low cost.

Customer toolkits based on gate-array technology offer the four major capabilities described earlier. They contain a range of tools, including those to test a design, that enable users to create their own prototypes through trial and error. They are customer-friendly in that they use Boolean algebra, which is the design language commonly taught to electrical engineers. They contain extensive libraries of pretested circuit modules. And they also contain information about production processes so that users can test their designs to ensure that they can be manufactured. Interestingly, more recent technology—chips called field programmable gate arrays (FPGAs)—enables the customer to become both the designer and the manufacturer. Essentially, FPGA toolkits contain design and simulation software and equipment that customers use to program chips for themselves.

THE BENEFITS AND CHALLENGES

Well-designed customer toolkits, such as those developed for the creation of custom semiconductor chips, offer several major advantages over traditional product development. First, they are significantly better at satisfying subtle aspects of customer need because customers know what they need better than manufacturers do. Second, designs will usually be completed much faster because customers can create them at their own site. Third, if customers follow the rules embedded in a toolkit (and if all the technological bugs have been worked out), their designs can be manufactured the first time around.

There are also ancillary benefits. Toolkits enable a company to do business with small customers that might have been prohibitively expensive to work with before, thus expanding the accessible market—and the number of product innovations. By serving these smaller clients, toolkits also reduce the pool of unserved, frustrated potential customers who might turn to competitors or to new entrants into the market. Furthermore, they allow companies to better serve their larger, preferred customers. That's a benefit most suppliers wouldn't expect, because they'd assume that their bigger customers would want the traditional hand-holding to which they're so accustomed. Experience shows, however, that such customers are often willing to use a toolkit, especially when fast product turnaround is crucial.

Of course, toolkits will not satisfy every type of customer. For one thing, they are generally not able to handle every kind of design. Also, they create products that are typically not as technically sophisticated as those developed by experienced engineers at a manufacturer using conventional methods. So manufacturers may continue to design certain products (those with difficult technical demands) while customers take over the design of others (those that require quick turnaround or a detailed and accurate understanding of the customer's need).

The business challenges of implementing a toolkit can be daunting. Turning customers into innovators requires no less than a radical change in management mind-set. Pioneers LSI Logic and VLSI Technology were successful because they abandoned a principle that had long dominated conventional management thinking at leading companies like IBM, Intel, and Fujitsu. For many years, these companies had assumed that their interests would best be served by keeping design expertise, tools, and technologies away from customers. In contrast, LSI, VLSI, and the other industry upstarts understood that they needed to do just the opposite by putting robust, user-friendly toolkits into customers' hands.

Such a dramatic shift in mind-set required a thorough rethinking of well-entrenched business practices. In essence, a company that turns its customers into innovators is out-sourcing a valuable service that was once proprietary, and the change can be traumatic if that capability has long been a major source of competitive advantage. For example, a common problem is resistance from sales and marketing departments, which have traditionally been responsible for managing relationships with customers and providing first-class service to them. With toolkits, computer-to-computer interactions replace intense person-to-person contact during product development. In other words, customers who design products themselves have little need for a manufacturer's sales or marketing department to determine what they need. If this change affects the compensation of sales representatives in the field, it could easily derail any efforts to alter the company's business model. As a result, senior management needs to face these issues head-on—for example, by determining how the sales and marketing functions should evolve and by using specific incentives to induce employees to support the transformation. (For more on how to adapt your business practices, see the feature box "Five Steps for Turning Customers into Innovators.")

To better understand these issues, consider GE Plastics, which recently made the bold move of introducing some elements of a Web-based customer toolkit. Doing so required GE Plastics to rethink its sources of competitive advantage and to develop new business models that forced major changes, including the ways in which its sales and marketing staff acquired new customers. The company's story holds several valuable lessons.

GE Plastics does not design or manufacture plastic products but sells resins to those that do, and the properties of those resins must precisely match that of both the end product (a cell phone, for instance) as well as the process used to manufacture that product. With the formation of the Polymerland division in 1998, GE Plastics allowed customers to order plastics online and later took the step of making 30 years of its in-house knowledge

Five Steps for Turning Customers into Innovators

1. Develop a user-friendly toolkit for customers.
   - The toolkit must enable customers to run repeated trial-and-error experiments and tests rapidly and efficiently.
   - The technology should let customers work in a familiar design language, making it cheaper for customers to adopt your toolkit.
   - The toolkit should include a library of standard design modules so customers can create complex custom designs rapidly.
   - The technology should be adapted to your production processes so that customer designs can be sent directly to your manufacturing operations without extensive tailoring.

2. Increase the flexibility of your production processes.
   Your manufacturing operations should be retooled for fast, low-cost production of specialized designs developed by customers.

3. Carefully select the first customers to use the toolkit.
   The best prospects are customers that have a strong need for developing custom products quickly and frequently, have skilled engineers on staff, and have little experience with traditional customization services. These customers will likely stick with you when you are working out the system's bugs.

4. Evolve your toolkit continually and rapidly to satisfy your leading-edge customers.
   Customers at the forefront of technology will always push for improvements in your toolkit. Investments in such advancements will likely pay off, because many of your customers will need tomorrow what leading-edge customers desire today.

5. Adapt your business practices accordingly.
   - Outsourcing product development to customers will require you to revamp your business models to profit from the shift. The change might, for instance, make it economically feasible for you to work with smaller, low-volume customers.
   - Toolkits will fundamentally change your relationship with customers. Intense person-to-person contact during product development will, for example, be replaced by computer-to-computer interactions. Prepare for these changes by implementing incentives to reduce resistance from your employees.

available on a Web site. Registered users were given access to company data sheets, engineering expertise, and simulation software. Customers could use that knowledge and technology to conduct their own trial-and-error experiments to investigate, for example, how a certain grade of plastic with a specific amount of a particular type of reinforcement would flow into and fill a mold. The approximate cost of bringing such sophisticated tools online: $5 million.

GE Plastics, of course, did not make the investment simply to be magnanimous. Through the Web site, the company identifies and tracks people likely to become customers. That information is then relayed to an e-marketing staff. Today, the Web site attracts about a million visitors per year who are automatically screened for potential sales; that information accounts for nearly one-third of all new customer leads, thus fueling much of GE Plastic's growth. And because the cost of acquiring new business has decreased, GE Plastics can now go after smaller customers it might have ignored in the past. Specifically, the sales threshold at which a potential customer becomes attractive to GE's field marketing has dropped by more than 60 percent.

The online tools have also enabled GE Plastics to improve customer satisfaction at a lower cost. Before the Web site, GE Plastics received about 500,000 customer calls every year. Today, the availability of online tools has slashed that number in half. In fact, customers use the tools more than 2,000 times a week. To encourage the rapid adoption of its toolkit, GE Plastics runs about 400 e-seminars a year that reach roughly 8,000 customers. The company hopes that this effort will help encourage product engineers to design parts made of plastic (and GE resins) when they might otherwise have opted for metal or other materials.

A PATTERN OF MIGRATION

Perhaps the most important lesson to be learned from GE Plastics is that a company that adopts the customers-as-innovators approach must adapt its business accordingly. Furthermore, we've found that because the value that toolkits generate tends to migrate, a company must continually reposition itself to capture that value.

When a supplier introduces a toolkit, the technology first tends to be company-specific: The designs can only be produced in the factory of the company that developed the toolkit. This creates a huge short-term advantage for the pioneering supplier, which can reduce its custom design costs because they are partially outsourced to customers. That, in turn, enables the supplier to serve more customers. And because the customer's designs must be produced on the supplier's system, the supplier doesn't risk losing any business.

But the loss of leverage by customers represents a fundamental shift. Traditionally, in the field of specialized industrial products, companies interested in a customer's business develop a custom design and submit it for evaluation. The customer picks the proposal from one supplier, and the others are saddled with a loss for their time and investment. A toolkit tied to a single supplier changes that dynamic: A customer that develops a design using the toolkit cannot ask for competing quotes because only one company can manufacture it.

Of course, customers would prefer the advantages of a toolkit without the associated loss of leverage. In the long run, this type of solution tends to emerge: Customer pressure induces third parties to introduce toolkits that can create designs to fit any supplier's manufacturing process. Or, in a slight variation, customers complain until a company that owns a dominant toolkit is forced to allow a spin-off to evolve the technology into a supplier-neutral form. Then, customers are free to shop their designs around to competing manufacturers.

In other words, one long-term result of customer toolkits is that manufacturers lose a portion of the value they have traditionally delivered. But if the conditions are ripe for the technology to emerge in a given industry and if customers will benefit from it—and our research shows that they will—then suppliers really don't have a choice. Some company will eventually introduce a toolkit and reap the short-term advantages. Then, others must follow. In the case of custom chips, Fujitsu initially resisted making its in-house design technology available to customers, thinking the move was too risky. (See **Exhibit 2,** "Creating Value with Customers as Innovators.") But after LSI introduced a toolkit and began to establish itself in the market, Fujitsu and others were forced to play catch-up.

What Mass Customization Is—and Isn't

Imagine a mass manufacturer that could customize products for each of its customers. Economically, that would require two things: first, learning how to design specialized products efficiently (the R&D problem), and, second, learning how to manufacture those goods cheaply and quickly (the production problem).

The second problem has been addressed by the popular concept of mass-customized production. In that approach, computerized process equipment or flexible assembly procedures can be adjusted quickly and inexpensively so companies can make single-unit quantities of one-of-a-kind products at a cost that is reasonably competitive with the manufacture of similar, mass-produced items. The classic example is Dell Computer: Consumers can buy a Dell computer by picking the major components they want (the size of the hard drive, the kind of monitor, the number and types of memory modules, and so on) from a menu on a Dell Web site. The company assembles and delivers the custom products in days.

But Dell's mass-customization approach does not address the first problem: learning how to design novel custom goods efficiently. The company's customers have only a limited number of standard components and combinations to choose from, leaving them little room for creativity or real innovation. What if someone wants a computer that cannot be assembled from those standard components, or what if that person is uncertain that a particular product will actually fulfill her needs? For instance, will the computer she's assembled be able to run the latest game software without crashing? Unless customers can test a computer design that they've assembled before placing the order, they can't perform the trial-and-error experiments needed to develop the product best suited to their needs. In other words, with mass customization, the cost of manufacturing unique products has dropped, but the cost of designing such items has not.

The approach presented in this article—using toolkits that enable customers to become innovators—targets the first problem; its goal is to provide customers with enough creative freedom to design innovative custom products that will truly satisfy their needs.

QUESTIONS OF VALUE

Predicting where value will migrate—and knowing how to capture it—will be crucial as customer toolkits become more widespread. So far, the customers-as-innovators approach has mainly emerged in the B2B field, but numerous signs indicate that it is also spreading to the B2C arena. Many companies already offer so-called "product configurators" that enable consumers to obtain a mass-customized version of a standard product. Dell customers, for example, can select various components (a disk drive, monitor, memory modules, and so on) from a menu to assemble the computer best suited to their needs. Eyeglass frames, automobiles, and even Barbie dolls can be similarly configured. In fact, no application seems too trivial. General Mills is planning to introduce a Web site that will allow consumers to mix and match more than 100 ingredients to create their own breakfast cereal. Although such product configurators are currently limited in what they can do (for one thing, they don't allow a user to try out a design, either through a prototype or a computer simulation), future versions could approach the functionality of true customer toolkits and allow for radically new innovations. (See the feature box "What Mass Customization Is—and Isn't.")

Producers of information products, especially software, will perhaps feel the biggest impact. Companies like Microsoft have long relied on customers to beta-test new products.

Now other companies have taken that concept to the next level. Stata, which sells a software package for performing complex statistical analyses, encourages its customers to write software add-on modules for performing the latest statistical techniques; the company then adapts and incorporates the best of those into its next release.

The danger to software companies is that production is essentially free, so the customer might one day mass-distribute copies of a custom program with the simple press of a button. If that practice becomes widespread, a truly effective toolkit might itself become the product, forcing companies to adapt quickly to the dramatic change. Or users might abandon their status as customers altogether, collaborating to design and build their own toolkits as well as their own specialized programs.

The growing popularity of open-source software could touch off such a revolution. Consider what has happened to companies that sell software for Linux, an operating system that is virtually free. Recently, IBM took the bold step of placing $40 million of in-house tools for developing software into the public domain to encourage people to write programs that run on Linux. IBM is hoping that the move will help make Linux a widespread standard and that the company will make money by selling specialized Linux software applications, the hardware to run them, and consulting services. Other Linux companies like Red Hat are focusing on packaging, distribution, and support.

Outsourcing a portion of the innovation task to customers can be an effective approach for speeding up the development of products better suited to customer needs. The approach also holds the power to turn markets topsy-turvy, creating and shifting value at three separate levels: the industry as a whole, companies that implement the technology, and customers that take advantage of it. Exactly where that value will be generated and how it might best be captured are the multimillion dollar questions facing companies competing in industries that are being transformed by customers as innovators.

EXHIBIT 1
A New Approach to Developing Custom Products

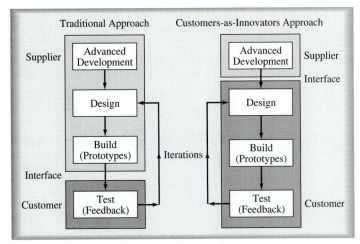

Traditionally, suppliers have taken on most of the work—and responsibility—of product development. The result has been costly and time-consuming iterations between supplier and customer to reach a satisfactory solution. With the customers-as-innovators approach, a supplier provides customers with tools so that they can design and develop the application-specific part of a product on their own. This shifts the location of the supplier-customer interface, and the trial-and-error iterations necessary for product development are now carried out by the customer only. The result is greatly increased speed and effectiveness.

EXHIBIT 2
Creating Value
with
Customers as
Innovators

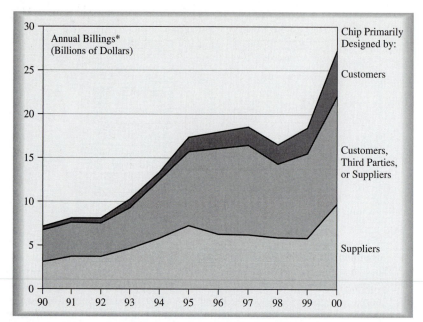

In the elctronics market, suppliers have traditionally been the designers of full-custom and application-specific integrated circuits (light gray, with a combined annual growth rate of about 12%). During the 1990s, toolkits based on gate-array and standard-cell technologies (medium gray, with a CAGR of about 13%) enabled customers and third parties to also become product innovators. With field programmable technology (dark gray, with a CAGR of about 29%), customers take on primary responsibility for custom circuit design, creating great value in the industry.

* Figures are from World Semiconductor Trade Statistics for custom metal-oxide semiconductor (MOS) logic, a dominant technology for digital circuits.

Managing Development Networks

Product (and service) development has increasingly become *distributed*. Research and development organizations can rarely access in-house all the knowledge, skills, personnel, and other resources that both spur and contribute to innovation. Even within very large firms (like Microsoft, which you meet in this module), R&D activities are at a minimum scattered among development groups separately located. Indeed, whether R&D activities are outsourced (i.e., to another firm) or divvied up among geographically dispersed organizations within the corporate fold, development teams almost never work in isolation.

An obvious contributing factor to this increasing distribution of R&D work is cost, particularly labor cost. Just as manufacturing activities began to be distributed several decades ago in order to lower costs, so R&D has followed the pattern. Searching for lower costs, of course, is not simply a relentless quest to exploit "cheap" labor; manufacturers were driven, as well, to move production "closer to the customer," and R&D makes similar claims. But labor-cost differentials (in both situations) are compelling, and the trend toward seeking these out will not end soon.

Another motivation toward distributed work is based on the desire to find "the best" source(s) of components or other inputs possible. These sources are dedicated, it is assumed, to perfecting their particular "product," and to doing the innovation needed to maintain a state-of-the-art status. Finding these sources has become literally a matter of mouse-clicking; the ability to learn about and connect with such potential suppliers, large and small, known and unknown, is fast and (by and large) transparent. In fact, the very ease with which it is possible to "link up" can create its own problems. The apparent simplicity of communication can mask highly complicated issues of coordinating actual activities, schedules, deliveries, etc., when projects are in full swing (the Sega case illustrates this). Suppliers are themselves invariably "dispersed"—*their* R&D and manufacturing activities are scattered among *other* suppliers and sources, making *their* coordination efforts complicated. If we imagine that many of these sub-suppliers may also have distributed activities, we reach a point of towering (even paralyzing) complexity very quickly.

The upshot is a tremendous premium placed on the ability to design and manage development networks—whether these are within a single firm or span multiple boundaries. Note, however, this is itself a tremendous topic, and in this module you are receiving only a "30,000-foot" look at the challenges involved, and only a few critically important solutions are possible.

A principal challenge of "dispersed development" is inherent in development itself: the fact that almost every firm (beyond the one that incorporated yesterday) has *multiple* projects going on. Some of these are highly preliminary—perhaps just a range of experiments being performed; some projects have gotten approval but are still being tweaked in fundamental ways; some may be reaching the point when components or inputs from "other" sources now must be integrated. In a perfect world, each of these projects is flawlessly adhering to a rigorous *predicted* schedule, where each effort within that schedule is totally monitored and easily determined. Managers can tell you about every project, its status, and when it will be completed. Well, it's not a perfect world. It is a rare project that is on schedule (or stays that way); and some organizations do not know either how many projects they have, much less each one's progress. One method for keeping track of projects—their number and status—is the Aggregate Project Plan or APP (which is discussed as part of Module Theme 1). What the APP enables—getting a handle on what is happening—is critical when the complexities of distributed work are contemplated.

Imagine, for instance, that your organization has 50 projects in various states; each of these involves an array of activities (which includes the people doing the work, the organizations responsible for the people, the work itself, the resources supporting all this, etc.), all over the planet. These activities must be coordinated with the state of the project, yet be flexible when there are changes—intended or unintended. To the degree that each project is unique, the coordination task swiftly becomes a nightmare. Thus a solution for many organizations has been *platforms* (discussed in Module Theme 1, which also addresses the APP). Parts (or other elements) are shared or relatively common across "families" of projects, and how these efforts are constituted and managed varies according to the novelty of the project goal. In other words, a carefully thought-through, well-designed platform can accommodate "extensions" and "breakthroughs," but the projects to develop them are differently constructed.

Surely all this must be a lot simpler if the bulk of project activities, and the people doing them, originate in-house. The more that is dispersed across firm boundaries (to organizations that themselves may be involved in crossing firm boundaries)—as is the case for outsourced work—the greater the coordination difficulties. But projects primarily staffed by company employees should be a lot easier to coordinate and manage; a development network, even if it consists of geographically separated teams, should be easier to maintain. As you will see, the Siemens case reveals how even within a single firm, one with a "dominant culture," unexpected challenges appear when it comes to the distribution of work, particularly geographically. (See Module Theme 2.)

People who study distributed work recognize the many assumptions that exist about what can be distributed. One is that work is easily divisible—that "activities" (like software development) can be easily, painlessly, and cost-effectively transferred from one location, organization, and/or geographical setting to another. The result of this assumption is that the work will proceed as if this transfer had not happened, and in most cases, the costs involved will be dramatically lower. Another related assumption is that people themselves are interchangeable. One software coder is equivalent to another elsewhere. A third assumption is that someone doing one task can easily take on another one, because the work of each is considered both divisible and bounded. You saw this in the Bank of America case. The people doing the "experiments" in the branches were to undertake this (discrete) activity, as if it were a separate task. Those folks, however, quickly realized that the work of the experiments impinged on the work that they were being paid for—and given bonuses for—and in no way, when push came to shove, were these separable activities.

A key challenge, then, in designing and managing networks of development is understanding whether activities that must eventually be connected as a project evolves can in fact be connected easily, i.e., that they have "interfaces" in common; or whether these activities are interdependent in ways that mean considerable time and effort (and money) must be devoted to their ongoing coordination. As Module Theme 3 suggests, thinking of each project in terms of platforms, and thinking of all the projects in terms of a portfolio, helps to sharpen the issues of what is interdependent and what can be truly considered separable. But this is no easy feat—even with such thinking. Even with "separable" activities (that is, ones that have interfaces in common), the vagaries of project development-in-action make coordination difficult. That is the challenge you are to wrestle with, the cutting-edge of product and service development.

The "take-aways" from this module include the following:

- Few organizations have only one project under development; most have any number of projects in various stages of progress. Moreover, each project is a maze of activities performed by various teams, within the organization and beyond it, in pieces, and at various stages of progress themselves. Coordination becomes pivotal as a managerial skill.

- Designing a network of development, however, can help alleviate some of this coordination problem, particularly if doing so incorporates notions of platform and portfolio. Platforms help in determining mechanisms that create "interfaces" among an array of project activities; portfolios help rationalize coordination among all projects. A network of development attempts to encompass both—what can be relatively easy to link, and what takes more "management" to coordinate.

- Product (service) development can be *complex!* But a lot of complexity—not all, by any means—can be anticipated. In Module One, we began by digging deeply into the dynamics of experimentation, learning how, when well designed and managed itself, a process of experimentation—and one moreover that leverages the *power* of new technologies—contributes to the innovation possibilities projects can embody. A critical aspect of experimentation is to help anticipate complexities. We then looked at approaches to development, adding the "complexity" of customers, those pesky people who have to buy what we develop. How do we bring those folks in—early—to ensure that they do buy it? And we've ended this module with the realization that it isn't only the customer who must be brought in early. Those whom we share development with are equal network partners, and they add another layer of complexity to the mix.

- As much as a process in product or service development must be attuned to "disciplined flexibility" (as you saw in Module Two), so must a network of development. Networks are not stage-gate structures, rigidly transferring one set of activities to another "place." Networks are dynamic, and must be designed to allow for changes en route, but not being destroyed in consequence.

MODULE STRUCTURE

Five cases and five supplemental articles comprise this module, which like the previous two, explores issues common to product and service development. This material will take you from a complex project at Microsoft to how a biotech company, Millennium, grappled with the major problems that accompany *integration*. That is, as much as networks imply managing a range of skills, resources, people, etc., they also demand that these be somehow corralled to end up with a product (or service) that customers want and purchase, and purchase at a desired point in time! Between those two case situations, you'll meet up with Siemens, which attempts to deal with the distribution of its product development efforts across its own organizational and country locations, and Sega, which tries to integrate, and manage, a combination of in-house and beyond-the-firm participants in its all-important Dreamcast development effort. Once again, while the situations are very different in all these cases, there are common elements—and thus "Managing Development Networks" provides core learning for network design and management within the context of a portfolio-of-projects universe across multiple fronts. See the **Exhibit** on page 405 for a synopsis of the cases.

THEMES

Three themes about the growing importance of networks in the development of new products and services as part of "project portfolios" are interwoven in the situations you will be encountering in this module. The first two examine how to design, build, and manage development networks *within* firms. The third theme addresses the management of multi-firm development networks.

Theme 1: Managing Product Networks: Platform Strategies

Developing new products in isolation, i.e., without considering how other related products may be affected, is an invitation to competitive *dis*advantage. Imagine a company that tried to develop a new car without leveraging the engineering work it had done on other projects *and* without any thought about how new efforts could contribute to other vehicles. Doing so would not only be costly, it would be out of step with today's automotive industry.[1] Most companies, in most industries, would like to leverage development work across an array of products, for doing so allows them to cover multiple market segments with minimal R&D cost. In other words, new projects should not be planned and managed as "one-shot" development efforts; rather, senior management should consider how they contribute to an entire network (or family) of products, thereby leading to higher R&D productivity.

Central to achieving such leverage is creating a product platform. Typically, platforms establish the basic architecture for a set of follow-on derivative projects that are much

---

[1] For recent research on platform strategies within the automotive industry, see Michael Cusumano and Kentaro Nobeoka, *Thinking Beyond Lean: How Multi-Project Management Is Transforming Product Development at Toyota and Other Companies* (Free Press/Simon & Schuster, 1998). The topic has also been addressed by earlier research such as Kim Clark and Takahiro Fujimoto, *Product Development Performance* (Harvard Business School Press, 1991).

narrower in scope.[2] By spending substantial resources on platforms up front, derivative projects can be completed at much lower cost and in less time and aimed at very specific market segments. There are multiple benefits to this approach: (a) the platform development can be amortized over many derivatives (through design/manufacturing reuse and purchasing economies); (b) more derivatives can cover more profitable market niches that otherwise would be too costly to address; and (c) the platform/derivative planning process itself adds much needed strategic focus to organizations. For example, when the German carmaker BMW develops a new 3-Series car, it doesn't just plan to design a single model.[3] Instead, senior management plans a platform, followed by a stream of derivatives that are developed and launched according to a predetermined "train schedule." The first car, a four-door sedan, becomes the platform while other models (two-door, convertible, station wagon, etc.) are the derivatives that reuse much of what has already been engineered.[4]

Although the logic of creating platform projects that capture organizational and technical learning from previous projects and leverage it across future ones is compelling, like everything else you've encountered so far, it's easier said than done. Some of the most sophisticated companies in the world struggle with the problems that arise. Technical and organizational factors go hand-in-hand; alignment is critical. Most important, it is the *platform* (architecture) that drives the activities that make such alignment possible. As such, alignment implies more than having project work arrayed as a set of activities. Instead, just as a final product is to operate seamlessly, so must the development of the product. In other words, the platform has to be planned in a way that ensures integrated work over time.

But the complexity doesn't stop there, as difficult as it is to achieve such alignment and integration. To maximize leverage and productivity, a firm must equally aim to manage multiple projects—across platform types and/or at varying stages of development within them. How do we even think about doing this? What factors should be emphasized when characterizing projects—projects that attempt to be designed in terms of platforms and integrated accordingly? Are managers to monitor *everything, all the time?*

A powerful framework for managing the relationship among development projects is the Aggregate Project Planning approach. Introduced and applied in the Medtronics case, the Aggregate Project Plan (APP) not only characterizes projects along the degree of product and process change but also establishes a clear method for matching projects with a company's strategic needs and resources (see **Figure 3-1**).[5] A key element of the approach is the

---

[2] See Steven Wheelwright and Kim Clark, *Revolutionizing Product Development* (The Free Press, 1992), Chapter 2 and 4; and Marc Meyer and Alvin Lehnerd, *The Power of Product Platforms* (The Free Press, 1997), and Karl Ulrich and Steven Eppinger, *Product Design and Development* (McGraw-Hill, 1994), Chapter 9.

[3] For more details, see the case study "BMW AG: The Digital Car Project" in the second module of this book.

[4] In automotive research with my colleague Takahiro Fujimoto at the University of Tokyo, we have used 80 percent of parts value designed as a rough estimate of whether a project is a platform or derivative. More specifically, if the total percentage value of newly designed parts was greater than 80 percent, we considered such projects as platforms. Depending on the technology constraints and required market differentiation, the total percentage value could be somewhat lower but shouldn't be under roughly 70 percent.

[5] For details on the APP and how it is applied to product development, see Steven Wheelwright and Kim Clark, *Revolutionizing Product Development* (The Free Press, 1992), Chapter 4.

FIGURE 3-1
The Aggregate
Project Plan:
Managing
Product
Networks

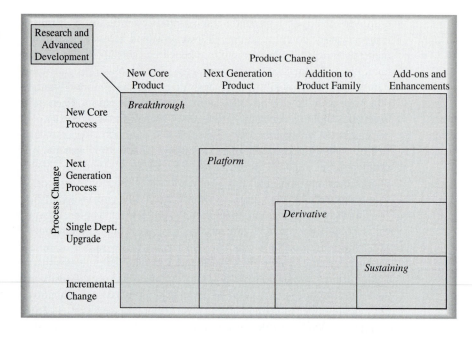

establishment of different team organizations (functional, lightweight, heavyweight, and autonomous) and their respective advantages and management challenges (see **Figure 3-2**).[6] That is, there is a conceptual link between project classifications and team organization. While derivative or incremental projects should by and large be managed through lightweight team organizations, successful platform projects often have heavyweight-type organizations. Autonomous teams that are organizationally separate generally match breakthrough-type efforts.

Theme 2: Managing Development Networks within Companies

In addition to managing diverse project portfolios, many large companies have also started to build and expand networks of global R&D sites: development becomes distributed. The companies do this to increase labor flexibility, to become closer to (global) customers, to access functional expertise, to lower labor and operating costs, and to take advantage of time zones—product development is potentially accelerated to "24/7." Not surprisingly, these various intentions, not to mention problems of physical and cultural distances, create their own challenges, as we will see in the Siemens AG case.

Management and Coordination of Projects

A pivotal challenge in managing global development networks comprises information flow, communication, and the coordination of various engineering and design activities such that projects are completed on time and budget. Specifications have to be developed and

---

[6] For an explanation of this figure, detailed research findings and how lightweight and heavyweight teams can be applied to product development, see Kim Clark and Takahiro Fujimoto, *Product Development Performance* (Harvard Business School Press, 1991), Chapter 9, and Steven Wheelwright and Kim Clark, *Revolutionizing Product Development* (The Free Press, 1992), Chapter 8.

FIGURE 3-2

Different Team Organizations: *Managing Project Execution*

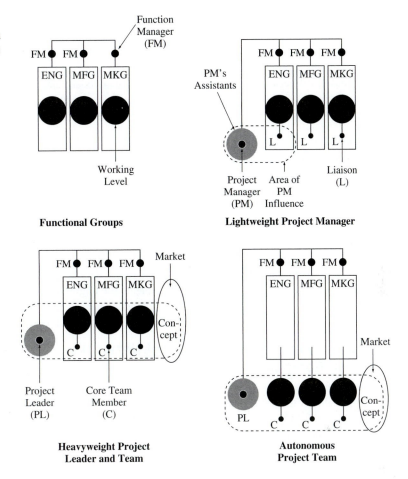

Functional Groups

Lightweight Project Manager

Heavyweight Project Leader and Team

Autonomous Project Team

understood by all, frequent team meetings have to be organized, integration of work must be facilitated, and problems—lots of problems—have to be solved rapidly. It is not enough to assume that "everything can be done by e-mail"!

Centralized versus Decentralized Decision Making and Control

Managing this tension between control and autonomy is one of the most difficult challenges for companies that build and run global development networks. Who "owns" what? Who's authorized to make changes—and how? Is everyone on the same page when it comes to assumptions about "what the customer wants"? Is everyone—across the planet—in agreement about "who's in charge"? Local managers? Headquarters? Without defined boundaries—of work, collaboration pathways, and authority—the dream of "24/7" can become a nightmare.

Task Interdependence and Partitioning

An effective way of addressing the distributed nature of global development is to pay close attention to interdependencies when large projects are partitioned into smaller tasks. Precisely where the boundaries between tasks are placed can have important consequences for project completion. For example, assigning two highly interdependent tasks to centers in different countries can have devastating effects. Design changes in one group will affect development work in the other group and vice versa. Such tasks and their boundaries are best kept within a single group. In contrast, relatively independent project tasks can and should be divided between development centers. Managers are usually aware of how task interdependence can affect projects, but other factors (such as the availability of engineering resources or local capabilities) tend to dominate decision making.[7]

Cultural Issues

A final but equally difficult challenge in managing global development networks is the issue of culture. "Culture" here runs the gamut from external factors—e.g., assumptions about everything from when vacations are taken to food in the cafeteria—to understanding customer needs. The farther from a company's core customer base its network is, the more carefully requirements must be specified—knowing that, in fact, it is impossible to specify every single project requirement in advance. Hence the importance of good communications, information flow, etc. In some cases cultural differences also resemble those found in many merger and acquisition situations. The face-paced culture meets the deliberative culture. Or the marketing culture meets the engineering one. In other words, cultural issues transcend obvious differences in language and local traditions; the management challenge is understanding and helping to bridge *all* the differences.

Theme 3: Managing Development Networks between Companies

The development of project platforms potentially enables more than leveraging learning and expertise over time and geography to maximize R&D productivity. Platforms can also be used to span firm boundaries. If you think about it, a product (or a technology) is in fact an interdependent network of components. These components, in turn, are themselves products—meaning the companies making them are often closely linked so that the result functions seamlessly. Thus, when one company invests in a new platform, its success will depend on others to develop complementary components that make the proverbial whole greater than the sum of its parts.[8] For example, the success of Intel's microprocessor technology depends on a complex network of companies developing products that make a computer valuable to an end user. Of course, it cuts the other way. Problems in one company in a network invariably affect other firms.[9]

A firm's external development network can be built in multiple ways, not simply among part manufacturers or between suppliers and users. In an increasing number of industries (as shown in the Sega and Millennium case studies), R&D activities are distributed among

---

[7] For literature on how task interdependence can be managed, see S. Eppinger, "Innovation at the Speed of Information," *Harvard Business Review,* January 2001; R. Smith and S. Eppinger, "A Prediction Model of Sequential Iteration in Engineering Design, *Management Science,* vol. 43 no. 8 (1997); and E. von Hippel, "Task Partitioning: An Innovation Process Variable." *Research Policy* 19:407–418 (1990).

[8] See Adam Brandenburger and Barry Nalebuff, *Co-opetition* (Currency-Doubleday, 1996); and Annabelle Gawer and Michael Cusumano, *Platform Leadership: How Intel, Microsoft, and Cisco Drive Industry Innovation* (HBS Press, 2002).

[9] See Venkatesh Shankar and Barry Bayus, "Network Effects and Competition: An Empirical Analysis of the Home Video Game Industry," *Strategic Management Journal,* 24 (2003).

a network of alliance partners to share risk, leverage diverse know-how and capabilities, and, once again, with the aim of speeding up development. However, management and coordination are neither simple nor straightforward activities. Alliance networks create complex issues of ownership, intellectual property rights, and value-capture; the design and monitoring of contracts (between firms and even project teams across them) become crucial.

Yet, as difficult as all these network-related challenges may appear, you have all along been confronting them in previous cases and readings. Think back on what did—and did not—work in various situations and you will discover "network problems," even if these were discussed solely in "management" terms. The bottom line is that in today's world of innovation and product development hardly any company anywhere goes it alone. We are all, to one degree or another, interconnected—as the well-known management consultant Ken Ohmae once put it, "We are all each other's suppliers." The winners in this networked world are those who understand how to leverage learning and expertise within their own firms through clever platform design and coordination *and* to effectively manage across firm boundaries at the same time.

DESCRIPTION OF CASES AND ARTICLES

The three module themes will be addressed in the various teaching cases and articles. The following summary of the material will prepare you for what you can expect to learn.

Microsoft Office: Finding the Suite Spot

By 1994, the market for suites of "productivity" application software, heretofore sold as individual products, had begun to coalesce. Like other developers of such software products, Microsoft faced the challenge of how such discrete projects could be integrated and competitively offered. Compounding this problem was the fact that despite its growing influence in the operating system market through Windows™, the company maintained a lively presence in other OS platforms (e.g., IBM, Apple). The case hones in on a particular issue that magnifies the larger problems involved in integrating a "network" of applications: integrating a network of people, "philosophies," and schedules. In addition, while the needs of individual development teams have to be considered, the demands customers increasingly make—and competitors are increasingly fulfilling—likewise must be addressed. Customers want something "seamless," but that may be very hard to deliver, given all the competing interests at Microsoft. You are challenged to figure out which development proposal outlined in the case is better, given the complexities involved. The case study will also introduce you to learning from project reviews. One successful approach is a postmortem review that is described in detail in the additional note, "Learning from Projects: Note on Conducting a Postmortem Analysis."

We've Got Rhythm! Medtronic Corporation's Cardiac Pacemaker Business

Medtronic is a best practice case in which you will learn how a team of managers transformed their business that had been in decline for a decade. It also highlights the complex network and interplay of "components" in a successful product and service development system. Using the concepts of Aggregate Project Planning (platform strategy, "train schedule", etc.), senior management patiently restored the competitiveness of Medtronic, whose market share eroded from about 70 percent in the early 1970s to below 30 percent in 1986. The product development problems that led to the decline can be found in many companies today and the case describes the transformation process that management followed, leading to a market share rebound to 50 percent by 1997. The *Harvard Business Review* article "Creating Project Plans to Focus Product Development" provides a conceptual foundation and detailed description of the Aggregate Project Planning method.

Siemens AG: Global Development Strategy

Siemens AG, one of the top five electronics and electrical engineering companies in the world, has been active in the global arena since its founding in 1847. In 2000, its roughly 464,000 employees were spread across 190 countries, with 57,000 employees working in R&D alone. Its largest division, Information and Communications Network (ICN), had spent decades building a network of 17 regional development centers (RDCs), supported by some 90 project managers based in Munich, Germany. When its fourth largest RDC, in Bangalore, India, took on more complex development responsibilities, German managers found it increasingly difficult to coordinate activities. The case provides an opportunity to closely examine the strategic and operational challenges of running complex development networks within Siemens in particular and to address the reality of global R&D management in general. Many companies have built global R&D networks and the *Harvard Business Review* article "Building Effective R&D Abroad" provides you with background information on the challenges and opportunities of being global.

Project Dreamcast: Serious Play at Sega Enterprises Ltd

Central to videogame industry player Sega's growth has been its successful arcade operations and machine sales, which have been bankrolling the company's development of its next-generation home videogame console, the Dreamcast platform. Because its previous console, Sega Saturn, was a financial disaster, senior management has focused on learning from past mistakes and doing everything right on Dreamcast's development. Set entirely in Japan, the case takes a close look at product development and market launch strategies in an extremely competitive environment characterized by strong network effects. It describes how Sega reaches the end of the Dreamcast development effort and has improved significantly at managing its complex network of game developers, retailers, and customers, and has also learned from its mistakes. The problem is, however, that it hasn't paid enough attention to its supplier, NEC, and now faces a serious chip shortage at market launch. This shortage could alienate retailers, customers, and independent game developers, who may not give Sega another chance. Because of the strong interdependence between network "nodes" (e.g., game developers), small mistakes can cause ripple effects for the company. As you will see in the case study, the dynamics and economics of the gaming industry are quite different than, for example, cars and the *Harvard Business Review* article "Increasing Returns and the New World of Business" not only shows you these differences but also provides guidance on how to operate in it as a manager.

Millennium Pharmaceuticals, Inc.

Millennium Pharmaceuticals, a leading biotechnology firm, has pharmaceutical and technology alliances with large firms, including Bayer AG, Monsanto, and Eli Lilly & Company. Central to its strategy and success in forming alliances is a technology platform for experimentation in drug discovery, considered to be one of the finest in the industry. At the same time, Millennium is using the technology platform to fundamentally rethink how it can discover new drugs and eventually become an integrated pharmaceutical company. This dual strategy—developing and selling its technology platform through alliances and leveraging these alliances to build downstream drug development capabilities—was challenged in August 1999, when the European agribusiness conglomerate Lundberg proposed a technology alliance to Millennium's senior management. The article "Mastering the Value Chain: An Interview with Mark Levin of Millennium Pharmaceuticals" will augment the case study with the perspective of the new company's CEO.

EXHIBIT
Themes of Cases in Module

Module 3: Managing Development Networks	
Microsoft Office: Finding the Suite Spot	• Product platform strategies • Platform-driven development and organizational design • Learning from projects using postmortem analysis • Reading: "Learning from Projects"
We've Got Rhythm! Medtronic Corporation's Cardiac Pacemaker Business	• Product and service networks with the firm • Aggregate Project Planning (APP) and development strategy • Building development systems • Reading: "Creating Project Plans to Focus Product Development" (*Harvard Business Review*)
Siemens AG: Global Development Strategy	• Managing global development networks *within* firm boundaries • Task partitioning and project management • Leading during technological transitions • Reading: "Building Effective R&D Abroad" (*Harvard Business Review*)
Project Dreamcast: Serious Play at Sega Enterprises Ltd.	• Linking development, supply chain, and operations strategies • Alliance networks *across* firm boundaries and development tools • Market launch strategies and lock-in effects • Reading: "Increasing Returns and the New World of Business" (*Harvard Business Review*)
Millennium Pharmaceuticals, Inc.	• R&D alliance strategies • Revolutionizing drug development through new technologies • Business model and alliance structure innovation • Reading: "Mastering the Value Chain" (*Harvard Business Review*)

Microsoft Office: Finding the Suite Spot

Chris Peters (ChrisP),[1] vice president of Office, and Jon DeVaan (JonDe), director of development for the Office Product Unit, gazed at the sunny weather illuminating Microsoft's campus in Redmond, Washington. On this late summer afternoon in 1994, the two were debating plans for the next release of Office.

The previous release, Microsoft Office 4.2,[2] had recently finished a tumultuous product cycle. The concept of Microsoft Office was to coordinate releases of integrated suites of personal productivity applications for both Microsoft Windows 3.1 and the Apple Macintosh. For the Windows release, this set of applications included Microsoft Word 6.0 (word-processing), Microsoft Excel 5.0 (spreadsheet), Microsoft PowerPoint 4.0 (presentation graphics), and in Microsoft Office Professional Edition, Microsoft Access 2.0 (database). Not only had the release been fraught with problems, the marketplace remained loaded with competitors; only Excel had gained significant market share. The marketplace for Windows applications was still smaller than the MS-DOS application market, though Windows customers were showing much interest in suites.

ChrisP and JonDe had a tough product plan to work out. Pete Higgins (PeteH), the senior vice president of the Applications Division, entrusted the two to build a product strategy and achieve consensus in the organization. Although the features and technical advances of the next products for Office had unknowns, there was a relative degree of certainty regarding changes; at the same time, decisions concerning product release strategy and development resources allocation all had alternatives. Given uncertainty in the software development process, the competitive landscape, and a number of internal issues, each

---

[1] In writing, long-time Microsoft employees generally referred to each other by their e-mail names, which were formed by a combination of first name and last initial. Internally, the e-mail domain@microsoft.com is omitted.

[2] Software versions are named according to the following scheme: *major_version.minor_revision update* (for example, 4.2c stands for major revision 4, minor revision 2, and update c).

Harvard Business School Case No. 9-699-046. Copyright 1998 President and Fellows of Harvard College. All rights reserved. For information: permissions@hbsp.harvard.edu.

This case was prepared by Steven Sinofsky and Stefan Thomke. HBS cases are developed solely for class discussion and do not necessarily illustrate effective or ineffective management.

alternative had substantial risks. Meanwhile, the troops were getting restless. As they often did, ChrisP and JonDe weighed their options over Coke and Mountain Dew, shunning Seattle's gourmet coffee in favor of more traditional programmer fuel.

MICROSOFT CORPORATION

Bill Gates (BillG) and Paul Allen (PaulA) founded Microsoft in 1975. From its inception, Microsoft's mission was to create software for the personal computer (PC) that empowered and enriched people in the workplace, at school, and at home. Microsoft was most well known for producing operating systems for personal computers, first MS-DOS and later Microsoft Windows. By fiscal 1994, the company's annual net revenue had reached US$4.65 billion.

Microsoft had three primary revenue streams. *Systems* revenue was based on sales of primarily MS-DOS and Windows (operating systems), development tools to support programmers developing for those operating systems, and the Microsoft BackOffice suite of enterprise server applications. The *OEM* revenue stream was based on sales of products, primarily operating systems, to PC manufacturers. The third major revenue source was the sale of personal productivity software sales for MS-DOS, Windows, and the Macintosh, known collectively as *applications*. In 1993, systems accounted for $1.52 billion, OEM for $1.18 billion, and applications for $2.93 billion.

Although most of the industry focused on the systems products, particularly Windows, it was the applications products that defined the typical customer experience. Most individuals and corporations used PCs for workplace productivity applications such as word processing and spreadsheets. These applications were becoming a major portion of Microsoft's revenues and an even greater portion of profits. Despite its leadership in systems, however, Microsoft had not yet achieved such a position in applications relative to the industry leaders of WordPerfect Corporation, Borland International, and Lotus Development Corporation.

MICROSOFT OFFICE FOR THE MACINTOSH: THE FIRST SUITE

In the mid-1980s, Microsoft released Microsoft Excel and Microsoft Word, both for the Macintosh. These were developed by the Applications Division, which also developed Microsoft Word for MS-DOS and Microsoft Multiplan (a spreadsheet) for MS-DOS. Microsoft realized moderate success with these MS-DOS products, stabilizing a secure second place in the market behind dominant products from WordPerfect Incorporated (WordPerfect word processor) and Lotus Development Corporation (Lotus 1-2-3 spreadsheet). The Applications Division, formally created in 1988, saw great success with the new Macintosh products, secured lead market share, and generated more revenue per computer for Macintosh software than for MS-DOS software. In addition, the engineering team developed the skills for creating programs employing the new graphical user-interface (GUI) that the Macintosh used. Not until 1989, with the release of Windows 3.0, were substantial numbers of Microsoft's operating system software customers using a GUI.

In 1989, the Macintosh business grew in both revenue and market share. Indeed, Microsoft Excel for the Macintosh had approximately 90 percent of the Macintosh spreadsheet market. The Macintosh word processing business was more fragmented; nonetheless, Microsoft

Word established a significant market share, becoming a *de facto* standard. Microsoft was the first company to compete successfully in multiple application categories, at least on the Macintosh.

MICROSOFT OFFICE FOR WINDOWS: NEW MARKET AND ROUGH START

Although the market for Windows applications was small, it was growing rapidly compared to that of applications for Microsoft's main operating system, MS-DOS. As such, Windows products were judged in comparison to their MS-DOS counterparts. In product reviews and in customer settings, Excel for Windows was compared to Lotus 1-2-3 for MS-DOS. Similarly, the word processing business was still nearly universally an MS-DOS business and WordPerfect had a dominating share. PC customers generally used only a single application; Macintosh customers, given the GUI's ease of use, often ran multiple applications simultaneously.

The development and sales efforts for applications products took place within business units. Word processing was engineered and marketed from the Word Business Unit, spreadsheet products from the Excel Business Unit, etc. This arrangement, which allowed the teams' engineering and business elements to focus on gaining market share and competing in the traditional categories, was successful. An *esprit de corps* developed in each unit, along with a healthy rivalry among teams. The Excel team, for instance, might have referred, jokingly of course, to a word processing document as a "spreadsheet with just one cell."

The marketing team working on Macintosh applications had meanwhile observed that customers purchased Word and Excel separately, if they purchased both products, and thus considered a *business package;* this would offer a convenient "suite" of common business applications, while increasing the amount of software purchased. The suite would comprise Microsoft Word, Microsoft Excel, plus the recently introduced Microsoft PowerPoint (presentation graphics), and Microsoft Mail (a corporate e-mail application). Named Microsoft Office for the Macintosh, the suite was released in 1989, to retail for around $895. Customers responded favorably, and the overall applications business grew. An updated Office for the Macintosh, version 2.0, was released the following year.

During the 1991–92 product cycle, Microsoft made plans for Office for Windows, a product that would pose some challenges. Not only was Windows 3.0 just gaining momentum among corporations, the marketplace remained fragmented among various MS-DOS (not GUI) applications, which most customers still used, and no company had substantial share in more than a single category. As a general surrogate for the marketplace, marketing often analyzed the sales of word processing product across the industry (see **Exhibit 1**).

Windows programming skills were being honed, however. The Excel team led the way with successful Windows development of three versions of Microsoft Excel, each released with corresponding Macintosh and OS/2 versions, thanks to a shared code strategy. Excel became the standard bearer for managing development schedules. Excel 3.0 finished less than two weeks later than originally planned, Excel 4.0 within four weeks.

For their part, the Word team struggled through an extremely difficult release of Windows Word 1.0, and a harder, and later, than expected version 2.0, released in late 1992; the PowerPoint team concentrated on Macintosh development, struggling with the relative complexities of development for Windows. The first release of PowerPoint for Windows, dubbed PowerPoint 3.0, was in mid-1992.

In late 1992 Microsoft finally released Microsoft Office for Windows, dubbed version 3.0 and often shortened to Office 3. The product met with relative success. Judging by industry reviews, however, the first generation of Windows Office was considered a suite of second-place products. As a result, Office 3 accounted for a small percentage of Desktop Applications' sales relative to individual application products.

THIRD TIME A CHARM

Nevertheless, individual applications grew more competitive with their MS-DOS competitors, suggesting that Windows was a viable way to run productivity software. And Windows customers, like their Macintosh counterparts, saw the benefits of using multiple applications simultaneously. Hence the concept of "suite" became more attractive with the mounting success of Windows. The combination of a Windows 3.0 GUI and the availability of powerful processors such as the Intel 386 facilitated multiple application scenarios.

In order to be successful in the individual categories, each independent business unit aimed the next series of products at its respective competitive situations.

Microsoft Word

The Word team targeted "ease of use," reacting to feedback on Windows Word 2 and to the complexities WordPerfect customers experienced using that much loved product. This led to such pioneering features as AutoCorrect, which automatically changed *teh* to *the* while typing. Although WordPerfect fell behind on its Windows version, the inertia behind its MS-DOS version and the specter of a Windows release kept the Utah firm competitive. Then, in 1991, a new competitor emerged, Ami Pro. The battle for the lead in Windows word processing was heating up.

The development of Word 6 did not go very smoothly.[3] The project's scale and the team's inability to predict the release date caused major tensions and, some said, bitterness throughout the product cycle. Excerpts from the team's *postmortem*[4] analysis follow:

- "Scheduling on [Word 6] was not done well and was seen later in the project as totally unrealistic. Milestones were left before they were really complete. This meant carrying bugs and work from the previous milestone over to the next. By the time we realized what shape we were in it was too late to make adjustments. [Word 6] milestones were longer milestones than on any other project; this should have been an indicator that there was a bigger problem." [**Word 6 development**]

- "Many of the problems with proposed features do not become obvious until development has starting working on it. By this time it is usually later in the project and program management has very little flexibility redesigning a feature." [**Word 6 development**]

---

[3] Office 4.2 included Word 6.0, Excel 5.0, and PowerPoint 3.0

[4] With each release of a Microsoft product, the product team conducted a *postmortem* to evaluate areas of the project that went well and those that did not. The report included suggestions for improving the product development process.

- "The project was too large with too many primary goals. We ended up touching too many areas of the product without consciously realizing it at the outset of the project. There were times individuals got so caught up in their feature, that it was hard to remember the priorities for the project as a whole ('what did I spend four days on that feature for?'). This highlighted the fact that the decision making process was not well defined. There was no one key person that would make the final decision when the team could not reach consensus on a problem." [**Word 6 program management**]

- "There were two principal reasons we were six months late in shipping: the inability to cut features and not know what to cut. We should have been more ruthless about cutting features in order to meet the schedule. People knew we were slipping (it was obvious after we missed the first Major Milestone), yet no one wanted to cut features. Development was concerned that it would hurt morale. When in fact, morale was hurt more by not being honest about the slipped date." [**Word 6 program management**]

- "The size and complexity of [Word 6] had changed dramatically from WinWord 2. 0. Yet it was never acknowledged that different processes and tools were needed to manage such a large project. It was planned and managed as a small project. Once again, care should be taken on the front end instead of full steam ahead and hoping that it will all work out." [**Word 6 testing**]

- "The schedule became everything. Individuals across all groups knew that the schedule was a myth but all were discouraged from communicating any slips in their work. Test knew where we were at with bugs, but this was not broadly communicated. Development Leads did not share this information with their team members because it was seen as de-motivating. It was pretty obvious that everyone knew what was going on, but nobody was willing to come forward and say "we're not going to make milestone." Even though everyone knew we wouldn't make schedule, it wasn't OK to talk about it. This was very demoralizing. Knowing the reality of ship dates affects quality of testing. One will compromise certain things when you only have a short amount of time. As a result of this schedule deception, poor decisions were made (i.e., quick fixes instead of well-thought-out changes, other trade-offs were managed very poorly) based on inaccurate schedule information. This deception was insulting to our intelligence." [**Word 6 testing**]

Microsoft Excel

The Excel team focused on the display and analysis of complex information, leveraging the strengths of the Windows GUI. The team also addressed ease of use, creating the innovative AutoSum feature that automatically created sum formulas for rows and columns. In general, however, the emphasis was on a higher-end customer who was interested in custom-programmable solutions. As such, Excel emphasized enhancing the power of the spreadsheet model; it included such features as PivotTable reports, which allowed data to be viewed in various aggregations. It also became the first application to incorporate Visual Basic for Applications (VBA), a cornerstone of Microsoft's programming language strategy. The spreadsheet marketplace was also a three-product race. Lotus 1-2-3 was mostly focused on its MS-DOS release as well as an immature Windows version. The Excel team braced for an updated, and improved, release of Lotus 1-2-3 for Windows. The third competitor, Borland Quattro Pro, enjoyed a legion of rabid customers who took their lead from Borland founder, Philippe Kahn (pkahn@borland.com); he positioned his company and products as "barbarians" that would beat Microsoft and Lotus.

The Excel 5 project was very difficult, and the Windows version of Excel 5 was finished three months later than originally planned. Although this was better than the Word 6 project, many felt burned out and expressed some major concerns in the *postmortem* document:

- "The schedule started out fairly ambitious. It had a good deal of development time in it, but it also had a good deal of development to be accomplished. This was OK as long as we remained honest about our schedule and our dates. We did an OK job of that, but there were significant periods where we were tacitly accepting missing a date and not making that information official. The slip from Thanksgiving to Christmas comes to mind. I think we need to continue to be as hard-core as possible about the dates. We were very flexible when VBA [Visual Basic for Applications] came in incredibly late. Instead of slipping our schedule or adjusting features, we just made up the time. While we are all in this together, we need to be honest when we are not hitting our targets. Honest with not only ourselves, but the rest of the company. Office, Word, [Localization], [Japan] and others are all trying to make decisions based on our ship date. While we still do one of the best jobs in the company of making it happen—and happen very close to our original estimates—we need to 'stick to the knitting' as Tom Peters would say, and be up front and honest." [**Excel 5 development**]

- "The milestones were not as closely adhered to as in the past. With many features spanning several milestones, it was difficult to get a good feel for the state of the product against the spec at any given time. Also, much of the milestone information contained in XL5NEW.XLS [the schedule] was incorrect, or incomplete. This made scheduling testing more problematic." [**Excel 5 testing**]

- "Cutting features until MM2 [Major Milestone 2] was painful—feature set should be better defined before MM1 [Major Milestone 1] starts." [**Excel 5 development**]

- "For as huge as the project was, the final ship was less stressful. We moved the date out early enough to make it a real date. Much better than [Excel 4] in that we didn't do the day-to-day slip. People kept up with the weekly mail on a consistent track rather than a huge crunch at the end. Spread out the hard work over a longer period of time, but not have the huge crunch. The last phase of Excel 5 was much more bearable than Excel 4." [**Excel 5 program management**]

Microsoft PowerPoint

The PowerPoint team, based in Cupertino, California, pioneered a technology called Object Linking and Embedding (OLE), which enabled one application to embed data, or files, from another, and also made it easy to edit such embeddings without leaving the user's current document. This technology was especially important for presentations containing information from various sources. PowerPoint was also in a competitive race with two other products. The established MS-DOS leader, Harvard Graphics (from Software Publishing), had a powerful Windows version. Lotus had recently acquired another rich presentation package, Freelance Graphics.

Gluing It Together

At this time, creating an integrated Office product fell to a small group within the Applications Division, the Application Interoperability Group (AIG)—a handful of program managers and some development and testing resources. AIG developed the Microsoft Office Manager (MOM), a small floating window that allowed users to easily launch each application. It also attempted consistency in user-interface elements, for example, in toolbars. Because such features were implemented differently in each individual application, AIG spent most of its time negotiating with the developers on each application team in an to attempt to "glue together" an integrated offering.

Marketing, meanwhile, zeroed in on making competitive inroads based on the suite concept, determining that it would lead its product launch activities with Office, rather than with the individual applications. As shown in **Exhibit 2,** it was reacting to a clear trend in the marketplace. The product teams were not in a good position to accomplish this, however.

The launch date for Office 4.0 was October 1993. Since the major applications were all on different schedules, they were nowhere near finishing at the same time. The call was made to announce and promote Microsoft Office 4.0 even though it would include only a new version of Microsoft Word and the older versions of Excel and PowerPoint. Customers purchasing Office 4.0 would receive coupons redeemable for the updated applications when they were released. Office 4 was off to a bumpy, and costly, start. Both reviews and customers expressed disappointment in the coupon strategy. Six months later, in April 1994, the first unified release of Microsoft Office 4 for Windows was done, christened Office 4.2 to signify that all the pieces were finally there. Yet the software was still not stable and reports of bugs plagued the release, particularly in Word. By October 1994, a full year after the announcement, the product was considered done and the release Office 4.2c was considered the final release of the Office 4 line.

The development teams had created some revolutionary advances, particularly in the new technology behind OLE and the architectural work supporting VBA. Yet considerable energy had been expended in wrestling with user-interface consistency across individual products—best highlighted by two infamous debates. One was a drop-down-drag-out fight between the Word and Excel Business Units over the height of toolbars. One team felt that toolbars should be 15 pixels high, the other 16. Office released with two different visuals. Another debate concerned cascading menus. This was a good user experience, the Excel team claimed; the Word team was dead-set against it. Office shipped with very different menu organizations.

Marketplace Reception

Office 4.2 was a blockbuster product for Microsoft and the industry (see **Exhibit 3**). For the first time, sales of suites outpaced those of individual applications. Reviews and analyses, however, continued to focus on applications. In fact, many in the industry were not very fond of suites. Many customers also felt that suites were not optimal for their use and were resistant to the notion of a one-stop-shopping approach.

COMPETITION IN THE MARKETPLACE: HOW SUITE IT IS

At the same time, many reviews extolled the virtues of Lotus SmartSuite, which emphasized workgroup computing. One influential industry publication noted that Microsoft Office was weak on workgroup features. Another observed that SmartSuite had greater consistency between applications and highly recommended it for customers who already used Lotus Notes.

SmartSuite had been introduced in 1992, making it the second complete suite on the market. Lotus 1-2-3 for Windows, the only component developed in house, received a disappointing reception when first released. Lotus subsequently purchased the Ami Pro word-processor from Samna Corporation, meaning that Microsoft now had a formidable competitor in both major application categories. Lotus SmartSuite for Windows included the Lotus 1-2-3 spreadsheet, Freelance Graphics for presentations, Ami Pro for word-processing, and the newly acquired Lotus Organizer personal information manager. Focusing on the suite market to strengthen its entry into Windows spreadsheets, Lotus also saw excitement around it revolutionary product, Lotus Notes, which promised to be a solution to the difficulties business faced in communicating and collaborating. Lotus Notes defined a new category called workgroup software and SmartSuite worked best with Notes. Lotus touted SmartSuite as a workgroup suite in contrast to Microsoft's suite aimed at individual productivity.

Behind SmartSuite's design lay the notion that a suite should be more than a collection of applications; it should seamlessly share important user-interface constructs. This was captured in the tagline "Working Together." Lotus touted four product design elements as evidence:

- Common appearance and behavior make the applications easy to learn and use.
- SmartIcons (a row of customizable graphical buttons along the top of the screen, or "toolbar") provide quick and consistent access to powerful functionality.
- Status bars (the information display at the bottom of the screen, indicating the current page number for example) that display and allow you to quickly change the current settings in your document, spreadsheet, or presentation.
- Support for the Windows clipboard (the functionality behind Cut/Copy/Paste), dynamic data exchange (the ability to automatically move data from one application to another), and object linking and embedding, which all help to copy, move, and share information among the applications.

From a product design perspective, the Lotus and Microsoft products had gone down different paths. Microsoft had emphasized building category leaders from its "second place" products, leading to application-specific innovation. Lotus had improved its flagship spreadsheet, shoring it up with a full assault on the new suite market. In fact, Lotus created a much-publicized development team focused entirely on the notion of suite. The team aimed to create the shared implementation of common features and to ensure that SmartSuite products had a level of user-interface consistency to support the "Working Together" theme.

Additionally, a third competitor was created from a tactical marketing agreement between Borland International and WordPerfect. That suite, Borland Office for Windows, comprised the WordPerfect word processor, the Borland Quattro Pro spreadsheet and Paradox database, as well as presentation graphics. Although this offering was clearly in third place, the industry felt that the powerful combination of best of breed showed potential for developing into a powerful, integrated work environment.

ORGANIZED TENSION

By mid-summer 1994, the key roles within the Desktop Applications organization were:

- **General Manager:** Managed a business unit and managed the multiple disciplines of the product team, with overall responsibility for delivering a product that succeeded in the category. The job was primarily one of product development, with little financial responsibility.

- **Software Design Engineer ("developer"):** Wrote the product's code and was responsible for overall technical architecture. The development function reported up through to the development manager, who reported to a GM of a business unit.

- **Program Manager:** Owned the product design, user-interface, and user-experience, as well as overall coordination and project management. "The voice of the customer," a PM drove customer research and created the feature list and specifications for the product. The PM function reported up through the group program manager, who reported to a GM of a business unit.

- **Software Test Engineer ("tester"):** Insured that the product met specification. "The conscience of the product," testers ultimately "signed off" and stated that the product was complete. The testing function reported up through the test manager, who reported to a GM.

- **Product Manager ("marketing"):** Communicated the product offerings and managed the sales and marketing channels. Ultimate financial responsibility for the business stood with marketing. Prior to Office 4, the marketing function reported to the GMs, but in an effort to focus the marketing efforts on the "suite," the marketing function was consolidated and now reported up through the director of Applications, Marketing, who reported to the vice president of Desktop Applications.

Meanwhile, as a response to the changing competitive landscape, Senior Vice President PeteH had created a business unit, within Desktop Applications, called the Office Product Unit (OPU); its sole purpose was to oversee the shared customer experience for Office—what exactly this implied in terms of engineering would be left to the new team's members. ChrisP, general manager of Word, became vice president of Office; JonDe was appointed director of development for the unit, moving from Excel. Both were among the most respected members of their applications teams and had more than 20 combined years of Microsoft experience. PeteH had formally and informally mentored the two for many years and trusted them with the huge responsibility of deciding major elements of the Office product.

The other disciplines in the Office team were subsequently filled with directors (across the division, directors were perceived as leaders of their disciplines). PeteH made a deliberate decision to move individuals from the Application Business Units to the OPU. At the same time, a 10-year veteran of Microsoft Word became the Excel development manager, while the Word development manager had several years of experience on Excel. This began a tradition of moving members of the entire development organization around the product. Both Testing and Program Management followed this same pattern.

The new organization faced many challenges, the first being staffing. As most members of the division had become accustomed to working on and identifying with an application, the idea of working for a "suite" was somewhat foreign, or at least uncomfortable; the new "Office group" was perceived with a great deal of skepticism. Rather than arbitrarily assign people to the Office team, the approach was to take volunteers who believed in the engineering of a suite. This had the unintended side effect of leaving the staunchest supporters of the individual products, those generally the most skeptical of suites, on the individual product teams.

Once the team was staffed, as shown in **Exhibit 4,** it faced the task of determining both the timing and content of the next release. Key challenges included:

- Establishing a timeframe for the next release.
- Creating a development process that could span the organization.
- Determining the focus and features of the next release.
- Winning in the individual application categories.
- Remaining nimble enough to respond to the anticipated changes in the application categories.
- Taking leadership in the increasingly important suite category through consistency of user-interface.
- Adding support for collaboration and workgroup computing.

PLANNING THE NEXT PRODUCT CYCLE

During the summer of 1994, PeteH, ChrisP, JonDe, the general managers of the individual applications, and the senior development and program managers brainstormed the merits of several approaches for the next product cycle, homing in on the need to make two major decisions: what would define the customer experience for the suite, and what should the release schedule be?

With each release of a software product, development team members dreamed up much more work than could ever be done on schedule. The constraining factor for a software project was the calendar time spent developing the release; there were no production-line, manufacturing, or other downstream considerations. Although Microsoft development teams were rarely limited by their ability to attract development and engineering talent, they were limited by their ability to manage the work of a large number of engineers. This became increasingly difficult as the development schedule lengthened; the chances for divergent implementations, increasing product integration challenges, changes in the marketplace, and the burdens of ongoing communication all created significant, possibly insurmountable, challenges. Therefore, when planning a release the first, and most important, issue was determining the product's overall timeline. Product features would then be scaled or cut back to fit within it.

The primary charter from PeteH and BillG was to improve the architecture of the code implementing the applications. To speed up the development process as well as make products more robust and feature-rich, how products were built would need to improve. It was generally felt that the component applications needed to share more code—that is, use one program element to implement functionality in several places in the products, rather than several implementations of the same feature in each product. Code-sharing had a dual advantage, in fact. It was more efficient to implement a feature only once, and it was also better for the customer since consistency would be guaranteed. At the same time, code reuse and sharing had been the Holy Grail of the software industry for decades. Integrating shared code into existing code bases not only was difficult, it often led to slower programs that were harder to test. The latter was a substantial concern of the individual application teams, especially Excel, for which performance had been a crucial design point. Excel had also had a less-than-positive experience in integrating the shared code that implemented Visual Basic for Applications (VBA).

There was, however, considerable opportunity to create a better suite experience for customers. As shown in **Exhibit 5,** users experienced very different user-interfaces in formatting text in each application. Even the basic look at start-up differed in the choice, layout, and size of buttons. The most trivial functions varied in each product, such as the dialog asking a user to save changes to a document. But implementing a consistent, shared set of functions, particularly in the user-interface area, would represent considerable effort.

Zeroing in on a release schedule would be an even bigger challenge. Each applications team had just come off product cycles that were anywhere from six months to one year late (see **Exhibit 6** for release dates). Each had varying levels of concerns about its category competition—there were rumors of an imminent update to the Lotus 1-2-3 for Windows product that worried the Excel team; the Word team worried that WordPerfect would better its Windows release.

An applications team customarily scheduled 12 or 18 months of work in three or four development milestones. Although each team conducted a project *postmortem* and identified a number of potential areas for improvement, no obvious solutions were found consistently across these reviews. The tension over competing in the feature-rich category battles versus the architectural improvements threatened to push the limits of scheduling, moreover. Although most teams were confident that they could add compelling category features in 12–18 months, they were doubtful that the architectural work could be accomplished in under 18–24 months.

A major external issue loomed as well. The Windows group had begun to solidify plans for Chicago, code name for the product released as Windows 95. A key feature was that applications would now be a full 32-bits, to take full advantage of Intel's microprocessor architecture. For an end-user a 32-bit operating system promised applications that would be faster and handle larger files, and an operating system that would better handle running multiple applications at one time. For Chicago to have these demonstrable benefits, applications would have to be converted from Windows 3.0's 16-bit architecture. Doing so was not well understood, and since Chicago was still under development the difficulties were compounded. Nevertheless, the company was making an enormous strategic bet on Chicago and the next release of Office would require Chicago's 32-bit functionality. Crucially, Office would be released simultaneously with Chicago in early spring of 1995.

A master at "walking the halls," ChrisP canvassed many people throughout the division to learn their concerns about the timing of the next release. There were consistent themes. The organization was unsure of the OPU's new role and unsure of the efforts required to significantly rearchitect elements of the products in order to share code. The work needed to build applications for Chicago was regarded as a moving target, and there was little support for this highly critical strategic initiative.

At Excel, GM Lewis Levin (LewisL) was very concerned by the imminent release of an updated Lotus 1-2-3 for Windows; he also headed the analysis of Lotus' workgroup efforts and Notes. Excel generally favored extreme focus on competing with Lotus to the exclusion of any other work.

Meanwhile, the Word Product Unit was desperate to prevent another difficult release. Peter Pathe (PPathe), the GM of Word, replacing Chris Peters, hoped to improve things without rocking the boat. WordPerfect was a resilient competitor and there were concerns about Ami Pro as well. Many on the Word team sought to significantly improve product's code base in order to improve the stability and robustness.

The PowerPoint team, headed by Vijay Vashee (VijayV), was still primarily focused on the Macintosh. Geographical separation made including the team difficult, and it often felt left out of decision-making processes. In order to deliver on simultaneous releases of Macintosh and Windows versions, however, PowerPoint determined that a major rearchitecture of its code was needed, which could take significant calendar time.

As for the Office Product Unit, that team was working to clarify its role. How would it push architectural advances? What features would define the customer experience for Office? How would the specification and development process work? Because the new organization was perceived as "taking" resources from core application efforts (see **Exhibit 7**) and introducing an unknown into a development machine achieving success in the market, the team was anxious to define schedule parameters so it could begin the hard job of feature and process definition.

ChrisP also talked with long-time Applications marketing director, Hank Vigil. HankV had headed the launch of Office 4.2 and was seeing the bet on Office pay handsomely. Initially, he was concerned over any product plan that might cause customers to delay upgrading to Office 4.2. But the competitive realities kicked in, and he hoped for a release sooner rather than later.

Meanwhile, PeteH counseled ChrisP and JonDe on the importance of making significant investments in the architecture of Office—improving the amount of shared code, creating a more robust development process, and modernizing the code base. BillG clearly expressed to PeteH the importance of betting, despite massive uncertainty, on Chicago. PeteH, a former product manager himself, expressed his concerns over losing sight of near-term competitive battles.

The "12/24" Proposal

Finally, JonDe had an insight that crystallized the debate—establish a small team within each application to create a release of Office that did the necessary amount of work to support Chicago along with a small number of category features. The bulk of the architectural work would be scheduled for 24 months of development. The proposal became known as *12/24* since it called for the Chicago release in 12 months, and a follow-up release 12 months later based on 24 months of work.

The logic of this plan was solid. The practical implications, and unknowns, were enormous:

- How would the focus shift from individual products as the primary goal to an integrated suite as the primary goal?
- How much work would building applications for Chicago entail?
- Would Chicago ship on time? If it shipped too late, would the releases of Office follow one another too closely?
- How would the teams be split? Traditionally the "whole" team worked on a release and never before had a team been split across two releases.
- Would there be a critical mass of resources for the short-term release? Would the release have a critical mass of features to be competitive with the threatened releases of WordPerfect and Lotus 1-2-3?

- How would the work of the 12-month effort be folded into the 24-month effort so the 24-month product represented a full superset of the 12-month product?
- How would the teams align their schedules and scheduling methodologies?
- Could the teams successfully execute on a two-year schedule?
- What architectural work would define the 24-month release?

If such a plan could be executed, it would allow the Chicago-specific work to progress, which pleased upper management and provided a release vehicle for competitive features—which pleased the GMs. It also provided a platform shift that BillG and PeteH had been pushing for.

The 15-Month Proposal

The alternative to 12/24 was to define a shared development schedule for all products, allowing product teams the most flexibility in addressing their competitive needs. The general feeling was that a schedule of approximately 15 months allowed for ample investment in competitive features. The upsides of such a product plan were well understood:

- Products could emphasize competitive features, working to gain market share.
- A longer schedule was much more comfortable for the developers and testers fresh off of the Office 4 release. They were just decompressing from releases that finished much later than originally scheduled.
- There would be ample time to complete the Chicago-specific work. To date this work was still an unknown quantity and many feared that it was being underestimated.
- Management would be focused on a single release and the entire team would be marching in the same direction on the same schedule.

The clock was ticking and a large development team would sit idle if a release schedule could not be agreed to. Once that was in place the product development process could start. Until then, the hallways and cafeterias filled with speculation, doubt, and uncertainty. ChrisP and JonDe were feeling the pressure.

EXHIBIT 1

Worldwide Sales of Word-Processors (Including Suites) for MS-DOS and Windows, 1993

Source: International Data Corporation.

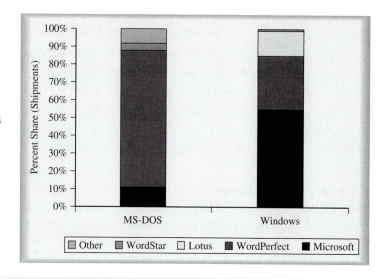

EXHIBIT 2

Windows-Based Word-Processors Shipments v. Suite Shipments (1990–1994)

Source: International Data Corporation.

	Windows-Based Word-Processors Forecast	Office Suite Shipments	Windows-Based Word-Processors Shipped in Suites (%)
1990	445,000	—	—
1991	2,236,000	—	—
1992	5,550,000	890,000	16.0
1993	9,295,000	3,200,000	34.4
1994	14,230,000	7,900,000	55.5

EXHIBIT 3

Distribution of Revenue for Microsoft Desktop Applications (Fiscal Year 1994)

Source: Microsoft Corporation.

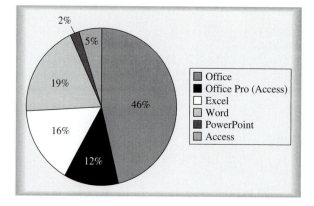

EXHIBIT 4   **Organization of the Desktop Applications Division (mid-1994)**

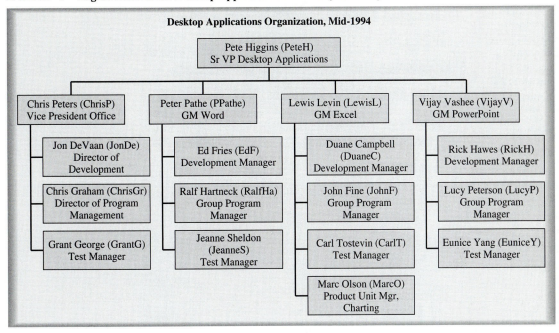

Source: Microsoft Corporation.

EXHIBIT 5
User Interface
Elements from
Office 4.2
Demonstrating
Lack of
Consistent
Product Design

Source: Microsoft
Corporation.

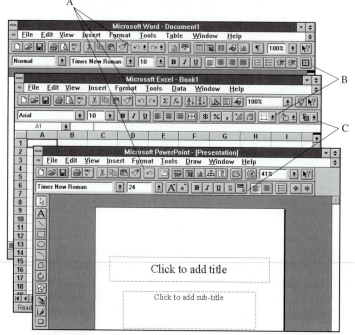

Note numerous inconsistencies in basic user-interface elements. For example:

A. Shows the multiple implementations of *Undo* functionality.
B. Shows two different methods for adding borders and outlines to text.
C. Shows two different methods for changing the color of text.

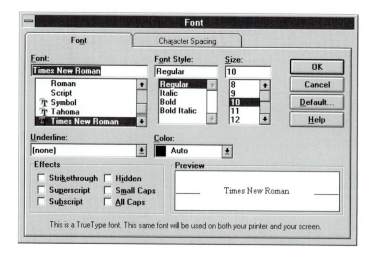

EXHIBIT 5
(*continued*)

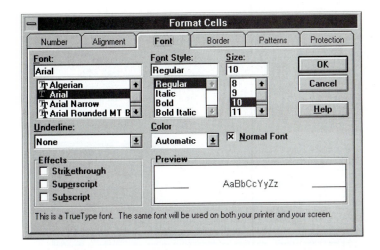

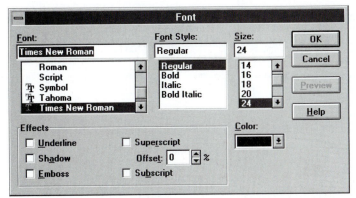

Basic character formatting dialogs for Word 6.0, PowerPoint 3.0, and
Excel 5.0 (clockwise). Note the inconsistent interface for the basic
operations.

Inconsistent message from each application asking the user to save a file
(above and right).
Menu structures for Format menu in each application. Note unique use
of hierarchical menu in Microsoft Excel (below).

EXHIBIT 5
(*continued*)

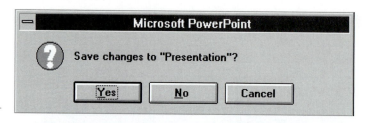

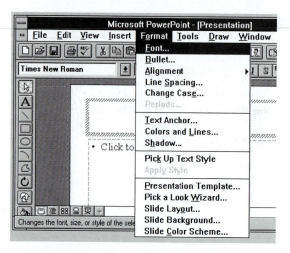

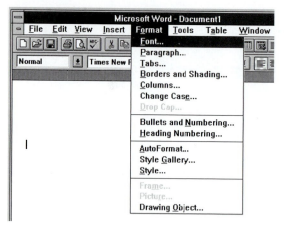

EXHIBIT 5
(*concluded*)

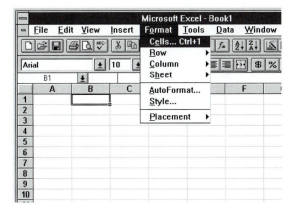

EXHIBIT 6   Key Product Release Dates

Product	Release Date	Notes
Microsoft PowerPoint 3.0	May 1992	First Windows release of PowerPoint
Microsoft Word 2.0	August 31, 1992	Second major release of Windows Word after the November 1989 release of Word 1.0
Microsoft Excel 4.0a	November 1, 1992	Release of Excel 4.0 for Office
Microsoft Word 2.0c	November 18, 1992	Third maintenance release of Word and release for Office 3
Microsoft Office 3.0 for Windows	December 1992	First full release of Office for Windows
Microsoft Office 4.0 for Windows	October 28, 1993	Consisted of Word 6.0 and coupons for updated Excel and PowerPoint
Microsoft Office 4.2 for Windows	April 3, 1994	Fully updated Windows Office (Word 6.0, Excel 5.0, PowerPoint 4.0)
Microsoft Word 6.0c	August 10, 1994	Third maintenance release of Word 6.0 and release for Office 4
Microsoft Excel 5.0c	August 31, 1994	Third maintenance release of Excel 5 and release for Office 4
Microsoft Office 4.2c	September 17, 1994	Final, and complete, release of Office 4.2
Lotus SmartSuite 1.0	April 6, 1992	First suite for Windows from Lotus Development
Lotus SmartSuite 2.1	September 15, 1993	Major update to SmartSuite included updated Lotus 1-2-3 for Windows
Lotus SmartSuite 3.0	June 29, 1994	Major update to SmartSuite included Lotus 1-2-3 for Windows Release 5
WordPerfect 5.2 for Windows	October 30, 1992	First widely used release of Windows WordPerfect
WordPerfect 6.0 for Windows	August 30, 1993	Update to Windows WordPerfect
WordPerfect 6.1 for Windows	November 8, 1994	Significant update corrected performance and stability concerns
Borland/WordPerfect Office 1.0	April 21, 1993	Co-marketing agreement provided both companies with suite entry
Borland/WordPerfect Office 2.0	November 17, 1993	Update to offering included latest WordPerfect and Quattro Pro

Source: Microsoft Corporation

EXHIBIT 7
Allocation of Resources Contributing to the Office Product Within the Desktop Applications Division (as of July 1994)

Source: Microsoft Corporation.

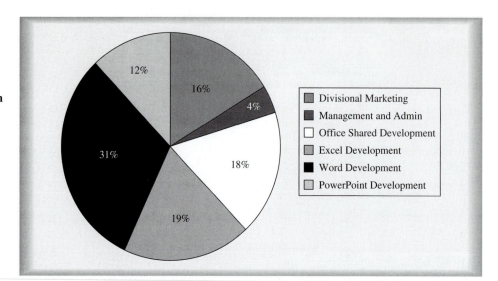

16%

4%

12%

31%

18%

19%

☐ Divisional Marketing
■ Management and Admin
☐ Office Shared Development
☐ Excel Development
■ Word Development
☐ PowerPoint Development

Note

Learning from Projects: Note on Conducting a Postmortem Analysis

The end of a project offers firms a window of opportunity to learn from the many things that went right and wrong over a project's duration. Unfortunately, many firms do not take full advantage of this unique opportunity, despite research that indicates that these post-project review activities play an instrumental role in feeding forward learning and improving overall project performance.[1] In one study, researchers found that the same design problem showed up repeatedly over three sequential automotive development projects. The purpose of this note is to describe in detail the process of postmortem analysis, which has been used very successfully by Microsoft and other software developers for learning from past projects.

WHAT IS A POSTMORTEM?

A postmortem is both a *process* and a *document* (or set of documents). The primary purpose of assembling a team and going through the postmortem process to produce a summary document is to identify what aspects of the project went well, what went poorly and what needs improvement. The secondary purpose of a postmortem is to provide closure to a project, which is particularly important for projects that have taken a great deal of time, effort, and commitment by the team members and organization.

---

[1] For a list of publications with empirical evidence and discussions, see the reference section at the end of the note.

This note provides a set of questions and a suggested process for guiding a team through a postmortem analysis. In order for a postmortem to be successful and valuable, it is imperative that the participants follow a few simple guidelines:

- **Be inclusive.** Postmortems should be inclusive of key disciplines, participants, and stakeholders. It is too easy to omit representation from a known "trouble area" in an effort to reduce the negatives in the process.
- **Be self-critical.** Participants should check their egos at the door. The postmortem will necessarily find "flaws" with processes and team members who executed (or failed to execute) aspects of the project.
- **Be professional.** Discussions should cover a broad range of team issues and dynamics, from process to product issues. However it should not under any circumstances become personal. Most projects have enough elements that need to improve that any mention of names or specific instances can best be skipped.
- **Be factual.** Documentation and data should be included in both the discussions and in the final report. Future projects will find it valuable to learn from project metrics and other project management data. The postmortem provides a good process for gathering that information and including it in the report.
- **Be brief.** Suggestions and commentary in the final report should be brief and agreed to by broad consensus. Although dozens or more issues will surface during the postmortem process, the next project will benefit more from a small number of very specific suggestions.

The following postmortem outline suggestions are based on successful postmortem practices at Microsoft Corporation.

THE POSTMORTEM MEETING

A postmortem meeting takes place after the project is complete. Most projects never quite finish (for example, there will always be subsequent maintenance releases), but most projects do have a point when the majority of participants feel like they are "done." It is good to wait a few weeks after a longer project in order for team members to distance themselves from the last few hectic weeks of a project; however, the team should not wait too long since the best information could be lost.

The postmortem meeting provides a chance for the team to get together and work through the important issues to create an action plan that will improve the development process for the team. The improvement may be targeted for the next milestone or for the next release.

Length

While some postmortem meetings are daylong events, it is better to keep them to four hours or less (even if it means breaking it into two different meetings). Quite a bit of the work can be done outside of the meeting.

Room

Choose a room with a round or oval shaped table so people can easily see each other and no one appears as the *boss* at the table's head. In fact, you may want to purposefully arrange for the leader of the meeting/project/group to sit on the long side of the table instead of at the head.

The room should be large enough to comfortably seat everyone. If you predict quite a bit of conflict among people, allow for more space since feeling "cramped" can increase the level of tension.

Who Should Attend?

Anyone who was involved in the project should be invited. If inviting everyone makes the group too large, consider having mini-postmortems with people who worked on specific parts of the project (usually by team discipline). Representatives from each of these mini-postmortems can then attend the final postmortem. Another alternative is to have people send in their comments on the agenda items to a few key players and have a postmortem with those people. When at all possible, you want to have everyone together for the post-mortem so they can speak for themselves.

Facilitator

An effective postmortem requires a neutral person to facilitate the meeting. Ideally, it should be someone who was not involved in the project and has no reason to be involved in the discussion. This person will be in charge of the process in the postmortem, making sure that:

- People stay on the topic.
- No one is personally attacked (keep comments constructive).
- The agenda items are covered.
- Everyone is equally involved in the discussion.
- Time is watched closely.

Recorder

The tool that makes postmortems most effective is creating a visual recording of the discussion. Taping large sheets of flipchart paper on walls or using white boards is very effective for recording information. This way everyone involved in the discussion automatically focuses on the recorded information (instead of on each other). The recorder should organize the information as well as record it. Some ideas are to

- **Use various colors** of markers to represent the type of comment (i.e., black=bad, green=good, red=warning flag, purple=idea, brown=neutral observation).
- **Use symbols** to reflect tone (i.e., !!!=feels strongly about this, *=everyone agreed with this, ?=not everyone agreed, lll=3 people mentioned this).

PREPARING FOR THE POSTMORTEM MEETING

As with any meeting, a postmortem should have an agenda. Since there is likely to be a lot of free-flowing discussion, it is a good idea to set time limits on portions of the meeting. If it seems like more discussion is warranted then by all means continue—do not let time limits steal from the opportunity to learn from past projects. The basic agenda for any postmortem is:

1. Reconstructing the timeline for the project, the players and percentage of their time contributed to the project.
2. Listing which aspects of the project and product went poorly.

3. Suggesting what should be done differently for future projects.

4. Listing what went well.

5. Brainstorming recommendations for future projects.

As long as these elements are included in some form in the postmortem process, it does not matter whether they all take place during the actual meeting. The timeline can be developed by one or two people ahead of time and distributed to others for review. Each person involved can report on his or her involvement/role, percentage of time spent on project, dates involved, etc. Typically, the timeline acts as a vehicle for focusing people on the entire project, rather than just the end or just when they were involved.

PREPARATION

Send out the agenda at least one week prior to the postmortem with instructions to begin thinking about the project with the agenda topics in mind. You may want people to send a list of "good" and "bad" parts of the project to the person organizing the postmortem one day in advance. That list can then become the "new" agenda, taking each topic and discussing the good, the bad, and the improvements needed. Otherwise, it is perfectly appropriate for people to simply think about the agenda and bring up their "good" and "bad" points during the postmortem. You should also have some of the team review old postmortems from your group if they exist. If possible, review some of the postmortems that exist for other projects. It can be very helpful to review postmortems from projects that were very similar to your own.

RUNNING THE POSTMORTEM MEETING

Opening

Open a postmortem with the person who organized it stating the reason for getting together. It is very important that everyone present understands that it is not a chance to "get back" at people, place blame, vent, or even to propose solutions to each and every problem. The purpose is to come up with recommendations for future projects based on the experience with the previous project. It is also important for people to understand that the comments made during the postmortem will not be reflected in their performance reviews, etc. The facilitator should explain his or her role, (i.e., keeping the discussion on topic, protecting people, etc.) as well as laying some ground rules (do not interrupt or attack another person). This will make it easier for the facilitator to intervene or refocus the discussion when necessary. The recording function should also be explained and everyone should be encouraged to correct the recorder when appropriate.

Timeline and Resources

The first topic of discussion is the timeline. This includes who was involved and the amount of time each person was involved in the project. If this information was generated ahead of time, it should be visibly displayed in the room. If this information was not generated ahead of time, use several sheets of paper to create a timeline for the project and begin filling in dates as people remember things. Either way will immediately focus on the project and remind participants of the entire timeframe to be discussed and how much discussion remains.

What Went Poorly/Should Be Done Differently?

It is usually best to start with what went poorly, because most people are more interested in talking about that anyway (plus, you get to end the meeting with what went well). If you have not collected a list of discussion topics ahead of time, the first task is to compile a list of everything that went wrong. This can be done using various techniques:

- **Brainstorm:** Participants say whatever comes to mind as they think of it.
- **Nominal technique:** Participants list individually what they thought went wrong (may have done this prior to the meeting) and then the facilitator asks each person to say one item from their list until everyone's lists are recorded.
- **Storyboarding:** Participants write their lists on index cards (one item per card), which are then combined together and sorted by topic to create a comprehensive list.

Deciding which technique to use should be based upon several factors: if certain people dominate a brainstorm, then use *nominal group;* if participants care that others know the source of their comment, use *storyboarding;* or if the team needs to know how many people think a particular issue was a problem, use *storyboarding* as well.

If the list of what went wrong was collected ahead of time, go over it now and ask for any additions. Once you have the list generated, the facilitator will need to prioritize the list so that the most important issues are discussed first (in case you run out of time or energy).

One simple technique is to have everyone "vote" on the top three issues. This can be done using little round stickers (each person gets three and places them on the list), having each person make a "tic mark" next to their top three items, or simple hand-raising.

Again, use the technique that works best with the concerns and dynamics of your group. Everything that is said should be recorded in some form. For each issue, the discussion should flow as follows:

- Why was this a problem? What went wrong?
- What were the signs that should have warned us?
- What should we have done differently?

What Went Well

This part of the postmortem is generally much easier to facilitate. The team simply needs to list what participants thought went well and record why it was successful. Some of the things listed might contradict what was discussed during the "what went poorly" part, which is okay. It is important to record that there were differences of opinion

Recommendations

This is a nice way to summarize the postmortem. Looking back at the information recorded for both the "good" and "bad" discussions summarize what the group would recommend for future projects. Sometimes the person writing the postmortem document does this after the meeting.

POSTMORTEM SUMMARY DOCUMENT

Documenting the postmortem is very important not just for future reference, but also for the people involved. Having a summary of the meeting serves as a project archive and closure, and also allows the team to spread lessons beyond the meeting attendees.

Ahead of time the team should decide who will be responsible for writing the document. The person should include the timeline, names of people involved, list of recommendations, and the information recorded from the discussion. To maintain accuracy there should be very little deleted from the information that was recorded during the meeting or from e-mail collected by the postmortem team. Before the document is published, it is very important that everyone involved has a chance to review and propose changes as appropriate.

One important addition to the final postmortem document is a summary of project metrics, or an analysis of project-tracking data. For example, once the list of project team members is known, it is often a good idea to document the full-time equivalents for each month of the project or the most important design problems (and their solutions) that the team discovered. For software projects, bug trends, code coverage for testing, code productivity over time, etc. all make useful postmortem information.

NEXT STEPS

One of the biggest traps to fall into after a postmortem is to put the document away and never refer to it. If a group is involved in another project with several of the same people from the postmortem, it is very effective to use the recommendations from the postmortem as a "self-check" on the new project. At various planned times throughout the next project, take out the list of recommendations and evaluate as a group how you are doing in those areas. This makes the time and effort of the postmortem seem more productive.

As an organizational tool, postmortems can be very useful. For example, if a project had some specific difficulties and these come out during a postmortem, the manager of a team can commit to specific remedies for the next project. This has the dual purpose of improving the development process and reinforcing the learning organization.

The postmortem process is effective in a wide variety of corporate settings. Traditionally, the process is applied to product development; however, some nontraditional uses of postmortems include marketing events (for example, a multi-city tour), a major presence at a trade show, a workshop held for customers, or even a relatively simple task such as creating a set of tools for use by the sales force. The postmortem process is beneficial in many ways, so do not hesitate to try it out.

SOME SELECTED REFERENCES

Adler, Paul, 1995, "Interdepartmental Interdependence and Coordination: The Case of the Design/Manufacturing Interface," *Organization Science*, vol. 6, no. 2, March–April.

Cusumano, M. and K. Nobeoka, 1998, *Thinking Beyond Lean: How Multi-Project Management Is Transforming Product Development at Toyota and Other Companies* (The Free Press, New York).

Cusumano, M. and R. Selby, 1995, *Microsoft Secrets* (The Free Press, New York).

Thomke, S. and T. Fujiomoto, 1999, "The Effect of 'Front-Loading' Problem-Solving on Product Development Performance," Working Paper, Harvard Business School, forthcoming *Journal of Product Innovation Management.*

Watkins, M. and Clark, K., 1994, "Strategies for Managing a Project Portfolio," Working Paper, Harvard Business School.

Wheelwright, S. and K. Clark, 1992, *Revolutionizing Product Development* (The Free Press, New York).

EXHIBIT 1

Sample Excerpts from Microsoft Word 6 Postmortem

Source: S. Sinofsky and S. Thomke, "Microsoft Office: Finding the Suite Spot," Harvard Business School Case No. 699-046.

As is often the case with complex projects, the development of Word 6 did not go very smoothly. The project's scale and the team's inability to predict the release date caused major tensions. Excerpts from the team's *postmortem* analysis follow:

- "Scheduling on [Word 6] was not done well and was seen later in the project as totally unrealistic. Milestones were left before they were really complete. This meant carrying bugs and work from the previous milestone over to the next. By the time we realized what shape we were in it was too late to make adjustments. [Word 6] milestones were longer milestones than on any other project, this should have been an indicator that there was a bigger problem." [**Word 6 development**]

- "Many of the problems with proposed features do not become obvious until development has starting working on it. By this time it is usually later in the project and program management has very little flexibility redesigning a feature." [**Word 6 development**]

- "The project was too large with too many primary goals. We ended up touching too many areas of the product without consciously realizing it at the outset of the project. There were times individuals got so caught up in their feature, that it was hard to remember the priorities for the project as a whole ('what did I spend four days on that feature for?'). This highlighted the fact that the decision making process was not well defined. There was no one key person that would make the final decision when the team could not reach consensus on a problem." [**Word 6 program management**]

- "There were two principal reasons we were six months late in shipping: the inability to cut features and not know what to cut. We should have been more ruthless about cutting features in order to meet the schedule. People knew we were slipping (it was obvious after we missed the first Major Milestone), yet no one wanted to cut features. Development was concerned that it would hurt morale. When in fact, morale was hurt more by not being honest about the slipped date." [**Word 6 program management**]

- "The size and complexity of [Word 6] had changed dramatically from WinWord 2.0. Yet it was never acknowledged that different processes and tools were needed to manage such a large project. It was planned and managed as a small project. Once again, care should be taken on the front end instead of full steam ahead and hoping that it will all work out." [**Word 6 testing**]

- "The schedule became everything. Individuals across all groups knew that the schedule was a myth but all were discouraged from communicating any slips in their work. Test knew where we were at with bugs, but this was not broadly communicated. Development Leads did not share this information with their team members because it was seen as de-motivating. It was pretty obvious that everyone knew what was going on, but nobody was willing to come forward and say 'we're not going to make milestone.' Even though everyone knew we wouldn't make schedule, it wasn't OK to talk about it. This was very demoralizing. Knowing the reality of ship dates affects quality of Testing. One will compromise certain things when you only have short amount of time. As a result of this schedule deception, poor decisions were made (i.e., quick fixes instead of well thought out changes, other tradeoffs were managed very poorly) based on inaccurate schedule information. This deception was insulting to our intelligence." [**Word 6 testing**]

EXHIBIT 2
Postmortem
Meeting
Checklist

Before Meeting

1. Send out copies of mini, functional postmortem results for review.
2. Ask for people to send lists of top issues to discuss—should be cross-functional issues that require the whole group in order to be resolved.
3. Send out agenda with a list of potential topics.
   a. Prioritize topics to discuss.
   b. Discuss each topic; emphasize what to do in future.
   c. Summarize and prioritize recommendations.
4. Reserve large room, tape flipchart paper to walls.
5. Compose list of discussion topics.

During Meeting

Note: If the recorder/facilitator needs to contribute to the discussion, give someone else the marker to record the information.

1. Start with reviewing and ranking topics to be discussed.
2. Begin with the top issue and record what went wrong as well as how to do it differently in future.
3. Stop "wrong" discussion after 5–7min. and start asking what to do differently.
4. Check that all functional groups have contributed.
5. Save time at the end to prioritize recommendations.

After Meeting

1. Send written-up notes to attendees for edits, then send to entire group.

EXHIBIT 3
**Sample
Questions for
Postmortem
Meetings**

Planning

- Were the goals of the project clear to you?
- Were the marketing goals clear to you?
- Were the development goals clear to you?
- How complete do you think the planning was prior to the actual commencement of work?
- How could planning be improved?
- What recommendations would you make for the planning process for our next release?
- Were customers adequately represented in the planning process?

Resources

- Were there enough resources assigned to the project, given the schedule constraints?
- How can we improve our methods of resource planning?
- What could have been done to prevent resource overload or under utilization?
- Do you think resources were managed effectively once the project started?

Project Management/Scheduling

- Was the schedule realistic?
- Was the schedule detailed enough?
- Looking over the schedule, which tasks could you have estimated better and how?
- Did having a series of milestones help in making and monitoring the schedule?
- What were the biggest obstacles to meeting the scheduled dates?
- How was project progress measured? Was this method adequate? How could it be improved?
- Was contingency planning apparent? How can we improve our contingency planning for the next release?
- How could scheduling have been done better or been made more useful?
- What would you change in developing future schedules?
- How were changes managed late in the cycle?
- Were the trade-offs between schedule and features handled well?

Design and Specifications

- Were there issues in the functional design and ownership?
- Were there issues involved in using component or with code sharing? How could this be done more effectively?
- Were the specifications completed on time? Did they contain adequate information for development to work from?
- Did the specifications ever reach a state of being "done"?

Communication

- Was communication in your group handled efficiently/effectively?
- Was communication between groups handled efficiently/effectively?
- Were the status meetings effective?
- Was communication with the external groups effective?

Team/Organization

- Did you understand who was on the team and what each member was responsible for?
- Was the role of the different groups clear to you?
- What would you do to alter the organization to more effectively put out product? Functional vs. Project team organization?
- Do you think the different groups fulfilled their roles?
- What was deficient in your group? Other groups?
- Did you have all the information you needed to do your job? If not, were you able to obtain the information.
- Did you think the team worked together well?

EXHIBIT 3
(*continued*)

Product

- In retrospect, could the work of your group have been done better? How?
- What needs to happen to avoid problems in the future?
- Are you satisfied with the product we shipped? If not, why?
- Are customers satisfied with the project?
- What elements of process failures are most evident in the resulting product?
- What would you do to improve the process of creating the product?

Management

- Did your manager help you do your job?
- Did you view management's role as useful?
- Were management decisions communicated to the team? Did you understand how decisions were made?
- Were external dependencies managed effectively?

Tools and Practices

- What tools did you employ for managing project and developing the product?
- What other tools do we need?
- What other improvements to we need with the existing tools that we have?

General

- List three things that went well (in order of importance)?
- List three things that need improvement (in order of importance)? Suggest methods of improvement.
- Any other issues you would like to raise?

We've Got Rhythm! Medtronic Corporation's Cardiac Pacemaker Business

The legacy of Medtronic Corporation, the company that created the cardiac pacemaker industry, is a proud one. Starting from its earliest pacemakers, which had to be carried outside the body, Medtronic had achieved dramatic improvements in the functionality, size, and reliability of these devices. In so doing it had extended the lives, and improved the quality of life, for hundreds of thousands of people in whom pacemakers had been implanted. The pacemaker has been designated as one of the ten most outstanding engineering achievements in the world over the past 50 years, along with the digital computer and the Apollo 11 moon landing.[1]

Medtronic, which in 1995 booked operating profit of $300 million on revenues of $1.7 billion, had been founded in 1957 in Minneapolis, Minnesota by Earl Bakken, a researcher and inventor who had to his credit patents on several of the crucial technologies that led to the modern heart pacemaker. Pacemakers were small, battery-powered devices that, when implanted within a patient, helped a malfunctioning heart to beat in a steady, fixed rhythm. Because Medtronic was the first entrant into the pacemaker field and built a strong technological lead, it enjoyed a substantial portion (over 70 percent) of the market share for cardiac pacing through the 1960s.

Building upon Medtronic's legacy of leadership was not easy, however. In the face of increasing competition, rapid technological change, and tightening market and regulatory demands for product quality, Medtronic saw its market share cut by more than half between 1970 and 1986. Though it had invested heavily in technology and product development

---

[1] This citation was made by the National Society of Professional Engineers in 1984.

Harvard Business School Case No. 9-698-004. Copyright 1997 President and Fellows of Harvard College. All rights reserved. For information: permissions@hbsp.harvard.edu.

This case was prepared by Clayton M. Christensen. HBS cases are developed solely for class discussion and do not necessarily illustrate effective or ineffective management.

over this period, much of that investment had been unproductive. Many projects failed to produce product designs that could be launched competitively, and the features and functionality of most of the products the company was able to launch lagged the competition. Several key employees left the company, seeing greater opportunity to develop their new pacemaker product ideas in new start-ups rather than within Medtronic. These competitors proved much faster than Medtronic at developing new products that advanced the state-of-the-art in pacemaking. Medtronic was also pummeled by two major product recalls related to product quality problems. Observers felt the company would have lost even more of the market during this period, were it not for its strong worldwide salesforce and the lingering legacy of its brand reputation amongst surgeons, the primary customer group.

Management changes that were initiated in the late 1980s, however, had sparked a dramatic reversal in the company's fortunes, and by 1996 the company had regained its position of product and market leadership. By all accounts, it was in front and pulling away from its competitors. On a pleasant Minneapolis spring afternoon in 1996, several members of the team that managed this turnaround—Steve Mahle, president of the Brady Pacing Business; Mike Stevens, general manager of the Pulse Generator & Programming Systems (PGPS) Division; Bill Murray, general manager of the MicroRel component manufacturing subsidiary; Director of Marketing Paula Skjefte (pronounced Sheftee); and Director of Product Development Technology Don Deyo—gathered to assess the progress they had made since they had taken the helm of the troubled division in the late 1980s. They were also anxious to understand whether the management structure and the processes, values, and resources they had created to achieve this turnaround were capable of maintaining the company's successful momentum in the future. This case recounts their achievements and concerns.

Medtronic's Brady Pacing Business

Medtronic's Brady Business Unit designed and built pacemakers that delivered a rhythm of electrical impulses, to remedy a disorder called Bradycardia, in which the heart's electrical system does not generate pulses to cause the heart to beat rapidly enough to sustain the body's normal activity, as described in Appendix 1.[2] Among its other businesses, Medtronic also had a Tachycardia Business Unit, whose products addressed the opposite malfunction—when the heart's electrical system generated too many beats. Because of the prevalence of Bradycardia relative to other disorders in cardiac patients, the Brady Business Unit historically had delivered most of Medtronic's revenues and an even larger share of its profits. Consequently, the health and vitality of the Brady Business strongly affected the corporation's overall financial performance.

The Brady Business Unit worked hand-in-glove with the component divisions of Medtronic in product development efforts, as shown in **Exhibit 1.** The Promeon Division, for example, developed new technologies to power pacemakers. In the early years of the industry's history in particular, battery technology had been a pivotal selling point because the battery could not be replaced: once it was depleted, a new pacemaker had to be implanted. Another division, MicroRel, designed and fabricated the critical hybrid microelectronic circuits in Medtronic's pacemakers. Located in Tempe, Arizona, it supplied proprietary circuitry to all of Medtronic's businesses. Work with MicroRel was viewed as a crucial

---

[2] The term "brady" derives from a Latin root meaning "slow." The opposite cardiac pacing disorder, tachycardia, took its name from a Latin root meaning "fast."

connection in the development of new pacemakers, because of the increasing importance that integrated circuit (IC) technology played within these devices. Perhaps the most critical division for the Brady Business was the Pulse Generators & Programming Systems (PGPS), headed by Mike Stevens. Unlike the other two component divisions that shared their services and output with other parts of Medtronic, PGPS focused on developing new products for Bradycardia pacing, by translating customer and market-based inputs into product designs, and then worked closely with manufacturing to produce the final products. This involved design and assembly of the pacemaker as well as the programming unit, which typically sat on a table in the cath lab or operating room where the implantation was performed. Programming units allowed physicians to tailor the firmware in the pacemaker so that the frequency of the pulses it generated and a number of other attributes of the device matched the needs of each individual patient. The leads that carried electrical impulses from the pulse generator to the wall of the heart were designed by a separate leads group within the Brady Pacing Business Unit, headed by Warren Watson.

HOW THE PACEMAKING LEADER LOST ITS RHYTHM

Product development at Medtronic historically had been supervised by its functional managers, who were intimately involved with each development effort during the company's early years. However, as the company grew, the functional managers became increasingly absorbed by operating responsibilities in their own functional organizations, making coordination across functions, in practice if not intent, a lower priority. The company responded by creating a group of project managers to coordinate the work of various functional groups. While this helped, most major decisions still had to be passed by the functional managers—"a legacy of how decisions had been made that still lingered in the organization," according to a long-time employee. The project managers' job was to try and get decisions to be made by the functional leadership—they only had minor authority to make decisions themselves.

"Planning new products is actually a lot more difficult in a business like this than it looks," reflected another experienced executive. "In some businesses the problem is a lack of great ideas. But in our situation—with rapidly changing technological possibilities, some darned good competitors, and thousands of cardiologists out there with ideas for all kinds of new features—the opposite is true: We've always had *too* many ideas for new products. In our functional organization, without a single, coordinated process or person to articulate a product plan or strategy, development projects just started everywhere. When you had a good idea, you'd mock up something—either a real prototype or something on paper—and carry it around with you. Then when you'd run into Earl Bakken or another powerful manager in the hall, you'd corner him, pull your idea out of your pocket, and try to get him to support it. If his reaction seemed positive, then you would use that leverage, to get a few friends to help you push it along. At some point you'd go to the engineering manager to get formal resources."

"The problem with this system was *not* that we were working on bad ideas. Most of them were technically sound and made market sense," commented Don Deyo, an experienced engineer and currently director of product development and technology. "We were trying to do too many things, and no project got the focus and attention needed to get it done right.

It was taking too long to get anything to market. We never got good at releasing new products, because you only get good at things you do a lot. Those that we did introduce often followed the lead of competitors. That's what happens when you continually try to respond to every new idea to come along."

"The problem then fed on itself," reflected Mike Stevens, general manager. "The development people would tell me that they could never get anything to market because marketing kept changing the product description in the middle of the projects. And the marketing people would say that it took so long for engineering to get anything done, that by the time they got around to completing something, the market demands would have changed. When customer requirements evolve faster than you can develop products, it becomes a vicious spiral."

"In environments like that, it is *very* difficult to plan product families," Stevens continued. "If the company launched a product that subsequently could be modified or extended to create derivative models, it was a stroke of luck." Because of the *ad hoc* way in which new product development projects were conceived, Medtronic's project pipeline was made up of incongruous development cycles. Projects were separated according to whether they were single- or dual-chamber platforms. Each new model had largely its own unique circuitry, components, testing programs, casing, and battery. Due to the high costs of developing all these parts of the pacemaker, project managers battled each other for resources.

Although the company's reputation and strong salesforce relationships with surgeons kept disaster at bay, the company's performance suffered as a result of its disabilities in development. Between 1970 and 1986, it was almost always a competitor, not Medtronic, that introduced major new improvements to the market. For example, Cordis introduced the world's first programmable pacemaker in 1972; Medtronic followed in 1980. Cardiac Pacemakers Inc., a Medtronic spin-off, pioneered the first pacemaker with a long-life lithium battery in 1974. Even though the technology was available from a third-party supplier, Medtronic did not get its lithium battery-powered product out the door until 1978.

Although Medtronic introduced its first dual-chamber pacemaker during this period, it did not follow it with an improved dual-chamber device for another eight years. Deyo explained, "We were working on next-generation dual-chamber products during all of those eight years. The problem was that just as we'd get ready to announce a new product, a competitor would come out with something better. So we'd force the funnel open again to allow for this new input, re-scope the project, and try to leap ahead of the competitor. Then just as we'd get ready with the improved version, a competitor would come in ahead of us with an even better product; and so on."

"I got so that I just didn't want to answer the phone because I was afraid there would be a salesman on the line wanting to know when we were going to come out with a product that was comparable to something a competitor had introduced," recalled Paula Skjefte, director of marketing. "I just couldn't give him an answer."

Field product failures compounded the problems caused by Medtronic's long development cycle. Its Xytron pacemaker line was recalled in 1976 after several units failed following implantation. And a few years later, physicians found that the leads on some pacemakers they had implanted had disintegrated, so that the pacemaker's output was not getting transmitted to their patients' hearts. In total, Medtronic was forced to issue four different product advisories to warn that certain models were susceptible to malfunction. The result of these factors was a massive loss of share, from 70 percent in 1970 to 29 percent in 1986, as shown in **Exhibit 2.** Still, however, due to significant growth in the market, the company continued to report record sales and profits over this period, and for many in the company there was no cause for alarm.

"Medtronic was a really nice Minneapolis company," Don Deyo noted. This reflected in many ways the values of Medtronic's founder, who had a genuine reverence for every employee's contributions to the company's success. "But somehow in the mid-1970s," Deyo noted, "this attitude got out of hand. We dominated the market, and were very profitable. Because there was so little pressure on the business, we lost our intensity and willingness to focus our efforts."

A Home Run Saves the Day

The company's decline was arrested in 1986—more by good fortune than any change in management practice, however. In the early 1980s a project leader, Ken Anderson, championed an idea for a "rate-responsive" pacemaker—a device that could sense when changes in body activity required the heart to beat faster or slower, and stimulated the heart to beat accordingly. Although most cardiologists Anderson spoke to thought the idea was impractical, and despite the indifference of most of Medtronic's staff, Anderson won the support of the general manager, and the two of them set up a dedicated team to pursue the idea. Its product, dubbed *Activitrax,* worked—technologically and in the marketplace. Cardiologists found its single-chamber design easy to implant, and its effect was nearly as good for patients as a dual-chamber pacemaker. Patients reported feeling stronger, because it would cause their hearts to beat more rapidly when they were working hard or exercising. And they reported feeling more rested in the morning, because Activitrax paced their hearts to beat more slowly when they were asleep.

The dramatic Activitrax therapeutic breakthrough literally saved Medtronic, because no other new platform products were ready for introduction until 1992. It did not, however, alter the way the company developed products.

THE TURNAROUND IN PRODUCT DEVELOPMENT

Though Medtronic's market position was helped by the success of Activitrax and by a serious product recall suffered by a principal competitor, the most dramatic changes in the company's market position were instigated when Mike Stevens was assigned to be vice president for product development of the PGPS Division in 1987. Stevens' career with Medtronic had begun in 1973, when Motorola decided to shut down its hybrid circuit manufacturing operation near Phoenix. Stevens and several other employees of the Motorola facility decided to continue the operation and obtained financing from Medtronic, which had been a major customer.

Stevens had watched Medtronic's struggles in product development from a supplier's viewpoint. "Though I didn't have a background in product development, I saw much of Medtronic's problem as Management 101. We had very strong functional roles. People were being measured by cost centers, and there was no accountability for the delay or failure of a new product. I felt the basic values and ethics of the company were still really strong. But what needed work were its *processes*. I felt if we could get those straightened out, then we could bring the Brady business back to its past glory."

Stevens summarized key elements of his management philosophy as follows:

1. Commitments are sacred. The more responsibility you give to people to control their destiny, the more you can and must hold them accountable.
2. Create a sense of urgency by contrasting the excitement of bringing new therapy to patients, versus the consequences if your competitors are there first with better solutions. Don't waste time with excess travel or off-site meetings.
3. Are happy employees productive, or are productive employees happy? Stevens believed the latter, whereas Medtronic management had been acting as if the former were true.
4. Do nothing that separates management and employees. Management means responsibility, not status.
5. You only get what you measure.
6. Focus on gaining market share. Over time, this is the most accurate measure of your success.

Managers in the PGPS Division got a taste of Stevens' belief that commitments are sacred when, shortly after arriving at Medtronic, he held management to the project milestones they had agreed upon at the beginning of fiscal year 1988. Their incentive compensation was tied to these objectives, and 1988 was the first year in memory that management did not receive year-end bonuses that were tied to objectives.

Measuring Product Development Performance

Stevens implemented his measurement philosophy by focusing on four measures of product development performance, which corresponded to the achievements he wanted the organization to focus upon. These are described in the following table.

Focus	Measure	Stevens' Comments
Speed	Cycle time	"This is the time required to get a new product into the market. If I measure this, there isn't much else I need to measure. It forces you to do the other things right in product development, because you can't make mistakes, and you can't waste time."
Cost	Fully allocated unit product costs	"The reason we focus on fully allocated cost, rather than just viewing functional costs or direct product costs, is that it gets you thinking about market share, and the impact that unit volumes can have on your financial success. This is healthy thinking."
Innovativeness	Product performance relative to competitors	"This translates into market share, pure and simple."
Product Quality	Field performance—defects per million	"In our business, you can't afford a field failure—because our patients count on us, and doctors can choose to go elsewhere."

Most people in PGPS welcomed Stevens' attitude. One commented, "I was just getting started as a project manager, and Mike was a breath of fresh air. His priorities were clear;

I knew where he stood. He had a very different management style: very firm, assertive, thoughtful, and focused. He was execution-oriented, and really held people accountable."

Processes and Practices

"This isn't a story about great management," Stevens emphasized. "It's a story about putting into place a set of processes that helped a great team of people be as productive as they could be." The processes Stevens instituted had the following features:

1. Speed

"Being fast to market eliminates *so* many other problems," commented Steve Mahle, who took over as president of the Brady Pacing Business in 1990. "The slowest part of our process was actually in deciding what needed to be done. We used to spend *lots* of time debating what we should do. One of Mike's greatest achievements was in cleaning up the front end. He did this by articulating very clearly what our strategy was, so that there was a well-defined criteria that could guide these decisions. Then he created a process to get those decisions made."

Exhibit 3 describes the process by which new products were defined. An assessment of the competitive and customer environment was combined with a technology assessment, to define the business objectives of each new product, and to clarify what the financial and competitive contributions of the new product needed to be. Stevens, who by 1991 had become division general manager, reviewed new product ideas according to their potential for meeting those business objectives. His staff, comprised of the managers of the division's marketing, research, development, technology, finance, human resources, and manufacturing functions, participated in this review with Stevens.

2. Platform Strategy

Since product ideas in the earlier regime had originated in disparate parts of the organization and were approved and funded in independent decisions, it was quite common that products that required significant investments of time and money were not leveraged with derivative products that could extend their life and market reach. The highly successful Activitrax model, for example, did not spawn a single derivative product that offered different features, performance, or price points to the market. To devise an effective product line architecture built around product platforms, Mahle established a product planning team comprised of himself, Mike Stevens, Paula Skjefte, Don Deyo, and Stan Myrum, vice president and general manager of the business unit's leads division. This team defined a platform strategy around three key elements.

The first element was that the initial platform product had to be designed to accommodate the full range of derivative models from it, without significant redesign. "In other words," Stevens explained, "We designed the highest-performance, most fully featured version of the product at the outset." Medtronic then created derivatives by de-featuring and de-rating certain elements of that design, so that it could address other tiers of the market as well.

The second element of the platform strategy was enabled by the first. Historically, Medtronic had introduced new pacemaker features on its single-chamber models first, because they were technologically simpler to design and build. Once the features were accepted and the technology perfected in the single-chamber platform, the features were then moved up-market onto the dual-chamber platform. "The effect of this," Paula Skjefte noted, "was to force a lot of our lead physicians to continue focusing on single-chamber devices just so they could utilize our newest features. Once we began designing the platform to accommodate the full range of derivative models we planned to spin off from it, we didn't face the same constraint—it was just as easy to put the most advanced features on the dual-chamber model. This gave us a much clearer progression from basic, simple devices for the low-end of the market to high-performance, fully featured models at the high end.

Skjefte continued, "The way we used to play in the low-end of the market was to discount the price of our old model, after we had introduced a new one. This was ironic. Because we were reducing the cost of our products with each generation, we sold our high-cost models at the lowest prices, and our low-cost, newest models at the highest prices." The result was that there was little incentive to maintain a strong presence in lower tiers of the market. Under the new strategy, Medtronic addressed lower price points in its market with the simplest versions of its new lower-cost platforms. Hence, even as Medtronic was assuming a leadership role in features and functionality in higher tiers of the market, it strengthened its position in the low end as well.

The third aspect of Medtronic's platform strategy was to change the way platforms were defined. Formerly, Medtronic had thought of platforms in terms of physical architecture. Hence, it was inconceivable that a dual-chamber device could have been levered off of a single-chamber device platform. The projects were executed by completely different teams, and their designs therefore diverged from the very beginning. Under the new strategy, advances in microelectronics technology enabled so many of the most important capabilities to be designed into the hybrid circuit, that the circuit design constituted the platform. This circuit could then be modified quite readily, often through firmware modifications, to enable or disable particular features in the design of derivative products.

"I couldn't say whether Medtronic's decision to integrate backward into hybrid circuit production by starting MicroRel was good luck or good management," Stevens reflected. "But at this point the expertise we have developed in circuit design and production is an enormous advantage. Our competitors outsource their hybrid circuits. But we have found that the hybrid is so integral to our functionality and our standards in quality and specifications, that suppliers just can't meet what we need. We can outsource things that are a little bit more modular—things that aren't so integral to the essence of our product. And being vertically integrated helps with speed. We can go down to MicroRel and shift priorities if something needs to be done quickly. We are also vertically integrated with our battery development and manufacturing."

Medtronic faced two particular challenges in implementing its platform strategy, Stevens reflected. "First, we learned that we needed to have the technology building blocks in place, before we could begin a platform project. Product development is not technology development—you can't have the uncertainties of advanced technology development on the critical path of a rhythmically executed product development project. Technology takes time to put into place, and it requires consistency in strategy and management methods, to tie advanced technology development with product development in a consistent, useful way. The second challenge we encountered was that platform projects required *much* more interaction and coordination amongst various individuals and groups in the company—within engineering, and across engineering, manufacturing, marketing and finance—than other projects. You can't have a 'one-size-fits-all' habit of organizing and managing development teams, if you're really serious about a platform strategy."

Indeed, Stevens' decision to vest platform development teams with much greater decision making authority—essentially making project managers the peers of functional managers—had a pervasive and sometimes disruptive impact on many in the organization. Heavyweight project managers with dedicated teams—from research, development, and marketing—oversaw the development of every platform. Other project managers, working under the supervision of the platform manager, took responsibility for derivative projects extending off of each platform. This represented a significant shift in the job of the company's functional managers. Their charge became providing trained, capable people to staff projects, and developing new technology platforms. "It became very clear, very quickly," observed Bill Murray, an electrical engineer-turned-project manager, "that project management was the path for career advancement. Even some of the functional managers left their positions to become project managers."

3. Project Documentation

Previous agreements to initiate a project were often made verbally. "It was amazing how many misunderstandings and disagreements seemed to survive those verbal contracts," Don Deyo recalled. "You could leave a meeting thinking you had agreed on something, and learn a few months later that you hadn't. Then when we had to change something, the marketing and engineering people were always accusing each other of violating an earlier agreement. It's amazing in a set-up like that, how easy it is legitimately and honestly to find someone else at fault." One way Stevens implemented his credo that commitments are sacred was to require two documents to be written at the start of the development phase of each project: a *Product Description* document, written by marketing, which detailed the customer requirements, product definition and clinical performance expectations of the product; and the *Product Specification* document, written by engineering. This detailed the technical and cost specifications that the product would have to meet in order to meet the Product Description. Stevens required marketing to sign off on the Product Specification, certifying that there was a technical specification corresponding to each requirement in the Product Description. Similarly, engineering had to sign off on the Product Description, as a double-check that marketing and engineering were synchronized.

4. Phase Definition

Stevens and Mahle defined a system of phases and project reviews to which all projects would be subject. Projects started in a *business analysis phase,* in which the Product Description was written and the financial benefits of the project to Medtronic were estimated. Following review of the business case, the project would enter the *demonstration phase.* Here, the technological feasibility of the project was probed to avoid putting the necessity of inventing something on the critical path of a development program. Rapid prototyping was emphasized in this phase to identify problems and possible solutions as quickly as possible. If a product idea required a technology that was not well developed, Medtronic would shelve the idea, preferring to wait until the approach had been developed and proven in other markets. The Product Specification was prepared during this phase, and consistency with the Product Description was verified.

The major executive review came after the demonstration phase, where the proposed product's technological potential, competitive activity and market needs, and its volume, profit and return on investment projections were rigorously reviewed. "I call this our *Commitment*

Review," noted Mahle. "I believe that language conveys intent. We had been plagued by waffling and compromise, and weren't doing what we said we would do." At one commitment review on a critical product, in fact, Mahle asked the team to stand up and make a verbal pledge to deliver to the customers and patients what they had said they would. "I believe in the power of personal commitment. Management tools are important, but tools alone won't do it."

Following the commitment review, projects went into the *development*, or *commitment phase*, of the process. "In the first two phases we have a lot of product ideas falling out or getting canceled, because we decide the market or technology just isn't there," Stevens commented. "But once projects enter the commitment phase, we expect 100 percent of them to be technically and commercially successful. There is no narrowing of the funnel after that."

The Product Planning Team, which as noted earlier was responsible for establishing the product line architecture, also had responsibility for conducting the major phase reviews for each project.

5. Rhythm

"There's a lot of uncertainty in new product development," noted Stevens. "You don't want to create additional uncertainty by the way you manage. The more predictability you can build into the development environment, the more productive your efforts will be." Stevens implemented this philosophy in two steps. First, he and Mahle fixed a date each month, a year in advance, when phase reviews would be held. Project teams approaching a review milestone thus could always count on Mahle and Stevens being available to review their progress. Second, the management team established a schedule, far into the future, according to which new products would be developed and launched. "Of course, we don't know what these specific products will be," said Stevens. "But we know the technology will always change, and we know the competition will always be trying to get ahead. It's like publishing a train schedule. It helps people to know when the next projects are scheduled to leave the station."

In retrospect, one benefit of setting a "train schedule" in advance was that there was less clamoring amongst Medtronic's marketers to revise objectives to include additional functionality or features after projects had begun. "In our troubled days," recalled Mahle, "no one knew when the next project was going to be started, let alone finished. Because of this, whenever a competitor came out with something, or an important physician came up with an important new idea, our marketing people were desperate to revise the charter of the product currently under development, to include that feature. If they didn't get it on this train, when would they ever get it? Once we had a train schedule, they could relax. If we froze the spec and their feature or idea didn't make it on this one, they knew that in another 18–24 months, another train would be leaving the station, and they could get their idea on that one."

6. Market Inputs

Medtronic also systematized the ways in which the company got input from customers, by revitalizing two eight-person physician review boards that had previously been functioning but that had lost their impact on company policy, for each of Medtronic's pacemaker lines. These boards met twice each year to give inputs on the performance of existing models, and suggest what functionality and features the company might incorporate in new models. "A big challenge with these boards," noted Paula Skjefte, was that "there is a strong tendency just to have experts on our boards. Life would be easier if we did that, but we wouldn't be getting the whole picture. Joe Average Cardiologist only spends about 2 percent of his practice on pacemakers. He's just not interested in spending a whole day on our board advising us about pacemakers. We want to be able to satisfy all the customers, from the experts who want do their own programming, to the cardiologists who just want to get the pacemaker going with no hassle. Taking the pulse of the less demanding end of the market is actually a huge challenge." Once these boards were properly constituted and functioning, they became critical to Medtronic's ability to define the right pacing systems to meet clinical and customer needs.

RESULTS TO DATE

The result of the Medtronic team's efforts to put discipline into the Brady Pacing Division's product development operations have been remarkable, as summarized in **Exhibits 2** and **4.** The time required to develop new platform products was reduced by 75 percent between 1986 and 1996. Fully allocated product cost per unit fell 30 percent. Manufacturing defects per million units dropped by a factor of 4; and the number of field failures over the life of an implant dropped by 90 percent. And the company's share of the Brady Pacemaker market increased from 29 percent in 1986, to 51 percent in 1996. Medtronic was the leader in every segment of the market.

From July 1995 to July 1996, Medtronic replaced 100 percent of its products with new models. It was able to access every segment of the market, and became the highest-volume competitor in each—with ten derivative products built around a single-platform technology.

"What's interesting," Paula Skjefte observed, "is now to see some of our competitors doing the same thing as we did in the past. There is a vicious cycle that almost got us, and is starting to hurt them. It looks like this: 1) When their share starts to decline, they start arguing over what needs to be done and how to do it. They start more and more projects into the system, to placate these diverse opinions. 2) Because they aren't focused, it causes delays, and Medtronic gets its product out first. 3) They have to redirect their project to respond to our product, which slows them down. 4) They panic because we are getting way ahead, and try to make sure that the flagship product they are trying to launch has all the features and functions that will boost it ahead of the competition. 5) This takes even longer—forcing them either to introduce products that are not functionally competitive, or to rush something into the market that is potentially faulty, just to get something out there. 6) The effect of this is that they spend all the money required to develop and launch products, but it is wasted because it does not generate profitable revenue."

Stevens added, "People ask us what the secret is, to make a development organization work effectively. I tell them there aren't any magic bullets that kill the problems. It's just discipline. You need to do what you say needs to be done. You need to be in it for the long haul. There are no quick fixes. It's interesting how many people leave these conversations and then go off in search of an easier answer from some guru somewhere. It's amazing that the obvious isn't so obvious."

Challenges for the Future

Success brought a new set of challenges to the Medtronic team, however. Internally, it was becoming clear that the job of changing company practices and culture would never be finished. Stevens noted, for example, that Medtronic's career path system constituted one of the most vexing challenges to implementing improvements. "When your best people are moving on every two or three years, you can never just sit back and say, 'It's working.'

Because we're always losing the people we've trained, the understanding of what we're doing and why we're doing it has a very short half-life. We have to keep training and teaching and coaching. I suppose that someday these values and processes will become so ingrained that working this way will just be a part of our culture. But we sure aren't there yet. And probably by the time it gets deeply ingrained here, we'll need to unlearn this because something even better has come along."

"The new marketing challenges are formidable as well," Skjefte remarked. "We've always measured the performance of our products in terms of their therapeutic benefit—the extent to which the pacemaker can mimic the normal functioning of the heart's electrical system. Now we have dual-chamber pacemakers whose rate varies with the patient's activity, whose batteries have a life far longer than the life expectancy of most implant recipients. Fifteen years ago pacemakers were not programmable. Today, our most advanced models have 200 parameters, which can be reprogrammed non-invasively using RF (radio frequency) technology. Today our models can sense and store all kinds of data about irregularities and other abnormal events in a patient's heart. Doctors can download this data with RF technology, simply by placing a device near the patient's chest. How much more do we need? I worry that we're getting to the point that 'better' will no longer be valued as 'better' by the mainstream cardiologists. How do you develop a stream of improved products if customers are genuinely happy with the performance and features in the products that they have today? In the future we'll need to change the rules of the game. We've got to figure out how to add value in different ways."

"Catching up to competitors was a very different challenge than it is now, to stay a generation *ahead* of them—because now we're the ones needing to define what the product generations must be," Don Deyo added.

Fortunately for Medtronic, experts continued to forecast strong growth for the pacemaker market into the foreseeable future, thanks to the bulge in the population most likely to need pacemakers created by the aging of the relatively prosperous "baby boom" generation in Western Europe, Japan, and North America. In addition to this growth, the large potential markets for pacemakers in other parts of Asia, Latin America, and Eastern Europe, where economic growth was making advanced medical technology more affordable, defined even greater growth possibilities. This was especially true if the price of pacemakers (currently priced between $2,000 and $7,500, depending upon features and functionality) could be reduced significantly.

It also appeared in 1996 that the industry's competitive landscape had stabilized. Whereas fifteen firms had entered the world pacemaker industry between 1965 and 1980, by 1996 only five of them remained. Medtronic claimed half of the market; St. Jude Medical (formerly Siemens) held 23 percent; Sulzer Intermedics 11 percent; and Guidant (recently divested by Eli Lilly) and Biotronik, a German firm focusing primarily in developing regions of the world, each accounted for 8 percent). Though several of these competitors were reeling from the rapid pace of product development that Medtronic had set, they were capable companies with substantial financial depth. In North America in particular, efforts of managed care providers to purchase larger volumes from fewer, highly capable suppliers with broad product lines, had substantially raised the barriers to future would-be entrants into the industry.

"We've set some very different goals," added Steve Mahle. "We want to bring pacing to less developed countries. This will be a challenge to Medtronic, because our culture won't allow us to bring them substandard therapy just to make it affordable. We've got to find a way to bring them *appropriate* therapy at an affordable price. This will likely involve *very* advanced technology, and a massive effort at physician education. And we've got to figure out how to do all of this profitably.

"In developed countries, where we do 95 percent of our volume, our goal is to see that every patient has access not just to pacemaking therapy, but to *optimum* therapy—where the technology in their pacemakers is matched to their disease. For example, ten years ago only 30 percent of patients were receiving dual-chamber pacemakers. Today we're at 50 percent, but 70 percent really need them. This requires that we no longer just sell devices," Mahle continued. "We have to educate physicians, and help insurance providers understand that they should reimburse patients for devices that provide optimum therapy."

Skjefte described another dimension of the marketing challenge: "Now that we've taken the technological lead, we've got to work much more closely with our customers to understand how to make *them* more successful and profitable by using our products. This means not just the *physician* customers—cardiologists, electrophysiologists, and surgeons—but hospital management, payors, and buying groups."

Helping these customers become more profitable by using Medtronic devices loomed as a huge challenge, because the priority each placed on various aspects of a pacing system was different, and because the customers themselves often weren't structured to understand what was profitable for them. As an example, Medtronic had recently lost a major account, the Intermountain Cardiology Clinic in Salt Lake City, to a competitor that had undercut Medtronic's pacemaker price by nearly $1,000 per device. Although the Medtronic device was easier to program as the pacemaker was being installed, those responsible for maximizing the profitability of the clinic's "cath lab" (the operating room where pacemakers were implanted) determined that they would nonetheless maximize the cath lab's profitability by using the less expensive pacemaker.

The follow-up of patients with newly implanted pacemakers at this clinic was managed by a different out-patient profit center, however, and for *them,* use of the competing pacemaker proved much *more* expensive. All new pacemakers required some adjustments a few weeks after implantation, to address unique aspects of each patient's disease and lifestyle. Because Medtronic's product recorded data about the patient's heart functions within the pacemaker itself and allowed physicians to download and analyze this data and adjust the pacemaker easily through an RF device held close to the patient's chest, all necessary adjustments could be done in a single, 30-minute visit. The competitor's system, in contrast, required the patient to visit the out-patient clinic twice for adjustments, taking approximately 1.5 hours per visit. In addition, during the time between these visits (about two weeks) the patient had to carry a $500 "holter monitor" on his or her belt 24 hours per day, which recorded the heart functions as detected by a set of electrodes taped to the patient's chest. These additional monitoring and adjustment costs overwhelmed the money saved by purchasing the cheaper pacemaker. But because the savings and added expenses were incurred within two different profit centers of the clinic, it took enormous effort for Medtronic's salesforce to win back the business.

"These customers not only speak a different language than our traditional physician customers, but their knowledge and preferences are very heavily influenced by what pieces of the therapeutic puzzle they have responsibility for. Somehow we've got to restructure our sales and marketing teams to better understand and address their concerns."

APPENDIX: THE CARDIAC PACEMAKER

Rhythmic contractions of the heart that pump blood through the body are stimulated by electrical impulses from the nervous system. Cardiac pacemakers either supplement or entirely replace the heart's own malfunctioning electric system. The heart contains four chambers—the right and left atria (singular: atrium) and the right and left ventricles. Blood flows from the veins of the body into the right atrium where it collects, and then is pumped into the right ventricle. The blood is pumped from the right ventricle to the lungs to obtain oxygen, and is then pumped into the left ventricle. The blood, now refreshed with oxygen, is then pumped from the left ventricle through arteries to all parts of the body.

To initiate the proper sequence of contractions, a normal electrical impulse originates in the sinoatrial (SA) node in the right atrium. This impulse then spreads throughout both atria and stimulates atrial contraction. The electrical signal continues on to the ventricles through the atrioventricular (AV) node, which delays the signal approximately 1/10 of a second to allow for the ventricles to fill with blood. When the ventricles complete their contraction, the signal is initiated once again in the SA node, creating a steady rhythm of heart beats.

Heart conditions necessitating a cardiac pacemaker can result from malfunction in any stage of this electrical system. Problems usually arise within the SA node and/or the AV conduction pathways, resulting in a slow, fast, or irregular heart rhythm. When the SA node malfunctions, the proper electrical impulses will not be generated to contract the atria and the ventricles at correct intervals. Patients with this condition suffer from Sinus Bradycardia: Their hearts beat at a persistently slow rate. When the AV node and its neurological pathways malfunction, the electrical signal that has just stimulated atrial contraction is blocked from initiating ventricle contraction. Consequently, a patient suffering from atrioventricular blockage would have a normal atrial beat but the ventricular rate would be too slow.

As diagrammed below, the main body of the pacemaker is called the pulse generator, comprised primarily of electrical circuitry and the battery. An insulated wire called the lead connects this circuitry to the inside wall of one of the heart's chambers. The electrical impulse is created by the pulse generator and then delivered to the heart's muscle through the lead.

The first pacemakers employed a single-chamber system: They had one lead that was attached to the right ventricle. These devices paced the heart at a fixed rate (usually 70 to 80 beats per minute), independently of the heart's intrinsic rhythm and changes in body activity. Because the heart and the implantable pacemaker were operating independently, the pacing was called "asynchronous."

The next generation of single-chamber pacemakers, which Medtronic invented in the mid-1960s, paced the heart on "demand," meaning that if the heart beat on its own, the pacemaker did not send a pacing impulse to the heart.

In 1981, Intermedics Corporation, an industry entrant whose founders included several former Medtronic employees, introduced the first dual-chamber pacemaker. This design utilized two leads—one in the right atrium and one in the right ventricle, which could sense and record the activity of both chambers and make sure that their contractions were synchronized. The dual-chamber pacemaker was capable of varying the heart rate by sensing or "tracking" atrial activity and then pacing the ventricle accordingly. Synchronizing atrial-ventricular contractions afforded the patient more flexibility in activity.

Pacemakers were implanted beneath the patient's skin near the heart, in a relatively simple proceedure. Immediately prior to implantation, most pacemakers were placed in a programming device that typically sat on a table in the cath lab or operating room where the implantation was performed. This allowed the physician to program the firmware in the pacemaker so that the frequency of the pulses it generated and a number of other attributes of the device could be tailored to the needs of each individual patient.

The lead on the single-chamber design was implanted into the right ventricle relatively easily. Attaching the lead of the dual-chamber pacemaker, however, required much greater surgical skill, because the locations in the atrium were tricky to access, and attaching the lead to the smooth atrial chamber wall was difficult. This difficulty, coupled with its higher cost, had kept the dual-chamber pacemaker's share of the total market at about 20 percent throughout the 1980s, despite its superior functionality. Device and procedural innovations in the 1990s had reduced these barriers, however, so that use of dual-chamber devices became much more common.

The Cardiac Pacemaker

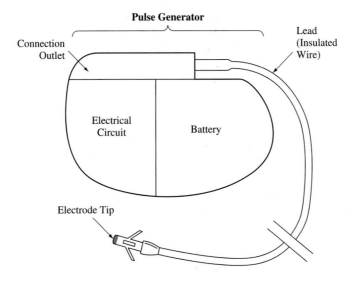

EXHIBIT 1
A Partial Organization Chart of Medtronic

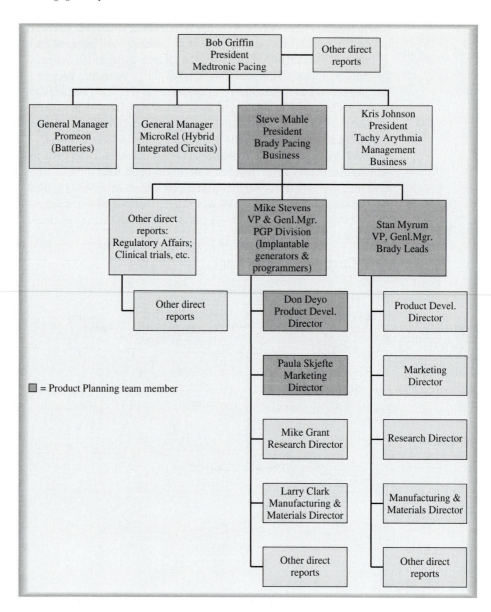

EXHIBIT 2
Changes in the Market Shares of Leading Pacemaker Manufacturers

Source: Casewriter's estimates, synthesized from data provided by the company, by investment analysts, and by David Gobeli and William Rudelius, in "Managing Innovation: Lessons from the Cardiac-Pacing Industry," *Sloan Management Review (26)*, Summer 1985, pp. 24–43.

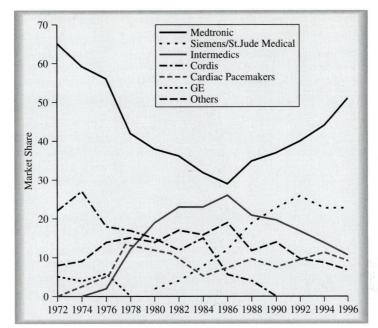

Note: Over this period, ownership of several of these companies changed hands. Intermedics was acquired by Sulzer in the early 1990s. St. Jude Medical acquired the pacemaker business of Siemens; and Cardiac Pacemakers, a division of Eli Lilly, was spun off along with other of Lilly's medical device companies, into an independent corporation called Guidant.

EXHIBIT 3
Process by Which New Product Concepts Were Defined at Medtronic

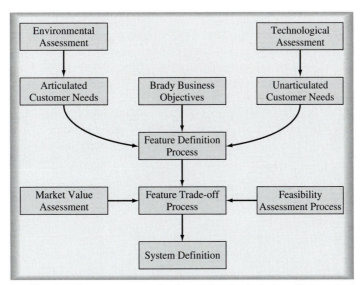

Note: Throughout this process, as customers' needs were balanced against business objectives and technological feasibility, the marketing members of the Medtronic development teams repeatedly sought customers' feedback to the trade-offs that were being contemplated.

EXHIBIT 4   Improvements in New Product Development Performance at Medtronic, 1986–1996

Year	Platform Name	Time* Req'd to Develop Platform	# of Derivative Models Designed from This Platform	Fully Allocated Manufacturing Cost* Per Unit	Manufacturing Defects* Per Million Units	Manufacturing Throughput Time (Days)
1986	Activitrax	160	1	140		30
1987						
1988						
1989						14
1990				120		
1991						
1992	Elite	140	1			
1993					270	
1994				110	150	8
1995	Thera	100	41	100	100	7

Note: To protect the company's proprietary interests, numbers in the third, fifth, and sixth columns, whose headings are denoted by an asterisk(*), are indexed, where 1995 = 100.

Article

Creating Project Plans to Focus Product Development

The long-term competitiveness of any manufacturing company depends ultimately on the success of its product development capabilities. New product development holds hope for improving market position and financial performance, creating new industry standards and new niche markets, and even renewing the organization. Yet few development projects fully deliver on their early promises. The fact is, much can and does go wrong during development. In some instances, poor leadership or the absence of essential skills is to blame. But often problems arise from the way companies approach the development process. They lack what we call an "aggregate project plan."

Consider the case of a large scientific instruments company we will call PreQuip. In mid-1989, senior management became alarmed about a rash of late product development projects. For some months, the development budget had been rising even as the number of completed projects declined. And many of the projects in the development pipeline no longer seemed to reflect the needs of the market. Management was especially troubled because it had believed its annual business plan provided the guidance that the marketing and engineering departments needed to generate and schedule projects.

To get to the root of the problem, the chief executive first asked senior managers to compile a list of all the current development projects. They discovered that 30 projects were under way—far more than anticipated, and, they suspected, far more than the organization could support. Further analysis revealed that the company had two to three times more development work than it was capable of completing over its three-year development planning horizon. (See **Exhibit 1,** "PreQuip's Development Predicament: Overcommitted Resources.")

With such a strain on resources, delays were inevitable. When a project ran into trouble, engineers from other projects were reassigned or, more commonly, asked to add the crisis

Steven C. Wheelwright and Kim B. Clark are both professors of business administration at the Harvard Business School, where they teach technology and operations management. This article is taken from their book, *Revolutionizing Product Development: Quantum Leaps in Speed, Efficiency, and Quality,* published by The Free Press in April 1992.

project to their already long list of active projects. The more projects they added, the more their productivity dropped. The reshuffling caused delays in other projects, and the effects cascaded. Furthermore, as deadlines slipped and development costs rose, project managers faced pressure to cut corners and compromise quality just to keep their projects moving forward.

The senior management team also discovered that the majority of PreQuip's development resources—primarily engineers and support staff—were not focused on the projects most critical to the business. When questioned, project leaders admitted that the strategic objectives outlined in the annual business plan had little bearing on project selection. Instead, they chose projects because engineers found the technical problems challenging or because customers or the marketing department requested them. PreQuip had no formal process for choosing among development projects. As long as there was money in the budget or the person making the request had sufficient clout, the head of the development department had no option but to accept additional project requests.

Many engineers were not only working on noncritical projects but also spending as much as 50 percent of their time on nonproject-related work. They responded to requests from manufacturing for help with problems on previous products, from field sales for help with customer problems, from quality assurance for help with reliability problems, and from purchasing for help with qualifying vendors. In addition to spending considerable time fixing problems on previously introduced products, engineers spent many hours in "information" and "update" meetings. In short, they spent too little time developing the right new products, experimenting with new technologies, or addressing new markets.

PreQuip's story is hardly unique. Most organizations we are familiar with spend their time putting out fires and pursuing projects aimed at catching up to their competitors. They have far too many projects going at once and all too often seriously overcommit their development resources. They spend too much time dealing with short-term pressures and not enough time on the strategic mission of product development.

Indeed, in most organizations, management directs all its attention to individual projects—it micromanages project development. But no single project defines a company's future or its market growth over time; the "set" of projects does. Companies need to devote more attention to managing the set and mix of projects. In particular, they should focus on how resources are allocated between projects. Management must plan how the project set evolves over time, which new projects get added when, and what role each project should play in the overall development effort.

The aggregate project plan addresses all of these issues. To create a plan, management categorizes projects based on the amount of resources they consume and on how they will contribute to the company's product line. Then, by mapping the project types, management can see where gaps exist in the development strategy and make more informed decisions about what types of projects to add and when to add them. Sequencing projects carefully, in turn, gives management greater control of resource allocation and utilization. The project map also reveals where development capabilities need to be strong. Over time, companies can focus on adding critical resources and on developing the skills of individual contributors, project leaders, and teams.

Finally, an aggregate plan will enable management to improve the way it manages the development function. Simply adding projects to the active list—a common practice at many companies—endangers the long-term health of the development process. Management needs to create a set of projects that is consistent with the company's development strategies rather than selecting individual projects from a long list of ad hoc proposals. And management must become involved in the development process before projects get started, even before they are fully defined. It is not appropriate to give one department—say, engineering or marketing—sole responsibility for initiating all projects because it is usually not in a position to determine every project's strategic worth.

Indeed, most companies—including PreQuip—should start the reformation process by eliminating or postponing the lion's share of their existing projects, eventually supplanting them with a new set of projects that fits the business strategy and the capacity constraints. The aggregate project plan provides a framework for addressing this difficult task.

HOW TO MAP PROJECTS

The first step in creating an aggregate project plan is to define and map the different types of development projects; defining projects by type provides useful information about how resources should be allocated. The two dimensions we have found most useful for classifying are the degree of change in the product and the degree of change in the manufacturing process. The greater the change along either dimension, the more resources are needed.

Using this construct, we have divided projects into five types. The first three—derivative, breakthrough, and platform—are commercial development projects. The remaining two categories are research and development, which is the precursor to commercial development, and alliances and partnerships, which can be either commercial or basic research. (See **Exhibit 2,** "Mapping the Five Types of Development Projects.")

Each of the five project types requires a unique combination of development resources and management styles. Understanding how the categories differ helps managers predict the distribution of resources accurately and allows for better planning and sequencing of projects over time. Here is a brief description of each category.

Derivative projects range from cost-reduced versions of existing products to add-ons or enhancements for an existing production process. For example, Kodak's wide-angle, single-use 35 mm camera, the Stretch, was derived from the no-frills Fun Saver introduced in 1990. Designing the Stretch was primarily a matter of changing the lens.

Development work on derivative projects typically falls into three categories: incremental product changes, say, new packaging or a new feature, with little or no manufacturing process change; incremental process changes, like a lower cost manufacturing process, improved reliability, or a minor change in materials used, with little or no product change; and incremental changes on both dimensions. Because design changes are usually minor, incremental projects typically are more clearly bounded and require substantially fewer development resources than the other categories. And because derivative projects are completed in a few months, ongoing management involvement is minimal.

Breakthrough projects are at the other end of the development spectrum because they involve significant changes to existing products and processes. Successful breakthrough projects establish core products and processes that differ fundamentally from previous generations. Like compact disks and fiber-optics cable, they create a whole new product category that can define a new market.

Because breakthrough products often incorporate revolutionary new technologies or materials, they usually require revolutionary manufacturing processes. Management should give development teams considerable latitude in designing new processes, rather than force them to work with existing plant and equipment, operating techniques, or supplier networks.

Platform projects are in the middle of the development spectrum and are thus harder to define. They entail more product and/or process changes than derivatives do, but they don't introduce the untried new technologies or materials that breakthrough products do. Honda's 1990 Accord line is an example of a new platform in the auto industry: Honda introduced a number of manufacturing process and product changes but no fundamentally new technologies. In the computer market, IBM's PS/2 is a personal computer platform; in consumer products, Procter & Gamble's Liquid Tide is the platform for a whole line of Tide brand products.

Well-planned and well-executed platform products typically offer fundamental improvements in cost, quality, and performance over preceding generations. They introduce improvements across a range of performance dimensions—speed, functionality, size, weight. (Derivatives, on the other hand, usually introduce changes along only one or two dimensions.) Platforms also represent a significantly better system solution for the customer. Because of the extent of changes involved, successful platforms require considerable upfront planning and the involvement of not only engineering but also marketing, manufacturing, and senior management.

Companies target new platforms to meet the needs of a core group of customers but design them for easy modification into derivatives through the addition, substitution, or removal of features. Well-designed platforms also provide a smooth migration path between generations so neither the customer nor the distribution channel is disrupted.

Consider Intel's 80486 microprocessor, the fourth in a series. The 486 introduced a number of performance improvements; it targeted a core customer group—the high-end PC/workstation user—but variations addressed the needs of other users; and with software compatibility between the 386 and the 486, the 486 provided an easy migration path for existing customers. Over the life of the 486 platform, Intel will introduce a host of derivative products, each offering some variation in speed, cost, and performance and each able to leverage the process and product innovations of the original platform.

Platforms offer considerable competitive leverage and the potential to increase market penetration, yet many companies systematically underinvest in them. The reasons vary, but the most common is that management lacks an awareness of the strategic value of platforms and fails to create well-thought-out platform projects. To address the problem, companies should recognize explicitly the need for platforms and develop guidelines for making them a central part of the aggregate project plan.

Research and development is the creation of the know-how and know-why of new materials and technologies that eventually translate into commercial development. Even though R&D lies outside the boundaries of commercial development, we include it here for two reasons: it is the precursor to product and process development; and, in terms of future resource allocation, employees move between basic research and commercial development. Thus R&D projects compete with commercial development projects for resources. Because R&D is a creative, high-risk process, companies have different expectations about results and different strategies for funding and managing it than they do for commercial development. These differences can indeed be great, but a close relationship between R&D and commercial development is essential to ensure an appropriate balance and a smooth conversion of ideas into products.

Alliances and partnerships, which also lie outside the boundaries of the development map, can be formed to pursue any type of project—R&D, breakthrough, platform, or derivative. As such, the amount and type of development resources and management attention needed for projects in this category can vary widely.

Even though partnerships are an integral part of the project development process, many companies fail to include them in their project planning. They often separate the management of partnerships from the rest of the development organization and fail to provide them with enough development resources. Even when the partner company takes full responsibility for a project, the acquiring company must devote in-house resources to monitor the project, capture the new knowledge being created, and prepare for the manufacturing and sales of the new product.

All five development categories are vital for creating a development organization that is responsive to the market. Each type of project plays a different role; each requires different levels and mixes of resources; and each generates very different results. Relying on only one or two categories for the bulk of the development work invariably leads to suboptimal use of resources, an unbalanced product offering, and eventually, a less than competitive market position.

PREQUIP'S PROJECT MAP

Using these five project types, PreQuip set about changing its project mix as the first step toward reforming the product development process. It started by matching its existing project list to the five categories. PreQuip's product line consisted of four kinds of analytic instruments—mass spectrometers, gas and liquid chromatographs, and data handling and processing equipment—that identified and isolated chemical compounds, gases, and liquids. Its customers included scientific laboratories, chemical companies, and oil refineries—users that needed to measure and test accurately the purity of raw materials, intermediate by-products, and finished products.

PreQuip's management asked some very basic questions in its attempt to delineate the categories. What exactly was a breakthrough product? Would a three-dimensional graphics display constitute a breakthrough? How was a platform defined? Was a full-featured mass spectrometer considered a platform? How about a derivative? Was a mass spectrometer with additional software a derivative?

None of these questions was easy to answer. But after much analysis and debate, the management team agreed on the major characteristics for each project type and assigned most of PreQuip's 30 projects to one of the five categories. The map revealed just how uneven the distribution of projects had become—for instance, less than 20 percent of the company's projects were classified as platforms. (See **Exhibit 3**, "Before: PreQuip's Development Process Was Chaotic. . . .")

Management then turned its attention to those development projects that did not fit into any category. Some projects required substantial resources but did not represent breakthroughs. Others were more complicated than derivative projects but did not fall into PreQuip's definition of platforms. While frustrating, these dilemmas opened managers' eyes to the fact that some projects made little strategic sense. Why spend huge amounts of money developing products that at best would produce only incremental sales? The realization triggered a reexamination of PreQuip's customer needs in all product categories.

Consider mass spectrometers, instruments that identify the chemical composition of a compound. PreQuip was a top-of-the-line producer of mass spectrometers, offering a whole series of high-performance equipment with all the latest features but at a significant price premium. While this strategy had worked in the past, it no longer made sense in a maturing market; the evolution of mass spectrometer technology was predictable and well defined, and many competitors were able to offer the same capabilities, often at lower prices.

Increasingly, customers were putting greater emphasis on price in the purchasing decision. Some customers also wanted mass spectrometers that were easier to use and modular so they could be integrated into their own systems. Others demanded units with casings that could withstand harsh industrial environments. Still others required faster operating speeds, additional data storage, or self-diagnostic capabilities.

Taking all these customer requirements into account, PreQuip used the project map to rethink its mass spectrometer line. It envisaged a single platform complemented with a series of derivative products, each with a different set of options and each serving a different customer niche. By combining some new product design ideas—modularity and simplicity—with some features that were currently under development, PreQuip created the concept of the C-101 platform, a low-priced, general-purpose mass spectrometer. In part because of its modularity, the product was designed to be simpler and cheaper to manufacture, which also helped to improve its overall quality and reliability. By adding software and a few new features, PreQuip could easily create derivatives, all of which could be assembled and tested on a single production line. In one case, a variant of the C-101 was planned for the high-end laboratory market. By strengthening the casing and eliminating some features, PreQuip also created a product for the industrial market.

Mapping out the new mass spectrometer line and the three other product lines was not painless. It took a number of months and involved a reconceptualization of the product lines, close management, and considerable customer involvement. To provide additional focus, PreQuip separated the engineering resources into three categories: basic R&D projects; existing products and customers, now a part of the manufacturing organization; and commercial product development.

To determine the number of breakthrough, platform, derivative, and partnered projects that could be sustained at any time, the company first estimated the average number of engineering months for each type of project based on past experience. It then allocated available engineering resources according to its desired mix of projects: about 50 percent to platform projects, 20 percent to derivative projects, and 10 percent each to breakthrough projects and partnerships. PreQuip then selected specific projects, confident that it would not overallocate its resources.

In the end, PreQuip canceled more than two-thirds of its development projects, including some high-profile pet projects of senior managers. When the dust had settled in mid-1990, PreQuip had just eleven projects: three platforms, one breakthrough, three derivatives, one partnership, and three projects in basic R&D. (See **Exhibit 4**, ". . . After: PreQuip's Development Process Was Manageable.")

The changes led to some impressive gains: between 1989 and 1991, PreQuip's commercial development productivity improved by a factor of three. Fewer projects meant more actual work got done, and more work meant more products. To avoid overcommitting resources and to improve productivity further, the company built a "capacity cushion" into its plan. It assigned only 75 full-time-equivalent engineers out of a possible 80 to the 8 commercial development projects. By leaving a small percent of development capacity uncommitted, PreQuip was better prepared to take advantage of unexpected opportunities and to deal with crises when they arose.

FOCUS ON THE PLATFORM

PreQuip's development map served as a basis for reallocating resources and for rethinking the mix of projects. Just as important, however, PreQuip no longer thought about projects in isolation; breakthrough projects shaped the new platforms, which defined the derivatives. In all four product lines, platforms played a particularly important role in the development strategy. This was not surprising considering the maturity of PreQuip's industry. For many companies, the more mature the industry, the more important it is to focus on platform projects.

Consider the typical industry life cycle. In the early stages of growth, innovative, dynamic companies gain market position with products that have dramatically superior performance along one or two dimensions. Whether they know it or not, these companies employ a breakthrough-platform strategy. But as the industry develops and the opportunity for breakthrough products decreases—often because the technology is shared more broadly—competitors try to satisfy increasingly sophisticated customers by rapidly making incremental improvements to existing products. Consciously or not, they adopt a strategy based on derivative projects. As happened with PreQuip, this approach ultimately leads to a proliferation of product lines and overcommitment of development resources. The solution lies in developing a few well-designed platform products, on each of which a generation of products can be built.

In the hospital bed industry, for example, companies that design, manufacture, sell, and service electric beds have faced a mature market for years. They are constantly under pressure to help their customers constrain capital expenditures and operating costs. Technologies are stable and many design changes are minor. Each generation of product typically lasts 8 to 12 years, and companies spend most of their time and energy developing derivative products. As a result, companies find themselves with large and unwieldy product lines.

In the 1980s, Hill-Rom, a leading electric-bed manufacturer, sought a new product strategy to help contain costs and maintain market share. Like other bed makers, its product development process was reactive and mired in too many low-payoff derivative projects. The company would design whatever the customer—a single hospital or nursing home—wanted, even if it meant significant commitments of development resources.

The new strategy involved a dramatic shift toward leveraging development and manufacturing resources. Hill-Rom decided to focus on hospitals and largely withdraw from the nursing home segment, as well as limit the product line by developing two new platform products—the Centra and the Century. The Centra was a high-priced product with built-in electronic controls, including communications capabilities. The Century was a simpler, less complex design with fewer features. The products built off each platform shared common parts and manufacturing processes and provided the customer with a number of add-on options. By focusing development efforts on two platforms, Hill-Rom was able to introduce new technologies and new product features into the market faster and more systematically, directly affecting patient recovery and hospital staff productivity. This strategy led to a less chaotic development cycle as well as lower unit cost, higher product quality, and more satisfied customers.

For companies that must react to constant changes in fashion and consumer tastes, a different relationship between platform and derivative projects makes sense. For example, Sony has pioneered its "hyper-variety" strategy in developing the Walkman: it directs the bulk of its Walkman development efforts at creating derivatives, enhancements, hybrids, and line extensions that offer something tailored to every niche, distribution channel, and competitor's product. As a result, in 1990, Sony dominated the personal audio system market with over 200 models based on just three platforms.

Platforms are critical to any product development effort, but there is no one ideal mix of projects that fits all companies. Every company must pursue the projects that match its opportunities, business strategy, and available resources. Of course, the mix evolves over time as projects move out of development into production, as business strategies change, as new markets emerge, and as resources are enhanced. Management needs to revisit the project mix on a regular basis—in some cases every six months, in others, every year or so.

STEADY STREAM SEQUENCING: PREQUIP PLANS FUTURE DEVELOPMENT

Periodically evaluating the product mix keeps development activities on the right track. Companies must decide how to sequence projects over time, how the set of projects should evolve with the business strategy, and how to build development capabilities through such projects. The decisions about changing the mix are neither easy nor straightforward. Without an aggregate project plan, most companies cannot even begin to formulate a strategy for making those decisions.

PreQuip was no different. Before adopting an aggregate project plan, the company had no concept of project mix and no understanding of sequencing. Whenever someone with authority had an idea worth pursuing, the development department added the project to its active list. With the evolution of a project plan, PreQuip developed an initial mix and elevated the sequencing decision to a strategic responsibility of senior management. Management scheduled projects at evenly spaced intervals to ensure a "steady stream" of development projects. (See **Exhibit 5**, "PreQuip's Project Sequence.")

A representative example of PreQuip's new strategy for sequencing projects is its new mass spectrometer, or C series. Introduced into the development cycle in late 1989, the C-101 was the first platform conceived as a system built around the new modular design. Aimed at the middle to upper end of the market, it was a versatile, modular unit for the laboratory that incorporated many of the existing electro-mechanical features into the new software. The C-101 was scheduled to enter manufacturing prototyping in the third quarter of 1990.

PreQuip positioned the C-l/X, the first derivative of the C-101, for the industrial market. It had a rugged casing designed for extreme environments and fewer software features than the C-101. It entered the development process about the time the C-101 moved into manufacturing prototyping and was staffed initially with two designers whose activities on the C-101 were drawing to a close.

Very similar to the C-1/X was the C-1/Z, a unit designed for the European market; the C-1/X team was expanded to work on both the C-l/X and the C-1/Z. The C-1/Z had some unique software and a different display and packaging but the same modular design. PreQuip's marketing department scheduled the C-101 to be introduced about six months before the C-l/X and the C-1/Z, thus permitting the company to reach a number of markets quickly with new products.

To leverage accumulated knowledge and experience, senior management assigned the team that worked on the C-l/X and the C-l/Z to the C-201 project, the next-generation spectrometer scheduled to replace the C-101. It too was of a modular design but with more computer power and greater software functionality. The C-201 also incorporated a number of manufacturing process improvements gleaned from manufacturing the C-101.

To provide a smooth market transition from the C-101 to the C-201, management assigned the remainder of the C-101 team to develop the C-101X, a follow-on derivative project. The C-101X was positioned as an improvement over the C-101 to attract customers who were in the market for a low-end mass spectrometer but were unwilling to settle for the aging technology of the C-101. Just as important, the project was an ideal way to gather market data that could be used to develop the C-201.

PreQuip applied this same strategy across the other three product categories. Every other year it planned a new platform, followed by two or three derivatives spaced at appropriate intervals. Typically, when a team finished work on a platform, management assigned part of the team to derivative projects and part to other projects. A year or so later, a new team would form to work on the next platform, with some members having worked on the preceding generation and others not. This steady stream sequencing strategy worked to improve the company's overall market position while encouraging knowledge transfer and more rapid, systematic resource development.

AN ALTERNATIVE: SECONDARY WAVE PLANNING

While the steady stream approach served PreQuip well, companies in different industries might consider alternative strategies. For instance, a "secondary wave" strategy may be more appropriate for companies that, like Hill-Rom, have multiple product lines, each with their own base platforms but with more time between succeeding generations of a particular platform.

The strategy works like this. A development team begins work on a next-generation platform. Once the company completes that project, the key people from the team start work on another platform for a different product family. Management leaves the recently introduced platform on the market for a couple of years with few derivatives introduced. As that platform begins to age and competitors' newer platforms challenge it, the company refocuses development resources on a set of derivatives in order to strengthen and extend the viability of the product line's existing platform. The wave of derivative projects extends the platform life and upgrades product offerings, but it also provides experience and feedback to the people working on the product line and prepares them for the next-generation platform development. They receive feedback from the market on the previous platform, information on competitors' platform offerings, and information on emerging market needs. Key people then bring that information together to define the next platform and the cycle begins again, built around a team, many of whose members have just completed the wave of derivative products.

A variation on the secondary wave strategy, one used with considerable success by Kodak, involves compressing the time between market introduction of major platforms. Rather than going off to work on another product family's platform following one platform's introduction, the majority of the development team goes to work immediately on a set of derivative products. This requires a more compressed and careful assessment of the market's response to the just-introduced platform and much shorter feedback loops regarding competitors' products. If done right, however, companies can build momentum and capture significant incremental market share. Once the flurry of derivative products has passed, the team goes to work on the next-generation platform project for the same product family.

Before 1987, Kodak conducted a series of advanced development projects to explore alternative single-use 35mm cameras—a roll of film packaged in an inexpensive camera. Once used, the film is processed and the camera discarded or recycled. During 1987, a group of Kodak development engineers worked on the first platform project which resulted in the market introduction and volume production of the Fling 35mm camera in January 1988. (The product was later renamed the Fun Saver.) As the platform neared completion, management reassigned the front-end development staff to two derivative projects: the Stretch, a panoramic, double-wide image version of the Fling, and the Weekend, a waterproof version.

By the end of 1988, Kodak had introduced both derivative cameras and was shipping them in volume. True to the definition of a derivative, both the Stretch and the Weekend took far fewer development resources and far less time than the Fling. They also required less new tooling and process engineering since they leveraged the existing automation and manufacturing process. The development team then went to work on the next-generation platform product—a Fun Saver with a built-in flash.

No matter which strategy a company uses to plan its platform-derivative mix—steady stream or secondary wave—it must have well-defined platforms. The most advanced companies further improve their competitive position by speeding up the rate at which they introduce new platforms. Indeed, in a number of industries we've studied, the companies that introduced new platforms at the fastest rate were usually able to capture the greatest market share over time.

In the auto industry, for example, different companies follow quite different sequencing schedules, with markedly different results. According to data collected in the late 1980s, European car companies changed the platform for a given product, on average, every twelve years, U.S. companies every eight years, and Japanese companies every four years. A number of factors explain the differences in platform development cycles—historical and cultural differences, longer development lead times, and differences in development productivity.[1]

In both Europe and the United States, the engineering hours and tooling costs of new products were much higher than in Japan. This translated into lower development costs for Japanese car makers, which allowed faster payback and shorter economic lives for all models. As a consequence, the Japanese could profitably conduct more projects and make more frequent and more extensive changes than both their European and U.S. competitors and thus were better positioned to satisfy customers' needs and capture market share.

THE LONG-TERM GOAL: BUILDING CRITICAL CAPABILITIES

Possibly the greatest value of an aggregate project plan over the long term is its ability to shape and build development capabilities, both individual and organizational. It provides a vehicle for training development engineers, marketers, and manufacturing people in the different skill sets needed by the company. For instance, some less experienced engineers initially may be better suited to work on derivative projects, while others might have technical skills more suited for breakthrough projects. The aggregate project plan lets companies play to employees' strengths and broaden their careers and abilities over time.

Thinking about skill development in terms of the aggregate project plan is most important for developing competent team leaders. Take, for instance, an engineer with five years of experience moving to become a project leader. Management might assign her to lead a derivative project first. It is an ideal training ground because derivative projects are the best defined, the least complex, and usually the shortest in duration of all project types. After the project is completed successfully, she might get promoted to lead a larger derivative project and then a platform project. And if she distinguishes herself there and has the other required skills, she might be given the opportunity to work on a breakthrough project.

In addition to creating a formal career path within the sphere of development activities, companies should also focus on moving key engineers and other development participants between advanced research and commercial development. This is necessary to keep the transfer of technology fresh and creative and to reward engineers who keep their R&D efforts focused on commercial developments.

Honda is one company that delineates clearly between advanced research and product development—the two kinds of projects are managed and organized differently and are approached with very different expectations. Development engineers tend to have broader skills, while researchers' are usually more specialized. However, Honda encourages its engineers to move from one type of project to another if they demonstrate an idea that management believes may result in a commercially viable innovation. For example, Honda's

---

[1] Based on research by Kim B. Clark and Takahiro Fujimoto. See their article, "The Power of Product Integrity," *Harvard Business Review*, November–December 1990, p. 107.

new lean-burning engine, introduced in the 1992 Civic, began as an advanced research project headed by Hideyo Miyano. As the project moved from research to commercial development, Miyano moved too, playing the role of project champion throughout the entire development process.

Besides improving people's skills, the aggregate project plan can be used to identify weaknesses in capabilities, improve development processes, and incorporate new tools and techniques into the development environment. The project plan helps identify where companies need to make changes and how those changes are connected to product and process development.

As PreQuip developed an aggregate project plan, for example, it identified a number of gaps in its capabilities. In the case of the mass spectrometer, the demand for more software functionality meant PreQuip had to develop an expertise in software development. And with an emphasis on cost, modularity, and reliability, PreQuip also had to focus on improving its industrial design skills.

As part of its strategy to improve design skills, the company introduced a new computer-aided design system into its engineering department, using the aggregate project plan as its guide. Management knew that one of the platform project teams was particularly adept with computer applications, so it chose that project as the pilot for the new CAD system. Over the life of the project, the team's proficiency with the new system grew. When the project ended, management dispersed team members to other projects so they could train other engineers in using the new CAD system.

As PreQuip discovered, developing an aggregate project plan involves a relatively simple and straightforward procedure. But carrying it out—moving from a poorly managed collection of ad hoc projects to a robust set that matches and reinforces the business strategy—requires hard choices and discipline.

At all the companies we have studied, the difficulty of those choices makes imperative strong leadership and early involvement from senior management. Without management's active participation and direction, organizations find it next to impossible to kill or postpone projects and to resist the short-term pressures that drive them to spend most of their time and resources fighting fires.

Getting to an aggregate project plan is not easy, but working through the process is a crucial part of creating a sustainable development strategy. Indeed, while the specific plan is extremely important, the planning process itself is even more so. The plan will change as events unfold and managers make adjustments. But choosing the mix, determining the number of projects the resources can support, defining the sequence, and picking the right projects raise crucial questions about how product and process development ought to be linked to the company's competitive opportunities. Creating an aggregate project plan gives direction and clarity to the overall development effort and helps lay the foundation for outstanding performance.

EXHIBIT 1
PreQuip's
Development
Predicament:
Overcommitted
Resources

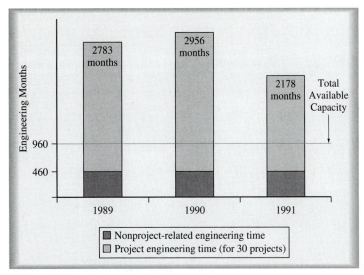

PreQuip had 960 engineering months each year to allocate to development work. But combining the time it would take to keep its current 30 projects on schedule with the time engineers spent doing nonproject development work, the company found it had overcommitted its development resources for the next three years by a factor of three.

EXHIBIT 2
Mapping the
Five Types of
Development
Projects

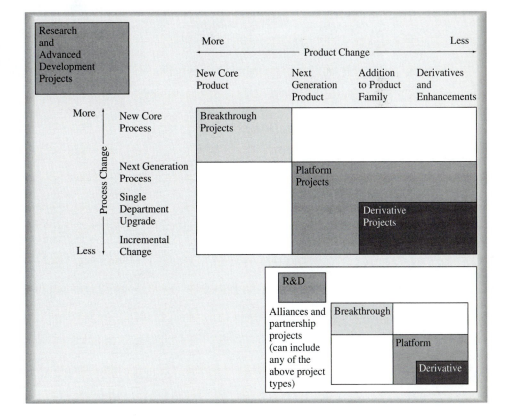

EXHIBIT 3

**Before:
PreQuip's
Development
Process Was
Chaotic ...**

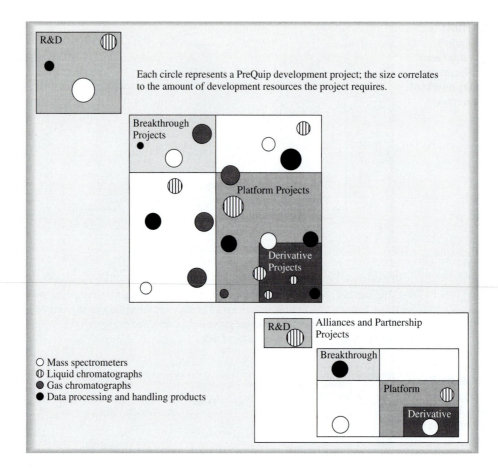

Each circle represents a PreQuip development project; the size correlates to the amount of development resources the project requires.

R&D

Breakthrough Projects

Platform Projects

Derivative Projects

R&D

Alliances and Partnership Projects

Breakthrough

Platform

Derivative

○ Mass spectrometers
◍ Liquid chromatographs
◕ Gas chromatographs
● Data processing and handling products

EXHIBIT 4
. . . After:
PreQuip's
Development
Process Was
Manageable

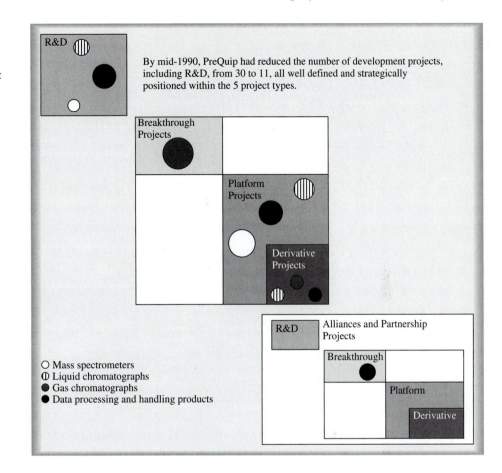

By mid-1990, PreQuip had reduced the number of development projects, including R&D, from 30 to 11, all well defined and strategically positioned within the 5 project types.

○ Mass spectrometers
⦶ Liquid chromatographs
● Gas chromatographs
● Data processing and handling products

EXHIBIT 5   **PreQuip's Project Sequence**

Project Type	Development Resources Committed at Mid-1990 (% of Total Engineering Time)	Project Description	Project Number	Sequencing 1990 — 1991
R&D	(Separate)	Advanced pump	RD-1	———————— ——————→
		Electronic sensors	RD-2	————————————
		Software	RD-3	————————
Breakthrough	12.5%	Fully automated self-diagnostic system for gas chromatograph	BX-3	————————————
Platform	52.5	Liquid chromatograph	A series	A-502 ——————→
		Gas chromatograph	B series	B-502
		Mass spectrometer	C series	C-101 C-201
		Data processing and handling equipment	D series	DX-52 DX-82 ——→
Derivative	18.75	Liquid chromatograph	A series	A-311 A-321 A-502X
		Gas chromatograph	B series	B-22 B-32
		Mass spectrometer	C series	C-1/X C-1/Z C-101X
		Data processing and handling equipment	D series	D-333 D-433
Partnership	10.0	Medical/chemical diagnostic system	VMH	————————————

Case **3-3**

Siemens AG: Global Development Strategy

It was the spring of 2000, but even under the afternoon shade of the palm trees at the Oberoi hotel in Bangalore, South India, it felt like summer. Horst Eberl sat contemplating the recommendations that he and his subdivisional co-head, Karl-Friedrich Hunke, would be preparing for the Siemens Information and Communications Networks (ICN) management board. Things were neat, tidy, and cool on this grassy side of the hotel. Just outside the main walls however lay the dust, pollution, and confusion of the Indian traffic. And if one took life in one's hands by darting through the traffic, across the street lay Siemens' regional development center in India, scattered among floors rented in three different office buildings. Two backup power generators, as well as battery backup for all computers, helped ensure a reliable infrastructure for the 600 personnel here.

What vexed Eberl and Hunke was that Deutsche Telekom, Siemens ICN's largest customer, was upset because of slow product delivery on a new telecommunications software product, the so-called NetManager. For a variety of reasons the project had rapidly mushroomed in size and scope beyond what had been initially envisioned. To solve the problem, Eberl, co-head of ICN's largest subdivision, had to travel some 7000 kilometers to this dusty corner of the world: despite the conveniences of e-mail, telephone, and fax, there was little substitute for face-to-face interaction.

The Germans and Indians regarded each other with mutual respect and camaraderie. The Indians marveled at the meticulousness of the Germans, which had allowed them over four decades to assemble one of the world's finest telecommunications systems. The Germans, in turn, appreciated the diligence and enthusiasm of Indian employees. Yet, both sides did at times find fault with each other. Quite often the Indians appeared more interested in pursuing entrepreneurial jobs rather than in working in one corner of the vast Siemens machine. And to the Indians, the Germans sometimes appeared disloyal by refusing to cancel pre-arranged long vacations at junctions critical to a project.

The Indians' lack of experience with large telecommunications systems had led them to make several wrong assumptions about the current project. Would more personal interaction

Harvard Business School Case No. 9-602-061. Copyright 2001 President and Fellows of Harvard College. All rights reserved. For information: permissions@hbsp.harvard.edu.

This case was prepared by Stefan Thomke and Ahok Nimgade. HBS cases are developed solely for class discussion and do not necessarily illustrate effective or ineffective management.

between the Munich headquarters and Bangalore throughout the project have prevented problems from escalating to this point? Or perhaps, the Indians simply needed more time and project autonomy before graduating to a Center of Competence—the highest distinction of experience and technical competence within the global Siemens R&D network. Solving the current crisis would pave the way for smoother R&D management across national borders in the rapidly changing field of telecommunications equipment. It could also help point out the direction for future growth of the Indian division, by now ICN's third-largest regional development center outside Germany.

TELECOMMUNICATIONS SYSTEMS: THE INVISIBLE HAND

Telecommunications systems of the turn-of-the-millennium would have evoked far stronger emotions than 167 years ago, when Samuel Morse ushered in the telegraph era of telecommunications with the words "What hath God wrought!" Over the decades, millions of engineering hours and thousands of patents had gone into creating systems that could automatically connect telephone calls via digital "carrier switches." These systems rapidly "routed" a call over a complex network of telephone lines in an optimal manner, while keeping track of each call for billing purposes. Consumers enjoyed low costs thanks to innovations such as digital switching and allowing dozens of conversations to be transmitted simultaneously over a single telephone line. Equally miraculous was the systems' reliability that allowed telephone users to take the presence of a dial tone for granted. Such was hardly the case decades earlier, or even in contemporary third world nations. (See **Exhibit 1** for background on the early history of telecommunications.)

Large telecommunications systems operated smoothly thanks to their installation and maintenance by multinational giants such as Siemens, Lucent, Ericsson, and Alcatel. A telephone system had hundreds if not thousands of different features, most of which were invisible to casual users but not to the large and often national telephone operators that ran these systems around the globe. For decades, providers of these large systems enjoyed a cozy relationship with their traditional customers, relationships that often outlasted the up to 30-year lifespan of a telephony system.

In the mid-1990s, telecommunications had reached a new inflection point. The Internet now allowed for the revolutionary possibility of voice and data transmitted over the same broadband lines using the same protocols. Phone calls or faxes were traditionally handled over telephone lines but could possibly be handled much more cheaply over data lines and lower cost equipment employed for computer networks (see **Exhibit 2** for information on service transaction cost). Siemens and other major telecommunications companies remained aware that over the next five to ten years, Internet-based voice transmission could dominate their industry if quality and reliability problems were solved. Already, the upcoming market fielded new terms such as "Voice over Internet Protocol (IP)" and customers could place telephone calls using their personal computers. Many at Siemens feared that the leap from old to new might prove too large for a company that, by admission of a U.S. board member himself, people viewed as a "slow-moving dinosaur."[1]

[1] M. Reardon, "Siemens' Haunted History—As the Company Shapes Its Future, It's Still Forced to Confront Its Past." Data Communications, August 7, 1999,

BUILDING AN INDUSTRIAL GIANT

In 1847 in Germany, Werner Siemens and J. Halske founded what was to be known as Siemens to manufacture and install telegraphic systems.[2] Early orders came from Germany, Russia, and England, with the company's London branch even helping lay the first deep-sea telegraphic cables connecting England with America as well as India. Over the years, the Siemens family capitalized on several emerging technologies ranging from the telephone to electric power generation to the X-ray tube, laying the foundation for the company's continued presence in these areas and leading *Fortune* magazine to typify Siemens' strategy as "second is best." The company was quick to produce an improved and patented version of Alexander Graham Bell's telephone. In 1909, the company built an automatic telephone exchange to serve Munich's 2500 telephone users.

The independence of Siemens's foreign subsidiaries was reinforced during World War I, when the British nationalized (temporarily) the London branch and Bolsheviks likewise appropriated the St. Petersburg branch. Throughout the twentieth century, however, Siemens continued its international growth, with its presence extending even as far as Mars, through development of space probe technologies for NASA. Siemens dominated in areas such as telecommunications, medical technology, data-processing systems, manufacture of heavy electrical equipment, nuclear plants, and railroad equipment. The company had developed a legendary ability to manage large, complex projects and prided itself on quality and durability—its early mobile telephones, for instance, could still function after being hurled across a room at a wall. By 2000, Siemens was one of the top five electronics and electrical engineering companies in the world, with annual revenues exceeding 130 billion Euros.[3] It could boast some 464,000 employees scattered across 190 countries, with 57,000 employees dedicated to R&D alone. In 2000, Siemens held some 120,000 patent rights and spent over 10 billion Euros on research and development. Its largest group, Information and Communications Networks (ICN), employed 53,000 people, operated in 160 countries, and had headquarters that spread over dozens of buildings at two fenced sites in suburban Munich, Germany (see **Exhibits 3** to **5** for financials and corporate structure).

Siemens expanded its markets on the basis of technological competence and close relations with large customers rather than aggressive marketing. Its conservatism extended even to consumer financing. "Siemens historically has guarded its credit rating," according to Peter Kröbel, a U.S.-based director of international business development. This approach had kept the company from falling prey to traps such as extending credit to unstable Latin American nations as well as aggressive Internet-related acquisitions that had ensnared many of its rivals.

In the 1990s, with a worldwide wave of deregulation affecting various industries including telecommunications, Siemens could no longer rely as heavily on its traditional relationships with large customers. With computer and telecommunications industries changing rapidly, productivity gains of as much as 10 percent a year were often canceled out by price declines. 1998 marked a crisis point when net income slumped two-thirds from

---

[2] Much of the early company history draws from "Siemens A.G." Mirabile, L. (Ed.) *International Directory of Company Histories,* V.II, Chicago and London: St. James Press, 1990.

[3] While the exchange rate between the Euro, German mark, and U.S. dollar fluctuated, the following rate roughly applied: 2 DM = 1 Euro = 0.90 US$.

a 1996 peak of $1.36 billion. Siemens CEO von Pierer acknowledged that "In Germany, competition was like a wind. Now, it's a storm. And it will become a hurricane!"[4]

Industry observers often linked the company's challenges to its geographic location: "Siemens' problems are Germany's problems. Its faults were typical of dozens of German manufacturers: great engineers, iffy marketing. High labor costs and taxes. Overregulation. Complacency after years of government coddling."[5] In response, Siemens shed some of the traditional German consensus-building style in favor of a U.S.-style of management that by CEO von Pierer's own admission was based on the General Electric model. The company officially launched a ten-point plan that called for, among other things: divesting poor-performing units in favor of strengthening remaining businesses with the potential to become world leaders in their field; setting tougher profit targets for managers; tying as much as 60 percent of managers' pay to performance; trimming the high-cost German workforce and management by as much as a third; reducing overtime pay; adopting U.S. accounting principles; and more aggressively incorporating marketing into its product development processes.

Amid this painful transition, the company bet much of its future on the vast but volatile telecommunications market as firms scrambled to build next-generation mobile networks and upgraded their networks to handle broadband multimedia services. With hundreds of billions of dollars at stake, players in this field faced costly consequences for misreading technology shifts. A conglomerate such as Siemens would have to battle New World telecom stars such as Nokia and Cisco (see **Exhibits 6a** and **6b** for switching equipment competitors and markets). By early 2000, von Pierer's strategic shifts appeared to have reaped dividends. Led in part by the mobile-phone business, its net income doubled in the first quarter of 2000 to $694 million on sales of $17 billion. A weak Euro had further helped by making its products cheaper overseas. Noticeably, the software component to Siemens' projects had grown to account for almost a fourth of its revenues now.

In the United States, Siemens now became the largest foreign employer, with 73,000 people employed at 700 locations in all 50 states. Thanks to its acquisition of Westinghouse, its products accounted for nearly half the U.S. power generation. In contrast, the ICN division's 10 percent market share was well below its 25 percent share of the world's telecommunications systems. As a result, the company sought to bolster its American presence through a series of strategic acquisitions such as Unisphere Networks. Like many very large firms, however, Siemens was still burdened with too many middle managers who resisted changes necessary in a rapidly changing industry.

SIEMENS INFORMATION AND COMMUNICATION NETWORKS (ICN)

Siemens ICN represented a natural outgrowth of Siemens' work in telegraphy and telephony. ICN could offer entire nations turnkey telecommunications switching systems based around its flagship product "EWSD,"[6] the best selling and most reliable telecommunications switch in the world. Each EWSD resembled a steel frame the size of a walk-in closet, with hundreds of horizontal slots containing removable modules (see **Exhibit 7**). An EWSD was

---

[4] J. Ewing, "Siemens Climbs Back: The German Electronics Giant Has Embraced Speed, Innovation, and the Art of Pleasing Customers," *BusinessWeek* (International Edition), June 5, 2000.

[5] Ibid.

[6] German acronym of *Elektronisches Wählsystem Digital* (in English: "Electronic Switching System Digital").

scaleable to accommodate all switching needs in the range of up to 240,000 telephone lines (or "ports"). Hence, it could cost anywhere between $500,000 and $10 million, with a marginal cost of up to $100 per port.

Although the EWSD did not represent a pioneering effort, it demonstrated the ability of Siemens to be a fast and very successful follower. The technology had started out in the early 1980s as a hybrid analog-digital switching system (which in turn grew out of the EWSA, where the "A" stood for "analog"). In 1981, because of technology breakthroughs by competitors such as AT&T, Siemens piloted its first hybrid switch in faraway South Africa. Despite advances in digital semiconductor technology in the early 1980s, the company hedged its bets by sticking to its hybrid approach, which relied on its decades-old expertise with electromechanical systems.

Then, one Friday afternoon in 1983, in a move highly unusual for Siemens, the head of ICN summoned all 1500 developers for an emergency meeting in the cafeteria, the only place where everyone could fit. He announced: "Stop all your work! As of today, all work on mechanical switches will cease; henceforth we will undertake only work on digital systems." The announcement sent shockwaves throughout the multinational corporation used to a more gradual, consensus-based approach to technological change.

Altogether, over the next two decades, Siemens ICN invested over 30,000 staff years to create the fully digital EWSD. Its bold move of 1983 was to pay off handsomely. By 2000, ICN equipment controlled almost 300 million telephone lines and routed one in five phone calls worldwide. In its homeland Germany alone, EWSDs controlled almost 50 million telephone lines—representing two-thirds of the German market. Telecommunications systems had to provide a reliability of 99.999 percent (referred to as the "five nines"), with a downtime of under five minutes per switch per year. Not surprisingly, the "fifth nine" was the hardest to achieve but also mattered the most to its large customers. To achieve this reliability while providing scores of new product features, ICN alone spent 270 million Euros on R&D per year.

EWSD hardware and software development followed a regular release cycle that was a major undertaking, utilizing up to 1,000 staff-years per release, with many subsystems developed from scratch. By the year 2000, ICN was already developing release 15.0, which would be made available to major customers around the world. Later system releases had offered new features such as voice recognition, traffic measurement, voice-mail boxes for end users, caller ID, and automatic dial back for missed calls. As a result of constant improvements, according to director of rapid prototyping Dr. Hermann Granzer, "even after a decade, at a customer's site an EWSD is similar to a brand new car with the new trunk, wheels, windows, and ignition system, and so on."

By 2000, three-fourths of ICN's 11 billion Euro revenues came from hardware and the remainder came from software. Siemens ICN employed about 53,000 people worldwide and was active in 160 countries where it sold telecommunications products with market cycles ranging from over a decade in third world nations such as Indonesia to as short as three months in Germany. Like its top competitors, ICN emphasized good service and maintained close links with its customers. It avoided outsourcing service work on its telecommunications systems to ensure the type of customer commitment that only its staff could provide over the years or decades to come. Its carrier switching (CS) subdivision, headed by Horst Eberl and Karl-Friedrich Hunke, accounted for roughly 25 percent of ICN's 11 billion Euro revenue and was the largest and most profitable unit (see **Exhibit 8** for ICN's organization).

To its wealthier customers in developed nations, Siemens offered almost yearly EWSD updates and other benefits such as free upgrades, discounts, or even free switches. For customers in developing nations, the most attractive offerings were reliability, durability, and prompt service. For many decades, Siemens even maintained at its Munich headquarters exact replicas of the large systems that it had installed in distant nations in order to expedite problem solving. Most field problems could be solved by customers reading through large product manuals, sometimes with help from local service teams. The harder problems would often have to be referred to any of Siemens' major R&D centers, a more expensive proposition, as it often pulled personnel away from new projects. The entire system of fault management was painstakingly monitored by "FEKAT," a proprietary fault management tool devised and honed by Siemens over the past two decades.

In many ways the traditional German system of work—long, if not lifetime, mutual commitment and loyalty on part of employer and employee—suited a large organization such as Siemens well. Individuals with this mindset would not mind dedicating their entire careers to tasks such as fault analysis monitoring or testing in a small corner of a giant ongoing system such as EWSD. A young employee could expect to work on an initial project lasting one to two years while being able to seek advice from a sea of experienced managers. The downside for employers was dealing with circumscribed workweeks and generous vacations. But as one manager himself put it, "Other people may live to work, but we Germans work to live!"

For Siemens ICN, however, gray clouds on the horizon loomed nearer with every year. Despite being a steady cash producer, EWSD faced a 0 percent growth rate in the developed world. By the mid-1990s, with the growing importance of the Internet, management realized that EWSD would ultimately die out. The speed with which the Internet would begin to replace traditional data transmission, however, would catch ICN and its competitors by surprise. "We always saw it as a niche market," according to board member Volker Jung.[7] Even industry veteran Horst Eberl admitted that "if transmission of voice over the Internet matches the quality and flexibility of regular telephone, EWSD will die." ICN, however, had no cash-out strategy except to sell as many EWSD units as it could, especially in fast growing developing markets such as China and Brazil. The company could also count on a large installed base that, especially in the developing world, might need servicing for years to come.

To prepare for the future, Siemens ICN launched a new hybrid platform named "SURPASS," which combined traditional EWSD and new broadband technology for data transmission that came in part from acquisitions in the U.S. Customers would be offered a very reliable and feature rich system solution that met all their data and voice transmission needs and thus resembled ICN's strategy during earlier technology shifts.

GLOBAL PRODUCT DEVELOPMENT AND PROJECT MANAGEMENT

Almost from its very inception Siemens viewed itself as a global organization. For two major reasons ICN conducted almost half its R&D efforts at 17 Regional Development Centers (RDCs) scattered across the globe (see **Exhibit 9** for locations). First, because of local labor shortages, ICN could simply not centralize all product development at Munich.

[7] W. Boston, "Too Big, Too Slow? Telecoms Titans Play Catchup on the Net(?)," *The Wall Street Journal,* Europe, March 15, 1999.

Second, having regionally based managers, engineers and technicians facilitated rapid response to local needs such as EWSD customization. A *de facto* partition thus emerged with Munich taking leadership for creating and maintaining new releases of the platform product (baseline projects) and some major RDCs focusing on customization projects and field service (customer projects). Baseline projects were partitioned into subprojects and then placed with regional centers under the project leadership in Munich. Over the years, however, Siemens had followed a strategy of shifting more autonomy to its regional centers to strengthen its global presence. An important consideration for increased autonomy was a center's technical and project management competence. As ICN's Carrier Switching co-head Hunke observed: "In contrast to developing consumer products, telecom system development requires long experience, deep technical skills and the ability to manage complex projects."

Out of a total of 60–70 customization projects per year, about 20 were self-financed by local companies' sales budgets and required no financial support. In such cases, technical managers would start by talking with customers in the early planning stages for new releases. Customers, in turn, gave new product feature "wish-lists," which often magically shrank in size after sales managers returned with a matching price estimate. Some leading customers served as test sites for new system features that gave ICN early feedback on problems.

Great variance existed between different centers: the Greek RDC, for instance, was flush with funds to the point of being able to buy out R&D centers from other companies; at the other extreme, the Hungarian RDC had plateaued in growth to sustain only 15–20 developers. The Indian RDC, though a relative newcomer, had grown to well over 600 people thanks to its access to a talented and inexpensive labor pool for software development. The Florida RDC was quite independent not only because it had been in operation for several decades but also because of its responsibility for North American marketing (see **Exhibit 10** for various cost comparisons between ICN's six largest RDCs).

Typically, German managers ran newly formed RDCs, but in later stages local managers gained more control. An ongoing tension was how much independence to provide each center: in general, the more customization an RDC provided for regional customers, the more independent it became. How much direction to provide developers working on subsystems in different RDCs also proved an ongoing issue. Having Munich specify all parameters of a project upfront decreased regional flexibility but ensured high product quality. In many projects involving a high degree of innovation, however, it was impossible to do so. Nor was this always desirable. As Dr. Jürgen Klunker, a deputy director in the Siemens Carrier Switching group, wryly observed: "A false sense of security can be created from specifying everything!"

Munich headquarters typically coordinated cooperation between RDCs through formal channels, including annual technical conferences at Munich involving representatives from different RDCs, as well as through facilitating informal, often serendipitous encounters between different RDC members at Munich. The biggest challenges in coordinating international efforts occurred because of interdependency of subprojects, delays in assembling crucial employees from differing countries, and international coordination overhead—which could cost as much as 15 percent of project budgets. The utopian ideal of "development around the clock" by exploiting time zone differences rarely appeared to pan out regardless of which countries were involved. Of course, the potential always existed for cultural or linguistic differences slowing down coordination of work.

Munich coordinated project work through a matrix structure. Generally, individuals worked in different so-called "Centers of Competence" (CoC) groups, which were divided along technical lines such as "systems architecture," "systems testing," "peripheral systems," or "core processing." Each CoC controlled budgets and milestones for projects in its technical domain. This structure allowed groups to work on new product releases while simultaneously troubleshooting for products as old as a decade or more.

Some 90 project managers acted as midwives for subprojects, bringing them to fruition in line with milestones. More than 40 of these managers held multiple project responsibilities and 20 were involved with customization projects. Although most engineers or software developers knew their personal responsibilities and their immediate supervisors, they could not always identify exactly who was ultimately in charge. They could rest assured, however, that two or three levels above them conflicts over milestones or technical feasibility would eventually get sorted out.

At its Munich headquarters, ICN emphasized the need for solving problems through finding "common understanding." Every other Monday, CoC heads met with senior project management for up to four hours to focus on critical issues, especially involving larger subprojects. Higher-level problems were resolved at a so-called "Development Board," which met biweekly. For projects involving other RDCs, Siemens ICN held meetings—either in Munich or at the RDC—every six weeks with all involved project managers. Unfortunately, decisions were often delayed for weeks because there wasn't enough time to resolve all major issues between CoC heads, project managers and senior executives. Complicating decision-making further was that some regional development centers reported directly to independent Siemens companies located in their respective home countries instead of business divisions such as ICN. In such cases, some conflicts had to be settled at the corporate management board level.

At its American RDC, the company had experimented with the use of strongly defined project teams for each release of a product. Managers claimed to find, however, a decline in quality, increased duplication of efforts, and difficulty in motivating individuals to troubleshoot problems with older product releases. Nonetheless, for critical and time-sensitive projects, ICN was now using two or three "strong" project leaders who were individuals being groomed for upper management.

The motivation for change came from its 14- to 16-month-long market cycles (in the form of new EWSD product releases), which had led analysts to worry about the company's future. One industry observer noted: "There's not much about Silicon Valley that will be familiar to Continental executives accustomed to gilded traditions of hierarchy, protected markets, and sacrosanct summer vacations."[8]

BOCA RATON, FLORIDA: AN OLD RDC IN THE NEW WORLD

Amid the stately palm trees and manicured lawns of Southern Florida, stood the second largest overseas outpost, the Boca Raton Regional Development Center (RDC), which was established in 1978. Some 2000 people (including 600 engineers and programmers) operated

[8] S. Baker, "Technology Phone Giants on the Prowl: Europe's Titans Are Devouring U.S. High-Tech Start-ups," *BusinessWeek* (International Edition), March 22, 1999.

primarily in warm Boca Raton, with access to three airports, and offered a fairly central location for the Americas and Munich. Technologically, Florida hosted the American space program and had served as birthplace of the IBM personal computer.

Inside the Boca Raton RDC, workers operated in individual cubicles and managerial offices with open doors—a contrast to Munich, where all personnel worked in offices, with junior members sharing office space. Although many of the workers at Boca Raton were foreign-born, they had been to various degrees "Americanized" and acclimated to an informal environment of golf shirts and Docker jeans. With personnel turnover averaging around 13 percent per year, newcomers could find plenty of experienced employees for help with what Boca Raton manager Kevin Holwell termed "bewildering tasks such as figuring out whom in the Siemens Munich telephone book to call."

As with all RDCs, the work of the Florida group centered around the EWSD. Munich engineers would transmit the software for each fresh release of EWSD by high-speed data lines to Florida. The Boca Raton center would then, under project groups as well as Centers of Competence, spend up to a half year customizing the system for the U.S. To coordinate activities at a senior level, Boca Raton and Munich held joint quarterly meetings with management, alternating between the two locations. Over the years, the center had accumulated the experience and technical skills to manage complex systems projects.

As a large RDC, catering primarily to the vast U.S. market with its unique industry standards, Boca Raton often drifted technologically apart from Munich. Widening this drift was the need to keep pace with fast-moving competitors. Technologists at Boca Raton would on several occasions act first and then inform Munich. Some managers admitted to the existence of the "NIH or 'Not Invented Here' syndrome," which led each side to duplicate certain efforts. As a result, the Boca Raton group had developed, for instance, some of its own fault analysis tools. One Munich manager described the situation thus: "If you ask an engineer in our Indian RDC to test 1, 2, 3, 4 . . . in a keypad, they will test 1, 2, 3, 4, and nothing else; but if you ask an engineer in our American RDC to test 1, 2, 3, 4 . . . , they will test 5, 6, 7, 8 . . . !"

Boca Raton, like other RDCs, also developed specific applications requested by local customers. A prominent example was the "Remote Switching Unit" (RSU), which served as a stripped-down, inexpensive "mini-switch" that could hook up to 5,000 lines in a remote community to one central EWSD via a "trunk" line. By linking several RSUs to one central EWSD a telephone service provider could minimize the length of expensive copper wiring needed. Several of Boca Raton's smaller customers had requested such a system to leverage telephone service coverage of their relatively few EWSDs. Many other Siemens centers such as the Indian RDC were not considered for the RSU project, as they lacked the prerequisite hardware system design capabilities.

Starting June 1997, Boca Raton invested close to 400 person-years on the project. It divided work on the tens of thousands of lines of computer programming into independent subsystems that usually correlated with different areas of technical competence. A project manager kept the entire effort on track, which involved coordinated development activities between the U.S., Germany, Austria and Portugal. System developers shuttled across the Atlantic, supplementing their efforts through biweekly video conferences that were viewed as much less effective. To speed up development, all RDCs had access to remote system testing facilities on a mainframe computer in Munich that allowed them to test their components 24 hours per day. Postmortem analysis showed, however, that over 5 percent of staff years on the project were spent just traveling. The analysis also indicated that the dream of around the clock development of complex products—taking advantage of the world's time zone differences—had remained just that . . . a dream.

Towards the end of the project, engineers worked 16- to 18-hour days. Intensive bonds developed during these periods between engineers, regardless of national origin, and each side could find much in their counterparts to admire. Many Germans, however, found the nonsmoking policies or the lack of public transportation in Florida stifling. For their part, several Americans found it difficult to match Munich beer-drinking abilities. In the Oktoberfest crowds, one American visitor vanished, only to be found, after a tense manhunt, supine in the mud and nodding to a Bavarian band.

Although the RSU project finished with only a few months of delay, Munich and Boca Raton created a "Convergence Group" to stem the divergence between project management styles. As one German manager observed, "We cannot get the Americans in line with our process; they don't analyze things at the beginning of a project the way we do. We want our road maps; they will just proceed and then see what happens. Sometimes a week after starting a subsystem project we would get an e-mail stating 'sorry, we can't do this!'"

Every several weeks, engineers and managers from both sides convened in either Florida or Munich. Both sides agreed to keep work styles on the EWSD base as similar as possible through, for instance, using similar testbeds and common Centers of Competence. With regard to software applications, in the words of Florida manager Keith Hohlin, however, they "agreed to disagree" and followed different development processes.

BANGALORE, INDIA: A NEW RDC IN THE OLD WORLD

After its independence from England in 1947—a hundred years after the founding of Siemens—India developed one of the world's three largest engineering work forces. Under a socialistic program, central government planners designated Bangalore in South India as the nation's computational technology center. By 1990, Indian communications engineers had developed a low cost indigenous switching device that could economically link even impoverished rural villages. Over the decades, however, the worldwide high tech explosion would lure away many programmers with substantially higher paying jobs. By the 1990s, up to a fifth of Microsoft software developers in the USA hailed from the Indian subcontinent.

Fears of a one-way "brain drain," however, were mitigated by nonresident Indians investing in their motherland technological firms as well as the burgeoning Indian population's ability to keep churning out talented programmers. Bangalore, with its relatively temperate climate thanks to an elevation of 1000 meters, good educational institutes, and growing cosmopolitanism became known as India's Silicon Valley. It soon hosted leading multinational corporations as well as domestic companies.

Siemens had had a presence in India for decades and enjoyed an excellent reputation. ICN's Bangalore RDC was set up in 1994 at least partly to avail itself of inexpensive—at 20 percent of the German labor costs—and readily available English-speaking software specialists. When work at Bangalore started, some German engineers admitted to feeling threatened by losing their jobs to low-cost Indian labor. To escape local corporate taxation, Siemens established the Bangalore center as an "Export Oriented Unit" that would not sell product into the Indian market. Starting with just 20 individuals, including 12 German expatriates, the Bangalore center eventually grew to over 600 strong to become ICN's fourth largest RDC worldwide.

The Bangalore center featured American-styled offices with employees in individual cubicles and managers in individual offices on the periphery. Siemens maintained an informal, relatively open atmosphere in which young employees could work without the pressures of bureaucracy. Only three layers of management existed here, as compared with seven in Munich. Overall, the Indian programmers, who were organized along the basis of projects, barely noticed organizational or management changes in Munich.

It took three or four months to get an Indian university recruit up to speed on a project, a year to get to full productivity, and up to a two years to gain proficiency in working with Siemens' technology. Because Indian programmers trained on inexpensive personal computers they relied heavily on German guidance for working on large systems. With wages skyrocketing, by 2000, a fresh programmer could earn—in addition to health, housing, and vehicle benefits—about $6000 a year, a considerable amount in India (more than twice that of university professors). Salaries could double in three years based on performance. The average programmer worked 40–45 hours/week, but, with no unions to restrict their activities, would often work longer during crunch times with no overtime benefits.

Young Indians regarded Siemens as one of the best employers to work for in Bangalore. However, with other competitors such as Lucent and Cisco bidding for newly minted software talent, the local job market heated up and Siemens could no longer count on having first pick. Already, by 2000, out of the top 30 most prestigious employers in Bangalore, Siemens had slipped from front-runner status to a middle-ranking.

EARLY EXPERIENCES AT BANGALORE

The first sizable software project conducted at Bangalore for Munich involved the so-called "Advanced Multifunctional Operator Service System" (ADMOSS) project. The purpose of ADMOSS was to allow modern call centers to increase their productivity through capabilities such as facilitating telemarketing, interfacing with non-Siemens equipment, or large conference calls (see **Exhibit 11** for product description). ADMOSS was to field some 500 features, chosen from customer "wish lists" compiled by Munich's marketing group. Because Munich engineers for decades had only programmed larger computers, ICN sought to develop ADMOSS elsewhere. The task ultimately fell upon Bangalore, with its strength in personal computer programming.

Work in India started right after the RDC's founding in 1994 and the project later peaked at 150 software developers. Initially, project management was "top-down," with specifications for various subsystems transmitted from Munich at a high managerial level to Bangalore. Each team of Indian software developers, generally under supervision of a German expatriate or a senior Indian manager, worked from specifications for an entire subsystem. Munich would then test and integrate the work with other subsystems. To complicate matters, specifications were adjusted and fine-tuned throughout the project through a flurry of e-mails and faxes between Germany and India.

With such a highly complex project, according to senior project managers, "not all specifications were finished by our Munich office since we ourselves were not given enough time!" The first real workshop involving middle and lower level managers and programmers only occurred in late 1995. Up to that point, according to Bangalore-based senior manager, A. Anuradha, "We were groping in the dark."

Like their brethren throughout the world, Indian software developers had faced the frustration of stopping work because of budgetary cuts or because of changing needs of customers. On one occasion work on a billing application was stopped midstream after a half-year's work because of the customer's changing needs. Although this type of work interruption involved only some 15–20 personnel at Bangalore each year, programmers admitted to feeling "demotivated," wondering about how much miscommunication might have been going on several thousand kilometers to the West.

Finally, when all two million lines of the ADMOSS computer code were melded together to attempt to create a seamless, integrated system, many problems surfaced. As it turned out, subsystems were far more interdependent than had been assumed. Since Bangalore developers worked thousands of kilometers away from the Munich test beds, testing of newly integrated system turned out to be a major obstacle. To worsen matters, visa restrictions and bureaucracy on the part of the German government made it extremely difficult to fly Indians developers to Munich.

For the few Indians who obtained visas, "the first trips were exciting," observed Anuradha. "In fact, there was no substitute for going: this way we could see the full behavior of the system. But with things not working out, we had mixed feelings!" On one occasion, Indians temporarily stationed in Munich were flown to Nuremberg to help solve a customer's problem that, on further investigation, could have been solved by the local service department, had it consulted the basic manuals more carefully. For the Indian team, however, this provided a welcome initial encounter with a Siemens customer.

ADMOSS was finally released to a German customer at the end of 1996—about a year late. "This was with some embarrassment," according to Hans Hauer, VP of software R&D, "because as Germans, we expect delivery on time and with quality!" The system turned out not to be fully stabilized and kept crashing. Other minor problems also emerged. The user interfaces designed by the young Indian programmers were sometimes found to be "flashy and distracting, resembling video game interfaces." "Overall, the customer was upset!" admitted Hauer. Munich immediately standardized user interfaces and also took control of documentation because customers found the Indian-written documents too technical.

ICN managers also found visits to Bangalore more productive with several small meetings. An initial large meeting, in fact, proved a disaster since Indian department heads found it impolite to speak their minds in front of everyone. The groups, however, could never get as small as the Germans would like primarily because of insufficient Indian personnel with large systems experience.

With time, the Indo-German team corrected the system faults and delivered a stable, working system to Munich. ADMOSS ended up highly popular with customers. The Bangalore site remained active with after-sales service, eventually correcting over 90 percent of ongoing faults. By 2000, a skeletal crew of about 50 programmers in Bangalore and 20 systems developers in Europe maintained the ADMOSS system and produced yearly updates.

EAST IS EAST, AND WEST IS WEST?

The ADMOSS project crystallized several problems in managing the Bangalore division. Primary among the problems was the high turnover rate among Indian programmers in the increasingly heated local job market (see Exhibit 10). With competing firms regarding Siemens experience highly, recruiters would entice young software developers with better salary offers. In this environment, annual turnover at the ICN Bangalore center could reach as much as one-third. Making it even harder to retain staff was the eagerness of Indian programmers to openly discuss salaries in the hallways or canteen. This surprised most Germans who had grown up viewing India as supposedly a "nonmaterialistic" culture. According to German expatriate Richard Bock, "The Bangalore programmers would even ask salary information of the Germans, who would become red in the face."

The career-related impatience of young Indian programmers also caught the Germans by surprise. The fresh recruits at Bangalore were sometimes shocked by the prospect of being on a project for over a year. For many of them, a "dream project" would preferably last less than a half-year and involve "leading-edge" areas such as mobile communications or Internet protocols (rather than areas such as quality testing or integration).

In every other way, however, the Germans found the Indians polite—almost too polite. Siemens managers observed that the Indians rarely said "no" to any request, even if it turned out beyond their capabilities. Feeling cultural issues might be involved, developer Richard Bock was asked to "decode" the Indian way of communication. Bock's three years in India had tinged his English with a head-turning South Indian accent and taught him that "the cultural awareness materials and role-playing exercises we engaged in at Munich were simplistic and out of date, and did not take into account the wide cultural variation within India. The warnings about Indian workers not being 'well-motivated' applied perhaps to factory workers [in a socialist system], and not at all to our Bangalore people."

Bock was soon able to explain that the phrase "there is no problem" meant to Indians that "we do not see any problems in the *sub-system* on which we have been working." To the Germans, however, it meant, "within the *entire system* there is no problem." A related issue involved the Indians' understanding of fault analysis. To the Indians, the top priority was to solve a fault and not to take an additional four annoying minutes to document each of the hundreds of faults. To the Germans, however, tracking the faults themselves was essential for monitoring the health of systems development and maintenance. It also allowed informing customers about whether a fault was in the "analysis phase" or in the "correction phase."

Bock also found little substitute for face-to-face interaction: "Sometimes you think a point has been settled on the phone, but then three days later you may get a phone call asking, 'why don't we try this other approach?' Programmers in Munich or Vienna will follow customer-defined specifications out of a sense of duty. But in India you have to give the workers a sense of belonging, through early workshops or other means; otherwise, if you ask for a fridge you might get a toaster!"

Few on either side, however, appeared willing to use cultural differences as an excuse for miscommunication, although such clashes were inevitable on occasion—for instance, when one orthodox Indian refused to pick up his official correspondence on astrologically "non-auspicious" occasions. Occasionally, Indians would interpret directness or bluntness on the part of a German as rudeness. Several Indian programmers admitted their frustration when, after learning to say "no," their exercise of this magic word in order to extend a subproject deadline was once met with, "That is not acceptable."

Overall, the Indians felt well-treated by their German employers. The Germans in turn remained relatively pleased by their enthusiastic, hard-working, and talented Bangalore programmers. Expatriates essayed their hand at subcontinental passions including cricket and Indian food. They did receive a bonus "hardship pay," which one expatriate earned after turning beet red from mistakenly swallowing an entire Indian hot pepper (a story the Indians relished in recalling). Expatriate manager Ralph Sussick gamely earned his bonus by spending his first weeks apart from his family in an unlit apartment still under construction. The perks, however, included personal chauffeurs and entry into the highest levels of Indian society. Over the years, one German couple gave birth while in Bangalore, and even a few Indo-German marriages occurred.

Noting a complementarity between the German and Indian approaches to work and life, Indian manager Sai "Charlie" Sreekanth M., stated: "The Germans manage depth well; we manage breadth well. We idolize our 'all-rounder'—the person who does well in sports, debate, and academics. And socially, we're happiest arguing about a great many things in coffeehouse settings!" This contrasted with observations that greatly amused Indians in Munich of certain German employees who with clockwork precision caught exactly the same commuter train every day.

Managing breadth well implied that the Indians could cover for each other to keep a project rolling even in the midst of vacations, illness, or job resignations on part of any team member. The complementarity between the German and Indian approaches to career, however, allowed Bangalore project manager Santosh Prabhu to observe: "When I was working on a subsystem, I definitely found it simpler to have my Munich counterpart—who had been working on it for well over five years and thus knew it inside-out—make corrections and provide feedback about its eventual performance."

THE NETMANAGER PROJECT

> The Germans created the world's most reliable telecommunications systems over a period of decades. Even they cannot be expected to produce a new system that is as highly reliable in just two or three years!
>
> —*Bangalore software developer*

By the mid-1990s, personal computers had grown in power and capabilities to the point of controlling access to an entire switching system responsible for routing tens of thousands of calls. At ICN, this realization gave birth to the "EWSD NetManager" project. The user-friendly and graphics-based software product would offer telecom customers a complete range of facilities for performing all operating, administration and maintenance functions on EWSD network nodes and networks (e.g., integration of new telephone subscribers, billing, enable "traffic studies" to understand customer needs, and provide system surveillance). Not surprisingly, NetManager development required a deep understanding of EWSD technology and its 6,000 or so functions.

Creating NetManager would entail, however, programming in desktop computer languages and systems with which Munich product developers lacked experience. ICN over the decades had, after all, developed and refined its own computer language "CHILL" for its large proprietary operating system. It would have taken months to get up to speed with Windows-based systems, let alone learning to deal with quirks of an entirely different system (e.g., memory space problems that necessitated frequent re-booting of computers). Because of budget cuts at Munich, ICN senior managers deliberated over which regional development center should develop the NetManager.

Boca Raton and Bangalore emerged near the top of the pile of contenders. Some argued in favor of Boca Raton because of its greater experience in working on large, complex systems and its knowledge of EWSD systems. Others argued in favor of India because of cost advantages. By now, however, the cost advantages of working in India were rapidly diminishing thanks to roughly 25 percent annual wage increases for developers in Bangalore. In fact, after factoring in other costs such as information transfer, travel, job-training, and management costs, working in Eastern Europe was now perhaps cheaper than working in India. The NetManager assignment eventually went to Bangalore because of staff availability, familiarity of the Indians with personal computer-based programming, and budgetary restrictions at Western RDCs. Work at Bangalore commenced in early 1996 with an initial force of 30 programmers. The June 1998 pilot release involved some 300,000 lines of code and proved a hit at the customer test sites. ICN then apprised several important clients including Deutsche Telekom about its forthcoming product.

The world of personal computing and telecommunications, however, had changed rapidly by now. What was envisioned as a simple, isolated, "low-end" product with low reliability gradually transformed into a complex and highly visible product for large customers. Where initially the NetManager was meant to allow one personal computer to control just one element of the system, now it had grown in scope to enabling one PC to control a network using 20 servers and 30 terminals. This implied that the entire project would no longer be shielded from the challenge of managing interdependencies with many other Siemens telecommunications products. It was no wonder that NetManager, by spring 2000, would involve 60 percent of the Bangalore center's staff.

Thanks to an old "testbed" sent by Munich after lessons learned from the ADMOSS experience, Indian programmers could now test subsystems as they were developed. By November 1999, Bangalore sent its complete NetManager Version 2 to Munich for testing. Typically Munich tested "stability" (or reliability) of new software by installing and launching it on a Friday afternoon and hoping to find no errors in the test log on Monday. NetManager Version 2, however, ran only one hour before crashing to a halt.

A check of the test logs ultimately revealed a staggering 700 faults hidden at various points along some 600,000 lines of computer programming code, with 100 categorized as serious "Level I" faults. Initial trouble-shooting indicated that each fault could not simply be corrected individually, since each correction could create ripple effects across the entire system. The Bangalore RDC quickly boosted its staffing on NetManager and software developers worked seven days a week to solve the crisis. Three Indian developers were sent to Munich for more than one month.

A late-November 1999 workshop in Bangalore involving managers from Munich and India tracked down the root cause of quality problems. As it turned out, the Indian group assumed, as in the case of most desktop computing applications, that the system would be shut off at night, and that it was acceptable for a desktop-based computer system to crash once a week. This assumption was further reinforced by an understanding that operation of the EWSD switch itself would not depend on NetManager. Furthermore, the Indian team underestimated system usage by an entire order of magnitude. "We were ignorant!" admitted an Indian programmer. "We didn't think of asking what loads to test with, but Munich was also at fault for not telling us!"

Some of these erroneous assumptions could ultimately be traced to different work schedules. In the crucial summer months, many Germans went ahead with their several weeks–long pre-booked family vacations—often without leaving contact information—stranding the Indians. During crisis periods, Indian programmers, in contrast, typically took only personal leaves of two or three days, and worked 70–80 hours per week or even more. Balanced against this, however, was the ongoing high attrition rate in Bangalore.

In January 2000, Siemens, with one Bangalore engineer present, went ahead with the planned demonstration of NetManager to Deutsche Telekom. But even the Munich testers did not appear well-prepped for the tests, leaving Bangalore programmers to wonder why it had commenced in the first place. The result proved disastrous: far too many reliability errors cropped up. Deutsche Telekom halted the tests immediately.

In February, postmortem analysis indicated that the old testbed sent to Bangalore was smaller than those used at present and thus could not detect all design problems. Another three Bangalore programmers went to Munich to help iron out the reliability wrinkles on larger testbeds. One of these was software manager Lalitha J. S., who recounted: "The Munich people were very nice. They did say that 'these problems are causing us commercial consequences,' but they never threatened our group or said, 'Hey Bangalore, what's up!' The face-to-face interactions helped; otherwise, back home we were sometimes thinking, 'were they making things up?'"

Senior management set the deadline of August 2000 for fixing all version 2 faults. The top managers decided that the version 3 release planned for July 2000 should be scrapped and merged into a fully reliable version 4 product, promised to customers for Spring 2001.

DEUTSCHE TELEKOM CALLS

Eberl and Hunke knew that immediate action would be needed. The NetManager Project had clearly mushroomed in size and strategic importance beyond that initially envisioned. Deutsche Telekom, ICN's largest customer, was demanding the product but also issued a warning that reliability problems would not be acceptable. As a result, some German executives had already suggested that NetManager development and project management should be moved to Austria, Belgium, or Portugal. In the shorter term, they argued that further delays were inevitable even if the project remained in Bangalore and that decisive action was long overdue. In the longer term, this would also bring the system developers and programmers closer to Siemens' major customers and smooth out coordination problems with India.

But already some 50 percent of NetManager resources, development and project management were based in Bangalore. Transferring these project activities back to Europe would involve a delay of several weeks during which time Indian and German software developers and managers would have to shuttle back and forth across the Arabian Sea. Relocating the NetManager project might also cast a pall over the Bangalore. Over the years, Indian managers had begun suggesting to change their RDC from a software development outpost for Munich into a center with status equal to that of, say, Boca Raton. As one Indian manager, C.R. Rao, observed: "We would like to climb up the value chain to work with customers, create growth and career opportunities, and start charting our own destiny." Such an evolution would, among other things, require major investments and a significant expansion of system-testing and hardware design capabilities.

As an alternative proposal to relocating core NetManager activities to Europe, some Siemens managers suggested moving major project responsibility and accountability to Munich but leaving all development activities in Bangalore. While travel and coordination cost would increase, this proposal ensured strict project management and quality control while keeping Indian software developers on NetManager. It was unclear, however, if a project of such complexity could be managed by people living thousands of miles away.

In the meantime, the late afternoon pollution thickened as the traffic weaved without the slightest regard for lane markings. If Bangalore was to grow into a world stature city, it would need to discipline its pollution and growing traffic.

EXHIBIT 1
History of
Telecommuni-
cations[a]

Prehistory +	Use of smoke signals, tom-toms, carrier pigeons, runners, horse-back messengers, and many other systems developed independently by many cultures for conveying messages across great distances.
Late 1700s	Visual systems used to convey messages over long distances. Semaphore system developed in France.
1820–1837	Hans Christian Orsted (Denmark) discovers that a wire carrying electric current can deflect a magnetic needle; Michael Faraday (Britain) and others refine science of electromagnetism.
1837	Cooke & Wheatstone (Britain) obtain patents for first telegraph. Samuel Morse, professor of painting and art in New York City, is granted patent on system for communicating information using electromagnets (represented on paper by dots and dashes). His first public transmission from Washington D.C. to Baltimore, "What hath God wrought!" ushers in telegraph era.
1847	Together with business partner Johann Georg Halske, Werner Siemens begins to manufacture pointer telegraphs, a product of his own invention, and lays the foundations for electrical engineering giant Siemens AG.
	Alexander Graham Bell patents telephone. Originally intended to supplant telegraphy, the two technologies coexist for decades to come.
1877	First public telephone exchange installed. The first system (New Haven, CT) allows up to 21 callers to contact one another and is manned by human operators who must physically connect the caller's line to the called party's line. Quite rapidly, the system grows to accommodate hundreds of users.
1913	First electromechanical switches installed. By 1974, one of these systems can handle up to 35,000 calls.
1918	"Modulated carrier" technology allows for many different messages to be transmitted simultaneously over a single telephone line. Vacuum tube circuits amplify and regenerate weak signals to allow for more efficient signal transmission.
1947	Transistor invented. Allows for smaller, faster switching devices based on electronic, rather than on electromechanical, components.
1960s	AT&T introduces Electronic Switching System (ESS) that combines numerous new technologies including semiconductors for switching. Allows for up to 65,000 calls per switch.
1976	Switching systems developed by AT&T that allow voice data to be digitized into smaller packets of information that can be sent from caller to called party through more flexible, efficient routes. These flexible systems allow for handling 100,000 lines and laid the basis for modern switching systems.
1980	Siemens ICN develops the EWSD digital electronic telephone switch, which would become the most reliable and best-selling voice switch in the world.

[a]Much of the timeline information is adapted from: *The New Encyclopaedia Britannica Macromedia*, v. 28, "Telecommunications Systems" 1997, pp. 473–504.

EXHIBIT 2
Cost per Service Transaction in Industrialized Countries (Estimate)

Source: Siemens AG.

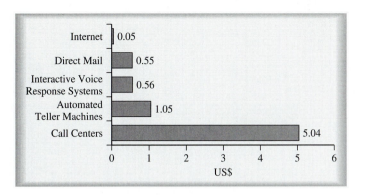

EXHIBIT 3
Siemens Statement of Income (German Marks in Millions)

Source: Siemens AG Annual Report 1999.

Siemens Worldwide Income (Year Ends Sept. 30)

Year	1999	1998
Net Sales	**134,134**	**117,696**
Cost of sales	(96,014)	(85,780)
Gross profit on sales	**38,120**	**31,916**
Research and development expenses	(10,240)	(9,122)
Marketing and selling expenses	(19,120)	(17,672)
General administration expenses	(5,185)	(3,616)
Other operating income	1,618	951
Other operating expenses	(2,570)	(883)
Net income from investment in other companies	544	474
Net Income from financial assets and marketable securities	1,807	1,451
Net interest income (expense) from Operations/Pension Fund	679	(451)
EBIT from Operations		
Other interest (expense) income	(40)	390
Income from ordinary activities before income taxes	**5,613**	**3,438**
Taxes on income from ordinary activities	(1,965)	(780)
Income before extraordinary items	**3,648**	**2,658**
Extraordinary items after taxes		(1,741)
Net Income	**3,648**	**917**

490

EXHIBIT 4 Siemens Corporate Structure

Corporate Structure

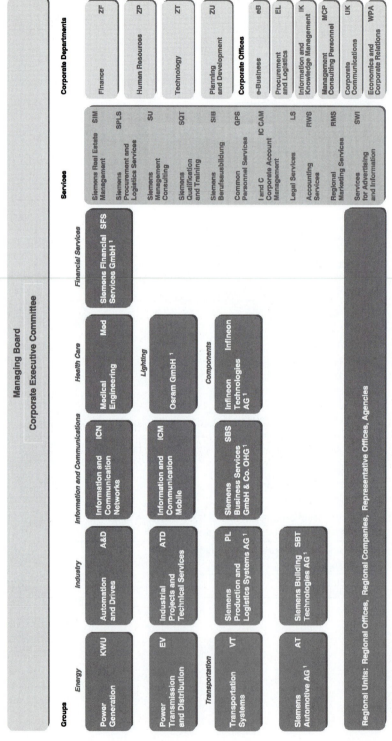

1 legally separate Group

ZU S 2 - September 29, 2000

Source: Siemens AG.

Issue: October 1, 2000

EXHIBIT 5   Siemens Financials by Segment (German Marks in Millions)

	External Sales		Intersegment Sales		Total Sales		EBIT	
	1999	1998	1999	1998	1999	1998	1999	1998
Operations								
Power Generation (KWU)	15,437	10,566	74	83	15,511	10,649	(261)	(196)
Power Transmission and Distribution (EV)	5,973	6,439	385	510	6,358	6,949	248	191
Automation and Drives (A&D)	11,567	11,368	2,253	2,378	13,820	13,746	1,447	1,385
Industrial Projects and Technical Services (ATD)	5,943	7,923	2,111	2,405	8,054	10,328	279	289
Production and Logistics Systems (PL)	2,136	2,239	375	334	2,511	2,573	150	111
Siemens Building Technologies (SBT) (1)	7,618		716		8,334		319	
Information and Communication Network (ICN)	**23,422**	**23,405**	**607**	**453**	**24,029**	**23,858**	**1,061**	**1,143**
Information and Communication Products (ICP)	16,677	15,179	2,468	2,582	19,145	17,761	956	501
Siemens Business Services (SBS)	4,273	3,852	2,782	2,355	7,055	6,207	8	(258)
Transportation Systems (VT)	5,794	5,029	14	17	5,808	5,046	(122)	(746)
Automotive Systems (AT)	6,380	5,560	9	8	6,389	5,568	310	293
Medical Engineering (Med)	7,887	7,414	93	58	7,980	7,472	660	283
Osram	6,799	6,530	359	28	7,158	6,558	680	643
Infineon (HL) (2)	6,986	5,636	1,275	1,058	8,261	6,694	101	(852)
Passive Components and Electron Tubes (PR)	2,474	2,230	314	353	2,788	2,583	283	327
Electromechanical Components (EC)	1,384	1,325	235	215	1,619	1,540	17	78
Eliminations and other (3)	2,823	2,643	(16,316)	(14,909)	(13,493)	(12,266)	(326)	6
Total	**133,573**	**117,338**			**131,327**	**115,266**	**5,810**	**3,198**

(1)Due to the short time of affiliation with Siemens, only the assets and liabilities of SBT were included in the consolidated financial statements at September 30, 1998.

(2)Comprising substantially all of the former HL activities.

(3)"Other" primarily refers to centrally managed equity investments (such as BSH Bosch and Siemens Hausgeräte GmbH, Munich), liquid assets of operations, corporate items relating to Regional Companies, and corporate headquarters.

Source: Siemens AG Annual Report 1999.

EXHIBIT 6a
Worldwide
Voice Switch
Equipment
Market
(1999)—By
Supplier

Source: Gartner
Dataquest (estimate),
Siemens AG.

Rank 1999	Supplier	Headquarters	Voice Ports Shipped (in Thousands)[a]	
			Worldwide Shipments	% Share
1	Alcatel	France	18,244	18.1%
2	Siemens	Germany	15,135	15.0%
3	Lucent	USA	13,083	13.0%
4	Ericsson	Sweden	10,051	10.0%
5	Nortel	Canada	8,361	8.3%
6	NEC	Japan	6,797	6.7%
7	Fujitsu	Japan	4,559	4.5%
8	Italtel	Italy	778	0.8%
9	Nokia	Finland	383	0.4%
10	Others		23,574	23.3%
			100,965	**100%**

[a]One voice port is equivalent to a single telephone line. Siemens EWSD systems are scalable to roughly 240,000 voice ports, with costs anywhere from $500,000 and $10 million, depending on the number of ports (with a marginal cost of up to $100 per port).

EXHIBIT 6b
Worldwide
Voice Switch
Equipment
Market
(1999)—By
Region and
Supplier

Source: Gartner
Dataquest (estimate),
Siemens AG.

Supplier	Europe	North America	Latin America	Middle East/Africa	Asia/Pacific
Alcatel	6,969	0	563	2,051	8,661
Siemens	7,319	610	247	2,203	4,756
Lucent	1,049	6,115	434	54	5,431
Ericsson	5,804	57	1,180	256	2,754
Nortel	1,263	4,507	558	627	1,406
NEC	404	731	740	635	4,287
Fujitsu	0	0	11	53	4,495
Italtel	727	0	46	0	5
Nokia	292	0	0	0	91
Others	1,623	13,512	4,911	5,879	73,162
Ports shipped	**25,450**	**12,767**	**4,345**	**5,879**	**52,524**
(in thousands)	(25.2%)	(12.6%)	(4.3%)	(5.8%)	(52.0%)

EXHIBIT 7
EWSD Digital Electronic Switching System

Source: Siemens AG.

Open EWSD system with flexible hardware and software architecture

The number of racks depends on the capacity of the system

EWSD platform can accommodate fixed and mobile communications networks

Open rack reveals a modular design

Multiple modules make up EWSD system

Each module frame consists of assembly rails, side section and guides for modules.

System capacity can be increased by adding modules to each frame

EWSD modules are controlled by software such as NetManager (developed in Bangalore)

EXHIBIT 8   Position of Carrier Switching Division (CS) Within the Siemens Organization

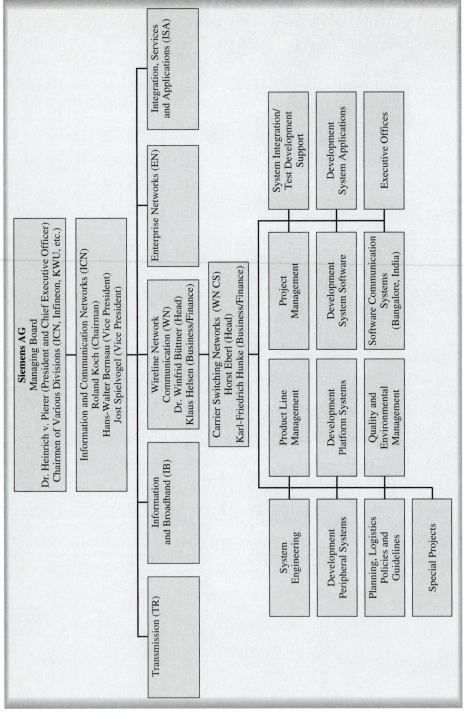

Source: Siemens AG.

EXHIBIT 9   **Siemens ICN Regional Development Centers (RDCs) and Manufacturing Sites Around the World**

○	Regional development centers in Europe, Asia, Africa, America, and Australia
●	Manufacturing sites in 20 countries

Source: Siemens AG.

EXHIBIT 10   **Internal Cost Benchmarks of Largest Regional Development Centers (1999)**

Regional Development Center (RDC)	Total Development Effort for Siemens ICN-Wireline[a]		Annual Cost of One Developer[b] (Thousand Euros)	Employee Turnover[c] (% of Total Staff)	Coordination Cost[d] (% of Total Effort)
	(Person-Years)	(Thousand Euros)			
Austria	500	50,000	100	4%	8%
USA	200	20,000	150	13%	3%
India	300	8,000	40	35%	15%
Belgium	100	10,000	100	12%	5%
Slovenia	90	5,000	60	5%	6%
Portugal	80	6,000	70	17%	6%

[a]Effort used by ICN only; total size of development center may be significantly larger

[b]Fully-loaded person-year (salary, benefits and overhead)

[c]Annualized turnover (or attrition) of development staff

[d]Travel, meetings, teleconferences, etc. incurred by Munich headquarters in supporting each RDC

Source: Siemens AG.

EXHIBIT 11
**The Evolution
of Call Centers
in the
Telephone
Industry**

Source: Siemens ICN.

Siemens transit exchange center

Berlin, Germany, 1906

Modern call center at major Telecom
operator using ADMOSS call service
software and EWSD telephone
switching system

Examples of ADMOSS (Advanced Multifunctional Operator Service System) Call Center Solution Features:

Call distribution system and queues (e.g., route call to operator with required language skills)

Switching features (e.g., conference calls of up to 25 participants)

Booking system (e.g., advance booking of calls between U.S. and India)

Directory assistance (e.g., number appears as SMS on mobile phone)

Charging features (e.g., cost information available prior to call)

Announcements (e.g., position of caller in queue)

Internet services (e.g., caller contacts operator through Internet link)

EXHIBIT 12   Terminology

ADMOSS	Abbreviation for Advanced Multifunctional Operator Service System. Siemens ICN software product used by call centers to manage telephone services such as directory assistance, billing, conference calls, etc. ADMOSS is designed to be used with EWSD voice technology.
Backbone	Part of the communications network that carries the heaviest traffic. The backbone interconnects the devices (switches and edge devices) to which customers are usually connected.
Bandwidth	Bandwidth is the width of a communication channel measured in "bits per second" or bps. High bandwidth implies that more information can be moved through a channel at the same time. Low bandwidth connections (e.g., phone dial-in) are typically fractions of 64 kbps (kilobits per second). High bandwidth connections usually supply several Mbps (megabits per second).
Broadband	Transmission facility providing high bandwidth. Such a facility can carry voice, video, and data channels simultaneously.
EWSD	Abbreviation for *Elektronisches Wählsystem Digital* or Electronic Switching System Digital. EWSD is a voice switch and Siemens ICN's flagship product.
Digital subscriber lines (DSL)	A technology that uses existing copper telephone lines to transmit voice and data at high speeds (up to 8 Mbps).
Integrated services digital network (ISDN)	Switched network allowing for provision of both voice and data services over copper wire (up to 128 kbps).
Internet protocol (IP)	The set of rules that specify how data is cut into packets, routed and addressed for delivery between different Internet nodes.
Packet switching	A way of sending data through a network to another location by subdividing the data into individual units or packets, each with a unique identification and destination address. Data is received by reassembling packets at destination.
Telecom Switch	A device that interconnects traffic (voice or data) from one port to another based on information within traffic (e.g., IP addresses), signaling (e.g., intervoice switch signaling) or predefined routes.
Voice switching	A way of sending and receiving voice through a network of telephone lines and switches. Voice switches reserve resources for the duration of a call, which ensures high quality of voice transmission. In contrast, packet switching usually does not reserve similar resources, leading to dropped packets and delays and thus lower voice transmission quality.

Sources: S&P Communications Equipment Industry Survey 2001, Siemens AG, case authors.

Article

Building Effective R&D Capabilities Abroad

An increasing number of companies in technologically intensive industries such as pharmaceuticals and electronics have abandoned the traditional approach to managing research and development and are establishing global R&D networks in a noteworthy new way. For example, Canon is now carrying out R&D activities in eight dedicated facilities in five countries, Motorola in fourteen facilities in seven countries, and Bristol-Myers Squibb in twelve facilities in six countries. In the past, most companies—even those with a considerable international presence in terms of sales and manufacturing—carried out the majority of their R&D activity in their home countries. Conventional wisdom held that strategy development and R&D had to be kept in close geographical proximity. Because strategic decisions were made primarily at corporate headquarters, the thinking went, R&D facilities should be close to home.

But such a centralized approach to R&D will no longer suffice—for two reasons. First, as more and more sources of potentially relevant knowledge emerge across the globe, companies must establish a presence at an increasing number of locations to access new knowledge and to absorb new research results from foreign universities and competitors into their own organizations. Second, companies competing around the world must move new products from development to market at an ever more rapid pace. Consequently, companies must build R&D networks that excel at tapping new centers of knowledge and at commercializing products in foreign markets with the speed required to remain competitive. And more and more, superior manufacturers are doing just that. (See **Exhibit 1**, "Laboratory Sites Abroad in 1995.")

In an ongoing study on corporate strategy and the geographical dispersion of R&D sites, I have been examining the creation of global research networks by 32 U.S., Japanese, and

European multinational companies.[1] The most successful companies in my study brought each new site's research productivity up to full speed within a few years and quickly transformed knowledge created there into innovative products. I found that establishing networks of such sites poses a number of new, complex managerial challenges. According to my research, managers of the most successful R&D networks understand the new dynamics of global R&D, link corporate strategy to R&D strategy, pick the appropriate sites, staff them with the right people, supervise the sites during start-up, and integrate the activities of the different foreign sites so that the entire network is a coordinated whole.

ADOPTING A GLOBAL APPROACH TO R&D

Adopting a global approach to R&D requires linking R&D strategy to a company's overall business strategy. And that requires the involvement of managers at the highest levels of a company.

Creating a Technology Steering Committee. The first step in creating a global R&D network is to build a team that will lead the initiative. To establish a global R&D network, the CEOs and top-level managers of a number of successful companies that I studied assembled a small team of senior managers who had both technical expertise and in-depth organizational knowledge. The technology steering committees reported directly to the CEOs of their respective companies. They were generally small—five to eight members—and included managers with outstanding managerial and scientific records and a range of educational backgrounds and managerial responsibilities. The committees I studied included as members a former bench scientist who had transferred into manufacturing and had eventually become the head of manufacturing for the company's most important category of therapeutic drugs; a head of marketing for memory chips who had worked before in product development in the same electronics company; and an engineer who had started out in product development, had moved to research, and eventually had become the vice president of R&D. Members of these committees were sufficiently senior to be able to mobilize resources at short notice; and they were actively involved in the management and supervision of R&D programs. In many cases, members included the heads of major existing R&D sites.

Categorizing New R&D Sites. In selecting new sites, companies find it helpful first to articulate each site's primary objective. (See **Exhibit 2,** "Establishing New R&D Sites.") R&D sites have one of two missions. The first type of site—what I call a *home-base-augmenting site*—is established in order to tap knowledge from competitors and universities around the globe; in that type of site, information flows *from* the foreign laboratory *to* the central lab at home. The second type of site—what I call a *home-base-exploiting site*—is established to support manufacturing facilities in foreign countries or to adapt standard products to the

[1] In a systematic effort to analyze the relationship of global strategy and R&D investments in technologically intensive industries, I have been collecting detailed data on all dedicated laboratory sites operated by 32 leading multinational companies. The sample consists of ten U.S., twelve Japanese, and ten European companies. Thirteen of the companies are in the pharmaceutical industry, and nineteen are in the electronics industry. Data collection includes archival research, a detailed questionnaire, and in-depth interviews with several senior R&D managers in each company. Overall, these companies operate 238 dedicated R&D sites, 156 of them abroad. About 60 percent of the laboratory sites abroad were established after 1984. I have used this sample, which is the most complete of its kind, as a basis for a number of quantitative and qualitative investigations into global strategy, competitive interaction, and R&D management.

demand there; in that type of site, information flows *to* the foreign laboratory *from* the central lab at home. (See **Exhibit 3,** "How Information Flows Between Home-Base and Foreign R&D Sites.")

The overwhelming majority of the 238 foreign R&D sites I studied fell clearly into one of the two categories. Approximately 45 percent of all laboratory sites were home-base-augmenting sites, and 55 percent were home-base-exploiting sites. The two types of sites were of the same average size: about 100 employees. But they differed distinctly in their strategic purpose and leadership style.[2] (See the feature box "Home-Base-Augmenting and Home-Base-Exploiting Sites: Xerox and Eli Lilly.")

Choosing a Location for the Site. Home-base-augmenting sites should be located in regional clusters of scientific excellence in order to tap new sources of knowledge. Central to the success of corporate R&D strategy is the ability of senior researchers to recognize and combine scientific advancements from different areas of science and technology. Absorbing the new knowledge can happen in a number of ways: through participation in formal or informal meeting circles that exist within a geographic area containing useful knowledge (a knowledge cluster), through hiring employees from competitors, or through sourcing laboratory equipment and research services from the same suppliers that competitors use.

For example, the Silicon Valley knowledge cluster boasts a large number of informal gatherings of experts as well as more formal ways for high-tech companies to exchange information with adjacent universities, such as industrial liaison programs with Stanford University and the University of California at Berkeley. In the field of communication technology, Siemens, NEC, Matsushita, and Toshiba all operate laboratory sites near Princeton University and Bell Labs (now a part of Lucent Technologies) to take advantage of the expertise located there. For similar reasons, a number of companies in the same industry have established sites in the Kanto area surrounding Tokyo. Texas Instruments operates a facility in Tsukuba Science City, and Hewlett-Packard operates one in Tokyo.

After a company has picked and established its major R&D sites, it might want to branch out. It might selectively set up secondary sites when a leading competitor or a university succeeds in building a critical mass of research expertise in a more narrowly defined area of science and technology outside the primary cluster. In order to benefit from the resulting miniclusters of expertise, companies sometimes establish additional facilities. For that reason, NEC operates a small telecommunications-oriented R&D facility close to a university laboratory in London, and Canon operates an R&D facility in Rennes, France, close to one of France Telecom's major sites.

Home-base-exploiting sites, in contrast, should be located close to large markets and manufacturing facilities in order to commercialize new products rapidly in foreign markets. In the past, companies from industrialized countries located manufacturing facilities abroad primarily to benefit from lower wages or to overcome trade barriers. Over time, however, many of those plants have taken on increasingly complex manufacturing tasks that require having an R&D facility nearby in order to ensure the speedy transfer of technology from

[2] My research on global R&D strategies builds on earlier research on the competitiveness of nations and on research on foreign direct investment, including Michael E. Porter, *The Competitive Advantage of Nations* (New York: The Free Press, 1990), and Thomas J. Wesson, "An Alternative Motivation for Foreign Direct Investment" (Ph.D. dissertation, Harvard University, 1993). My research also builds on an existing body of knowledge about the management of multinational companies. See, for example, Christopher A. Bartlett and Sumantra Ghoshal, *Managing Across Borders* (New York: The Free Press, 1989).

Home-Base-Augmenting and Home-Base-Exploiting Sites: Xerox and Eli Lilly

The particular type of foreign R&D site determines the specific challenges managers will face. Setting up a *home-base-augmenting site*—one designed to gather new knowledge for a company—involves certain skills. And launching a *home-base-exploiting site*—one established to help a company efficiently commercialize its R&D in foreign markets—involves others. The cases of Xerox and Eli Lilly present an instructive contrast.

Xerox established a home-base-augmenting laboratory in Grenoble, France. Its objective: to tap new knowledge from the local scientific community and to transfer it back to its home base. Having already established, in 1986, a home-base-augmenting site in Cambridge, England, Xerox realized in 1992 that the research culture in continental Western Europe was sufficiently different and complementary to Great Britain's to justify another site. Moreover, understanding the most advanced research in France or Germany was very difficult from a base in Great Britain because of language and cultural barriers. One senior R&D manager in the United States notes, "We wanted to learn firsthand what was going on in centers of scientific excellence in Europe. Being present at a center of scientific excellence is like reading poetry in the original language."

It was essential that managers from the highest levels of the company be involved in the decision-making process from the start. Senior scientists met with high-level managers and entered into a long series of discussions. Their first decision: to locate the new laboratory at a center of scientific excellence. Xerox also realized that it had to hire a renowned local scientist as the initial laboratory leader. The leader needed to be able to understand the local scientific community, attract junior scientists with high potential, and target the right university institutes and scholars for joint research projects. Finally, Xerox knew that the laboratory would have an impact on the company's economic performance only if it had the critical mass to become an accepted member of the local scientific community. At the same time, it could not become isolated from the larger Xerox culture.

Xerox considered a number of locations and carefully evaluated such aspects as their scientific excellence and relevance, university liaison programs, licensing programs, and university recruiting programs. The company came up with four potential locations: Paris, Grenoble, Barcelona, and Munich. At that point, Xerox also identified potential laboratory leaders. The company chose Grenoble on the basis of its demonstrated scientific excellence and hired as the initial laboratory leader a highly regarded French scientist with good connections to local universities. Xerox designed a facility for 40 researchers and made plans for further expansion. In order to integrate the new laboratory's scientists into the Xerox community, senior R&D management in Palo Alto, California, allocated a considerable part of the initial laboratory budget to travel to other Xerox sites and started a program for the temporary transfer of newly hired researchers from Grenoble to other R&D sites. At the same time, the Grenoble site set out to integrate itself within the local research community.

In 1989, Eli Lilly considered establishing a home-base-exploiting laboratory in East Asia. The company's objective was to commercialize its R&D more effectively in foreign markets. Until then, Eli Lilly had operated one home-base-augmenting laboratory site abroad and some small sites in industrialized countries for clinical testing and drug approval procedures. But in order to exploit Lilly's R&D capabilities and product portfolio, the company needed a dedicated laboratory site in East Asia. The new site would support efforts to manufacture and market pharmaceuticals by adapting products to local needs. To that end, the management team decided that the new laboratory would have to be located close to relevant markets and existing corporate facilities. It also determined that the initial laboratory leader would have to be an experienced manager from Lilly's home base—a manager with a deep understanding of both the company's local operations and its overall R&D network.

The team considered Singapore as a potential location because of its proximity to a planned Lilly manufacturing site in Malaysia. But ultimately it decided that the new home-base-exploiting laboratory would have the strongest impact on Lilly's sales if it was located in Kobe, Japan. By establishing a site in the Kobe-Osaka region—the second-largest regional market in Japan and one that offered educational institutions with high-quality scientists—Lilly would send a signal to the medical community there that the company was committed to the needs of the Japanese market. Kobe had another advantage: Lilly's corporate headquarters for Japan were located there, and the company was already running some of its drug approval operations for the Japanese market out of Kobe. The city therefore was the logical choice.

The team assigned an experienced Lilly researcher and manager to be the initial leader of the new site. Because he knew the company inside and out—from central research and development to international marketing—the team reasoned that he would be able to bring the new laboratory up to speed quickly by drawing on resources from various divisions within Lilly. In order to integrate the new site into the over-all company, some researchers from other Lilly R&D sites received temporary transfers of up to two years to Kobe, and some locally hired researchers were temporarily transferred to other Lilly sites. It took about 30 months to activate fully the Kobe operation—a relatively short period. Today the site is very productive in transferring knowledge from Lilly's home base to Kobe and in commercializing that knowledge throughout Japan and Asia.

research to manufacturing. A silicon-wafer plant, for example, has to interact closely with product development engineers during trial runs of a new generation of microchips. The same is true for the manufacture of disk drives and other complex hardware. For that reason, Hewlett-Packard and Texas Instruments both operate laboratories in Singapore, close to manufacturing facilities.

The more complex and varied a manufacturing process is, the more often manufacturing engineers will have to interact with product development engineers. For example, in the case of one of Toshiba's laptop-computer-manufacturing plants, a new model is introduced to the manufacturing line every two weeks. The introduction has to happen seamlessly, without disturbing the production of existing models on the same line. In order to predict and remedy bugs during initial production runs, development engineers and manufacturing engineers meet several times a week. The proximity of Toshiba's laptop-development laboratory to its manufacturing plant greatly facilitates the interaction.

ESTABLISHING A NEW R&D FACILITY

Whether establishing a home-base-augmenting or a home-base-exploiting facility, companies must use the same three-stage process: selecting the best laboratory leader, determining the optimal size for the new laboratory site, and keeping close watch over the lab during its start-up period in order to ensure that it is merged into the company's existing global R&D network and contributes sufficiently to the company's product portfolio and its economic performance.

Selecting the Best Site Leader. Identifying the best leader for a new R&D site is one of the most important decisions a company faces in its quest to establish a successful global

R&D network. My research shows that the initial leader of an R&D site has a powerful impact not only on the culture of the site but also on its long-term research agenda and performance. The two types of sites require different types of leaders, and each type of leader confronts a particular set of challenges.

The initial leaders of home-base-augmenting sites should be prominent local scientists so that they will be able to fulfill their primary responsibility: to nurture ties between the new site and the local scientific community. If the site does not succeed in becoming part of the local scientific community quickly, it will not be able to generate new knowledge for the company. In addition to hiring a local scientist, there are a variety of other ways to establish local ties. For example, Toshiba used its memory-chip joint venture with Siemens to develop local ties at its new R&D site in Regensburg, Germany. The venture allowed Toshiba to tap into Siemens's dense network of associations with local universities. In addition, it helped Toshiba develop a better understanding of the compensation packages required to hire first-class German engineering graduates. Finally, it let the company gain useful insights into how to establish effective contract-research relationships with government-funded research institutions in Germany.

In contrast, the initial leaders of home-base-exploiting sites should be highly regarded managers from within the company—managers who are intimately familiar with the company's culture and systems. Such leaders will be able to fulfill their primary responsibility: to forge close ties between the new lab's engineers and the foreign community's manufacturing and marketing facilities. Then the transfer of knowledge from the company's home base to the R&D site will have the maximum impact on manufacturing and marketing located near that site. When one U.S. pharmaceutical company established a home-base-exploiting site in Great Britain, executives appointed as the initial site leader a manager who had been with the company for several years. He had started his career as a bench scientist first in exploratory research, then in the development of one of the company's blockbuster drugs. He had worked closely with marketing, and he had spent two years as supervisor of manufacturing quality at one of the company's U.S. manufacturing sites. With such a background, he was able to lead the new site effectively.

However, the best candidates for both home-base-augmenting and home-base-exploiting sites share four qualities: they are at once respected scientists or engineers and skilled managers; they are able to integrate the new site into the company's existing R&D network; they have a comprehensive understanding of technology trends; and they are able to overcome formal barriers when they seek access to new ideas in local universities and scientific communities.

Appointing an outstanding scientist or engineer who has no management experience can be disastrous. In one case, a leading U.S. electronics company decided to establish a home-base-augmenting site in the United Kingdom. The engineer who was appointed as the first site leader was an outstanding researcher but had little management experience outside the company's central laboratory environment. The leader had difficulties marshaling the necessary resources to expand the laboratory beyond its starting size of fourteen researchers. Furthermore, he had a tough time mediating between the research laboratory and the company's product development area. Eleven of the fourteen researchers had been hired locally and therefore lacked deep ties to the company. They needed a savvy corporate advocate who could understand company politics and could promote their research results within the company. One reason they didn't have such an advocate was that two of the three managers at the company's home base—people who had promoted the establishment of the new R&D lab—had quit about six months after the lab had opened because they disagreed about the company's overall R&D strategy. The third manager had moved to a different department.

In an effort to improve the situation, the company appointed a U.S. engineer as liaison to the U.K. site. He realized that few ideas were flowing from the site to the home base; but he attributed the problem to an inherently slow scientific-discovery process rather than to organizational barriers within the company. After about two years, senior management finally replaced the initial laboratory leader and the U.S. liaison engineer with two managers—one from the United Kingdom and one from the United States. The managers had experience overseeing one of the company's U.S. joint ventures in technology, and they also had good track records as researchers. Finally, under their leadership, the site dramatically increased its impact on the company's product portfolio. In conjunction with the increase in scientific output, the site grew to its projected size of 225 employees and is now highly productive.

In the case of both types of sites, the ideal leader has in-depth knowledge of both the home-base culture and the foreign culture. Consider Sharp's experience. In Japan, fewer corporate scientists have Ph.D.'s than their counterparts in the United Kingdom; instead they have picked up their knowledge and skills on the job. That difference presented a management challenge for Sharp when it established a home-base-augmenting facility in the United Kingdom. In order to cope with that challenge, the company hired a British laboratory leader who had previously worked as a science attaché at the British embassy in Japan. In that position, he had developed a good understanding of the Japanese higher-education system. He was well aware that British and Japanese engineers with different academic degrees might have similar levels of expertise, and, as a result, he could manage them better.

The pioneer who heads a newly established home-base-augmenting or home-base-exploiting site also must have a broad perspective and a deep understanding of technology trends. R&D sites abroad are often particularly good at combining knowledge from different scientific fields into new ideas and products. Because those sites start with a clean slate far from the company's powerful central laboratory, they are less plagued by the "not-invented-here" syndrome. For example, Canon's home-base-augmenting laboratory in the United Kingdom developed an innovative loudspeaker that is now being manufactured in Europe for a worldwide market. Senior researchers at Canon in Japan acknowledge that it would have been much more difficult for a new research team located in Japan to come up with the product. As one Canon manager puts it, "Although the new loudspeaker was partially based on knowledge that existed within Canon already, Canon's research management in Japan was too focused on existing product lines and would probably not have tolerated the pioneering loudspeaker project."

Finally, leaders of new R&D sites need to be aware of the considerable formal barriers they might confront when they seek access to local universities and scientific communities. These barriers are often created by lawmakers who want to protect a nation's intellectual capital. Although foreign companies do indeed absorb local knowledge and transfer it to their home bases—particularly in the case of home-base-augmenting sites—they also create important positive economic effects for the host nation. The laboratory leader of a new R&D site needs to communicate that fact locally in order to reduce existing barriers and prevent the formation of new ones.

Determining the Optimal Size of the New R&D Site. My research indicates that the optimal size for a new foreign R&D facility during the start-up phase is usually 30 to

40 employees, and the best size for a site after the ramp-up period is about 235 employees, including support staff. The optimal size of a site depends mainly on a company's track record in international management. Companies that already operate several sites abroad tend to be more successful at establishing larger new sites.

Companies can run into problems if their foreign sites are either too small or too large. If the site is too small, the resulting lack of critical mass produces an environment in which there is little cross-fertilization of ideas among researchers. And a small R&D site generally does not command a sufficient level of respect in the scientific community surrounding the laboratory. As a result, its researchers have a harder time gaining access to informal networks and to scientific meetings that provide opportunities for an exchange of knowledge. In contrast, if the laboratory site is too large, its culture quickly becomes anonymous, researchers become isolated, and the benefits of spreading fixed costs over a larger number of researchers are outweighed by the lack of cross-fertilization of ideas. According to one manager at such a lab, "Once people stopped getting to know one another on an informal basis in the lunchroom of our site, they became afraid of deliberately walking into one another's laboratory rooms to talk about research and to ask questions. Researchers who do not know each other on an informal basis are often hesitant to ask their colleagues for advice: they are afraid to reveal any of their own knowledge gaps. We realized that we had crossed a critical threshold in size. We subsequently scaled back somewhat and made an increased effort to reduce the isolation of individual researchers within the site through communication tools and through rotating researchers among different lab units at the site."

Supervising the Start-Up Period. During the initial growth period of an R&D site, which typically lasts anywhere from one to three years, the culture is formed and the groundwork for the site's future productivity is laid. During that period, senior management in the home country has to be in particularly close contact with the new site. Although it is important that the new laboratory develop its own identity and stake out its fields of expertise, it also has to be closely connected to the company's existing R&D structure. Newly hired scientists must be aware of the resources that exist within the company as a whole, and scientists at home and at other locations must be aware of the opportunities the new site creates for the company as a whole. Particularly during the start-up period, senior R&D managers at the corporate level have to walk a fine line and decide whether to devote the most resources to connecting the new site to the company or to supporting ties between the new site and its local environment.

To integrate a new site into the company as a whole, managers must pay close attention to the site's research agenda and create mechanisms to integrate it into the company's overall strategic goals. Because of the high degree of uncertainty of R&D outcomes, continuous adjustments to research agendas are the rule. What matters most is speed, both in terms of terminating research projects that go nowhere and in terms of pushing projects that bring unexpectedly good results.

The rapid exchange of information is essential to integrating a site into the overall company during the start-up phase. Companies use a number of mechanisms to create a cohesive research community in spite of geographic distance. Hewlett-Packard regularly organizes an in-house science fair at which teams of researchers can present projects and prototypes to one another. Canon has a program that lets researchers from home-base-augmenting sites request a temporary transfer to home-base-exploiting sites. At Xerox, most sites are linked by a sophisticated information system that allows senior R&D managers to determine within minutes the current state of research projects and the number of researchers working on those projects. But nothing can replace face-to-face contact between active researchers. Maintaining a global R&D network requires personal meetings, and therefore many researchers and R&D managers have to spend time visiting not only other R&D sites but also specialized suppliers and local universities affiliated with those sites.

Failing to establish sufficient ties with the company's existing R&D structure during the start-up phase can hamper the success of a new foreign R&D site. For example, in 1986, a large foreign pharmaceutical company established a biotechnology research site in Boston, Massachusetts. In order to recruit outstanding scientists and maintain a high level of creative output, the company's R&D management decided to give the new laboratory considerable leeway in its research agenda and in determining what to do with the results—although the company did reserve the right of first refusal for the commercialization of the lab's inventions. The new site was staffed exclusively with scientists handpicked by a newly hired laboratory leader. A renowned local biochemist, he had been employed for many years by a major U.S. university, where he had carried out contract research for the company. During the start-up phase, few of the company's veteran scientists were involved in joint research projects with the site's scientists—an arrangement that hindered the transfer of ideas between the new lab and the company's other R&D sites. Although the academic community now recognizes the lab as an important contributor to the field, few of its inventions have been patented by the company, fewer have been targeted for commercialization, and none have reached the commercial stage yet. One senior scientist working in the lab commented that ten years after its creation, the lab had become so much of an "independent animal" that it would take a lot of carefully balanced guidance from the company to instill a stronger sense of commercial orientation without a risk of losing the most creative scientists.

There is no magic formula that senior managers can follow to ensure the success of a foreign R&D site during its start-up phase. Managing an R&D network, particularly in its early stages, is delicate and complex. It requires constant tinkering—evaluation and reevaluation. Senior R&D managers have to decide how much of the research should be initiated by the company and how much by the scientist, determine the appropriate incentive structures and employment contracts, establish policies for the temporary transfer of researchers to the company's other R&D or manufacturing sites, and choose universities from which to hire scientists and engineers.

Flexibility and experimentation during a site's start-up phase can ensure its future productivity. For example, Fujitsu established a software-research laboratory site in San Jose, California, in 1992. The company was seriously thinking of establishing a second site in Boston but eventually reconsidered. Fujitsu realized that the effort that had gone into establishing the San Jose site had been greater than expected. Once the site was up and running, however, its productive output also had been higher than expected. Furthermore, Fujitsu found that its R&D managers had gained an excellent understanding of the R&D community that created advanced software-development tools. Although initially leaning toward establishing a second site, the managers were flexible. They decided to enlarge the existing site because of its better-than-expected performance as well as the limited potential benefits of a second site. The San Jose site has had a major impact on Fujitsu's software development and sales—particularly in Japan but in the United States, too. Similarly, at Alcatel's first foreign R&D site in Germany, senior managers were flexible. After several months, they realized that the travel-and-communications budget would have to be increased substantially beyond initial projections in order to improve the flow of knowledge from the French home base. For instance, in the case of a telephone switchboard project, the actual number of business trips between the two sites was nearly twice as high as originally projected.

INTEGRATING THE GLOBAL R&D NETWORK

As the number of companies' R&D sites at home and abroad grows, R&D managers will increasingly face the challenging task of coordinating the network. That will require a fundamental shift in the role of senior managers at the central lab. Managers of R&D networks must be global coordinators, not local administrators. More than being managers of people and processes, they must be managers of knowledge. And not all managers that a company has in place will be up to the task.

Consider Matsushita's R&D management. A number of technically competent managers became obsolete at the company once it launched a global approach to R&D. Today managers at Matsushita's central R&D site in Hirakata, Japan, continue to play an important role in the research and development of core processes for manufacturing. But the responsibility of an increasing number of senior managers at the central site is overseeing Matsushita's network of 15 dedicated R&D sites. That responsibility includes setting research agendas, monitoring results, and creating direct ties between sites.

How does the new breed of R&D manager coordinate global knowledge? Look again to Matsushita's central R&D site. First, high-level corporate managers in close cooperation with senior R&D managers develop an overall research agenda and assign different parts of it to individual sites. The process is quite tricky. It requires that the managers in charge have a good understanding of not only the technological capabilities that Matsushita will need to develop in the future but also the stock of technological capabilities already available to it.

Matsushita's central lab organizes two or three yearly off-site meetings devoted to informing R&D scientists and engineers about the entire company's current state of technical knowledge and capabilities. At the same meetings, engineers who have moved from R&D to take over manufacturing and marketing responsibilities inform R&D members about trends in Matsushita's current and potential future markets. Under the guidance of senior project managers, members from R&D, manufacturing, and marketing determine timelines and resource requirements for specific home-base-augmenting and home-base-exploiting projects. One R&D manager notes, "We discuss not only why a specific scientific insight might be interesting for Matsushita but also how we can turn this insight into a product quickly. We usually seek to develop a prototype early. Prototypes are a good basis for a discussion with marketing and manufacturing. Most of our efforts are targeted at delivering the prototype of a slightly better mousetrap early rather than delivering the blueprint of a much better mousetrap late."

To stimulate the exchange of information, R&D managers at Matsushita's central lab create direct links among researchers across different sites. They promote the use of videoconferencing and frequent face-to-face contact to forge those ties. Reducing the instances in which the central lab must act as mediator means that existing knowledge travels more quickly through the company and new ideas percolate more easily. For example, a researcher at a home-base-exploiting site in Singapore can communicate with another researcher at a home-base-exploiting site in Franklin Park, Illinois, about potential new research projects much more readily now that central R&D fosters informal and formal direct links.

Finally, managers at Matsushita's central lab constantly monitor new regional pockets of knowledge as well as the company's expanding network of manufacturing sites to determine whether the company will need additional R&D locations. With 15 major sites around the world, Matsushita has decided that the number of sites is sufficient at this point. But the company is ever vigilant about surveying the landscape and knows that as the landscape changes, its decision could, too.

As more pockets of knowledge emerge worldwide and competition in foreign markets mounts, the imperative to create global R&D networks will grow all the more pressing. Only those companies that embrace a global approach to R&D will meet the competitive challenges of the new dynamic. And only those managers who embrace their fundamentally new role as global coordinators and managers of knowledge will be able to tap the full potential of their R&D networks.

EXHIBIT 1

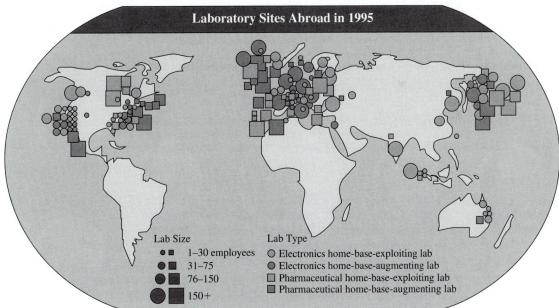

Laboratory Sites Abroad in 1995

Lab Size
- 1–30 employees
- 31–75
- 76–150
- 150+

Lab Type
- ○ Electronics home-base-exploiting lab
- ◐ Electronics home-base-augmenting lab
- □ Pharmaceutical home-base-exploiting lab
- ■ Pharmaceutical home-base-augmenting lab

EXHIBIT 2   Establishing New R&D Sites

Types of R&D Sites	Phase 1 Location Decision	Phase 2 Ramp-Up Period	Phase 3 Maximizing Lab Impact
Home-Base-Augmenting Laboratory Site Objective of establishment: absorbing knowledge from the local scientific community, creating new knowledge, and transferring it to the company's central R&D site	–Select a location for its scientific excellence –Promote cooperation between the company's senior scientists and managers	–Choose as first laboratory leader a renowned local scientist with international experience—one who understands the dynamics of R&D at the new location –Ensure enough critical mass	–Ensure the laboratory's active participation in the local scientific community –Exchange researchers with local university laboratories and with the home-base lab
Home-Base-Exploiting Laboratory Site Objective of establishment: commercializing knowledge by transferring it from the company's home base to the laboratory site abroad and from there to local manufacturing and marketing	–Select a location for its proximity to the company's existing manufacturing and marketing locations –Involve middle managers from other functional areas in start-up decisions	–Choose as first laboratory leader an experienced product-development engineer with a strong company-wide reputation, international experience, and knowledge of marketing and manufacturing	–Emphasize smooth relations with the home-base lab –Encourage employees to seek interaction with other corporate units beyond the manufacturing and marketing units that originally sponsored the lab

EXHIBIT 3   How Information Flows Between Home-Base and Foreign R&D Sites

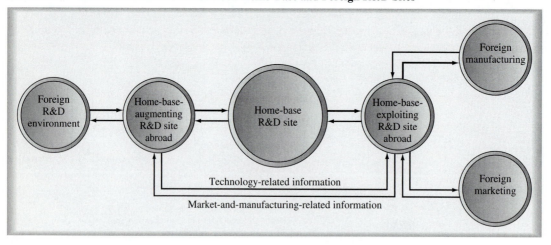

Project Dreamcast: Serious Play at Sega Enterprises Ltd.

Ueno Kunihisa, chief of operational planning in Sega's Consumer Business Group, had just returned to his office following his daily staff meeting, where he had been assured that preparations for the launch of Sega's Dreamcast™ home video game platform were on track. Satô Hideki, head of the development and production group for consumer goods and the project's guiding light, indicated that the hardware design had been finalized for production, while game software development remained on schedule both inside and outside the company. Large retailers had begun to place significant orders for the year-end gift-giving season in Japan, and it seemed that enough hardware and game software would be in the market by then for Sega to recoup some of the huge financial investment the project had entailed. Finally, the marketing group had initiated the press and television advertising campaigns to bring public interest to a crescendo for the system's November 27, 1998 launch—a very short eight weeks from today.

All in all, Ueno was pleased with his staff's work and optimistic about Dreamcast's prospects. This was all the more pleasing because the Saturn™ game system, Sega's previous generation of home video game hardware, had not been successful—and Ueno was not going to allow that to happen again.

Then the phone rang. It was Satô, with news he had just received about production figures for Dreamcast's graphics engine chip, the Power VR2. Designed by VideoLogic, a British company, and produced by NEC at a state-of-the-art plant in Kyûshû, the graphics engine gave the Dreamcast system the computational power needed to render and animate in three-dimensions the thousands of Sega characters, such as Sonic the Hedgehog and the Virtual Fighters. Despite NEC's continuing claims that production goals would be met, Satô's new figures suggested that NEC would only be able to provide one-third of the Power VR2 chip production necessary for product launch. Alarmed by the news, Satô recommended that Ueno, Sega president Irimajiri and he go to Kyûshû to learn the complete truth behind the numbers. For if they were accurate, Ueno and the whole Sega organization

Harvard Business School Case No. 9-600-028. Copyright 1999 President and Fellows of Harvard College. All rights reserved. For information: permissions@hbsp.harvard.edu.

This case was prepared by Stefan Thomke and Andrew Robertson. HBS cases are developed solely for class discussion and do not necessarily illustrate effective or ineffective management.

would face a very tough choice: either delay the launch date or reduce the supply of machines available at launch.

As he pondered Satô's call, Ueno recalled the daring and very successful promotional campaign—known as "Yukawa Ganbare!"—that he and his staff had organized to separate the Sega name from the very public failings of its Saturn game system. Playing off both the surreal quality of home video games and the genuine suffering that Saturn's failure had caused Sega's executives, a series of commercials had described the fall and abasement of Yukawa Hidekazu, an actual corporate manager at Sega. Teased by children—"Wow, Saturn really sucks!"—beaten by thugs, taunted by child demons, and eventually reduced to a stammering, nervous wreck hiding under his desk, Yukawa Hidekazu only found the will to live in the promise of Dreamcast. Not only had the campaign generated considerable public interest, its final episode was scheduled to initiate the launch of the Dreamcast system. Changing the launch date to accommodate the hardware shortage would mean revising the associated marketing campaign. Launching without sufficient hardware to feed the demand generated by the marketing campaign would result in an inefficient use of marketing resources. Moreover, both options could generate significant resentment in potential customers and game software suppliers.

SEGA ENTERPRISES, LTD.

Founded by two Americans in 1951 to import arcade games for U.S. armed forces in Japan, Sega remained for many years an importer of pinball machines and jukeboxes. Acquired by Gulf + Western in 1969, the successful small trading company's brush with international capital stimulated a period of strenuous growth. Under Gulf + Western's policy of diversification, Sega developed its own domestic manufacturing capabilities and by the late 1970s entered the amusement arcade business both as a supplier of machines and manager of arcades. Unfortunately, lacking the necessary marketing expertise, Sega floundered. In December 1978 Gulf + Western purchased Esuko Bôeki, a mid-sized trading company in the game equipment industry, and merged it with Sega. Nakayama Hayao, president of Esuko, became Sega's vice president for Marketing. By 1983, revenues had tripled, to 24.3 billion yen, and Nakayama had become Sega's president.[1]

In that same year, with growth slowing in the arcade business, Nakayama decided to enter the home video market with an 8-bit game system called the SG-1000. Much to the alarm of Gulf + Western's corporate management, Sega developed an aggressive strategy to expand this business. Having watched the American home video game market implode in 1983, Gulf + Western's management took a dim view of these plans. In response, Nakayama searched for a corporate parent more supportive of Sega's high tech adventures. By May 1984, he had convinced CSK, a Japanese computer and electronics manufacturer, to purchase 70 percent of Sega's stock. Nakayama purchased the rest. With CSK's technical support, Sega now had the expertise to enter the home video game market. Although, in the end, the SG-1000 sold only haltingly in both the United States and

---

[1] Some of the information comes from A. Brandenburger, "Power Play (B): Sega in 16-bit Video Games," Harvard Business School, Case No. 795-103, pp. 2–3; I. Nonaka, M. Osaka, E. Fukushima, "Sega Entâpuraisesu—Sofuto Ichiba Sôzô," Keiei Academî, Shakai Keizai Seisan Honbu Kêsu No. 29, 1.

Japan, the success of the second generation Mega Drive™ would prove Nakayama's faith in the market.

Sega launched the 16-bit Mega Drive in Japan in October 1983. Despite a significant technical advantage over the market-leading Nintendo Famicon™ game system, the Mega Drive struggled to attract customers. Unable to convince third-party software houses to write game software for its system, Sega sales in Japan languished. Few of Nintendo's game aficionados wanted to give up the plethora of titles produced for the Nintendo system in exchange for the performance advantages of Sega. When Nintendo released its next generation 16-bit machine, the Super Famicon, in Japan in November 1990, Mega Drive's fate was sealed. By 1992, it held only 8 percent of the domestic market. Overseas, however, it proved extremely profitable. Marketed under the name Genesis™ in Europe and the U.S., Nakayama's brainchild benefited from better software and Nintendo's delay in marketing the Super Famicon. Propelled by European and American hunger for Sonic the Hedgehog and his friends—Sega's first blockbuster video game—net sales expanded at an annual rate of 58 percent between 1989 and 1993, with sales of home video game–related products leading the way at an annual growth rate of 74 percent. By 1993, fully 92 percent of its home video game revenue came from exports to European and American markets. Pundits remarked that Sega should consider relocating its corporate headquarters to its Sega of America operations in California.[2]

But suddenly, from 1993 to 1997, Sega's North American market share dropped from over 60 percent to less than 10 percent. In 1994, Sega had released its successor to Genesis, the 32-bit Sega Saturn™, which defined the state of the art in home video game hardware. At the same time, pressured by Sega of America management, Nakayama ordered the development of 32X, an alternate 32-bit machine exclusively for the U.S. and European market; its performance was lower, but it was compatible with the older Genesis machines and its software. Because Sega lacked the financial clout to support dual marketing and software development, both machines struggled. Finally, when Sony Computer Entertainment entered the market in September 1995 with its Sony PlayStation™, a low-cost, high-performance 32-bit system with very popular game software, it rapidly took market share away from Sega and Nintendo. By 1997, despite some initial success in Japan, Sega Saturn was also in retreat in the face of strong PlayStation competition. As one Sega executive put it, given the cost, marketing, and software problems associated with Sega Saturn, "we did well to last as long as we did."

In April 1998, after 15 years at the helm, Nakayama stepped down as the president of the company. Into his boots, stepped Irimajiri Shôichirô, a young, forceful executive vice president. To rescue the company's fortunes in the development of its next generation of game hardware, Irimajiri pressed for a return to Sega's core competency, digital creativity. Recognizing that cutting-edge hardware and mind-blowing game software were not the only criteria for success, Irimajiri demanded from his employees a reorientation of priorities towards customers, merchants, and software developers. Mimicking the Zero Defect quality control programs so widespread in Japanese businesses, he summed up Sega's new management philosophy in his "Three Zeroes": 1) Zero distance to customers; 2) Zero delay in responding to customers; and 3) Zero disappointment in dealing with customers.[3]

---

[2] Sega Enterprises Ltd., Annual Report, 1994.

[3] Ibid.

COMPETITIVE BATTLES IN THE WORLD VIDEO GAME MARKETS

The economic downturn that had hung over the Japanese market for seven long years had finally blossomed into full-grown recession by 1997. For the first time since the oil shocks of the early 1970s, the economy shrank, and domestic consumption dropped. Unlike those days, however, the nation seemed paralyzed, unable to decide upon a politically and economically coherent course of action. For a nation only a decade earlier dreaming of a Japanese twenty-first century, the humiliation was almost unendurable. Pessimism was rife, fomenting comparisons, admittedly ill-conceived, with the desolation of the immediate postwar period. In the home video game market, a price war erupted between Sega, Sony Computer Entertainment, and Nintendo (see **Exhibit 4**). Low demand—over 90 percent of households with teenage children owned a video game system already—coupled with the general economic contraction led to a 29.3 percent reduction in the size of the Japanese market.[4] At the same time, however, growth in the world video game markets continued to be very impressive. Projections indicated that 1999 hardware and game software revenue would be in excess of US$15 billion in the U.S. and Japan alone, with most of the gains coming from the thriving U.S. economy (see **Exhibit 3b**).

Despite these dislocations, Sony Computer Entertainment further tightened its grip on the home video game market. Only recently, its corporate parent, Sony, had seemed to be another slow-moving conglomerate unable to diversify—losing billions in its investments in Hollywood—and incapable of reviving growth in its core television and stereo industries. It had posted its first-ever loss—US$2.8 billion—in 1994. But by 1997, Sony was enjoying record sales and profits. Key to this transformation had been the repositioning of Sony and its products undertaken by its iconoclastic, Porsche-driving president, Idei Nobuyuki. Appointed in 1994, Idei decided to focus on the development of high margin, premium price products that leveraged both Sony's strength in design and manufacturing and its reputation for quality and value. As one component of this strategy, Idei had continued support for the development of Sony's first product for the home video game industry, the Sony PlayStation.[5]

Launched in September 1995, the PlayStation mobilized Sony's considerable hardware, software and manufacturing expertise in consumer operations. Sony also developed a significant new approach to the gaming business. Reducing the cost of game development with a combination of better technical support and better and cheaper game development software, Sony offered customers a huge range of game software choices. Because the company had reduced the cost of game development, it could also position the PlayStation to enter an untouched market, one ignored by Sega and Nintendo in their pursuit of teenagers and comprising tens of millions of older, more sophisticated twenty-somethings who had either stopped or never started gaming. Hirai Kazuo, a Sony Computer Entertainment executive, described the shift: "PlayStation is more than a toy. It's our dream to see a PlayStation console in every house, just like VCRs and CD players." Holding over 57 percent

---

[4] "Goodbye Hashimoto," *The Economist,* vol. 348, no. 8077 (July 18, 1998), 17; K. Yokota, "Sega Casts Game System Dreams with New 128-bit Machine: Analysts Say Sales Will Depend on Titles, Market Likely to Fade," *Nihon Keizai Shinbun* (September 7, 1998), 1.

[5] P. Abrahams, "The Greatest Challenge Yet Lies Ahead: Nobuyuki Idei: This Year May Be a Difficult One for Sony's Quick-Thinking President," *Financial Times* (London) (November 30, 1998), 4.

of the domestic home video game hardware market, 53 percent of the American market, and 65 percent of the European market, and possessing a software line with titles numbering in the thousands, in 1997 it looked like Hirai's dream could possibly come true.[6]

Meanwhile, Nintendo, the longstanding champion of the home video game industry, deployed its Nintendo 64 game system, the first to allow full 3D graphics. This came at a price, however. Production problems with the Silicon Graphics–designed graphics processor delayed its launch. When finally released in June 1996, the system was almost a year late. Having splendid 64-bit graphics and allowing users to maneuver characters through a virtual, three-dimensional world, the Nintendo 64 offered a transcendent experience for game designers and players.

But independent game software suppliers, like Square and Namco, shunned development for the Nintendo 64. The hardware's complexity made game software development risky and expensive—which was compounded by Nintendo reserving the right to block release of a game it determined to be of insufficient quality. Indeed, Sony's current stimulation of the software market appalled Nintendo executives. Nintendo's president, Yamauchi Hiroshi, complained, "Those who believe that 'the more games the better' are just ignorant of the actual market situation . . . . The current flood of thousands of games each year is surely ruining the market." Nintendo set the bar high, and many companies had seen costly game development projects derailed by seemingly arbitrary decisions from Nintendo's management. Thus, although way behind schedule, at launch the Nintendo 64 had only three games to run on it. Engrossing as these were, by comparison competitors already had software titles numbering in the hundreds. By virtue of strong sales of its Game Boy, a handheld game unit for children aged 7 to 12, Nintendo could still claim 31 percent of the domestic home video game market. In the 32/64-bit sector of the hardware market, however, it held only 14 percent compared to Sony's 73 percent share.[7]

The same fate befell Sega and its 32-bit offering, the Sega Saturn. Launched in November 1994, it initially grabbed market share from the aging Nintendo Super Famicon technology. In 1995, Sega finally seized leadership of the domestic home video game market from Nintendo. The elation was short-lived. Like Nintendo, Sega suffered in comparison to the Sony PlayStation, in terms of price and software. Although not as authoritarian as Nintendo in relations with its game software developers, Sega relied for the majority of its software development on in-house games created for its arcade business; consequently, it did not wholeheartedly support external game developers like Sony did. Although Sega marketed a greater range of software than Nintendo, by 1997 its share of the total hardware market had dropped to an anemic 9.8 percent. Its share of the 32/64-bit sector was little better at 12.5 percent.[8]

With the advent of the PlayStation, the organization of the Japanese home video game industry underwent a profound shift. Sony Computer Entertainment now stood as the

[6] I. Kunii, S. Brull, P. Burrows, E. Baig, "The Games Sony Plays," *BusinessWeek* (June 15, 1998), 129; P. Roberts, "Sony Changes the Game," *Fast Company* (August–September, 1997), 122; Yokota, "Sega Casts," 1.

[7] A. Pollack, "Nintendo Chief Is All Work, No Play; Seeking a Turnaround with Souped Up Machines and a Few New Games," *The New York Times* (August 26, 1996), D1; "Video Games: Nintendo Wakes Up," *The Economist* (August 3, 1996), 55; *Toy Journal,* Tokyo Toys and Dolls Wholesalers Association (July, 1998).

[8] *Toy Journal,* Tokyo Toys and Dolls Wholesalers Association (July, 1998).

single dominant company, with the traditional powers, Nintendo and Sega, a distant second and third. In November 1998 Sega stood poised to roll the dice again, betting on the success of its 128-bit Dreamcast platform, which sported 3D processing power ten times that of the PlayStation and the Nintendo 64. But the issue of technical support for the game manufacturers remained critical. "The problem, that Sega has, is that they have burned people before,"[9] remarked an industry expert commenting on the millions invested and lost on game development for the Sega Saturn. Still, with the successor to the Sony PlayStation not expected until late 1999 and Nintendo's still later, a well-executed launch of a new product could blindside both companies. The risks were high. Usui Okitane, a vice president at Sega, described Sega's situation:

> Frankly, I would characterize this business as "Go Big or Go Home." You either make a $500 million profit or as easily a $500 million loss. There is no middle ground.

Despite deep pockets from its operations in the arcade business, another catastrophe like Sega Saturn would certainly put an end to what remained of the company's reputation as a manufacturer of home video game hardware. And it could conceivably push the company into severe financial distress.

HARDWARE AND GAME SOFTWARE DEVELOPMENT

The home video game industry is characterized by two complementary areas: hardware and game software. The main game hardware players, Sony Computer Entertainment, Nintendo, and Sega Enterprises, all competed in the same key markets in Japan, U.S.A, and Europe. Because of differences in customer tastes and consumption patterns, in addition to developing its own game software products, each manufacturer built ties to local game software producers. In Japan, these were Namco, Capcom, Square, Bandai, and ASCII. In the United States, the prominent game software companies were Midway, THQ, Electronic Arts, and Acclaim. Software companies were not contractually held to a given hardware producer and thus were free to transport a game from one game system to a competing hardware platform.

Essentially a dedicated computer, optimized for graphics and sound processing, a typical home video game system comprised a handheld controller and a processing unit. Commands from the player were interpolated with program data loaded into the processing unit and the result displayed on a television set. Unlike computers, however, these machines lacked hard drives and monitors. Given the cost sensitivity of the targeted audience—overwhelmingly male and generally aged between 10 and 30—such additions were undesirable. Still, recent innovations in hardware design included separate graphics and sound processors, CD program storage, and modems. Despite the complexity of the product, cost constraints demanded that these systems be developed, manufactured, assembled, packaged, distributed, and promoted for a unit price only a little more than one-tenth that of Dell's top of the line laptop computer (see **Exhibit 6**).

Each company's software was proprietary. Likewise, succeeding generations of any given manufacturer's hardware tended not to be backwardly compatible—Sega Genesis

---

[9] J. Angwin, "Gamemakers Girding for Video Battle," *The San Francisco Chronicle* (May 28, 1998), Business, D1.

games would not run on the Sega Saturn. Sega attempted to take advantage of backward compatibility in designing its 32X system to run Sega Genesis games, but maintaining backward compatibility increased cost and reduced performance. Finally, all hardware producers used security circuitry in their hardware to enforce market discipline. Thus, Sega Saturn games released in the Japanese market could not run on machines destined for America. This allowed hardware manufacturers to develop independent software development and marketing strategies for the American, European, and Japanese markets. Not surprisingly, there was a small but vigorous black market on the Internet for the purchase of chips to circumvent these security measures.

Given a lack of standardization across product lines both inside and outside companies, the development cycle averaged about five years—a long time in an industry using components that as a rule doubled in performance every 18 months. Hardware designers had to remain flexible to take advantage of unpredictable shifts in technological capabilities. At the same time, because hardware platforms and game software were developed nearly simultaneously, hardware designers needed to specify in advance the data standards and protocols to be used.

High quality game software was key to successfully launching a new hardware system. Without a good software base and the promise of more to come, hardware manufacturers would have a hard time attracting converts to their game platforms, no matter how technically sophisticated. At the same time, manufacturers lured software developers through a large installed base of machines and thus a large base of captive customers (see **Exhibit 3**). Sony and more recently Sega and Nintendo had escaped this dilemma in three ways: by aggressively pricing their home video game hardware, often below manufacturing costs; by building close technical support ties with software companies well prior to a new system's launch; and by developing game software in-house. If a new system did not sell briskly, getting the software houses to continue investing in game development became an increasingly difficult proposition. Profits and revenue for hardware manufacturers derived mostly from the sale of their own game software and royalties from the sale of games by software companies.

On average, a game required one year, one million dollars, and a team of 10 to 20 programmers to develop; it had a product life of about three months, during which development costs had to be recouped. Game software had to be released essentially perfect—there was rarely a "Version 2.0" of a game. Furthermore, young players were very unforgiving of products that gained poor reputations. Whether the issue was buggy code or "uncoolness," the game would not sell—indeed, it could not even be given away and would usually be off the shelves in weeks. On the other hand, blockbusters like Sega's "Virtual Fighter" or Square's "Final Fantasy" might remain in shops for years and spawn multiple spin-offs. Such products were often more expensive and time-consuming to develop, requiring 100 or more programmers, a budget of $8–10 million, and as much as three years, but could also generate hundreds of millions of dollars in revenue.[10]

---

[10] K. Sunagawa, "Nihon Gêmu Sangyô ni Miru Kigyôsha Katsudô no Keiki to Gijutsu Senryaku–Sega to Namuko ni Okeru Sofutouea Kaihatsu Soshiki no Keisei," *Keiei Shigaku* (1997) vol. 32, no. 4; R. Kohashi and K. Tadao, "The Exchanges and Development of Images: A Study of the Japanese Video Game Industry," Unpublished Paper, August 11, 1995, 14–15; Roberts, "Sony Changes," 126.

Game software design demanded artistic talent, imagination, and inventiveness to generate these worlds of wonder (see **Exhibit 2**). Successful game developers were stars—and supporting stars within the regimented environment of an engineering company was tricky. Many emulated the movie industry. Each major genre of game software—sports, action, role-playing games—was assigned to a studio. Headed by a virtuoso producer, every studio had multiple teams of 10–20 developers, each assigned to a different product and managed by a game director. A team was divided into three design specialties: graphics, programming, and sound, which allowed a fairly informal and consensual management approach. Marketing experts also worked closely with both producer and director. At the team level, management balanced scheduling and quality concerns against the freedom and initiative necessary to create free-wheeling video game "madness."[11]

PRODUCT DEVELOPMENT AT SEGA: CAPABILITIES AND RIGIDITIES

Sega's approach to home video game development was strongly influenced by its extensive arcade business and the close ties between the research and development organizations supporting it. During the slow, painful collapse of the Sega Saturn from 1995 to 1998, while the consumer goods division shrank by 60 percent, the amusement arcade operations and machine sales grew by 23 percent and 67 percent respectively. Though insufficient to stem the hemorrhaging caused by Sega Saturn, especially in its final phase, the active and robust arcade and arcade machinery businesses provided Sega with the financial resources to bankroll its next generation hardware platform development.

The support was not only financial. Since its inception in 1983, Sega's home video game business had drawn technical support, especially in game design, from Sega's arcade business. Sega ported libraries of arcade game software to its home video game hardware. While fiscally prudent, this reliance on its arcade game software had very real effects on Sega's positioning within the home video game market. Arcade games had to be sufficiently difficult to separate teenagers quickly from their money, 100 yen at a time. At the same time, the games had to be not so challenging that players would lose interest and not invest in becoming more skillful at a given game. Sega had to strike a delicate balance, and its developers had learned over many years to "get it just right." By contrast, home video games needed simply to sustain a player's interest in play for as long as possible, a very different development goal that could be achieved with a far larger range of games and play strategies than in the arcade business. Although Sega benefited from the popularity of its arcade games in marketing home video game software, the range of games available tended to suffer in comparison to its competitors, both of which lacked arcade businesses. Also, to attract players, arcade games had splashy graphics, good sound, and high powered processors that ramped up game difficulty quickly. Transferring game software from these machines forced Sega to push the envelope on home video game technology to insure the processing power necessary to make game software look as good in the living room as it did in the arcade. To support this, Sega developed a corporate culture strongly oriented towards hardware development and product lines that were consistently the most technically advanced in the market.

---

[11] Sunagawa, "Nihon Gêmu," 17.

Given its in-house focus, Sega did not develop strong ties to independent game software developers. Management believed that they already had a complete line of games and saw independent game developers as potential competitors in the high margin game software business. As a consequence, game software companies did not receive good product development support from Sega. The libraries and software for designing Sega game software were expensive and would arrive late, sometimes six months after Sega's internal game developers had acquired them, if at all. This problem was especially pronounced in the Saturn generation of machines. Third-party game developers found programming the dedicated graphics engine (named SPRITE) an exasperating, time-consuming chore. Rather than absorb these costs themselves, they chose simply not to develop game software for Saturn.

Less emphasis on design-to-cost was another consequence of the close ties between Sega's home video game and arcade businesses. Arcade machines were owned by corporate entities like Sega whereas home video game machines were primarily sold to teenagers and young adults. As a result of costlier designs, Sega machines tended to be relatively expensive at product launch. A possibly apocryphal story described how the chief engineer for the Sony PlayStation opened a Sega Saturn to inspect its production engineering. He derisively exclaimed, "Nattô!" (a Japanese food famous for its smell and sticky, glutinous quality). Realizing Saturn's complexity and hence production cost, he envisioned a simpler, less costly PlayStation design. In any event, Sega Saturn's price usually hovered about 5,000 yen above the PlayStation's (see **Exhibit 4a**).

SERIOUS PLAY: PROJECT DREAMCAST

Dreamcast is driven by two overall goals—to deliver the best gaming experience the industry has ever seen through the most versatile console ever and to win back the No. 1 position in the home video game console category. In quantitative terms, our goal is to capture more than 50 percent of the next-generation home-gaming market. In other words, we are aiming to blow away not only video game players but also our video game industry competitors.[12]

—*Irimajiri Shôichirô, President* Sega Enterprises

Development of next-generation Sega game hardware began in January 1995. Code named "Katana" after the larger of the two swords traditionally carried by Japanese *samurai,* Dreamcast was to embody the weapon's technical perfection and fighting spirit. Although work progressed throughout 1995, driven by Hitachi's desire to specify and produce a new controller for the system, not until Sony's release of PlayStation in late 1995 did development go into high gear.

Satô Hideki and his engineers realized that the primary difficulty in marketing Saturn stemmed from an unwillingness to listen to the needs of both the customer and the game software producers. Guiding the new system's development would be the concept of "Communication and Play," drawn from the notion that all game playing—competition or

---

[12] Sega Enterprises Ltd., Annual Report, 1998.

collaboration—was a basis for communication. Dreamcast would evoke a community of digital adversaries and allies, software producers and hardware partners, and customers and suppliers. Satô explained:

> Basically, a game is a communications tool. Without sympathetic exchange between the game producers and the game players, Sega is isolated and cannot understand the strengths of our games. Where there is miscommunication, our customers will reject our games.

Satô alluded to the Japanese language's word for information, *jôhô*, and the meanings of the two ideograms forming the word—"emotion" (jô) and "disseminate" (hô). As a basis for the display, manipulation, and transmission of information, Dreamcast would foster a virtual community. Within this community, the sharing of information would become an act of emotional intimacy.

DREAMCAST DESIGN: COSTS, COOPERATION, AND STANDARDIZATION

The strategy for designing Dreamcast had three elements: to minimize manufacturing costs, to improve relations with third-party game software developers, and to standardize hardware across arcade, home video, and PC play systems.

All design work started with a study of its effect on the system's target price of 29,800 yen. Satô's engineers worked backwards from that price, trading system capabilities on their ability to add value while coming in under budget. For example, if Dreamcast had a modem, players could access the Internet and play networked games. In Japan, where personal computer penetration was substantially lower than in the United States, Internet access would make Dreamcast interesting to parents as well as their children. By establishing the Sega Web site as the default gateway for all Dreamcast users, Sega could also enter the rapidly growing electronic commerce business. But a modem would add about 3,000 yen to the machine's cost—a problem given customers' price sensitivity (see **Exhibit 4b**). As for the American market, where PC ownership was more common, a modem of moderate performance—only 33.6 kbaud—would not attract much attention.

In its management of relations with software companies, Sega engaged them right from the beginning of the development process (see **Exhibit 7**). Simply by asking for advice on Dreamcast's hardware and game development libraries, Sega signaled its willingness to change. Later, as the companies geared up to begin new game design, Sega provided external developers with its latest and most powerful development software for testing and development. Likewise, to provide direct software development support, Sega established a formal game software support section within the hardware design unit and even stationed Sega engineers at the game developers' laboratories. While the software houses responded positively, suspicions stemming from the Saturn experience lingered.

To induce game designers to adopt Dreamcast for game development work, Sega opted to develop the Dreamcast core 3D graphics technology as the standard for game development in the home video game, arcade, and personal computer markets. Given a potential combined annual volume for hardware estimated at 154 million units in 1999 and 182 million in 2000, a standard that allowed game developers to market one game across three markets could reduce game development costs sharply. For players, finding their favorite arcade games so quickly available on Dreamcast would enhance their gaming experience. To accomplish this in Dreamcast, Sega created a consortium of high technology companies—Hitachi, NEC, VideoLogic, Microsoft, and Yamaha—to produce the graphics, acoustics, and programming environment standards that would allow interchangeability across these different markets.[13]

THE COLLABORATION WITH NEC AND VIDEOLOGIC

Sega's previous SPRITE graphics processor had proved a problem from the release of Saturn in mid-1994. Although providing Saturn with higher quality graphics than its Sony competitor, third-party software houses found it difficult to program. Sega evaluated a number of different graphics engines as replacements and in mid-1996 eventually settled on the Voodoo Graphic Accelerator, a chip designed by the American company, 3Dfx. In early 1997, Sega's software development team completed the initial version of the in-house library software, called Ninja, for Dreamcast. Sega software engineers defined the API (Application Program Interface), which specified exactly how Dreamcast software and hardware would interact, and released the first round of development tools to the game software companies for evaluation. By April, the feedback received was not good.

While a game system standard designed to operate in all three segments of the game industry seemed eminently reasonable at first, the technology required to do this demanded that game developers cede control over some aspects of the programming process. Sega would provide general versions of the most basic library functions to allow rapid porting of game software. This did not resonate well with the game designers, long used to optimizing their software by programming in complex assembly language directly on the game hardware. Without this option available to them, their fortunes were more closely tied to the raw processing power available in the graphics hardware. 3Dfx's Voodoo chip, however, did not impress them with overwhelming processing power.

The images Dreamcast would manipulate comprised millions of microscopic polygons, each shaded, shaped, and oriented to provide the illusion of continuity and depth. How many and how quickly a graphics engine could process these polygons determined its computational power. With a rendering rate of around 400,000 polygons per second, Voodoo provided only a ten-fold increase in processing speed over its SPRITE predecessor. Sega had opted for the 3Dfx graphics engine based on the promise of lower production costs through the integration of multiple designs on a single chip. To achieve lower costs, however, 3Dfx had to work closely with two other semiconductor firms, Hitachi and VLSI, which were becoming increasingly estranged. This lack of cooperation started to get Sega's management worried about the Voodoo's chip performance and reliability. After all, the graphics engine was a core component of its next generation game platform. Satô Hideki explained:

> We didn't think their technology could carry Sega into the twenty-first century. Moreover, because 3Dfx is a design company, we could not get them to take responsibility for the

---

[13] "Dreamcast Power VR Driven," *Business Wire,* May 21, 1998; "Microsoft and Sega Collaboration," *Business Wire,* May 21, 1998.

production—and thus cost—of the chip. Their attitude was, "This is not our problem. We can recommend a foundry, but the risk associated with production is your problem." We were very concerned about who would be responsible for product failure. We wanted more of a guarantee.

Fortunately, while developing the 3Dfx chip's hardware and support software, Sega had also continued research on a competing graphics engine, the Power VR1 chip. Designed by the British company VideoLogic and manufactured by NEC, the Power VR1 chip appeared full of potential. Its design simplified Dreamcast production and the expected second generation of Power VR technology promised a five- to ten-fold performance improvement over VR1. In July 1997, Sega decided to shift to this technology, and in August the second-generation chip became available. With a polygon rendering rate of three to four million polygons per second, it promised to be the industry's most powerful 3D-graphics processor on which Satô could build Sega's fortunes in the twenty-first century.

The decision to change graphics engines was not made lightly. 3Dfx sued, claiming breach of contract and damages of US$155 million for loss of intellectual property rights but eventually settled for US$10 million. Significantly, however, the decision meant redesigning not only Power VR2 but also the larger Dreamcast hardware platform. Sega engineers became fixtures at VideoLogic's London headquarters—a group of six spent the month of December 1997 completing the final design and simulation of the Power VR2 chip and drinking warm English ale. Yet, the Power VR2 underwent further changes. Rumors about the graphics capability of Sony's next generation PlayStation led to a major redesign in February 1998. Sega stabilized the Power VR2 design in April and completed the Dreamcast platform in August, three months prior to launch.[14]

Convincing game designers to program with predefined libraries reduced the amount of redesign necessary to change graphics engines. Programmers continued game development more or less safe in the knowledge that a library call would respond identically whether operating on Voodoo, Power VR1, or Power VR2. As Sega incrementally updated its software libraries between August 1997 and August 1998, adapting game software to Dreamcast design changes required nothing more than recompiling the game software with the new libraries and loading them onto the new hardware.

GAME DEVELOPMENT TOOLKITS: THE COLLABORATION WITH MICROSOFT

On May 21, 1998, Microsoft announced its collaboration with Sega Enterprises in the development of a flexible, versatile game development environment suitable for porting Dreamcast games onto PCs. "We are confident," said Sega's President Irimajiri, "that our collaboration with Microsoft will create an unequalled environment for developers that will lead to the greatest selection of high-quality game titles ever seen on a home video game system."[15] The two companies had worked since mid-1996 to perfect Windows CE for the Dreamcast system. The goal was to enhance both the portability of PC-based games and the

---

[14] "3Dfx Adds VideoLogic to Others Named in Suit," *Electronic News* (November 3, 1997), vol. 43, no. 2192, 14.

[15] "Microsoft and Sega Collaboration," *Business Wire,* May 21, 1998.

productivity of game developers by allowing PC-based game development. In addition to the game environment, Sega redesigned Dreamcast to be able to communicate with Microsoft's library protocol. The new environment, named DragonOS, provided a standardized interface, so Dreamcast software could easily be ported to and from PC environments.

The performance of game software using the Microsoft system, however, was about half that of Sega's Ninja library system, thus making it more suitable for slower and less complex software such as internet browsers. For game developers both inside and outside Sega, this performance penalty was unacceptable. They admired the artistry of jagged light splashing off racing space ships or the fall of a silk sleeve from a princess' arm and anything reducing their ability to produce these effects was despised. Microsoft also fell behind in its development schedule, recognizing that the design of an operating system for a home video game was more difficult than anticipated. Thus, of the 40-odd games scheduled to be available within the first six months of Dreamcast's launch, only one, Rally Racer, used the joint Sega-Microsoft DragonOS toolkit; the others used Ninja.

As with its graphic engine, Sega had had a contingency plan for failure in the development of the Microsoft software. Although the Sega Game Library had been roundly criticized when initially released for the Sega Saturn, it was completely revised in January 1997 during extensive consultation between Ninja's developers, Sega's in-house game software designers, and various prominent third-party game software designers.

PRODUCTION PROBLEMS AT NEC

The news about production problems at NEC's state-of-the-art plant in Kyûshû was most disappointing to Ueno; it came at a time when Sega's marketing campaign was in high gear and had been extremely well received by retailers and potential new customers. In particular the "Yukawa Ganbare!" promotional campaign had brought Sega's history and future to the forefront of national attention. Before making any changes to Sega's launch strategy, Ueno and Satô, together with Sega President Irimajiri, decided to go on a fact finding trip to NEC. The meetings in Kyûshû added much needed clarity to Sega's supply problem: NEC's production of the Power VR2 graphics engine would definitely not meet the contractually agreed-upon minimum for launch. NEC, like Microsoft, had underestimated the complexity of the technology contained in these "toys." With 10 million transistors on a die approximately 1.2 cm (about ½ inch) on each side, the Power VR2 was NEC's most complicated semiconductor project to date. Although the prototype graphics engines functioned well, the transition to mass production proved extremely difficult. Sega wanted several hundred thousand chips per month and a million in total by the end of March 1999. NEC had assigned sufficient production facilities to produce at these levels, assuming production yields similar to those NEC experienced when transferring its traditional DRAM[16] memory chips to mass production. The complexity of the graphics processor design, however, demanded a larger number of aluminum layers—five against the two or three typical of most memory designs—to allow superior data communication throughout the chip. Lacking experience in the manufacture of chips with five aluminum layers, NEC suffered unusually low yield rates that improved only slowly.

---

[16] Dynamic Random Access Memory—a memory technology used for high-speed access in computers.

Satô and Ueno worried what this shortfall in production might mean for the Dreamcast project. Sega could either delay the launch or launch without the product to satisfy expected demand. The inescapable fact was that, either way, hardware sales would be behind sales projections. Without hardware to run software, the game software houses might choose to save marketing and sales costs for unsellable products and postpone the release of Dreamcast game software. From experience, Sega knew that by itself it could not produce a sufficient range of high quality game software to satisfy the market. External software developers were key in Sega's new strategy. Without an extensive range of spectacular game software, customers would opt for the visually less spectacular, but also less speculative, Sony PlayStation. In the worst-case scenario, instead of the virtuous circle of investment, game development, profit and more investment pulled forward by Dreamcast's increasing customer base, third-party software houses might instead remember the futility of developing for the Saturn system and opt to curtail general game development for Dreamcast.

Priced at 29,800 yen[17] (about US$250), Sega's sales projections called for one million Dreamcast units sold by the end of its fiscal year (March 1999), with an additional 2.5 to 3 million sold by the following December—an installed base that would give them the momentum to start the next millennium on a high note.

---

[17] In October 1998, one U.S. dollar was worth about 115 Japanese yen.

EXHIBIT 1   Dreamcast System and Game Characters in Action

Dreamcast™

(Game platform logo)

Sonic, the Hedgehog, and his pal Tails take to the sky

Elliot Ballade, the Blue Stinger, battles the dread mutant Nefilim in twenty-first century Mexico City.

The Dreamcast System:
Control Panel, Dreamcast and Virtual Memory

Source: Sega Enterprises, Ltd.

EXHIBIT 2   **Sega Enterprises Ltd.: Selected Financials and Operating Data (Unconsolidated)[1]**

	1995	1996	1997	1998
Workforce	3,758	3,764	3,872	3,982
Income Statement (million yen)				
Net Sales				
Consumer products	188,486	169,524	164,395	74,375
Domestic (%)	30	59	59	78
Export (%)	70	41	41	22
Amusement center operations	74,204	82,136	88,191	90,958
Amusement machine sales	61,400	84,976	98,241	101,890
Domestic (%)	67	65	67	68
Export (%)	33	35	33	32
Royalties on game software	9,233	9,546	9,103	4,252
Total net sales	333,323	346,182	359,930	271,475
Other Income				
Other operating income	(4,598)	2,557	1,842	(40,046)
Net investment income	1,757	(22,826)	(19,535)	(9,459)
Net interest income	1,897	1,886	721	662
Total other income	(944)	(18,383)	(16,972)	(48,843)
Total Revenues	332,379	327,799	342,958	222,632
Cost of sales	257,371	270,968	285,146	216,596
Selling, general and administrative expenses	44,744	45,578	43,555	41,172
Net Income Before Taxes	30,264	11,253	14,257	(35,136)
Taxes	16,179	5,949	8,685	8,164
Net Income	14,085	5,304	5,572	(43,300)
Exchange rate: 1 US$ = _____ yen	89.35	106.35	124.10	132.10

[1]Sega's fiscal year ends March 31 (e.g. fiscal 1998 ended on March 31, 1998).

Source: Sega Enterprises, Annual Reports 1995–1998.

EXHIBIT 3 **Selected Market Data in the Home Video Game Industry**

(a) Game Platform Industry (Hardware Only); by Manufacturer and Country[1]

	Sega Saturn	Nintendo 64	Sony PlayStation	Total Market
Japan				
Market Share (hundred million yen)				
1994	314	—	239	1,795
1995	574	—	551	1,843
1996	420	494	822	2,072
1997	144	116	846	1,464
Total Installed Base (1000 units)				
1994	840	—	600	1,440
1995	2,500	—	2,450	4,950
1996	4,800	2,040	6,500	13,340
1997	5,600	3,150	11,450	20,200
U.S.A.				
Market Share (million dollars)				
1995	70	—	150	220
1996	154	380	484	1,018
1997	70	660	750	1,480
1998	8	650	970	1,628
Total Installed Base (1000 units)				
1995	200	—	500	700
1996	900	1,900	2,700	5,500
1997	1,300	6,300	7,700	15,300
1998	1,350	11,000	14,700	27,050

[1]Total market includes sales of 16-bit and hand-held machines.

(b) Game Industry Market Size (Hardware and Game Software); by Country

	1995	1996	1997	1998 (est.)	1999 (est.)
Japan (hundred million yen)	7,400	7,362	7,294	8,023	8,825
U.S. (million dollars)	4,500	5,100	6,500	7,200	9,500

Sources: Tokyo Toys and Dolls Wholesalers Association, *Tokyo Journal* (July 1998); "The U.S. Market for Video Games and Interactive Electronic Entertainment" by DFC Intelligence, San Diego, California, 1999; Electronic Industries Association, *Electronic Market Data Book* (1997), 27; N. Konish, "Video Game Giants are Neck to Neck for the Profit," *Electronic Design* (September 14, 1998); Y. Yokota, "Sega Casts Game System Dreams with New 128-Bit Machine," *The Nikkei Weekly* (September 7, 1998); casewriter estimates.

EXHIBIT 4
Game Platform Pricing in Japan

(a) Evolution of Pricing for Competing Platforms

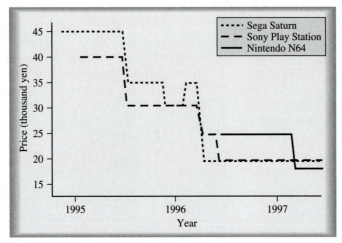

Source: Various company press releases.

(b) Estimated Relationship Between Price and Inclination to Purchase

Hardware Unit Price		Inclination to Purchase (Estimate)
30,000 yen	→	15%–20%
25,000 yen	→	30%–40%
20,000 yen	→	Most customers in target market

("Inclination to Purchase" is defined as the percentage of a focus group inclined to purchase Dreamcast.)

Source: Sega Enterprises Ltd.

EXHIBIT 5
Price Structure
of Third-Party
Game Software
(in Yen)

Source: Sega Enterprises Ltd.; casewriter estimates.

	Sega Saturn	Sony PlayStation	Nintendo Super Famicon
Average retail price of software	¥5,800	¥5,800	¥9,800
Manufacturing costs	2,610	2,240	2,500
Software maker's profit	1,276	950	3,000
Wholesaler's profit	464	1,160	1,500
Retailer's profit	1,450	1,450	2,800
Game development costs:			
Average duration	1 year		
Average cost:	¥100–¥200 million		
Manpower:	10–20 engineers		

EXHIBIT 6   **Hardware and Price Comparison of the Sega Dreamcast to the Dell Computer**

	Sega Dreamcast Hardware Platform	Dell Dimension XPS R450
CPU:	128 Bit SH4 RISC CPU (64 Bit Data Bus)	32-bit Pentium II CISC CPU
Clock speed:	200 MHz	450 MHz
Graphics:	Power VR2 DC	3D TNT 16 MB Graphic Card
Rendering:	Over 3,000,000 polygons/second	(other options available)
Colors:	16.77 million simultaneously	
Sound Processor:	32-bit RISC CPU, 3D Sound Support 64 Channels	Turtlebeach 3D 64 Sound Card
Operating System:	Microsoft Windows CE Custom	Microsoft Windows '98
Memory:	26 MB	128 MB
Modem:	33.6 Kbps	56 Kbps
Hard Drive:	—	Up to 17.2 GB
CD-ROM:	~1 GB	DVD (~17 GB)
Price:	29,800 yen (about $250; in Japan)	About US$2,000 (in U.S.)

Sources: Sega Enterprises Ltd., 1998; Dell Computer Web site, January 25, 1999, http://www.dell.com.

EXHIBIT 7
**Supplier
Cooperation
for Software
Game
Development
Toolkit**

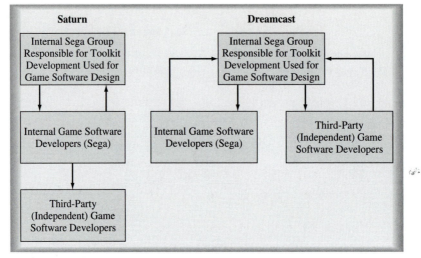

Changes:
• Engineer/designer exchanges with third-party software houses.
• Creation of software support within hardware design section.
• Participation by third-party software houses in design of hardware and software development toolkits.
• Internal and third-party game software developers receive the same priority for toolkit software releases.

EXHIBIT 8
**Organizational
Chart for Sega
Enterprises,
1998**

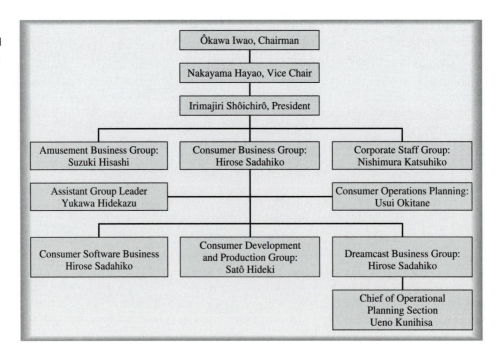

Article

Increasing Returns and the New World of Business

Our understanding of how markets and businesses operate was passed down to us more than a century ago by a handful of European economists—Alfred Marshall in England and a few of his contemporaries on the continent. It is an understanding based squarely upon the assumption of diminishing returns: products or companies that get ahead in a market eventually run into limitations, so that a predictable equilibrium of prices and market shares is reached. The theory was roughly valid for the bulk-processing, smokestack economy of Marshall's day. And it still thrives in today's economics textbooks. But steadily and continuously in this century, Western economies have undergone a transformation from bulk-material manufacturing to design and use of technology—from processing of resources to processing of information, from application of raw energy to application of ideas. As this shift has occurred, the underlying mechanisms that determine economic behavior have shifted from ones of diminishing to ones of increasing returns.

Increasing returns are the tendency for that which is ahead to get further ahead, for that which loses advantage to lose further advantage. They are mechanisms of positive feedback that operate—within markets, businesses, and industries—to reinforce that which gains success or aggravate that which suffers loss. Increasing returns generate not equilibrium but instability: If a product or a company or a technology—one of many competing in a market—gets ahead by chance or clever strategy, increasing returns can magnify this advantage, and the product or company or technology can go on to lock in the market. More than causing products to become standards, increasing returns cause businesses to work differently, and they stand many of our notions of how business operates on their head.

Mechanisms of increasing returns exist alongside those of diminishing returns in all industries. But roughly speaking, diminishing returns hold sway in the traditional part of the economy—the processing industries. Increasing returns reign in the newer part—the knowledge-based industries. Modern economies have therefore bifurcated into two interrelated worlds of business corresponding to the two types of returns. The two worlds have different economics. They differ in behavior, style, and culture. They call for different management techniques, strategies, and codes of government regulation.

They call for different understandings.

ALFRED MARSHALL'S WORLD

Let's go back to beginnings—to the diminishing-returns view of Alfred Marshall and his contemporaries. Marshall's world of the 1880s and 1890s was one of bulk production: of metal ores, aniline dyes, pig iron, coal, lumber, heavy chemicals, soybeans, coffee—commodities heavy on resources, light on know-how. In that world it was reasonable to suppose, for example, that if a coffee plantation expanded production it would ultimately be driven to use land less suitable for coffee. In other words, it would run into diminishing returns. So if coffee plantations competed, each one would expand until it ran into limitations in the form of rising costs or diminishing profits. The market would be shared by many plantations, and a market price would be established at a predictable level—depending on tastes for coffee and the availability of suitable farmland. Planters would produce coffee so long as doing so was profitable, but because the price would be squeezed down to the average cost of production, no one would be able to make a killing. Marshall said such a market was in perfect competition, and the economic world he envisaged fitted beautifully with the Victorian values of his time. It was at equilibrium and therefore orderly, predictable and therefore amenable to scientific analysis, stable and therefore safe, slow to change and therefore continuous. Not too rushed, not too profitable. In a word, mannerly. In a word, genteel.

With a few changes, Marshall's world lives on a century later within that part of the modern economy still devoted to bulk processing: of grains, livestock, heavy chemicals, metals and ores, foodstuffs, retail goods—the part where operations are largely repetitive day to day or week to week. Product differentiation and brand names now mean that a few companies rather than many compete in a given market. But typically, if these companies try to expand, they run into some limitation: in numbers of consumers who prefer their brand, in regional demand, in access to raw materials. So no company can corner the market. And because such products are normally substitutable for one another, something like a standard price emerges. Margins are thin and nobody makes a killing. This isn't exactly Marshall's perfect competition, but it approximates it.

THE INCREASING-RETURNS WORLD

What would happen if Marshall's diminishing returns were reversed so that there were *increasing* returns? If products that got ahead thereby got further ahead, how would markets work?

Let's look at the market for operating systems for personal computers in the early 1980s when CP/M, DOS, and Apple's Macintosh systems were competing. Operating systems show increasing returns: if one system gets ahead, it attracts further software developers and hardware manufacturers to adopt it, which helps it get further ahead. CP/M was first in the market and by 1979 was well established. The Mac arrived later, but it was wonderfully easy to use. DOS was born when Microsoft locked up a deal in 1980 to supply an operating system for the IBM PC. For a year or two, it was by no means clear which system would prevail. The new IBM PC—DOS's platform—was a kludge. But the growing base of DOS/IBM users encouraged software developers such as Lotus to write for DOS. DOS's prevalence—and the IBM PC's—bred further prevalence, and eventually the DOS/IBM combination came to dominate a considerable portion of the market. That history is now well known. But notice several things: It was not predictable in advance (before the IBM deal) which system would come to dominate. Once DOS/IBM got ahead, it locked in the market because it did not pay for users to switch. The dominant system was not the best: DOS was derided by computer professionals. And once DOS locked in the market, its sponsor, Microsoft, was able to spread its costs over a large base of users. The company enjoyed killer margins.

These properties, then, have become the hallmarks of increasing returns: market instability (the market tilts to favor a product that gets ahead), multiple potential outcomes (under different events in history, different operating systems could have won), unpredictability, the ability to lock in a market, the possible predominance of an inferior product, and fat profits for the winner. They surprised me when I first perceived them in the late 1970s. They were also repulsive to economists brought up on the order, predictability, and optimality of Marshall's world. Glimpsing some of these properties in 1939, English economist John Hicks warned that admitting increasing returns would lead to "the wreckage of the greater part of economic theory." But Hicks had it wrong: the theory of increasing returns does not destroy the standard theory—it complements it. Hicks felt repugnance not just because of unsavory properties but also because in his day no mathematical apparatus existed to analyze increasing-returns markets. That situation has now changed. Using sophisticated techniques from qualitative dynamics and probability theory, I and others have developed methods to analyze increasing-returns markets. The theory of increasing returns is new, but it already is well established. And it renders such markets amenable to economic understanding.

In the early days of my work on increasing returns, I was told they were an anomaly. Like some exotic particle in physics, they might exist in theory but would be rare in practice. And if they did exist, they would last for only a few seconds before being arbitraged away. But by the mid-1980s, I realized increasing returns were neither rare nor ephemeral. In fact, a major part of the economy was subject to increasing returns—high technology.

Why should this be so? There are several reasons:

Up-front Costs. High-tech products—pharmaceuticals, computer hardware and software, aircraft and missiles, telecommunications equipment, bioengineered drugs, and suchlike—are by definition complicated to design and to deliver to the marketplace. They are heavy on know-how and light on resources. Hence they typically have R&D costs that are large relative to their unit production costs. The first disk of Windows to go out the door cost Microsoft $50 million; the second and subsequent disks cost $3. Unit costs fall as sales increase.

Network Effects. Many high-tech products need to be compatible with a network of users. So if much downloadable software on the Internet will soon appear as programs written in Sun Microsystems' Java language, users will need Java on their computers to run them. Java has competitors. But the more it gains prevalence, the more likely it will emerge as a standard.

Customer Groove-in. High-tech products are typically difficult to use. They require training. Once users invest in this training—say, the maintenance and piloting of Airbus passenger aircraft—they merely need to update these skills for subsequent versions of the product. As more market is captured, it becomes easier to capture future markets.

In high-tech markets, such mechanisms ensure that products that gain market advantage stand to gain further advantage, making these markets unstable and subject to lock-in. Of course, lock-in is not forever. Technology comes in waves, and a lock-in such as DOS's can last only as long as a particular wave lasts.

So we can usefully think of two economic regimes or worlds: a bulk-production world yielding products that essentially are congealed resources with a little knowledge and operating according to Marshall's principles of diminishing returns, and a knowledge-based part of the economy yielding products that essentially are congealed knowledge with a little resources and operating under increasing returns. The two worlds are not neatly split. Hewlett-Packard, for example, designs knowledge-based devices in Palo Alto, California, and manufactures them in bulk in places like Corvallis, Oregon, or Greeley, Colorado. Most high-tech companies have both knowledge-based operations and bulk-processing operations. But because the rules of the game differ for each, companies often separate them—as Hewlett-Packard does. Conversely, manufacturing companies have operations such as logistics, branding, marketing, and distribution, which belong largely to the knowledge world. And some products—like the IBM PC—start in the increasing-returns world but later in their life cycle become virtual commodities that belong to Marshall's processing world.

THE HALLS OF PRODUCTION AND THE CASINO OF TECHNOLOGY

Because the two worlds of business—processing bulk goods and crafting knowledge into products—differ in their underlying economics, it follows that they differ in their character of competition and their culture of management. It is a mistake to think that what works in one world is appropriate for the other.

There is much talk these days about a new management style that involves flat hierarchies, mission orientation, flexibility in strategy, market positioning, reinvention, restructuring, reengineering, repositioning, reorganization, and re-everything else. Are these new insights or are they fads? Are they appropriate for all organizations? Why are we seeing this new management style?

Let us look at the two cultures of competition. In bulk processing, a set of standard prices typically emerges. Production tends to be repetitive—much the same from day to day or even from year to year. Competing therefore means keeping product flowing, trying to improve quality, getting costs down. There is an art to this sort of management, one widely discussed in the literature. It favors an environment free of surprises or glitches— an environment characterized by control and planning. Such an environment requires not just people to carry out production but also people to plan and control it. So it favors a hierarchy of bosses and workers. Because bulk processing is repetitive, it allows constant improvement, constant optimization. And so, Marshall's world tends to be one that favors hierarchy, planning, and controls. Above all, it is a world of optimization.

Competition is different in knowledge-based industries because the economics are different. If knowledge-based companies are competing in winner-take-most markets, then managing becomes redefined as a series of quests for the next technological winner— the next cash cow. The goal becomes the search for the Next Big Thing. In this milieu, management becomes not production-oriented but mission-oriented. Hierarchies flatten not because democracy is suddenly bestowed on the workforce or because computers can cut out much of middle management. They flatten because, to be effective, the deliverers of the next-thing-for-the-company need to be organized like commando units in small teams that report directly to the CEO or to the board. Such people need free rein. The company's future survival depends upon them. So they—and the commando teams that report to them in turn—will be treated not as employees but as equals in the business of the company's success. Hierarchy dissipates and dissolves.

Does this mean that hierarchy should disappear in meatpacking, steel production, or the navy? Contrary to recent management evangelizing, a style that is called for in Silicon Valley will not necessarily be appropriate in the processing world. An aircraft's safe arrival depends on the captain, not on the flight attendants. The cabin crew can usefully be "empowered" and treated as human beings. This approach is wise and proper. But forever there will be a distinction—a hierarchy—between cockpit and cabin crews.

In fact, the style in the diminishing-returns Halls of Production is much like that of a sophisticated modern factory: the goal is to keep high-quality product flowing at low cost. There is little need to watch the market every day, and when things are going smoothly the tempo can be leisurely. By contrast, the style of competition in the increasing-returns arena is more like gambling. Not poker, where the game is static and the players vie for a succession of pots. It is casino gambling, where part of the game is to choose which games to play, as well as playing them with skill. We can imagine the top figures in high tech—the Gateses and Gerstners and Groves of their industries—as milling in a large casino. Over at this table, a game is starting called multimedia. Over at that one, a game called Web services. In the corner is electronic banking. There are many such tables. You sit at one. How much to play? you ask. Three billion, the croupier replies. Who'll be playing? We won't know until they show up. What are the rules? Those will emerge as the game unfolds. What are my odds of winning? We can't say. Do you still want to play? High technology, pursued at this level, is not for the timid.

In fact, the art of playing the tables in the Casino of Technology is primarily a psychological one. What counts to some degree—but only to some degree—is technical expertise, deep pockets, will, and courage. Above all, the rewards go to the players who are first to make sense of the new games looming out of the technological fog, to see their shape, to cognize them. Bill Gates is not so much a wizard of technology as a wizard of precognition, of discerning the shape of the next game.

We can now begin to see that the new style of management is not a fad. The knowledge-based part of the economy demands flat hierarchies, mission orientation, above all a sense of direction. Not five-year plans. We can also fathom the mystery of what I've alluded to as *re-everything*. Much of this "re-everything" predilection—in the bulk-processing world—is a fancy label for streamlining, computerizing, downsizing. However, in the increasing-returns world, especially in high tech, re-everything has become necessary because every time the quest changes, the company needs to change. It needs to reinvent its purpose, its goals, its way of doing things. In short, it needs to adapt. And adaptation never stops. In fact, in the increasing-returns environment I've just sketched, standard optimization makes little sense. You cannot optimize in the casino of increasing-returns games. You can be smart. You can be cunning. You can position. You can observe. But when the games themselves are not even fully defined, you cannot optimize. What you *can* do is adapt. Adaptation, in the proactive sense, means watching for the next wave that is coming, figuring out what shape it will take, and positioning the company to take advantage of it. Adaptation is what drives increasing-returns businesses, not optimization.

PLAYING THE HIGH-TECH TABLES

Suppose you are a player in the knowledge-industry casino, in this increasing-returns world. What can you do to capitalize on the increasing returns at your disposal? How can you use them to capture markets? What strategic issues do you need to think about? In the processing world, strategy typically hinges upon capitalizing on core competencies, pricing competitively, getting costs down, bringing quality up. These are important also in the knowledge-based world, but so, too, are other strategies that make use of the special economics of positive feedbacks.

Two maxims are widely accepted in knowledge-based markets: it pays to hit the market first, and it pays to have superb technology. These maxims are true but do not guarantee success. Prodigy was first into the online services market but was passive in building its subscriber base to take advantage of increasing returns. As a result, it has fallen from its leading position and currently lags the other services. As for technology, Steve Jobs's NeXT workstation was superb. But it was launched into a market already dominated by Sun Microsystems and Hewlett-Packard. It failed. A new product often has to be two or three times better in some dimension—price, speed, convenience—to dislodge a locked-in rival. So in knowledge-based markets, entering first with a fine product can yield advantage. But as strategy, this is still too passive. What is needed is active management of increasing returns.

One active strategy is to discount heavily initially to build up an installed base. Netscape handed out its Internet browser for free and won 70 percent of its market. Now it can profit from spin-off software and applications. Although such discounting is effective—and widely understood—it is not always implemented. Companies often err by pricing high initially to recoup expensive R&D costs. Yet even smart discounting to seed the market is ineffective unless the resulting installed base is exploited later. America Online built up a lead of more than 4.5 million subscribers by giving away free services. But because of the Internet's dominance, it is not yet clear whether it can transform this huge base into later profits.

Let's get a bit more sophisticated. Technological products do not stand alone. They depend on the existence of other products and other technologies. The Internet's World Wide Web operates within a grouping of businesses that include browsers, online news, e-mail, network retailing, and financial services. Pharmaceuticals exist within a network of physicians, testing labs, hospitals, and HMOs. Laser printers are part of a grouping of products that include computers, publishing software, scanners, and photo-input devices. Unlike products of the processing world, such as soybeans or rolled steel, technological products exist within local groupings of products that support and enhance them. They exist in mini-ecologies.

This interdependence has deep implications for strategy. When, in the mid-1980s, Novell introduced its network-operating system, NetWare, as a way of connecting personal computers in local networks, Novell made sure that NetWare was technically superior to its rivals. It also heavily discounted NetWare to build an installed base. But these tactics were not enough. Novell recognized that NetWare's success depended on attracting software applications to run on NetWare—which was a part of the ecology outside the company's control.

So it set up incentives for software developers to write for NetWare rather than for its rivals. The software writers did just that. And by building NetWare's success, they ensured their own. Novell managed these cross-product positive feedbacks actively to lock in its market. It went on to profit hugely from upgrades, spin-offs, and applications of its own.

Another strategy that uses ecologies is linking and leveraging. This means transferring a user base built up upon one node of the ecology (one product) to neighboring nodes, or products. The strategy is very much like that in the game Go: you surround neighboring markets one by one, lever your user base onto them, and take them over—all the time enhancing your position in the industry. Microsoft levered its 60-million-person user base in DOS onto Windows, then onto Windows 95, and then onto Microsoft Network by offering inexpensive upgrades and by bundling applications. The strategy has been challenged legally. But it recognizes that positive feedbacks apply across markets as well as within markets.

In fact, if technological ecologies are now the basic units for strategy in the knowledge-based world, players compete not by locking in a product on their own but by building webs—loose alliances of companies organized around a mini-ecology—that amplify positive feedbacks to the base technology. Apple, in closing its Macintosh system to outsiders in the 1980s, opted not to create such a web. It believed that with its superior technology, it could hold its increasing-returns market to itself. Apple indeed dominates its Mac-based ecology. But this ecology is now only 8 percent of the personal computer business. IBM erred in the other direction. By passively allowing other companies to join its PC web as clones, IBM achieved a huge user base and locked in the market. But the company itself wound up with a small share of the spoils. The key in web building is active management of the cross-company mutual feedbacks. This means making a careful choice of partners to build upon. It also means that, rather than attempting to take over all products in the ecology, dominant players in a web should allow dependent players to lock in their dependent products by piggybacking on the web's success. By thus ceding some of the profits, the dominant players ensure that all participants remain committed to the alliance.

Important also to strategy in knowledge-based markets is psychological positioning. Under increasing returns, rivals will back off in a market not only if it is locked in but if they *believe* it will be locked in by someone else. Hence we see psychological jockeying in the form of preannouncements, feints, threatened alliances, technological preening, touted future partnerships, parades of vaporware (announced products that don't yet exist). This posturing and puffing acts much the way similar behavior does in a primate colony: it discourages competitors from taking on a potentially dominant rival. No moves need be made in this strategy of premarket facedown. It is purely a matter of psychology.

What if you hold a losing hand? Sometimes it pays to hold on for residual revenue. Sometimes a fix can be provided by updated technology, fresh alliances, or product changes. But usually under heavy lock-in, these tactics do not work. The alternatives are then slow death or graceful exit—relinquishing the field to concentrate on positioning for the next technology wave. Exit may not mean quitting the business entirely. America Online, Compuserve, Prodigy, and Microsoft Network have all ceded dominance of the online computer networking market to the Internet. But instead of exiting, they are steadily becoming adjuncts of the Net, supplying content services such as financial quotations or games and entertainment. They have lost the main game. But they will likely continue in a side game with its own competition for dominance within the Net's ecology.

Above all, strategy in the knowledge world requires CEOs to recognize that a different kind of economics is at work. CEOs need to understand which positive and negative feedback mechanisms are at play in the market ecologies in which they compete. Often there are several such mechanisms—interbraided, operating over different time frames, each needing to be understood, observed, and actively managed.

WHAT ABOUT SERVICE INDUSTRIES?

So far, I've talked mainly about high tech. Where do service industries such as insurance, restaurants, and banking fit in? Which world do they belong to? The question is tricky. It would appear that such industries belong to the diminishing-returns, processing part of the economy because often there are regional limits to the demand for a given service, most services do consist of "processing" clients, and services are low-tech.

The truth is that network or user-base effects often operate in services. Certainly, retail franchises exist because of increasing returns. The more McDonald's restaurants or Motel 6 franchises are out there geographically, the better they are known. Such businesses are patronized not just for their quality but also because people want to know exactly what to expect. So the more prevalent they are, the more prevalent they can become. Similarly, the larger a bank's or insurance company's customer base, the more it can spread its fixed costs of headquarters staff, real estate, and computer operations. These industries, too, are subject to mild increasing returns.

So we can say more accurately that service industries are a hybrid. From day to day, they act like bulk-processing industries. But over the long term, increasing returns will dominate—even though their destabilizing effects are not as pronounced as in high tech. The U.S. airline business, for example, processes passengers day to day. So it seemed in 1981 that deregulation should enhance competition, as it normally does under diminishing returns. But over the long term, airlines in fact experience a positive feedback: under the hub-and-spoke system, once an airline gets into trouble, it cannot work the feeder system for its routes properly, its fleet ages, it starts a downward spiral, and it loses further routes. The result of deregulation over the long term has been a steady decline in large carriers, from fifteen airlines in 1981 to approximately six at present. Some routes have become virtual monopolies, with resulting higher fares. None of this was intended. But it should have been predicted—given increasing returns.

In fact, the increasing-returns character of service industries is steadily strengthening. One of the marks of our time is that in services everything is going software—everything that is information based. So operations that were once handled by people—designing fancy financial instruments or automobiles or fashion goods, processing insurance claims, supplying and inventorying in retail, conducting paralegal searches for case precedents—are increasingly being handled by software. As this reengineering of services plays out, centralized software facilities come to the fore. Service providers become hitched into software networks, regional limitations weaken, and user-base network effects kick in.

This phenomenon can have two consequences. First, where the local character of service remains important, it can preserve a large number of service companies but clustered round a dominant software provider—like the large numbers of small, independent law firms tied in to the dominant computer-search network, Lexis-Nexis. Or physicians tied in to an

HMO. Second, where locality is unimportant, network effects can transform competition toward the winner-take-most character we see in high tech. For example, when Internet-based retail banking arrives, regional demand limitations will vanish. Each virtual bank will gain in advantage as its network increases. Barring regulation, consumer banking will then become a contest among a few large banking networks. It will become an increasing-returns business.

Services belong to both the processing and the increasing-returns world. But their center of gravity is crossing over to the latter.

THOUGHTS FOR MANAGERS

Where does all this leave us? At the beginning of this century, industrial economies were based largely on the bulk processing of resources. At the close of the century, they are based on the processing of resources and on the processing of knowledge. Economies have bifurcated into two worlds—intertwined, overlapping, and different. These two worlds operate under different economic principles. Marshall's world is characterized by planning, control, and hierarchy. It is a world of materials, of processing, of optimization. The increasing-returns world is characterized by observation, positioning, flattened organizations, missions, teams, and cunning. It is a world of psychology, of cognition, of adaptation.

Many managers have some intuitive grasp of this new increasing-returns world. Few understand it thoroughly. Here are some questions managers need to ask themselves when they operate in knowledge-based markets:

Do I understand the feedbacks in my market? In the processing world, understanding markets means understanding consumers' needs, distribution channels, and rivals' products. In the knowledge world, success requires a thorough understanding of the self-negating and self-reinforcing feedbacks in the market—the diminishing- and increasing-returns mechanisms. These feedbacks are interwoven and operate at different levels in the market and over different time frames.

Which ecologies am I in? Technologies exist not alone but in an interlinked web, or ecology. It is important to understand the ecologies a company's products belong to. Success or failure is often decided not just by the company but also by the success or failure of the web it belongs to. Active management of such a web can be an important magnifier of increasing returns.

Do I have the resources to play? Playing one of the increasing-returns games in the Casino of Technology requires several things: excellent technology, the ability to hit the market at the right time, deep pockets, strategic pricing, and a willingness to sacrifice current profits for future advantage. All this is a matter not just of resources but also of courage, resolution, will. And part of that resolution, that courage, is also the decisiveness to leave the market when increasing returns are moving against one. Hanging on to a losing position that is being further eroded by positive feedbacks requires throwing reinforcements into a battle already lost. Better to exit with financial dignity.

What games are coming next? Technology comes in successive waves. Those who have lost out on this wave can position for the next. Conversely, those who have made a killing on this cycle should not become complacent. The ability to profit under increasing returns is only as good as the ability to see what's coming in the next cycle and to position oneself for it—technologically, psychologically, and cooperatively. In high tech, it is as if we are moving slowly on a ship, with new technologies looming, taking shape, through a fog of unknowingness. Success goes to those who have the vision to foresee, to imagine, what shapes these next games will take.

These considerations appear daunting. But increasing-returns games provide large payoffs for those brave enough to play them and win. And they are exciting. Processing, in the service or manufacturing industries, has its own risks. Precisely because processing is low-margin, operations must struggle to stay afloat. Neither world of business is for the fainthearted.

In his book *Microcosm,* technology thinker George Gilder remarked, "The central event of the twentieth century is the overthrow of matter. In technology, economics, and the politics of nations, wealth in the form of physical resources is steadily declining in value and significance. The powers of mind are everywhere ascendant over the brute force of things." As the economy shifts steadily away from the brute force of things into the powers of mind, from resource-based bulk processing into knowledge-based design and reproduction, so it is shifting from a base of diminishing returns to one of increasing returns. A new economics—one very different from that in the textbooks—now applies, and nowhere is this more true than in high technology. Success will strongly favor those who understand this new way of thinking.

IN THE CASE OF MICROSOFT . . .

What should be legal in this powerful and as yet unregulated world of increasing returns? What constitutes fair play? Should technology markets be regulated, and if so in what way? These questions have come to a head with the enormous amount of publicity generated by the U.S. Justice Department's current antitrust case against Microsoft.

In Marshall's world, antitrust regulation is well understood. Allowing a single player to control, say, more than 35 percent of the silver market is tantamount to allowing monopoly pricing, and the government rightly steps in. In the increasing-returns world, things are more complicated. There are arguments in favor of allowing a product or company in the web of technology to dominate a market, as well as arguments against. Consider these pros and cons:

Convenience. A locked-in product may provide a single standard of convenience. If a software company such as Microsoft allows us to double-click all the way from our computer screen straight to our bank account (by controlling all the technologies in between), this avoids a tedious balkanizing of standards, where we have to spend useless time getting into a succession of online connection products.

Fairness. If a product locks in because it is superior, this is fair, and it would be foolish to penalize such success. If it locks in merely because user base was levered over from a neighboring lock-in, this is unfair.

Technology Development. A locked-in product may obstruct technological advancement. If a clunker such as DOS locks up the PC market for ten years, there is little incentive for other companies to develop alternatives. The result is impeded technological progress.

Pricing. To lock in, a product usually has been discounted, and this established low price is often hard to raise. So monopoly pricing—of great concern in bulk-processing markets—is therefore rarely a major worry.

Added to these considerations, high tech is not a commodity industry. Dominance may consist not so much in cornering a single product as in successively taking over more and more threads of the web of technology, thereby preventing other players from getting access to new, breaking markets. It would be difficult to separate out each thread and to regulate it. And of course it may be impracticable to regulate a market before it forms—before it is even fully defined. There are no simple answers to antitrust regulation in the increasing-returns world. On balance, I would favor a high degree of regulatory restraint, with the addition of two key principles:

- **Do not penalize success.** Short-term monopolization of an increasing-returns market is correctly perceived as a reward or prize for innovation and risk taking. There is a temptation to single out dominant players and hit them with an antitrust suit. This reduces regulation to something like a brawl in an Old West saloon—if you see a head, hit it. Not a policy that preserves an incentive to innovate in the first place.
- **Don't allow head starts for the privileged.** This means that as a new market opens up—such as electronic consumer banking—companies that already dominate standards, operating systems, and neighboring technologies should not be allowed a ten-mile head start in the land rush that follows. All competitors should have fair and open access to the applicable technologies and standards.

In practice, these principles would mean allowing the possibility of winner-take-all jackpots in each new subindustry, in each new wave of technology. But each contender should have access to whatever degree possible to the same technologies, the same open standards, so that all are lined up behind the same starting line. If industry does not make such provisions voluntarily, government regulation will impose them.

Case 3-5

Millennium Pharmaceuticals, Inc.

"Great meeting" were the words echoing in the halls of Millennium's new headquarters in Cambridge, Massachusetts, as a dozen people in business suits swarmed out of the meeting room, shaking hands and slapping backs. Their dark suits contrasted sharply with the daily informal wear at the fast-moving biotechnology firm where even the CEO often appeared in loud Hawaiian shirts. Six of the meeting participants representing the European agribusiness conglomerate Lundberg had flown in by private plane. Their eagerness to access Millennium's genetic technology for agricultural applications showed throughout the meeting. The proposed alliance enjoyed support from the very highest levels at Lundberg; in fact, C. Marie Lundberg, heiress to the closely held family business and a senior vice president herself, had attended this August 1999 meeting.

The real question, however, that CEO Mark Levin pondered was the amount of middle-level support from Lundberg for the deal. Although no specific amount of money had been discussed, both sides remained aware that since 1993, Millennium had graduated to multi–hundred million dollar technology and drug discovery deals. The firm was currently involved with a half-dozen technology and pharmaceutical deals worth over a billion dollars. In fact, even without a single drug even close to clinical development, just on the basis of its technology and drug discovery deals alone, Millennium had broken into the ranks of the top biotechnology firms. Just one year ago, it had created history by signing a half-billion dollar alliance with the German multinational company Bayer AG—the largest deal ever between a biotechnology and a pharmaceutical firm.

Over the past year, Millennium's stock had skyrocketed, creating unexpected fortunes for its staff, which received part of its compensation as stock options. But continued performance on Wall Street meant pleasing both investors and analysts who wanted to see the company continue its highly successful alliance stream (see **Exhibit 1** for financials). Already many biotech firms were starving for money and a clear sense of strategic direction.

Although the firm attracted some of the world's leading human genetics experts, it viewed itself as operating in a much larger context; in the words of its CEO and founder

Harvard Business School Case No. 9-600-038. Copyright 1999 President and Fellows of Harvard College. All rights reserved. For information: permissions@hbsp.harvard.edu.

This case was prepared by Stefan Thomke and Ashok Nimgade. HBS cases are developed solely for class discussion and do not necessarily illustrate effective or ineffective management.

Mark Levin, "I never thought of Millennium as just a technology company." Millennium, in fact, sought to break into the ranks of the giant pharmaceutical firms. And it planned to do so by revolutionizing drug development—a process as notoriously lengthy as it was unpredictable. As chief technology officer Michael Pavia, Ph.D., outlined his vision, "Developing drugs ought to be managed like any other complex development process; some day, we will make it as predictable as developing and making automobiles." To accomplish this vision would require time and a lot of cash.

THE BIOTECHNOLOGY REVOLUTION(S)

In the mid-1970s, stunning biological breakthroughs set the stage for the modern biotechnology industry. Scientists could now cut and paste snippets of deoxyribonucleic acid (DNA), the blueprint of life and the longest known molecule in the universe. In fact, if all the DNA in any given human cell were laid end to end, it would span over a meter across. Since there are trillions of cells in the human body, all of the DNA in a given adult would easily stretch from earth to the sun and back, *several times over*. This provides just one index of the complexity of the human body. Each second in the body, millions of basic compounds are being synthesized and thousands of interrelated biochemical reactions occur. These all rely ultimately on the accuracy with which DNA in each cell is being deciphered to create proteins, vital building blocks of the body. A small misstep virtually anywhere in these processes can potentially result in morbidity and mortality.

By gaining the power to revise DNA and create new protein products, biologists in the laboratory could more precisely manipulate the primary biological molecules of life. In the 1970s and 1980s, commercial possibilities for the new technologies were seen well in advance of the ability to deliver on them. In these decades, Wall Street and individual speculators poured millions of dollars into new biotech firms, often even without the faintest idea of what differentiated a gene from its homonym.

Part of the excitement stemmed from the fact that the traditional way of finding cures for diseases was extremely effort-intensive and expensive. Large pharmaceutical companies spent up to 15–20 percent of sales in R&D. In the United States, as part of an extensive, highly regulated safety approval process, each drug had to pass three phases of clinical trials under the scrutiny of the U.S. Food and Drug Administration (FDA): Phase I, which tested clinical safety; Phase II, which assessed drug efficacy; and Phase III, which tested adverse effects from long-term use. For each successful product the sponsoring drug firm typically spent more than $230 million, with the average time to market being 14.8 years—over twice as long as it took the U.S. space program to get a man on the moon. (See **Exhibit 2** for a description of drug development.)

Metaphorically, drugs were molecular-sized "keys" that had to fit "locks" or targets; chemists were the locksmiths. Indeed, they were effectively semi-blind locksmiths, for they had to make up thousands of different keys to find the one that matched. Newly synthesized molecular keys were then tested by biologists, typically using animals that served as models for a disease (for example, a mouse with a neurological problem similar to Parkinsonism). Most compounds would show no activity or be too toxic for further evaluation. A few, however, might show promise, and chemists would modify these "lead compounds" until a good clinical candidate emerged. Typically, for each successful drug that made it to market, a firm began with roughly 10,000 starting compounds. Of these, only 1000 would make it to more extensive *in vitro* trials (i.e. outside living organisms in settings such as a test tube), of which 20 would be tested even more extensively *in vivo* (i.e. in the body of a living organism such as a mouse) before ten compounds made it to human clinical trials. The entire process represented a long and costly commitment, with the human trials closely monitored by the U.S. government.

Biotechnology, by promising a shortcut through the cumbersome and risky drug development process, promised investors wealth. It attracted entrepreneurs and maverick scientists. The hub of biotech activity was near academic centers like San Francisco and Cambridge (some observers even transformed the old Boston-Cambridge moniker "beantown" into "genetown"). In the 1980s the guiding principle behind quicker drug discovery was "rational drug design." By finding out about the disease causing receptor in the body on which a potential drug compound acts, scientists hoped to make better compounds. The analogy would be to find out about key features of a lock before designing a properly fitting key rather than a brute force strategy of making keys at random with the hope that one might eventually fit.

But rational drug design often turned out difficult to implement because of the subtle complexities of biological systems and the difficulties of finding the right receptors. In fact, the biotech industry generally disappointed investors in the 1980s partly because of the hype, and partly because biotechnology firms were not large enough to absorb the high rate of failures in drug development. A crushing blow to a biotech firm might be absorbed like a gnat's sting by a pharmaceutical firm. The crushing blows, unfortunately, came usually late in the drug development process during human clinical trials, after considerable investments of time and money had been made. Following announcements of negative human clinical trial outcomes, stock prices for biotech firms dipped by an average of a third—quite often they remained depressed for the following half-year.[1] Thus, even with the newest technologies up their sleeves, small biotech firms often played David to the pharmaceutical Goliaths, with a few exceptions such as the California firm Amgen.

Here, however, Biblical parallels end, for most biotech upstarts wanted nothing more than to become fully integrated pharmaceutical giants themselves. But after more than a decade of inflated promises made by biotech firms, investors became increasingly wary. Biotech firms established primarily for product discovery often disappointed investors. As a result, many biotech firms were forced to form partnerships with pharmaceutical firms or even merged with one another.

In the 1990s, the nascent fields of "combinatorial chemistry" and "high throughput screening" breathed new life into the industry by allowing scientists to create and screen prodigious numbers of novel compounds. Returning to the lock-and-key metaphor, scientists could now churn out keys by the thousands and test them almost equally rapidly. Drug companies, however, would still need to muster as many biochemical tricks as they could to identify worthwhile pharmaceutical "targets" (the industry parlance for the "locks" in the lock-and-key metaphor).

While technologies evolved, so did industry dynamics. Biotech firms in the late 1990s wove more intricate alliances with their pharmaceutical partners, often leveraging these relationships to gain access to Wall Street money and gaining downstream synergies for manufacturing and marketing infrastructures. The giant firms, in return, gained access to emerging technologies that could often be protected; furthermore, they could add to their product pipelines. For a pharmaceutical giant with $10 billion annual revenues to continue growing at 10 percent a year would require three to four new products a year (a typical

[1] *Biotech 98: Tools, Techniques, and Transition*, G. S. Burrill, San Francisco: Burrill & Co., 1998.

product generating $300–$400 million annually). Even more would be needed to cover drugs going off patent. With internal pipelines producing less than one significant product a year, big firms increasingly needed to partner with smaller firms.

Many newer generation biotech firms began emphasizing sales of drug development technologies more than pharmaceutical products. These firms, sometimes termed "tool companies," hoped to generate revenue faster by providing services to drug discovery companies, thus avoiding the high cash "burn-rates" involved in searching for drugs. Many of these firms developed multiple relationships with different drug firms, thus blurring the line between sales and strategic partnerships. By the late 1990s, two decades into the biotech revolution, about 300 biotech-based drugs were on the market, and nearly 450 were in clinical trials.[2] These seemingly impressive numbers paled in comparison to the over 1,300 biotech firms actually in existence. The year 1997 saw 228 new biotech-pharmaceutical collaborations, valued at $4.5 billion.[3] Those biotech firms unable to create products or merge with other companies often foundered, leaving their investors holding worthless stock. In such an environment, pharmaceutical firms could often "cherry-pick" drug candidates from financially troubled smaller companies. Only a half-dozen U.S. biotech firms had marketed major drugs without selling majority stakes to pharmaceutical firms. Of these, only Amgen, a California firm with a market valuation of over $30 billion, had emerged as a major drug company with very successful drugs. Onto this sea of broken dreams and treacherous regulatory currents Millennium set sail in 1993.

BIRTH OF A NEW MILLENNIUM

When Mark Levin interviewed early in his career at the pharmaceutical giant Eli Lilly without socks, his staid recruiters thought him "a little weird." Even as CEO, he continued raising eyebrows, taking family outings to the local horse racetrack, and appearing annually at Millennium Halloween parties in drag—in a recent year he appeared, wife and daughter in tow, dressed as a French maid in a low-cut dress. Photographs of Levin in any of his large collection of colorful shoes, including zebra-patterned, adorned investor publications.

A one-time Midwestern shoe salesman and former donut shop owner, Levin leveraged his training in chemical engineering to climb his way out of small-town obscurity. After helping start up a beer-brewing plant and getting exposure to the pharmaceutical world through Lilly (he did get the job), Levin quickly found his niche in the emerging biotech industry of the early 1980s. While working for Genentech, the pioneering California-based biotech firm, Levin's brilliance in managing complex projects won him a job at Mayfield Fund, a San Francisco venture capital firm. Here Levin founded some 10 biotech firms—serving as interim CEO of five. His crown jewel, however, proved to be Millennium Pharmaceuticals (see **Exhibit 3** for historical milestones).

Levin's concept for Millennium proved so new and strange that an extensive executive search concluded that only Levin could head up the proposed company. According to Grant Heidrich, general partner at Mayfield, Levin "has tremendous vision for what is looming

[2] D. Stipp, "Hatching a DNA giant," *Fortune,* May 24, 1999.
[3] *Biotech 98: . . . ,* op. cit.

out there. For most people, there are those elements that are hidden in the fog bank. But Mark finds these disconnected pieces and just pulls them together."[4] The plan was to build a drug development company around findings emerging from the Human Genome Project, an ambitious international effort to identify and map every bit of human DNA (which in its entirety is termed the "genome").

Genes causing disease could prove potential targets for drug development. These targets could then be used to develop families of new drugs the world has never seen before. Mapping the human genome "may be the most important step we've taken in science," according to Nobel laureate James Watson, co-discoverer of the DNA structure.[5] Since every disease has a genetic component, deciphering the "Book of Life," as some scientists refer to the genome, promised to revolutionize medical research over decades to come. Even if only 5–10 percent of all estimated 30,000 to 100,000 human genes would yield viable drug targets, it could still open up a rich lode of pharmaceutical drug leads. For the past 100 years, after all, the painstaking efforts involved in drug research had limited medicines developed to less than 500 targets. Even several decades after Watson and Crick discovered the structure of DNA, scientists of the 1980s took years to find and sequence just a single gene or a stretch of DNA of particular interest. For drug companies in 1999, the new revolution could not have been better timed because patents on some 30 major drugs were to expire in the next three years, placing pressure to add to the product pipeline.

With this vision in mind, starting in 1993 with $8.5 million in venture capital funding, Levin set up the company in Cambridge, Massachusetts, in order to court the nation's leading genome scientists. Even without a written business plan or formal organizational charts Levin sold his vision for a new Millennium well. "The reason spectacular scientists want to come to Millennium is that spectacular scientists work at Millennium," according to Professor Eric Lander, a scientific founder of Millennium and himself one of the leading genome experts in the world. "Mark saw that from the beginning."[6] Levin and his team leveraged off the star scientist reputations to raise large amounts of funding with which to create far better research facilities than even the finest universities.

The firm's roster of brilliant technologists included its chief technology officer, Michael Pavia, a pioneer in the combinatorial chemistry revolution. Pavia wanted to leverage the lessons he learned as former head of research at Sphinx Pharmaceuticals, another Cambridge-based biotech firm that was acquired by Eli Lilly, and also wanted to take part in the next revolution: that of transforming the drug development process itself. Millennium also recruited top business people and legal counsel, some of whom were high-performing mavericks in larger pharmaceutical firms and many of whom had nontraditional backgrounds. The company's chief business officer, Steven Holtzman, for instance, is an Oxford-trained Rhodes Scholar whose philosophy training in making fine distinctions helped craft partnership deals that left Millennium with sizable shares of finely cut pies.

Senior management strategically highlighted technology development from the very start. Levin and Holtzman wanted to avoid the mistakes of other biotech firms, which often found themselves stranded in the vise of big pharmaceutical firms because of not having

---

[4] "Millennium's Chief Found His Calling Starting Up New Biotechnology Firms," *Boston Business Journal,* December 5–11, 1997.

[5] A. Zitner, A. and R. Saltus, *The Boston Globe,* Sept 26, 1999, p 1+.

[6] K. Blanton, op. cit.

resources to market drug compounds or not having a broad enough technology platform to avoid becoming research boutiques. If risk diversification for a biotech firm proved difficult on the basis of different products, then at least it should occur on the basis of leading edge technologies.

The initial vision of Millennium was to marry molecular biology with automation and informatics. This would allow for discovering and processing huge amounts of information about genes, making thousands of new targets possible. A dramatic increase in targets would also require quicker screening technologies in order to test many more compounds. Proprietary lab technology included software for analyzing gene function and machines that decode DNA sequences. Harking back on Levin's background as a chemical engineer with work experience in process control, the *Economist* noted:

> Whereas biologists tend to see biotech as the search for a compound, Mr. Levin thinks of it as a complex production process. While they concentrate on the bio, he also thinks hard about the technology. Mr Levin focuses on trying to make each link in the discovery chain as efficient as possible. . . . He has assembled an impressive array of technologies—including robotics and information systems as well as molecular biology. He then enhances them and links them together in novel ways to create what the engineer in him likes to call "technology platforms," [which] should help drug searchers to travel rapidly on their long and tortuous journey from gene to treatment. And Mr Levin is prepared—keen, even—to use or buy other people's technology to help in the struggle to keep up to date. One observer has called him the "Mao Zedong" of biotech, a believer in continuous revolution in both technology and organization.[7]

By creating a technology platform considered the finest available, the firm generated capital for updating the platform to keep ahead of the competition. Biotechnology promised a shortcut for finding cures for human genetic diseases. It allowed for skirting the traditional time-consuming study of family trees of diseased individuals in order to track down the responsible genes. Since these genes could be anywhere along the vast expanse of human DNA, some firms tried to take advantage of rulings that allowed for filing patents on naturally occurring gene sequences as fast as they could find them. "The important thing is to get California instead of Appalachia" in this pharmaceutical land grab, according to Millennium executive John Maraganore.[8] To find these prime pieces of genetic real estate, researchers analyzed hundreds of gene sequences simultaneously using miniature "DNA probes" that could ferret out promising stretches of DNA. These probes were derived through research on DNA samples from people suffering from diseases of particular interest.

Not only could a gene sequence be patented, but also the specific protein produced by that gene as well as the engineered drug produced by splicing the gene into a microbe for production could be. In addition, patents could be filed for the use of the gene in diagnostics tests as well as in drugs targeted at the gene. By 1999, although every large drug company had incorporated combinatorial chemistry into its R&D arsenal, such was not the case with genomics. In April 1999, several large drug companies including the two giant firms Glaxo Wellcome and Bayer AG started a collaboration to locate tens of thousands of areas on the genome that may be implicated with disease and put these in the public domain.[9] Skeptics view this as an effort of the Goliaths to thwart growth of the biotech Davids.

[7] Anonymous, "Millennium's Bugs," *The Economist,* Sept 26, 1998, p. 70.

[8] D. Stipp, op. cit.

[9] I. Amato, "Industrializing the Search for New Drugs," *Fortune,* May 10, 1999.

Millennium's genomics-based approach reversed the traditional process by first identifying and understanding the role of genes implicated in causing a disease. This should allow for selecting drug candidates based on their ability to intervene in disease initiation and progression—thus targeting the root genetic basis of illness. The firm's strategy relied on using many advanced biotech technologies as well as other computer and robotics technology advances based on the Human Genome Project (see **Exhibit 4** for some of the technology).

Some experts warned that the new interest in genomics might turn out to be another disappointment just as rational drug design of the 1980s had. According to genomics entrepreneur Craig Venter, himself involved with co-founding of the leading-edge genomics firm Celera, "genomics has been oversold, although it does mark a 'new starting point.'"[10]

MANAGING GROWTH

Millennium's vision is to focus on activities that allow us to take the highest downstream share of a drug's profit—wherever these profits may occur. How much you participate in downstream activities and what you have to do has changed and will continue to change in this industry.

—*Steven Holtzman, chief business officer*

From its genesis in 1993 with only 20 individuals, Millennium grew rapidly, drawing upon its founders' willingness to experiment and try new strategies, and systematically learn from failures of other firms. Itself a small company, its rapid growth stemmed from research collaborations with dozens of other biotech firms and university scientists. Although the company prided itself on avoiding the trappings of hierarchy—no formal organizational charts existed—several divisions and subsidiaries evolved over time. By the late 1990s, Millennium saw itself as a family of the different groups working toward a common end of developing expertise in genomics as well as revolutionizing drug development (see **Exhibit 5**).

Central to its success and growth, however, was its ability to attract good employees based on scientific merit and interpersonal skills. "You get interviewed about 12 times before they hire you," stated Kenneth Conway, who was recruited to head the predictive medicine subsidiary in 1997. "First they want to know if you have the drive and intelligence to do the job. Then they reinterview you six times to find out if you'll fit in personally."[11] According to Vincent Miles, vice president of business and technology management, "In spite of a tight labor market, we have managed to get to 800 excellent employees without major politics. At a small biotech firm I worked at previously, there were always two camps of seven individuals each, and the CEO would have to act as tie-breaker. Here, people will cover for each other."

Many workers attributed the relative lack of internal politics to top management's low-key approach in running the company. At meetings, Levin often remained in the background, speaking primarily to keep the discussion from going off-track. His office, a modest affair with wall-mounted shelves underlined the flat structure of the organization. Levin, Holtzman

---

[10] Ibid.

[11] D. Stipp, op. cit.

and Pavia also set the pace for the hard-working environment, usually arriving every morning to their spartan offices before 5:00 or 6:00 A.M. Employees arriving early enough were often treated to the sight of their CEO working with headphones to the beat of rock music. All employees received stock options that had resulted in very significant capital gains after the Millennium's stock started to skyrocket in mid-1998.

Through its half-dozen years in existence, senior management realized it needed to chart its own destiny despite its need for large partners. According to Miles, "We did not want to be managed by remote control by committees of larger firms." Indeed, biotech managers often complained of the manner in which large companies dragged their feet. A life-or-death decision for a biotech firm, after all, could represent an hour's revenues for a pharmaceutical giant. Scientists at biotech companies were often demoralized by these delays, since it frequently meant delaying their valued scientific publications because of patent considerations.

To achieve its goals of independence senior management adopted several strategies. First, it intended to eschew the traditional full-time equivalent (FTE) model of funding favored by many biotech firms. In the FTE system, biotech firms would charge their partners for the time spent on alliance specific activities—similar to the way a consulting firm would bill its client for time spent on a project. Although this FTE system tied funding for individual researchers to specific partnership deals and generated predictable cash flow, it often led to a "clock puncher" attitude, with researchers focused on meeting goals of individual partnership projects rather than on the growth and mission of the company itself. Second, Millennium sought partnerships that would fund the type of R&D that would bring it closer to becoming a major drug development firm. Third, as much as possible, it signed only those partnership deals that would enhance, rather than stymie, its ambitious goals for future growth. (See **Exhibit 6** for its revenue structure.)

Management's negotiating strategy for strategic alliances reflected the company's long-term goals by carefully carving out enough choice cuts for the firm itself. Because countless other biotech firms had been frustrated by the slow pace of their larger partners, Millennium crafted agreements that held the feet of its larger partners to the fire, making them answerable for unmet scheduled milestones. For instance, in a recent Millennium alliance, once it found a potential drug target, the partner would need to screen it within a given time; otherwise the rights to the target would revert back to Millennium.

Millennium also sought to retain rights to unforeseen discoveries in the course of a partnership. "We grant select rights of high value to our partners," according to Miles, "while retaining new knowledge and the remaining rights to ourselves." Focusing on such select rights actually worked well with pharmaceutical partners, largely because the big company executives tended to think along divisional lines and focused on rights that fell within their strategic focus. This allowed Millennium to reserve some rights for its own future drug development, such as selected geographic markets or particular therapeutic applications, that were not of immediate interest to its alliance partners. Millennium's contracts were long and explicit, drawing upon some of the most talented lawyers in biotechnology as well as upon Holtzman's attention to both big picture issues and small but crucial details. For instance, in the field of cancer, senior management carved out separate arrangements with three different firms in a manner that eventually boosted its revenues by tens of millions of dollars. At the same time, few of its partners complained. In the words of Paul Pospisil, associate director of business development and strategy, "Large companies salivate over parts of our state-of-the-art technology platform, and our negotiating team is smart enough not to discuss money prematurely."

Millennium underwent one merger when, in 1997, it bought neighboring biotech firm ChemGenics for $90 million. At that time, it had five alliances with drug firms for finding specific gene targets (the "locks"). Through these alliances, Millennium began to realize that it lacked expertise in going from drug targets to actual lead compounds (the "keys")—a major weakness if the firm itself wanted to develop its own drugs some day or simply validate the feasibility of targets that it supplied to its larger partners. Buying ChemGenics with its expertise in lead discovery was a step towards addressing this weakness and would also allow Millennium to negotiate with big firms from a position of greater strength. There was also a feeling among senior executives that general drug targets were becoming increasingly commoditized. Validated targets, on the other hand, where evidence for downstream drug development potential could be demonstrated early were still rare.

Thus, when Millennium realized that ChemGenics was planning an initial public offering, it essentially bought out ChemGenics. A bonus was ChemGenics's expertise in the area of infectious disease—an attractive area for drug development with more predictable and shorter clinical trials than newer therapeutic areas such as central nervous diseases. Culturally, too, the companies appeared compatible. Both, having been launched next to the Cambridge Brewery, were imbued with the very same spirit—the hard-working, hard-playing, high-tech ethos.

By drawing on world-class personnel, and through tough negotiating strategies that led to key mergers, acquisitions, and value-adding relationships with universities and other firms, Millennium had vaulted into the front rank of biotech firms. Unlike most other biotech firms, it posted profits early. For three of its first six years—not counting a one-time charge for the ChemGenics acquisition—Millennium had posted profits.

Being a pioneer in a new field, Millennium got surprisingly little heat from direct competition. Somewhere between two and three dozen genomics biotech firms existed, with a market value of the leading 14 firms of $4.7 billion. Only two of these biotech firms, however, could be considered the firm's peers: Human Genome Sciences (HGS) in Rockville, Maryland, and Incyte Pharmaceuticals in Palo Alto, California.

In the late 1990s, HGS rode high after finding more disease-related gene targets for its pharmaceutical partner SmithKline Beecham (under their original 1993 $125 million agreement) than even one multinational drug company could use. HGS had also negotiated to retain several targets for itself, and by spring 1999 one HGS compound was already undergoing human trials with 25 other candidates to follow suit. HGS also claimed to have applied for patents on 3,000 genes.[12] Incyte, on the other hand, used an entirely different strategy to become a leading genomics firm. It sold drug companies' information in user-friendly databases about the genome. Despite licensing out this information nonexclusively it reaped subscription fees well over $100 million in 1998 alone.

Part of what shielded Millennium from direct competition with other biotech firms was its own success in attracting large partners to create record-breaking alliances, which generally had either a pharmaceutical or technology focus or sometimes a combination of both (see **Exhibit 7** for a list of alliances).

Technology Alliances: The Monsanto Deal

For thousands of years, farmers have crossbred crops and herders have crossbred livestock. Agriculturists, unencumbered by human genetic ethics or the long life span of humans,

---

[12] Ibid.

could experiment with crops in ways not possible with humans. Darwin, in fact, drew upon the accumulated centuries of knowledge gleaned from agriculture in explaining the theory of evolution through natural selection. Thus, agriculture should have drawn upon biotechnology earlier than pharmaceutical companies. Surprisingly, however, agricultural firms were slow to do so despite the fact that in the late 1990s the 1.5 percent world population growth rate outstripped the rate of growth of agricultural productivity (<1 percent) in a global setting of decreased availability of fresh water and arable land.[13] The slowness of agribiotech to bloom, however, stemmed partly from tremendous technical challenges facing agricultural biotechnologists: unlike human researchers, agriculturalists diffused their research efforts across dozens of different species, some of which possessed genomes even larger than human genomes.

One of the first of the giant multinational giants to realize the potential of biotechnology, however, was the Midwestern U.S. firm Monsanto. In 1997, Monsanto approached Millennium to gain access to state-of-the-art genomics technologies. The acquisition of ChemGenics had made it even more attractive to Monsanto. (ChemGenics had already been talking with agricultural firms in a preliminary fashion.) Millennium, in turn, was looking to leverage the integrated platform for agriculture and create near-term value.

The challenge to senior management, however, was to avoid being distracted from its focus on human therapeutics, particularly at a time when the staff was already extended. Millennium contemplated several structures for its partnership including a typical biotech-pharmaceutical partnership, a joint venture, and a technology transfer. To avoid being distracted from its focus on human health, Millennium sought the last option. By agreement with Monsanto, it agreed to replicate or "clone" its technology platform in an agricultural milieu through creating Cereon Genomics, a Monsanto subsidiary. Even the local character was preserved by basing Cereon in Cambridge.

Millennium would receive up to $218 million ($118 million in an up-front fee, and the remainder in yearly $20 million increments based on achieving milestones over the next five years). The milestones were set to be "80 percent achievable." This was to avoid the game of the biotech firm being conservative and the pharmaceutical firm being aggressive. Examples of milestones included: number of DNA lanes sequenced over a given time period; total sequencing capabilities of Cereon by certain time intervals; and software to be set up.

Millennium involved 100 of its scientific staff to help deliver the technology to Monsanto. Nonetheless, the firm learned quickly that the venture would require hiring new staff largely in order to help Cereon *receive* the technology. Technology transfer, after all, always takes place at both ends of the transfer mechanism. Monsanto, however, had generally underestimated the size, infrastructure and training of its technological staff that were necessary to make full use of genomics technology. The middle-ranking scientists and technologists generally found the technology transfer relationship symbiotic; the transfer process, for instance, forced Millennium to document its protocols and software more formally—steps that would help its own new staff members. In the course of working out glitches, useful new information also flowed back to Millennium. Socially, strong bonds were formed through weekend activities such as a joint softball team that consisted of Millennium and Cereon employees.

Over the course of the Monsanto alliance and other deals, Millennium grew from 400 to 700 employees, with 30 new applicants arriving each Monday for five interviews each, and

---

[13] *Biotech 98: . . . ,* op. cit.

eventually added over $20 per share to its stock. It achieved all the milestones agreed with Monsanto, thus obtaining the maximum fees outlined in its contract. According to Miles, "This was our first value-based deal. We thought we could replicate this model over and over again. We were blown away by our success at replicating our technology platform." But only a string of success stories could keep the stock price continuing upward.

Pharmaceutical Alliances: The Bayer Deal

With the ink still drying on the Monsanto-Cereon deal, Millennium underwent a period of soul-searching. It realized that its staff was increasingly stretched across a variety of medical areas in terms of upstream drug target development. Although the Monsanto-Cereon deal indicated that Millennium could go on creating new technology deals, the company still lacked the capabilities to take drugs all the way to market and a robust pipeline of drug development opportunities to pursue on its own behalf. It would have to look for strategic alliances with drug firms to make up for these weaknesses.

At the same time, across the Atlantic, Bayer AG, a large German research firm with 145,000 employees worldwide—best known for introducing Aspirin—was also undergoing a soul-searching exercise termed internally the "Vision 2000" initiative. In 1997, pharmaceuticals accounted for a third of Bayer's $30 billion business but senior management realized that it lagged behind in terms of target discovery and biotechnology. To address this, the company surveyed hundreds of biotech companies for acquisition or partnership deals. With a large war chest it could easily broker deals with a dozen or more biotech firms.

In late October 1997, Bayer invited 55 senior managers from leading biotech companies to what industry insiders termed a "biotech beauty pageant." Millennium, a leading contender, had a prime place on the roster. This came as no surprise, since as early as June of 1996, a Bayer manager had put out "feelers" (i.e., tentative approaches) to a Millennium executive in Paris. A few days later, Bayer invited the firm to partner with it in several areas. With Millennium, Vision 2000 had recognized a natural partnership—one that extended far beyond the similarity of names—and which would allow for "one-stop-shopping" for both sides.

The two companies signed an agreement under which Millennium would find 225 new drug targets for Bayer—an impressive number considering that over the past century, all of the world's drug discoverers combined had found around 500 drug targets. In effect, Millennium would take responsibility for finding half of all targets going into Bayer's drug development pipeline. Areas to be covered included cancer, cardiovascular diseases, pain, osteoporosis, viral infections, and blood disorders. Consistent with its strategy, Millennium would also retain rights to several targets found in the course of the collaboration.

In return for up to $465 million over five years, Bayer would also obtain a 14 percent equity stake in Millennium. The Bayer deal ended up becoming the largest alliance ever between a biotech firm and a pharmaceutical firm. Again, Millennium's stock jumped, creating remarkable capital gains for its stockholders inside and outside the firm.

A NEW DRUG DEVELOPMENT PARADIGM

When Mark hired me, he told me that I had five years to revolutionize drug development. I have about four and a half years left.

—*Michael Pavia, Ph.D., chief technology officer, July 1999*

Fundamental to Millennium's strategy was its ability to revolutionize drug development, which, in the late 1990s, was still long, costly and very risky. In 1997, CEO Mark Levin hired Michael Pavia as chief technology officer with the charter to help make the drug development process "twice as fast and half as expensive" within five years, with the countdown starting in the beginning of 1999. As Pavia translated his charter for industrializing the drug discovery process, "the only way to achieve such an aggressive goal is to question everything and to hire people that challenge assumptions held by the industry for decades."

Millennium was by no means the only company thinking along these bold lines. Most large pharmaceutical firms had initiatives under way to shorten the development cycle significantly and make drug development more predictable. Current practice seemed unsustainable. Pharmaceutical firms would bring several successful drugs to market each year and bear the cost of failure in the very long and expensive clinical phase where only one out of ten drug candidates would make it to the market. Eli Lilly, for instance, had announced its internal goal of "2000 days by the year 2000," implying an aggressive compression of the traditional 12- to 14-year drug development cycle into less than seven years.

Nonetheless, recruits were often attracted to Millennium because of their frustration with the slow progress of large firms. The revolutionary technology platform they saw mirrored the very different training and mindset of the firm's founders. Millennium, being new and unencumbered by corporate inertia—let alone formalized plans—could learn from the mistakes of prior firms and aggressively challenge conventional wisdom. For instance, could traditional drug makers drive costly drug failures to the early phases of development when failure was relatively inexpensive? After all, drug discovery would always involve trial and error. But errors discovered in late development were very costly and could only be absorbed by large firms.

Many lessons in drug development were brought in through recruits from larger companies. It was an experienced job candidate interviewee, for instance, who pointed out that the Federal Drug Administration (FDA) nowhere mandates that pre-clinical trials must be done in defined sequential phases in lock-step. (Perhaps, therefore, attempts to "frontload" problems—one of Millennium's development strategies—might lead it to reshuffle the order in which drugs would be tested.)

To revolutionize drug development, Pavia's group aggressively approached its task using the following three strategies: (1) speed up individual steps of the development process, including rapid feedback on critical tests such as toxicology; (2) carry out serial steps in parallel wherever possible; and (3) "front-load" drug failure modes through the use of new technologies. More will be said about each of these strategies below:

1. *Speed up individual steps of the process:* For the early research phase of drug discovery, scientists and engineers sought to speed up the various steps involved in isolating, characterizing and understanding DNA. By drawing on automation experts and engineers with manufacturing experience, Millennium sought to automate truly complex process steps and create an industrial "R&D factory" (see Exhibit 4), using robots and other equipment often used in advanced production of other products. To achieve this, engineers opportunistically outsourced and modified emerging technologies, often creating machines envied even by leading universities. Like other firms, Millennium also planned to use combinatorial chemistry and high-throughput screening to reduce the time required in the laborious, traditional random search process for drug candidates. Interestingly, no matter how much each step was sped up, however, a crucial bottleneck in the entire R&D

process remained: the ability of scientists to assimilate and make sense of the staggering amount of information made available. To address this, Pavia felt that an increased focus on the rapidly growing field of bioinformatics was essential for Millennium.

2. *Carry out serial steps in parallel wherever possible:* In early 1999, Pavia established a group that reviewed the entire drug development process, using basic principles of operations management, for ways to compress the drug development timeline by allowing more steps to be conducted in parallel. This shift in thinking could save considerable time during drug discovery as well as human clinical trials when drug developers evaluated each candidate compound for *target validity, organ-specificity* (i.e., was the target specific to the organ of interest), *bioavailability* (i.e., would the compound be absorbed appropriately by the body), and *toxicity.* Rather than addressing each of these issues one by one in the traditional sequential fashion, Millennium decided it would seek to do a series of several "quick and dirty" tests on minute quantities of each candidate compound in a fairly simultaneous fashion to see if a candidate was even in the "right ballpark." This was analogous to prescreening job candidates over the telephone in parallel so that only a smaller batch of higher yield candidates would be invited in for in-depth interviews.

3. *Find new technologies that could "front-load" critical problems, thus eliminating less-promising drug candidates early:* In the 1990s, only one out of ten drug candidates typically made it through clinical development—by far the costliest phase of drug development. Pavia wanted to improve these odds by at least half. His staff sought to diminish this wastage by trying to find the potential failure modes through, for instance, prescreening drug candidates as discussed above. Gaining information about, say, the toxicological profile of a drug early on could significantly improve the predictability of its likely success. Pavia's group also decided that it would systematically seek to use other failed drug candidates to see if new technologies could indeed pick up these "failures" earlier (for an example of such a new technology, see Exhibit 8). Pavia charged Paul Pospisil, a chemist trained at Harvard who also had strategic responsibilities, to scour conventions and trade fairs for cutting-edge technologies that would provide earlier feedback on candidate drugs. The point was not necessarily to avoid failure, but to shift failures to earlier phases in the process.

Thus, in terms of reducing the product development cycle, much potential for technological improvement existed alongside the uncertainties inherent in all drug development projects. Like most of the major pharmaceutical firms aiming to shorten the drug development cycle, Millennium realized it would have to focus on many, if not all, links in the drug development process. Focusing on just early drug development through combinatorial chemistry and high-throughput screening, for instance, could save only an estimated half-year to one year. Thus, downstream phases would also need to be shortened. These downstream changes could be achieved through administrative as well as technological changes. For instance, reviewing toxicology data as it was generated might compress the traditional nine-month cycle for a toxicology review into as little as a month.

TAKING STOCK

At Millennium we believe that nothing is impossible.

—*Millennium Corporate Value Statement*

With the Bayer deal, Millennium entered the realm of very large pharmaceutical alliances and now basked in the glow of Wall Street's approval. Unlike other biotech firms, however, it resisted the temptation to sell stock after going public, preferring instead to live off its deals. It did not want to get locked into the traditional pattern of seeking up-front funding in return for royalties—the type of arrangement that pleased investors but did not necessarily build up a biotech firm's long-term capabilities. With Millennium's stock price now at unprecedented heights—having doubled to $60 per share from spring through the summer of 1999, *Fortune* magazine observed, "No drug company wannabe has mustered as much value with as little red ink."[14]

By 1999, the company had grown to about 800 scientists. Millennium remained aware that the current tight job market did not apply to it. In fact, a recent newspaper ad for jobs for mid-level research personnel led to a line well over a block long just for the privilege of dropping off resumes. Many had come from other local biotech firms. Nonetheless, senior management now planned for its growth, at least for the foreseeable future, to plateau at 1,000 scientists.

But even at that size the company dynamics would have to change, despite the best of efforts to retain its small company roots. CEO Levin exclaimed in a 1999 press interview, "It was a lot easier to walk out the bathroom with my [Halloween] costume on when there were 30 people in the company and I knew them all well. Now I walk out into this crowd of 800 wondering if most of them are thinking, 'Who is this idiot?' But it's fun."[15]

But signs of strain in the organization were showing throughout all levels. According to Pavia, "Growing the organization from 100 to 200 was relatively easy; doubling from there to 400 was a bit harder but manageable; but to think of growing beyond 800 would place all sorts of new strains and would need re-thinking on how we do things." With growth, high-ranking scientists had to supervise more people while contending with having their skills marketed to more outside partners. Indications of increased stress at lower levels came from the Human Relations department's latest semi-annual survey from March 1999. It showed that despite general high employee satisfaction, the areas that scored the lowest were in terms of workload, expectations, and manageability of stress. These areas scored a hairline lower than a half-year ago.

"I absolutely love what I am doing," one worker commented on the questionnaire, "but the workload sometimes is unmanageable. . . . Sometimes you don't know whether you are swimming or sinking." Another worker added, "I think my workload and the expectations are higher than in the other industrial settings where I've worked—I've worked for three other companies." Yet another worker quantified this frustration: "I am currently committed to do two scientists' worth of work. Consequently I feel that I have to make a choice between trying to do it all in a mediocre way, or I can only do part of it well and leave the rest undone—if I take the latter route, there is no good decision mechanism to tell me what is the most important: I'm told 'Everything is important!'"

To manage stress within the firm, the company's human relations department under Peter McLaughlin wanted to avoid stopgap measures such as occasional stress-reduction seminars. Instead, in early 1999, it sought to make all managers responsible for having regular one-to-one sessions with subordinates to discuss such issues. How this change in approach

[14] I. Amato, op. cit.

[15] D. Stipp, op. cit.

would work had yet to be seen. In any case, the company was more aware that money alone could not buy its way out of the stress dilemma. According to Miles, vice president of business and technology management:

> In the past we were driven by financing. We made commitments without detailed planning. For example, the Bayer deal was so huge that we would do whatever they wanted. Now we are pickier. Our strategy just two years ago was not as clearly defined as now. But we realized that technology alliances could be either financing vehicles or distractions. Every time we thought about a new deal we worried about several tensions: were we biting off more than we could chew? After all, we were already quite extended. Were we in danger of losing our focus? Several other prominent biotech firms have a hard time stating exactly what they do.

Without a formal plan, Millennium had found its path to its present prosperity. Its vision had encompassed becoming a genomics firm and helping revolutionize the drug development process. Already, with these two visions not even fully implemented, its managers and scientists were talking about what could only be whispered at most other biotech firms: the prospect of growing into a fully integrated pharmaceutical firm.

BIG DEAL

In June 1999, after a presentation at an industry conference, a Millennium senior executive was quietly approached by an executive from Lundberg, a multinational agribusiness concern and one of the largest privately held companies in Europe. Despite not being a household name, Lundberg impacted the daily lives of most Europeans through its dealings in livestock and agricultural produce. It was ironic, therefore, that a company that made fortunes in the futures market from one-cent price swings of commodities sold by the ton now approached a firm that operated on the scale of milligrams.

Through Millennium, Lundberg sought access to genomics technology, much in the manner of the Millennium-Monsanto deal. Lundberg specifically sought access to technology that would help identify plant genes as well as for high throughput screening capabilities. For Lundberg, the applications were limitless. It would, for instance, allow for facile manipulation of the fat content of livestock or the carbohydrate content of grain. For Millennium's senior management, three issues loomed large in their minds as they thought about a potential deal with Lundberg: strategic fit, impact on its R&D productivity, and potential conflict with its prior relationship with Monsanto.

If the Lundberg deal did not fit strategically with Millennium's own goals, the company decided it would consider the deal a distraction. Strategic fit would have to be analyzed by considering impact on the entire company. For instance, although at first glance informatics did not appear to be directly involved, the firm would have to help create software for the new venture. This was no small venture, because the Millennium software platform was orders of magnitude larger than commercial office software and would require frequent upgrades. On the other hand, through a partnership with Lundberg, it could pay for some of the work it needed to do for itself anyway. For instance, software documentation for Lundberg would also help Millennium internally.

In terms of the impact of the Lundberg deal on Millennium's own productivity, many variables remained unclear. If a deal with Lundberg were to hamper productivity, it could stifle growth several years later. For instance, it was clear that Lundberg did not possess an infrastructure for receiving any transferred genomics technology, and therefore Millennium would have to set up a system that would allow Lundberg to receive the technology. This implied using Millennium's senior staff to interview and hire new personnel on Lundberg's behalf. On the other hand, once the interviewing was done, Millennium's top-level staff would be minimally distracted by the Lundberg deal. Furthermore, Millennium's staff generally appeared confident it could repeat its first agribiotechnology technology transfer even quicker the second time, building on experience and expertise that was built as a result of the Monsanto alliance.

Potential conflict with the Monsanto deal turned out not to be an important consideration. The Monsanto agreement allowed for considerable areas of collaboration between Millennium and any other agricultural concern. For instance, while Millennium could not help manipulate the fat content for plant foods because of its relationship with Monsanto, it could do so for livestock.

While Millennium grappled with the issues discussed above, eight senior Lundberg executives created time on their busy calendars to come to Cambridge. No figures were quoted by either party, although Millennium's senior management hinted from the outset that the alliance would have to be at least as large as the Monsanto deal. As these issues were discussed in the meeting, Levin and Holtzman were surprised to learn that Lundberg, for its part, had done little due diligence; it had not even examined the SEC filings for the Monsanto-Millennium collaboration. It was also unclear how the company expected to receive the technology platform as its middle management had not been involved in any of the discussions. On the other hand, Lundberg's senior management, led by a family member that held a majority position in the privately held firm, showed strong consensus and were ready to make a major financial commitment right away.

The business development team that had prepared the meeting for Levin felt very good—the discussions showed little conflict or disagreement between the two senior executive teams. Announcement of the deal would please Wall Street analysts and probably add a quarter billion dollars or more of cash to Millennium's financial coffer. After the meeting, Levin sat down in his office and reflected on his company's future. In a few minutes, several key executives, including Holtzman and Pavia, would come to his office to discuss the final decision on whether to pursue the Lundberg alliance. Counting the chairs in his modest office, he wondered whether there would be enough room for the small group.

EXHIBIT 1

Selected Financials for Millennium Pharmaceuticals

Source: Financial Reports.

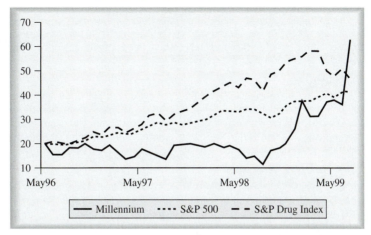

Millennium Pharmaceuticals Stock Price

Selected Financial Data (Dollars in Millions, Except Per-Share Data)

	1995	1996	1997	1998
Sales	22.9	31.8	89.9	133.7
Cost of goods sold	19.4	38.9	81.6	125.0
Gross profit	3.5	−7.1	8.4	8.7
Operating Income Before Depreciation	3.5	−7.1	8.4	8.7
Depreciation, Depletion & Amortization	1.7	3.9	12.2	16.3
Operating Profit	1.7	−11.0	−3.8	−7.6
Net income	1.2	−8.8	−81.2[a]	10.3
Other data:				
EPS (Primary)	0.07	−0.39	−2.87	0.34
Dividends per share	0	0	0	0
ROA (%)	5.1%	−10%	−56%	4%
ROE (%)	9.8%	−13%	−88%	5%
Market value ($ Mil.)		415.5	554.2	903.6

[a] Includes acquisition of ChemGenics

EXHIBIT 2   **Summary of Drug Development in the United States**

New drug development is a costly affair with high failure rates. For each therapeutic drug entering the market, pharmaceutical firms invest more than $230 million (estimates go up to $359 million) and 14.8 years (up from 14.3 years in the 1970s). Estimated costs include out-of-pocket expenses, costs of failed projects, and opportunity costs. A brief outline of the drug development process follows:

Basic Research (About Two Years)

This phase typically starts through the initial screening of plants, microorganisms, and other naturally occurring substances to find a "hit" or "lead" compound. In a painstaking iterative process, organic chemists would then make analogues or modifications of existing leads. Although this stage typically cost a firm $30–50 million, it represented a point of great leverage for speeding up a firm's drug development process. Only 40 out of an initial 10,000 compounds might make it to the next stage of pre-clinical testing.

Pre-Clinical (Biological) Screening (About Three Years)

Pre-clinical trials, which often overlapped the basic research phase, involved animal testing to assess drug safety and to gather data on biological effects (e.g., absorption, metabolism, and excretion). Only one in four drugs typically made it through this phase to enter human clinical testing as "Investigational New Drugs" (INDs).

Human Clinical Trials (About Six Years)

Investigational New Drugs faced the FDA's regulatory hurdles, the most stringent and time-consuming approval process for therapeutic drugs in the world. Total costs for conducting clinical trials topped $200 million, but with increasing proportions of this cost occurring with each of the three successive phases describe below.

- **Phase I Safety Trials (One Year):** In Phase I trials, researchers determined highest tolerated doses, toxicities, and safe ranges in one or two dozen healthy volunteers. This phase also yielded invaluable information on absorption, metabolism, and excretion of the drug in humans.
- **Phase II Efficacy Trials (Two Years):** Phase II tested efficacy of drug candidates in up to several hundred volunteer patients based at test sites composed of participating hospitals. To ensure statistically relevant data, from this point onward, a portion of the volunteers received the drug while the others received placebos. Roughly one-third of all drug candidates survived Phases I and II.
- **Phase III Long-Term Efficacy Trials (Three Years):** In the longest and most expensive phase of drug testing, researchers monitored drug use in thousands of volunteer patients for long term safety, optimum dosage levels, and subtler adverse effects. Only about a fourth of all drug candidates survived Phases I, II, and III, and moved on to the FDA review stage.

FDA Review (About Two to Three Years)

Despite a trend toward computer-assisted applications, the hundreds of thousands of pages submitted in the New Drug Application (NDA) to the FDA represented a tribute to the pharmaceutical industry's data-generating capacity. The NDA included data on each patient, as well as on the company's plans for producing and stocking the drug. The FDA committee took up to three years to review the NDA. Even after approval, however, post-marketing surveillance by the FDA continued. Only one-tenth of all drug candidates entering clinical trials ultimately reached the market.

Sources: J.A. DiMasi (1995), "New Drug Development: Cost, Risk, and Complexity," *Drug Information Journal,* May; FDA (1995), "From Test Tube to Patient: New Drug Development in the United States," *FDA Consumer,* Special Issue, January; Kenneth I. Kaitin, and Hub Houben (1995), "Worthwile Persistence: The Process of New Drug Development," Odyssey, *The Glaxo-Wellcome Journal of Innovation in Healthcare,* June.

EXHIBIT 3
Important Milestones for Millennium

1865	Austrian monk Gregor Mendel's plant breeding experiments find evidence for hereditary transmission of traits. He postulates building-blocks of heredity that later scientists would term "genes." Mendel's findings collect dust for decades.
1869	Swiss scientist Miescher discovers an abundant and seemingly useless material in the cell nucleus that he terms "nuclein." Later known as DNA, nuclein's role in transmitting genetic information would not be appreciated until later.
1953	Structure of deoxyribonucleic acid (DNA) elucidated by Watson and Crick who would later receive a Nobel prize for their work.
Early 1970s	Biotech industry starts, primarily in California and Massachusetts, based on discoveries that allow scientists to excise and recombine bits of DNA.
1990	Human Genome Project launched by U.S. government with the mission of identifying every bit of human DNA including all 100,000 or so human genes. Technological advances accelerate anticipated project completion date (by three years to 2002) in a manner worth emulating by other government initiatives.
1993	Millennium founded with Mark Levin as CEO in Cambridge, Massachusetts and with $8.5 million in venture capital funding.
March 1994	Millennium signs its first major pharmaceutical deal with Hoffman-LaRoche. The deal centers around finding new drug targets in obesity and diabetes.
October 1995	Millennium signs equity funding and research deal with Eli Lilly & Co.—the first of several deals with Millennium CEO Mark Levin's old employer.
February 1997	Millennium acquires neighboring biotech firm ChemGenics for $90 million. This expands Millennium's downstream capabilities for developing drug targets into leads and boosts Millennium's bargaining power with big firms.
October 1997	Millennium signs agreement with Monsanto and creates Cambridge-based Cereon to transfer the genome technology platform for agricultural purposes.
September 1998	Millennium announces the biggest biotech-pharma alliance ever: the nearly half-billion-dollar deal with Bayer AG. The agreement covers drug target identification in several medical fields.
August 1999	Case setting: Current offer from Lundberg for a technology deal paralleling the Monsanto alliance.

EXHIBIT 4
Millennium's
R&D
Factories:
Automated
DNA
Sequencing

Source: Millennium
Pharmaceuticals.

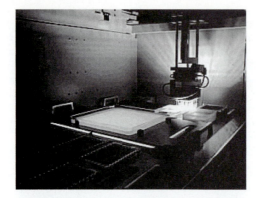

Colony Picking: "Libraries" of DNA corresponding to healthy and diseased individuals are grown in bacteria and picked up by robot arm for DNA sequencing.

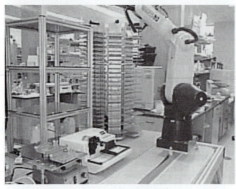

DNA Preparation: The DNA molecules are isolated from the rest of the bacterial materials.

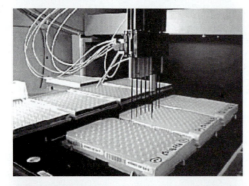

Reaction Assembly: Pure DNA materials are dispensed for automatic sequencing.

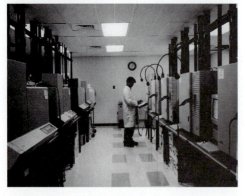

DNA Sequencing: The identity of DNA molecules is "read" by an automated sequencing process.

EXHIBIT 5
Millennium's Corporate Structure

Millennium saw itself as a family of the following groups working toward a common end of developing expertise in genomics as well as gearing toward ultimate drug development:

- *Pharmaceutical Division:* This division worked on providing pharmaceutical companies with high-value drug targets and drug leads. Scientists here generally focused on small therapeutic molecules. Customers included multinationals such as Hoffman-LaRoche, Lilly, Astra, Wyeth-Ayerst, and Pfizer. The 1997 acquisition of ChemGenics (see below) greatly extended the downstream drug development capabilities.
- *Millennium BioTherapeutics, Inc (MBio):* Millennium's first subsidiary, launched in 1997, used biotech and genomics technologies to discover and develop larger therapeutic molecules such as proteins and gene products for drug companies. From the very beginning, Lilly invested $20 million in MBio for an 18 percent ownership interest. Millennium retained rights to half the drug candidates identified by the research collaborations with Lilly.
- *Technology Division:* This division provided to other branches of Millennium as well as third-party clients, high-value R&D technologies pertaining to genomics and related fields such as high-throughput screening, combinatorial chemistry. Despite a preference for technologies based on internal efforts, the division actively scanned the industry for external acquisition of technologies useful for enhancing the company's technology platform. Many of this division's customers overlapped with those of MPharma.
- *Millennium Predictive Medicine, Inc. (MPMx):* This subsidiary, launched in 1997, focused on genomics-based products and technologies for improving the diagnosis and prediction of disease. By elaborating the relationship between genes and patients' reactions to drugs, this group would hopefully help physicians with deciding with tailoring therapeutics toward individual patients.
- *Cereon Genomics:* This wholly-owned subsidiary of Monsanto marked Millennium's foray into agriculture. This allowed for making the company's technology platform available to a partner in an area far removed from Millennium's general province of human healthcare: plant agriculture.

EXHIBIT 6   Millennium's Revenue Structure

Consolidated Revenue (Dollars in 000s; 12/31/94 Through 6/30/99)

	1994	1995	1996	1997	1998	6/30/99
Contract (FTE)	5,963	11,250	23,171	44,569	51,983	25,226
License Fees (One Time)	2,000	11,130	6,250	43,438	20,000	15,000
Milestones	—	500	1,400	1,100	23,350	3,625
Bayer Alliance	—	—	—	—	33,400	42,500
Reimbursed Collaborations/Support	—	—	944	827	4,949	1,913
Total	7,963	22,880	31,764	89,933	133,682	88,264

Source: Millennium Pharmaceuticals

EXHIBIT 7 Lists of Millennium's Alliances (by Company, Year, Therapeutic Area, Dollar Amount)

Date	Alliances	Terms	Focus
3/94	Hoffmann-LaRoche Inc.	Equity: $6 M; Full-Time Equivalent (FTE) Funding: $10 M/yr over 5 yrs.; milestone fees and royalties	Obesity, Type II diabetes
10/95 & 3/96	Eli Lilly and Company	Equity: $8 M; Up-front Licensing Fee: $4 M; FTE Funding: $10 M/yr over 5 years; milestone fees and royalties	Atherosclerosis & oncology
12/95	Astra AB	Up-front Licensing Fee: $10 M; FTE Funding: $8 M/year over 5–7 years; milestone fees and royalties	Inflammatory respiratory diseases
6/96	American Home Products (Wyeth-Ayerst)	Up-front Licensing Fee: $10M; FTE Funding: $10 M/yr over 5–7 years; milestone fees and royalties	Central Nervous System disorders
2/97	ChemGenics Pharmaceuticals, Inc.	4,783,688 shares CG common stock	Antibacterial small molecule drug targets
5/97	MBio	Joint funding with Eli Lilly; share rights to discoveries (see below)	(see below)
5/97	Eli Lilly	Research Funding: $8–$10 M/yr over 3 years (option to renew for 2 years); $20 M MBio stock; 18 percent equity interest in MBio; licensing and milestone fees' royalties	Therapeutic proteins
10/97	Monsanto Company	Up-front Licensing Fee: $38 M; Technology Fees: $180 M over 5 years; royalties; exclusive rights to plant agritechnology; nonexclusive rights to nonagritechnology	Agritechnology (via Cereon)
9/98	Bayer AG	Up-front Licensing Fee: $33.4 M; Ongoing Licensing Fee and Research Funding: $219 M; Performance Target Delivery: up to $116 M; $96.6 M (4.96M shares) Millennium common stock	Cardiovascular disease; Oncology (separate. from Eli Lilly targets); Osteoporosis; Liver fibrosis; Hematology; Viral Infections 225 targets over five-year period

Source: S. Matthews and M. Watkins, "Strategic Deal-Making at Millennium Pharmaceuticals," Harvard Business School Case No. 899-242 (1999).

EXHIBIT 8   **Genomics Technology in Drug Discovery: Front-Loading Toxicology Assessment Through Transcriptional Profiling**

Extreme diseases demand severe cures.
—Hippocrates

Hippocrates notwithstanding, in a world where most drugs have undesired side effects, modern drug makers continually sought kinder, gentler drugs. To achieve this goal, drug makers screened compound candidates for those with a high margin of safety between doses producing the desired, therapeutic effects and doses producing toxic doses. Sometimes, as in the case of anti-cancer chemotherapies, for lack of better alternatives, physicians were forced to use rather toxic drugs.

To understand and assess the potential damage wrought by drug compounds in the body, we must examine the liver, since most of the body's detoxification occurs here. Liver cells, often described as the body's factory, use a variety of mechanisms to rid the body of toxins. All detoxification steps in the specific mechanism are ultimately controlled by specific genes. Toxins that cannot be removed may ultimately damage the liver itself over time, leading, for example, to the liver cirrhosis of excessive alcohol drinkers.

The classic approach to examining the liver's actions against a drug involved studying drug metabolism in lab animals at the pre-clinical stage. This proved a long and expensive process, since weeks or months would pass before the effects on the animal livers could be assessed. Newer methods, however, allow for exposing liver tissue slices to the test chemicals to assess for drastic effects such as cell death on liver tissue. In the late 1990s, this was routinely done. Through increasing biochemical finesse, however, researchers sought to discover which of the many important detoxification mechanisms in the liver were being used in order to create strategies for modifying the chemical compound to less toxic forms.

A powerful genomics technology for assessing toxicology is "transcriptional profiling." Transcriptional profiling is a technology that allows for assessing what genes are active (i.e., being "transcribed" by the cell's genetic machinery into genetic messages that would serve as architectural blueprints for making proteins, the building blocks of the body). The DNA in each human cell contains the same set—or genome—of about 100,000 genes, of which about 15,000 different genes will be active during a cell's life-time. Different combinations of genes would be active in different cell types, with the highly active liver cells likelier to activate a large number of genes.

To identify the set of genes in liver cells associated with detoxifying a specific class of drugs, genomics researchers compare the "transcriptional profile" of a dormant liver cell with liver cells actively metabolizing the drugs in question. Any discrepancies likely reflect the use of genes specifically activated for ridding the body of the specific toxins. (To ferret out these discrepancies, copies of all known genes are placed in a systematic array on a surface. The cellular genetic "messages" churned out by the activated liver cells would then combine in a "like-seeks-like" fashion with the genes on these arrays most like their parent genes.) By thus identifying the genes most relevant for detoxifying a given compound, drug makers could now quickly understand how difficult a drug might prove to be to detoxify.

Transcriptional profiling, thus, can potentially provide a quick way to "front-load" failure modes early in the drug development process and thus steer a company away from a likely unfruitful avenue of research at a stage when it was still inexpensive and quick to switch course.

EXHIBIT 9 Glossary

Analog

A structural variation of a parent molecule. Useful analog compounds may exhibit fewer adverse effects or might be therapeutic in smaller doses.

Assay

A test to determine properties of a chemical entity such as strength or purity or activity in a biological system.

Chemical Library

A collection of differing compounds (analogous to a library of books), usually maintained for further study. Drug firms often maintain libraries of all compounds synthesized in the past by their scientists.

Combinatorial Chemistry

A branch of synthetic chemistry developed that allows for systematically generating large numbers of chemically diverse but related compounds. Combinatorial chemistry, thus, potentially allows drug makers to rapidly generate and explore thousands of compounds in just weeks in order to find promising compounds.

Compound

A distinct chemical entity formed by the union of two or more ingredients in a distinctive proportion. Drug compounds are formed from a distinctive proportion of differing chemical elements.

Molecular Diversity

The importance of molecular diversity—analogous to diversity found within the human race—stems from the fact that even minor changes in molecular structure can tremendously alter function. As a result, drug makers seek to adequately explore molecular diversity of a promising drug's analogues in order to field the best possible drug, (just as a good company recruits from an adequate diversity of candidates).

Receptor

A specialized protein located on or within cells in the body capable of detecting specific environmental changes. Receptors in the nervous system, once activated by neurotransmitters, will often trigger specific responses within the body.

Rational Drug Design

An approach that uses very advanced scientific methods such as x-ray crystallography and/or nuclear-magnetic resonance (NMR) spectroscopy to determine the three dimensional shape and structure of a target that they wish to influence with a drug. With the aid of computer simulation, scientists would then be able to design drug molecules that bind to the target receptor.

Screening

A process of systematically examining a collection of compounds to find those with the most promise for a given purpose (such as drug development). "High throughput screening" refers to the ability to screen a large number of compounds in a short time period—a capability needed to successfully apply combinatorial chemistry.

Synthetic Chemistry

The branch of chemistry dealing with the creation of compounds in the laboratory

Target

A receptor, enzyme or molecule associated with a particular disease. The goal of drug discovery is to find or create compounds that will bind to a particular target with a required degree of tenacity (binding affinity) and, at the same time, not bind to other targets that may be structurally similar but have different functions.

Article

Mastering the Value Chain: An Interview with Mark Levin of Millennium Pharmaceuticals

As today's business leaders are all too aware, a new scientific or technological breakthrough can quickly transform an industry's competitive landscape. The upheaval is often traumatic for the companies involved, forcing them to rethink their strategies and redefine their boundaries in response to seismic shifts in value along the industry supply chain. New, tech-savvy specialists rush in to capitalize on new sources of value, while established companies scramble to acquire new capabilities.

The pharmaceutical industry exhibits all the symptoms of this kind of strategic dislocation. The race to unlock the secrets of the human genome has produced an explosion of scientific knowledge and spurred the development of new technologies that are altering the economics of drug development. Billions of dollars of investment capital have poured into the industry, resulting in the creation of a host of high-tech start-ups. At the same time, the big drug companies, with their deep pockets, have begun acquiring and forming partnerships with abandon, hoping to ride out the storm with their leadership positions intact.

Millennium Pharmaceuticals sits at the nexus of the strategic forces shaping the industry. Founded in 1993, the high-tech, high-risk new venture specialized in performing basic research on genes and proteins using automated R&D technologies. Today it is repositioning itself in the value chain, pursuing a strategy that more closely resembles that of an established player than of an entrepreneurial upstart. Through a series of ambitious partnerships, the company has migrated down the value chain and across product categories. Millennium's goal is to be a dominant player in the pharmaceutical industry of tomorrow.

In a recent interview, conducted at Millennium's headquarters in Cambridge, Massachusetts, founder and CEO Mark Levin described his vision of the future of the drug business and the central role Millennium hopes to play in it. Levin, who holds degrees in chemical and bio-chemical engineering and has also worked as a venture capitalist, explains how the company is leveraging its capabilities as a technology pioneer to expand its reach across the value chain. The vigorous approach he takes to balancing long-term strategy with short-term tactics offers important lessons to any executive facing an industry upheaval.

The conclusion of the Human Genome Project seems to mark a strategic inflection point, to borrow a phrase from Andy Grove, for the pharmaceutical industry. Would you agree?
Absolutely. We're seeing fundamental changes not only in the nature of drugs and drug making but also in the way value is created and profits are distributed throughout the indus-try. Drug development is an extremely time-consuming and expensive process—a typical drug takes 15 years and $500 million to bring to market—and a company's position in that process is critical in determining its profit potential. When Millennium was founded eight years ago, we situated ourselves at the furthest upstream end of the industry value chain: doing basic research into genes and proteins and selling our findings to big pharmaceutical companies. But as the distribution of value in the industry has changed, we've moved down-stream, toward the patients who actually use and pay for the drugs.

When you say the distribution of value in the industry has changed, what do you mean?
To answer that question, I'll have to give you a brief history lesson. The distribution of value in our industry—in any industry, I'd argue—is shaped to a considerable degree by forces that are beyond the control of any single company and that often play out over the course of many years. To understand those forces, you can't just look at a snapshot of the present. You have to see what's come before and imagine how that will shape what comes next. In the case of the pharmaceutical industry, I believe we're at its third major inflection point.

The modern industry came into being in the early nineteenth century, when scientists realized that the herbs and potions people took to treat illnesses worked because they contained specific active ingredients. Several German companies began to systematically isolate those ingredients, test them for efficacy, and sell them as pills. Those three steps—research, testing, and delivery—defined the industry's value chain for the next 100 years. The major drugs companies that began to emerge—companies like Pfizer and Eli Lilly—participated in each of the activities, either directly or, in the case of research, through partnerships with universities. To thrive, companies had to pursue a strategy of vertical integration along the value chain.

The industry's second inflection point came during the 1960s. In the wake of Crick and Watson's discoveries about DNA, people began to realize that certain diseases were closely linked to genetic makeup. By relating slight changes in the proteins produced by specific genes in specific parts of the body to cancer or diabetes or asthma, companies realized that they might be able to develop products that would treat the causes, rather than just the symptoms, of those diseases. Suddenly, basic research was seen as much more valuable. A company that owned scientific knowledge about certain genes or proteins could own the cures developed from them.

The Drug Development Process

Pills and serums are the end products of a long, complex discovery process. It starts with an identification of the genes involved in a particular disease. Next, you identify and validate the proteins—or targets—that different genes produce in different parts of the body. It's those targets that cause the malfunctions in cells that become diseases. Third, you try to identify small molecules that will attach to the target protein and prevent it from causing the disease. After you've identified these leads, you enter the testing phase. The leads are tested first on animals and then on humans. Finally, you have to find ways of economically manufacturing the drugs on a large scale and marketing them successfully to doctors and patients. (In some instances, the problem may be the absence of proteins—such as a growth hormone, for example—in which case, the challenge is to find ways to synthesize and deliver the missing proteins. But these "large molecule" treatments account for only 10% of the industry.)

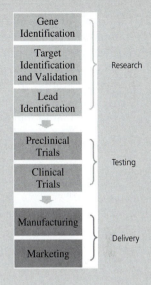

The genetics revolution effectively brought two new upstream steps to the pharmaceutical industry's value chain: research into the genes associated with a disease and identification of the proteins those genes produced. Billions of dollars were poured into these activities, and a host of more specialized high-tech companies such as Amgen and Genentech were created. This upstream end was and remains highly fragmented. But even so, the benefits of these investments have been tremendous, and the companies involved have made huge contributions to our basic knowledge about genes and proteins. Indeed, without their involvement, we'd still be decades away from a map of the human genome.

Millennium was a child of this revolution as well. Our main contribution thus far has been advances in research technologies: we've found ways to speed up the search for genes and proteins through information technologies and automation. Our biosensor technology, for instance, uses customized microchips to analyze interactions among proteins and between proteins and small molecules in tiny samples, far smaller than was previously the norm.

But we've become increasingly aware that we cannot afford to remain a research company because the value in our industry is shifting again. We're at the third inflection point. For the moment, at least, it looks as though most of the really big leaps in basic scientific knowledge have been made. We've mapped the genome, and the information is publicly available. We're awash in basic information about genes. As a result, that stage of the value chain is no longer as lucrative as it was seen to be just a few years ago. Value has started to migrate downstream, toward the more mechanical tasks of identifying, testing, and manufacturing molecules that will affect the proteins produced by genes, and which become the pills and serums we sell. At Millennium, we've anticipated this shift by expanding into downstream activities across several major product categories. Our ultimate goal is to develop capabilities and a strong presence in every stage of the industry's value chain—from gene to patient. (See the feature box in the previous page, "The Drug Development Process.")

So you want to shift from being a specialist to being a generalist? That seems counterintuitive. The value chain for other high-tech products has, after all, tended to break down into a few separate, largely independent industries. Take the computer business: there's chip manufacturing, computer assembly and delivery, and software: Intel, Dell, and Microsoft coexist where IBM used to dominate. Why is the pharmaceutical industry different?

It's because there's still only one really valuable product you can sell: the pill or serum that the patient takes. The discrete stages that specialist companies can carve out ultimately do not carry enough of the product's value, so margins tend to be quite small. Say I find a target protein for obesity; that target is still $500 million away from doing anybody any good. Even if I find a molecule that actually hits the target, it's not valuable unless I've got hundreds of others to offer as well. The vast majority of promising molecules—we call them leads—never make it through testing. I'm not saying that you can't make a good steady business by being a niche player—there are, for instance, very profitable companies that just do preclinical and even clinical testing. But no company will ever create any serious long-term value in our industry by staying in just one or two stages of the value chain.

So you plan to build Millennium into a fully integrated pharmaceutical company?

We prefer to call it a biopharmaceutical company, but basically, yes. From the start, we've believed that the industry's future lies in personalized medicine. One day, everyone will have their own genomes mapped out and stored in memory chips, and doctors will look at the information in those chips and prescribe accordingly: "Mary, you should take this drug, but Mark, you should take that drug, because different things in your genes are causing your asthma." We want to be the leader in personalized drug therapies. In fact, our expressed goal is to be the first company to deliver health care tailored to the patient's genetic profile. To achieve that goal, we need to reach all the way to the doctors and the patients.

Given the downstream strength of the pharmaceutical companies, aren't you at a huge disadvantage having started at the less valuable end of the chain?

Not entirely. One major weakness of traditional pharmaceutical development was that companies all tended to focus on the same targets—those identified in the academic literature. This created a me-too phenomenon. It's why we have 60 birth control pills on the market, and so many calcium channel blockers, and so on. Because we have the ability to find our own targets, we have an advantage. We can avoid the me-too competition that drives down profit margins.

Millennium's Partnerships

As the following table shows, Millennium has amassed an enviable portfolio of alliances. In the last three years, it has acquired an increasing ownership stake in the end products of its collaborations.

Year	Partner	Value (in millions)	Terms	Role of Millennium
1994	Hoffmann-La Roche	$70	Equity investment and fees from partner	Gene/target research
1995	Eli Lilly I	$50	Equity investment and fees from partner	Gene/target research
1996	Astra AB	$60	Fees from partner	Gene/target research
	Eli Lilly II	$30	Fees from partner	Extension of previous deal
1997	AHP (Wyeth-Ayerst)	$90	Fees from partner	Gene/target research
	ChemGenics	$90	Acquisition	Acquisition of lead research capability
	Eli Lilly III	$20	Equity investment and fees from partner	Extension of previous deal
	Monsanto	$218	Fees from partner	Technology transfer to partner
1998	Bayer	$465	Equity investment and fees from partner; ownership of targets not retained by Bayer	Gene/target research
1999	LeukoSite	$750	Acquisition	Acquisition of lead research capabilities, product development pipeline, and near-market products
	Becton-Dickinson	$68	Equity investment and fees from partner	Gene/target research
	Bristol-Myers Squibb	$32	Fees from partner	Gene/target research
2000	Aventis	$450	Equity investment and fees from partner; 50-50 ownership of end products	Full codevelopment of drug; cocommercialization in North America
	Cambridge Discovery Chemistry	$50	Acquisition	Acquisition of chemistry capability
2001	Abbott Laboratories	$250	Equity investment from partner; 50-50 ownership of end products	Full codevelopment of drug; cocommercializaton

Expanding downstream in the pharmaceutical industry is a huge challenge, requiring big investments and new capabilities. How will you pull it off?

We've always relied heavily on partnerships—both to broaden our capabilities and to gain funding—and we'll continue to do so. The structure of our partnerships, though, will change. At first, we were more or less contract researchers: in return for investment in our R&D, we gave away ownership of any targets we identified, retaining only a royalty interest. We raised about $1.8 billion that way, which, together with equity raised from the investment community, helped us develop our R&D platform.

But as we've begun to move down the value chain, we've changed the nature of these partnerships, retaining more control over the products of our research. Many of our partnerships now are 50-50 alliances, and instead of just equity investment and R&D support, we're getting an ownership stake in products. At the same time, we're also involved in downstream development and marketing. We've just signed such a deal with Abbott Laboratories. Roughly 225 scientists from our companies will research the genes and proteins involved in obesity and diabetes. We'll treat those proteins on the molecular level, and then test our results together, first on animals in the lab, and then on humans in the clinic. Any drugs that we come up with we'll sell jointly in the United States, splitting the revenues 50-50. Abbott will commercialize them globally. We think the profits from this partnership will provide a steady cash flow for future growth. Last year, we signed a similar deal with Aventis for treatments in rheumatoid arthritis, asthma, multiple sclerosis, and other major inflammatory diseases.

Our long-term strategy, however, is to move beyond having a 50 percent stake in our products to owning them 100 percent. We've already started to develop a few of our own drugs for metabolic diseases such as obesity and Type II diabetes, as well as some of the major cancers. In some of these areas, we've brought in the missing capabilities through share-financed acquisitions rather than partnerships. In 1997, for instance, we acquired ChemGenics, based here in Cambridge, because of its technology for high-speed chemical screening of molecules. That gave us the ability to quickly identify promising leads.

Our acquisition of LeukoSite in 1999 brought us capabilities further downstream. The company, also based in Cambridge, was already testing its own drugs on humans and was working with the FDA to win approval. So we bought not only the leads that it had developed fairly far downstream but also the people who had done that development. Our acquisition of the British company Cambridge Discovery Chemistry has brought in skilled medicinal chemists—people who can work out how to synthetically produce the molecules that we own, which is what makes mass production possible. I expect that we'll be doing a lot more acquisition in the future, especially as the revenues from our partnership drugs start to flow. Indeed, as we grow and compete with the established drugs companies, acquisitions will overtake partnerships as our main way to build a pipeline and add new capabilities.

Your strategy will bring you into direct competition with the large pharmaceutical companies. Why would they want to partner with you?
Because we've developed an R&D platform that has the potential to completely change the economics of drug development. At the moment, drug development is essentially a hugely expensive trial-and-error process. For every 50 targets, you might find just 25 leads. Of those 25 leads, only ten will make it through preclinical trials. Of those ten, just five will reach clinical testing. Only one will end up as a marketable drug.

With those kinds of economics, it's difficult for even the largest pharmaceutical companies to keep themselves where they are—let alone grow at 10 percent to 15 percent a year, as the market seems to expect. Just keeping a drug pipeline full involves investing $2 billion to $5 billion a year in research, and that doesn't include production and distribution costs. That's just not sustainable, which is why all the major pharmaceutical companies are merging; buying someone else's pipeline is a quick way to beef up your own. But the M&A mating game can't go on forever, and companies must find ways to make the entire drug-development process—finding and testing leads—much faster and more cost effective.

That's what our R&D technology can do. We've already dramatically accelerated the process of identifying leads. It wasn't too long ago that a scientist might spend half a year working on just one lead. She'd sit at a bench, do a few experiments, and report the results six months later. But thanks to our technology, our scientists can spend their time designing automated experiments and analyzing results rather than carrying out the experiments manually. Indeed, if you go into any Millennium-run laboratory, you're not going to see a lot of scientists at work because the process has become so automated that most of the actual experimentation is carried out by robots. One scientist can now look at dozens of experiments in the space of a week rather than just the one she did.

We can even leverage our gene-finding technologies to improve productivity in the testing stages of the value chain. Let's say we run a preclinical study on 100 people in a particular stage of a disease and find that a particular lead works in 80 percent of that population, but that one or two people have a toxic reaction to it. Traditionally, work on the lead would stop right there. The one or two people would almost certainly turn into thousands if the drug were to come to market, and some of them might die. No company would invest $50 million to $100 million on clinical tests for a drug that had such a high risk. But gene identification technology like ours rescues these leads. Companies can work out a marker test that enables companies to identify the people with the genetic disposition to react badly to a lead. That means it is safe for companies to develop the lead to the benefit of the 80 percent of the population who might be well served by it. The overall result is that we can use more of the drugs we develop, making the whole process much more productive. These efficiency gains are extremely attractive to our partners.

If you fulfill your strategy of becoming an integrated biopharmaceutical company, you'll obviously become a much larger organization. Aren't you afraid you will lose your entrepreneurial spirit?
This is our number one challenge, and we spend a tremendous amount of time on it. It was easy to be entrepreneurial years ago, when we had just 30 people in the company; everybody could sit around one table. Of course, it's impossible to perfectly duplicate the intensity and passion of a start-up, but you have to act like you can.

At first, we tried to stay nimble by keeping our operating units separate. For instance, when we struck our deal with Eli Lilly in 1995 to develop large-molecule drugs—drugs that supply missing proteins rather than treat existing ones—we set up the new venture as an independent business, not as an operating unit. We called it MBio, and Eli Lilly was a coinvestor. The idea was to replicate the entrepreneurial Millennium model in another business with another small group of highly qualified people. We did the same with our diagnostics venture, MPMx, and Becton Dickinson came in as a coinvestor. But as Millennium evolved and we formulated the overall vision of a gene-to-patient business, we came to see that a loose confederation of specialists wasn't enough; we needed to integrate many of these capabilities. So in the past two years, we've brought the independent businesses back into the parent company.

Since then, we've tried to keep the entrepreneurial spirit alive by putting together a group of 70 leaders from across the organization. These leaders include senior managers such as myself, Craig Muir (the VP of process technology), and Glenn Betchelder (our VP of operations). But most of them are operational managers, responsible for small teams of

20 to 30 people. Some of them run small labs; others are in administrative functions, like internal accounts. Each month, we all get together and brainstorm—the idea is to re-create the passion and fanaticism we had when everyone at Millennium could sit around the one table. Each leader is responsible for communicating what we've discussed to his or her group—and for kindling their enthusiasm, too. As a result, we have lots of small get-togethers and parties at Millennium. We also take the whole company on an off-site every quarter, where we brainstorm about our strategy in an open forum and in workshops.

But you can go only so far with structure. What really makes a company entrepreneurial, I think, is its people. Once you've got good people, they'll look for other good people: last year, 35 percent of new hires were referred by employees. The overriding thing we look for in these hires is passion—passion for making a difference in people's lives. That's always a big part of the discussions we have with one another at Millennium. At our last off-site, for instance, we brought in doctors we were working with on clinical trials and the patients who would be taking our drugs. Reminding ourselves that real people are affected by what we do keeps us aware of the importance and relevance of the work. It's also healthy for us to remember that we've still got a ways to go—for all our scientific and business achievements, we haven't yet cured a disease.

What do you think has been your personal contribution to the company's development?
I spend a lot of time thinking about our goals. Before starting Millennium, I spent three years talking to the leading genome scientists. I still talk to a wide array of industry thought leaders around the world, and I've integrated many of their ideas into our vision of Millennium as a personalized, gene-to-patient health care company. Articulating a broad vision, though, is only a first step—you need to map out a course to get there. The way I do it is to give our people a specific vision or theme for each year. In fact, this is probably one of the reasons why we've managed to stay entrepreneurial. If you have a new vision every 12 months, you become, in effect, a new company every 12 months.

Our original theme in 1994, our first full year of operations, was "Nothing's impossible." The idea was to get ourselves to open our minds, put fear behind us, and believe that we were going to make something happen. Had we started with any less ambitious a mind-set, we could never have gotten Millennium off the starting block, let alone make it the bio-pharmaceutical company of the future. Since then, the themes have often anticipated our movement down the value chain. In 1996, for instance, the theme was "Perspicacious targetization." That was when we knew we couldn't focus only on genes anymore; we had to focus on targets and molecules. In 1999, we adopted "Genetically defined, clinically inclined" as our motto. That's the year we took our own molecules into the clinic for the first time.

The themes have also guided our organizational and cultural evolution. In 1995, our motto came from Bob Marley: "Jammin'." At the time, we had grown to over 100 people, and for the first time, everybody didn't know everybody else really well. Personality issues were developing, and distinct departmental cultures were forming. To deal with this, we tried to think of ourselves as a band of musicians coming together spontaneously in a jam session. We even wrote our own version of the Marley song and worked with a local reggae band; they play for us every Thanksgiving. A couple of years later, when we set up the leaders group, we chose as our motto "Validated leaders." At that point, we had hundreds of people at Millennium, and we realized that we couldn't operate as a group of jammin' individuals any more. We needed leaders to step up and make things happen. Our most recent

A History in T-shirts

Each year Millennium hands out T-shirts emblazoned with the company's annual theme, reflecting the organizational and strategic challenges the company wants to address in that year.

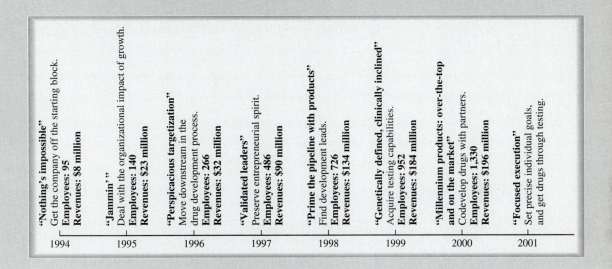

1994 — **"Nothing's impossible"** Get the company off the starting block. Employees: 95 Revenues: $8 million

1995 — **"Jammin'"** Deal with the organizational impact of growth. Employees: 140 Revenues: $23 million

1996 — **"Perspicacious targetization"** Move downstream in the drug development process. Employees: 266 Revenues: $32 million

1997 — **"Validated leaders"** Preserve entrepreneurial spirit. Employees: 486 Revenues: $90 million

1998 — **"Prime the pipeline with products"** Find development leads. Employees: 726 Revenues: $134 million

1999 — **"Genetically defined, clinically inclined"** Acquire testing capabilities. Employees: 952 Revenues: $184 million

2000 — **"Millennium products: over-the-top and on the market"** Codevelop drugs with partners. Employees: 1,330 Revenues: $196 million

2001 — **"Focused execution"** Set precise individual goals, and get drugs through testing.

motto, "Focused execution," also has a strong organizational aspect to it. We're trying to tell people that everyone must have specific goals and that we're counting on each person to make those goals happen. (See the feature box "A History in T-shirts.")

Of course, I don't claim to think up the company's strategy and vision all by myself. We brainstorm throughout the company all the time—in the leaders meetings, in one-on-ones, and at the off-sites. At the end of the day, though, someone has to draw a conclusion and say: "I've listened to what everyone has to say, and this is where I think we've got to go for now." It's difficult, but it's a challenge I welcome.

Index